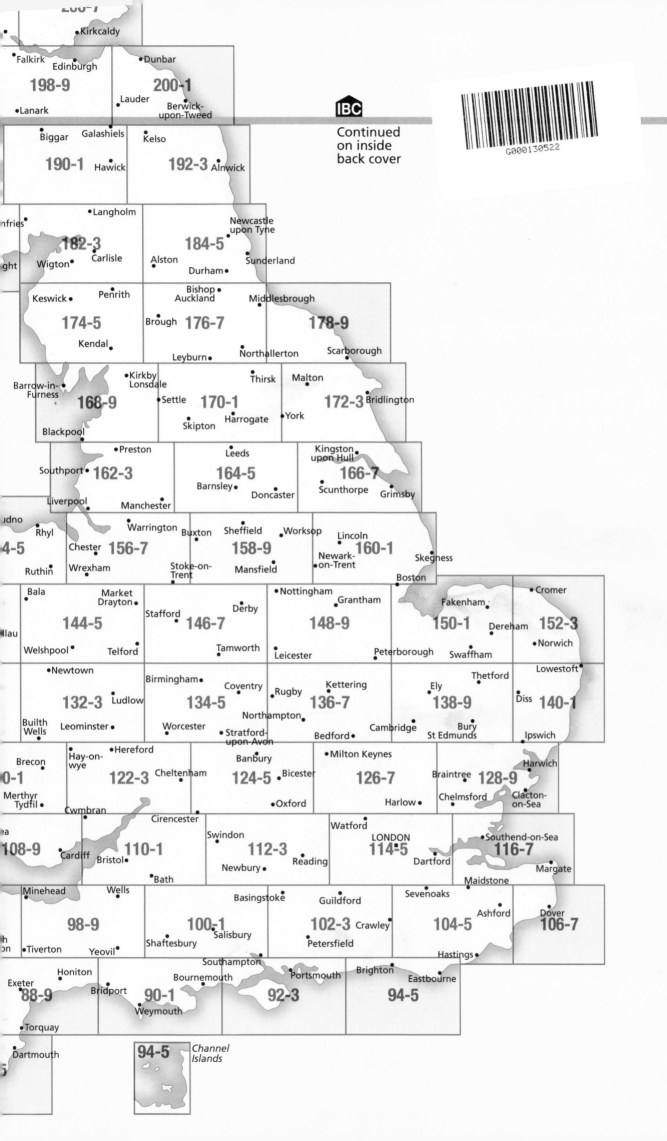

200-7

Kirkcaldy

Falkirk
Edinburgh • Dunbar
198-9 **200-1**
Lauder Berwick-
Lanark upon-Tweed

Biggar Galashiels Kelso
190-1 Hawick **192-3** Alnwick

IBC

Continued
on inside
back cover

G000130522

• Langholm Newcastle
upon Tyne
nfries **182-3** **184-5**
ght Wigton • Carlisle Alston Sunderland
Durham •

Keswick • Penrith Bishop Middlesbrough
Auckland
174-5 Brough • **176-7** **178-9**
Kendal • Northallerton Scarborough
Leyburn •

Barrow-in- • Kirkby Thirsk Malton
Furness Lonsdale
168-9 • Settle **170-1** **172-3** Bridlington
Skipton • Harrogate • York
Blackpool

• Preston Leeds Kingston
upon Hull
Southport • **162-3** **164-5** **166-7**
Barnsley • Scunthorpe Grimsby
Liverpool • Manchester Doncaster

udno Warrington Buxton Sheffield Worksop Lincoln
Rhyl
4-5 Chester **156-7** **158-9** **160-1**
Ruthin Wrexham Stoke-on- Mansfield Newark- Skegness
Trent on-Trent
Boston

Bala Market • Nottingham Grantham Fakenham • • Cromer
Drayton Derby
144-5 Stafford **146-7** **148-9** **150-1** Dereham **152-3**
lau Swaffham • Norwich
Welshpool • Telford Tamworth Leicester Peterborough

• Newtown Birmingham • Coventry Kettering Ely Thetford Lowestoft
132-3 Ludlow **134-5** Rugby **136-7** **138-9** Diss **140-1**
Builth Leominster • Worcester Northampton Cambridge Bury
Wells • Stratford- Bedford • St Edmunds Ipswich
upon-Avon

Brecon Hay-on- • Hereford Banbury • Milton Keynes Harwich
wye
0-1 **122-3** Cheltenham **124-5** Bicester **126-7** Braintree **128-9**
Merthyr Harlow • Chelmsford Clacton-
Tydfil • Cwmbran • Oxford on-Sea

Cirencester Watford
ea Swindon LONDON • Southend-on-Sea
108-9 Cardiff **110-1** **112-3** **114-5** **116-7**
Bristol Newbury • • Reading Dartford Margate
• Bath Maidstone

Minehead Wells Basingstoke Sevenoaks
Guildford Ashford Dover
98-9 **100-1** **102-3** Crawley **104-5** **106-7**
• Tiverton Yeovil Shaftesbury Salisbury Petersfield Hastings •

Honiton Southampton
Exeter Bournemouth Portsmouth Brighton Eastbourne
88-9 Bridport **90-1** **92-3** **94-5**
• Torquay Weymouth

Dartmouth **94-5** *Channel
Islands*

EST.1905

DRIVER'S ATLAS

BRITAIN & IRELAND

ROAD ATLAS, TOURING GUIDE
AND MOTORING HANDBOOK

DRIVER'S ATLAS
BRITAIN & IRELAND

Road atlas, touring guide and motoring handbook

1st edition October 2008

© Automobile Association Developments Limited 2008

Cartography:
All cartography in this atlas edited, designed and produced by the Mapping Services Department of AA Publishing (A03760).

 This product includes mapping data licensed from Ordnance Survey® with the permission of the Controller of Her Majesty's Stationery Office. © Crown copyright 2008. All rights reserved. Licence number 100021153.

 This atlas includes Northern Ireland mapping. This material is based upon Crown Copyright and is reproduced with the permission of Land and Property Services under delegated authority from the Controller of Her Majesty's Stationery Office, © Crown copyright and database rights LA59 © Crown copyright 2008. Permit No. 80043.

© Ordnance Survey Ireland/Government of Ireland Copyright Permit No. 8430

Publisher's Notes:
Published by AA Publishing (a trading name of Automobile Association Developments Limited, whose registered office is Fanum House, Basing View, Basingstoke, Hampshire RG21 4EA, UK. Registered number 1878835).

ISBN: 978 0 7495 6021 8

A CIP catalogue record for this book is available from The British Library.

Disclaimer:
The contents of this atlas are believed to be correct at the time of the latest revision, it will not contain any subsequent amended, new or temporary information including diversions and traffic control or enforcement systems. The publishers cannot be held responsible or liable for any loss or damage occasioned to any person acting or refraining from action as a result of any use or reliance on material in this atlas, nor for any errors, omissions or changes in such material. This does not affect your statutory rights.

The publishers would welcome information to correct any errors or omissions and to keep this atlas up to date. Please write to the Atlas Editor, AA Publishing, The Automobile Association, Fanum House, Basing View, Basingstoke, Hampshire RG21 4EA, UK. E-mail: roadatlasfeedback@theaa.com

Acknowledgements:
AA Publishing would like to thank the following for their assistance in producing this atlas:

RoadPilot® Information on fixed speed camera locations provided by RoadPilot © 2008 RoadPilot® Driving Technology. Information on truckstops and transport cafés kindly provided by John Eden (www.transportcafe.co.uk). Cadw, English Heritage, English Nature, Forestry Commission, Historic Scotland, Johnsons, National Trust and National Trust for Scotland, RSPB, Scottish Natural Heritage, The Countryside Agency, The Countryside Council for Wales (Britain road maps).

The Environment & Heritage Service, Heritage of Ireland, RSPB, Department of Agriculture & Rural Development,

An Roinn Gnóthaí Pobail, GaelSaoire, Tuaithe agus Gaeltachta, Coillte Teoranta, The National Trust, An Taisce, Roads Service and The National Roads Authority (Ireland road maps).

Crown copyright material (pages 26–28) reproduced under licence from the Controller of HMSO and the Driving Standards Agency.

Republic of Ireland traffic signs courtesy Road Safety Authority, Ballina, Co. Mayo.

Relief map image (page 31) supplied by Mountain High Maps® Copyright © 1993 Digital Wisdom, Inc.

Cover design ey communications ltd (www.eysite.com)

Picture credits:
The Automobile Association would like to thank the following photographers and libraries for their assistance in the preparation of this book.

Abbreviations for the picture credits are as follows: (t) top; (b) bottom; (l) left; (r) right; (AA) AA World Travel Library.

16tr David Ducros/Science Photo Library; 30tr AA/G Rowatt; 30ct AA/L Whitwam; 30cr Courtesy of Midland Expressway Ltd; 30bl SwindonWeb; 31tr AA/S Day; 31ctr AA/M Taylor; 31cbr AA/S Day; 31cr AA/J Welsh; 31cl AA/J Henderson; 31bl AA/I Burgum; 31br AA/R Mort; 81 C Bamber; 83l AA/J Wood; 83tr AA/R Moss; 83br AA/J Wood; 85l AA/J Wood; 85tr AA/C Jones; 85cr AA/N Hicks; 85br AA/C Jones; 87tl AA/J Wood; 87bl AA/R Moss; 87tr AA/N Hicks; 87br AA/J Wood; 89tl AA/P Baker; 89tr AA/N Hicks; 89br AA/N Hicks; 91tl AA/M Jourdan; 91tr AA/R Newton; 91cr AA/M Jourdan; 91br AA/M Jourdan; 93tl AA/A Burton; 93bl AA/W Voysey; 93tr AA/A Burton; 93br AA/A Burton; 95tl AA/J Miller; 95bl AA/M Trelawny; 95tr AA/J Miller; 95br AA/J Miller; 97tl AA/N Hicks; 97tr AA/J Wood; 97cr AA/T Teegan; 97br AA/N Hicks; 99tl AA/J A Tims; 99tr AA/T Teegan; 99b AA/R Hall; 101tl AA/E Meacher; 101bl AA/S Day; 101tr AA/D Forss; 101br AA/C Jones; 103tl AA/P Brown; 103tr AA/J Miller; 103bl AA/M Moody; 103bc AA/J Miller; 103br AA/P Brown; 105tl AA/D Noble; 105tr AA/T Souter; 105br AA/J Miller; 107tl AA/D Forss; 107tr AA/R Strange; 107cr AA/J A Tims; 107br Photodisc; 109tl AA/C Jones; 109tr AA/M Moody; 109bc AA/I Burgum; 109br AA/I Burgum; 111tl AA/D Hall; 111tr AA/I Burgum; 111cr AA/D Hall; 111br AA/A Baker; 113tl AA/D Hall; 113bc AA/C Jones; 113tr AA/F Stephenson; 113br AA/D Croucher; 115tl AA/R Turpin; 115br AA/J A Tims; 117tl AA/P Baker; 117bc AA/S & O Mathews; 117tr AA/M Busselle; 117br AA/M Busselle; 119tl AA/I Burgum; 119bl AA/J Gravell; 119br AA/M Moody; 121tl AA/C Molyneux; 121tr AA; 121br AA/I Burgum; 123tl AA/I Burgum; 123tr AA/D Hall; 123br AA/C Jones; 125tl AA/C Jones; 125tr AA/D Hall; 125br AA/S Day; 127tl AA/M Moody; 127tr AA/M Birkitt; 127br AA/M Birkitt; 129tl AA; 129tr AA/W Voysey; 129cr AA/M Trelawny; 129b AA/T Mackie; 131tl AA/C Molyneux; 131tr AA; 131br AA/N Jenkins; 133tl AA/C Jones; 133br AA/M Hayward; 135tl AA/C Jones; 135br AA/M Moody; 137tl AA/M Birkitt; 137tr AA/M Birkitt; 137b AA/M Birkitt; 139tl AA/T Mackie; 139cr AA/T Mackie; 139br AA/T Mackie; 141tl AA/S & O Mathews; 141tr AA/T Mackie; 141b AA/T Mackie; 143tl AA/I Burgum; 143tr AA/G Matthews; 143b AA/P Aithie; 145tl AA/N Jenkins; 145tr AA/N Jenkins; 145br AA/D Croucher; 147tl Alton Towers; 147br AA/J Welsh; 149tl AA/P Baker; 149tr AA/M Birkitt; 149b AA/M Birkitt; 151tl AA/T Mackie; 151br AA/T Mackie; 153tl AA/T Mackie; 153tr AA/T Mackie; 153b AA/T Souter; 155tl AA/G Matthews; 155br AA/W Voysey; 157tl AA/L Whitwam;157b AA/I Burgum; 159tl AA/M Birkitt; 159br AA/P Baker; 161tl AA; 161tr AA/M Birkitt; 161br AA/M Birkitt; 163tl AA/S

Day; 163tr AA/T Griffiths; 163b AA/M Trelawny; 165tl AA/T Mackie; 165tr AA/P Wilson; 165br AA/L Whitwam; 167tl AA/P Wilson; 167tr AA/P Wilson; 167br AA/M Birkitt; 169tl AA/C Jones; 169br AA/P Sharpe; 171tl AA/T Mackie; 171b AA/M Kipling; 173tl AA/P Bennett; 173br AA/P Wilson; 175tl AA/A J Hopkins; 175tr AA/E A Bowness; 175br AA/A Mockford & N Bonetti; 177tl AA/T Mackie; 177br AA/S & O Mathews; 179tl AA/T Mackie; 179b AA/M Kipling; 181tl AA/S Anderson; 181tr AA/S Anderson; 181b AA/J Beazley; 183tl AA/M Alexander; 183tr AA/M Alexander; 183b AA/E A Bowness; 185tl AA/J Beazley; 185tr AA/J Beazley; 185br AA/R Coulam; 187tl Mark Salter/Alamy; 187tr AA; 187b Derek Croucher/Alamy; 189tl AA/P Sharpe; 189tr AA/K Paterson; 189cr AA/K Paterson; 189br AA/S Anderson; 191tl AA/S Anderson; 191bl AA/K Paterson; 191tr AA/S Anderson; 191br AA/J Beazley; 193tl AA/R Coulam; 193tr AA/R Coulam; 193br AA/R Coulam; 195tl Navin Mistry/ Alamy; 195tr Scottish Viewpoint/Alamy; 195cr Navin Mistry/ Alamy; 195b Navin Mistry/Alamy; 197tl AA/J Carnie; 197bl AA/S Anderson; 197tr AA/K Paterson; 197br AA/S Anderson; 199tl AA/K Paterson; 199tr AA/S J Whitehorne; 199b AA/J Smith; 201tl AA/K Paterson; 201tr AA/D Forss; 201b AA/R Coulam; 203tl AA/S Anderson; 203tr AA/R G Elliott; 203b AA/S Anderson; 205tl AA/D W Robertson; 205bl AA/J Carnie; 205tr AA/J Smith; 205c AA/D W Robertson; 207tl AA/J Smith; 207br AA/J Smith; 209tl AA/J Henderson; 209tr AA/S J Whitehorne; 209b AA/J Carnie; 211tl AA/J Henderson; 211tr AA/J Smith; 211br AA/S J Whitehorne; 213tl AA/K Paterson; 213tr AA/J Henderson; 213b AA/R Weir; 215tl AA/E Ellington; 215tr AA/K Paterson; 215b AA; 217l AA/S J Whitehorne; 217br AA/J Henderson; 219tl AA/S Anderson; 219tr AA/S Anderson; 219b AA/E Ellington; 221tl AA/E Ellington; 221tr AA/S J Whitehorne; 221c AA/S J Whitehorne; 221b AA/J Henderson; 223tl AA/S J Whitehorne; 223bl AA/J Henderson; 223tr AA/E Ellington; 223br AA/E Ellington; 225l AA/S Hill; 225tr AA/S Hill; 225br AA/J Blandford; 227l AA/S McBride; 227tr AA/S McBride; 227b AA/S McBride; 229tl AA/C Jones; 229bl AA/J Blandford; 229br AA/C Jones; 231l AA/D Forss; 231b AA/S McBride; 233l AA/P Zollier; 233tr AA/S Day; 233br AA/C Jones; 235l AA/S Hill; 235tr AA/C Jones; 235br AA/S McBride; 237l AA/SlideFile; 237tr AA/C Jones; 237b AA/M Short; 239tl AA/L Blake; 239bl AA/M Diggin; 239tr AA/L Blake; 239br AA/S McBride; 241tr AA/L Blake; 241tr AA/L Blake; 241br AA/S Day; 243l AA/C Jones; 243b AA/S Day; 245tl AA/C Coe; 245tr AA/C Hill; 245br AA/L Blake; 247l AA/C Hill; 247tr AA/C Coe; 247br AA/C Coe; 249l AA/G Munday; 249b AA/I Dawson; 251l AA/G Munday; 251b AA/I Dawson; 253tl AA/C Hill; 253tr AA/D Forss; 253br AA/C Coe; 255l AA/S Smith; 255t AA/B Smith; 255b AA/C Sawyer; 256t AA/R Strange; 256b AA/M Jourdan; 306 AA/P Baker; 307 AA/C Coe; 313 AA/R G Elliott; 314 AA/S J Whitehorne; 319 AA/S Day; 320 Francisco Martinez/Alamy; 322 AA/C Jones; 324 AA/W Voysey; 330/1 AA/T Souter; 330/1 AA/T Souter; 333t ; 333c ; 333b ; 335t © SOUTH WEST NEWS SERVICE; 335c ; 335b ; 336t ; 336c © SOUTH WEST NEWS SERVICE; 336b

Every effort has been made to trace the copyright holders, and we apologise in advance for any accidental errors. We would be happy to apply the corrections in the following edition of this publication.

Printer:
Printed in Italy by Nuovo Istituto Italiano d'Arti Grafiche S.p.A, Bergamo.

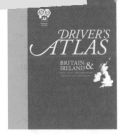

Atlas contents

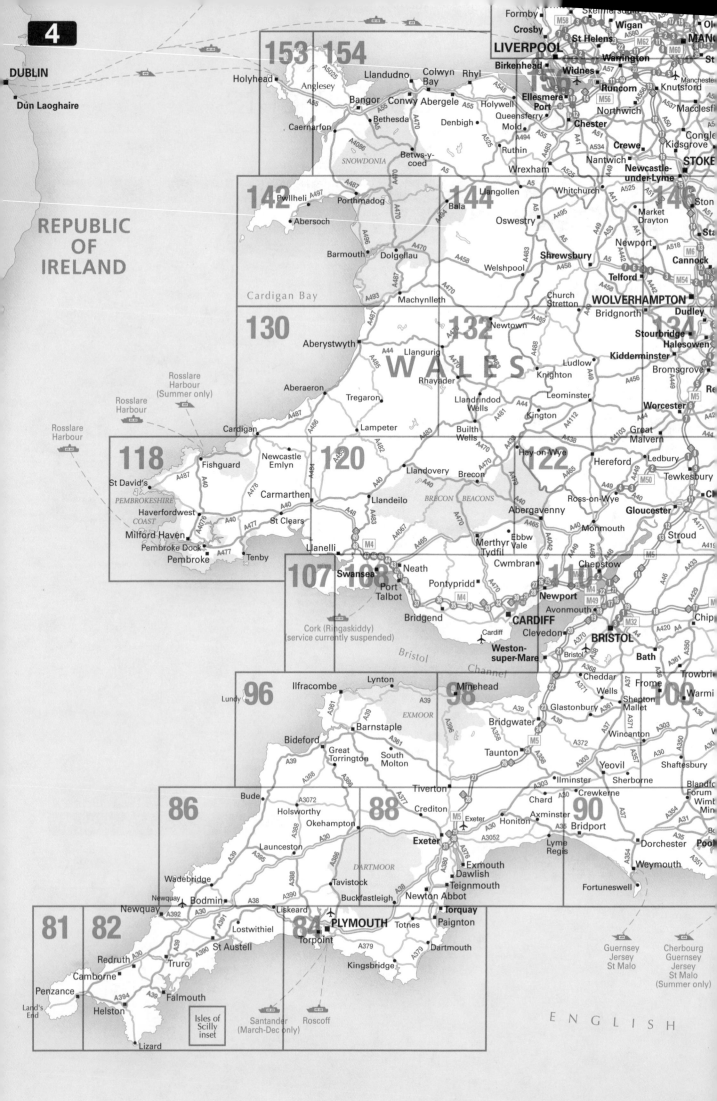

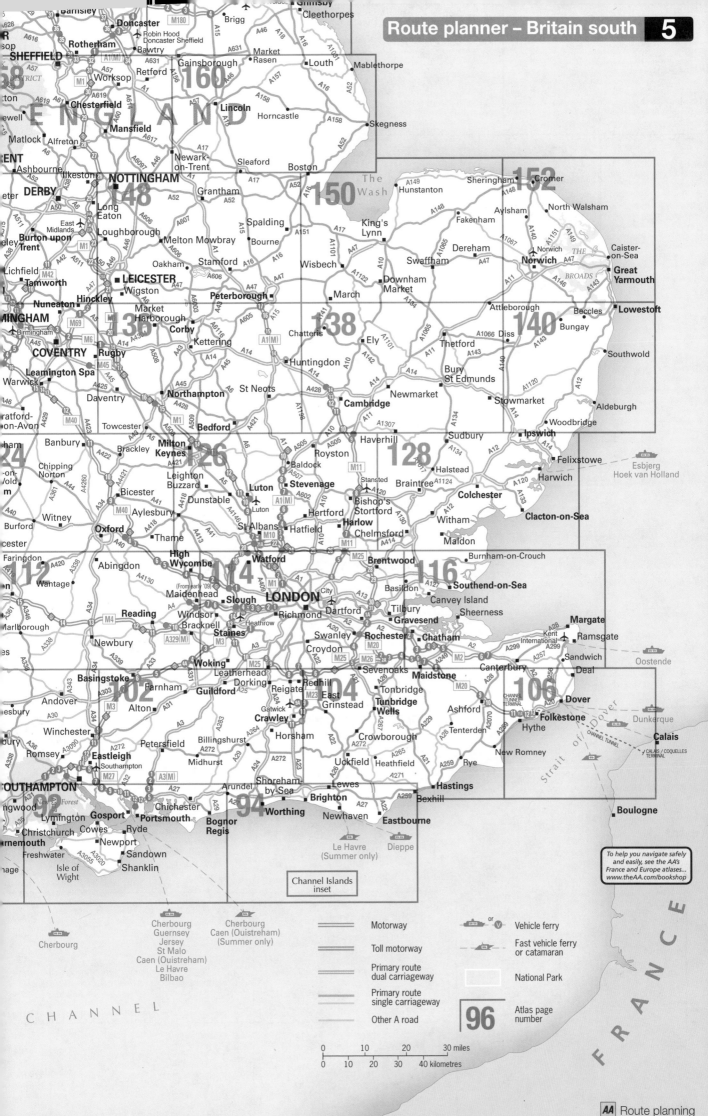

Motorway
Toll motorway
Primary route dual carriageway
Primary route single carriageway
Other A road
Vehicle ferry
Fast vehicle ferry or catamaran
National Park
96 Atlas page number

To help you navigate safely and easily, see the AA's France and Europe atlases... www.theAA.com/bookshop

AA Route planning

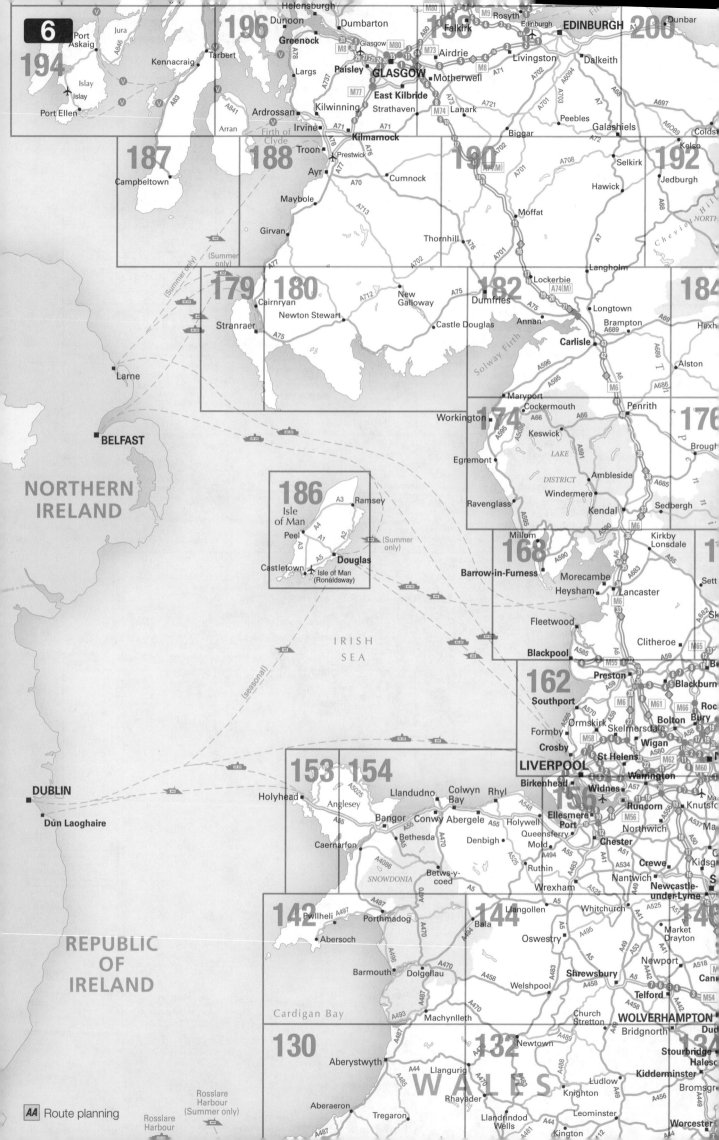

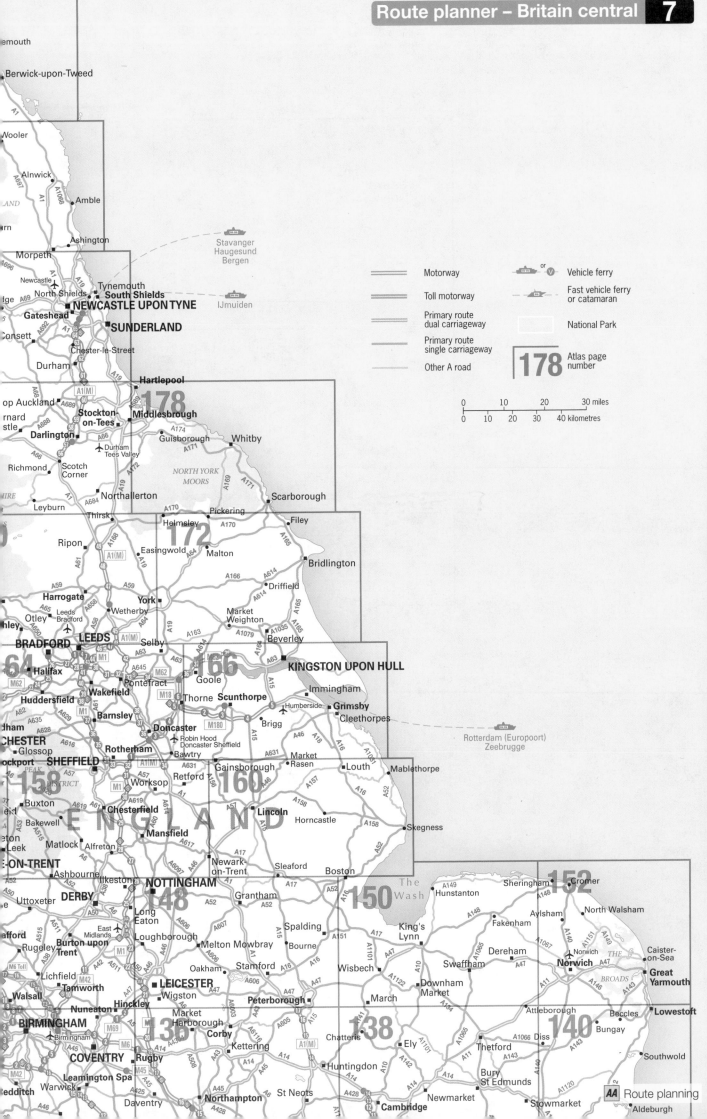

Legend:

— Motorway

— Toll motorway

— Primary route dual carriageway

— Primary route single carriageway

— Other A road

Vehicle ferry

Fast vehicle ferry or catamaran

National Park

178 Atlas page number

0   10   20   30 miles
0   10   20   30   40 kilometres

AA Route planning

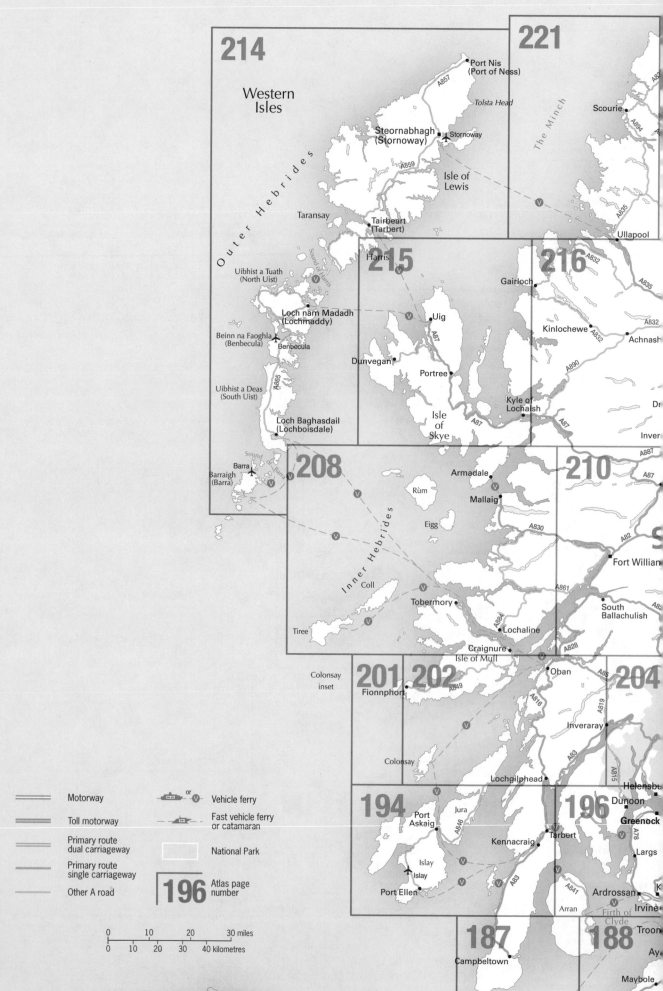

214

Western Isles

221

Port Nis
(Port of Ness)

Tolsta Head

Scourie

A894

Steornabhagh
(Stornoway)

Stornoway

The Minch

Isle of
Lewis

A859

Outer Hebrides

Taransay

A832

Ullapool

A835

Tairbeart
(Tarbert)

215

216

Harris

Gairloch

A832

Uibhist a Tuath
(North Uist)

Sound of Harris

Uig

Kinlochewe

A832

Achnash

Loch nam Madadh
(Lochmaddy)

Dunvegan

A87

Portree

A890

Dr

Beinn na Faoghla
(Benbecula)

Benbecula

Kyle of
Lochalsh

Inver

Uibhist a Deas
(South Uist)

A865

Isle
of
Skye

A87

A87

Loch Baghasdail
(Lochboisdale)

A887

Barra

208

Armadale

210

Barraigh
(Barra)

Sound of Barra

Rùm

Mallaig

A87

Eigg

Inner Hebrides

A830

A82

S

Fort Willian

Coll

A861

Tobermory

South
Ballachulish

A82

Tiree

A884

Lochaline

A828

Craignure

Isle of Mull

Oban

A85

204

Colonsay
inset

201

202

A849

A85

A819

Inveraray

Fionnphort

A816

Lochgilphead

A815

Helensbu

Colonsay

A83

196

Dunoon

194

Jura

Greenock

Port
Askaig

A846

Tarbert

A78

Kennacraig

Largs

Islay

A83

Islay

A841

Ardrossan

K

Port Ellen

Arran

Irvine

*Firth of
Clyde*

Troon

187

188

Campbeltown

Ay

Maybole

Girvan

Motorway

Vehicle ferry

Toll motorway

Fast vehicle ferry
or catamaran

Primary route
dual carriageway

National Park

Primary route
single carriageway

196 Atlas page
number

Other A road

0   10   20   30 miles
0 10 20 30 40 kilometres

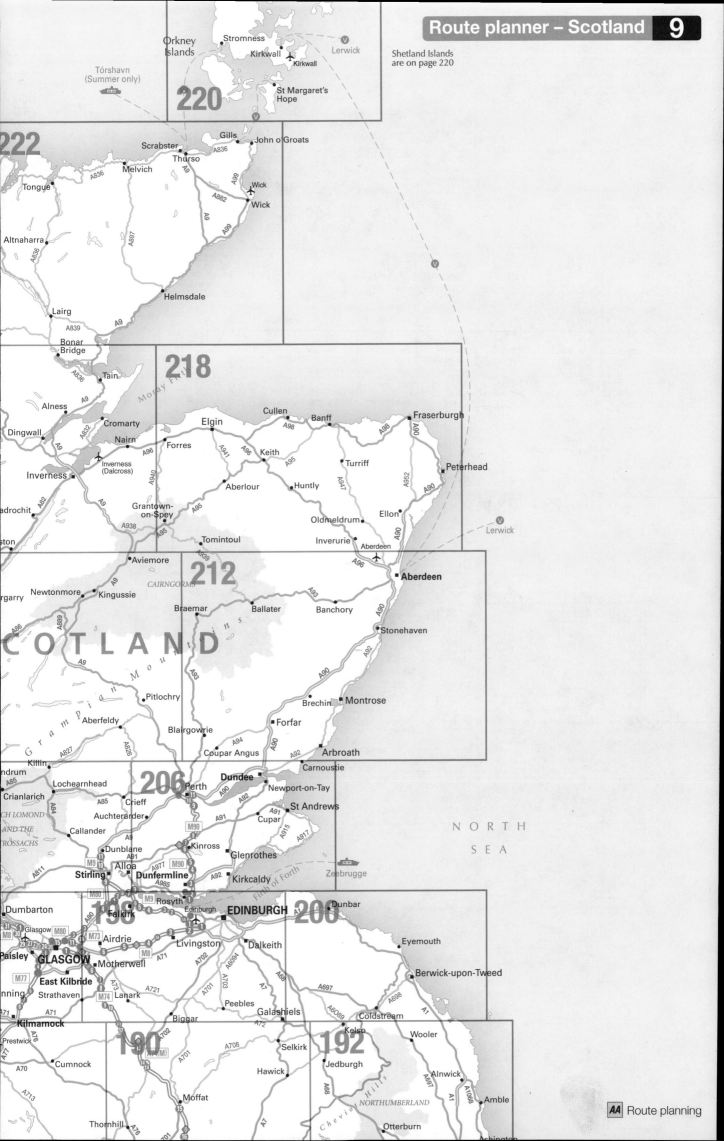

Shetland Islands
are on page 220

Tórshavn
(Summer only)

Orkney
Islands

220

Stromness
Kirkwall
Kirkwall
Lerwick
St Margaret's
Hope

222

Gills
Scrabster
A836
John o'Groats
Thurso
A9
Melvich
A99
Tongue
A882
Wick
A836
Wick

Altnaharra
A897
A9

Helmsdale
A9

Lairg
A839
Bonar
Bridge
A836
Tain

218

Moray Firth

Alness
A9
Cromarty
Cullen
Banff
Fraserburgh
Elgin
A98
A98
A90
Dingwall
A832
Nairn
Forres
A941
Keith
Turriff
Peterhead
Inverness (Dalcross)
A96
A96
A95
A952
A90
Inverness
A940
Aberlour
Huntly
A947
adrochit
A82
A9
Grantown-
on-Spey
Oldmeldrum
Ellon
ston
A938
A95
Inverurie
Aberdeen
A90
Tomintoul
A96

Aviemore
212
Aberdeen
rgarry
Newtonmore
Kingussie
CAIRNGORMS
A93
A889
A339
Braemar
Ballater
Banchory
A86
S C O T L A N D
Grampian Mountains
A90
Stonehaven
A9
A93
A92
Pitlochry
Aberfeldy
Brechin
Montrose
A827
A826
Blairgowrie
Forfar
Killin
A94
A90
A92
Arbroath
ndrum
Lochearnhead
Coupar Angus
A85
206
Carnoustie
Crianlarich
Perth
Dundee
CH LOMOND
A84
Crieff
A90
A92
Newport-on-Tay
AND THE
Auchterarder
A91
St Andrews
TROSSACHS
Callander
A91
Cupar
A9
M90
A915
A917
Dunblane
Kinross
NORTH
A811
M9
Alloa
A977
M90
Glenrothes
SEA
Stirling
Dunfermline
A92
Kirkcaldy
Firth of Forth
Zeebrugge
A985
M9
Dumbarton
198
Rosyth
Falkirk
Edinburgh
EDINBURGH
200
Dunbar
M80
Glasgow
M80
Airdrie
M73
Eyemouth
M8
M8
Livingston
Dalkeith
GLASGOW
Motherwell
A71
Berwick-upon-Tweed
Paisley
A702
A6094
East Kilbride
M77
A73
A701
A703
A7
A68
A698
A1
nning
Strathaven
A721
Peebles
A697
M74
Lanark
Galashiels
Kilmarnock
A72
A6089
Coldstream
A76
Biggar
A708
190
192
Kelso
Prestwick
A702
Selkirk
Wooler
Cumnock
A701
Jedburgh
A70
Hawick
A68
Alnwick
A697
A1068
Amble
A713
Moffat
NORTHUMBERLAND
Cheviot Hills
Thornhill
A76
Otterburn

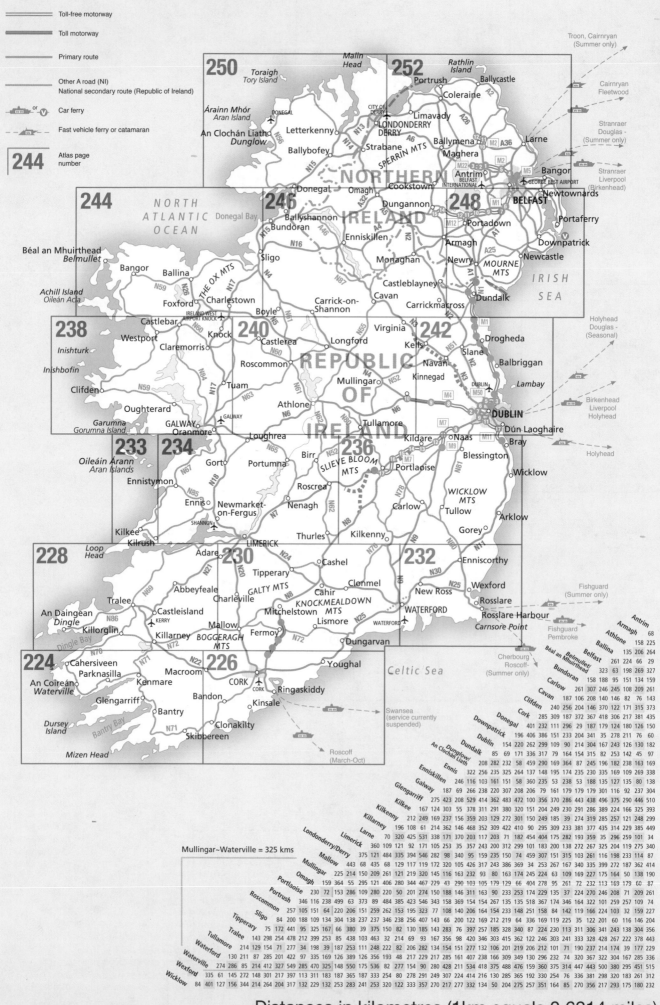

Toll-free motorway

Toll motorway

Primary route

Other A road (NI)
National secondary route (Republic of Ireland)

Car ferry

Fast vehicle ferry or catamaran

244 Atlas page number

Mullingar~Waterville = 325 kms

Distances in kilometres (1km equals 0.6214 miles)

The mileage chart shows distances in miles between two towns along AA-recommended routes. Using motorways and other main roads this is normally the fastest route, though not necessarily the shortest.

The journey times, shown in hours and minutes, are average off-peak driving times along AA-recommended routes. These times should be used as a guide only and do not allow for unforeseen traffic delays, rest breaks or fuel stops.

For example, the 378 miles (608 km) journey between Glasgow and Norwich should take approximately 7 hours 28 minutes.

Journey times

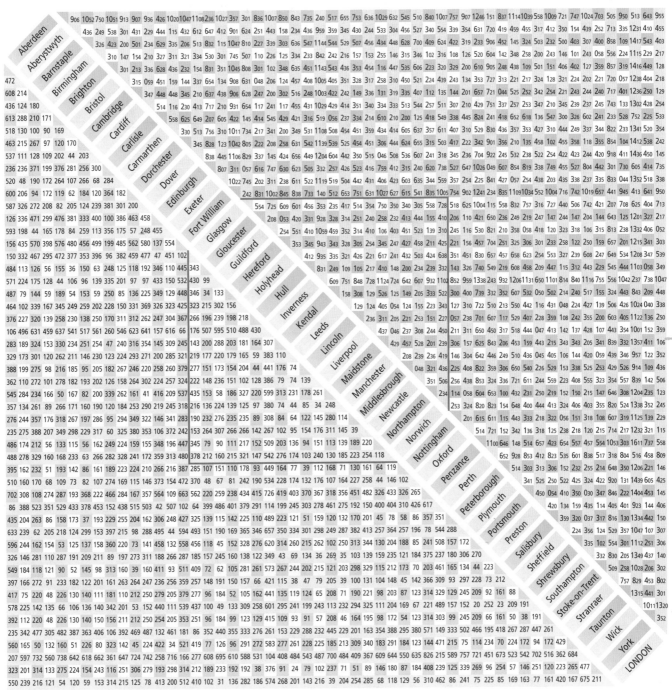

Distances in miles (one mile equals 1.6093km)

M1 London - Leeds

Junction	Northbound	Southbound
2	Access only from A1 (northbound)	Exit only to A1 (southbound)
4	Access only from A41 (northbound)	Exit only to A41 (southbound)
6A	Access only from M25 (no link from A405)	Exit only to M25 (no link from A405)
7	Access only from M10	Exit only to M10
17	Exit only to M45	Access only from M45
19	Exit only to northbound M6	Access only from M6
21A	Exit only to A46	Access only from A46
23A	Access only from A42	Exit only to A42
24A	Access only from A50	Exit only to A50
35A	Exit only to A616	Access only from A616
43	Exit only to M621	Access only from M621
48	Exit only to A1(M) (northbound)	Access only from A1(M) (southbound)

M2 Rochester - Faversham

Junction	Westbound	Eastbound
1	Exit only to A289 (eastbound)	Access only from A289 (westbound)

M3 Sunbury - Southampton

Junction	Southwestbound	Northeastbound
8	Exit only to A303	Access only from A303
10	Access only from Winchester & A31	Exit only to Winchester & A31
13	Access only to M27 (westbound) & A33	No restriction
14	Exit only to M27 (eastbound) & A33	Access only

M4 London - South Wales

Junction	Westbound	Eastbound
1	Access only from A4 (westbound)	Exit only to A4 (eastbound)
4A	No exit to A4 (westbound)	No restriction
21	Exit only to M48	Access only from M48
23	Access only from M48	Exit only to M48
25	Exit only to B4596	Access only from B4596
25A	Exit only to A4042	Access only from A4042
29	Exit only to A48(M)	Access only from A48(M)
38	Exit only to A48	No restriction
39	Access only from A48	No access/exit

M5 Birmingham - Exeter

Junction	Southwestbound	Northeastbound
10	Exit only to A4019	Access only from A4019
11A	Exit only to A417 (eastbound)	Access only from A417 (westbound)
18A	Access only from M49	Exit only to M49
29	Access only from A30 (westbound)	No restriction

M6 Toll motorway

Junction	Northbound	Southbound
T1	Access only	No access or exit
T2	No access or exit	Exit only
T3	Staggered junction; follow signs - access only from A38	Staggered junction; follow signs - no restriction
T5	Access only from A5127 (southbound)	Exit only to A5148 (northbound)
T7	Exit only	Access only
T8	Exit only	Access only

M6 Rugby - Carlisle

Junction	Northbound	Southbound
3A	Exit only	Access only
4	No access from M42 (southbound). No exit to M42 (northbound)	No access from M42 (southbound). No exit to M42
4A	Access only from M42 (southbound)	Exit only to M42
5	Exit only to A452	Access only from A452
10A	Exit only to M54	Access only from M54
11A	Access only	Exit only
20A (with M56)	No restriction	No access from M56 (westbound)
20	Access only from A50	No restriction
24	Access only from A58	Exit only to A58

M8 Edinburgh - Bishopton

Junction	Westbound	Eastbound
8	No access from M73 (southbound) or from A8 (eastbound) & A89	No exit to M73 (northbound) or to A8 (westbound) & A89
9	Access only	Exit only
13	Access only from M80 (southbound)	Exit only to M80 (northbound)
14	Access only	Exit only
16	Exit only to A804	Access only from A879
17	Exit only to A82	No restriction
18	Access only from A82 (eastbound)	Exit only to A814
19	No access from A814 (westbound)	Exit only to A814 (westbound)
20	Exit only	Access only
21	Access only	Exit only to A8
22	Exit only to M77 (southbound)	Access only from M77 (northbound)
23	Exit only to B768	Access only from B768
25	No access or exit from or to A8	No access or exit from or to A8
25A	Exit only	Access only
28	Exit only	Access only
28A	Exit only to A737	Access only from A737

M9 Edinburgh - Dunblane

Junction	Northwestbound	Southeastbound
1A	Exit only to A90	Access only from A90
2	Access only	Exit only
3	Exit only	Access only
6	Access only from A904	Exit only to A905
8	Exit only to M876 (southwestbound)	Access only from M876 (northeastbound)

M10 St Albans - M1

Junction	Northwestbound	Southeastbound
with M1 (jct 7)	Exit only to M1 (northbound)	Access only from M1 (southbound)

M11 London - Cambridge

Junction	Northbound	Southbound
4	Access only from A406	Exit only to A406
5	Exit only to A1168	Access only from A1168
9	Exit only to A11	Access only from A11
13	Exit only to A1303	Access only from A1303
14	Exit only to A14 (eastbound)	Access only from A14

M20 Swanley - Folkestone

Junction	Southeastbound	Northwestbound
2	Staggered junction; follow signs - exit only to A227	Staggered junction; follow signs - access only from A227
3	Access only from M26 (eastbound)	Exit only to M26 (westbound)
5	For access follow signs - exit only to A20	Access only from A20
6	For exit follow signs	No restriction
11A	Exit only	Access only

M23 Hooley - Crawley

Junction	Southbound	Northbound
7	Access only from A23 (southbound)	Exit only to A23 (northbound)
10A	Exit only to B2036	Access only from B2036

M25 London orbital motorway

Junction	Clockwise	Anticlockwise
1B	No direct access, use slip road to Jct 2. Exit only to A296	Access only from A296. No exit - use jct 2
5	No exit to M26	No access from M26
19	Exit only to A41	Access only from A41
21	Access only from M1 (southbound). Exit only to M1 (northbound)	Access only from M1 (southbound). Exit only to M1 (northbound)
31	No exit (use slip road via jct 30)	For access follow signs

M26 Sevenoaks - Wrotham

Junction	Eastbound	Westbound
with M25 (jct 5)	Access only from anticlockwise M25 (eastbound)	Exit only to clockwise M25 (westbound)
with M20 (jct 3)	Exit only to M20 (southeastbound)	Access only from M20 (northwestbound)

M27 Cadnam - Portsmouth

Junction	Eastbound	Westbound
4	Staggered junction; follow signs - access only from M3 (southbound). Exit only to M3 (northbound)	Staggered junction; follow signs - access only from M3 (southbound). Exit only to M3 (northbound)
10	Access only from A32	Exit only to A32
12	Staggered junction; follow signs - access only from M275 (northbound)	Staggered junction; follow signs - exit only to M275 (southbound)

M40 London - Birmingham

Junction	Northwestbound	Southeastbound
3	Exit only to A40	Access only from A40
7	Exit only to A329	Access only from A329
8	Exit only to A40	Access only from A40
13	Exit only to A452	Access only from A452
14	Access only from A452	Exit only to A452
16	Access only from A3400	Exit only to A3400

M42 Bromsgrove - Measham

Junction	Northeastbound	Southwestbound
1	Access only from A38	Exit only to A38
7	Exit only to M6 (northwestbound)	Access only from M6 (northwestbound)
7A	Exit only to M6 (southeastbound)	No access or exit
8	Access only from M6 (southeastbound)	Exit only to M6 (northwestbound)

M45 Coventry - M1

Junction	Eastbound	Westbound
unnumbered (Dunchurch)	Exit only to A45 & B4429	Access only from A45 & B4429
with M1 (jct 17)	Exit only to M1 (southbound)	Access only from M1 (northbound)

M53 Mersey Tunnel - Chester

Junction	Southeastbound	Northwestbound
11	Access only from M56 (westbound). Exit only to M56 (eastbound)	Access only from M56 (westbound). Exit only to M56 (eastbound)

M54 Telford

Junction	Westbound	Eastbound
with M6 (jct 10A)	Access only from M6 (northbound)	Exit only to M6 (soutbound)

M56 North Cheshire

Junction	Westbound	Eastbound
1	Access only from M60 (westbound)	Exit only to M60 (eastbound) & A34 (northbound)
2	Exit only to A560	Access only from A560
3	Access only from A5103	Exit only to A5103 & A560
4	Exit only	Access only
9	Exit to M6 (southbound) via A50 interchange	Access from M6 (northbound) via A50 interchange
15	Exit only to M53	Access only from M53

M57 Liverpool outer ring road

Junction	Northwestbound	Southeastbound
3	Access only from A526	Exit only to A526
5	Access only from A580 (westbound)	Exit only to A580

M58 Liverpool - Wigan

Junction	Eastbound	Westbound
1	Access only	Exit Only

M60 Manchester orbital

Junction	Clockwise	Anticlockwise
2	Access only from A560	Exit only to A560
3	No access from M56	Access only from A34 (northbound)
4	Access only from A34 (northbound). Exit only to M56	Access only from M56 (eastbound). Exit only to A34 (southbound)
5	Access and exit only from and to A5103 (northbound)	Access and exit only from and to A5103 (southbound)
7	No direct access, use slip road to jct 8. Exit only to A56	Access only from A56. No exit - use jct 8
14	Access from A580 (eastbound)	Exit only to A580 (westbound)
16	Access only from A666	Exit only to A666
20	Exit only to A664	Access only from A664
22	No restriction	Exit only to A62
25	Exit only to A6017	No restriction
26	No restriction	No access or exit
27	Access only from A626	Exit only to A626

M61 Manchester - Preston

Junction	Northwestbound	Southeastbound
3	No access or exit	Exit only to A666
with M6 (jct 30)	Exit only to M6 (northbound)	Access only from M6 (southbound)

M62 Liverpool - Kingston upon Hull

Junction	Eastbound	Westbound
23	Exit only to A640	Access only from A640

M65 Preston - Colne

Junction	Northeastbound	Southwestbound
1	Access and exit to M6 only	Access and exit to M6 only
9	Exit only to A679	Access only from A679
11	Access only	Exit only

M66 Bury

Junction	Southbound	Northbound
with A56	Access only from A56 (southbound)	Exit only to A56 (northbound)
1	Access only from A56	Exit only to A56

M67 Hyde bypass

Junction	Eastbound	Westbound
1	Exit only to A6017	Access only from A6017
2	Access only	Exit only to A57
3	No restriction	Exit only to A627

M69 Coventry - Leicester

Junction	Northbound	Southbound
2	Access only from B4669	Exit only to B4669

M73 East of Glasgow

Junction	Northbound	Southbound
2	No access from or exit to A89. No access from M8 (eastbound).	No access from or exit to A89. No exit to M8 (westbound)
3	Exit only to A80 (northeastbound)	Access only from A80 (southwestbound)

M74 and A74(M) Glasgow - Gretna

Junction	Southbound	Northbound
2	Access only from A763	Exit only to A763
3	Exit only	Access only
7	Exit only to A72	Access only from A72
9	Exit only to B7078	No access or exit
10	Access only from B7078	No restrictions
11	Exit only to B7078	Access only from B7078
12	Access only from A70	Exit only to A70
18	Access only from B723	Exit only to B723
21	Exit only to B6357	Access only from B6357
with B7076	Access only	Exit only
Gretna Green	Exit only	Access only
with A75	Access only from A75	Exit only to A75
with A6071	Exit only to A74 (southbound)	Access only from A74 (northbound)

M77 South of Glasgow

Junction	Southbound	Northbound
with M8 (jct 22)	No access from M8 (eastbound)	No exit to M8 (westbound)
4	Exit only	Access only
6	Exit only	Access only

M80 Stepps bypass

Junction	Northeastbound	Southwestbound
1	Access only	No restriction
3	Exit only	Access only

M80 Bonnybridge - Stirling

Junction	Northbound	Southbound
5	Exit only to M876 (northeastbound)	Access only from M876 (southwestbound)

M90 Forth Road Bridge - Perth

Junction	Northbound	Southbound
2A	Exit only to A92 (eastbound)	Access only from A92 (westbound)
7	Access only from A91	Exit only to A91
8	Exit only to A91	Access only from A91
10	No access from A912. No exit to A912 (southbound)	No access from A912 (northbound). No exit to A912

M180 Doncaster - Grimsby

Junction	Eastbound	Westbound
1	Exit only A18	Access only from A18

M606 Bradford spur

Junction	Northbound	Southbound
2	Exit only	No restriction

M621 Leeds - M1

Junction	Clockwise	Anticlockwise
2A	Access only	Exit only
4	Exit only	No restriction
5	Access only	Exit only
6	Exit only	Access only
with M1 (jct 43)	Exit only to M1 (southbound)	Access only from M1 (northbound)

M876 Bonnybridge - Kincardine Bridge

Junction	Northeastbound	Southwestbound
with M80 (jct 5)	Access only from M80 (northbound)	Exit only to M80 (southbound)
2	Exit only to A9	Access only from A9
with M9 (jct 8)	Exit only to M9 (eastbound)	Access only from M9 (westbound)

A1(M) South Mimms - Baldock

Junction	Northbound	Southbound
2	Exit only to A1001	Access only from A1001
3	No restriction	Exit only to A414
5	Access only	No access or exit

A1(M) East of Leeds

Junction	Northbound	Southbound
44	Access only from M1 (northbound)	Exit only to M1 (southbound)

A1(M) Scotch Corner - Newcastle upon Tyne

Junction	Northbound	Southbound
57	Exit only to A66(M) (eastbound)	Access only from A66(M) (westbound)
65	No access Exit only to A194(M) & A1 (northbound)	No exit Access only from A194(M) and A1 (southbound)

A3(M) Horndean - Havant

Junction	Southbound	Northbound
1	Exit only to A3	Access only from A3
4	Access only	Exit only

A48(M) Cardiff spur

Junction	Westbound	Eastbound
29	Access only from M4 (westbound)	Exit only to M4 (eastbound)
29A	Exit only to A48 (westbound)	Access only from A48 (eastbound)

A66(M) Darlington spur

Junction	Eastbound	Westbound
with A1(M) (jct 57)	Access only from A1(M) (northbound)	Exit only to A1(M) (southbound)

A194(M) Newcastle upon Tyne

Junction	Northbound	Southbound
with A1(M) (jct 65)	Access only from A1(M) (northbound)	Exit only to A1(M) (southbound)

A12 M25 - Ipswich

Junction	Northeastbound	Southwestbound
13	Access only from B1002	No restriction
14	Exit only	Access only
20A	Access only to B1137	Access only from B1137
20B	Access only B1137	Exit only to B1137
21	No restriction	Access only from B1389
23	Exit only to B1024	Access only from B1024
24	Access only from B1024	Exit only from B1024
27	Exit only to A113	Access only from A113
unnumbered (with A120)	Exit only A120	Access only from A120
29	Access only from A120 and A1232	Exit only to A120 and A1232
unnumbered	Exit only	Access only

A14 M1 - Felixstowe

Junction	Eastbound	Westbound
With M1/M6 (jct19)	Access only from M6 and M1 (southbound)	Exit only to M6 and M1 (northbound)
4	Access only from B669	Exit only to B669
31	Access only from A428 & M11. Exit only to A1307	Exit only to A428 & M11. Access only from A1307
34	Exit only to B1047	Access only from B1047
unnumbered	No access from or exit to A1303	Access only from A1303
36	Access only from A11	Exit only to A11
38	Exit only to A11	Access only from A11
39	Access only from B1506	Exit only to B1506
49	Exit only to A1308	Access only from A1308
61	Exit only to A154	Access only from A154

A55 Holyhead - Chester

Junction	Eastbound	Westbound
8A	Access only from A5	Exit only to A5
23A	Exit only	Access only
24A	No access or exit	Exit only
33A	No access from or exit to B5126	Exit only to B5126
33B	Access only from A494	Exit only to A494
35A (west)	Exit only A5104	Access only from A5104
35B (east)	Access only from A5104	Exit only to A5104

Ireland

M1 Belfast - Dungannon

Junction	Eastbound	Westbound
3	Access only	Exit only

M1 Dublin - Dundalk

Junction	Northbound	Southbound
with R152	Exit only	Access only
at Donore	No restriction	Exit only
with R132	Access only	Exit only
with R170	Exit only	Access only

M2, M22 Belfast to Randalstown

Junction	Westbound	Southbound
2	No restriction	No exit to M5

M7 Naas and Newbridge bypass

Junction	Eastbound	Westbound
11	Access only from M9 (northbound)	Exit only from M9 (southbound)

M50 Dublin ring road

Junction	Northbound	Southbound
14	Exit Only	No restriction
17	No restriction	No exit to M11 (north)

Refer also to atlas pages 114–115

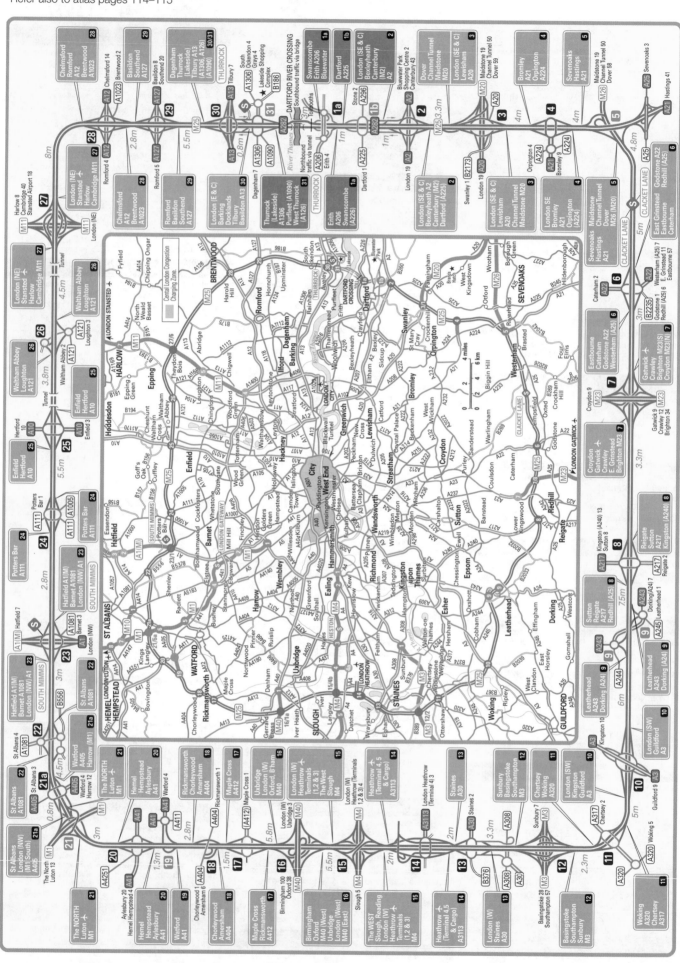

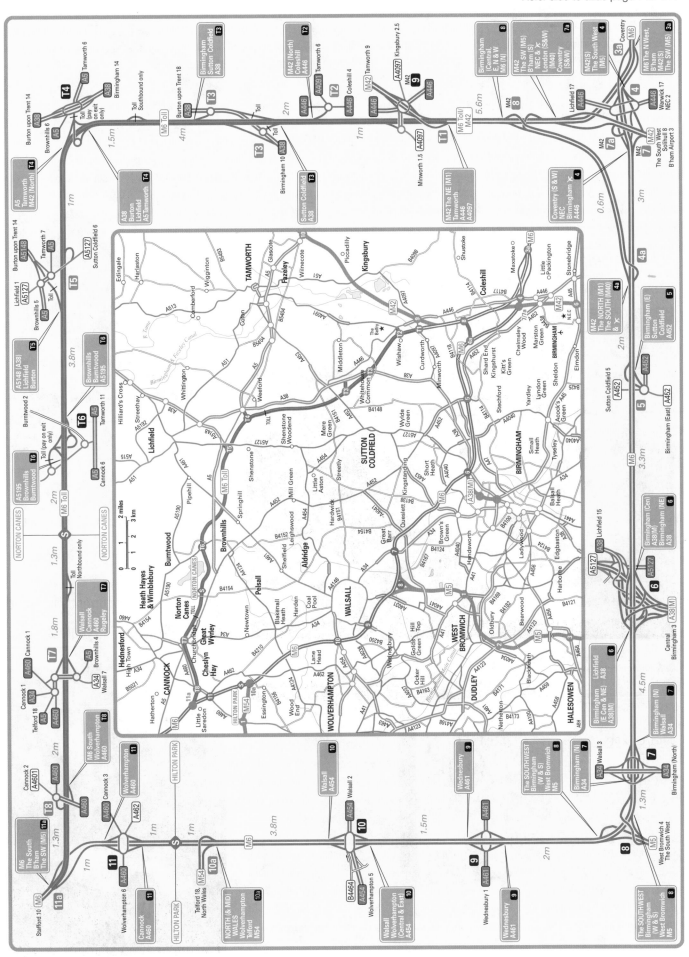

RoadPilot

RoadPilot is the developer of one of the largest and most accurate databases of speed camera locations in the UK and Europe. It has provided the speed camera information in this atlas. RoadPilot is the UK's pioneer and market leader in GPS (Global Positioning System) road safety technologies.

microGo (pictured below) is RoadPilot's latest in-car speed camera location system. It improves road safety by alerting you to the location of accident black spots, fixed and mobile camera sites.

RoadPilot's microGo does not jam police lasers and is therefore completely legal.

RoadPilot's database of fixed camera locations has been compiled with the full co-operation of regional police forces and the Safety Camera Partnerships.

For more information on RoadPilot's GPS road safety products, please visit **www.roadpilot.com** or telephone 0870 240 1701.

Global Positioning System (GPS)

Relaying information from a series of 24 satellites orbiting the earth, a GPS device listens for the signals of four or more satellites at a time in order to work out an accurate location.

SPEED READING

RoadPilot is dedicated to creating and maintaining the most accurate database of safety cameras in Europe.

A team of surveyors visit and accurately record the exact position and attributes of each and every camera in the RoadPilot database. On average 400 new locations/modifications are added every month.

■ Countries currently included

■ Planned / In progress

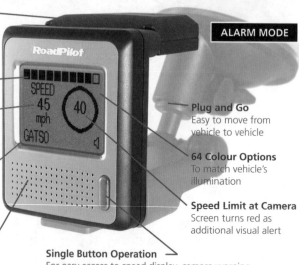

ALARM MODE

GPS Antena
microGo is directional, it only alerts you to cameras on your side of the road

Visual Countdown
To camera location

Your Speed
The speed you are travelling when approaching camera

Camera Types Located
Gatso, Specs, Truvelo, TSS/DSS, Traffipax, mobile camera sites, accident black spots, congestion charges, tolls

Voice Warnings
Only if you are exceeding the speed limit at the camera

Single Button Operation
For easy access to speed display, camera warning, rescue me location, trip computer, congestion charge, max speed alarm, date and time

Plug and Go
Easy to move from vehicle to vehicle

64 Colour Options
To match vehicle's illumination

Speed Limit at Camera
Screen turns red as additional visual alert

RoadPilot®
RoadPilot Surveyors add approximately 400 new locations every month

Road safety and mobile speed cameras

Breaking the speed limit is illegal and can cost lives. The AA advises drivers to follow the legal speed limit at all times.

Both the AA and the British Government believe that speed cameras should be operated within a transparent system. By providing information relating to road safety and speed hotspots, the AA believes that the driver is better placed to be aware of speed limits and can ensure adherence to them, thus making the roads safer for all users. For this reason the AA has compiled a list of more than 3,000 regularly policed mobile camera sites, based on Britain and Northern Ireland's official regional Safety Camera and Casualty Reduction Partnership sources. In the Republic of Ireland accurate locations of mobile patrols are not available.

Mobile cameras are also deployed, generally on a temporary basis, at other sites and at roadworks. Due to the nature and purpose of mobile speed control devices the list cannot be exhaustive or completely accurate all of the time and **we advise drivers to always follow the signed speed limits**.

Britain and Ireland's speed camera regions

Speed Limits

Types of vehicle	Built up areas* MPH (km/h)	Single carriageways MPH (km/h)	Dual carriageways MPH (km/h)	Motorways MPH (km/h)
 **Cars & motorcycles** (including car derived vans up to 2 tonnes maximum laden weight)	30 (48)	60 (96)	70 (112)	70 (112)
 **Cars towing caravans or trailers** (including car derived vans and motorcycles)	30 (48)	50 (80)	60 (96)	60 (96)
 **Buses, coaches and minibuses** (not exceeding 12 metres (39 feet) in overall length)	30 (48)	50 (80)	60 (96)	70 (112)
Goods vehicles (not exceeding 7.5 tonnes maximum laden weight)	30 (48)	50 (80)	60 (96)	70† (112)
 **Goods vehicles** (exceeding 7.5 tonnes maximum laden weight)	30 (48)	40 (64)	50 (80)	60 (96)

* The 30mph (48km/h) limit usually applies to all traffic on all roads with street lighting unless signs show otherwise.

† 60mph (96km/h) if articulated or towing a trailer.

Region-by-region list of mobile camera sites

Road number	Location	Speed limit (mph)
ENGLAND		
Avon and Somerset		
A4	Newbridge Rd, Bath	30
A4	Anchor Rd, Bristol	30
A4	Bath Rd, Bristol (at Totterdown Bridge)	30
A4	Portway, Bristol (near Sea Mills)	50
A4	Portway, Bristol (near A4176 Bridge Valley Rd)	30
A4	Keynsham Bypass (at A4174 jct)	50
A30	Cricket St Thomas	50
A30	East Chinnock	30
A30	Roundham	40
A30	Sherborne Rd, Yeovil	30
A30	Hospital Roundabout, Yeovil	40
A37	Wells Rd, Bristol (near A4174 Airport Rd)	30
A37	Wells Rd, Totterdown, Bristol (near St John's La)	30
A37	Chilthorne Domer	60
A37	Emborough (south of B3139)	50
A37	Fosse Way (north of Podimore Roundabout)	60
A37	Gurney Slade	30
A37	Lydford, near Hornblotton (northbound)	60
A37	Lydford (southbound)	40
A37	Shepton Mallet	30
A38	Bathpool	30
A38	Heatherton Grange, Bradford-on-Tone	50
A38	Taunton Rd, Bridgwater	30
A38	Bedminster Down Rd/West St, Bedminster, Bristol	30
A38	Bedminster Down Rd, Bristol (near Bishopsworth Rd)	40
A38	Bridgwater Rd, Bedminster Down, Bristol	40
A38	Cheltenham Rd/Gloucester Rd, Bristol (near B4054 Cranbrook Rd)	30
A38	Gloucester Rd, Bristol (near B4052 Ashley Down Rd)	30
A38	Stokes Croft, Bristol	30
A38	Churchill to Lower Langford	40
A38	Cross	40
A38	North Petherton	30/40
A38	Aztec West, Patchway (near Bradley Stoke Way)	40
A38	Gloucester Rd, Patchway (near Highwood Rd)	40
A38	Gloucester Rd North, Patchway (near B4057 Gypsy Patch La)	40
A38	Pawlett	50
A38	Redhill	50

Road number	Location	Speed limit (mph)
A38	Rooks Bridge	30
A38	Sidcot (near A371 jct)	30
A38	East Reach/Toneway, Taunton	30
A38	Wellington Rd, Taunton	30
A38	West Huntspill	30
A39	Ashcott	30
A39	Bilbrook	30
A39	Bath Rd, Bridgwater	30
A39	North Broadway, Bridgwater (near A38, Taunton Rd)	30
A39	Quantock Rd, Bridgwater	30
A39	North Broadway/Broadway/ Monmouth St, Bridgwater	30
A39	Chewton Mendip	30
A39	Coxley	40
A39	Green Ore	50
A39	Bath Rd, Horsey	40
A39	Walton	30
A46	Tormarton	60
A46	Dunkirk	40
A303	Buckland St Mary	50
A303	Downhead (near Ilchester)	50
A303/ A358	Southfields Roundabout (near Ilminster)	60
A303/ A3088	Cartgate Roundabout (near Martock)	70
A357	Templecombe	30
A358	Ashill	60
A358	Donyatt	30
A358	Henlade (near M5, jct 25)	30
A358	Hornsbury Mill	40
A358	Pen Elm (3km west of Taunton)	40
A358	Greenway Rd, Taunton	30
A358	Priorswood Rd, Taunton	30
A358	Staplegrove Rd, Taunton (near A3065)	30
A359	Mudford	30
A361	Doulting	30
A361	Durston	40
A361	Frome Bypass	60
A361	Othery	30
A361	Pilton	30
A361	West Pennard	30
A362	Terry Hill (near A366 jct)	40
A367	Bear Flat, Bath	30
A367	Green Park Rd, Bath	30
A367	Wells Rd, Radstock	30
A369	Abbots Leigh	40
A369	Martcombe Rd, Easton-in-Gordano	60
A370	Backwell	30

Road number	Location	Speed limit (mph)
A370	Cleeve Village	30
A370	Station Rd/Bristol Rd, Congresbury	30
A370	Flax Bourton (near B3130)	30
A370	Long Ashton Bypass, Bristol end	40
A370	Beach Rd, Weston-super-Mare	30
A370	Herluin Way, Weston-super-Mare (near Winterstoke Rd)	50
A370	Somerset Ave, Weston-super-Mare (M5 to A371)	50
A370	Winterstoke Rd, Weston-super-Mare	30
A371	Draycott	30
A371	Priestleigh	40
A372	Aller	30
A372	Red Post (at B3151, Kingsdon)	50
A378	Curry Rivel	30
A378	Wrantage	40
A403	Avonmouth Docks	40
A420	Clouds Hill Rd/Bell Hill Rd, St George, Bristol	30
A420	High St/London Rd, Warmley, Bristol (near A4175)	30
A420	Lawrence Hill, Bristol	30
A420	Old Market, Bristol (near Temple Way/ Bond St)	30
A420	Wick/Tog Hill	60
A431	Bath Rd, Longwell Green, Bristol (near Willsbridge)	30
A432	Badminton Rd, Bristol (near A4174 Avon Ring Rd)	40
A432	Fishponds Rd, Bristol (near B4048 Lodge Causeway)	30
A432	Fishponds Rd, Bristol (at B4469 Muller Rd)	30
A432	Fishponds Rd, Bristol (near B4469 Royate Hill)	30
A432	Stapleton Rd, Bristol (near A4320 Easton Way)	30
A432	Kendleshire	40
A432	Station Rd/B4059 Stover Rd, Yate	30
A3033	Devonshire Rd, Weston-super-Mare	30
A3088	Lysander Rd, Yeovil	30
A3259	Monkton Heathfield	30
A4018	Black Boy Hill/Whiteladies Rd, Bristol	30
A4018	Falcondale Rd, Westbury-on-Trym, Bristol	30
A4018	Park Row/Perry Rd, Bristol	30
A4018	Westbury Rd, Bristol (near B4054 North View)	30
A4018	Whiteladies Rd into Queens Rd, Bristol	30
A4018	Catbrain (near Cribbs Causeway)	40
A4018	Cribbs Causeway (at jct 17 M5)	30
A4044	Temple Way, Bristol	30
A4162	Sylvan Way/Dingle Rd/Canford La, Westbury-on-Trym, Bristol	30
A4174	Avon Ring Rd (near M32 jct 1)	50
A4174	Avon Ring Rd, Bromley Heath (west of A432)	50
A4174	Filton Rd/Avon Ring Rd (near Coldharbour La)	50
A4174	Hartcliffe Way, Bristol	30
A4174	Hengrove Way/Airport Rd, Bristol (near Creswicke Rd)	40
A4174	Station Rd, Filton (near Great Stoke Way)	40
A4320	St Philips Causeway, Bristol (near A4 Bath Rd)	30
B3124	Walton Rd, Clevedon	30
B3130	Stockway North/Chapel Ave, Nailsea	30
B3130	Wraxall	30/40
B3139	Chilcompton	30
B3139	Mark Causeway	30
B3141	East Huntspill	30
B3151	Compton Dundon	30
B3151	Ilchester	30
B3151	Somerton Rd, Street	30
B3153	Keinton Mandeville	30
B3170	Shoreditch Rd, Taunton	30
B3440	Locking Rd, Weston-super-Mare	30
B4054	Avonmouth Rd, Shirehampton, Bristol	30
B4054	Linden Rd, Westbury Park, Bristol	30
B4054	Shirehampton Rd, Sea Mills, Bristol	30
B4056	Southmead Rd, Bristol	30
B4057	Crow La, Henbury, Bristol (near Passage Rd)	30
B4057	Winterbourne Rd, Great Stoke (near B4427)	40
B4057	Gypsy Patch La, Stoke Gifford (near Hatchet Rd)	30
B4058	Frenchay Park Rd, Bristol	30
B4058	Winterbourne Hill/High St, Winterbourne	30
B4059	Goose Green Way, Yate	30
B4060	Station Rd/Bowling Hill/Rounceval St, Yate/ Chipping Sodbury	30
B4061	Bristol Rd, Thornbury	30
B4061	Gloucester Rd, Thornbury (near Morton Way)	30
B4465	Staplehill Rd/High St, Fishponds, Bristol	30
B4465	Broad St, Mangotsfield, Bristol	30
-	Berrow; Coast Rd	30
-	Bristol; Bishport Ave, Hartcliffe	30
-	Bristol; Broadwalk, Knowle	30
-	Bristol; Hawkfield Rd, Hartcliffe (near A4174 Hengrove Way)	30
-	Bristol; Kingsway, St George	30
-	Bristol; Long Cross, Lawrence Weston	30
-	Bristol; Northumbria Dr, Westbury Park	30
-	Bristol; Redcliffe Way	30
-	Bristol; Stoke Hill/Stoke Rd, Clifton (near Saville Rd)	30
-	Bristol; Sturminster Rd, Stockwood	30
-	Bristol; Whitchurch La/Hareclive Rd, Bishopsworth	30
-	Clevedon; Central Way	30
-	Taunton; Cheddon Rd	30
-	Taunton; Chestnut Dr	30
-	Taunton; Lisieux Way	30
-	Taunton; Trull Rd	30
-	Watergore; Harp Rd (near Over Stratton)	50
-	Weston-super-Mare; Locking Rd/Alexandra Pde/Regent St	30
-	Yeovil; Combe St	30

Bedfordshire and Luton

Road number	Location	Speed limit (mph)
A1	Sandy	50
A5	Battlesden	60
A5	Hockliffe	40
A5	Kensworth (near B4540)	60
A6	New Bedford Rd, Luton	30
A6	Pulloxhill	60
A6	near Silsoe	60
A421	Brogborough/Aspley Guise	50
A421	Wootton	60
A428	Bromham Rd, Bedford	30
A428	Goldington Rd, Bedford	30
A505	Luton Rd, Dunstable	30
A505	Leighton Buzzard Bypass	60
A505	Park Viaduct, Luton	30
A507	near Clifton	60
A507	Ridgmont	30
A603	Cardington Rd, Bedford	30
A603	Willington	40
A1081	Airport Way, Luton	60
A4146	Billington Rd, Leighton Buzzard	30
A5120	High St, Flitwick	30
A5120	Harlington	40
A5120	Bedford Rd, Houghton Regis	40
A5120	Station Rd, Toddington	30
A5134	High St, Kempston	30
B531	Bedford Rd, Kempston	30
B1040	Potton Rd, Biggleswade	30
B1042	Wrestlingworth	30
B4540	Markyate Rd, Slip End, Luton	30
-	Arlesey; Hitchin Rd	30
-	Aspley Guise; Bedford Rd/West Hill	30
-	Bedford; Park Ave	30
-	Bedford; Roff Ave	30
-	Bedford; Wentworth Dr	30
-	Bromham; Stagsden Rd	30
-	Bromham; Village Rd	30
-	Caddington; Dunstable Rd	30
-	Clapham; High St	30
-	Cranfield; High St	30
-	Eaton Bray; The Rye	30
-	Harlington; Barton Rd	30
-	Heath and Reach; Woburn Rd	30
-	Leighton Buzzard; Heath Rd	30
-	Luton; Crawley Green Rd	30
-	Luton; Dunstable Rd	40
-	Luton; Leagrave High St	30
-	Luton; Waller Ave	30
-	Luton; Whitehorse Vale	30
-	Upper Caldecote; Hichin Rd	30
-	Wrestlingworth; High St	30

Cambridgeshire

Road number	Location	Speed limit (mph)
A1	Little Paxton to Southoe (northbound)	NSL
A1	south of Carpenter's Lodge Roundabout (B1081, south of Stamford)(northbound)	NSL
A10	Melbourn Bypass	NSL
A14	Jct 15 to 17 (eastbound)	NSL
A14	Jct 18 to 19 (westbound)	NSL
A14	Jct 20 (eastbound)	NSL
A14	West of jct 21 (A1) (eastbound)	NSL
A14	Jct 23 (eastbound)	NSL
A14	Girton to jct 31 (A1307) (westbound)	NSL
A14	Fen Ditton	NSL
A14	east of jct 35 (A1303) (westbound)	NSL
A14	Bottisham (westbound)	NSL
A14	north-east of jct 36 (A11) (eastbound)	NSL
A15	London Rd, Peterborough (New Rd to Rivergate)	30
A15	Paston Pkwy, Peterborough (northbound)	NSL
A47	Soke Pkwy, Peterborough (eastbound)	NSL
A47	west of Thorney Toll	NSL
A141	Huntingdon Northern Bypass	NSL
A141	at B1040 jct, south of Warboys (southbound)	NSL
A141	north-east of Warboys	NSL
A141	Clews Corner (south-west of Chatteris)	NSL
A141	Wimblington/Doddington Bypass	NSL
A142	Soham Bypass (southbound)	NSL
A142	Witchford Bypass (eastbound)	NSL
A428	St Neots Bypass	NSL
A505	east of Royston	NSL
A505	Thriplow	NSL
A603	Little Eversden	NSL
A605	Elton	NSL
A605	Oundle Rd, Peterborough (near Nene Pkwy jct)	30
A605	Kings Dyke (west of Whittlesey)	40
A605	Coates Rd, Eastrea	30
A1073	Masons Bridge/Steam House Farm (north of Eye)	NSL
A1101	Mildenhall Rd, Littleport	NSL
A1123	Houghton Hill, St Ives, east of B1090 (eastbound)	40
A1123	St Audrey La, St Ives	30
A1123	Needingworth Bypass	NSL
A1123	Wilburton bends to east of village	40
A1134	Trumpington Rd, Cambridge	30
A1198	Graveley/Hilton jcts	NSL
A1198	south of B1046 jct	NSL
A1303	near A1304 jct, Newmarket	NSL
A1307	Huntingdon Rd, Cambridge	40
A1307	Hills Rd, Cambridge (Gonville Pl to Worts' Cswy)(southbound)	30
A1307	Linton Bypass (westbound)	NSL
A1307	Bartlow Crossroads (dual carriageway)	NSL
A1309	Milton Rd, Chesterton, Cambridge	30
B198	Lynn Rd, Wisbech (north-east end)	40
B645	Tilbrook bends	40
B1061	Dullingham Rd, Newmarket	NSL
B1099	Wisbech Rd, March	30
-	Cambridge; Cherry Hinton Rd (at Cherry Hinton Hall)	30
-	Cambridge; Coldham's Lane (by airport)	40
-	Chatteris; Doddington Rd	40
-	Ramsey Forty Foot; Forty Foot Bank (2.5km east of village)	50

Cheshire

Road number	Location	Speed limit (mph)
A50	Manchester Rd/Toft Rd, Knutsford (Woodvale Rd to Garden Rd)	30
A50	Knutsford Rd, Grappenhall, Warrington (Heath Field Park to Cliff La)	30
A50	Long La, Warrington (Fisher Ave to Longfield Rd)	30
A54	Kelsall Rd, Ashton (west of B5393 Ashton La to Hollands La overbridge)	60/70
A56	Camsley La, Lymm (Deans La to M6 overbridge)	40
A57	New Manchester Rd, Paddington, Warrington (Larkfield Ave to Greymist Ave)	40
A523	London Rd, Poynton (South Park Dr to Clifford Rd)	30
A532	Coppenhall La/West St, Crewe (Marshfield Ave to Peel St)	30
A533	Booth La, Middlewich (Long La South to 320m south-east of Cledford La)	40
A533	Northwich Rd, Runcorn (A56 Chester Rd to Rivington Rd)	30
A537	Buxton New Rd, near Cat and Fiddle (100m north-west of Buxton Old Rd to A54)	50
A5019	Mill St/Vernon Way, Crewe (A532 Earle St to A534 Nantwich Rd)	30
A5032	Chester Rd, Whitby, Ellesmere Port (A5117 to 130m south of Dunkirk La)	30
A5034	Mereside Rd, Mere	60
A5104	Hough Green, Chester (A483 to Cliveden Rd)	30
B5071	Gresty Rd, Crewe (South St to 500m south of Davenport Ave)	30
B5078	Sandbach Rd North, Alsager (The Avenue to Leicester Ave)	30
B5082	Middlewich Rd, Northwich (East Ave to Pullman Dr)	30
B5132	Overpool Rd/Rivacre Rd, Ellesmere Port (B5132 Sutton Way to Netherpool Rd)	30
B5155	Runcorn, Heath Rd (Halton Rd to Boston Ave)	30
B5419	Widnes, Birchfield Rd (Pit La to Rose View Ave)	30
B5463	Station Rd, Little Sutton	30
B5470	Hurdsfield Rd/Rainow Rd, Macclesfield (Fence Ave to Well La)	30
-	Burtonwood; Lumber La (Green La to Melrose Ave)	30
-	Ellesmere Port; Overpool Rd (Wycliffe Rd to Fairview Rd)	30
-	Runcorn; Astmoor Rd (Lister Rd to Chadwick Rd)	40
-	Runcorn; Boston Ave (Morval Cres to Heath Rd)	30
-	Runcorn; Halton Rd (Daresbury Expressway overbridge to Boston Ave)	30
-	Runcorn; Heath Rd (Halton Rd to Boston Ave)	30
-	Runcorn; Moughland La/Clifton Rd (Greenway Rd to Beaufort Close)	30
-	Runcorn; Warrington Rd (Manor Park to Eastgate Rd)	30
-	Warrington; Battersby La, Howley	30
-	Warrington; Harpers Rd, Fearnhead (Pasture La to Freshfield Dr)	30
-	Warrington; Lovely La, Whitecross (Monks St to Clap Gates Rd)	30
-	Widnes; Hough Green Rd (B5178 Liverpool Rd to Arley Dr)	30
-	Widnes; Prescot Rd, Hough Green (Hough Green Rd to borough boundary)	30
-	Wilmslow; Hough La (northern end)	30
-	Winsford; Bradford La (either side of School Rd)	40
-	Winsford; St John's Dr (Brunner Pl to Forest Rd)	30
-	Winsford; Woodford Lane/Delamere St (southern end)	30

Cleveland

Road number	Location	Speed limit (mph)
A135	Yarm Rd, Eaglescliffe	30
A171	Charltons (near Margrove Park)	50
A171	Ormesby Bank, Ormesby	30
A172	Marton Rd, Middlesbrough (Longlands to St Lukes Hosp)	30
A172	Marton Rd, Middlesbrough (St Lukes to Marton crossroads)	40
A172	Dixons Bank, Nunthorpe (Guisborough Rd to Captain Cook's Cres)	40
A174	Carlin How (near Loftus)	30
A177	Durham Rd, Stockton-on-Tees (from Savacentre to county boundary)	50/60
A178	Coronation Drive, Hartlepool	40/30
A178	The Front, Seaton Carew	30
A179	Easington Rd/Powlett Rd, Hartlepool	30/ 40/50
A689	Stockton Rd, Hartlepool (from Sappers Corner)	50/40
A1027	Bishopton Ave, Stockton-on-Tees	30
A1032	Acklam Rd, Brookfield (Blue Bell to Crematorium)	40
A1032	Acklam Rd, Linthorpe	30
A1042	Kirkleatham La, Redcar	30/40
A1085	High St, Marske-by-the-Sea	30
A1130	Acklam Rd, Thornaby-on-Tees	30
A1130	Mandale Rd, Acklam	30
B1269	Redcar La, Redcar	30
B1274	Junction Rd, Stockton-on-Tees	30
B1276	Seaton La, Hartlepool	30
B1276	Station La, Seaton Carew	30
B1380	High St, Eston	30
B1380	Ladgate La, Marton (Marton crossroads to Ormesby Rd)	40
B1380	Normanby Rd, Ormesby	30
-	Acklam; Trimdon Ave	30
-	Billingham; Thames Rd	30
-	Billingham; White House Rd	30
-	Eston; Church La	30
-	Eston; Normanby Rd	30
-	Hartlepool; Catcote Rd	30
-	Hartlepool; Elwick Rd (York Rd to Elwick Rise)	30
-	Hartlepool; King Oswy Dr	30
-	Hartlepool; Owton Manor La	30
-	Hartlepool; Oxford Rd	30
-	Hartlepool; Raby Rd	30
-	Hartlepool; Throston Grange La	30
-	Hartlepool; Winterbottom Ave	30
-	Hartlepool; Wynyard Rd	30
-	Middlesbrough; Ormesby Rd	30
-	Normanby; Bankfields Rd	30
-	Normanby; Flatts La	30
-	Redcar; Broadway, Dormanstown	30
-	Redcar; Greenstones Rd	30
-	Redcar; Redcar Rd	30
-	Redcar; West Dyke Rd	30
-	Stanghow; Stanghow Rd	30
-	Stockton-on-Tees; Bishopton Rd West	30
-	Stockton-on-Tees; Darlington La	30
-	Stockton-on-Tees; Harrowgate La	30
-	Thornaby-on-Tees; Cunningham Ave	30
-	Thornaby-on-Tees; Thornaby Rd	30

Cumbria

Cumbria Safety Cameras no longer publish the locations of mobile safety camera sites and are developing new sites.

Road number	Location	Speed limit (mph)
M6	Jct 36 to 40	70
A6	London Rd, Carlisle	30
A6	Garnett Bridge north to Hollowgate	60
A6	Milnthorpe Rd, Kendal	30
A6	Shap Rd, Kendal	30
A6	Scotland Rd, Penrith	30
A6	Thiefside (south of High Hesket)	60
A7	Westlinton crossroads	60
A65	Burton Rd/Lound Rd/Kendal Lound Rd/ Oxenholme Rd, Kendal	30
A65	Devil's Bridge, Kirkby Lonsdale	40
A65	Hollin Hall to Hornsbarrow, Kirkby Lonsdale (north-west of town)	60
A66	Brough Hill, Warcop	60
A66	Brigham/Broughton to Bridgefoot	60
A66	Crackenthorpe	60
A66	Dubwath/Bassenthwaite Lake	60
A66	Sandford (either side of B6259 jct)	60
A66	Troutbeck (either side of A5091 jct)	60
A69	Aglionby (west of Warwick, single carr)	60
A69	Scarrow Hill (near Lanercost)	60
A74	Floriston (Todhills to River Esk)	70
A590	Bouth road ends (north of A5092 jct)	60
A590	Haverthwaite/Backbarrow	60
A590	Levens (A6 jct to west of A5074 jct)	70
A590	Newland, Ulverston	60
A592	Rayrigg Rd, Bowness	30/40
A595	Wigton Rd, Carlisle	30
A595	Greenhill Hotel, Red Dial	60
A595	West Woodside/Curthwaite jct	60
A595	Loop Rd, Whitehaven	40
A595	Wreaks End, Broughton-in-Furness	60
A596	Micklethwaite	60
A683	Cautley to Middleton	60
A685	Appleby Rd, Kendal	30
A686	Penrith to Gilderdale Forest	60
A5087	Ulverston	30
A6071	Smallstown Farm (near Longtown)	n/a
B5277	Lindale Rd, Grange-over-Sands	30
B5299	Dalston Rd, Carlisle	40
B5305	Sowerby Row	n/a
-	Barrow-in-Furness; Abbey Rd	30
-	Barrow-in-Furness; Michelson Rd	30
-	Carlisle; Blackwell Rd/Durdar Rd	30

Derbyshire

Road number	Location	Speed limit (mph)
A6	Duffield Rd, Allestree, Derby	30
A6	Allestree to Duffield	50
A6	Duffield	30/40
A6	Milford to Belper	40
A6	Belper	30
A6	Belper to Ambergate	50
A6	north of Crich to Cromford	50
A6	Cromford	40
A6	Matlock Bath	30
A6	Matlock Bath to Matlock	40
A6	Matlock (town centre)	30
A6	Dimple, Matlock	40
A6	Northwood	40
A6	Rowsley to Bakewell	50
A6	Bakewell	30
A6	Ashford in the Water	50
A6	Taddington to Buxton	50
A6	Buxton	30
A6	Buxton to Dove Holes	50
A6	Dove Holes	30
A6	Dove Holes to Chapel-en-le-Frith Bypass	50
A6	Furness Vale	40
A6	Furness Vale to Newtown	40
A6	London Rd, Derby (A5111 to Ascot Dr)	30
A52	Ashbourne Rd, Derby	30
A52	Mackworth, Derby	40
A52	east of Brailsford	50
A52	Shirley Hollow (5km south-east of Ashbourne)	50
A57	Snake Rd (at Ladybower Resr)	60
A514	Swadlincote (Darklands Rd to A511)	30
A514	Swadlincote to Hartshorne	40
A514	Hartshorne	30
A514	Ticknall	30
A514	Stanton by Bridge	40
A515	Alsop en le Dale	60
A515	north of A50 jct (for 2.5km)	50
A516	Uttoxeter New Rd, Derby	30/40
A601	Abbey St, Derby	30
A608	Smalley	30
A609	Kilburn to Horsley Woodhouse	30
A609	Stanley Common	40
A610	Bullbridge/Ridgeway to B6013	40
A610	Codnor	30
A615	Matlock Green, Matlock	30
A615	Tansley	30
A615	Tansley to Wessington	60
A616	Clowne	30
A616	Cresswell	30
A617	Bramley Vale (1km east of M1 jct 29)	40
A617	Glapwell to Pleasley	NSL
A619	west of Wadshelf	60
A623	Calver	40
A623	Stoney Middleton	30
A623	Stoney Middleton to Peak Forest	NSL
A623	Peak Forest	40
A623	Peak Forest to A6 jct	NSL
A624	Glossop (A57 to A6106)	30
A624	Chunal to Little Hayfield	50
A624	Hayfield to Chinley	50
A628	Tintwistle to county bdy	NSL
A632	Station Rd, Bolsover	30
A632	Hady to Calow (east of Chesterfield)	40
A632	Matlock	30
A5111	Warwick Ave, Derby	40
A6005	Draycott to Breaston	40
A6005	Breaston to Long Eaton (B6002 jct)	40
A6007	Codnor to Heanor	30
A6175	Holmewood	30
A6175	North Wingfield	30
B600	Somercotes	30
B5010	London Rd, Shardlow	30
B5010	Shardlow to Thulston (A6 jct)	60
B5020	Station Rd, Mickleover	30
B5353	Park Rd, Newhall, Swadlincote	30
B6051	Newbold Rd, Chesterfield (town centre to B6150)	30
B6052	Old Whittington, Chesterfield	30
B6057	Sheffield Rd, Stonegravels, Chesterfield	30
B6062	Buxton Rd, Chinley	30
B6179	Little Eaton	30
B6179	Little Eaton to Lower Kilburn	50
B6179	Lower Kilburn	40
B6179	Denby	40
B6179	Marehay to Ripley	30
-	Charlesworth; Long La	30
-	Chesterfield; Boythorpe Rd	30
-	Chesterfield; Old Rd	30
-	Derby; Shardlow Rd, Alvaston	30/40
-	Derby; Blagreaves La	30
-	Derby; Burton Rd, Littleover (Hillsway to A5111)	30
-	Derby; Kedleston Rd (A6 to A38)	30
-	Derby; London Rd (Litchurch La to A6)	30
-	Derby; Stenson Rd, Normanton (Village St to Sunnyhill Ave)	30
-	Derby; Stenson Rd, Stenson Fields (Wragley Way to Grampian Way)	40
-	Swadlincote; Hearthcote Rd	30

Devon and Cornwall

Road number	Location	Speed limit (mph)
A30	Chiverton Cross (A390/A3075 jct)	60
A30	Highgate	70
A30	Highgate Hill (A39 jct at Indian Queens)	70
A30	Monkton	40
A30	Sowton, Exeter	40
A30	Temple	60
A38	Lee Mill	70
A38	near Lower Clicker (B3251 jct, south-east of Liskeard)	70
A38	Deep Lane jct, Plympton	70
A38	Smithaleigh (4km west of Ivybridge)	70
A38	Smithaleigh (overbridge) (4km west of Ivybridge)	70
A38	Wrangaton-Bittaford straight	70
A39	Barras Moor (near Perranarworthal)	60
A39	Valley Truckle, Camelford	30
A39	Perranarworthal	40
A361	Ashford	50
A361	Eastern Ave, Barnstaple	30
A361	Knowle	40
A361	Knowle (Westerland)	30
A361	Wrafton	30
A374	Plymouth Rd, Plymouth	40
A374	Antony Rd, Torpoint	30
A376	Ebford	30
A376	Exeter Rd, Exmouth	30
A377	Copplestone	30
A377	Western Rd, Crediton	30
A377	Alphington Rd, Exeter	30
A379	Brixton	30
A379	Dartmouth Rd, Paignton	30
A379	Starcross	30
A379	Teignmouth Rd, Teignmouth	30
A379	Babbacombe Rd, Torquay	30

Road number	Location	Speed limit (mph)
A379	Yealmpton	30
A380	Newton Rd, Kingskerswell	40
A381	East St, Newton Abbot	30
A385	Totnes Rd, Collaton St Mary	30
A385	Ashburton Rd, Totnes	30
A386	Chub Tor (2km south of Yelverton)	60
A386	Outland Rd, Plymouth	30
A386	Roborough Down, Plymouth	60
A386	Tavistock Rd, Plymouth	40
A388	Kelly Bray (north of Callington)	30
A390	Penstraze (1.5km east of A30)	60
A390	Sticker Bypass	60
A394	Kenneggy Downs (near Praa Sands)	40
A396	Rewe	30
A396	Exeter Rd, Stoke Canon	30
A3015	Topsham Rd, Exeter	30
A3047	Trevenson Rd, Pool, Camborne	30
A3047	Tuckingmill, Camborne	30
A3058	Trewoon, St Austell	30
A3064	St Budeaux Bypass, Plymouth	30
A3074	Carbis Bay, St Ives	30
A3075	Rosecliston, near Newquay	60
B3165	Crewkerne Rd, Raymonds Hill (near A35)	30
B3174	Barrack Rd, Ottery St Mary	30
B3183	Heavitree Rd, Exeter	30
B3183	New North Rd, Exeter	30
B3212	Dunsford Rd, Exeter	30
B3212	Pinhoe Rd, Exeter	30
B3213	Wrangaton village	30
B3233	Bickington Rd, Barnstaple	30
B3250	North Hill, Plymouth	30
B3284	Liskey, Perranporth	30/60
B3344	Station Hill, Chudleigh	30
B3396	Milehouse Rd, Plymouth	30
B3416	Glen Rd, Plympton	30
B3432	Novorossisk Rd, Plymouth	40
-	Avonwick village	30
-	Castle-an-Dinas (4km east of St Columb Major)	60
-	Exeter; Buddle La	30
-	Exeter; Exwick La	30
-	Fraddon village	30
-	Ivybridge; Exeter Rd	30
-	Paignton; Colley End Rd	30
-	Paignton; Preston Down Rd	30
-	Plymouth; Beacon Park Rd	30
-	Plymouth; Church Hill, Eggbuckland	30
-	Plymouth; Devonport Rd, Stoke	30
-	Plymouth; Eggbuckland Rd	30
-	Plymouth; Glen Rd	30
-	Plymouth; Grenville Rd, St Judes	30
-	Plymouth; Haye Rd, Elburton	30
-	Plymouth; Honicknowle La	30
-	Plymouth; Lipson Rd	30
-	Plymouth; Mannamead Rd	30
-	Plymouth; Molesworth Rd	30
-	Plymouth; North Prospect Rd	30
-	Plymouth; Pomphlett Rd	30
-	Plymouth; Shakespeare Rd, Honicknowle	30
-	Plymouth; Southway Dr	30
-	Plymouth; St Levan Rd	30
-	Plymouth; Tamerton Foliot Rd	30
-	Plymouth; Union St	30
-	Plymouth; Weston Park Rd	30
-	Plymouth; Wolseley Rd	30
-	Saltash; Callington Rd	30

Dorset

Road number	Location	Speed limit (mph)
A30	Babylon Hill (1.5 km east of Yeovil)	70
A30	Long Cross, Shaftesbury	40
A31	Winterbourne Zelston	40
A35	Sea Rd South, Bridport	50
A35	Christchurch Bypass	70
A35	Lyndhurst Rd, Christchurch (near A337 jct)	60
A35	Friary Press, west of Dorchester	60
A35	Kingston Russell	60
A35	Baker's Arms Roundabout, Lytchett Minster, to roundabout with A350	70
A35	Upton Rd, Poole	30
A35	near Sherford/Slepe	60
A35	Vinney Cross (near Uploders)	60
A35	Whiteway Cross (2.5km west of Kingston Russell)	60
A37	Long Ash La, Frampton	60
A37	Holywell Cross, Holywell	60
A37	Staggs Folly (near Chalmington)	60
A338	Spur Rd (north of Hurn)	70
A338	Wessex Way, Bournemouth (near A3060 jct)	50
A348	Ringwood Rd, Bear Cross, Bournemouth (near A341 jct)	40
A349	Gravel Hill, Poole	40
A350	Holes Bay Rd, Poole	50
A350	Poole Rd (A31 to A35)	60
A350	Shaston Rd, Stourpaine	30
A350	Upton Country Park (east of Upton)	70
A352	Dorchester Rd, Wool	30
A354	Dorchester Rd, Ridgeway Hill (3km south of A35)	60
A354	Dorchester Rd, Upwey	30
A354	Dorchester Rd (Manor Roundabout to Weymouth Hospital)	30
A354	Dorchester Rd, Redlands, Weymouth	40
A354	Buxton Rd, Weymouth	30
A354	Winterbourne Whitechurch	30
B3065	Pinecliff Rd, Poole	30
B3065	The Avenue, Poole	30
B3073	Christchurch Rd, West Parley	30
B3073	Oakley Hill, Wimborne Minster	30
B3074	Higher Blandford Rd, Broadstone, Poole	30
B3081	Ringwood Rd, Ebblake, Verwood	30
B3082	Blandford Rd (near Badbury Rings)	60
B3092	Colesbrook, Gillingham	40
B3157	Portesham	30
B3157	Limekiln Hill, West Bexington (east of Clay La)	50
B3157	Chickerell Rd, Weymouth	30
B3157	Lanehouse Rocks Rd, Weymouth	30
B3369	Sandbanks Rd, Poole	30
B3369	Shore Rd, Poole	30
-	Blandford Forum; Salisbury Rd	30
-	Bournemouth; Branksome Wood Rd	30
-	Bournemouth; Carbery Ave	30
-	Bournemouth; Littledown Ave	30
-	Bournemouth; Southbourne Overcliff Dr	30
-	Ferndown; Wimborne Rd East, Stapehill	40
-	Poole; Constitution Hill Rd	30
-	Poole; Old Wareham Rd	30
-	Portland; Weston Rd	30
-	Upton; Poole Rd	30

Durham Constabulary area

Road number	Location	Speed limit (mph)
A66	Bowes Moor/Galley Bank/Greta Bridge	n/a
A167	North Rd, Darlington	n/a
A167	Durham (Merryoaks to Sniperley)	n/a
A690	Willington	n/a
A690	West Rainton, Durham	n/a
A693	Chester Rd, Stanley	n/a
A1086	Horden to Blackhall	n/a
B6168	Annfield Plain (to A692 jct)	n/a
B6280	Yarm Rd, Darlington	n/a
B6282	Woodhouse La, Bishop Auckland	n/a
B6284	Etherley La, Bishop Auckland	n/a
-	Darlington; McMullen Rd	n/a
-	Durham; Finchale Rd/Pit La	n/a
-	Peterlee; Essington Way	n/a

Essex

Road number	Location	Speed limit (mph)
A12	Overbridge, near Kelvedon interchange	70
A13	High St, Hadleigh (towards London)	30
A13	North Shoebury	n/a
A13	Ness Rd, Shoeburyness	30
A13	Bournes Green Chase, Southend-on-Sea	n/a
A13	Southchurch Blvd, Southend-on-Sea	n/a
A113	High Rd, Chigwell	30
A120	Harwich Rd, (Wix Arch Cottages to Cansey La, Goose Green)	n/a
A120	Horsley Cross (south-west to Park Rd)	n/a
A121	Goldings Hill, Loughton (at Monkchester Cl)	30
A121	High Rd, Loughton	30
A123	Fenpiece Rd, Grange Hill	30
A126	London Rd, Grays	30
A126	Montreal Rd, Tilbury	30
A128	High St, Chipping Ongar	30
A128	Brentwood Rd, Ingrave/Herongate	30
A128	Ongar Rd, Kelvedon Hatch	40
A129	Crays Hill, Basildon	30
A129	Southend Rd, Billericay	30
A129	London Rd, Rayleigh	30
A129	London Rd, Wickford	30
A129	Southend Rd, Wickford	30
A130	Long Rd, Canvey Island	30
A130	Canvey Way, South Benfleet	60
A131	Bournebridge Hill (near Halstead)	n/a
A133	Clacton Rd, Elmstead Market	30
A133	Colchester Rd (near Weeley)	n/a
A134	Nayland Rd, Great Horkesley	40
A137	Wignall St, Lawford	30
A414	Malden Rd, Danbury	30
A1016	Waterhouse La, Chelmsford	30
A1023	London Rd, Brentwood	30
A1023	Shenfield Rd/Chelmsford Rd, Brentwood	30
A1025	Second Ave, Harlow	40
A1025	Third Ave, Harlow	40
A1060	Lower Rd, Little Hallingbury	30
A1090	London Rd, Purfleet	30
A1090	Tank Hill Rd, Purfleet	30
A1124	Lexden Rd, Colchester	30
A1124	Hedingham Rd, Halstead	n/a
A1158	Southbourne Grove, Westcliff-on-Sea, Southend-on-Sea	30
A1168	Rectory La, Loughton	30
A1169	Southern Way, Harlow	40
A1232	Ipswich Rd, Colchester	30
A1235	Cranes Farm Rd, Basildon (at Honywood Rd)	40
B170	Chigwell Rise, Chigwell	30
B170	Roding La, Loughton	n/a
B172	Coppice Row, Theydon Bois	30
B173	Lambourne Rd, Chigwell	30
B184	Snow Hill, Great Easton	40
B186	South Rd, South Ockendon	30
B1002	High St, Ingatestone	30
B1007	Laindon Rd/High St/Stock Rd, Billericay	30
B1007	Galleywood Rd/Stock Rd, Chelmsford	n/a
B1008	Broomfield Rd, Chelmsford	30
B1013	Main Rd, Hawkwell	30
B1013	High Rd, Hockley	30
B1013	Southend Rd, Hockley/Hawkwell	30
B1013	High Rd, Rayleigh	30
B1014	Benfleet Rd, South Benfleet	30
B1016	Ness Rd, Shoeburyness	30
B1018	The Street, Latchingdon	30
B1018	The Causeway, Maldon	30
B1019	Maldon Rd, Hatfield Peveral	30
B1021	Church Rd, Burnham-on-Crouch	30
B1022	Maldon Rd, Colchester	30
B1022	Shrub End Rd, Colchester	30
B1022	Maldon Rd, Heckfordbridge	30
B1022	Colchester Rd, Maldon	30
B1027	St Osyth Rd, Alresford	40
B1027	St John's Rd, Clacton-on-Sea	30
B1027	Valley Rd/Old Rd, Clacton-on-Sea	30
B1027	Pump Hill, St Osyth	30
B1027	Brightlingsea Rd, (near Wivenhoe)	40
B1028	Colchester Rd, Wivenhoe	30
B1028	The Avenue, Wivenhoe	30
B1033	Frinton Rd, Kirby Cross	30
B1335	Stifford Rd, South Ockendon	30
B1352	Main Rd, Harwich	n/a
B1383	London Rd, Newport	30
B1383	Cambridge Rd, Stansted Mountfitchet	30
B1389	Hatfield Rd, Witham	30
B1393	High Rd, Epping	30
B1393	Palmers Hill, Epping	30
B1441	London Rd, Clacton-on-Sea	30
B1441	Clacton Rd, Weeley Heath	n/a
B1442	Thorpe Rd, Clacton-on-Sea	30
B1464	Clay Hill Rd, Basildon	30
B1464	London Rd, Bowers Gifford	30
-	Aveley; Purfleet Rd	30
-	Basildon; Ashlyns	30
-	Basildon; Clay Hill Rd	30
-	Basildon; Felmores	30
-	Basildon; Rectory Rd, Pitsea	30
-	Basildon; Sandon Rd, Barstable	30
-	Basildon; Vange Hill Dr	30
-	Basildon; Wash Rd, Laindon	30
-	Basildon; Whitmore Way	30
-	Basildon; Wickford Ave	30
-	Billericay; Mountnessing Rd	30
-	Braintree; Coldnailhurst Ave (Alexander Rd towards Church La)	30
-	Brentwood; Eagle Way (Clive Rd to Warley Rd)	30
-	Buckhurst Hill; Buckhurst Way/Albert Rd	30
-	Canvey Island; Dovervelt Rd	30
-	Canvey Island; Link Rd	30
-	Canvey Island; Thorney Bay Rd	30
-	Chadwell St Mary; Brentwood Rd	30
-	Chadwell St Mary; Linford Rd	30
-	Chadwell St Mary; River View	30
-	Chelmsford; Baddow Rd	30
-	Chelmsford; Chignall Rd	30
-	Chelmsford; Copperfield Rd	30
-	Chelmsford; Longstomps Ave	30
-	Chelmsford; New Bowers Way, Springfield	30
-	Clacton-on-Sea; Burrs Rd	30
-	Clacton-on-Sea; Kings Parade	30
-	Clacton-on-Sea; Marine Parade East	30
-	Clacton-on-Sea; St Osyth Rd, Rush Green	n/a
-	Colchester; Abbot's Rd	30
-	Colchester; Avon Way	30
-	Colchester; Bromley Rd	30
-	Colchester; Old Heath Rd	30
-	Daws Heath; Daws Heath Rd	30
-	Grays; Blackshots La	30
-	Grays; Lodge La	30
-	Harlow; Abercrombie Way (towards Southern Way)	40
-	Harlow; Howard Way	40
-	Hawkwell; Rectory Rd	30
-	Hullbridge; Coventry Hill	30
-	Leigh-on-Sea; Belton Way East (Marine Parade to Belton Gdns)	30
-	Leigh-on-Sea; Belton Way West	30
-	Leigh-on-Sea; Blenheim Chase	30
-	Leigh-on-Sea; Grand Parade/Cliff Parade	30
-	Leigh-on-Sea; Hadleigh Rd	30
-	Leigh-on-Sea; Highlands Blvd	30
-	Leigh-on-Sea; Manchester Dr	30
-	Leigh-on-Sea; Mountdale Gdns	30
-	Leigh-on-Sea; Western Rd	30
-	Loughton; Alderton Hill	30
-	Loughton; Loughton Way	30
-	Loughton; Valley Hill	30
-	Maldon; Fambridge Rd	30
-	Maldon; Holloway Rd	30
-	Maldon; Mundon Rd	30
-	North Benfleet; Pound Lane	n/a
-	Rayleigh; Bull La	30
-	Rayleigh; Down Hall Rd	30
-	Rayleigh; Trinity Rd (near Church Rd)	30
-	Rochford; Ashingdon Rd	30
-	Southend-on-Sea; Barnstaple Rd, Thorpe Bay	30
-	Southend-on-Sea; Bournemouth Park Rd	n/a
-	Southend-on-Sea; Chalkwell Ave, Westcliff-on-Sea	30
-	Southend-on-Sea; Green La (at Kendal Way), Eastwood	30
-	Southend-on-Sea; Hamstel Rd	30
-	Southend-on-Sea; Kenilworth Gdns, Prittlewell	30
-	Southend-on-Sea; Kings Rd, Westcliff-on-Sea	30
-	Southend-on-Sea; Lifstan Way	30
-	Southend-on-Sea; Prittlewell Chase, Prittlewell	30
-	Southend-on-Sea; Thorpe Hall Ave, Thorpe Bay	30
-	Southend-on-Sea; Western Approaches (at Rockall), Eastwood	30
-	Southend-on-Sea; Western Esplanade	30
-	South Woodham Ferrers; Hullbridge Rd	30
-	South Woodham Ferrers; Inchbonnie Rd	30
-	Stanford le Hope; London Rd	30
-	Stanford le Hope; Southend Rd, Corringham	30
-	Stanford le Hope; Springhouse Rd, Corringham	30
-	Theydon Bois; Piercing Hill	30
-	Waltham Abbey; Farm Hill Rd	30
-	Waltham Abbey; Paternoster Hill	30
-	Waltham Abbey; Sewardstone Rd	30
-	West Thurrock; London Road West Thurrock	30
-	Witham; Powers Hall End	30

Gloucestershire

Road number	Location	Speed limit (mph)
A38	Twigworth	40
A40	Andoversford (between A436 jcts)	60
A40	Gloucester Rd, St Marks, Cheltenham	40
A40	Churcham	50
A40	Farmington	60
A40	Hampnett	60
A40	Hazleton	60
A40	Little Barrington	60
A40	Northleach	60
A40	Whittington	60
A46	Ashchurch	30
A46	north of Nailsworth	40
A48	Stroat	60
A417	Burford Junction, Cirencester (north of A429 jct)	70
A417	Gloucester Rd, Corse	30
A417	Dartley Bottom (north-west of Cirencester)	70
A417	Lechlade on Thames	40
A417	Maisemore	30
A417	north of Hartpury	40
A419	Oldends La to Stonehouse Court, Stonehouse	40
A429	south-west of Bourton-on-the-Water	60
A429	Fossebridge	40
A430	Hempstead Bypass, Gloucester	40
A435	Colesbourne	60
A436	at jct with B4068	60
A4013	Princess Elizabeth Way, Arle, Cheltenham	30
A4013	Princess Elizabeth Way, Hester's Way, Cheltenham	30
A4019	Uckington	50
A4136	Brierley	40
A4136	Lower La, Coleford	40
A4136	Harrow Hill (near Nailbridge)	40
A4136	Little London	40
A4151	Steam Mills (north of Cinderford)	40
A4173	near St Peter's School, Tuffley, Gloucester	30
B4008	Bristol Rd, Olympus Park area, Quedgeley	30
B4008	Bristol Rd, Quedgeley (south of Tesco roundabout)	30
B4008	Gloucester Rd, Stonehouse	30
B4060	Kingswood (near B4058 jct)	30
B4215	south-east of Rudford	50
B4215	south of Newent Bypass	50
B4221	Kilcot Village	40
B4221	Picklenash School, Newent	30
B4226	Speech House (Forest of Dean)	60
B4228	Old Station Way, Coleford	30
B4228	Perrygrove, south of Coleford	40
B4231	Coleford Rd, Bream	30
B4633	Gloucester Rd, Cheltenham (near train station)	30
-	Cheltenham; St Georges Rd	30
-	Cheltenham; Swindon La	30
-	Cheltenham; Wyman's Lane	30
-	Cirencester; Chesterton La	30
-	Gloucester; Abbeymead Ave	30
-	Gloucester; Barrow Hill; Churchdown	30
-	Lydney; Highfield Rd	30
-	Minchinhampton Common	40
-	Parkend; Fancy Rd	30
-	Siddington	30
-	Tewkesbury; Gloucester Rd	40

Greater Manchester

Greater Manchester Casualty Reduction Partnership no longer make mobile safety camera sites freely available and are developing new sites.

Road number	Location	Speed limit (mph)
A6	Buxton Rd, Hazel Grove	30
A6	Buxton Rd, High Lane	30
A6	Stockport Rd, Manchester	30
A6	Wellington Rd North, Stockport	30
A6	Manchester Rd, Swinton	30
A34	Kingsway, Cheadle	40
A34	Birchfields Rd, Rusholme, Manchester	30
A34	Kingsway, Didsbury, Manchester	40
A49	Wigan Rd, Standish	30
A49	Warrington Rd, Marus Bridge, Wigan	30
A56	Jubilee Way, Bury	30
A56	Manchester Rd, Bury	30
A56	Walmersley Rd, Bury	30
A56	Bury New Rd, Manchester	30
A56	Chester Rd, Old Trafford (at White City Way)	30
A56	Bury New Rd, Prestwich	30
A56	Whalley Rd, Shuttleworth	30
A56	Manchester Rd, Whitefield	30
A57	Liverpool Rd, Eccles	30
A57	Manchester Rd, Hyde	30
A57	Mottram Rd, Hyde	30
A57	Hyde Rd/Manchester Rd, Manchester	30
A58	Lily La, Bamfurlong, Abram	30
A58	Liverpool Rd, Ashton-In-Makerfield	30
A58	Bury Rd, Bolton	30
A58	Wigan Rd, Deane, Bolton	30
A58	Wigan Rd, Hunger Hill, Bolton	40
A58	Angouleme Way, Bury	30
A58	Bolton Rd, Bury	30
A58	Rochdale Rd, Bury	30
A58	Bury and Bolton Rd, Radcliffe	40
A58	Halifax Rd, Rochdale	30
A62	Oldham Rd, Failsworth	30
A62	Oldham Rd, Manchester	30
A62	Manchester Rd, Werneth, Oldham	30
A62	Oldham Way, Oldham	40
A560	Shaftesbury Avenue,Timperley, Altrincham	40
A560	Mottram Old Rd, Hyde	30
A560	Crookilley Way, Stockport	50
A560	Wood St, Stockport	30
A571	Pemberton Rd, Winstanley, Wigan	30
A571	Victoria St, Newtown, Wigan	30
A572	Chaddock La, Astley, Tyldesley	30
A572	Newton Rd, Lowton (near Leigh)	30/40
A573	Wigan Rd, Golborne	30
A574	Warrington Rd, Leigh	30
A575	Walkden Rd, Worsley	30
A576	Middleton Rd, Crumpsall	30
A579	Atherleigh Way, Leigh	50
A580	East Lancashire Rd, Leigh	70
A580	East Lancashire Rd, Swinton/Worsley	50
A626	Marple Rd, Offerton, Stockport	30
A627	Oldham Rd, Ashton-under-Lyne	30
A627	Ashton Rd, Oldham	30
A627	Chadderton Way, Oldham	40
A635	Mancunian Way, Ardwick, Manchester	40
A635	Ashton Old Rd, Openshaw, Manchester	30
A635/ A6018	Stamford St, Stalybridge	30
A662	Ashton New Rd, Manchester	30
A663	Broadway, Failsworth	40
A664	Rochdale Rd, Manchester	30
A664	Manchester Rd, Castleton, Rochdale	30
A665	Bury Old Rd, Prestwich	30
A665	Cheetham Hill Rd, Manchester	30
A665	Water St/Blackburn St/Pilkington Way, Radcliffe	30
A665	New Rd, Radcliffe	30
A665	Higher La, Whitefield	30
A665	Radcliffe New Rd, Whitefield	30
A666	Blackburn Rd, Bolton	30
A666	St Peter's Way, Bolton	50
A666	Manchester Rd, Swinton	30
A667	Ringley Rd West, Whitefield	30
A670	Mossley Rd, Ashton-under-Lyne	30
A673	Chorley New Rd, Bolton	40
A676	Bolton Rd, Hawkshaw	30
A676	Bolton Rd West, Holcombe Brook, Ramsbottom	30
A676	Stubbins La, Ramsbottom	30
A680	Edenfield Rd, Rochdale	30
A5014	Talbot Rd, Stretford	30
A5079	Slade La, Levenshulme, Manchester	30
A5103	Princess Pkwy (M60 to M56)	40/50
A5103	Princess Rd, Manchester	30/40
A5106	Chorley Rd, Standish	30
A5143	Bridge La, Bramhall	30
A5143	Jacksons La, Hazel Grove	30
A5145	Edge La, Stretford	30
A5181	Mosley Rd, Trafford Park	30
A5209	Crow Orchard Rd, Shevington Moor	30
A5209	Almond Brook Rd, Standish	30
A6010	Alan Turing Way, Manchester	30
A6010	Pottery La, Manchester	30
A6017	Ashton Rd, Bredbury, Stockport	40
A6018	Mottram Rd, Stalybridge	30
A6033	Todmorden Rd, Littleborough	30
A6044	Hilton La, Prestwich	30
A6044	Sheepfoot La, Prestwich	30
A6045	Manchester Rd, Heywood	30
A6045	Heywood Old Rd, Middleton	30
A6046	Hollin La, Middleton	30
A6053	Dumers La, Radcliffe	30
A6104	Victoria Ave, Blackley, Manchester	30
A6144	Warburton La, Partington	30
A6144	Harboro Rd, Sale	30
A6144	Old Hall Rd, Sale Moor	30
A6145	Hulton La, Bolton	30
B5158	Lostock Rd, Urmston	30
B5160	Park Rd, Bowdon	30
B5165	Park Rd, Timperley, Altrincham	30
B5166	Ashton La, Ashton upon Mersey	30
B5166	Styal Rd, Heald Green, Gatley	30
B5206	Upholland Rd, Billinge	30
B5213	Church Rd, Flixton, Urmston	30
B5217	Seymour Grove, Old Trafford	30
B5218	Upper Chorlton Rd, Chorlton cum Hardy	30
B5237	Bickershaw La, Bickershaw, Abram	30
B5238	Scot La, Aspull	30
B5239	Bolton Rd, Aspull	30
B5239	Haigh Rd, Aspull	30
B5239	Dicconson La, Cooper Turning, Bolton	30
B5375	Miles La, Shevington	30
B5397	Dane Rd, Sale	30
B6101	Strines Rd, Marple	30
B6167	Gorton Rd, Reddish	30
B6177	Stamford Rd, Mossley	30
B6194	Abbey Hills Rd, Oldham	30
B6194	Broad La, Rochdale	30
B6196	Ainsworth Rd, Bury	30
B6196	Church St, Ainsworth, Bury	30
B6196	Cockey Moor Rd, Ainsworth, Bury	30
B6196	Hardy Mill Rd, Harwood, Bolton	30
B6199	Plodder La, Farnworth	30
B6213	Bury Rd, Tottington	30
B6213	Turton Rd, Tottington	30
B6214	Brandlesholme Rd, Bury	30
B6214	Helmshore Rd, Holcombe, Ramsbottom	30
B6214	Longsight Rd, Holcombe Brook, Ramsbottom	30

Road number	Location	Speed limit (mph)
B6215	Brandlesholme Rd, Greenmount, Ramsbottom	30
B6222	Bury Rd, Rochdale	30
B6225	Milnrow Rd, Littleborough	30
B6225	Wildhouse La, Milnrow	50
B6226	Chorley Old Rd, Bolton	30
B6226	Chorley Old Rd, Horwich	30
B6292	Ainsworth Rd, Radcliffe	30
B6292	Starling Rd, Radcliffe	30
B6377	Shawclough Rd, Rochdale	30
-	Bolton; Stitch-Mi-La	30
-	Bolton; Tottington Rd, Harwood	30
-	Bury; Croft La, Hollins	30
-	Bury; Radcliffe Rd	30
-	Bury; Walshaw Rd	30
-	Cheadle; Bird Hall La	30
-	Cheadle; Councillor La	30
-	Cheadle; Schools Hill	30
-	Cheadle Hulme; Carr Wood Rd	30
-	Hazel Grove; Chester Rd	30
-	Heywood; Bury Old Rd	30
-	Heywood; Queens Park Rd	30
-	Horwich; Lever Park Ave	30
-	Leigh; Queensway	30
-	Manchester; Blackley New Rd, Crumpsall	30
-	Manchester; Hazelbottom Rd/Waterloo St, Crumpsall	30
-	Mellor; Longhurst La	30
-	Pendlebury; Langley Rd	30
-	Radcliffe; Stand La	30
-	Rochdale; Bagslate Moor Rd	30
-	Rochdale; Caldershaw Rd	30
-	Rochdale; Smithybridge Rd, Smithy Bridge	30
-	Romiley; Sandy La	30
-	Sale; Glebelands Rd	30
-	Sale; Hope Rd	30
-	Sale; Norris Rd	30
-	Salford; Belvedere Rd	30
-	Stockport; Dialstone La, Offerton	30
-	Stockport; Harrytown, Bredbury	30
-	Stretford; Kings Rd	30
-	Trafford Park; Westinghouse Rd	30
-	Westhoughton; The Hoskers	30

Hampshire and the Isle of Wight

Road number	Location	Speed limit (mph)
A27	Portchester to Titchfield	30/40
A27	Parkgate to A3024	30/40
A30	Blackwater	30/40
A30	Hook	30/40
A33	Riseley to Basingstoke	50
A33	Millbrook Rd, Southampton	50
A33	The Avenue, Southampton	30
A325	Farnborough/Aldershot, Hawley La (B3272) to Cranmore La (B3008)	30/40/60/70
A325	Whitehill to county boundary near Farnham	30/40/60
A334	Wickham, A32 to B2177	n/a
A335	Eastleigh	30/40
A337	Lymington Rd/Christchurch Rd, New Milton	30/40
A337	Pennington, Lymington to Balmerlawn, Brockenhurst	30/40/50/60
A338	Fordingbridge to county boundary	40/60
A338	Ringwood to Ibsley	40/60
A339	Lasham	60
A340	Pamber End to Tadley	30/60
A2047	Fratton Rd, Portsmouth	30
A3020	Blackwater (IOW)	n/a
A3020	Blackwater Rd, Newport (IOW)	40
A3021	York Ave, East Cowes (IOW)	30
A3024	Bursledon Rd, Southampton	30/40
A3024	Northam Rd/Bitterne Rd West, Southampton	30
A3054	Binstead Hill, Binstead (IOW)	30
A3054	Fairlee Rd, Newport (IOW)	30/40
A3054	High St/Lushington Hill, Wootton Bridge (IOW)	30/40
A3055	High St/New Rd, Brading (IOW)	30
A3056	Blackwater (IOW)	n/a
B2149	New Rd, Havant	30
B2149	Petersfield Rd, Havant	40
B2177	A334 to Winchester Rd, Bishop's Waltham	30/40/60
B3037	Fair Oak to Eastleigh	30/40
B3055	Brockenhurst to A35	30/40
B3272	Yateley	30/40
B3321	Victoria Gr, East Cowes (IOW)	30
B3323	Carisbrooke Rd, Newport (IOW)	30
B3395	Sandown to Yaverland (IOW)	30
-	Basingstoke; Tobago Close	30
-	East Cowes; Adelaide Gr (IOW)	30
-	Gosport; Grange Rd	40
-	Newport; Long La (IOW)	30
-	Newport; Staplers Rd (IOW)	30
-	Portsmouth; Clarence Esplanade	30

Hertfordshire

Road number	Location	Speed limit (mph)
A119	North Rd, Hertford (at St Josephs School)	30
A409	Heathbourne Road, Bushey (at Bupa Hospital)	30
A411	London Rd, Bushey (east of Grange Rd)	30
A411	Barnet La, Elstree (at Edgwarebury La)	30
A411	Hempstead Rd, Watford (at Glen Way)	30
A414	St Albans Rd, Hemel Hempstead (at Longlands)	40
A414	St Albans Rd, Hemel Hempstead (near Rant Meadow)	40
A414	Hertingfordbury Rd, Hertford (at Valeside)	40
A505	Cambridge Rd, Hitchin (100m south-west of Queenswood Dr)	30
A505	Royston Rd, Baldock (at Slip End Farm)	70
A600	Bedford Rd, Hitchin (at Times Close)	30
A600	Bedford Rd, Hitchin (75m south of north jct of Wellingham Ave)	30
A602	Stevenage Rd, Hitchin	40
A602	Broadhall Way, Stevenage (A1072 to Shephalbury Park)	40
A602	Monkswood Way, Stevenage (100m north of Broadhall Way)	40
A1000	Barnet Rd, Ganwick Corner, Potters Bar (at Wagon Rd)	40
A1057	Hatfield Rd, St Albans (near Beechwood Ave)	30
A1057	St Albans Rd West, Hatfield (near Poplar Ave)	40
A1170	High Rd Wormley, Wormley	30
A4125	Sandy La, South Oxhey (180m south of Batchworth La)	30
A4147	Leverstock Green Rd, Hemel Hempstead (west of Bartel Cl)	30
A4251	London Rd, Bourne End	30
A5183	Elstree Hill South, Elstree	30
A5183	Park Street	30
A6141	Letchworth Gate, Letchworth (250m north-west of Baldock La)	40
B156	Goffs La, Cheshunt (at Goffs School)	30
B176	High St, Cheshunt (near Warwick Dr)	30
B197	London Rd, Baldock (at Hillcrest)	30
B197	North Rd, Stevenage (south of Rectory La)	30
B462	Aldenham Rd, Watford (at Met Police Club)	30
B487	Redbourn La, Hatching Green, Harpenden (at Oakfield Rd)	30
B487	Queensway, Hemel Hempstead (near Highfield La)	40
B488	Icknield Way, Tring (at Little Tring Rd)	40
B556	Mutton La, Potters Bar (near Albermarle Ave)	30
B1004	Windhill, Bishop's Stortford (west of Windhill Old Rd)	30
B1197	London Rd, Hertford Heath (north of Woodland Rd)	30
B1502	Stanstead Rd, Hertford (east of Foxholes Ave)	30
B4505	Chesham Rd, Bovingdon (near Hyde La)	30
B4630	Watford Rd, Chiswell Green, St Albans	30
B5378	Allum La, Borehamwood (at Lodge Ave)	30
B6426	Cavendish Way, Hatfield	30
-	Cheshunt; Hammondstreet Rd (west of Peakes La)	30
-	Hemel Hempstead; Bennetts End Rd (near Reddings)	30
-	Hemel Hempstead; High St Green	30
-	Hemel Hempstead; Long Chaulden	30
-	Hoddesdon; Essex Rd (at Pindar Rd)	30
-	Letchworth; Pixmore Way (at Shott La)	30
-	Royston; Old North Rd (York Way to Orchard Rd)	30
-	South Oxhey; Hayling Rd (Gosforth La to Arbroath Green)	30
-	St Albans; Sandpit La (at Gurney Court Rd)	30
-	Stevenage; Clovelly Way (Scarborough Ave to Eastbourne Ave)	30
-	Stevenage; Grace Way	30
-	Stevenage; Gresley Way, Poplars	30
-	Watford; Radlett Rd (north of Colonial Way)	30
-	Watford; Tolpits La (at Scammell Way)	30
-	Welwyn Garden City; Heronswood Rd (south of Linces Way)	30
-	Welwyn Garden City; Howlands (at garages at entrance to hospice)	30

Humberside

Road number	Location	Speed limit (mph)
M180	West of River Trent	70
A18	Barton Street (near Grimsby)	NSL
A18	Doncaster Rd, Scunthorpe	40
A18	Queensway, Scunthorpe	40
A46	Clee Rd, Cleethorpes	30
A46	Laceby Rd, Grimsby	30
A46	Weelsby Rd, Grimsby	30
A63	Castle St, Kingston upon Hull	40
A63	Daltry Street Flyover, Kingston upon Hull	40
A159	Ashby Rd, Scunthorpe	30
A159	Messingham Rd, Scunthorpe	30
A161	High Street, Belton	30
A163	Holme upon Spalding Moor	30
A164	Leconfield	30
A165	Beeford	30
A165	Kingsgate, Bridlington	30
A165	Coniston	40
A165	Freetown Way, Kingston upon Hull	30
A165	Holderness Rd, Kingston upon Hull	40
A165	Skirlaugh	30
A180	Great Coates junction	70
A614	Airmyn Rd, Goole	30
A614	Holme upon Spalding Moor	40
A614	Thorpe Rd, Howden	30
A614	Middleton on the Wolds	30
A614	Shiptonthorpe (both sides of roundabout)	60
A1031	Tetney Rd, Humberston	30
A1033	Thomas Clarkson Way, Kingston upon Hull	40
A1033	Thorngumbald	30
A1033	Withernsea	30
A1035	Hull Bridge Rd, Beverley	30
A1038	Quay Rd/St John's St, Bridlington	30
A1077	Barrow Rd, Barton-upon-Humber	30
A1079	Barmby Moor	50
A1079	Beverley Bypass (A1039 to Dunswell)	NSL
A1079	Beverley Rd, Kingston upon Hull (Desmond Ave to Riverdale Rd)	30
A1079	Beverley Rd, Kingston upon Hull (Sutton Rd to Mizzen Rd)	40
A1079	Beverley Rd, Kingston upon Hull (near Mizzen Rd)	40
A1079	Bishop Burton	30
A1079	Market Weighton Bypass	NSL
A1084	Bigby High Rd, Brigg	30
A1105	Boothferry Rd, Kingston upon Hull	40
A1136	Cromwell Rd, Grimsby	30
A1136	Great Coates Rd, Grimsby	30
A1174	Beverley Rd, Dunswell	30
A1174	Woodmansey	30
A1243	Louth Rd, Grimsby	30
B1203	Waltham Rd, Grimsby	30
B1206	Wold Rd, Barrow-upon-Humber	30
B1207	High St, Broughton	30
B1230	Gilberdyke	40
B1230	Newport	40
B1231	Anlaby Rd, Kingston upon Hull	30
B1232	Beverley Rd, Hessle	30
B1237	Leads Rd, Kingston upon Hull	30
B1237	Saltshouse Rd, Kingston upon Hull	30
B1238	Main Rd, Bilton, Kingston upon Hull	30
B1242	Rolston Rd, Hornsea	30
B1398	Greetwell	40
B1501	Grange La South, Ashby, Scunthorpe	30
-	Belton; Westgate Rd	30
-	East Halton; College Rd	30
-	Grimsby; Cromwell Rd	30
-	Immingham; Pelham Rd	30
-	Kingston upon Hull; Bricknell Ave	30
-	Kingston upon Hull; Bude Rd	30
-	Kingston upon Hull; Greenwood Ave	30
-	Kingston upon Hull; Hall Rd	30
-	Kingston upon Hull; John Newton Way	30
-	Kingston upon Hull; Marfleet La	30
-	Kingston upon Hull; Marfleet Ave	30
-	Kingston upon Hull; Priory Rd	30
-	Kingston upon Hull; Spring Bank West	40
-	Kingston upon Hull; Wawne Rd	30
-	Scunthorpe; Ashby Rd (near Pittwood House)	30
-	Scunthorpe; Cambridge Ave	30
-	Scunthorpe; Cottage Beck Rd	30
-	Scunthorpe; Doncaster Rd	40
-	Scunthorpe; Luneburg Way	30
-	Scunthorpe; Moorwell Rd, Yaddlethorpe	30
-	Scunthorpe; Rowland Rd	30
-	South Killingholme; Top Rd	30

Kent and Medway

Road number	Location	Speed limit (mph)
A2	Dunkirk to Upper Harbledown (eastbound)	70
A2	Guston (A256 to A258)	60
A2	Lydden (Wick La to Coxhill Rd, coastbound)	70
A2	London Rd, Strood, Rochester (opposite Lancelot Ave)	40
A21	Kipping's Cross	60
A21	Sevenoaks Bypass	70
A21	Castle Hill, Tonbridge	60
A25	Seal Rd, Sevenoaks (near Mill Pond)	30
A26	Maidstone Rd, Hadlow (Great Elms to Lonewood Way)	40
A28	Ashford Rd, Bethersden (near Kiln La)	40
A224	London Rd/Tubs Hill, Sevenoaks (Argyle Rd to Shoreham La)	30
A225	Sevenoaks Rd, Otford (Warham Rd to Old Otford Rd)	30
A226	Chalk, Gravesend	50
A226	Higham	40
A226	Shorne	50
A227	Culverstone Green	30
A227	Istead Rise	40
A227	Meopham Green	30
A228	Sundridge Hill, Cuxton	40
A228	Ratcliffe Highway, Chattenden	40
A228	Seven Mile Lane (A26 jct to south of Martin's La)	30
A229	Hartley Rd/Angley Rd, Cranbrook (Turnden Rd to High St)	40
A229	Blue Bell Hill, Maidstone (Tyland La to Chatham Rd)	50
A229	Linton Rd/Loose Rd, Loose, Maidstone (Linton Rd to Lancet La)	40/30
A229	City Way, Rochester	30
A249	South Street (Chalky Rd to Rumstead La)	70
A249	Chestnut Street (northbound, near slip rd to A2 Key St roundabout)	70
A256	Betteshanger	70
A256	Tilmanstone	70
A258	Dover Rd, Ringwould (north of Church La)	50
A259	Guldeford La (south-west of Brookland)	60
A259	High St, New Romney (near West St)	30
A259	St Mary's Bay (near Jefferstone La)	40
A260	Dover Rd, Folkestone (Wear Bay Rd to Southern Way)	30
A262	High St, Biddenden	30
A268	Queen St, Sandhurst	30
A289	Medway Tunnel, Chatham (near Vanguard Way)	50
A289	Wainscott Bypass (A228 to B2000)	70
A290	Blean	30
A291	Canterbury Rd, Herne (Lower Herne Rd to A299)	30
A299	Canterbury Road West, Cliffsend	30
A2990	Thanet Way, Swalecliffe, Whitstable (east of Chestfield roundabout)	60
B258	Barn End La, Wilmington, Dartford	30
B2000	Lower Rochester Rd, Rochester (north of A289)	40
B2005	Mill Way, Sittingbourne (Tribune Dr to Cooks La)	30
B2015	Maidstone Rd, Nettlestead Green (near Station Rd)	40
B2017	Badsell Rd, Five Oak Green (Whetstead Rd to Capel Grange Farm)	30
B2019	Seal Hollow Rd, Sevenoaks (A25 to Bayham Rd)	30
B2097	Maidstone Rd, Rochester (Horwood Close to Valley View)	30
-	Chatham; Street End Rd	30
-	Chatham; Walderslade Rd (Snodhurst Ave to Chestnut Ave)	30
-	Gillingham; Beechings Way (Bradbourne Ave to Beechings Green)	30
-	Herne Bay; Mickleburgh Hill	30
-	Longfield; Hartley Rd/Ash Rd (Castle Hill to Station Rd)	30
-	Margate; Shottendane Rd	30
-	Rainham; Maidstone Rd (Drury Dr to Thames Rd)	30
-	Rochester; Esplanade (Shorts Way to Hathaway Ct)	30
-	Sheerness; Marine Parade	30/40
-	Sole Street; Sole St (near Scratton Fields)	30
-	Teynham; Lower Rd (Station Rd to New Cottages)	30

Lancashire

Road number	Location	Speed limit (mph)
A6	Bolton Rd, Chorley	30/40
A6	Garstang Rd, Broughton (north of M55)	40
A6	Garstang Rd, Fulwood, Preston (north of Blackpool Rd)	30
A6	Garstang Rd, Fulwood, Preston (south of M55)	30
A6	Greaves Rd, Lancaster	30
A6	Scotforth Rd, Bailrigg, Lancaster (near Burrow La)	50
A6	North Rd, Preston	30
A6	Ringway, Preston	30
A56	Albert Rd, Colne	30
A56	Burnley Rd, Colne	30
A56	Leeds Rd, Nelson	30
A59	Gisburn Rd, Gisburn	60
A59	Liverpool Rd, Hutton	50
A59	New Hall La, Preston	30
A65	Cowan Bridge	40/60
A570	Southport Rd, Scarisbrick (at Brook House Farm)	40
A581	Southport Rd, Newtown	40
A583	Church St, Blackpool	30
A583	Whitegate Dr, Blackpool	30
A584	Promenade, Blackpool	30
A584	West/Central Beach, Lytham	30
A584	Lytham Rd, Warton	30/50
A587	East/North Park Dr, Blackpool	30
A587	Fleetwood Rd, Blackpool	30
A587	Rossall Rd/Crescent East, Cleveleys	30
A588	Lancaster Rd, Cockerham (at Gulf La)	60
A588	Head Dyke La, Preesall/Pilling	60
A666	Blackburn Rd, Earcroft, Darwen	30
A666	Blackburn Rd (Gr Manchester bdy to Bull Hill, Darwen)	50
A666	Bolton Rd, Darwen (near Cross St)	30
A666	Duckworth St, Darwen	30
A671	Whalley Rd, Read	30
A674	Preston Old Rd, Cherry Tree, Blackburn	30
A675	Belmont Rd (north of Belmont village)	50
A675	Belmont Rd (south of Belmont village)	50
A675	Bolton Rd, Abbey Village, Chorley (Dole La to Calf Hey Bridge)	30/60
A680	Rochdale Rd, Edenfield	40/60
A682	Gisburn Rd, Barrowford (near Moorcock Inn)	60
A682	Colne Rd, Brierfield	30
A682	Burnley Rd, Crawshawbooth	40
A682	Gisburn Rd, Gisburn	60
A682	Long Preston Rd, north of Gisburn	60
A683	Morecambe Rd, Lancaster	30
A5073	Waterloo Rd, Blackpool	30
A5085	Blackpool Rd, Lane Ends, Preston	30
A5209	Course La/Ash Brow, Newburgh	30
A6062	Livesey Branch Rd, Blackburn (near Green La)	30
A6068	Barrowford Rd, Barrowford	50
A6114	Casterton Ave, Burnley	30
B5192	Preston St, Kirkham	30
B5242	Bescar Brow La/Hall Rd, Scarisbrick	30
B5251	Pall Mall, Chorley	30
B5254	Leyland Rd/Watkin La, Lostock Hall	30
B5254	Leyland Rd, Penwortham, Preston (Talbot Rd to A59)	30
B5256	Turpin Green La, Leyland	30
B5266	Newton Dr, Blackpool	30
B5269	Whittingham La, Goosnargh	40
B6231	Union Rd, Oswaldtwistle	30
B6232	Haslingden Rd/Elton Rd (Belthorn to Grey Mare Inn, Blackburn)	40/50
B6232	Grane Rd, Haslingden (west of B6235)	50
B6243	Preston Rd, Longridge	50
-	Belmont; Egerton Rd	60
-	Blackburn; East Park Rd	30
-	Blackburn; Revidge Rd (near Pleckgate)	30
-	Blackburn; Whalley Old Rd, Sunny Bower (near A6119)	30
-	Blackpool; Dickson Rd (Queen St to Pleasant St)	30
-	Burnley; Burnley Rd, Harle Syke, Brierfield	30
-	Darwen; Lower Eccleshill Rd	30
-	Galgate; Bay Horse Rd	60
-	Nelson; Netherfield Rd	30
-	Preston; Lytham Rd	30
-	Preston; St George's Rd	30
-	St Annes; Church Rd/Albany Rd (near High School)	30

Leicester, Leicestershire and Rutland

Road number	Location	Speed limit (mph)
A1	Empingham	70
A1	Stretton	70
A5	Watling St, Hinckley (M69 to A47)	n/a
A5	Watling St, Hinckley (B578 to M69)	60
A5	Watling St, Sharnford (B4455 to B4114)	70
A6	Loughborough Rd, Birstall	40
A6	Abbey La, Leicester	40
A6	London Rd, Leicester (near A6030 jct)	30
A6	Derby Rd, Loughborough	30
A6	Glen Rd/Harborough Rd, Oadby	40
A47	Peterborough Rd, Barrowden	60
A47	Bisbrooke/Glaston	60
A47	Hinckley Rd, Earl Shilton	30
A47	1km west of Billesdon	50
A47	Uppingham Rd, Houghton on the Hill	40
A47	Hinckley Rd, Leicester	30
A47	Humberstone Rd, Leicester	30
A47	Glaston Rd, Morcott	50
A47	Uppingham Rd, Leicester	30
A50	Groby Rd/Leicester Rd, Glenfield, Leicester	40
A50	Woodgate/Frog Island, Leicester	30
A426	Lutterworth Rd, Dunton Bassett	50
A426	Leicester Rd, Lutterworth	60
A426	Leicester Rd, Glen Parva, Leicester	40
A426	Lutterworth Rd, Whetstone	60
A444	Atherstone Rd, Fenny Drayton	50
A444	Norton Juxta Twycross	50
A444	Main Rd, Twycross village	30
A447	Hinckley Rd, Cadeby	60
A447	Wash La/Melbourne Rd, Ravenstone	40
A512	Ashby Rd, Loughborough	30
A512	Ashby Rd Central, Shepshed	30
A563	Asquith Way, Leicester	30
A563	Attlee Way, Leicester	30
A563	Colchester Rd/Hungarton Blvd, Leicester	30
A563	Krefeld Way, Leicester	40
A563	New Parks Way, Leicester	30
A563	Glenhills Way, Leicester	30
A594	St Georges Way, Leicester	30
A606	Stamford Rd, Barnsdale (east of Oakham)	60
A606	Broughton	60
A606	Stamford Rd, Tinwell (west of A1)	60
A607	Melton Rd, Leicester	30
A607	Newark Rd, Thurmaston, Leicester	50
A607	Melton Rd, Waltham on the Wolds	60
A4304	Lubbenham Hill, Market Harborough	30
A5199	Welford Rd, Leicester	30
A5199	Bull Head St, Wigston	30
A5199	Leicester Rd, Wigston	30
A5460	Narborough Rd, Leicester	40
A6004	Alan Moss Rd, Loughborough	30
A6030	Wakerley Rd/Broad Ave, Leicester	30
A6121	Stamford Rd, Ketton	30
B568	Victoria Park Rd, Leicester	30
B581	Broughton Way/Station Rd, Broughton Astley	30
B582	Little Glen Rd, Blaby	30
B590	Rugby Rd, Hinckley	30
B591	Loughborough Rd, Charley (3km south-east of Shepshed)	60
B4114	Leicester Rd/King Edward Ave, Enderby/Narborough	40
B4114	Sharnford	30
B4666	Coventry Rd, Hinckley	30
B5366	Saffron La, Leicester	30
B6416	East Park Rd, Leicester	30
-	Ashby-de-la-Zouch; Tamworth Rd	30
-	Barrow-upon-Soar; Sileby Rd	30
-	Blaby; Lutterworth Rd	30
-	Ibstock; Leicester Rd	30
-	Leicester; Beaumont Leys La	30
-	Leicester; Fosse Rd South	30
-	Leicester; Station Rd, Glenfield	30
-	Loughborough; Forest Rd	30
-	Loughborough; Nanpantan Rd	30
-	Norris Hill; Ashby Rd (west of Ashby-de-la-Zouch)	40
-	Shepshed; Leicester Rd	30

Lincolnshire

Road number	Location	Speed limit (mph)
A15	Ashby Lodge (2km north of B1191)	60
A15	Aswarby	60
A15	B1191 to Dunsby Hollow	60
A16	Tytton La, Boston	60
A16	Burwell	40
A16	Grainsby to Holton le Clay	60
A16	Market Deeping Bypass	50/60
A16	North Thoresby	60
A16	Stickney (north of village)	60
A17	Fleet Hargate	60
A17	Hoffleet Stow (north of B1181)	60
A17	Moulton Common (south of B1357)	60
A52	Bridge End	60
A52	Swaton (west of B1394)	60
A52	Ropsley	60
A153	Billinghay	40
A153	Tattershall	50
A158	Scremby to Candlesby	40/50
A631	Dale Bridge near West Rasen	60
A631	Hemswell Cliff	50/60
B1188	Branston	30
B1188	Canwick (at Highfield House)	60
B1188	Potterhanworth (near B1178 jct)	60
B1191	Martin Dales	60

London

Road number	Location	Speed limit (mph)
M11	Woodford (near jct4)	n/a
M25	Jct 10 - 16	n/a
A1	Upper St, Islington	n/a
A1	Holloway Rd, Upper Holloway	n/a
A2	East Rochester Way, Bexley	n/a
A2	Old Kent Rd	n/a
A3	Clapham High St, Clapham	n/a

Road number	Location	Speed limit (mph)
A3	Kennington Park Rd, Kennington	n/a
A3	Kingston Bypass	n/a
A3	Malden Way, New Malden	n/a
A3	Kingston Rd, Roehampton	n/a
A3	Clapham Rd, South Lambeth	n/a
A4	Great West Rd, Chiswick/Brentford/Hounslow	n/a
A5	Edgware Rd, Cricklewood/Hendon	n/a
A5	Maida Vale, Maida Vale	n/a
A5	The Broadway, West Hendon	n/a
A10	Great Cambridge Rd, Edmonton	n/a
A10	Stamford Hill, Stoke Newington	n/a
A11	Bow Rd, Bow	n/a
A11	Mile End Rd, Stepney	n/a
A12	Colchester Rd, Romford	n/a
A12	Eastern Ave, Romford	n/a
A13	Alfred's Way, Barking	n/a
A13	Ripple Rd, Barking/Dagenham	n/a
A20	Sidcup Rd, Eltham/New Eltham	n/a
A20	Lee High Rd, Lewisham	n/a
A20	Lewisham Way, New Cross	n/a
A20	Sidcup Bypass, Sidcup	n/a
A21	Bromley Common	n/a
A21	Bromley Rd, Catford	n/a
A21	Rushey Green, Catford	n/a
A21	Bromley Rd, Downham	n/a
A22	Godstone Rd, Purley/Kenley	n/a
A23	Brixton Rd, Brixton	n/a
A23	Brixton Hill, Brixton	n/a
A23	Streatham High Road, Streatham	n/a
A23	Thornton Rd, Croydon	n/a
A24	Morden Rd, Merton	n/a
A24	High St Colliers Wood, Tooting	n/a
A40	Westway, Paddington/Shepherd's Bush	n/a
A40	Western Ave, Perivale	n/a
A40	Western Ave, Greenford	n/a
A40	Western Ave, Northolt	n/a
A40	Western Ave, Ruislip	n/a
A41	Gloucester Pl, Marylebone	n/a
A41	Park Rd, St John's Wood	n/a
A102	Homerton High St, Hackney	n/a
A105	Green La, Finsbury Park	n/a
A107	Cambridge Heath Rd, Bethnal Green	n/a
A107	Upper Clapton Rd, Clapton	n/a
A107	Clapton Common, Stamford Hill	n/a
A109	Bounds Green Rd, Bowes Park	n/a
A109	Oakleigh Rd South, Friern Barnet	n/a
A110	Enfield Rd, Enfield	n/a
A112	Chingford Rd, Walthamstow	n/a
A112	Hoe St, Walthamstow	n/a
A118	Romford Rd, Forest Gate	n/a
A118	London Rd, Romford	n/a
A124	Barking Rd, East Ham	n/a
A124	Barking Rd, Plaistow	n/a
A124	Rush Green Rd, Romford	n/a
A200	Creek Rd, Greenwich	n/a
A202	Camberwell New Rd, Camberwell	n/a
A202	Vauxhall Bridge Rd, Westminster	n/a
A205	Brownhill Rd, Catford	n/a
A205	Stanstead Rd, Catford	n/a
A205	Well Hall Rd, Eltham	n/a
A205	Upper Richmond Rd, Putney/Roehampton	n/a
A205	Upper Richmond Rd West, Richmond/Sheen	n/a
A206	Erith Rd, Belvedere	n/a
A206	Woolwich Rd, Belvedere	n/a
A206	Thames Rd, Crayford	n/a
A206	Woolwich Church St, Woolwich	n/a
A206	Beresford St, Woolwich	n/a
A207	Bellegrove Rd, Welling	n/a
A207	Great Western Rd, Westbourne Park	n/a
A208	Court Rd, Eltham	n/a
A208	Well Hall Rd, Eltham	n/a
A212	Gravel Hill, Croydon	n/a
A212	Grange Rd, South Norwood	n/a
A212	Westwood Hill, Sydenham	n/a
A213	Croydon Rd, Penge	n/a
A214	Elmers End Rd, Beckenham	n/a
A214	Trinity Rd, Wandsworth	n/a
A215	Denmark Hill, Camberwell	n/a
A215	Beulah Hill, Upper Norwood	n/a
A217	London Rd, Mitcham	n/a
A217	St Dunstan's Hill, Sutton	n/a
A217	Garratt La, Wandsworth	n/a
A218	Haydon's Rd, Wimbledon	n/a
A219	Fulham Palace Rd, Fulham	n/a
A219	Scrubs La, Willesden	n/a
A219	Parkside, Wimbledon	n/a
A221	Penhill Rd, Blackfen	n/a
A222	Long La, Addiscombe	n/a
A222	Bromley Rd, Beckenham	n/a
A223	North Cray Rd, Sidcup	n/a
A224	Sevenoaks Way, St Paul's Cray	n/a
A232	Croydon Rd, Wallington	n/a
A232	Cheam Rd, Sutton	n/a
A233	Main Rd, Biggin Hill	n/a
A234	Beckenham Rd, Beckenham/Penge	n/a
A234	Crystal Palace Park Rd, Sydenham	n/a
A236	Croydon Rd, Mitcham	n/a
A237	Smitham Bottom La, Purley	n/a
A238	Coombe La, Coombe	n/a
A239	Central Rd, Morden	n/a
A240	Kingston Rd, Tolworth/Stoneleigh	n/a
A298	Bushey Rd, Raynes Park	n/a
A307	Kew Rd, Kew	n/a
A307	Portsmouth Rd, Kingston upon Thames	n/a
A307	Richmond Rd, Kingston upon Thames	n/a
A308	Hampton Court Rd/Upper Sunbury Rd, Hampton	n/a
A311	High St, Teddington	n/a
A312	Harlington Rd West, Feltham	n/a
A312	Uxbridge Rd, Hampton	n/a
A312	near Southall	n/a
A313	Park Rd/Hampton Rd, Teddington	n/a
A314	Hanworth Rd, Hounslow	n/a
A315	High St, Brentford	n/a
A315	Staines Rd, Feltham	n/a
A315	Hammersmith Rd, Hammersmith	n/a
A315	Kensington Rd, Kensington	n/a
A316	Lower Richmond Rd, North Sheen	n/a
A400	Junction Rd, Holloway	n/a
A400	Fortress Rd, Kentish Town	n/a
A400	Kentish Town Rd, Kentish Town	n/a
A402	Bayswater Rd, Bayswater	n/a
A402	Holland Park Ave, Notting Hill	n/a
A404	Hillside, Harlesden	n/a
A404	Watford Rd, Harrow	n/a
A404	Harrow Rd, Kensal Green	n/a
A404	Rickmansworth Rd, Northwood	n/a
A404	George V Ave, Pinner	n/a
A404	Watford Rd, Wembley	n/a
A406	Barking Relief Rd, Barking	n/a
A406	Southend Rd (North Circular), South Woodford	n/a
A406	North Circular Rd, Finchley	n/a
A406	North Circular Rd, Dollis Hill	n/a
A406	North Circular Rd, Neasden/Stonebridge	n/a

Road number	Location	Speed limit (mph)
A408	Cowley Rd, Uxbridge	n/a
A408	High Rd, Cowley	n/a
A408	Stockley Rd, West Drayton	n/a
A410	Uxbridge Rd, Harrow Weald	n/a
A410	Fryent Way, Kingsbury	n/a
A501	Euston Rd, St Pancras	n/a
A501	Pentonville Rd, Pentonville	n/a
A503	Seven Sisters Rd, Finsbury Park/South Tottenham	n/a
A1000	High Rd, Totteridge	n/a
A1010	Fore St, Edmonton	n/a
A1020	Royal Docks Rd, Beckton	n/a
A1020	North Woolwich Rd, Silvertown	n/a
A1055	Watermead Way, Tottenham	n/a
A1112	Rainham Rd North, Dagenham	n/a
A1112	Romford Rd, Hainault	n/a
A1112	Dagenham Rd, South Hornchurch	n/a
A1153	Porters Ave, Becontree	n/a
A1199	St Paul's Rd, Islington	n/a
A1199	Woodford Rd, South Woodford	n/a
A1206	Manchester Rd, Isle of Dogs	n/a
A1206	Westferry Rd, Poplar/Isle of Dogs	n/a
A1261	Aspen Wall, Poplar	n/a
A1400	Woodford Ave, Gants Hill	n/a
A2000	Perry St, Crayford	n/a
A2022	Foxley La, Purley	n/a
A2043	Cheam Common Rd, North Cheam	n/a
A2043	Malden Rd, Cheam	n/a
A2043	Cambridge Rd/Kingston Rd, Kingston upon Thames	n/a
A2206	Southwark Park Rd, Bermondsey	n/a
A2212	Burnt Ash La, Plaistow, Bromley	n/a
A2215	Peckham Rye	n/a
A3002	Boston Rd, West Ealing	n/a
A3205	Battersea Park Rd, Battersea	n/a
A3212	Chelsea Embankment, Chelsea	n/a
A3212	Millbank, Westminster	n/a
A3216	Sloane St, Belgravia	n/a
A3220	Latchmere Rd, Battersea	n/a
A4000	Horn La, Acton	n/a
A4006	Kenton Rd, Harrow/Kenton	n/a
A4006	Kingsbury Rd, Kingsbury	n/a
A4020	Uxbridge Rd, Shepherd's Bush	n/a
A4020	Uxbridge Rd, Southall	n/a
A4020	Uxbridge Rd, Hayes	n/a
A4020	Hillingdon Hill, Uxbridge	n/a
A4090	Imperial Dr, Harrow	n/a
A4090	Alexandra Ave, South Harrow	n/a
A4090	Whitton Ave East, Sudbury	n/a
A4127	Greenford Rd, Greenford	n/a
A4127	Greenford Rd, Southall	n/a
A4140	Honeypot La, Queensbury	n/a
A4180	Ducks Hill Rd, Northwood	n/a
A4180	West End Rd, South Ruislip	n/a
A4180	Ruislip Rd, Yeading	n/a
A5109	Totteridge Common, Totteridge	n/a
B112	Homerton Rd, Hackney	n/a
B155	Belmont Rd, Harringay	n/a
B160	Larkshall Rd, Chingford	n/a
B175	Orange Tree Hill, Havering-atte-Bower	n/a
B175	Havering Rd, Collier Row, Romford	n/a
B178	Ballards Rd, Dagenham	n/a
B187	St Mary's La, Upminster	n/a
B205	Salter Rd, Rotherhithe	n/a
B210	Hillreach, Greenwich	n/a
B213	Abbey Rd, Abbey Wood	n/a
B213	Lower Rd, Belvedere	n/a
B214	Albany Rd, Walworth	n/a
B218	Brockley Rd, Brockley/Crofton Park	n/a
B218	Brockley Rise, Forest Hill	n/a
B221	Kings Ave, Clapham Park	n/a
B229	Bolingbroke Grove, Balham	n/a
B238	Peckham Rye	n/a
B243	Park Hill Rd, Croydon	n/a
B266	Brigstock Rd, Thornton Heath	n/a
B272	Beddington La, Croydon	n/a
B272	Foresters Dr, South Beddington	n/a
B275	Upper Selsdon Rd, Croydon	n/a
B276	Marlpit La, Coulsdon	n/a
B278	Green La, Morden	n/a
B279	Tudor Dr, Morden Park	n/a
B282	West Barnes La, Raynes Park	n/a
B286	Martin Way, Morden	n/a
B302	Royal Hospital Rd, Chelsea	n/a
B349	Mill Hill Rd, Barnes	n/a
B353	Sandycombe Rd, Kew	n/a
B358	Church Gr, Hampton Wick	n/a
B358	Sixth Cross Rd, Strawberry Hill	n/a
B358	Nelson Rd/Hospital Bridge Rd, Whitton	n/a
B415	Kensington Park Rd, Notting Hill	n/a
B450	Ladbroke Gr, Notting Hill	n/a
B454	Church La, Kingsbury	n/a
B455	Ealing Rd, Brentford	n/a
B461	Whitchurch La, Stanmore	n/a
B466	Eastcote Rd, Ruislip	n/a
B472	Joel St, Northwood Hills/Eastcote	n/a
B483	Park Rd, Uxbridge	n/a
B550	Friern Barnet La, Friern Barnet	n/a
B1335	Wennington Rd, Rainham	n/a
B1421	Ockendon Rd, Upminster	n/a
B1459	Chase Cross Rd, Collier Row	n/a
B2030	Coulsdon Rd, Coulsdon	n/a
B2230	Brighton Rd, Sutton	n/a
B2230	Rose Hill, Sutton	n/a
-	Balham; Atkins Rd	n/a
-	Beckenham; Wickham Way	n/a
-	Bedfont; Hatton Rd	n/a
-	Bexleyheath; Pickford La	n/a
-	Brixton; Herne Hill Rd	n/a
-	Brondesbury Park; The Avenue	n/a
-	Bushy Park; Chestnut Ave	n/a
-	Caterham; Coulsdon Rd	n/a
-	Catford; Whitefoot La	n/a
-	Collier Row; Pettits La North	n/a
-	Coulsdon; Chaldon Way	n/a
-	Coulsdon; Portnalls Rd	n/a
-	Coulsdon; St Andrew's Rd	n/a
-	Coulsdon; Woodplace La	n/a
-	Cricklewood; Crest Rd	n/a
-	Croydon; Farley Rd	n/a
-	Croydon; Shirley Hills Rd	n/a
-	Eastcote; Eastern Ave	n/a
-	East Wickham; King Harolds Way	n/a
-	Elmer's End; The Glade	n/a
-	Eltham; Glenesk Rd	n/a
-	Eltham; Rochester Way	n/a
-	Enfield; Lincoln Rd	n/a
-	Gidea Park; Heath Dr	n/a
-	Golders Green; Hampstead Way	n/a
-	Grove Park/Lee; Burnt Ash Hill	n/a
-	Hainault; Manford Way	n/a
-	Ham; Dukes Ave/Riverside Dr	n/a
-	Hampton; Broad La	n/a
-	Hanworth; Castle Way	n/a
-	Hanworth; Oak Ave	n/a
-	Hanworth; Swan Rd	n/a

Road number	Location	Speed limit (mph)
-	Harefield; Church Hill	n/a
-	Harefield; Northwood Rd	n/a
-	Harrow; Harrow View	n/a
-	Harrow; Porlock Ave	n/a
-	Harrow Weald; Courtenay Ave	n/a
-	Harrow Weald; Long Elmes	n/a
-	Hayes; Kingshill Ave	n/a
-	Herne Hill; Sunray Ave	n/a
-	Heston; North Hyde La	n/a
-	Hillingdon; Charville La	n/a
-	Honor Oak; Brenchley Gdns	n/a
-	Hornchurch; Minster Way	n/a
-	Hornchurch; Parkstone Ave	n/a
-	Hornchurch; Wingletye La	n/a
-	Kenton; Woodcock Hill	n/a
-	Kilburn; Christchurch Ave	n/a
-	Morden; Buckfast Rd	n/a
-	Morden Park; Hillcross Ave	n/a
-	New Addington; Featherbed La	n/a
-	New Addington; King Henry's Dr	n/a
-	New Beckenham; Worsley Bridge Rd	n/a
-	North Harrow; Whittington Way	n/a
-	North Kensington; Barlby Rd	n/a
-	North Kensington; Chesterton Rd	n/a
-	North Kensington; Latimer Rd	n/a
-	North Kensington; St Helen's Gardens	n/a
-	Old Malden; Manor Dr North	n/a
-	Peckham Rye	n/a
-	Peckham; Linden Gr	n/a
-	Pinner; Bridle Rd	n/a
-	Pinner; The Ridgeway	n/a
-	Purley; Pampisford Rd	n/a
-	Purley; Woodcote Valley Rd	n/a
-	Queensbury; Camrose Ave	n/a
-	Rainham; Lamb's La South	n/a
-	Romford; Balgores La	n/a
-	Romford; Brentwood Rd	n/a
-	Romford; Crow La	n/a
-	Romford; Mashiters Hill	n/a
-	Romford; Slewins La	n/a
-	Ruislip; King's College Rd	n/a
-	Ruislip; Park Ave	n/a
-	Ruislip; Southbourne Gardens	n/a
-	Shirley; Orchard Ave	n/a
-	Shirley; Upper Shirley Rd	n/a
-	Sidcup; Faraday Ave	n/a
-	South Ruislip/Eastcote; Field End Rd	n/a
-	Southall; Lady Margaret Rd	n/a
-	Southall; Park Ave	n/a
-	St Helier, Morden; Middleton Rd	n/a
-	Twickenham; Waldegrave Pk	n/a
-	Upminster; Hall La	n/a
-	Upminster; Ingrebourne Gdns	n/a
-	Wallington; Parkgate Rd	n/a
-	Wallington; Sandy La	n/a
-	Wandsworth; Bolingbroke Grove	n/a
-	West Dulwich; Alleyn Park	n/a
-	West Kensington; Holland Villas Rd	n/a
-	Willesden Green; Mount Pleasant Rd	n/a
-	Wimbledon; Church Rd	n/a
-	Wimbledon; Ridgeway Pl	n/a
-	Wood Green; White Hart La	n/a

Merseyside

Road number	Location	Speed limit (mph)
A57	East Prescot Rd, Knotty Ash, Liverpool	40
A58	Prescot Rd, St Helens	30
A506	Longmoor La, Fazakerley, Liverpool	30
A551	Leasowe Rd, Wallasey	40
A553	Laird St, Birkenhead	30
A561	Speke Rd/Speke Blvd, Speke, Liverpool	40
A562	Parliament St/Upper Parliament St, Toxteth, Liverpool	30
A572	Common Rd, Newton-le-Willows	30
A580	East Lancashire Rd (near A57 jct), St Helens	60
A580	Townsend Ave, Norris Green, Liverpool	30
A5038	Southport Rd, Bootle	30
A5080	Bowring Park Rd/Roby Rd, Court Hey, Liverpool	30
A5098	Hornby Rd, Walton, Liverpool	30
B5136	New Chester Rd, Bebington	30
B5189	Green La, Tuebrook, Liverpool	30
-	Liverpool; Great Homer St, Everton	30
-	Liverpool; Lower House La/Dwerryhouse La, Dog & Gun	30
-	Liverpool; Muirhead Ave, West Derby	30
-	Liverpool; Netherfield Rd North, Everton	30
-	Liverpool; Park La, Aintree	30
-	Liverpool; Utting Ave East, Norris Green	30

Norfolk

Road number	Location	Speed limit (mph)
A10	Downham Market to Setchey	n/a
A11	Ketteringham	70
A11	Roudham Heath (A1075/B1111)	70
A11	Spooner Row (near B1172 jct)	70
A12	Hopton on Sea	70
A17	Terrington St Clement	60
A47	Wisbech to King's Lynn	n/a
A47	East Winch	60
A47	Narborough	60
A47	Swaffham to Dereham	n/a
A47	Tuddenham to Easton	n/a
A47	Postwick	70
A47	Burlingham to Great Yarmouth	60
A134	Mundford to Whittington	n/a
A134	Thetford (south)	30
A140	Scole to Long Stratton	n/a
A140	Saxlingham Thorpe	40
A140	Aylsham Road, Norwich	30
A140	Norwich (Ring Road) to A149 jct	n/a
A143	Scole to Harleston	n/a
A143	B1062 jct to Earsham	60
A143	Broome Bypass	60
A143	Gillingham to Toft Monks	60
A143	Haddiscoe (bends)	30
A146	Hales	60
A146	Stockton	60
A147	Riverside Rd/Bishop Bridge Rd, Norwich	30
A148	Grimston Rd, King's Lynn	40
A148	Wootton Rd, King's Lynn	30
A148	West Rudham	30
A148	Sculthorpe to Bale	n/a
A148	Sharrington to Letheringsett	60
A148	Bodham	60
A148	Pretty Corner (near A1082/Sheringham)	60
A149	Kings Lynn (A10/A47 to B1145)	60
A149	Knights Hill (King's Lynn) to Hunstanton	n/a
A149	Sheringham	30
A149	Cromer to A140 jct	n/a
A149	A140 jct to B1436 jct	60
A149	A1151 jct to Great Yarmouth	n/a
A1065	Weeting	60
A1065	Hilborough	60
A1065	South Acre	60
A1066	Mundford Rd, Thetford	40
A1066	Rushford	60
A1066	South Lopham	60
A1066	Roydon & Diss	30
A1067	Drayton to Foxley	n/a
A1075	East Wretham (heath)	60
A1078	Edward Benefer Way, South Wootton, King's Lynn	40
A1122	Swaffham/Beachamwell	60
A1151	near A149 jct	n/a
B1108	Earlham Rd, Norwich	30
B1140	Plumstead Rd, Norwich	30
B1149	Horsford Woods (north of Horsford)	60
B1150	Scottow	40
B1150	Westwick	50
B1332	Ditchingham	50
-	Caister-on-Sea; Ormesby Rd	30
-	Drayton/Thorpe Marriot; Reepham Rd	50
-	Harleston	30
-	Norwich; Fifers La	30
-	Norwich; Hall Rd (near A146 jct)	30/40
-	Norwich; Plumstead Rd East	30
-	Norwich; Salhouse Rd, Sprowston	n/a
-	Norwich; Spixworth Rd, Old Catton	30
-	Wymondham (A11) to B1113 (Wreningham/Bracon Ash)	50

Northamptonshire

Road number	Location	Speed limit (mph)
A5	Towcester	30
A5	Long Buckby to Watford	60
A5	Kilsby	30
A5	near M1, jct 18	60
A5	Lilbourne	60
A6	Burton Latimer Bypass	60
A43	Broughton to Kettering	60
A43	Weldon (near Corby)	50
A43	Duddington	60
A43	Main Rd, Collyweston	30
A43	Collyweston to Easton on the Hill	40
A43	Easton on the Hill	30
A45	Flore	30
A361	Daventry Rd, Kilsby	30
A361	Welton	60
A422	Brackley Bypass	60
A422	Brackley (west)	60
A427	Oakley Rd/Weldon Rd, Corby	40
A427	Oundle Rd, Upper Benefield	30
A428	East Haddon	60
A428	Harlestone Rd, Northampton	30
A428	Little Houghton	60
A428	Brafield on the Green	30
A508	Broad St, Northampton	30
A508	Harborough Rd, Northampton	30
A508	Grafton Regis	30
A508	Stoke Bruerne to Yardley Gobion	60
A509	Kettering Rd, Isham	30
A605	Thrapston	40
A605	Thorpe Waterville	60
A605	Barnwell	60
A605	Oundle Bypass	60
A605	Tansor	40
A4256	Eastern Way, Daventry	40
A4500	Ecton Brook	40
A5028	Northampton Rd, Rushden	30
A5076	Redhouse Rd, Moulton Park, Northampton	40
A5095	Kingsley Rd/Kingsthorpe Gr, Northampton	30
A5095	St Andrew's Rd, Northampton	30
A5193	Harrowden Rd, Wellingborough	30
A5193	London Rd, Wellingborough	40
A6003	Kettering to Great Oakley	50
A6014	Oakley Rd, Corby	40
A6116	Brigstock	60
A6116	Geddington Rd, Corby	40
A6116	Steel Rd, Corby	40
B526	Horton	30
B569	Station Rd/Wollaston Rd, Irchester	30
B569	Knuston Vale, Rushden	50
B570	Gipsy La, Irchester	30
B576	Harborough Rd, Desborough	30
B576	Rothwell Rd, Desborough	30
B4036	Eastern Way, Daventry	40
B4100	Croughton Rd, Aynho	30
B4525	Helmdon	60
B4525	Thorpe Mandeville	40
B5385	Main St, Watford	30
-	Boughton; Moulton La	30
-	Barton Seagrave; Cranford Rd	40
-	Cranford St John; High St	30
-	Daventry; Royal Oak Way South	30
-	Islip; Kettering Rd	30
-	Northampton; Rowtree Rd, East Hunsbury	30
-	Overstone; Sywell Rd	30
-	Wellingborough; Doddington Rd	30
-	Yarwell; Nassington Rd/Wansford Rd	30

Northumbria

Road number	Location	Speed limit (mph)
A1	Berwick Bypass near Dunns jct	60
A68	Colt Crag (reservoir)	60
A69	Haltwhistle Bypass	60
A69	Nafferton (near B6309)	70
A69	Two Mile Cottage, Hexham	70
A182	Houghton Rd, Houghton-le-Spring	30
A183	Chester Rd/The Broadway, Sunderland	30
A184	Western Terrace, West Boldon	30
A186	City Rd, Newcastle	30
A186	West Rd, Denton Burn, Newcastle (A1 to A191)	40
A186	Westgate Rd, Newcastle (west of Elswick Rd jct)	30
A189	Haddricks Mill Rd, South Gosforth	30
A189	Cramlington	70
A190	Seghill	n/a
A191	Whitley Rd, Longbenton	30
A191	Springfield Rd, Blakelaw, Newcastle	30
A192	near Plessey Woods Country Park, Cramlington	30
A193	Shields Road Bypass, Byker	40
A193	Beresford Rd, Seaton Sluice	30
A193	Church Bank, Wallsend	30
A194	Newcastle Rd, Simonside (north-east of A1300 jct)	40
A194	Western Approach, South Shields (at Laygate)	30
A196	Blackclose Bank, Ashington	30
A690	Durham Rd, Houghton-le-Spring (at Stony Gate)	50
A690	Durham Rd, Sunderland	30
A692	Church St, Marley Hill (near Sunniside)	30
A694	Station Rd, Rowlands Gill	30
A694	Winlaton Mill	40
A695	Crawcrook Bypass	60
A695	Prudhoe Bypass (east)	40
A696	Belsay village	30
A696	Kirkwhelpington	60
A696	West Rd, Ponteland	30
A696	south-east of Otterburn	60
A697	Morpeth (1km north of A1 jct)	60
A697	Wooperton	60
A698	at B6470 jct	60
A1018	Ryhope Rd, Grangetown, Sunderland	30

Road number	Location	Speed limit (mph)
A1052	Dairy La, Houghton-le-Spring	30
A1058	Jesmond Rd, Jesmond, Newcastle	30
A1068	Amble Industrial Estate	30
A1068	The Wynd, Amble	30
A1147	Gordon Terr, Stakeford (near Ashington)	30
A1171	Dudley La, Cramlington	30
A1290	Vermont, Washington	30
A1300	Prince Edward Rd, South Shields	30
A6085	Lemington Rd, Lemington, Newcastle	40
A6127	Durham Rd, Barley Mow, Birtley	30
B1288	Leam Lane, Gateshead (near A195)	40
B1296	Old Durham Rd (Sheriffs Hwy), Gateshead	30
B1297	Blackett St/Western Rd, Jarrow	30
B1298	New Rd, Boldon Colliery	30
B1301	Dean Rd/Laygate, South Shields	30
B1316	Lynn Rd, North Shields	30
B1318	Bridge St, Seaton Burn	30
B1404	Seaham Rd, Houghton-le-Spring	30
B1426	Sunderland Rd, Felling	30
B1505	Great Lime Rd, West Moor, Longbenton	30
B1523	Plessey Rd, Blyth	30
B6315	Hookergate La, High Spen	30
B6317	Main Rd, Ryton	30
B6317	Whickham Highway, Whickham	30
B6318	Military Rd, Whitchester (east of Harlow Hill)	60
B6318	Military Rd, Whittington Fell (west of A68)	60
B6322	Haltwhistle	60
B6324	Stamfordham Rd, Westerhope, Newcastle	40
B6918	Woolsington Village	30
-	Ashington; College Rd	30
-	Ashington; Station Rd	30
-	Bedlington; Barrington Rd	30
-	Blaydon; Shibdon Bank	30
-	Blyth; Amersham Rd	30
-	Boldon Colliery; Hedworth La/Abingdon Way	40
-	Chopwell; Mill Rd	30
-	Crawcrook; Greenside Rd	30
-	Dinnington; Dinnington Rd (north of Brunton La)	60
-	Gateshead; Askew Rd West	30
-	Gateshead; Saltwell Rd South	30
-	Gateshead; Split Crow Rd	30
-	Hebburn; Campbell Park Rd	30
-	Longbenton; Coach La	30
-	Newcastle; West Denton Way, West Denton (east of Linhope Rd)	40
-	North Shields; Norham Rd	30
-	Shiney Row; Success Rd	40
-	South Shields; Harton La, Harton	30
-	South Shields; Nevinson Ave, Whiteleas	30
-	Sunderland; North Hylton Rd, Southwick (near Castletown Way)	40
-	Sunderland; North Moor La, Farringdon	40
-	Sunderland; St Luke's Rd, Pallion/South Hylton	30
-	Sunderland; Silksworth Rd, New Silksworth (near Rutland Ave)	30
-	Sunderland; Springwell Rd	30
-	Sunderland; Warwick Ter, New Silksworth	30
-	Wallsend; Battle Hill Dr	30
-	Whickham; Fellside Rd	30

North Yorkshire

There is currently no safety camera partnership.

Nottinghamshire

Road number	Location	Speed limit (mph)
A52	Clifton Blvd, Nottingham (at Nottingham Univ Hospital)	40
A52	Derby Rd, Nottingham (A6514 to A6464)	30
A60	Carlton in Lindrick	30
A60	Cuckney to Market Warsop	60
A60	Nottingham Rd, Mansfield	30
A60	Nottingham (Mapperley to Trent Bridge)	30
A60	Ravenshead	50
A609	Ilkeston Rd/Wollaton Rd/Russel Dr/Trowell Rd, Nottingham	30
A610	at Bobber's Mill, Nottingham	30
A611	Derby Rd, Annesley	40
A611	Hucknall Rd, Nottingham (A60 to A6002)	30
A612	Nottingham Rd, Southwell (Halloughton to Westgate)	30
A614	Ollerton Rd, Burntstump, Arnold (north of A60 jct)	60
A616	Ollerton Rd, Caunton	60
A620	Welham Rd, Retford	30
A631	Beckingham Bypass	50
A631	west of Beckingham	50
A631	Flood Plain Rd, west of Gainsborough	50
A6002	Bilborough Road, Nottingham	60
A6005	Castle Blvd/Abbey Bridge/Abbey St/Beeston Rd, Nottingham	30
A6008	Canal St, Nottingham	30
A6130	Gregory Blvd, Nottingham	30
A6130	Radford Blvd/Lenton Blvd, Nottingham	30
A6191	Chesterfield Rd South, Mansfield	30
A6200	Derby Rd, Nottingham	30
B679	Wilford La, West Bridgford	30
B682	Sherwood Rise/Nottingham Rd/Vernon Rd, Basford, Nottingham	30
B6004	Strelley Rd/Broxtowe La, Broxtowe	30
B6004	Oxclose La, Arnold, Nottingham	40
B6010	Nottingham Rd, Giltbrook, Eastwood	30
B6020	Kirklington Rd, Rainworth	30
B6040	Retford Rd, Worksop	30
B6033	Bath La/Ravensdale Rd, Mansfield	30
B6166	Lincoln Rd/Northgate, Newark	30
B6326	London Rd, Newark	40
-	Hucknall; Nottingham Rd/Portland Rd/Annesley Rd	30
-	Newark; Hawton La, Balderton	30
-	Nottingham; Beechdale Rd	30
-	Nottingham; Bestwood Park Drive	30
-	Nottingham; Ridge Way/Top Valley Drive	30
-	Nottingham; Wigman Rd	30

South Yorkshire

Road number	Location	Speed limit (mph)
A18	Carr House Rd, Doncaster (east of A6182)	40
A18	Tudworth Rd (near Hatfield)	60
A57	Mosborough Parkway, Sheffield (B6053 to B6064)	60
A57	Worksop Rd, South Anston	40
A60	Worksop Rd, Tickhill (near Friars Lane)	30
A61	Park Rd, Worsbrough Bridge, Barnsley	30
A61	Chesterfield Rd, Sheffield (near Tadcaster Way)	30
A61	Chesterfield Rd South, Sheffield (near Lowedges Rd)	40
A61	Halifax Rd, Sheffield	30
A61	Meadowhead, Norton, Sheffield	30
A628	Pontefract Rd, Lundwood/Cudworth	40
A628	Barnsley Rd, Penistone (at Nether Mill)	40
A629	Burncross Rd, Burncross, Chapeltown	30
A629	Wortley Rd, Kimberworth, Rotherham	30
A629	Upper Wortley Rd, Thorpe Hesley (near M1 jct 35)	40
A629	Halifax Rd, Wortley (at A616 overbridge)	40
A630	High Rd, Balby, Doncaster	40
A630	Wheatley Hall Rd, Doncaster	40
A630	Centenary Way, Rotherham (near Ickles Roundabout)	50
A630	Doncaster Rd, Thrybergh	40
A630	Sheffield Rd, Warmsworth	40
A631	Rotherham Rd, Maltby	30
A631	Bawtry Rd, Wickersley (west to A6021 jct)	40
A633	Rotherham Rd, Athersley South, Barnsley (near A61 jct)	30
A633	Rotherham Rd, Monk Bretton, Barnsley	40
A633	Barnsley Rd, Wombwell (near Aldham House La)	40
A635	Doncaster Rd, Ardsley, Barnsley	40
A638	Bawtry Rd, Doncaster (at racecourse)	40
A638	Great North Rd, Scawthorpe/Adwick-Le-Street	50
A638	York Rd, Scawthorpe/Sunnyfields, Doncaster	40
A6022	Rowns La, Swinton	30
A6023	Doncaster Rd, Mexborough	30
A6023	Mexborough Relief Rd (dual carr section)	40
A6101	Rivelin Valley Rd, Sheffield	30/40
A6102	Oughtibridge	30
A6102	Middlewood Rd, Sheffield (at ambulance station)	30
A6109	Meadow Bank Rd, Rotherham (near Oakdale Rd)	40
A6123	Herringthorpe Valley Rd, Rotherham (near Far La)	40
A6135	Ecclesfield Rd, Chapeltown	40
B6059	Kiveton Park/Wales	30
B6066	Whitehill La, Brinsworth, Rotherham	30
B6082	Carlisle St East, Sheffield	30
B6090	Wentworth Rd, Kilnhurst, Swinton	30
B6096	Station Rd, Wombwell	30
B6100	Hunningley La, Barnsley	30
B6200	Handsworth Rd/Retford Rd, Handsworth/Orgreave, Sheffield	30
B6411	Houghton Rd, Thurnscoe	30
B6463	Stripe Rd (south of New Rossington)	60
-	Armthorpe; Hatfield La	30
-	Armthorpe; Nutwell La, Nutwell	30
-	Auckley; Hurst La (near Hayfield La)	40
-	Barnsley; Fish Dam La, Carlton	30
-	Barnsley; Pogmoor Rd	30
-	Chapeltown; Park View Rd	30
-	Conisbrough; Old Rd (Chestnut Gr to Gardens La)	30
-	Doncaster; Thorne Rd (near St Mary's Rd)	30
-	Doncaster; Urban Rd, Hexthorpe	30
-	Grimethorpe; Brierley Rd	30
-	New Edlington; Broomhouse La	30
-	Sheffield; Shirecliffe Rd, Shirecliffe	30
-	Sheffield; Wordsworth Ave (near Buchanan Rd)	30
-	Sprotbrough; Melton Rd	30
-	Stainforth; Station Rd/Church Rd	30
-	Thorne; Marshland Rd, Moorends	30
-	Wath upon Dearne; Doncaster Rd	30

Staffordshire

Road number	Location	Speed limit (mph)
A5	Weston-under-Lizard	40
A5	from M6 jct 12 to A460/A4601	50
A5	South Cannock, from A460/A4601 to A34 (Churchbridge)	30/50
A5	South Cannock, from A34 (Churchbridge) to B4154 (Turf Pub island)	30/ 60/70
A5	Brownhills, from Hanney Hay/Barracks La island to A461	60/70
A5	from A461 to A5127/A5148	70
A5	from A5127/A5148 to A38	60
A5	from A38 to B5404 Tamworth	40/50
A34	Talke, from A5011 to A500	30/60
A34	Newcastle-under-Lyme to Talke, from B5369 to A500	40/70
A34	Newcastle-under-Lyme (north), from B5369 to B5368	30/70
A34	Newcastle-under-Lyme (south), from Barracks Rd (A527) to Stoke City boundary (signed)	40
A34	Trent Vale, from A500 to London Rd Bowling Club	30/40
A34	Stone Rd, Hanford, from A5035 to A500	30/40
A34	north of Stafford, from A513 to Lloyds island/Eccleshall Rd	n/a
A34	Stafford (south), from A449 to Acton Hill Rd	30/40
A34	Cannock (north), from north of Holly La to A34/B5012 roundabout	30
A34	Cannock (south), through Great Wyrley from A5 to Jones La	30
A34	Cannock (south), from Jones La to county boundary	30/50
A50	Kidsgrove, from city boundary to Oldcott Dr	30
A51	Weston, from New Rd to 500m north-west of Sandy La	40/ 50/60
A51	Pasturefields, from Amerton La to Hoomill La	50
A51	Rugeley (north), from A460 (Sandy La) to Bower La	30/40
A51	Rugeley (south), from A460 (Sandy La) to Brereton island (A513)	30/40
A51	Longdon	60/70
A51	from A5127 (Birmingham Rd) to Heath Rd, Lichfield	30/40
A51	Tamworth Rd/Dosthill Rd, Tamworth, from Peelers Way to Ascot Dr	30
A52	Stoke-on-Trent (east), from A5272 to A520	30/40
A53	Baldwin's Gate	30
A53	Blackshaw Moor (north of Leek)	50
A53	Leek New Rd, Endon, from Nursery Ave to Dunwood La jct	30/ 40/60
A53	Longsden, from Dunwood La jct to Wallbridge Dr, Leek	60/ 40/30
A53	Leek New Rd, from A5272 (Hanley Rd) to B5051 at Endon	30/40
A444	Stanton Rd, Burton on Trent, from St Peters Bridge to Derbyshire boundary	30
A449	Stafford (south) from A34 to Gravel La	30
A449	Penkridge, from Lynehill La to half mile north of Goods Station La	40
A449	Gailey, from Rodbaston Dr to Station Dr (Four Ashes)	60/70
A449	Coven, from Station Dr (Four Ashes) to M54	40/70
A449	Stourton (Dunsley Rd to Ashwood Lower La)	40/ 50/60
A454	Bridgnorth Rd, Trescott, from Brantley La to Shop La	50
A460	Rugeley Rd/Uxbridge St, Hednesford	n/a
A460	Sandy La/Hednesford Rd, Rugeley, from A51 to south of Stile Cop Rd	30
A511	Burton upon Trent (north), from A5121 to Anslow La	30/40
A511	Burton upon Trent (south), from A5121 to Derbyshire boundary	30
A513	Weeping Cross (A34 jct) to Milford	30
A518	Stafford (west), from M6 to Bridge St	30
A518	Stafford (east), from Riverway to Blackheath La	30/40
A519	Clayton Rd, Newcastle-under-Lyme	40
A520	Weston Rd, Longton, from A50 north to city boundary	30
A520	Sandon Rd, Meir, Stoke-on-Trent, from Grange Rd to A50	30
A521	Cheadle Rd, Forsbrook	30
A4601	Avon Rd, Cannock, from A34 (Walsall Rd) to Longford island	30
A4601	Wolverhampton Rd, Cannock, from Longford island toward jct 11 to Saredon Rd	30/40
A4601	Old Hednesford Rd, Cannock, from A5190 (Lichfield Rd) to A460 (Eastern Way)	30
A5005	Lightwood Rd, Stoke-on-Trent, from A50 to A520	30/40
A5035	from A34 (Trentham) to A50 (Longton)	30
A5121	Burton upon Trent, from Borough Rd to B5108, Branston	30/ 40/50
A5121	Burton upon Trent, from Byrkley St, Horninglow, to Hillfield La, Stretton	30
A5127	Lichfield, from Upper St John St to Burton Rd	30
A5189	Burton upon Trent, from Wellington Rd (A5121) to Stapenhill Rd (A444)	30/40
A5190	Cannock Rd/Bridge Cross Rd, Burntwood, from Attwood Rd to Stockhay La	30
A5190	Cannock, from Five Ways island to Hednesford Rd	n/a
A5272	Dividy Rd from A52 to B5039	30
B5044	Silverdale, Newcastle-under-Lyme, from Sneyd Terrace to B5368	30
B5051	Stoke-on-Trent, from Smallthorne to Brown Edge	30
B5080	Pennine Way, Tamworth, from B5000 to Pennymoor Rd	30/40
B5404	Lichfield St, Tamworth, from A4091 to A453	30/40
B5404	Watling St, Tamworth, from A51 to A5	30
-	Burton upon Trent; Rosliston Rd, Stapenhill, from A5189 to county boundary	30
-	Cannock; Pye Green Rd, from A34 (Stafford Rd) to Brindley Rd	30
-	Crackley; Cedar Rd, from Crackley Bank to B5500 (Audley Rd)	30
-	Stoke-on-Trent; Oxford Rd/Chell Heath Rd, from A527 to B5051	30

Suffolk

Road number	Location	Speed limit (mph)
A11	Red Lodge to Elveden	n/a
A12	Stratford St Mary to Copdock (A14)	n/a
A12	Lound to Nacton (A14)	n/a
A14	Newmarket to Felixstowe	n/a
A134	Barnham to Nayland	n/a
A137	Brantham	30
A140	A14 jct to A143 jct	n/a
A143	Bury St Edmunds (near B1066)	30
A143	Chedburgh	30
A143	Stanton Bypass	40
A143	Highpoint Prison, Stradishall	40
A144	Ilketshall St Lawrence	40
A146	Beccles to Lowestoft	n/a
A1065	Eriswell	40
A1071	A134 jct to Ipswich	n/a
A1092	Stoke by Clare to Long Melford	n/a
A1101	Flempton	30
A1156	Foxhall, Ipswich (Felixstowe Rd)	40/ NSL
A1156	Norwich Rd, Ipswich	30
A1214	London Rd, Ipswich	40
A1302	Bury St Edmunds	30
A1304	Golf Club, Newmarket	NSL
B1078	Barking	30
B1078	Needham Market	30
B1106	Fornham	30
B1113	Bramford	40
B1115	Chilton	40
B1375	Corton (A12 jct) to Lowestoft	n/a
B1438	Melton Hill, Woodbridge	30
B1506	Kentford	40
-	Carlton Colville	30
-	Felixstowe; Grange Farm Ave	30
-	Felixstowe; Trinity Ave	30
-	Ipswich; Ellenbrook Rd	30
-	Ipswich; Foxhall Rd	30
-	Ipswich; Landseer Rd	30
-	Ipswich; Nacton Rd	30
-	Ipswich; Ropes Dr, Kesgrave	30

Surrey

Road number	Location	Speed limit (mph)
A23	Brighton Rd, Horley	30
A23	Brighton Rd, Salfords	40
A31	Hogs Back, Guildford (central and eastern sections)	60
A244	Copsem La, Esher	n/a
A307	Portsmouth Rd, Thames Ditton	n/a
A308	Staines Bypass, Staines	50
A318	Byfleet Rd/Oyster La, New Haw	n/a
-	Staines; Kingston Rd	30

Sussex

Road number	Location	Speed limit (mph)
A22	High St, Nutley	30
A27	Hammerpot, Angmering (east of Dapper's La)	70
A27	Upper Brighton Rd, Lancing (near Grand Ave)	40
A27	Holmbush, Shoreham (near A270 jct)	70
A29	Shripney Rd, Bognor Regis	40
A29	Westergate St, Westergate/Woodgate	30
A259	Marine Dr, Black Rock, Brighton	30
A259	Brighton Rd, Lancing	30
A259	Hotham Way, Bognor Regis	30
A259	Main Rd, Fishbourne	30
A259	Marine Dr, Saltdean	30
A271	North Trade Rd, Battle	30
A271	Hailsham Rd, Herstmonceux	30
A280	Patching	40
A281	Guildford Rd, Horsham	30
A283	Northchapel	30
A283	Lower St (east), Pulborough	30
A285	Stane St, Halnaker	40
A285	Station Rd, Petworth	30
A2032	Littlehampton Rd/Poulter's La, Worthing	30
A2038	Hangleton Rd, Hove	30
A2270	Eastbourne Rd, Willingdon	40
B2066	New Church Rd, Hove	30
B2070	London Rd, Rake (near Petersfield)	40
B2093	The Ridge, Hastings	30
B2100	Crowborough Hill, Crowborough	30
B2104	Ersham Rd, Hailsham	30
B2111	Lewes Rd, Lindfield, Haywards Heath	30
B2123	Falmer Rd, Woodingdean, Brighton	30
B2138	Lower St, Fittleworth	30
B2166	Aldwick Rd, Bognor Regis	30
B2203	Hailsham Rd, Heathfield	30
-	Bognor Regis; Chalcraft La	30
-	Brighton; Carden Ave	30
-	Crawley; Gatwick Rd (near Hazelwick Flyover)	30
-	Crawley; Gossops Dr	30
-	Crawley; Manor Royal	30
-	Eastbourne; Brodrick Rd, Hampden Park	30
-	Horsham; Pondtail Rd	30
-	Hove; Shirley Dr	30
-	Worthing; Marine Pde	30
-	Worthing; The Boulevard	30

Thames Valley

Road number	Location	Speed limit (mph)
A4	Bath Rd, Calcot, Reading	40
A4	Bath Rd, Maidenhead (near All Saints Ave)	30
A4	Bath Rd, Speen, Newbury	30
A4	Berkeley Ave, Reading	30
A4	London Rd, Slough	40
A4	Sussex Pl, Slough	30
A4	Bath Rd, Thatcham	30
A4	Bath Rd, Woolhampton	30
A30	London Rd, Sunningdale	30
A34	Chieveley	70
A34	Kennington	70
A34	Radley	70
A40	Cassington	60
A40	Forest Hill	70
A40	Oxford Rd, Denham	30
A40	West Wycombe Rd, High Wycombe	30
A41	Gatehouse Rd, Aylesbury	30
A44	Over Kiddington	50
A44	London Rd, Chipping Norton	40/60
A308	Braywick Rd, Maidenhead	40
A322	Bagshot Rd, Bracknell (near A332 jct)	70
A329	Shooters Hill, Pangbourne	30
A329	Kings Rd, Reading	30
A329	Vastern Rd, Reading	30
A329	Wokingham Rd, Reading	30
A329	London Rd, Wokingham	30
A330	Brockenhurst Rd, Sunninghill	40
A355	Farnham Rd, Slough	30
A361	Burford Rd, Chipping Norton	30
A404	Marlow Bypass (near A4155 jct)	70
A404	Marlow Hill, High Wycombe	30/40
A412	North Orbital Rd, Denham	40
A412	Uxbridge Rd, Slough	40
A413	Buckingham Rd, Aylesbury	30
A413	Gravel Hill, Chalfont St Peter	30
A413	Walton St, Aylesbury	30
A413	Wendover Rd, Aylesbury	30
A413	Wendover Bypass, Wendover	60
A417	Charlton Rd, Wantage	30
A417	Faringdon Rd, Stanford in the Vale	30
A418	Oxford Rd, Tiddington	30
A420	Headington Rd, Oxford	30
A420	London Rd, Oxford	30
A421	Standing Way, Woughton on the Green, Milton Keynes	70
A421	Tingewick Bypass, Tingewick	70
A422	Newport Rd, Hardmead	60
A422	Stratford Rd, Buckingham	30/40
A509	Emberton Bypass	60
A4010	Aylesbury Rd, Monks Risborough	30
A4010	New Rd, High Wycombe	30
A4074	Woodcote Rd, Caversham, Reading	30
A4074	Nuneham Courtenay	50
A4095	Bampton Rd, Curbridge	40
A4095	Witney Rd, Freeland	40
A4130	Nuffield	60
A4130	Remenham Hill	40
A4155	Henley Rd, Reading	30
A4157	Oakfield Rd, Aylesbury	30
A4183	Oxford Rd, Abingdon	30
A4260	Banbury Rd, Rousham	60
A4260	Banbury Rd, Shipton-on-Cherwell	50
A4260	Oxford Rd, Kidlington	30
A4260	Steeple Aston	60
B480	Watlington Rd, Blackbird Leys, Oxford	30
B481	Peppard Rd, Sonning Common	30
B3018	Binfield Rd, Bracknell	30
B3349	Barkham Rd, Barkham	30
B3350	Wilderness Rd, Earley	30
B3430	Nine Mile Ride, Bracknell	50
B4009	Ewelme	50
B4011	Bicester Rd, Long Crendon	30
B4017	Drayton Rd, Abingdon	30
B4034	Buckingham Rd, Bletchley	30
B4044	Oxford Rd, Farmoor	40
B4447	Cookham Rd, Maidenhead	30
B4495	Windmill Rd, Oxford	30
-	Bracknell; Opladen Way	30
-	High Wycombe; Sawpit Hill, Hazlemere	30
-	High Wycombe; Holmers Farm Way	30
-	Maidenhead; Greenways Dr	30
-	Milton Keynes; Avebury Blvd	30
-	Milton Keynes; Midsummer Blvd	30
-	Milton Keynes; Silbury Blvd	30
-	Reading; Park La	30
-	Reading; Kentwood Hill, Tilehurst	30
-	Reading; Overdown Rd, Tilehurst	30
-	Reading; The Meadway, Tilehurst	30
-	Slough; Cippenham La	30
-	Slough; Buckingham Ave	30
-	Slough; Parlaunt Rd	30
-	Witney; Corn St	30
-	Woodley; Loddon Bridge Rd	30

Warwickshire

Road number	Location	Speed limit (mph)
A5	Churchover (north-west of A426)	NSL
A5	Grendon to Hinckley	50
A45	near Ryton-on-Dunsmore	50
A46	Stratford northern Bypass, near Snitterfield	60
A46	Kenilworth Bypass at Stoneleigh	70
A47	Hinckley Rd, Nuneaton	30
A47	The Long Shoot, Nuneaton	40
A422	Alcester Rd, Stratford-upon-Avon	30
A423	near Fenny Compton	60
A423	Marton village	30
A423	near Marton	60
A423	south of Southam	60
A425	Radford Semele	30
A425	Ufton	30
A426	Dunchurch Rd, Rugby	30
A426	near Stockton	60
A428	Rugby Rd, Binley Woods	30
A428	Church Lawford	60
A428	Long Lawford	40
A429	Stretton on Fosse	60
A429	south of Wellesbourne	60
A435	Mappleborough Green, Redditch	40
A439	Stratford-upon-Avon to A46	50
A446	Allen End	60
A452	Greys Mallory, near Bishop's Tachbrook	60
A452	Europa Way, Royal Leamington Spa	60
A3400	Alderminster	50
A3400	Little Wolford	60
A3400	north of Henley in Arden	40
A3400	Pathlow	50
A4091	Middleton	NSL

Road number	Location	Speed limit (mph)
A4189	Outhill to Lower Norton	60
B4089	Arden Rd, Alcester	30
B4098	Tamworth Rd, Corley	40
B4100	near jct 13, M40	60
B4100	Gaydon	60
B4102	Arbury Rd, Nuneaton	30
B4112	Ansley Rd, Nuneaton	40
B4113	Coventry Rd, Hill Top, Nuneaton	30
B4114	Lutterworth Rd, Burton Hastings	60
B4114	Church End	60
B4114	Coleshill Rd, Ansley Common (near Chapel End)	30
B4114	Tuttle Hill, Nuneaton	30
B4429	Ashlawn Rd, Rugby	40
B4455	Fosse Way, south of Princethorpe	60
B5414	Clifton Rd, Rugby	30
-	Nuneaton; Donnithorne Ave	30
-	Warwick; Primrose Hill	30

West Mercia

Road number	Location	Speed limit (mph)
A5	Aston (2km south-east of A483 jct)	60
A5	Montford Bridge	60
A5	Moreton Bridge (1.5km south of Chirk)	60
A5	West Felton	60
A40	Pencraig	50
A41	Albrighton Bypass	40/60
A41	Chetwynd	60
A41	Ternhill	40
A41	Whitchurch Bypass	60
A44	Bromyard Rd, Worcester	30
A44	Wickhamford	40
A46	Beckford	50
A46	Evesham Bypass	60
A49	Ashton	60
A49	Dorrington	30
A49	Harewood End	40
A417	Parkway (1km south of Ledbury)	40
A438	Staunton-on-Wye	60
A441	Evesham Rd, Astwood Bank	30
A442	Crudgington	40
A448	Kidderminster Rd, Bromsgrove	30
A456	Blakedown	30
A456	Newnham Bridge	30
A458	Morville	40
A458	Much Wenlock	30
A465	Allensmore	60
A491	Sandy La (west of M5, jct 4)	60
A491	Stourbridge Rd (both sides of B4188 jct)	50
A528	Ellesmere Rd, Shrewsbury	30
A4103	Lumber La to Lugg Bridge, Hereford (at and east of A465 jct)	60
A4103	Newtown Cross	40
A4103	Stifford's Bridge to Storridge	50
A4104	Drake St, Welland	30
A4104	Marlbank Rd, Welland	30
A4110	Three Elms Rd, Hereford	30
A5064	London Rd, Shrewsbury	30
B4084	Cropthorne	40
B4096	Old Birmingham Rd, Marlbrook	30
B4190	Habberley La, Kidderminster	30
B4208	Welland	30
B4211	Church St/Barnard's Green Rd, Great Malvern	30
B4373	Castlefields Way, Telford	40
B4373	Wrockwardine Wood Way, Oakengates, Telford	40
B4368	Hungerford (near Broadstone)	40
B4638	Woodgreen Dr, Worcester	30
B5060	Castle Farm Way, St George's, Telford	40
B5062	Edgmond Rd, Newport	60
B5062	Sundorne Rd, Shrewsbury	30
-	Hereford; Yazor Rd	30
-	Newport; Wellington Rd	30
-	Redditch; Alders Dr, Winyates	40
-	Redditch; Bromsgrove Rd	30
-	Redditch; Coldfield Dr	40
-	Redditch; Studley Rd	30
-	Shrewsbury; Longden Rd (rural)	30
-	Shrewsbury; Monkmoor Rd	30
-	Telford; Britannia Way, Hadley	30
-	Telford; Stafford Park 1	40

West Midlands

Road number	Location	Speed limit (mph)
A41	Warwick Rd, Solihull	30
A452	Collector Rd, Castle Bromwich/Kingshurst	50
A4034	Oldbury Rd, Blackheath	30
A4036	Pedmore Rd, Dudley	40
A4040	Bromford La, Hodgehill	30
A4123	Birmingham New Rd, Tipton Green (near A457)	40
A4600	Ansty Rd, Wyken, Coventry	40
B425	Lode La, Solihull	30
B4114	Washwood Heath Rd, Ward End	30
B4121	Barnes Hill, Selly Oak	40
B4121	Shenley La, Selly Oak	40
B4135	Heath St, Smethwick	30
-	Solihull; Widney Manor Rd	30
-	Wolverhampton; The Droveway	30

West Yorkshire

Road number	Location	Speed limit (mph)
M606	At jct 1/26	50
A58	Easterly Rd, Leeds (east of B6159 Harehills La)	40
A61	Harrogate Rd, Alwoodley	40
A61	Scott Hall Rd, Leeds	40
A61	Wakefield Rd, Leeds (M621 to A654)	40
A62	Gelderd Rd, Birstall (A643 to M62)	30
A62	Linthwaite to Marsden	30
A62	Manchester Rd, Huddersfield	30
A64	York Rd, Leeds (A64(M) to B6159)	40
A65	Ilkley Rd (north-west of Burley in Wharfedale)	40
A65	Otley Rd, Guiseley	30
A616	Armitage Bridge to Brockholes	40/30
A629	Halifax Rd, Cullingworth	30
A629	Halifax Rd, Keighley (Dorothy St to Victoria Rd)	30
A629	Ovenden Rd, Ovenden, Halifax (Ovenden Way to Shay La)	30
A629	Skircoat Rd, Halifax	30
A635	Holmfirth Rd, New Mill	30
A638	Ossett Bypass (B6128 to M1)	50
A640	Westbourne Rd, Huddersfield	30
A642	Northfield La, Horbury	30
A644	Huddersfield Rd, Dewsbury	30
A644	Keelham (A629 to Deep la)	30
A645	Pontefract Rd, Featherstone	30
A645	Wakefield Rd, Featherstone	30
A646	Burnley Rd, Cornholme	30
A646	Halifax Rd, Todmorden	30
A646	Luddenden Foot	30
A647	Bradford Rd, Pudsey	40
A647	Great Horton Rd, Bradford (Moore Ave to B6147 Cooper La)	30
A650	Bradford Rd, Frizinghall, Bradford (Emm La to A6038)	30
A650/ A6037	Shipley Airedale Rd, Bradford	40
A651	Bradford Rd, Birkenshaw	30
A653	Leeds Rd, (Chidswell to M62)	40
A657	Leeds Rd, Thackley, Shipley	30
A6025	Elland Rd, (Brighouse to Elland)	40/50
A6036	Bradford Rd, Northowram	30
A6037/ A650	Shipley Airedale Rd, Bradford	40
A6038	Otley Rd, Baildon, Shipley	40
A6038	Otley Rd, Esholt (near Guiseley)	40
A6120	Station Rd, Cross Gates, Leeds	30
A6177	Ingleby Rd, Bradford	30
A6177	Rooley La, Bradford (east of M606 jct)	40
A6186	Asdale Rd, Durkar	30
B6144	Haworth Rd, Daisy Hill, Bradford (west of B6269 jct)	30
B6144	Toller La, Bradford (near A6177)	30
B6145	Thornton Rd, Bradford	30
B6265	Bradford Rd, Stockbridge, Keighley (A650 to Kingsway)	30
B6273	Wakefield Rd, Kinsley	30
B6380	Beacon Rd, Bradford (Stephen Rd to Wibsey rbt)	30
-	Bradford; Cutler Heights La	30
-	Bradford; Dick La	30
-	Bradford; Gain La	30
-	Bradford; Moore Ave	30
-	Halifax; Crag La, Ovenden	30
-	Huddersfield; Long La, Dalton	30
-	Leeds; Broad La, Moorside	30
-	Leeds; Low La, Horsforth	30
-	Leeds; Otley Old Rd, Lawnswood/Holt Park	30
-	Leeds; Willow Rd/Cardigan Rd, Headingley	30
-	Wakefield; Balne La/Batley Rd	30

Wiltshire and Swindon

Road number	Location	Speed limit (mph)
M4	approx 7km east of jct 15	70
M4	both sides of jct 15	70
M4	approx 1.8km west of jct 15	70
M4	approx 3km east of jct 16	70
M4	approx 8.5km west of jct 16	70
M4	approx 8.5km east of jct 17	70
M4	approx 2.5km east of jct 17	70
A4	Froxfield	40
A4	West Overton	60
A30	Fovant	40
A30	The Pheasant Hotel (1km west of A343 jct)	60
A36	Brickworth (at A27 jct)	60
A36	Hanging Langford	60
A36	Knook	50
A36	Wilton Rd, Salisbury	30
A36	Thoulstone (south of A3098 jct)	60
A36	south of Whaddon	60
A303	Chicklade	50
A303	near Cholderton	70
A303	Folly Bottom (2km east of A345 jct)	70
A303	Mere Bypass	70
A303	west of Winterbourne Stoke	60
A303	Willoughby Hedge (1.5km west of A350 jct)	60
A303	Wylye Bypass	70
A338	Boscombe	40
A338	Downton Rd, Salisbury	30
A338	Little Woodbury (Britford) (1.5km south of Salisbury)	30
A338	near Southgrove Copse (1.5km south of Burbage)	60
A342	Ludgershall	30
A344	Airmans Cross (at A360 jct)	60
A345	Salisbury Clumps (south of Amesbury)	60
A345	south of Highpost	60
A346	Chiseldon Firs (3.5km south of M4)	60
A346	Whitefield (4.5km south of M4)	60
A350	Chippenham Bypass (south of A4)	60
A350	near Hart Hill Farm (2.5km north of Shaftesbury)	50
A350	Heywood	60
A350	Pretty Chimneys (2km south of M4)	70
A354	Coombe Bissett	30
A360	Airmans Cross (at A344 jct)	60
A361	Devizes to Beckhampton	60
A361	Inglesham	60
A361	near jct with B3101, west of Devizes	70
A361	Southwick	30
A361	Frome Rd, Trowbridge	30
A363	Trowbridge Rd, Bradford-on-Avon	30
A363	Trowle Common (north of Trowbridge)	40
A419	near Covingham, Swindon (south of A420 jct)	70
A419	near Broad Blunsdon	70
A420	Ford	40
A420	Giddeahall to Ford	60
A420	The Shoe (3km east of Marshfield)	50
A3026	Tidworth Rd, Ludgershall	40
A3028	Larkhill Rd, Durrington	30
A3102	south of Hilmarton	50/60
A3102	Lyneham	30
A3102	Sandridge Rd, Melksham	30
A3102	Tockenham (north of Lyneham)	60
A3102	High St, Wootton Bassett	30
A4259	near Coate, Swindon	50
A4259	Queens Dr, Swindon (at Rushton Rd)	40
A4361	Broad Hinton	60
A4361	Swindon Rd, Wroughton	30
A4361	Uffcott crossroads	60
B390	Maddington Farm (2km west of Shrewton)	60
B3098	Bratton	30
B3105	Hill St/Marsh Rd, Hilperton	30
B3106	Hammond Way, Hilperton	30
B3107	Holt Rd, Bradford-on-Avon	30
B4006	Marlborough Rd, Swindon	40
B4006	Swindon Rd, Stratton St Margaret	30
B4006	Ermin St/Hyde Rd, Swindon	30
B4006	Whitworth Rd, Swindon	30
B4040	Leigh (near Cricklade)	50
B4041	Station Rd, Wootton Bassett	30
B4141	Hyde Rd, Swindon	30
B4143	Bridge End Rd, Swindon	30
B4289	Great Western Way, Swindon (near Bruce St Bridges)	40
B4528	Hungerdown La, Chippenham	30
B4553	Tewkesbury Way, Swindon	40
B4587	Akers Way, Swindon	30
-	Bulford Camp; Bulford Rd	30
-	Bulford Camp; Marlborough Rd	30
-	Calne; Oxford Rd	30
-	Corsham; Park La	30
-	Larkhill; The Packway	40
-	Swindon; Merlin Way	30
-	Swindon; Moredon Rd	30
-	Trowbridge; Wiltshire Dr	30
-	Trowbridge; Woodmarsh, North Bradley	30

SCOTLAND

Central Scotland

Road number	Location	Speed limit (mph)
M9	at M876 (northbound)	70
M9	Polmont (northbound)	70
M9	Stirling (northbound)	70
M80	Denny (northbound)	70
M876	Torwood, Larbert (northbound)	70
A9	Dunblane (southbound)	70
A82	Crianlarich	30
A706	Linlithgow Rd, Bo'ness	30
A907	Cambus	40
A908	Devonside, Tillicoultry	30
A908	Sauchie	30
A993	Dean Rd, Bo'ness	30

Dumfries and Galloway

Road number	Location	Speed limit (mph)
A74(M)	Multiple sites	70
A7	south of Langholm	60
A75	Multiple sites	n/a
A76	Auldgirth/Blackwood	60
A76	Closeburn to Thornhill	60
A76	Gateside (3km east of Kirkconnel)	60
A76	Glasgow Rd, Dumfries	30
A77	Balyett (south of Innermessan)	60
A77	Cairnryan (north for 2km)	30
A77	Whiteleys (1km south of Stranraer)	60
A701	south of Moffat	30
A701	north and south of St Ann's	60
A709	Burnside (1.5km west of Lochmaben)	60
A711	Tongland Rd, Kirkcudbright	30
A716	north of Stoneykirk	60
A718	Craichmore (1km south-east of B798 jct)	60
B721	Eastriggs	30

Fife

Road number	Location	Speed limit (mph)
A91	Deer Centre to Stratheden (Hospital) jct	60
A91	Guardbridge to St Andrews	60
A92	Cadham (Glenrothes) to New Inn (near A912/A914 jct)	50
A92	Cardenden overbridge to A910 jct	70
A92	Cowdenbeath to Lochgelly	70
A92	Freuchie to Annsmuir (south of A91 jct)	60
A92	A91 jct to 1.5km north of Fernie	60
A92	Rathillet (south) to Easter Kinnear (1km south-west of B946)	60
A823	St Margaret Dr, Dunfermline	40
A823	Queensferry Rd, Dunfermline	30
A907	Halbeath Rd, Dunfermline	30
A911	Glenrothes to Leslie	n/a
A911	Glenrothes to Milton of Balgonie	60
A914	Forgan (near A92) to St Michaels (A919 jct)	60
A914	Kettlebridge to Kingskettle	60
A914	Pitlessie to Cupar	60
A915	Checkbar jct (Coaltown of Wemyss) to B930 jct	60
A921	Esplanade, Kirkcaldy	30
A921	High St/The Path, Kirkcaldy	30
A921	Rosslyn St/St Clair St, Kirkcaldy	30
A955	Methilhaven Rd, Buckhaven	30
A955	Methilhaven Rd, Methil	30
A955	Dysart to Coaltown of Wemyss	40
A977	Feregait, Kincardine	30
A985	Culross (west) to Valleyfield	60
A985	Admiralty Rd, Rosyth	30
A985	Waulkmill (east of Crombie) to Brankholm (Rosyth)	60
B914	Redcraigs to Greenknowes (east of A823)	60
B920	Crosshill to Ballingry	30
B933	Glenlyon Rd, Leven	30
B942	east of Colinsburgh	60
B980	Castlandhill Rd, Rosyth	30
B981	Broad St, Cowdenbeath	30
B981	Dunnikier Way, Kirkcaldy	40
B9157	north of Aberdour	60
B9157	east of Balmule	60
B9157	east of Kirkcaldy	60
-	Dunfermline; Townhill Rd/Kingseat Rd	30
-	Dunfermline; Masterton Rd	30
-	Glenrothes; Formonthills Rd	30
-	Glenrothes; Woodside Rd	30
-	Glenrothes; Woodside Way	30
-	Kirkcaldy; Hendry Rd	30

Lothian and Borders

Road number	Location	Speed limit (mph)
A7	Crookston (near B6368)	60
A7	north of Galashiels (Buckholmside to Bowland)	NSL
A7	Commercial Rd/Wilton Hill, Hawick	30
A7	Stow to Bowland	30
A8	Ratho Station, Edinburgh	40
A68	Jedburgh	30
A68	Soutra Hill	NSL
A70	Balerno	30
A71	Breich	30
A71	Polbeth	30
A72	Castlecraig (near Blyth Bridge)	NSL
A72	Innerleithen Rd, Peebles	30
A72	Holylee (near Walkerburn)	NSL
A89	West Main St, Armadale	30
A90	Cramond Bridge (Burnshot flyover to Cammo Rd) (southbound)	40
A697	Greenlaw and southern approach	30
A697	Ploughlands to Hatchednize (either side of B6461)	NSL
A697	Orange La (at B6461)	NSL
A697	Coldstream	30
A698	Denholm to A6088 jct	NSL
A698	Crailing to Eckford	NSL
A699	Maxton village	40
A701	Blyth Bridge to Cowdenburn (1km north-east of Lamancha)	NSL
A701	Rachan Mill, Broughton to A72	30
A702	Comiston Rd, Edinburgh	30
A702	Dolphinton north to Medwyn Mains	NSL
A703	Eddleston and approaches	30
A703	Leadburn south to Shiplaw	NSL
A703	Edinburgh Rd, Peebles	30
A703	Peebles north to Milkieston	30
A705	Whitburn to East Whitburn	30
A706	Longridge Village	30
A706	Whitburn (at Cairnie Pl)	30
A720	City Bypass, east of Gogar roundabout, Edinburgh	50
A899	south of Deer Park roundabout (M8 jct 3) Livingston	50
A899	north of Lizzie Bryce roundabout, Livingston	50
A901	Lower Granton Rd, Edinburgh	30
A6091	Melrose Bypass	NSL
A6105	Gordon and approaches	30
B6374	Galashiels, Station Bridge to Lowood Bridge	30
B7015	Howden South Rd, Livingston	30
B7069	West Main St, Whitburn	30
-	Edinburgh; Muirhouse Parkway	30
-	Edinburgh; West Approach Rd (Morrison St to Dundee St)	40
-	Edinburgh; West Granton Rd	30

North East Scotland

Road number	Location	Speed limit (mph)
A90	Ellon Rd, Aberdeen	30
A90	Newtonhill to South Damhead, Kincorth, Aberdeen	70
A90	South Damhead to Whitestripes Ave Roundabout, Aberdeen	40
A90	south of Leys (near Ellon) to Blackhills (near Longhaven)	60
A90	Upper Criggie (3km south-west of A92 jct) to Mill of Barnes (2.5km south-west of A937 jct)	70
A92	Johnshaven to Inverbervie	60
A92	Kinneff, north to Mill of Uras	60
A93	Banchory, east from caravan site	40
A93	Banchory, west from church	30
A93	Kincardine O'Neil, south-east to Haugh of Sluie	60
A93	Aboyne	30
A93	Aboyne to Dinnet	60
A93	Dinnet to Cambus o'May	60
A95	Cornhill	30
A95	Keith to Davoch of Grange	60
A96	Great Northern Rd, Aberdeen	30
A96	Haudagain Roundabout to Chapel of Stoneywood, Aberdeen	30
A96	south of Port Elphinstone	70
A96	north of Inverurie	60
A96	Old Rayne to 2.5km east of Bainshole	60
A96	near Thomastown	60
A96	Huntly (A920 to B9002)	60
A96	approx 2.5km north-west of Cairnie	60
A96	Fochabers to Forgie	60
A96	Mosstodloch to Lhanbryde (east)	60
A98	Fochabers to Mill of Tynet	60
A98	Mill of Tynet to Barhill Rd jct, Buckie	60
A98	from Carnoch Farm Rd, Buckie to Cullen	60
A98	Banff	30
A941	Elgin to Lossiemouth	60
A941	Elgin to Rothes	60
A944	Gairloch (B9126 jct) to Westhill Roundabout	60/ 40/30
A947	Fyvie to Tulloch	60
A947	Whiterashes to Newmacher	60
A948	Ellon to Auchnagatt	60
A952	New Leeds to A90	60
A956	Ellon Rd, Aberdeen	30
A956	King St, Aberdeen	30
A956	North Esplanade West, Aberdeen	30
A956	Wellington Rd, Aberdeen	40
A978	St Machar Dr, Aberdeen	30
B9005	Craigs Rd, Ellon	30
B9040	Silver Sands Caravan Park, Lossiemouth to B9012 jct	60
B9077	Great Southern Rd, Aberdeen	30
B9089	Kinloss north-east to Roseisle Maltings crossroads	60
-	Aberdeen; Beach Blvd/Wales St/Links Rd	30
-	Aberdeen; Springhill Rd	30
-	Aberdeen; West Tullos Rd	40

Northern Scotland

Road number	Location	Speed limit (mph)
A9	Cuaich, north-east of Dalwhinnie	60
A9	near Dalwhinnie (either side of A889 jct)	60
A9	Daviot	70
A9	Caulmaillie Farm, near Golspie	60
A9	south of The Mound (Loch Fleet near Golspie)	60
A9	Altnasleanach, near Inverness	60
A9	North Kessock jct	70
A9	near Fearn jct, south of Tain	60
A82	3km north of Temple Pier, Drumnadrochit	60
A82	1.5km north of Kings House Hotel, Glencoe	60
A82	Invergarry Power Station	60
A82	1.5km south of Alltsigh Youth Hostel, north of Invermoriston	60
A82	near White Corries, Rannoch Moor	60
A87	1.5km west of Bun Loyn jct (A887)	60
A95	Drumuillie, near Boat of Garten	60
A95	approx 5km north of Cromdale	60
A95	Congash Farm, near Speybridge, Grantown-on-Spey	60
A96	Auldearn Bypass, western jct	60
A96	Auldearn Bypass, eastern jct	60
A96	west of Allanfearn jct (near Culloden)	60
A96	Gollanfield	60
A99	Hempriggs, south of Wick	60
A834	near Fodderty Bridge, west of Dingwall	60
A834	Strathpeffer Rd, Dingwall	30
A835	Inverlael straight, south of Ullapool	60
A939	Dava Moor	60
B9006	Sunnyside, Culloden	60

Strathclyde

Road number	Location	Speed limit (mph)
M74	Jct 13 (Abington), northbound	70
A70	East Tarelgin (approx 5km west of Ochiltree)	60
A73	Carlisle Rd, Airdrie	30
A76	near Lime Rd, New Cumnock	30
A78	Main Rd, Fairlie	30
A82	Bridge of Orchy (Loch Tulla)	60
A82	Dumbarton Rd/Stirling Rd, Milton	40
A85	5.5km west of Tyndrum	60
A89	Forrest St, Airdrie	30
A706	south of Forth	60
A730	Blairbeth Rd, Rutherglen	30
A730	Glasgow Rd, Rutherglen	30
A730	Mill St, Rutherglen	30
A737	New St/Kilwinning Rd, Dalry	30
A749	East Kilbride Rd, (Cathkin Rd (B759) to Cairnmuir Rd)	40
A761	Glasgow Rd, Paisley at Newtyle Rd	30
A807	Balmore Rd, Bardowie	30
A809/ A810	Drymen Rd/Duntocher Rd, Bearsden	30
A814	Glasgow Rd, Clydebank	30
A814	Cardross Rd, Dumbarton	30
A815	near Ardkinglas (near A83 jct)	60
B749	Craigend Rd, Troon	30
B768	Burnhill St, Rutherglen	30
B803	Coatbridge Rd, Glenmavis	30
B814	Duntocher Rd, Clydebank (Singer Rd to Overton Rd)	30
B7078	Blackwood	30
B8048	Waterside Rd, Kirkintilloch	30
-	Barrhead; Aurs Rd	30
-	Bishopbriggs; Woodhill Rd	30
-	Coatbridge; Townhead Rd	30
-	East Kilbride; Maxwellton Rd	30
-	Johnstone; Beith Rd	30
-	Neilston; Kingston Rd	30
-	Newton Mearns; Mearns Rd	30

Tayside

Road number	Location	Speed limit (mph)
M90	Jct 6	70
A9	north-east of Aberuthven	70
A9	Cairnie Braes (south-west of B934)	70
A9	Tibbermore jct	70
A9	near Inveralmond Industrial Est, Perth	70
A9	Killiecrankie	60
A90	near M90 jct 11	70
A90	Westown (4km west of Inchture)	70
A90	Inchture	70
A90	Kingsway West, Dundee (Myrekirk Rd to Gourdie Pl)	50

Road number	Location	Speed limit (mph)
A90	Kingsway West, Dundee (west of A923 to Strathmartine Rd)	50
A90	Kingsway, Dundee (Caird Park)	50
A91	Dalqueich (2.5km west of M90 jct 7)	60
A92	East Dock St, Dundee	40
A92	Greendykes Rd, Dundee (Arbroath Rd to Craigie Ave)	30
A92	West Newton (2km north of Marywell)	60
A92	Inverkeilor	60
A92	Hawkhill (3km north of Inverkeilor)	60
A93	Scones Lethendry (3.5km south of Guildtown)	60
A93	Cargill	60
A93	Meikleour	60
A94	Perth Aerodrome	60
A94	Balbeggie	60
A94	Burrelton	60
A822	Drummond Castle	60
A923	River Isla bridge	60
A923	Kettins	60
A923	Leys	60
A923	Lundie	60
A933	Colliston Mill	60
A933	Legaston (1km south of Friockheim)	60
A933	Redford (4km south of Brechin)	60
A935	Montrose to House of Dun	60
A972	Kingsway East, Dundee (Forfar Rd to Pitairlie Rd)	40
A977	Balado House (2.5km west of M90, jct 6)	60
B961	Drumgeith Rd, Dundee	30
B996	Gairney Bank (north of B9097)	60
-	Dundee; Broughty Ferry Rd	30
-	Dundee; Charleston Dr	30
-	Dundee; Laird St	30
-	Dundee; Old Glamis Rd (A90 to Gilburn Rd)	30
-	Dundee; Perth Rd	30
-	Dundee; Strathmartine Rd (A90 to Balgowan Ave)	30

WALES

Mid and South Wales

Road number	Location	Speed limit (mph)
M4	Toll Plaza	50
M4	3km east of jct 24, Llanmartin overbridge	70
M4	approx 5km east of jct 32, Cherry Orchard Rd overbridge	70
M4	1km east of jct 32, Rhiwbina Hill overbridge	70
M4	1.1km east of jct 33, Llantrisant Rd overbridge	70
M4	2km east of jct 35 (overbridge)	70
M4	east of jct 36 (overbridge)	70
A40	Bancyfelin Bypass	70
A40	opposite Llangattock Lodge (southeast of Abergavenny)	70
A40	Llanhamlach	60
A40	Llansantffraed	60
A40	Rhosmaen (B4302 jct to national speed limit)	40
A40	Scethrog	60
A44	Forest Bends (5km south-east of Llandegley)	60
A44	Llanbadarn Fawr, Aberystwyth	30
A44	Sweet Lamb (west of Llangurig)	60
A48	Dinas Baglan Rd, Baglan	30
A48	Castleton (near motel)	50
A48	south of Cwmgwili	70
A48	Foelgastell	70
A48	Chepstow Rd, Langstone	40
A48	Llanddarog	70
A48	Clasemont Rd, Morriston, Swansea	30
A48	Nant-y-Caws	70
A48	Parkwall (near B4525 jct, Caldicot)	60
A48	north of Pont Abraham (M4 jct 49)	70
A48	Bolgoed Rd, Pontarddulais	30
A48	Margam Rd, Port Talbot (near Rhanallt St)	30
A438	Three Cocks	40
A449	Cat's Ash, Newport	70
A449	Llandenny	70
A458	Cefn Bridge	60
A458	Llanfair Caereinion (Neuadd Bridge)	60
A458	Trewern	40
A466	Chepstow (High Beech Roundabout to Old Hospital)	30
A466	Hereford Rd, Monmouth	30
A466	St Arvans	30
A467	Aberbeeg Rd, north-east of Aberbeeg	30
A467	Aberbeeg Rd, Abertillery	60
A467	Abertillery Rd, Blaina	40
A468	Caerphilly Rd, Rhiwderyn	30
A469	Lower Rhymney Valley Relief Rd, Llanbradach	70
A469	New Rd, Tir-y-Birth (north of Hengoed)	30
A470	Aberfan (overbridge)	70
A470	Aberduhonw (2km east of Builth Wells)	60
A470	near Alltmawr (south of Builth Wells)	60
A470	Argoed Mill (south of Rhayader)	60
A470	Beacons Reservoir (near A4059 jct)	60
A470	2.5km south of A4215 jct	60
A470	Ash Gr, Whitchurch, Cardiff	40
A470	north of Cilfynydd (overbridge)	70
A470	Erwood (south)	60
A470	Llandinam to Caersws jct	60
A470	Llanidloes to Llandinam	60
A470	Newbridge to Rhayader	60
A470	Rhydyfelin (overbridge, Dynea Rd)	70
A470	near Taffs Well	70
A470	Ysgiog (4km south of Builth Wells)	60
A472	Hafod-yr-ynys Rd, Hafodyrynys	30
A472	Main Rd, Maesycwmmer	30
A472	Monkswood	60
A472	Pontymoel Gyratory	50
A472	Ystrad Mynach to Nelson	30
A473	Bryntirion Hill, Bridgend	30
A473	New Rd, Bryncae	30
A473	Main Rd, Church Village	30
A473	Penybont Rd, Pencoed	30
A474	Graig Rd, Alltwen	40
A474	Glanffrwd Estate jct to 40mph speed limit, Garnant	30
A474	Briton Ferry Rd, Neath	50
A474	Penywern Rd, Neath	30
A474	Commercial St, Rhyd-y-fro	30
A475	Pentrebach, Lampeter	40
A475	Lampeter (central)	30
A475	Llanwnnen	30
A476	Carmel north to NSL, Temple Bar	40
A476	Ffairfach	30
A476	Thomas Arms, Llanelli to NSL, Swiss Valley	30
A476	Erw Non jct to Clos Rebecca jct, Llannon	30
A476	Llannon Rd/Bethania Rd, Upper Tumble	30
A478	Llandissilio	40
A478	Pentlepoir	30
A482	Lampeter Rd, Aberaeron	30
A482	Lampeter (central)	30
A483	Pen-y-banc Rd, Ammanford	30
A483	north of Crossgates	60
A483	Ffairfach	30
A483	Garthmyl	60
A483	Rhosmaen St, Llandeilo	30
A483	Midway Bends, Llandrindod Wells to Crossgates	60
A483	Fabian Way, Swansea (western end)	40
A484	Cenarth	30
A485	Cwmann (from A482 jct to NSL)	30
A484	Cwmffrwd (first bend on entering from the north)	40
A484	Idole (from B4309 jct to NSL)	40
A484	Sandy Rd, Llanelli (Wauneos Rd to Denham Ave)	30
A484	Llanelli (Trostre Roundabout to Berwick Roundabout)	60
A484	Newcastle Emlyn (from 80m west of New Rd jct east to NSL)	30
A485	Llanllwni	40
A486	Well St, Llandysul	30
A486	New Quay (central)	30
A487	Aberaeron (central)	30
A487	Aberystwyth (at A4120 jct)	30
A487	Penglais Hill/Waunfawr, Aberystwyth	30
A487	Bow Street	30
A487	Eglwyswrw	30
A487	Furnace	40
A487	Alma St, Llanarth	40
A487	Llanfarian	30
A487	Llanrhystud (southern approach)	40
A487	Newgale	30
A487	Newport	30
A487	Penparc	40
A487	Rhydyfelin	40
A487	Rhyd-y-pennau	30
A487	Tal-y-bont	30
A489	Caersws jct to Penstrowed	60
A489	Glanmule (at garage)	60
A489	Newtown to Penstrowed	60
A489	Newtown (west of Hafren College)	40
A4042	Mamhilad (near A472 jct)	60
A4043	Cwmavon Rd, Abersychan	40
A4043	St Lukes Rd, Pontnewynydd, Pontypool	30
A4046	College Rd, Ebbw Vale	30
A4046	Ebbw Vale (near Tesco)	30
A4046	Station Rd, Waunllwyd	30
A4047	Beaufort Hill/King St, Brynmawr	30
A4048	Blackwood Rd, Pontllanfraith	30
A4050	Jenner Rd, Barry	30
A4054	Cardiff Rd, Merthyr Vale	30
A4054	Cardiff Rd, Upper Boat	30
A4054	Oxford St, Nantgarw	30
A4054	Pentrebach Rd, Pontypridd	30
A4055	Gladstone Rd, Barry	30
A4058	The Broadway, Pontypridd	30
A4058	Trehafod	30
A4059	New Rd, Mountain Ash	30
A4061	Cemetery Rd/Blackmill Rd, Ogmore Vale	30
A4063	Sarn Bypass near jct with Bryncoch Rd	50
A4067	Abercraf	60
A4067	Crai	60
A4067	Mumbles Rd, Swansea (Sketty La to St Helens Sports Ground)	40
A4069	Station Rd, Brynamman (county bdy to Remploy factory)	30
A4069	Brynamman Rd, south of Brynamman	30
A4069	Broad St, Llandovery	30
A4075	Carew	30
A4076	Johnston	30
A4076	St Lawrence Hill, Milford Haven	30
A4076	Steynton Rd, Milford Haven	40
A4093	Gilfach Rd, Hendreforgan (near B4564 jct)	30
A4102	Goatmill Rd, Merthyr Tydfil	30
A4107	High St, Abergwynfi	30
A4109	Glynneath	30
A4119	Llantrisant Rd (at M4)	60
A4139	Orange Way, Pembroke	30
A4139	Bush St, Pembroke Dock	30
A4139	Marsh Rd, Tenby	30
A4216	Cockett Rd, Cockett, Swansea	30
A4222	Cowbridge Rd, Brynsadler	30
B4223	Gelli Rd, Gelli (Rhondda)	30
B4223	Maindy Rd, Ton Pentre (Rhondda)	30
B4236	Caerleon Rd, Llanfrechfa	30
B4237	Cardiff Rd, Newport (at hospital)	30
B4237	Chepstow Rd, Newport (near Aberthaw Rd)	30
B4237	Chepstow Rd, Newport (near Royal Oak Hill)	30
B4237	Maes-glas, Newport	30
B4237	Wharf Rd, Newport	30
B4239	Lighthouse Rd, Maes-glas, Newport	30
B4245	Leechpool (near Caldicot)	60
B4245	Magor (west)	30
B4245	west of Rogiet (at Green Farm bend)	40
B4246	New Rd, Garndiffaith, Abersychan	30
B4248	Garn Rd, Blaenavon	40
B4251	Kendon Rd, Oakdale	30
B4254	Church Rd, Gelligaer	30
B4254	Pengam Rd, Penpedairheol (near Gelligaer)	30
B4265	Llantwit Major Bypass	50
B4267	Leckwith Rd, Cardiff	30
B4275	Abercynon Rd, Abercynon	30
B4278	Dinas Rd, Dinas (near Tonypandy)	30
B4278	Penrhiw-fer Rd, Tonyrefail	30
B4282	Bridgend Rd/Castle St, Maesteg	30
B4283	Heol Fach, North Cornelly, Pyle	30
B4290	New Rd, Jersey Marine	30
B4290	Burrows Rd, Skewen, Neath	30
B4293	Devauden	30
B4293	Monmouth Rd, Trellech	30
B4295	Cwmbach Rd, Cockett, Swansea	30
B4295	New Rd, Crofty	30
B4296	Goetre Fawr Rd, Killay, Swansea	30
B4297	Bynea (Loughor Bridge Roundabout to Station Rd jct)	30
B4297	Capel Hendre	30
B4297	Llangennech (Cleviston Park to Park La)	30
B4297	Llwynhendy (Capel Soar to the Police Station)	30
B4303	Dafen Roundabout to Felinfoel Roundabout, Llanelli	30
B4304	Copperworks Roadbridge to Morfa Roundabout, Llanelli	40
B4304	Lower Trostre Rd Roundabout to Trostre Rd Roundabout, Llanelli	30
B4309	Cynheidre	30
B4314	Moorfield Rd, Narberth	30
B4320	Hundleton	30
B4325	Honeyborough Rd, Neyland	30
B4336	Llanfihangel-ar-Arth	30
B4436	Northway, Bishopston	40
B4337	Talsarn	40
B4350	north-east of Glasbury	60
B4471	Commercial Rd, Llanhilleth	30
B4478	Letchworth Rd, Pleasant View, Ebbw Vale	30
B4486	Steelworks Rd, Ebbw Vale	30
B4548	Aberystwyth Rd, Cardigan	30
B4556	Cae'r bryn, near Ammanford	30
B4591	High Cross, Newport (near jct 27)	30
B4591	Risca Rd, Pontymister, Risca (at Welsh Oak pub)	30
B4591	Risca Rd, Pontymister, Risca (opposite power station)	30
B4596	Caerleon Rd, Newport (south of M4)	30
B4596	Caerleon Rd, Newport (east of Beaufort Rd)	30
B4599	Ystradgynlais	30
B4603	Clydach Rd, Ynystawe	30
B4623	Mountain Rd, Caerphilly	30
-	Abergavenny; Hereford Rd	30
-	Abergwili (Ambulance Station to the Bypass roundabout)	30
-	Aberystwyth; Park Ave	30
-	Ammanford; New Rd/Pantyffynnon Rd	30
-	Barry; Barry Rd	30
-	Barry; Buttrills Rd	30
-	Barry; Winston Rd	30
-	Beaufort; Bryn Awelon	30
-	Beddau; Gwaunmiskin Rd	30
-	Bridgend; Brackla Way, Brackla	30
-	Caldicot; Chepstow Rd/Sandy La	30
-	Cardiff; Colchester Ave, Pen-y-lan	30
-	Cardiff; Maes-y-Coed Rd, Heath	30
-	Cardiff; Excalibur Dr, Thornhill	30
-	Cardiff; Lake Rd East, Roath Park	30
-	Cardiff; Lake Rd West, Roath Park	30
-	Cardiff; Wentloog Ave, Rumney	30
-	Cardiff; St Fagans Rd, Fairwater	30
-	Cardiff; Willowbrook Dr, St Mellons	30
-	Carmarthen; Lime Grove Ave/Fountain Head Terrace	30
-	Cefneithin (west of Gorslas)	30
-	Chepstow; Mathern Rd	30
-	Church Village; Station Rd	30
-	Cwmbran; Avondale Rd	30
-	Cwmbran; Thornhill Rd	30
-	Cwmbran; Ty Gwyn Way/ Greenmeadow Way	30
-	Ebbw Vale; New Church Rd	30
-	Gorseinon; Frampton Rd	30
-	Haverfordwest; Pembroke Rd, Merlin's Bridge	30
-	Llanbradach; Coed-y-Brain Rd	30
-	Llanelli; Heol Goffa (A476 to A484)	30
-	Llangybi (south of Usk)	30
-	Llantwit Major; Llanmaes Rd	30
-	Merthyr Tydfil; High St, Dowlais	30
-	Merthyr Tydfil; Swansea Rd, Gellideg	30
-	Merthyr Tydfil; Pant Rd	30
-	Merthyr Tydfil; High St, Pen-y-Darren	30
-	Merthyr Tydfil; Rocky Rd	30
-	Milford Haven; Priory Rd	30
-	Nant-y-caws (from Heol Login along Nant-y-caws Hill)(east of Carmarthen)	60
-	Neath; Crymlyn Rd, Skewen	30
-	Newport; Corporation Rd	30
-	Pontypool; Leigh Rd	30
-	Pontypool; Newport Rd	30
-	Pontypool; Sunnybank Rd, Griffithstown	30
-	Port Talbot; Village Rd, Sandfields	30
-	Rogerstone; Tregwillym Rd	30
-	Swansea; Llethri Rd, Felinfoel	30
-	Swansea; Pentregethin Rd, Cadle (near Farm Shop)	30
-	Swansea; Mynydd Garnllwyd Rd/Caemawr Rd/Parry Rd/ Vicarage Rd	30
-	Swansea; Mynydd Newydd Rd	30

North Wales

Road number	Location	Speed limit (mph)
A5	Bangor to Llandygai	30/40
A5	Froncysyllte to Betws-y-Coed (seasonal)	30/ 40/60
A5	London Rd, Holyhead	30
A5	Menai Bridge to Gwalchmai	30/ 40/60
A5/ A483	Chirk to Ruabon	60
A5/ A5025	Holyhead to Llanfachraeth	50
A458	Cwm-Cewydd east to county boundary (seasonal)	60
A470	Dolgellau (A496 to east of A494)	40/60
A470	Llansanffraid Glan Conwy to Betws-y-Coed	30/60
A470	Llandudno to A55, jct 19	30/ 40/60
A470	Mallwyd to A487 (seasonal)	30/ 40/60
A470	North of Rhiwbrifdir to Congl-y-wal, Blaenau Ffestiniog	30/ 40/60
A483/A5	Ruabon to Chirk	60
A487	Caernarfon to Dolbenmaen	30/40/ 50/60
A487	Pantperthog to A470 (seasonal)	30/ 40/60
A487	Penmorfa to Gellilydan	30/ 40/60
A494	Bala to Glan-yr-afon	40/60
A494	Llyn Tegid (Bala Lake)	30
A494	Ruthin to Corwen (seasonal)	30/ 40/60
A494	Ruthin to Llanferres	40/60
A496	Harlech to Llanbedr	30/ 40/60
A499	Pwllheli to Penrhos	30/ 40/60
A525	Llanfair Dyffryn Clwyd to Llandegla (near B5430)	30/ 40/60
A525	Ruthin to Denbigh	40/60
A525	St Asaph to Trefnant	30/ 40/60
A525	Vale Rd/Rhuddlan Rd, Rhyl	30
A525	Wrexham to Minera	30/60
A525	Wrexham to Redbrook	30/ 40/60
A534	Holt Rd, Wrexham	30
A539	Mill St, Llangollen	30/60
A539	Trevor to Erbistock (A528 jct)	30/ 40/60
A541	Caergwrle to Wrexham	30/40/ 60/70
A541	Mold to Caergwrle	30/40/ 60/70
A541	Mold Rd, Wrexham	30
A541	Trefnant to Bodfari	30/ 40/60
A542	Horseshoe Pass (seasonal)	60
A543	Denbigh to Pentrefoelas (seasonal)	30/60
A545	Menai Bridge to Beaumaris	30/40
A547	Colwyn Bay to Old Colwyn	30/ 40/50
A547	Prestatyn to Rhuddlan	30/ 40/60
A548	Dundonald Ave, Abergele	30
A548	Gronant to Flint (Oakenholt)	30/ 40/50/ 60/70
A548	Rhyl to Prestatyn	30/40
A548	Abergele to Kinmel Bay	30/40
A549	Mynydd Isa to Buckley	30/60
A550	Hawarden	30
A4080	Brynsiencyn to Rhosneigr (seasonal)	30/ 40/60
A4086	Cwm-y-Glo to Llanrug	30/ 40/60
A4086	Llanberis (seasonal)	30/ 40/60
A4212	Bala	30/60
A4212	Trawsfynydd to Llyn Celyn	60
A4244	Cwm-y-Glo to B4547	60
A5025	Amlwch to Menai Bridge	30/40/ 50/60
A5025/ A5	Llanfachraeth to Holyhead	50
A5104	Coed-Talon to Leeswood (A541 to B5101)	30
A5104	Coed-Talon to A494 (seasonal)	30
A5119	Flint to Mold	30/ 50/60
A5152	Chester Rd, Wrexham	30
A5152	Rhostyllen	30/40
A5154	Victoria Rd, Holyhead	30
B4501	Denbigh to Cerrigydrudion (seasonal)	30/ 40/60
B4545	Kingsland to Valley (via Trearddur Bay)	30/40
B5105	Ruthin to Cerrigydrudion (seasonal)	30/ 40/60
B5108	Brynteg to Benllech	30/60
B5109	Llangefni towards Bodffordd	30
B5113	Kings Rd/Kings Dr, Colwyn Bay	30
B5115	Llandudno Promenade to Penrhyn Bay	30/40
B5115	Llandudno Rd, Llandrillo-yn-Rhos	30
B5118	Rhyl Promenade, Rhyl	30
B5120	Pendyffryn Rd, Prestatyn	30
B5125	Hawarden	30
B5129	Kelsterton to Saltney Ferry	30/60
B5420	Menai Bridge (Four Crosses to Menai Bridge Sq)	30
B5425	Wrexham to Llay	30/60
B5445	Rossett	30
B5605	Johnstown to Ruabon	30/ 40/60
-	Holyhead; Prince of Wales Rd	30
-	Penrhyn Bay to Rhos Point (coast road)	30
-	Kinmel Bay; St Asaph Ave	30/60

NORTHERN IRELAND

Road number	Location	Speed limit (mph)
A1	Upper Lisburn Road, Belfast (at Musgrave Park Hosp)	30
A1	Lisburn (M1 jct7) to border	40/50/ 60/70
A2	Belfast to Bangor	30/40/ 50/60
A2	Bangor Ring Rd	40
A2	Culmore Rd, Londonderry (Buncrana Rd jct to Culmore)	30/ 40/60
A2	Dundrum Rd, Newcastle	60
A2	south of Newcastle (Bloody Bridge to Ballymartin)	30/ 40/60
A2	Dublin Rd, Newry	30/40
A2	Ballyreagh Rd, Portrush	30/40
A2	Newry Rd, Warrenpoint	30
A3	Armagh to east of Middletown	30/60
A3	Portadown to Armagh	30/60
A4	Dungannon (west of jct 15)	60
A4	Enniskillen to Lisbellaw	60
A5	Doogary to Ballygawley	60
A6	west of Dungiven (B74 jct to Ballymoney)	60
A6	Dungiven Rd, Londonderry	30
A6	Glenshane Rd, Londonderry	60
A6	west of Maghera (Glen to B42 jct)	60
A6	Antrim Rd, Glengormley, Newtownabbey (Hightown Rd to O'Neill Rd)	30
A7	Belfast Rd/Saintfield Rd, Carryduff	30/ 40/60
A8	Larne, south-west to Moss Rd	40/ 60/70
A8	Ballyclare Rd, Glengormley, Newtownabbey (Manse Rd to A8(M))	40
A20	south of Greyabbey to Ardkeen	30/60
A20	Portaferry Rd, Newtownards (near airport)	40
A21	Bangor Rd, Newtownards (near North Rd jct)	30/40
A22	Comber Rd, Dundonald	30
A23	Castlereagh Rd, Belfast (south of Beersbridge Rd)	30
A24	Saintfield Rd, Carryduff	40
A24	Saintfield Rd, Newtownbreda, Belfast (both sides of A55 jct)	30
A25	Mill Hill, Castlewellan	30/40
A25	Newry to Belleek	30/ 40/60
A26	north of Ballymena to Ballymoney (Frosses Rd)	50/ 60/70
A27	Tandragee Rd, Newry (1km north of Newry Bypass)	40/60
A27	Warrenpoint Rd, Newry	70
A29	Armagh to Cookstown	60
A29	Tobermore Rd, Maghera	30
A32	Corngrade Rd, Enniskillen	30
A37	west of Coleraine (either side of Macosquin)	60
A42	Galgorm Rd, Ballymena	40/60
A44	Moyarget Rd, Ballycastle	30/60
A52	Crumlin Rd, Belfast (near Ballysillan Rd)	30
A55	Ballysillan Rd, Ballysillan, Belfast	30
A55	Outer Ring, Belfast (Holywood Rd to Balmoral Ave)	30/40 50/60
A55	Springfield Rd, Belfast	30
A501	Falls Rd, Belfast	30
A501	Glen Rd, Belfast	30
A505	Drum Rd, Cookstown (Cookstown to west of Drum Manor)	30/60
A505	Omagh to Mountfield	60
A509	Derrylinn to Mackan	60
A520	Knockmore Rd, Lisburn	50
-	Dublin Rd, Antrim (2km north of airport)	60
B10	Scarva Rd, Banbridge	30
B21	Donaghadee Rd, Bangor	30
B23	University Rd/Malone Rd, Belfast	30/ 40/50
B38	Springfield Rd, Belfast	30
B58	Woodburn Rd, Carrickfergus	30
B62	Ballybogy Rd, Ballymoney (north to B17 jct)	40/60
B62	Ballycastle Rd, Coleraine	30
B67	Moyarget Rd (at Ballinlea Rd), south-west of Ballycastle	60
B68	Ballyquin Rd, Limavady	30/60
B102	Andersonstown Rd/Stewartstown Rd, Belfast	30
B194	Racecourse Rd, Londonderry	30
-	Belfast; Cliftonville Rd, Cliftonville	30
-	Belfast; Old Holywood Rd	30
-	Londonderry; Springtown Rd	30

Key to listing

- Motorway
- Primary route
- Other A road
- B road
- Minor road

Identifying a vehicle's country of origin

Member states that have undertaken to comply with the Conventions on Road Traffic are required to notify the United Nations of the distinguishing signs used on vehicles from their country while travelling abroad. Official UN signs are labelled in regular type together with some unofficial signs which are labelled in *italic*.

British and European signs

(A)	Austria	(FL)	*Liechtenstein*	(MC)	*Monaco*
(AL)	Albania	(FR)	Faeroe Islands	(MD)	*Moldova*
(AND)	Andorra	(GB)	United Kingdom	(MK)	Macedonia
(B)	Belgium	(GBG)	Guernsey	(MNE)	*Montenegro*
(BG)	Bulgaria	(GBJ)	Jersey	(N)	Norway
(BIH)	Bosnia & Herzegovina	(GBM)	Isle of Man	(NL)	Netherlands
(BY)	Belarus	(GBZ)	Gibraltar	(P)	Portugal
(CH)	Switzerland	(GR)	Greece	(PL)	Poland
(CY)	Cyprus	(H)	Hungary	(RO)	Romania
(Cymru)	*Wales*	(HR)	Croatia	(RSM)	San Marino
(WAL)		(I)	Italy	(RUS)	Russian Federation
(CZ)	Czech Republic	(IRL)	Republic of Ireland	(S)	Sweden
(D)	Germany	(IS)	Iceland	(SCO)	*Scotland*
(DK)	Denmark	(Kernow)	*Cornwall*	(SK)	Slovakia
(E)	Spain	(L)	Luxembourg	(SLO)	Slovenia
(EST)	Estonia	(LT)	Lithuania	(SRB)	*Serbia*
(F)	France	(LV)	Latvia	(TR)	Turkey
(FIN)	Finland	(M)	Malta	(UA)	Ukraine
				(V)	Holy See

The rest of the world (complying countries)

AM	Armenia	IL	Israel	RCA	Central African Republic
AUS	Australia	IND	India	RCB	Congo
AZ	Azerbaijan	IR	Iran	RCH	Chile
BD	Bangladesh	J	Japan	RH	Haiti
BDS	Barbados	JA	Jamaica	RI	Indonesia
BH	Belize	LB	Liberia	RL	Lebanon
BRN	Bahrain	K	Cambodia	RM	Madagascar
BS	The Bahamas	KS	Kyrgyzstan	RMM	Mali
BR	Brazil	KWT	Kuwait	RN	Niger
BRU	Brunei	KZ	Kazakhstan	RNR	Zambia
BUR	Burma (Myanmar)	LAO	Laos	ROK	South Korea
BW	Botswana	LS	Lesotho	ROU	Uruguay
CDN	Canada	MA	Morocco	RP	Philippines
CI	Ivory Coast	MAL	Malaysia	RWA	Rwanda
CL	Sri Lanka	MEX	Mexico	SD	Swaziland
CR	Costa Rica	MGL	Mongolia	SME	Surinam
DOM	Dominican Republic	MS	Mauritius	SN	Senegal
DY	Benin	MW	Malawi	SGP	Singapore
DZ	Algeria	NAM	Namibia	SY	Seychelles
EAK	Kenya	NIC	Nicaragua	SYR	Syria
EAT	Tanzania	NZ	New Zealand	T	Thailand
EAU	Uganda	PE	Peru	TG	Togo
EC	Ecuador	PK	Pakistan	TJ	Tajikistan
ET	Egypt	PNG	Papua New Guinea	TM	Turkmenistan
FJI	Fiji	PY	Paraguay	TN	Tunisia
GCA	Guatemala	RA	Argentina	TT	Trinidad & Tobago
GE	Georgia	RC	Taiwan	USA	United States of America
GH	Ghana			UZ	Uzbekistan
GUY	Guyana			WAG	The Gambia
HKJ	Jordan			WAL	Sierra Leone
				WAN	Nigeria
				WG	Grenada
				WL	St Lucia
				WS	Samoa
				WV	St Vincent and the Grenadines
				YV	Venezuela
				ZA	South Africa
				ZRE	Democratic Republic of Congo
				ZW	Zimbabwe

A car displaying the DK sticker is from Denmark.

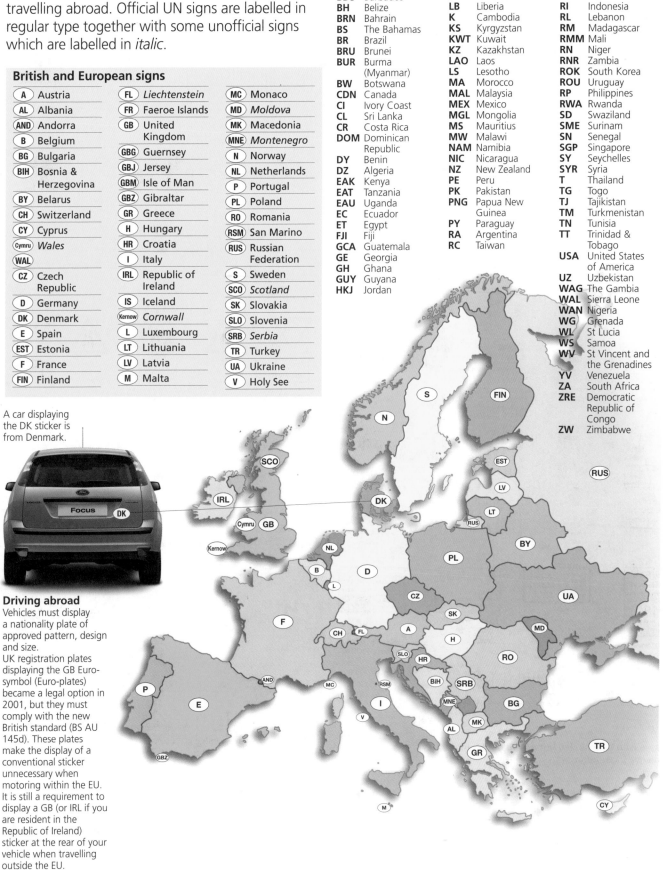

Driving abroad
Vehicles must display a nationality plate of approved pattern, design and size.
UK registration plates displaying the GB Euro-symbol (Euro-plates) became a legal option in 2001, but they must comply with the new British standard (BS AU 145d). These plates make the display of a conventional sticker unnecessary when motoring within the EU. It is still a requirement to display a GB (or IRL if you are resident in the Republic of Ireland) sticker at the rear of your vehicle when travelling outside the EU.

Traffic signs (Britain and Northern Ireland)

Signs giving orders

**Signs with red circles are mostly prohibitive.
Plates below signs qualify their message.**

 Entry to 20mph zone

 End of 20mph zone

 Maximum speed

 National speed limit applies

 School crossing patrol

 Mini-roundabout (roundabout circulation – give way to vehicles from the immediate right)

 Route to be used by pedal cycles only

 Segregated pedal cycle and pedestrian route

 Minimum speed

 End of minimum speed

 Stop and give way

 Give way to traffic on major road

 Manually operated temporary STOP and GO signs

GO

 No entry for vehicular traffic

 Buses and cycles only

 Trams only

 Pedestrian crossing point over tramway

One-way traffic (note: compare circular 'Ahead only' sign)

 No vehicles except bicycles being pushed

 No cycling

 No motor vehicles

 No buses (over 8 passenger seats)

 No overtaking

 With-flow bus and cycle lane

 Contraflow bus lane

With-flow pedal cycle lane

No towed caravans

No vehicles carrying explosives

No vehicle or combination of vehicles over length shown

No vehicles over height shown

No vehicles over width shown

Warning signs

Mostly triangular

 Distance to 'STOP' line ahead

 Dual carriageway ends

 Road narrows on right (left if symbol reversed)

 Road narrows on both sides

Distance to 'Give Way' line ahead

 Give way to oncoming vehicles — Give priority to vehicles from opposite direction

 No right turn

No left turn

No U-turns

No goods vehicles over maximum gross weight shown (in tonnes) except for loading and unloading

 Crossroads

 Junction on bend ahead

 T-junction with priority over vehicles from the right

 Staggered junction

 Traffic merging from left ahead

The priority through route is indicated by the broader line.

 WEAK BRIDGE — No vehicles over maximum gross weight shown (in tonnes)

 Permit holders only — Parking restricted to permit holders

 RED ROUTE No stopping at any time except buses — No stopping during period indicated except for buses

 URBAN CLEARWAY Monday to Friday — No stopping during times shown except for as long as necessary to set down or pick up passengers

 Double bend first to left (symbol may be reversed)

 Bend to right (or left if symbol reversed)

 Roundabout

 Uneven road

 REDUCE SPEED NOW — Plate below some signs

 No waiting

No stopping (Clearway)

 Two-way traffic crosses one-way road

 Two-way traffic straight ahead

 Opening or swing bridge ahead

 Low-flying aircraft or sudden aircraft noise

 Falling or fallen rocks

**Signs with blue circles but no red border mostly give
positive instruction.**

 Ahead only

 Turn left ahead (right if symbol reversed)

 Turn left (right if symbol reversed)

 Keep left (right if symbol reversed)

Vehicles may pass either side to reach same destination

Traffic signals not in use

Traffic signals

Slippery road

Steep hill downwards

Steep hill upwards

Gradients may be shown as a ratio i.e. 20% = 1:5

Tunnel ahead

Trams crossing ahead

Level crossing with barrier or gate ahead

Level crossing without barrier or gate ahead

Level crossing without barrier

Downward pointing arrows mean 'Get in lane'
The left-hand lane leads to a different destination from the other lanes.

School crossing patrol ahead (some signs have amber lights which flash when crossings are in use)

Frail (or blind or disabled if shown) pedestrians likely to cross road ahead

Pedestrians in road ahead

Zebra crossing

Overhead electric cable; plate indicates maximum height of vehicles which can pass safely

The panel with the inclined arrow indicates the destinations which can be reached by leaving the motorway at the next junction

Available width of headroom indicated

Signs on primary routes - green backgrounds

At the junction

Sharp deviation of route to left (or right if chevrons reversed)

Light signals ahead at level crossing, airfield or bridge

Miniature warning lights at level crossings

On approaches to junctions

Route confirmatory sign after junction

On approaches to junctions

On approach to a junction in Wales (bilingual)

Blue panels indicate that the motorway starts at the junction ahead.
Motorways shown in brackets can also be reached along the route indicated.
White panels indicate local or non-primary routes leading from the junction ahead.
Brown panels show the route to tourist attractions.
The name of the junction may be shown at the top of the sign.
The aircraft symbol indicates the route to an airport.
A symbol may be included to warn of a hazard or restriction along that route.

Cattle

Wild animals

Wild horses or ponies

Accompanied horses or ponies

Cycle route ahead

Primary route forming part of a ring road

Risk of ice

Traffic queues likely ahead

Distance over which road humps extend

Other danger; plate indicates nature of danger

Soft verges

Signs on non-primary and local routes - black borders

Side winds

Hump bridge

Worded warning sign

Quayside or river bank

Risk of grounding

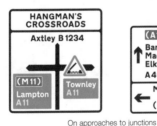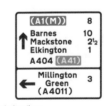
On approaches to junctions

At the junction

Direction to toilets with access for the disabled

Green panels indicate that the primary route starts at the junction ahead.
Route numbers on a blue background show the direction to a motorway.
Route numbers on a green background show the direction to a primary route.

Direction signs

Mostly rectangular

Signs on motorways – blue backgrounds

At a junction leading directly into a motorway (junction number may be shown on a black background)

On approaches to junctions (junction number on black background)

Route confirmatory sign after junction

Note: Although this road atlas shows many of the signs commonly in use, a comprehensive explanation of our signing system is given in the Department of Transport's booklet *Know Your Traffic Signs*, which is on sale at booksellers. The booklet also illustrates and explains the vast majority of signs the road user in likely to encounter. The signs illustrated in this road atlas are not all drawn to the same scale. In Wales, bilingual versions of some signs are used including Welsh and English versions of place names. Some older designs of signs may still be seen on the roads.

Traffic signs (Britain and Northern Ireland)

Other direction signs

Picnic site

Ancient monument in the care of English Heritage

Direction to a car park

'Countdown' markers at exit from motorway (each bar represents 100 yards to the exit). Green-backed markers may be used on primary routes and white-backed markers with black bars on other routes. At approaches to concealed level crossings white-backed markers with red bars may be used. Although these will be erected at equal distances the bars do not represent 100 yard intervals.

Motorway service area sign showing the operator's name

Zoo
Tourist attraction

Direction to camping and caravan site

Advisory route for lorries

Route for pedal cycles forming part of a network

Recommended route for pedal cycles to place shown

Route for pedestrians

Traffic has priority over oncoming vehicles

Hospital ahead with Accident and Emergency facilities

Tourist information point

No through road for vehicles

Symbols showing emergency diversion route for motorway and other main road traffic

Diversion route

Recommended route for pedal cycles

Home Zone Entry

Area in which cameras are used to enforce traffic regulations

Bus lane on road at junction ahead

Information signs

All rectangular

Entrance to controlled parking zone

Entrance to congestion charging zone

Greater London Low Emission Zone (LEZ)

Advance warning of restriction or prohibition ahead

Parking place for solo motorcycles

With-flow bus lane ahead which pedal cycles and taxis may also use

Lane designated for use by high occupancy vehicles (HOV) - see rule 142

Vehicles permitted to use an HOV lane ahead

End of motorway

Start of motorway and point from which motorway regulations apply

Appropriate traffic lanes at junction ahead

Traffic on the main carriageway coming from right has priority over joining traffic

Additional traffic joining from left ahead. Traffic on main carriageway has priority over joining traffic from right hand lane of slip road

Traffic in right hand lane of slip road joining the main carriageway has priority over left hand lane

Roadworks signs

Road works

Loose chippings

Temporary hazard at roadworks

Temporary lane closure (the number and position of arrows and red bars may be varied according to lanes open and closed)

Slow-moving or stationary works vehicle blocking a traffic lane. Pass in the direction shown by the arrow.

Mandatory speed limit ahead

Roadworks 1 mile ahead

End of roadworks and any temporary restrictions including speed limits

Signs used on the back of slow-moving or stationary vehicles warning of a lane closed ahead by a works vehicle. There are no cones on the road.

450 yds

Lane restrictions at roadworks ahead

One lane crossover at contraflow roadworks

Traffic signs (Republic of Ireland)

Warning signs

Dangerous corner ahead

Dangerous bend ahead

Series of dangerous corners ahead

Series of dangerous bends ahead

Crossroads

T-junction

Y-junction

Junction ahead with road or roads of equal importance

End of dual carriageway

Roundabout ahead

Crossroads

Side road

Junction ahead with roads of less importance

Y-junction

Staggered Junction ahead with roads of equal importance

with roads of less importance

Crossroads

T-junction

Advance warning (where vision is limited) of a major road ahead

Accompanied horses and ponies

Unprotected quay, canal or river ahead

Slippery road ahead

Sharp rise ahead (e.g. hump-back bridge)

Sharp dip ahead

Series of bumps or hollows ahead

Steep ascent ahead

Steep descent ahead

Roadworks ahead

School ahead

Children crossing (in residential area)

Traffic signals ahead

3.86 m
Low bridge ahead (height restriction shown)

Level crossing ahead unguarded by gates or lifting barriers

guarded by gates or lifting barriers

Signs giving orders

Stop and give way

Major road ahead- yeild or give way to traffic on it

GÉILL SLÍ

School warden's stop sign

Approaching traffic must stop as long as this sign is exhibited by a school warden

50 km/h
Max speed limit (km/h)

No entry

Parking permitted

Parking prohibited

Periods etc. for which parking is permitted or prohibited may be shown on a plaque placed beneath the sign

Clearway - stopping or parking prohibited

Information signs

National road advance direction sign

National road direction sign

Entry to motorway

End of motorway

Regional road direction sign

Advanced indication of bollards

City, town or village sign

Traffic lay-by ahead

Traffic lay-by

Road records

Since 1910 AA maps and atlases have become as trusted as AA Patrols and the Cartography Department of the AA has always been the primary source of answers to AA members' enquiries and questions. Here are some of the more interesting answers:

Highest main road
Cutting through the Grampians, the A93 reaches its summit at Cairnwell Pass, 665m (2182ft) above sea level.

Lowest bridge height
The Forth & Clyde Canal aqueduct bridges over Auchendavie Road in Kirkintilloch, giving a vehicle clearance height of just 1.3m (4ft 9 inches).

Highest motorway
Cutting across the Pennines, the M62 reaches its summit at junction 22 on Moss Moor more than 350m (1,148ft) above sea level.

First motorway
The short 5-mile (8km) Preston bypass (M6) opened in December 1958, 11 months before the more extensive section of the M1 opened north of Watford.

Longest road tunnel
Opened in 1934, the Mersey Tunnel is 2.87 miles (4.62km) in length including approaches and branch tunnels.

Biggest interchange
18 routes on six levels give junction 6 on the M6 motorway the apt title of 'Spaghetti Junction'.

▲ Most infamous roundabout
Built in 1972, Swindon's 'Magic Roundabout' is a central island surrounded by five mini-roundabouts. Local drivers swear it works.

Longest bridge
Opened in 1966 and of box girder construction, the A92 Tay Road Bridge stretches 1.4 miles (2.2km) across the Firth and remains Britain's longest road bridge.

Geographic centre
Britain's most central location is Dunsop Bridge, off the B6478, just north of Clitheroe.

▲ Steepest drivable road
Chimney Bank on the Hutton-le-Hole road just south of Rosedale Abbey is a 1:3 gradient.

▲ Longest suspension bridge
The world's longest when it opened in 1981 the A15 Humber Bridge, with a span of 0.88 miles (1.4km), remains Europe's longest single-span suspension bridge.

Longest straight road
The A15 between the M180 at Scawby and Scampton Airfield, just north of Lincoln is 15.1 miles (24.3km) in length.

▲ First toll motorway
The 27-mile M6 Toll motorway opened in December 2003 to bypass the busiest section of the M6 around Birmingham (Ireland's M1 Drogheda bypass opened in June 2003).

Lowest 'A' road
The A1101 between Bury St Edmunds and Long Sutton is barely above sea level for much of its length.

Busiest motorway
The M25 between junctions 14 and 15, A3133 to the M4 at Heathrow, carries 165,000 vehicles per day (in both directions).

Road records continued

Britain

Car number plates – Number plates, just three letters long, were first introduced in August 1932.

Cat's Eyes – 29 April 1935 saw inventor Percy Shaw's unique glass reflectors first used on British roads.

First main road – In *circa* AD50 the Romans built the Fosse Way to link Exeter and Lincoln.

Land's End to John o' Groats – The distance is 876 miles (1,410km) by main road or 602 miles (969km) as the crow flies.

Largest car park – Birmingham's National Exhibition Centre car park has capacity for 20,000 vehicles.

Longest 'A' road – At 403 miles (648km) in total length, linking London to Edinburgh, the A1 is the longest.

Longest motorway – The M6 from its junction with the M1 at Rugby to the Scottish border north of Carlisle is 236 miles (380km) long.

Longest ring road – The M25 London Orbital Motorway is 121.5 miles (195.5km) long.

Shortest street – Elgin Street in Bacup, Lancashire, is just 5.2m (17ft) in length.

Traffic lights – On the 15 December 1931, following their success in central London, traffic lights were introduced throughout the country.

White lines – September 1925 saw the introduction of white lines painted on roads to help reduce accidents.

Ireland

Longest road bridge – Opened in 1984 the elegant Foyle Bridge on the A2 north of Londonderry is 947 yards (866m) in length. Due to open in 2011 the new N25 New Ross bridge is planned to be Ireland's longest.

Longest road tunnel – When it opened on 20th December 2006 the M50 Dublin Port Tunnel, at 2.8 miles (4.5km), was Europe's longest urban motorway tunnel.

Geo facts

The biggest, longest, narrowest, highest, deepest, tallest and shortest of Britain and Ireland's geographical features.

Highest waterfall
Eas a' Chual Aluinn's slender cascade drops 201m (658ft) making it Britain's tallest.

Deepest lake
At its deepest point Loch Morar plunges to 310m (1,017ft).

Narrowest strait
Seil Sound narrows to just 6m (20ft) wide where its short bridge is said to span the North Atlantic.

Longest lake
Loch Ness stretches 24.2 miles (39km) along The Great Glen from Fort Augustus towards Inverness.

Highest lake
Lochan Buidhe, at the head of Glen Avon, is 1,097m (3,600ft) above sea level.

▲ Highest mountain
Ben Nevis rises skyward to 1,343m (4,406ft) above sea level.

▲ Longest rail bridge
Completed in 1887, the Tay Bridge is 2.2 miles (3.5km) long.

Largest lake ▶
Loch Lomond is 27.5 miles² (71km²) in area and 22.6 miles (36km) long.

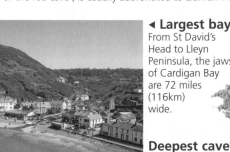

▲ Longest fiord
Loch Fyne, Scotland's longest sea loch, penetrates 42 miles (67.6km) into the West Highlands.

Shortest place name
The village of 'Ae' 8 miles north of Dumfries.

Longest place name
The village of **Llanfairpwllgwyngyllgogerychwyrndrobwllllantysiliogogogoch**, meaning 'St Mary's Church in the hollow of the white hazel near a rapid whirlpool and the Church of St Tysilio of the red cave', is usually abbreviated to Llanfair PG

▲ Highest village
'Flash' in Staffordshire's Peak District is 465m (about 1,518ft) above sea level.

◀ Largest bay
From St David's Head to Lleyn Peninsula, the jaws of Cardigan Bay are 72 miles (116km) wide.

Deepest cave
Ogof Ffynnon Ddu is 308m (1,010ft) deep.

Longest river
Rising on the slopes of Plynlimon the Severn flows 220 miles (354km) through the Vale of Powys and into the Bristol Channel.

Longest rail tunnel
The Channel Tunnel is 31 miles (50km) long, with 23 miles (38km) under the sea.

▲ Tallest building
At 243.8m (800ft) tall, Canary Wharf Tower dominates London Dockland's skyline.

Geo facts continued

Definitions
United Kingdom: Denotes the political union of England, Scotland, Wales and Northern Ireland. It does not include the Isle of Man or the Channel Islands.

Great Britain: Denotes the political entity of England, Scotland and Wales. It does not include the Isle of Man, the Channel Islands or Northern Ireland. It is often abbreviated to 'Britain'.

British Isles: Unofficial term for the geographical entity comprising the United Kingdom, the Republic of Ireland, the Isle of Man and the Channel Islands.

Largest island: Mainland Britain's area is 90,504 miles² (234,411km²).

England
Capital: London.
Highest peak: Scafell Pike 978m (3,210ft).
Highest waterfall: Cauldron Snout 61m (200ft).
Longest river: Thames 215 miles (346 km).
Largest lake: Windermere 5.7 miles² (14 km²) in area, 10.5 miles (17km) long, Lake District.
Deepest lake: Wast Water 78m (258ft), Lake District.
Deepest cave: Peak Cavern 248m (814ft).

Scotland
Capital: Edinburgh
Highest village: Wanlockhead 424.6m (1,393ft).
Longest river: Tay 117 miles (188km).

Wales
Capital: Cardiff
Highest peak: Snowdon 1,085m (3,560ft).
Highest village: Garn-yr-erw 400.8m (1,315ft).
Highest waterfall: Pistyll Rhaeadr 73m (240ft).
Longest river: Towy (Tywi) 64 miles 103km).
Largest lake: Llyn Tegid 1.7 miles² (4.5km²) in area.

Ireland
Capital: Belfast (Northern Ireland), Dublin (Republic of Ireland).
Highest Peak: Carrauntoohil 1,039m (3,409ft).
Highest waterfall: Powerscourt Falls 106m (348ft)
Longest River: Shannon 161 miles (259km)
Largest Lake: Lough Neagh 147miles² (381km²) in area.

Scotland

Abers	**Aberdeenshire**
Ag & B	**Argyll & Bute**
Angus	**Angus**
Border	**Scottish Borders**
C Aber	**City of Aberdeen**
C Dund	**City of Dundee**
C Edin	**City of Edinburgh**
C Glas	**City of Glasgow**
Clacks	**Clackmannanshire (1)**
D & G	**Dumfries & Galloway**
E Ayrs	**East Ayrshire**
E Duns	**East Dunbartonshire (2)**
E Loth	**East Lothian**
E Rens	**East Renfrewshire (3)**
Falk	**Falkirk**
Fife	**Fife**
Highld	**Highland**
Inver	**Inverclyde (4)**
Mdloth	**Midlothian (5)**
Moray	**Moray**
N Ayrs	**North Ayrshire**
N Lans	**North Lanarkshire (6)**
Ork	**Orkney Islands**
P & K	**Perth & Kinross**
Rens	**Renfrewshire (7)**
S Ayrs	**South Ayrshire**
Shet	**Shetland Islands**
S Lans	**South Lanarkshire**
Stirlg	**Stirling**
W Duns	**West Dunbartonshire (8)**
W Isls	**Western Isles**
W Loth	**West Lothian**

Northern Ireland

Antrim	**Antrim**
Armagh	**Armagh**
Belfst	**Belfast**
Down	**Down**
Ferman	**Fermanagh**
Lderry	**Londonderry**
Tyrone	**Tyrone**

Republic of Ireland

Carlow	**Carlow**
Cavan	**Cavan**
Clare	**Clare**
Cork	**Cork**
Donegl	**Donegal**
Dublin	**Dublin**
Dublin	**Dublin City (62)**
Dublin	**Dún Laoghaire-Rathdown (63)**
Dublin	**Fingal (64)**
Dublin	**South Dublin (65)**
Galway	**Galway**
Kerry	**Kerry**
Kildre	**Kildare**
Kilken	**Kilkenny**
Laois	**Laois**
Leitrm	**Leitrim**
Limrck	**Limerick**
Longfd	**Longford**
Louth	**Louth**
Mayo	**Mayo**
Meath	**Meath**
Monhan	**Monaghan**
Offaly	**Offaly**
Roscom	**Roscommon**
Sligo	**Sligo**
Tippry	**Tipperary North**
Tippry	**Tipperary South**
Watfd	**Waterford**
Wmeath	**Westmeath**
Wexfd	**Wexford**
Wicklw	**Wicklow**

England

BaNES	**Bath & N E Somerset (18)**
Barns	**Barnsley (19)**
Beds	**Bedfordshire**
Birm	**Birmingham**
Bl w D	**Blackburn with Darwen (20)**
Bmouth	**Bournemouth**
Bolton	**Bolton (21)**
Bpool	**Blackpool**
Brad	**Bradford (22)**
Br & H	**Brighton and Hove (23)**
Br For	**Bracknell Forest (24)**
Bristl	**City of Bristol**
Bucks	**Buckinghamshire**
Bury	**Bury (25)**
C Derb	**City of Derby**
C KuH	**City of Kingston upon Hull**
C Leic	**City of Leicester**
C Nott	**City of Nottingham**
C Pete	**City of Peterborough**
C Plym	**City of Plymouth**
C Port	**City of Portsmouth**
C Sotn	**City of Southampton**
C Stke	**City of Stoke**
Calder	**Calderdale (26)**
Cambs	**Cambridgeshire**
Ches	**Cheshire**
Cnwll	**Cornwall**
Covtry	**Coventry**
Cumb	**Cumbria**
Darltn	**Darlington (27)**
Derbys	**Derbyshire**
Devon	**Devon**
Donc	**Doncaster (28)**
Dorset	**Dorset**
Dudley	**Dudley (29)**
Dur	**Durham**
E R Yk	**East Riding of Yorkshire**
E Susx	**East Sussex**
Essex	**Essex**
Gatesd	**Gateshead (30)**
Gloucs	**Gloucestershire**
Gt Lon	**Greater London**
Halton	**Halton (31)**
Hants	**Hampshire**
Hartpl	**Hartlepool (32)**
Herefs	**Herefordshire**
Herts	**Hertfordshire**
IoS	**Isles of Scilly**
IoW	**Isle of Wight**
Kent	**Kent**
Kirk	**Kirklees (33)**
Knows	**Knowsley (34)**
Lancs	**Lancashire**
Leeds	**Leeds**
Leics	**Leicestershire**
Lincs	**Lincolnshire**
Lpool	**Liverpool**
Luton	**Luton**
M Keyn	**Milton Keynes**
Manch	**Manchester**
Medway	**Medway**
Middsb	**Middlesbrough**
NE Lin	**North East Lincolnshire**
N Linc	**North Lincolnshire**
N Som	**North Somerset (35)**
N Tyne	**North Tyneside (36)**
N u Ty	**Newcastle upon Tyne**
N York	**North Yorkshire**
Nhants	**Northamptonshire**
Norfk	**Norfolk**
Notts	**Nottinghamshire**
Nthumb	**Northumberland**
Oldham	**Oldham (37)**
Oxon	**Oxfordshire**
Poole	**Poole**
R & Cl	**Redcar and Cleveland**
Readg	**Reading**
Rochdl	**Rochdale (38)**
Rothm	**Rotherham (39)**
Rutlnd	**Rutland**
S Glos	**South Gloucestershire (40)**
S on T	**Stockton-on-Tees (41)**
S Tyne	**South Tyneside (42)**
Salfd	**Salford (43)**
Sandw	**Sandwell (44)**
Sefton	**Sefton (45)**
Sheff	**Sheffield**
Shrops	**Shropshire**
Slough	**Slough (46)**
Solhll	**Solihull (47)**
Somset	**Somerset**
St Hel	**St Helens (48)**
Staffs	**Staffordshire**
Sthend	**Southend-on-Sea**
Stockp	**Stockport (49)**
Suffk	**Suffolk**
Sundld	**Sunderland**
Surrey	**Surrey**
Swindn	**Swindon**
Tamesd	**Tameside (50)**
Thurr	**Thurrock (51)**
Torbay	**Torbay**
Traffd	**Trafford (52)**
W & M	**Windsor & Maidenhead (53)**
W Berk	**West Berkshire**
W Susx	**West Sussex**
Wakefd	**Wakefield (54)**
Warrtn	**Warrington (55)**
Warwks	**Warwickshire**
Wigan	**Wigan (56)**
Wilts	**Wiltshire**
Wirral	**Wirral (57)**
Wokham	**Wokingham (58)**
Wolves	**Wolverhampton (59)**
Worcs	**Worcestershire**
Wrekin	**Telford and Wrekin (60)**
Wsall	**Walsall (61)**
York	**York**

Wales

Blae G	**Blaenau Gwent (9)**
Brdgnd	**Bridgend (10)**
Caerph	**Caerphilly (11)**
Cardif	**Cardiff**
Carmth	**Carmarthenshire**
Cerdgn	**Ceredigion**
Conwy	**Conwy**
Denbgs	**Denbighshire**
Flints	**Flintshire**
Gwynd	**Gwynedd**
IoA	**Isle of Anglesey**
Mons	**Monmouthshire**
Myr Td	**Merthyr Tydfil (12)**
Neath	**Neath Port Talbot (13)**
Newpt	**Newport (14)**
Pembks	**Pembrokeshire**
Powys	**Powys**
Rhondd	**Rhondda Cynon Taff (15)**
Swans	**Swansea**
Torfn	**Torfaen (16)**
V Glam	**Vale of Glamorgan (17)**
Wrexhm	**Wrexham**

Channel Islands & Isle of Man

Guern	**Guernsey**
Jersey	**Jersey**
IoM	**Isle of Man**

How to use this atlas

Each road map spread has a fold-out flap on the right-hand page. This makes it easier for you to follow west-east routes across the country, removing the risk of losing your place when you turn the page. It also opens to reveal a guide to places to visit covered by the map spread.

Following west-east routes

 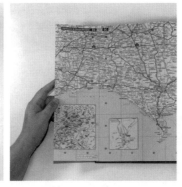

If you keep the map flap closed (left-hand picture) you can see a village or other landmark in relation to the routes westward, and if you open it as you turn the page (right-hand picture) you can see the same landmark in relation to the routes eastward.

Guide to places to visit

The fold-out flap on the right-hand page opens to reveal a guide to places of interest, specially selected to give you a flavour of the area covered by each map spread.

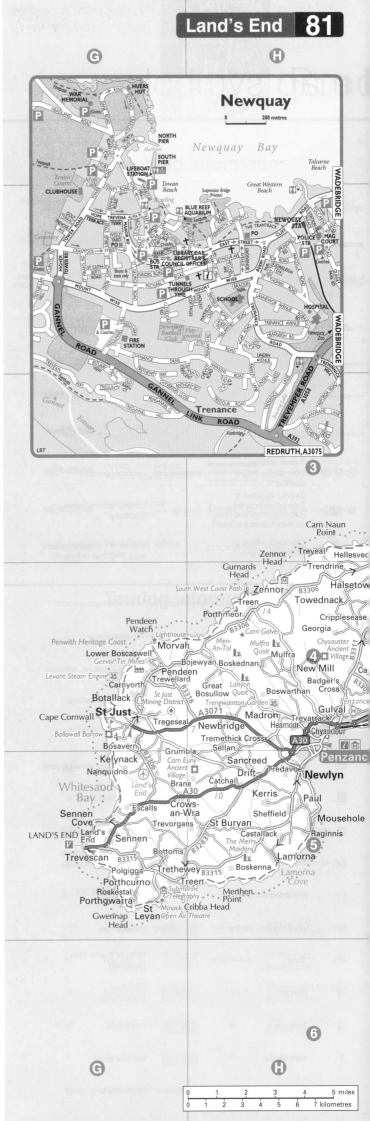

86

A **B** **C** **D**

1

Bedruthan Steps
Carnewas
Trenance Downhill Erva
Ilva
Berryls Point
Griffins Point Mawgan Porth
Trevarrian St Ma
Carloggas
Watergate Tregurrian Newquay
Bay A3059
Towan Head Newquay St Columb Tregaswith
Minor Trevithick
Newquay Porth A30
Fistral Bay Colan
West Kelsey Head Pentire Treninnick Mountjoy
Holywell Crantock Pentire Trevemper Quintrell St Colu
Bay Trenowah Lane Downs Retyn
Penhale Point Tresean Rosecliston Kestle Mill Troan
Holywell Treveal Trevoll Trerice Dairyland St Ender
Ligger Point Mount Newlyn Gummow's Shop Chap
Cubert East Lappa Valley
Ligger or Treamble Rejerrah Trevilson
Perran Bay Rose Trevorgan St Ender
Perranporth Goonhavern Carland
Cligga Point Bolingey Cocks World in Miniature Cross Trelasick
Trevellas Perranwell Carnkiet B3285 Trende
Downs Penhallow Perranzabuloe Zelah St Trelassick
St Agnes St Barkla Shop Callestick Marazanvose Treworgan Allen Ladock
Heritage Coast Agnes Cross Mithian Treverbyn
ST AGNES HEAD Coombe Goonbell Allet Common Idless St Erme Tresawle
Wheal Coates Goonvrea Coldharbour Silverwell Bodrean
St Agnes Mount Shortlanesend Kenwyn Penair Tresillian
Mining District Hawke Three Burrows Kenwyn Merther
Porthtowan Mawla Menagissey Wheal B3284 Truro
Mawla Rose Blackwater Three St Clement
Godrevy-Portreath Cambrose Wheal Peevor Milestone Higher Malpas St Michael
Heritage Coast Portreath B3300 Chacewater Saveock Town Penkevil
Navax North Water Newbridge P+R Calenick Old Kea Lamorran
Godrevy Point Illogan Country A30 Scorrier Baldhu Kea Porthkea Trewor
Godrevy Point Paynter's Mount St Day Cross Lanes Killiow Playing Coombe Trelissick Treworth
Tehidy Park Lane End Ambrose Twelveheads Chyeowling Place Penelewey Trelissick Philleigh
Coombe South Bottom Carn Frogpool Bissoe Garden
Gwealavellan Tehidy Cornish Brea Carharrack Gwennap Carnon Penpol Trevilla Treluggan
St Ives Reskadinnick Treswithian Tuckingmill Redruth Trevarth Downs Feock Trewithian
Gwithian Kehelland Roseworthy Carn Brea Lanner Perranwell Devoran Carclew Carg
Upton Towans Camborne Carnkie A393 Angarrack Mylor Restronguet Rose
St Ives Connor Downs Penponds Bolenowe Penhalurick Perran Bridge St Just-in Portsca
Carbis The Phillack Barripper Four Penhalvean Wharf Lower Mylor Roseland Gerrans
Bay Towans Angarrack Carnhell Troon Lanes Ponsanooth Stockdale Treluswell St Gluvia's Tregew Greeb
Hayle Green Rosewarne Hendra Burnthouse Trelew Flushing
Lelant Copperhouse Praze-an Stithians Carnkie Longdowns Mabe Penryn St Mawes
Brunnion High Gwinear Beeble Tregolls Burnthouse A39 Bohortha
Canonstown Lanes Wall Horsedown Blackrock Farms Porkellis Rame Trenoweth Budock Penjerrick South West Coast Pat
Whitecross St Erth Fraddam Common Lezerea Edgcombe Treverva Water Falmouth ZONE
le Gate St Erth Praze Leedstown Crowan Wendron Treverva Lamanva Pendennis POINT
Cockwells Kerthen Mining District Seworgan Penjerrick Point
Crowlas Wood Townshend Drym Nancegollan Trenear Poldark Mine Brill Barreppa Maenporth
Ludgvan Tregonning, Gwinear Godolphin Prospidnick Trevarno A394 High Carlidnack Mawnan Smith
Longrock & Trewavas Cross Wendron Manhay Cross Constantine ROSEMULLION HEAD
Marazion Mining District Crowntown Sithney Lower Coverack Porth Navas Mawnan
Goldsithney Millpool Balwest Carleen Green Town Bridges Gweek Helford Passage Durgan Toll Point
Perranuthnoe Newtown Trescowe Sithney Brill Helford St Anthony
St Michael's Rosudgeon Germoe Trew Breage Common Helston Gweek Helford Gillan Nare Point
Mount Kenneggy Ashton Lower Mawgan Gear Manaccan Carne Lestowder
Prussia Cove Praa Rinsey Croft A394 Sithney Garras St Martin Roskorwell
Sands Rinsey Common Trelowarren Tregidden Porthallow
Cudden Rinsey Trewavas Porthleven Higher Halliggye Newtown Tregarne Trenance
Point Head Pentire Fogou in-St Martin Porthoustock
MOUNT'S BAY Chyvarloe Berepper White Cury Treleague Manacle Point
Gunwalloe Cross Cross Lanes Traboe Rosenithon
Chyanvounder Garras Goonhilly Satellite Zoar St Keverne
Angrouse Earth Station
Poldhu Point Trewoon GOONHILLY
Marconi Memorial DOWNS Trelan Lowland Point
Mullion Cove Mullion Penhale Ponsongath North Corner
Mullion Gwenter Coverack
Island Ruan Trewillis
Predannack Major Kuggar Treleaver
Wollas St Trewrickle Black Head
Predannack Head Mount Hermon Ruan
Vellan Head St Poltescoe
The Lizard Heritage Coast Grade Ruan Minor Devil's Frying Pan
Lizard Head South West Cadgwith
Kynance Cove Coast Path Church Cove
Lizard Lighthouse
LIZARD POINT Bass Point

2

3

4

5

6

A **B** **C** **D**

Town plan: Newquay p.81

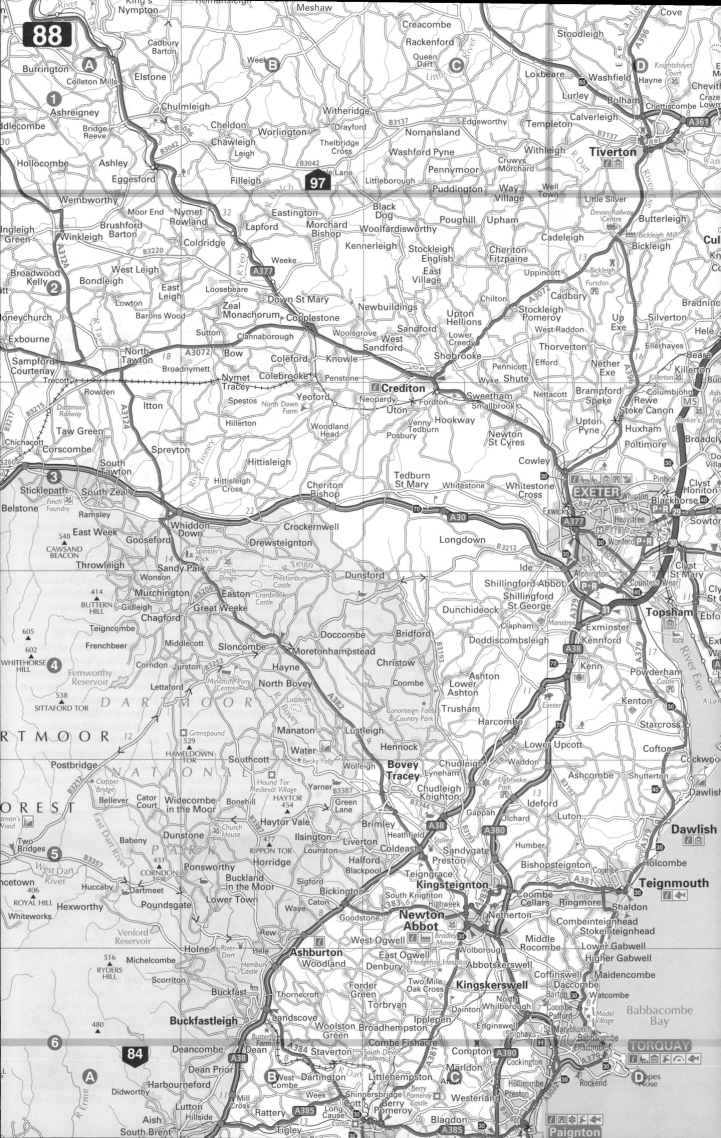

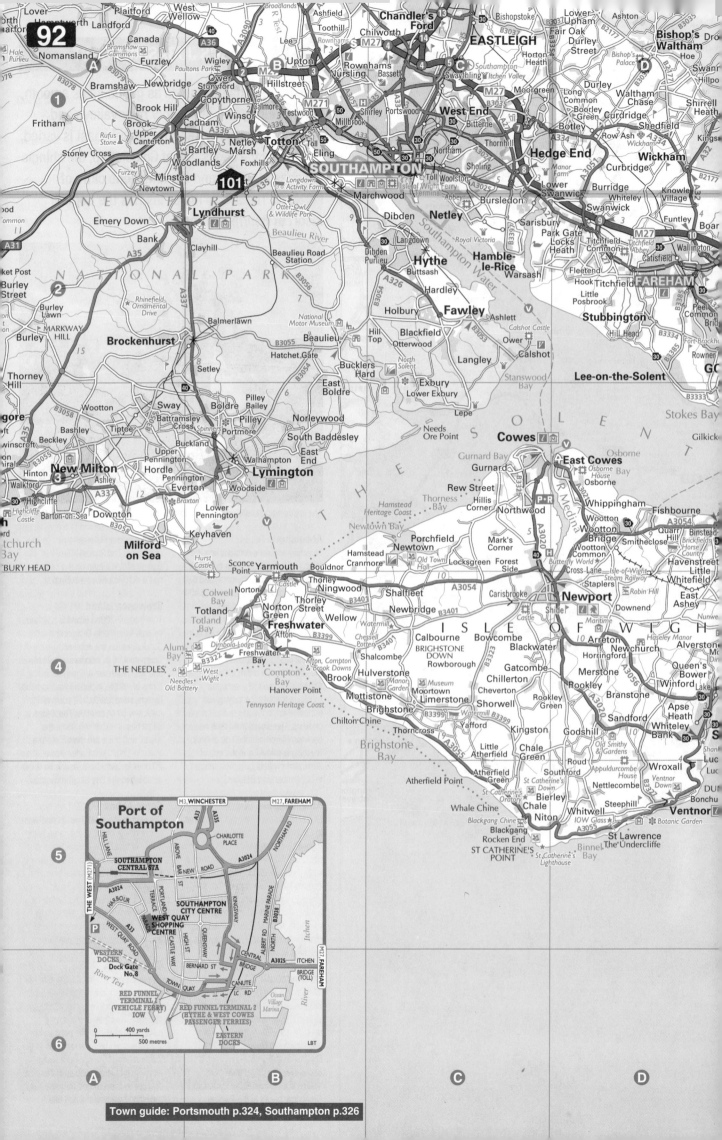

Meonstoke
OLD WINCHESTER HILL
SALT HILL
BUTSER HILL
Buriton
Elsted
Cocking Causeway
South Lavington
South Ambersham
Coultershaw Bridge
Egdean

Brockbridge
Chidden
Clanfield
War Down
Queen Elizabeth Country Park
South Harting
East Harting
Trey
Depton
LINCH DOWN
Cocking
Heyshott
Norwood
Graffham
Duncton

Soberton
E
Hambledon
Butser Ancient Farm
Chalton
Compton
North Marden
South Downs Way
G
12
East Lavington
255
DUNCTON HILL
H
Sutton
Barlavington

Soberton Heath
Catherington
F
East Marden
Chilgrove
Singleton
West Dean
LEVIN DOWN 170
DUNCTON HILL
Bignor
Roman Villa

Hoe Gate
Anthill Common
Blendworth
Up Marden
West Marden
Charlton
East Dean
Goodwood
Weald & Downland Open Air Museum
206
The Trundle
THE TRUNDLE
Upwaltham
BIGNOR HILL 225

Worlds End
Furzeley Corner
Horndean
1
Finchdean
Forestide
Deanlane End
Stoughton
Bow Hill
Kingley Vale
Charlton
Halnaker Hill 144
NORE HILL
103

Denmead
Anmore
2
Lovedean
Rowland's Castle
Walderton
East Lavant
Waterbeach
Eartham
Slindon

WATERLOOVILLE
Southwick
Cowplain
102
Staunton
Lordington
Aldsworth
Funtington
Woodend
West Stoke
Mid Lavant
Strettington
Westerton
Halnaker
Priory
Fontwell
A27

Purbrook
Stakes
Widley
Bedhampton
HAVANT
Westbourne
Woodmancote
West Ashling
East Ashling
Summersdale
Goodwood
Boxgrove
Crockerhill
Norton
Tangmere
Fontwell

Ports Down
Royal Armouries
Drayton
Earlsdon
Brockhampton
Hermitage
Hambrook
Southbourne
Broadbridge
Roman Palace
Shopwyke
Westhampnett
Westergate
Binsted
Walberton

hester
Castle
Port Solent
12
Cosham
12
Langstone
Emsworth
Prinsted
Nutbourne
Walton
Fishbourne
Chichester
Oving
Woodgate
30
Barnham
Eastergate
North End

30
Hilsea
Northney
Chidham
Bosham
Dell Quay
Apuldram
Merston
Runcton
Colworth
Shripney
Yapton
A259

Harbour
Continental Ferry Terminal
North End
North Hayling
Stoke
Tye
HAYLING ISLAND
Fleet
THORNEY ISLAND
Bosham Hoe
West Thorney
Donnington
Hunston
North Mundham
South Mundham
Elbridge
Bersted
North Bersted
South Bersted
Flansham
Bilsham
Ancton

RT
Portsea
Fratton
South Hayling
West Town
Chichester Harbour
West Itchenor
Birdham
Sidlesham Common
Fisher
Street End
Runcton
Felpham
Middleton-on-

Southsea
Spinnaker Tower
Eastney
Fort Cumberland
Shipton Green
Somerley
Sidlesham
Rose Green
BOGNOR REGIS

PORTSMOUTH
Hayling Bay
West Wittering
Highleigh
Nyetimber
Aldwick

Spitbank Fort
Bracklesham
East Wittering
Earnley
Almodington
Pagham Harbour
Pagham
3

THEAD
Bracklesham Bay
Church Norton

Puckpool Point
Nettlestone Point
Seaview
Selsey

Nettlestone
SELSEY BILL

St Helens
The Duver
(Summer Only)
4

Bembridge
FORELAND
Bembridge Windmill
Lifeboat Station
Cherbourg
Guernsey
Jersey
St Malo
Caen (Ouistreham)
Bilbao
Le Havre
Cherbourg
Caen (Ouistreham)

ding
Steyne Cross
Whitecliff Bay

Yarbridge
Yaverland
Culver Cliff

andown
ndown Bay

lin

Village
hine

Portsmouth Harbour

M27, SOUTHAMPTON, CHICHESTER

0 ___ 800 yards
0 ___ 500 metres

CONTINENTAL FERRY PORT
HM NAVAL BASE
Portsea

PORTSMOUTH HARBOUR STA & IOW PASSENGER FERRY
Passenger Ferry to Gosport
ISLE OF WIGHT CAR FERRY TERMINAL
Passenger Ferry to Ryde IOW
HOVERCRAFT TERMINAL
SOUTHSEA

PORTSMOUTH CITY CENTRE
PORTSMOUTH & SOUTHSEA STA
FRATTON STA

A2030
WINSTON AVENUE
CHURCHILL
GOLDSMITH AVE
B2154
KING'S RD
ELM GROVE
B2154
B2155
LBT

---

0 1 2 3 4 5 miles
0 1 2 3 4 5 6 7 kilometres

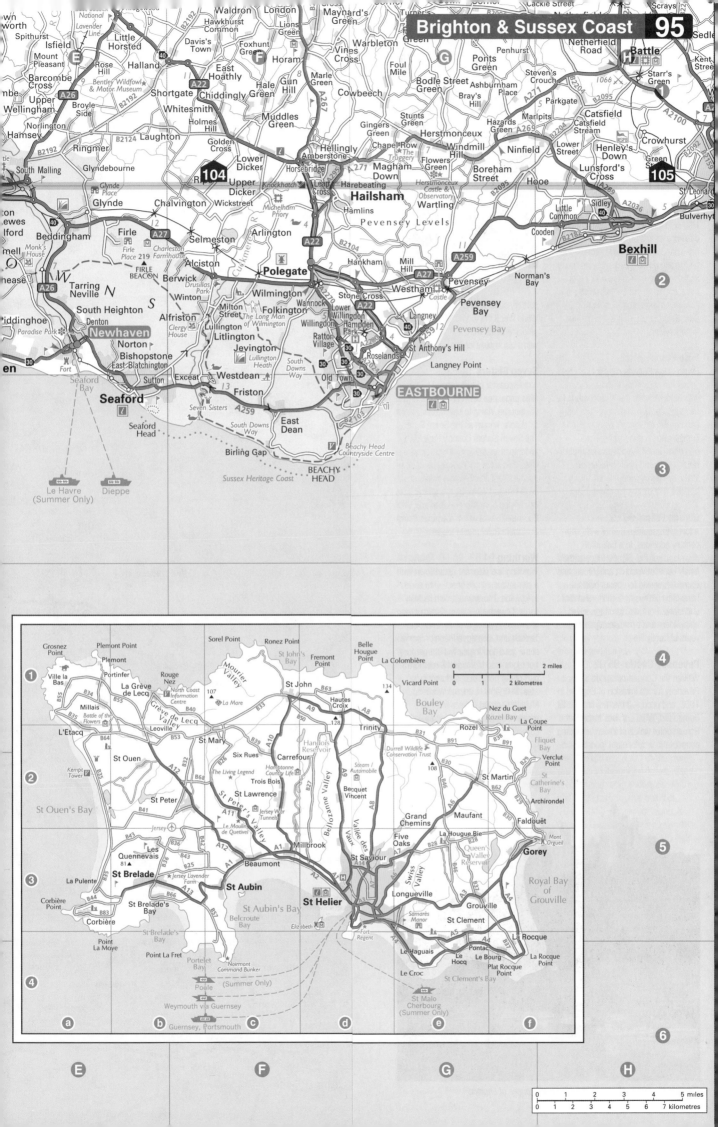

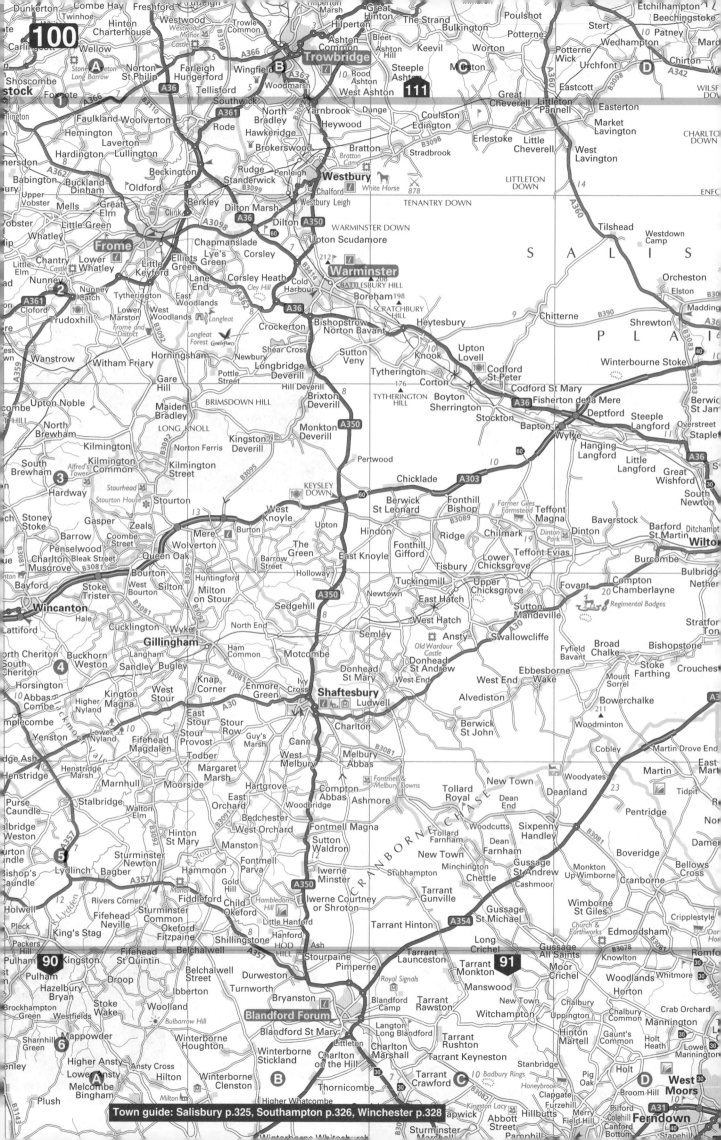

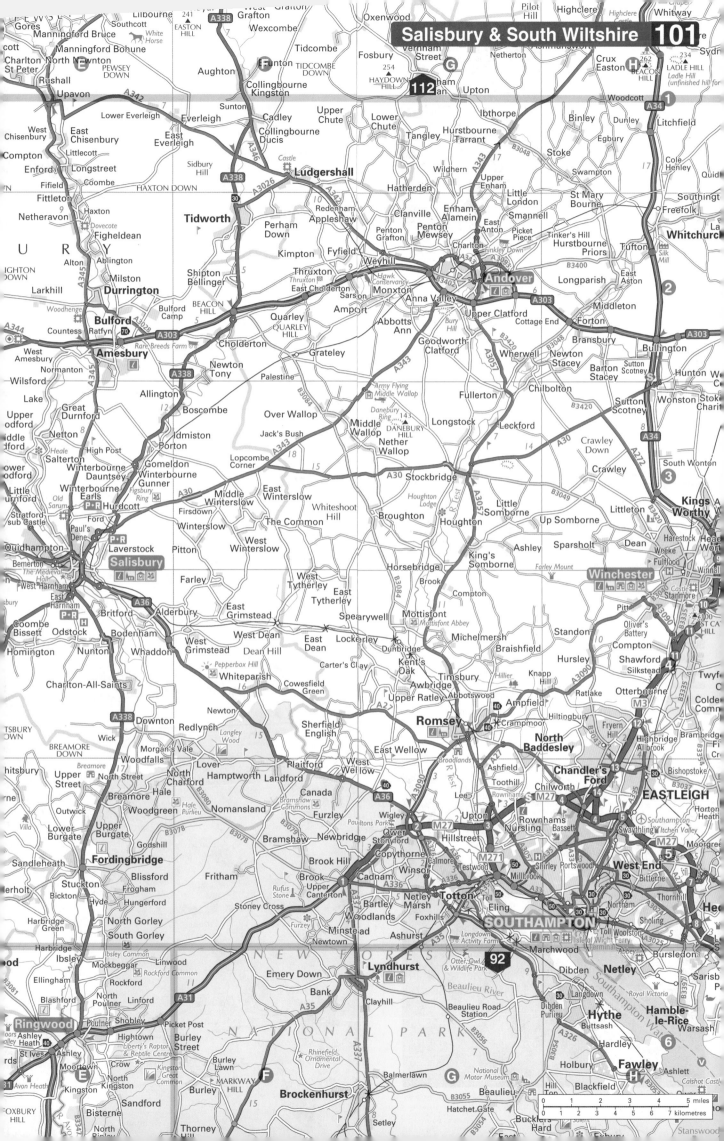

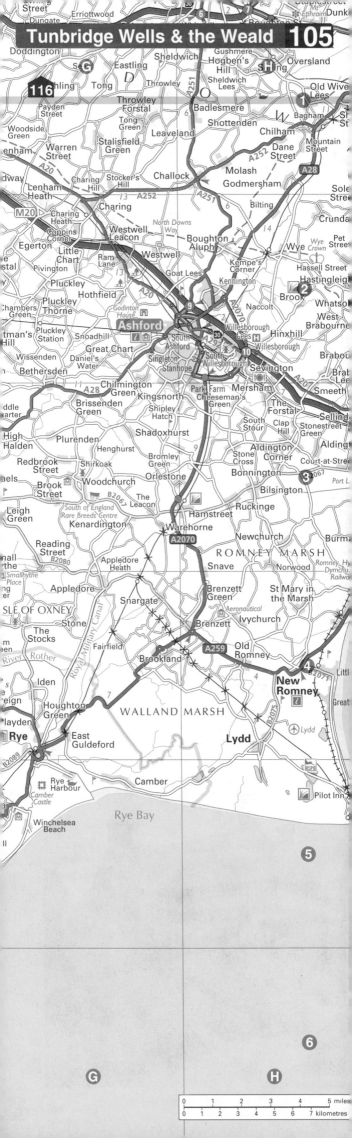

elegant Georgian buildings, with the most photogenic spots along Mermaid Street. The antiques shops and galleries are great for browsing. Parts of the 14th-century defences still remain, such as the Landgate Arch and Ypres Tower, a 13th-century lookout that houses the Rye Castle Museum.

Sheffield Park 104 B4

Sheffield Park was originally landscaped by 'Capability' Brown, in about 1775 to create a beautiful park with four lakes and cascades. Further extensive planting took place at the beginning of the 20th century, to give emphasis to autumn colour among the trees. In May and June masses of azaleas and rhododendrons bloom and later there are magnificent water lilies on the lakes. Autumn brings stunning colours from the many rare trees and shrubs.

Wakehurst Place

Sissinghurst Castle Garden 105 F3

The writer Vita Sackville-West and her husband, the diplomat and author Sir Harold Nicolson, created this famous Wealden garden in the 1930s around the ruin of a moated Elizabethan mansion. Sissinghurst, a major influence on garden design, consists of a series of small, enclosed compartments that between them provide an outstanding display of hues through the seasons. The brick front range (*c*1490) and the four-storey tower (*c*1565) are all that survive of the house.

Tunbridge Wells Museum & Art Gallery 104 C3

This combined museum and art gallery tells the story of the borough of Tunbridge Wells. There are collections of costume, art, dolls and toys along with natural and local history from dinosaur bones to the original Pantiles. There is also a large collection of Tunbridge ware, the intricate wooden souvenirs made for visitors to the wells. The art gallery features a changing programme of contemporary and historic art, touring exhibitions, and local art and craft.

Wakehurst Place 104 A3

The country offshoot of the Royal Botanic Gardens at Kew is a beautiful creation in its own right. A picturesque watercourse links lakes and ponds, and the gardens surround an Elizabethan mansion with a rural exhibition. This is one of the country's most varied gardens, with a worldwide collection, an arboretum, and year-round colour. The Millennium Seed Bank, an £80-million international conservation project, safeguards the world's most endangered plant species in massive underground seed vaults.

Winchelsea 105 G5

Winchelsea, a medieval Cinque Port, began life at sea level until its destruction in a storm in 1287. It was rebuilt to a grid pattern (the first example of town planning in medieval England) on the clifftop, fortified with walls and gateways against French invaders. Most buildings have 17th- and 18th-century façades but many are much older. Three gates survive of the medieval defences. Medieval Court Hall, restored in the 16th century, houses the local museum.

Flowers of every hue welcome you to the gardens of Great Dixter

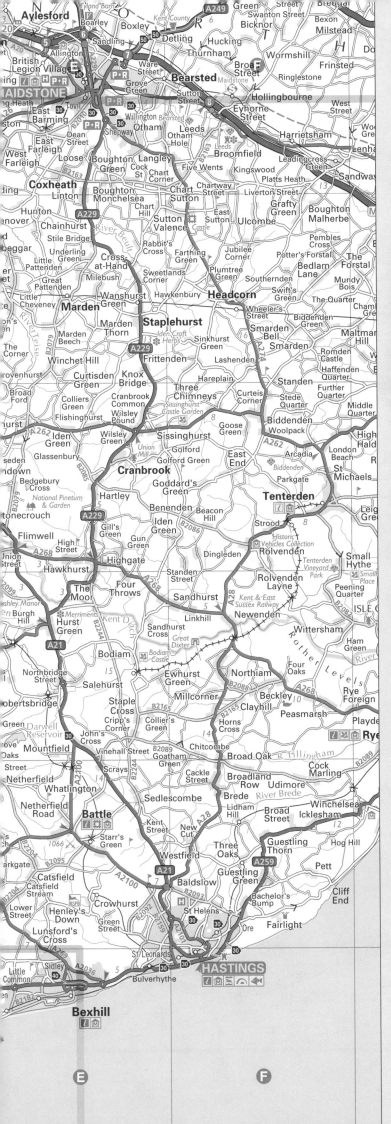

TUNBRIDGE WELLS & THE WEALD

At the heart of the Weald is Royal Tunbridge Wells – an elegant old spa town that entertained the royals of Regency days. To the south are the flat marshlands around the ancient towns on Winchelsea and Rye and the handsome town of Hastings, each with a markedly different character.

The Pantiles, a tree-lined promenade, stands at the heart of Tunbridge Wells

Battle of Hastings Abbey & Battlefield 105 E5
Explore the site of the Battle of Hastings, where on 14 October 1066, one of the most famous events in English history took place. There is a free interactive wand tour of the battlefield and atmospheric abbey ruins.

Bodiam Castle 105 E4
With its tall drum towers at each corner and walls rising virtually to their original height over a wide, water lily-filled moat, this substantial ruin recalls a fairytale castle. Bodiam was built by Sir Edward Dalnygrigge in 1385, both as a defence and a comfortable home. There is also a small museum.

Chartwell 104 B1
This Victorian house was the country home of Britain's prime minister during World War II, Sir Winston Churchill, from 1924 until his death in 1965. The rooms look as if he has just stepped outside: there are books, maps, pictures, photographs and personal belongings, including hats, uniforms and Churchill's famous cigars. He and his wife, Lady Clementine Spencer-Churchill, added several features to the grounds, including a small lake and Churchill's studio, where he loved to paint. The studio is still full of his works, some of which display a definite talent.

Great Dixter 105 F4
The highly respected gardening author Christopher Lloyd created one of the most experimental, exciting and constantly evolving gardens of our time at Great Dixter. Yew topiary, riotous mixed borders, an exuberant Exotic Garden, carpets of meadow flowers, a formal pool and natural ponds contribute to the overall effect. The house, Lloyd's birthplace and home, dates from around 1450, but was restored and enlarged by architect Sir Edwin Lutyens in 1912.

Hastings 105 F6
Forever associated with the Norman invasion, Hastings is a mix of faded seaside resort and attractive fishing port. The old town, a labyrinth of narrow streets, lies east of the centre. The Victorian East Hill Cliff Railway climbs to the sandstone cliffs for coastal walks to Fairlight Cove. Across the valley, the Norman ruins of Hastings Castle crown West Hill.

Herstmonceux Observatory 104 D5
From the 1950s to the 1980s this was part of the Royal Greenwich Observatory, and was used by astronomers to observe and chart movements in the night sky. Visitors can learn about astronomy along with other areas of science in a series of interactive and engaging displays. There are also exhibitions, a discovery park, and a collection of unusual giant exhibits.

Leeds Castle 105 F1
Set on two islands in the middle of a lake, Leeds Castle was originally a Norman stronghold and was a royal residence from 1278 to 1552, for no fewer than six medieval queens. It was fortified and enlarged by a series of royal incumbents and became a firm favourite of Henry VIII and his first queen, Catherine of Aragon. The landscaped grounds consist of formal gardens, a maze leading to a secret grotto, a vineyard and an aviary.

Rye 105 G4
Rye, of the five medieval Cinque Ports, is a huddle of cobbled streets, medieval half-timbered, red-tiled houses and

Canterbury

Sandwich

Deal

DOVER

FOLKESTONE

Hythe

STRAIT OF DOVER

Port of Dover

DEAL   CANTERBURY

DOVER CASTLE

DOVER PRIORY STATION

TRAVEL CENTRE

FERRY & PASSENGER TERMINAL

EASTERN DOCKS

Outer Harbour

Prince of Wales Pier

WESTERN DOCKS

PRINCE OF WALES ROUNDABOUT

LIMEKILN ROUNDABOUT

CRUISE TERMINAL

CRUISE TERMINAL 2

0   800 yards
0   500 metres

Folkestone Terminal

Peene

Newington

PASSENGER TERMINAL

FREIGHT SERVICES CENTRE

FRONTIER CONTROLS

PETROL STATION

CHECK IN

POLICE STA.

PETROL STATION

PETROL STATION

Cheriton

Departures to France follow →
Arrivals from France follow ←

0   400 yards
0   500 metres

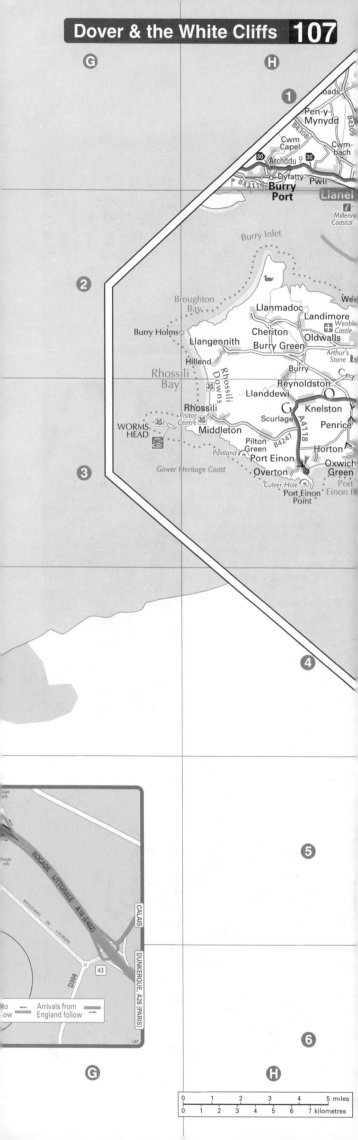

G   H

1

oads

Pen-y-Mynydd

Cwm Capel

Cwm-bach

30 Arddu 9 30

B4308

B4309

B4311

Dyfatty

Pwll

Burry Port

Llanel

Millenn Coastal

2

Burry Inlet

Broughton Bay

Llanmadoc

Landimore

Weoble Castle

Burry Holms

Cheriton

Oldwalls

Llangennith

Burry Green

Hillend

Burry

Arthur's Stone

Rhossili Bay

Rhossili Downs

Reynoldston

Ce

Llanddewi

Rhossili

Knelston

Scurlage

Penrice

Visitor Centre

B4247

B4118

WORMS HEAD

Middleton

Pilton Green

Horton

Paviland

Port Einon

Oxwich Green

Gower Heritage Coast

Overton

Port Einon B

Culver Hole

Port Einon Point

3

4

5

ROCADE LITTORALE A16 (E402)

BOULEVARD DE L'EUROPE

43

CALAIS

DUNKERQUE, A26 (PARIS)

to ow

← Arrivals from → England follow

LBT

6

| 0 | 1 | 2 | 3 | 4 | 5 miles |
| 0 | 1 | 2 | 3 | 4 | 5 | 6 | 7 kilometres |

A steam-hauled train on the Romney, Hythe and Dymchurch Railway

library where the Treaty of Paris was signed after World War I. Visit the Spencer Roberts mural room and the Martin Jordan animal mural room.

Romney, Hythe & Dymchurch Railway 105 H5–106 A3

The world's smallest public railway has its headquarters here. The concept of two enthusiasts coincided with Southern Railway's plans for expansion, and so the 13.5-mile stretch of 15-inch gauge railway came into being, running from Hythe through New Romney and Dymchurch to Dungeness Lighthouse.

Walmer Castle 106 C2

Originally built by Henry VIII as a formidable and austere fortress, the castle has since been transformed into an elegant stately home, formerly used by HM The Queen Mother. Many of the rooms used by the Queen Mother are open to view. Gardens surrounding the house include a wildlife garden and a woodland walk.

MacFarlane's colourful butterflies

Many rare and endangered animals can be seen at Port Lympne

Map (Calais region)

E   F

CALAIS

Calais/Coquelles Terminal

Coquelles

A16 (E402)

D243E

BOULOGNE

A16 (E402) ROCADE LITTORALE

BOULEVARD DE L'EUROPE

BOULEVARD DE LA CÔTE D'OPALE

CITÉ DE L'EUROPE

PASSENGER TERMINAL

PETROL STATION

CHECK-IN

FRONTIER CONTROLS

HGV FUEL STATION

FREIGHT TERMINAL

EUROTUNNEL ADMINISTRATION HEADQUARTERS

Arrivals Platforms

Departure Platforms

Freight only

42

41

400 yards
500 metres

Departures to England follow

E   F

DOVER & THE WHITE CLIFFS

East Kent is England's front door to continental Europe and it was for thousands of years the obvious way in for invaders. A formidable fortresses and a World War II museum testify to past conflicts. The White Cliffs of both Dover and Calais remind us that Britain and France were once joined – a link which the Channel Tunnel has now restored.

Cannons guard the bastions of Tudor Deal Castle

Deal 106 C1

A fishing port and seaside resort, Deal is a delightful jumble of narrow lanes which make doglegs to divert the driving winds from the Channel. The past is brought to life in the local history museum and visitors can explore formidable Deal Castle and discover the history of the castle with its long, dark passages that once linked a garrison of 119 guns.

Dymchurch Martello Tower 106 A4

This artillery tower, now fully restored and re-equipped with its cannon, formed part of a chain of strongholds intended to resist invasion by Napoleon.

Folkestone 106 B3

Beyond the great white cliffs and the downland behind them lies Folkestone, an attractive seaside resort with spacious clifftop esplanades and solid, harmonious Victorian terraces and crescents. Folkestone is also home to the Channel Tunnel Terminal.

Gateway to the White Cliffs Visitor Centre 106 C2

The visitor centre has spectacular views over both the historic landmark and the world's busiest shipping lanes towards France. At the centre visitors are introduced to 5 miles of coast and countryside through imaginative displays, videos and stunning photography. There is also a café and a National Trust shop.

Kent Battle of Britain Museum 106 B3

Once a Battle of Britain Station, today it houses the largest collection of relics and related memorabilia of British and German aircraft involved in the fighting. Also shown are full-size replicas of the Hurricane, Spitfire and Me109 used in Battle of Britain films. The Armoury building displays a collection of both ground-based and airborne weapons and 1940s uniforms. Artefacts on show, recovered from over 600 Battle of Britain aircraft, form a lasting memorial to all those involved in the conflict.

MacFarlane's Butterfly Centre 106 B2

This tropical greenhouse garden is home to scores of colourful butterflies from all over the world free flying among exotic plants such as bougainvillea, oleander and banana.

Port Lympne Wild Animal Park, Mansion & Garden 106 A3

This 243ha wild animal park houses hundreds of rare animals: African elephants, rhinos, wolves, bison, snow leopards, Siberian and Indian tigers, gorillas and monkeys. Features include a glass-fronted lion enclosure and an open-topped woodland home for the Colobus monkeys. The mansion designed by Sir Herbert Baker is surrounded by 6ha of spectacular gardens. Inside, notable features include the restored Rex Whistler Tent Room, a Moroccan patio, and the hexagonal

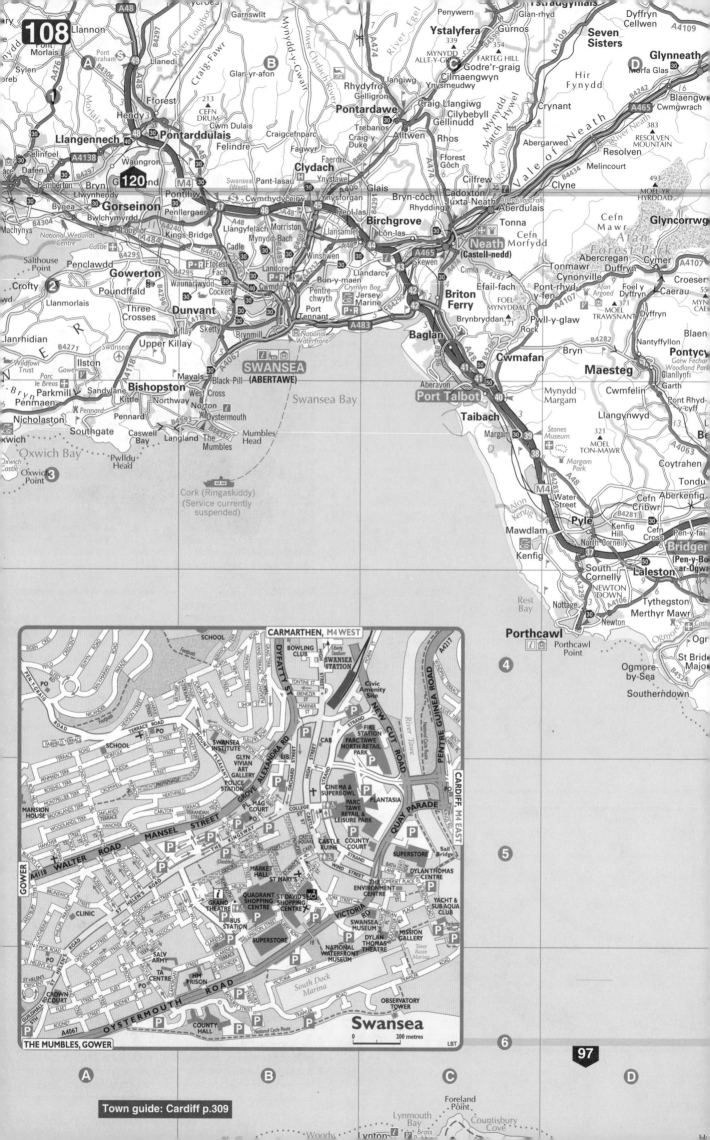

Old Beaupre Castle 108 F4

This medieval manor house, now a substantial ruin, was rebuilt during the Tudor period. Its most notable feature is a magnificent Renaissance three-storied porch.

Rhondda Heritage Park 109 F2

Based at the former Lewis Merthyr Colliery, this heritage park evokes the sounds, smells and sights of what life was like in a coal mine leading up to the large-scale closures of South Wales' mines in the 1970s and 80s. The underground tour, led by ex-miners, vividly recreates working conditions on a shift, there is even a simulated explosion. The multimedia exhibition Black Gold uses the lives of a real miner and his predecessors to illustrate the Rhondda's coal industry from the 1850s, and there are displays about the mining valley communities.

Rhossili 107 H3

At the western end of the peninsula facing Carmarthen Bay, Rhossili is the pride of Gower: a perfect, gently arcing sandy beach flanked by sandstone cliffs and the steep grassy flanks of Rhossili Down. On many days the breeze is up and the bay is full of surfers riding the waves. When the tide is out you'll see the wooden skeleton of the coaster, *Helvetia*, driven ashore by the gales of 1887. Rhossili village has one large hotel and a National Trust information centre and shop. A large car park gives access to the long beach and to Worms Head. Tides are of the utmost importance for those wanting to scramble across the rocky causeway to the headland: consult the timetables posted on the National Trust shop and at the coastguard's station.

St Fagans: National History Museum 109 G4

A stroll around the indoor galleries and 40ha of beautiful grounds will give you a fascinating insight into how people in Wales have lived, worked and spent their leisure hours since Celtic times. You can see people practising the traditional means of earning a living, the animals they kept and at certain times of year, the ways in which they celebrated the seasons.

Rhossili Bay's sweeping sands

Swansea 108 B2

This industrial city on the south coast boasts two fine museums, virtually adjacent in the regenerated dockland district. The National Waterfront Museum opened in time for the 200th anniversary of Nelson's victory at Trafalgar in 1805. The theme is mostly industrial history, Nelson's fleet was kitted out with copper hulls and cannonballs from the city's giant metal manufacturers, and a focal point among the modern interactive displays is a tin-plate rolling mill. The nearby Swansea Museum tells the city's own story, with floating exhibits as well as graphic accounts of the Blitz in World War II, the Mumbles lifeboat and the Cape Horn coal trade.

Tredegar House 109 H3

Regarded as the finest Restoration house in Wales, Tredegar was the seat for 500 years of the Morgan family, and they had it built in red brick around two sides of a courtyard. One wing survives from the original 15th-century building, while interior highlights include the Brown Room, completely furnished in 17th-century oak with elaborate and grotesque carvings, and the King's Room, furnished as it was in the 1930s and 40s, when it was occupied by Evan Morgan, the last member of the family to live here.

Weobley Castle 107 H2

This 12th- to 14th-century fortified manor house has an exhibition on the history of Weobley and other historic sites on the Gower peninsula.

Caerphilly is one of the largest and best-preserved castles in Britain

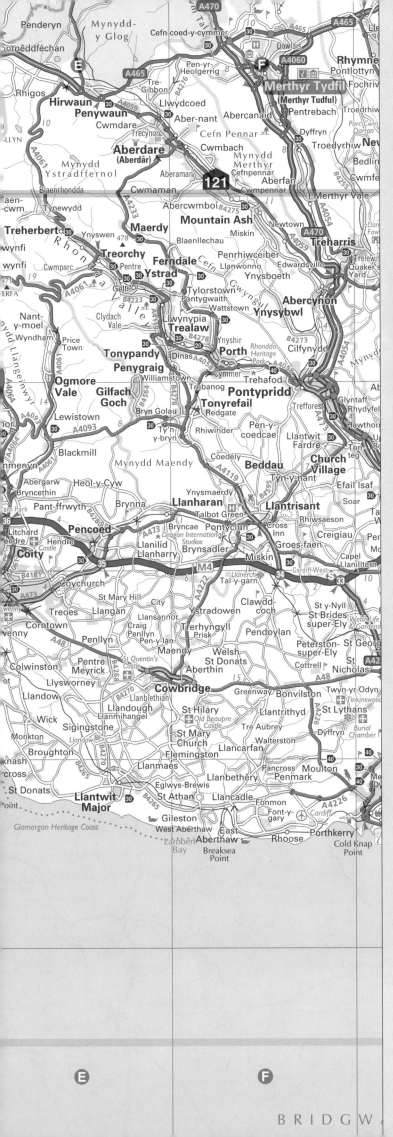

SWANSEA & SOUTH WALES

The limestone cliffs and golden sandy bays of the Gower peninsula are a protected Area of Outstanding Natural Beauty. Further east, Cardiff is in every sense the capital of Wales. It has a rich industrial, commercial and cultural heritage, and has evolved into a modern, vibrant and cosmopolitan city.

Aberdulais Falls have been a source of power to local industries for over 300 years

Aberdulais Falls 108 C2

The water thunders into a natural amphitheatre of rock in a wooded setting, and has powered industry for over 400 years. The copper-smelting works founded in 1584 later gave way to flour and grist mills, then tinplate works from 1830 to 1890, and today a hydroelectric plant is installed here. Displays (including letters and engravings) in the information section and turbine house trace the long history of this industrial site.

Caerphilly Castle 109 G3

The concentrically planned castle was begun in 1268 by Gilbert de Clare and completed in 1326. It is the largest in Wales, and has extensive land and water defences. A unique feature is the ruined tower – the victim of subsidence – which manages to out-lean even Pisa. The south dam platform, once a tournament-field, now displays replica medieval siege engines.

Castell Coch 109 G3

On the edge of Cardiff is this unfinished Victorian Gothic fantasy, designed in 1875 by William Burges (who also designed Cardiff Castle) for John Patrick Crichton Stuart, third Marquess of Bute, as a hunting lodge. Burges created a fairytale place with sharp conical roofs and outrageously lavish interiors with painted ceilings and walls, sculpted and gilded figures, and elaborate furnishings. Look for the clever details in the wall decoration of the drawing room – such as the painted ribbons that seem to support the family portraits, and the frog holding a bottle of cough mixture for the frog in its throat.

Llancaiach Fawr 109 G2

Step back in time to the Civil War period at this fascinating living history museum. The year is 1645 and visitors are invited into the manor to meet the servants, some puritanical, others gossipy, of 'Colonel' Edward Prichard.

National Wetlands Centre Wales 108 A2

One of nine centres in Britain to be run by the Wildfowl and Wetlands Trust, this reserve lies on the east side of Carmarthen Bay. Hundreds of ducks, geese, swans and flamingoes enjoy life here, some are tame enough to be fed by hand. There are observatory hides for birdwatchers, as well as a Millennium Discovery Centre, Millennium Wetlands play area with Water Vole City tunnels and Swans Maze.

Castell Coch, Cardiff

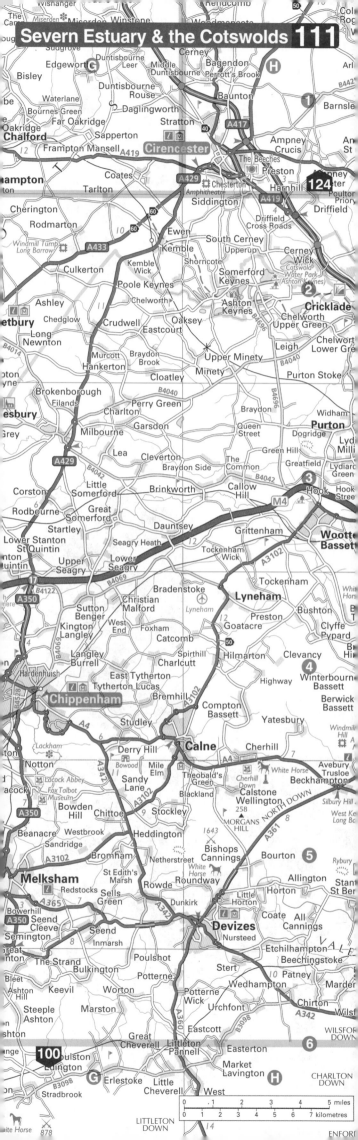

Corsham Court 111 F4

Set in the small Cotswold town of Corsham is this Elizabethan manor of 1582, altered over the centuries and largely the work of architects John Nash and Thomas Bellamy. The current owners, the Methuen family, bought the manor in 1745. The State Rooms and Picture Gallery display works by Reynolds, Rubens and Van Dyck. Landscaped by 'Capability' Brown, the peacock-embellished grounds feature formal lawns edged with flowering shrubs and herbaceous borders, avenues of mature trees, a lake and a Gothic bathhouse.

Lacock Abbey 111 G5

Lacock Abbey was founded in 1232 and retains much of its medieval fabric, including the cloisters, sacristy and nuns' chapter house. After the Dissolution of the Monasteries in the mid-16th century, it became a family home, and later acquired an octagonal Tudor tower, 17th-century hall and brewery. Owned largely by the National Trust and immaculately preserved, the village of Lacock is mostly grey-stone houses and half-timbered thatched cottages dating from medieval times to the 19th century. Nearby, The Fox Talbot Museum commemorates abbey resident and photographer William Fox Talbot, who in 1840 invented the positive/negative process that led to the development of modern photography.

Westonbirt Arboretum 111 F2

Worth visiting at any time of year but especially magnificent in autumn, this is among the largest and most diverse collections of trees and shrubs in Europe. The 18,000 trees, set in 240ha of landscaped, wooded grounds criss-crossed with trails (many suitable for visitors in wheelchairs), were planted from 1829 to the present day and come from all over the world. There is a visitor office with an exhibition and video. Various events are held throughout the year, from concerts to open-air plays in summer to autumn.

A family day out at Chepstow Castle

Wotton-under-Edge 111 E2

Wotton-under-Edge is perhaps one of the most interesting small towns in the Cotswolds. In the Middle Ages Wotton was an important wool town entitled to hold markets and fairs and the Chipping, part of which is now a car park, was the site for them. The old fire station in the Chipping is now an interesting heritage centre, showing the history of the town and the surrounding area.

Autumn at Westonbirt Arboretum

Lacock Abbey, now in the care of the National Trust, has fine medieval cloisters

Modern motorways span the Severn Estuary linking England with South Wales, but this region is at its busiest around Bristol and Bath. Bristol is full of historic features and cultural adventure and in Bath you can discover the city's outstanding Georgian architecture. To the east are the pretty villages of the Cotswolds.

Beautiful terraced gardens complement the castle at Berkeley

Berkeley Castle 110 D2

Dominating the village of Berkeley and home of the Berkeleys for almost 850 years, this 12th- and 14th-century castle is a rambling fortress surrounded by walls 3m thick and graced by Elizabethan terraced gardens and a vast park. The Great Hall, with its original timber roof, marks where the rebel barons of the West Country met in 1215 before going on to Runnymede to force King John to seal the Magna Carta. In the keep are the dungeons, including the cell where Edward II was brutally murdered in 1327 after his deposition.

Bowood 111 G4

The family home of the Marquis and Marchioness of Lansdowne since 1754 stands in parkland created by the 18th-century landscape gardener 'Capability' Brown. Built in 1624, the house was finished by the architect Robert Adam (among others) in the 18th century. The main draws of Bowood, however, are the gardens and grounds which feature terraced rose gardens, an arboretum, a cascade waterfall, Hermit's Cave and woodland and rhododendron walks. For children, there is a playground and a soft pay area.

Bradford-on-Avon 111 F5

Almost every route into this hillside town is down a steep incline lined with mellow Bath-stone weavers' cottages, old inns and flower-decked shops. The tall but tiny Saxon Church of St Laurence is one of the most complete examples from that time, while The Hall (1610) is a fine example of Jacobean architecture.

Caerleon Roman Fortress & Baths 110 A2

One of three Roman legionary bases in Britain founded in AD 75, Caerleon retains a well-preserved rectangular fortress, with a 6,000-seat amphitheatre and excavated remains of the barracks. Amid the modern town and preserved under cover are the baths, which included an open-air pool, heated changing rooms and an exercise hall. Excavated items are on display at Caerleon Legionary Museum. Demonstrations of a Roman legionary's life take place in the museum's Capricorn Centre, with a reconstructed barrack room, food preparation and replica armour to try on.

Caldicot Castle 110 B3

Set in a country park, Caldicot is a restored 13th-century castle on a Norman motte, built by Humphrey de Bohun, Earl of Hereford. Its elaborate defences included portcullises, heavy gates and murder holes. Although the castle was restored by the antiquary J R Cobb from 1855, much of the original stonework is still intact. Other surviving architectural details include latrine turrets, a hooded fireplace and window-seats.

Chepstow 110 C2

Guarding a vital crossing point into Wales and at the foot of the hilly town of Chepstow, the impressive fortress of Chepstow Castle was built in 1067 as the Norman invaders pushed westwards. The stone keep is original, but the towers, walls, gatehouses and barbicans were added later. It was adapted for musketry and cannon after the Civil War.

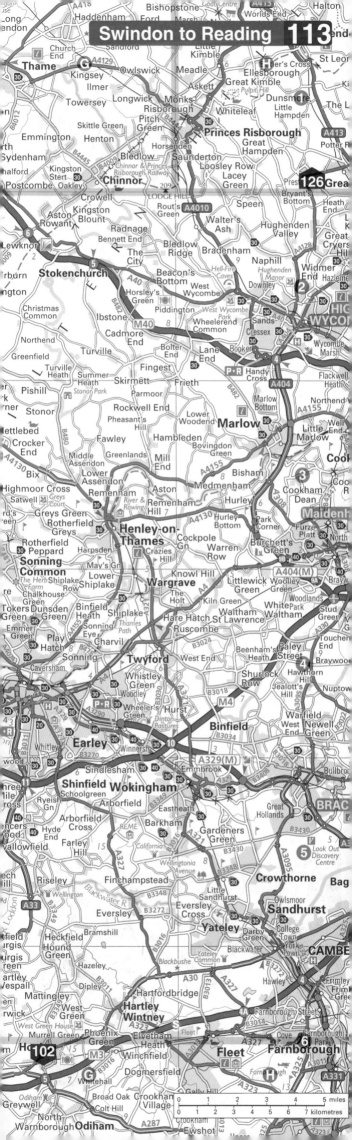

members were reputed to have held outrageous and blasphemous parties in the caves, which extend approximately half a mile underground. The entrance, from a large forecourt, is a brick tunnel that leads into the caves, where tableaux and curiosities are exhibited.

Reading 113 G4
Reading has a long history, with a 12th-century Cluniac abbey and a borough charter of 1542, but you have to search for visible signs of it. The Museum of Reading in the Town Hall is a good place to start. The Riverside Museum at Blake's Lock tells the story of Reading's two rivers – the Kennet and the Thames.

Open parkland at the front of Stonor

River & Rowing Museum 113 G3
The award-winning River and Rowing Museum has galleries dedicated to rowing and the quest for speed, from the Greek Trireme to modern Olympic rowing boats, plus the River Thames from source to sea with its rich history and varied wildlife. See the boats that won gold in Sydney and the riverside town of Henley featuring the Royal Regatta. The permanent *Wind in the Willows* exhibition recreates the drawings of E H Shepard in a walk-through attraction using models, lighting and sound to bring the classic book to life.

Stonor 113 G3
The house dates back to 1190 but features a Tudor façade. It has a medieval Catholic chapel that is still in use today, and shows some of the earliest domestic architecture in Oxfordshire. Its treasures include rare furniture, paintings, sculptures and tapestries from Britain, Europe and America. The house is set in beautiful gardens with commanding views of the surrounding deer park.

Swindon 112 A3
The main visitor attraction in Swindon is STEAM: Museum of The Great Western Railway which tells the story of the men and women who built, operated and travelled on the Great Western Railway. Hands-on displays, world-famous locomotives, archive film footage and the testimonies of

ex-railway workers bring the story to life. A reconstructed station platform, posters and holiday memorabilia re-create the glamour and excitement of the golden age of steam.

Uffington White Horse 112 C3
At Uffington, on the Ridgeway, the stylised form of the great White Horse, finest of all the carved figures that pepper the chalk landscape, overlooks the Vale of the White Horse where it runs its broad course along the edge of the Berkshire Downs. The 115m prehistoric figure is thought to be about 3,000 years old.

The Vyne 113 F6
Built in the early 16th century for Lord Sandys, The Vyne was visited by Henry VIII at least three times. The house later became home to the Chute family for 350 years. The building is a fascinating microcosm of architectural and design fads and fashions through the centuries. Visitors can view the family's original collection of art and sculpture, and the garden and grounds are very popular for walking. A wetlands area with a new bird hide attracts a wide diversity of wildlife.

Wellington Country Park 113 G5
Set in 142ha of parkland, Wellington Country Park has nature trails, lakeside walks, barbeque and picnic areas, a miniature railway and children's play areas.

The Vyne was a Parliamentarian stronghold during the Civil War

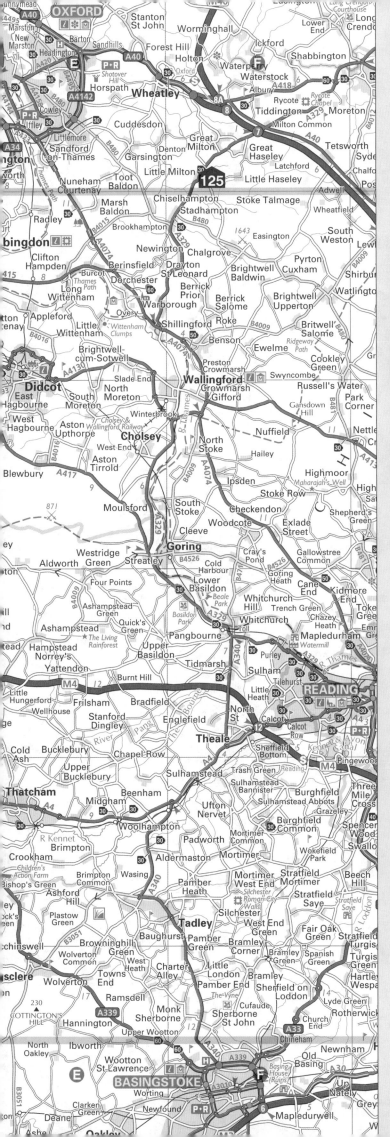

SWINDON TO READING

The rolling scenery around the chalk downlands, cut through by the ancient Ridgeway, is home to many strange shapes and sites including the stone circles of Avebury and the white horses cut into the chalk. Swindon owes its importance to the Great Western Railway while modern Reading lies on the River Thames.

Cotswold Water Park is popular with nature lovers and watersports' enthusiasts

Avebury 112 A5

Set in an area of chalk downlands and now a World Heritage Site, the village of Avebury is enclosed by the largest prehistoric stone circle in the British Isles. Built of local sarsen stones between 2600 BC and 2100 BC, it consists of two stone circles surrounded by a larger henge (a banked circular enclosure) along which stand 200 huge standing stones. A wide processional avenue of megaliths once led 1.5 miles beyond West Kennet to the site of The Sanctuary, a temple complex from around 3000 BC.

Beale Park 113 F4

Beale Park is home to an extraordinary collection of birds and animals including peacocks, swans, owls and parrots. It also offers a steam railway, rare breeds of farm animals, a great pet corner, meerkats, wallabies, ring-tailed lemurs, a deer park, three splash pools, a huge adventure playground, acres of gardens, and sculptures in a traditional, family park beside the Thames. There are summer riverboat trips and excellent lake and river fishing.

Cotswold Water Park 112 A2

Ashton Keynes, 5 miles south of Cirencester, is best known for the series of flooded gravel pits that make up the Cotswold Water Park. Broadly speaking there are two sections, one between Cricklade and Kemble (where Ashton Keynes is situated), the other between Fairford and Lechlade, which provide facilities for nature lovers, birders and sportsmen alike. There are seven nature reserves and the wetlands attract millions of wildfowl, particularly in the winter. The various activities coexist happily on 140 lakes.

Didcot Railway Centre 113 E2

Based around the original GWR engine shed, the Centre is home to the biggest collection anywhere of Great Western Railway steam locomotives, carriages and wagons. A typical GWR station has been re-created and a section of Brunel's original broad gauge track relaid, with a replica of the *Fire Fly* locomotive of 1840. There is a full programme of steam days, including the now-traditional Thomas the Tank Engine and Santa specials.

Hell-Fire Caves 113 H2

The entrance to West Wycombe caves is halfway up the hill that dominates the village. On the summit stands the parish church and the mausoleum of the Dashwood family. The caves are not natural but were dug on the orders of Sir Francis Dashwood between 1748 and 1752. Sir Francis, the Chancellor of the Exchequer, was also the founder of the Hellfire Club, whose

Beale Park on the banks of the Thames

Westminster, Richmond or Kingston upon Thames. The Maze, planted in 1690, is fiendishly frustrating.

Kensington Palace 114 D3

A royal home for more than 300 years, 17th-century Kensington Palace is probably most famous as the home of Diana, Princess of Wales. The Royal Ceremonial Dress Collection includes some of her dresses. The Queen's Apartments, including Queen Mary's Bedchamber, and King's Apartments are of interest for their opulence.

Kenwood House 114 D3

At the northern end of Hampstead Heath is Kenwood House, built in 1616 and remodelled by Robert Adam in 1764 for the Earl of Mansfield. It was left to the nation in 1927 by the first Earl of Iveagh, along with its outstanding collection of paintings. Here you will find Rembrandt's brooding *Portrait of the Artist* (c1665) and Vermeer's *The Guitar Player* (c1676), among other important works by English and Dutch masters.

Kew Gardens 114 C4

There's something to see all year round at Kew's Royal Botanic Gardens, which were created under George III and developed into one of the world's foremost facilities for horticultural research. The Temperate House, once the world's largest greenhouse, has an elevated gallery from where to view the plants, including the Chilean wine palm, planted in 1846. The Princess of Wales Conservatory opened in 1987; here arid desert moves gradually to orchid-filled tropics.

Lullingstone Roman Villa 115 G5

Possibly the luxury summer house of an important Roman official, the villa's mostly 4th-century remains include painted walls and fine mosaic floors. Around AD 390, Lullingstone's occupiers converted to Christianity and installed a chapel in one of the rooms.

This is one of the earliest surviving Christian chapels in England. The free interactive audio tour paints the picture of the occupants. Combine this with a visit to Lullingstone Castle close by, a Tudor and Queen Anne family mansion.

Runnymede 114 A4

Partly designated as a Site of Special Scientific Interest, Runnymede is an area of meadows, grassland and woodland that sits alongside the Thames. It is best known as the site where King John signed the Magna Carta in 1215. Also there are the Fairhaven Lodges, designed by Edward Lutyens, one of which is now an art gallery.

Thorpe Park 114 B5

For hard core adrenaline junkies, Thorpe Park is the must-do destination with some incredible rides. Pick up a park map to help you find your way around the loops, spins, vertical drops and incredible speeds of over 25 rides.

Twickenham 114 C4

At the Museum of Rugby & Twickenham Stadium Tours you can combine a behind-the-scenes guided tour of the world's most famous rugby stadium with a visit to the museum. The tour includes breathtaking views from the top of the North Stand, a visit to the England dressing room, and ends by walking through the players' tunnel to pitch side. The multi-media museum appeals to enthusiasts of all ages and charts the history and world-wide growth of rugby.

Wisley 114 B6

The flagship of the Royal Horticultural Society opened as a place of gardening excellence in 1904. Wisley demonstrates British gardening at its best, offering a blend of landscaped gardens and horticultural tips for keen gardeners. Much of the most important work takes place in trial fields, while elsewhere a series of model gardens serves the needs of a variety of conditions.

Cacti, agaves and aloes thrive in the Dry Tropics Zone at Kew Gardens

Visitors to London may not automatically think of visiting the outer boroughs or suburbs. There are, however, not only many pleasant green areas but also plenty of attractions to visit. For those keen on the river, cruise a little upstream and make a trip out to Kew, with its famous gardens, to Richmond, magnificent Hampton Court and Windsor. To the east is Greenwich, with its maritime traditions, and the Thames Barrier.

The imposing West Front entrance of Hampton Court Palace

Bekonscot Model Village
114 A2

A miniature world depicting rural England in the 1930s. A gauge I model railway meanders through six little villages, each with its own tiny population. Rides on the sit-on miniature railway take place weekends and local school holidays.

Cliveden 114 A3

The 150ha of garden and woodland overlook the River Thames, and include a magnificent parterre, topiary, lawns with box hedges, and water gardens. The palatial house, former home of the Astors, is now a hotel. The Great Hall and French Dining Room can be visited on certain afternoons.

Down House 115 F5

Charles Darwin, one of the most influential scientists of modern times, occupied Down House from 1842 until his death. On the ground floor, the drawing room, dining room, billiard room and study have been furnished and decorated to portray the domestic daily life of his family. In the study are his writing desk and chair, where he wrote the ground-breaking *On the Origin of Species by Means of Natural Selection* (published 1859), along with objects associated with his research.

Greenwich 115 E4

Historic buildings and the museums are the big draw here, but it's also worth browsing the craft stalls at the weekend market. The sleek tea clipper *Cutty Sark*, anchored by Greenwich Pier, was built in 1869 to carry cargo

between Britain and the Orient. The monumental Old Royal Naval College was created by Sir Christopher Wren in 1664 as a hospital for sailors. Two areas are open to the public: the Painted Hall and the chapel.

New galleries have given the National Maritime Museum more space to tell the story of Britain's maritime history, from the failed 16th-century invasion by the Spanish Armada to the 19th century. Among the collection is the jacket Nelson was wearing when he was fatally wounded at the Battle of Trafalgar in 1805.

The Royal Observatory was founded by Charles II in 1675 to tackle the problem of finding longitude at sea. Take a look through the telescopes and time-measuring instruments. The Gate Clock measures Greenwich Mean Time, the standard by which time is set around the world. Stand astride the Greenwich Meridian, marked by a brass strip, and you'll have one foot in the eastern hemisphere and the other in the western.

Hampton Court Palace 114 C5

This magnificent Tudor palace on the banks of the River Thames was begun in 1514 as a country residence for Cardinal Thomas Wolsey, Lord Chancellor to Henry VIII. Fourteen years later, Wolsey presented it to the king, and for centuries it was home to British monarchs. Costumed guides and audio tours lead the way through corridors, grand apartments, lavish bedrooms and vast kitchens that remain much as they were when in use. In summer you can arrive by riverboat from

G   H

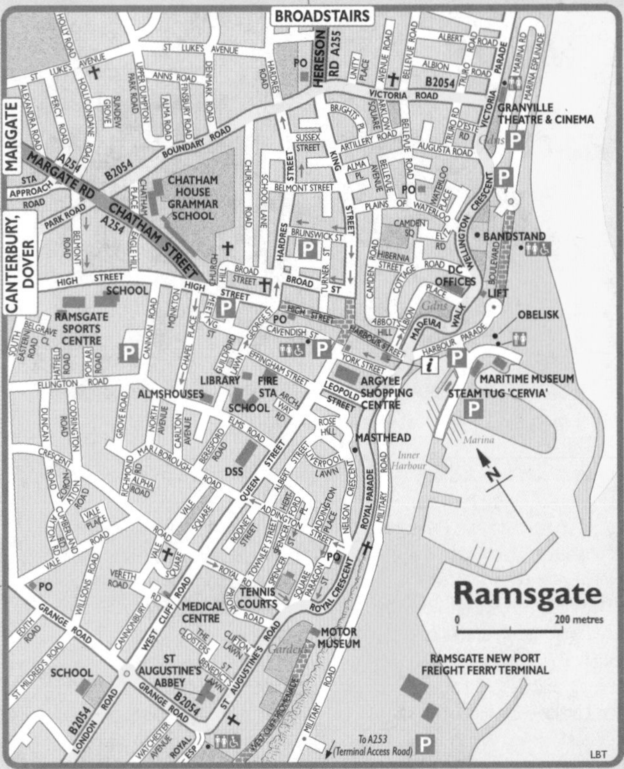

BROADSTAIRS

MARGATE

CANTERBURY, DOVER

CHATHAM HOUSE GRAMMAR SCHOOL

CHATHAM STREET

GRANVILLE THEATRE & CINEMA

BANDSTAND

OBELISK

LIFT

DC OFFICES

RAMSGATE SPORTS CENTRE

LIBRARY

FIRE STA

SCHOOL

DSS

ALMSHOUSES

ARGYLE SHOPPING CENTRE

MASTHEAD

MARITIME MUSEUM
STEAM TUG 'CERVIA'

Inner Harbour

Marina

TENNIS COURTS

MEDICAL CENTRE

ST AUGUSTINE'S ABBEY

MOTOR MUSEUM

SCHOOL

PO

Ramsgate

0   200 metres

RAMSGATE NEW PORT
FREIGHT FERRY TERMINAL

To A253
(Terminal Access Road)

LBT

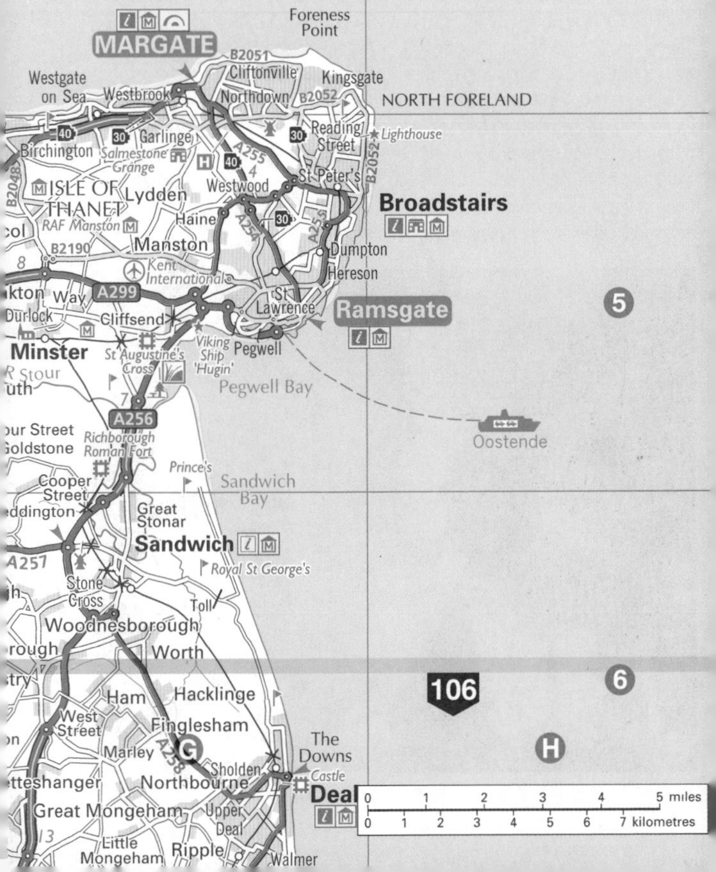

4

Foreness Point

MARGATE

Westgate on Sea   Westbrook

Cliftonville
Northdown

Kingsgate

NORTH FORELAND

Birchington   Garlinge

Salmestone Grange

Reading Street

Lighthouse

ISLE OF THANET

Lydden

RAF Manston

Haine

Westwood

St Peter's

Broadstairs

Manston

Kent International

Dumpton

Hereson

Way

Durlock

Cliffsend

St Lawrence

Ramsgate

5

Minster

St Augustine's Cross

Viking Ship 'Hugin'

Pegwell

R Stour

Pegwell Bay

Oostende

Goldstone

Richborough Roman Fort

Prince's

Cooper Street

Sandwich Bay

Great Stonar

Sandwich

Royal St George's

Stone Cross

Woodnesborough

Worth

Toll

106

Ham   Hacklinge

Finglesham

The Downs

H

West Street   Marley

Sholden

Northbourne

Upper Deal

Deal

Great Mongeham

Little Mongeham

Ripple

Walmer

0   1   2   3   4   5 miles

0   1   2   3   4   5   6   7 kilometres

Margate still attracts holidaymakers to its excellent beaches

many small cats and rare monkeys and the world's largest group of Western Lowland gorillas. Glass fronted tiger enclosures, the children's adventure playground and the new Jurassic Mine with ice and gem cave are not to be missed. Visit the Natureworks Arts and Craft Studio for painting, pottery, arts and crafts and the open-topped Javan Langur enclosure where the endangered monkeys can be seen in a natural environment.

Margate 117 G4

Margate is a big and brash seaside resort, with traditional funfairs, amusement arcades and donkey rides. Behind the beaches and bright lights is Margate old town where 17th- and 18th-century buildings, one housing the local history museum, huddle around the harbour.

Ramsgate 117 G5

Ramsgate is a busy maritime centre and its maritime museum is housed in the early 19th-century Clock House, focal point of the town's historic Royal Harbour. Four galleries explore the maritime heritage of east Kent. Themes include the fishing industry, transport, shipwreck and salvage, the area during two World Wars and the archaeology of the Goodwin Sands. A fifth display and conservation room features a 17th-century naval gun. Parts of the town are conservation areas with some fine architecture.

Richborough Roman Fort 117 G5

Explore the site of the first Roman landing in Britain and visit the museum with its collection of artefacts uncovered on site. See the remains of the huge triumphal arch, once 25m high.

Rochester 116 A5

Rochester, on the Medway, still has pockets of charm and a huge castle keep built by Henry I to defend the Medway crossing against invaders. Nowadays it has an easier time watching over the yachts and dinghies that skim around the estuary waters. The Guildhall Museum has collections covering local history and archaeology, fine and decorative art. There is a gallery devoted to the prison hulks of the River Medway, and a room detailing the links between Charles Dickens and the Medway Towns.

Sandwich 117 G6

The sea has receded from what was once England's major port, but Sandwich is still one of the best-preserved medieval towns in Britain. The Guildhall Museum covers the history of Sandwich. Walk beside the River Stour on the earth ramparts to the Old Toll Bridge, from where the Sandwich River Bus takes you to Richborough Roman Fort. Dating to the Roman invasion of AD 43, the fortified walls and foundations of a triumphal arch remain.

Rochester Castle's great Norman keep dominates the skyline

Margate

[map of Margate showing streets, landmarks and surrounding areas including Herne Bay, Canterbury, Sturry, and coastal towns]

THAMES ESTUARY

Historic Canterbury with its great cathedral and atmospheric old streets, Henry VIII's historic dockyards at Chatham, and the Thanet resorts of Margate, Broadstairs and Ramsgate are among the highlights of the region. To the north of the Thames Estuary is the seaside resort of Southend-on-Sea and the coastal town of Burnham-on-Crouch.

Bleak House in Broadstairs was the seaside home of novelist Charles Dickens

Broadstairs 117 G5

With its seven sandy bays, Broadstairs is a bewitching combination of a sedate, old-fashioned resort and a fishing port with winding streets and ancient fishermen's cottages. Writer Charles Dickens was a regular visitor from 1837. Dickens House Museum, on Victoria Parade, was once the home of Mary Pearson Strong, on whom Dickens based the character of Miss Nancy Trotwood for his novel *David Copperfield*. The parlour re-creates the scenes of the book, much as in the original illustrations by H K Browne ('Phiz'). The novel was written nearby at Dickens' seafront home, which is now called Bleak House.

Burnham-on-Crouch 116 C2

This attractive coastal town offers wildlife trips along the sheltered creeks by Wallasea Island to see birds and seals in their natural habitat. The local museum, situated on the Quay, has displays covering maritime, agricultural, industrial and social history.

Chatham Historic Dockyard 116 A5

Chatham is the world's most complete dockyard to survive from the age of sail and was once England's most important naval dock. It closed in 1984 to become a working museum. In dry dock are three battleships, while the Wooden Walls exhibition recreates the sights, sounds and smells of the Royal Dockyard from 1758. Inside the working Ropery, traditional techniques are used to make rope to rig the world's greatest sailing ships. The Museum of the Royal Dockyard celebrates 400 years of the history of Chatham and the Royal Navy.

Faversham 116 D5

Expanded and updated, and housed in 16th-century premises, the Fleur de Lis Heritage Centre features colourful displays and room settings that vividly evoke the 2,000 year history of Faversham. Special features include the Gunpowder Experience and a working old-style village telephone exchange, one of only two remaining in Britain. In July, during the Faversham Open House Scheme, over 20 historic properties in the town are opened to the public.

Howletts 117 E6

Set in 36ha of parkland, Howletts is home to some of the world's most rare and endangered animals. Howletts boasts the UK's largest group of African elephants, Indian and Siberian tigers,

Chatham Historic Dockyard

118

Fishguard Harbour

FISHGUARD HARBOUR STATION

FERRY TERMINAL

VEHICLE CHECK IN

Goodwick

Fishguard

FISHGUARD TOWN CENTRE

A40

A487

A487

A40

B4313

CARDIGAN

ST DAVID'S

HAVERFORDWEST

0 ½ mile
0 1km

LBT

Rosslare Harbour (Summer Only)

Rosslare Harbour

Dinas Heritage

STRUMBLE HEAD

Carregwastad Head

Pen Brush

Llanwnda

Fishguard Bay

Pwll Deri

Goodwick Ocean Lab

Pembrokeshire Coast Path

Trefasser

Lower Town

Fishguard (Abergwaun)

Manorowen

St Nicholas

Panteg

Scleddau

Ynys Daullyn

Granston

A40

Jordanston

Trecwn

Carreg Sampson

Abercastle

Llangloffan

Porthgain

Trefin

Mathry

16

A487

Castle Morris

B4331

Little Newcastle

Abereiddy

Llanrhian

Square & Compass

Letterston

Welsh Hook

St Dogwe

Berea

Croes-goch

B4330

Treffynnon

15

Tretio

Treglemais

River Solva

Llandeloy

Wolf's Castle

Rinaston

ST DAVID'S HEAD

Treleddyd-fawr

Carnhedryn

Cerbyd

Tancredston

Pont-yr-hafod

Triffl

Whitesand Bay

Rhodiad-y-brenin

Caer Farchell

Hayscastle

Hayscastle Cross

Treffgarne

Spittal

Bishop's Palace

B4583

Whitchurch

Middle Mill

Treffgarne Owen

Brawdy

St David's

Nine Wells

Solva

A487

Pen-y-cwn

178 DUDWELL MT

Leweston

Scolton

RAMSEY ISLAND

Ramsey Sound

Newgale

16

Roch

Wolfsdale

Great Rudbaxton

RSPB

St David's Peninsula Heritage Coast

PEMBROKESHIRE COAST NATIONAL PARK

Roch Gate

Simpson Cross

Camrose

Pembrokeshire County

Poy Cro

A40

Rickets Head

Nolton Haven

Keeston

Tangiers

Crundale

St Brides Bay

Nolton

A487

Pelcomb Cross

Pelcomb

St Brides Bay Heritage Coast

Druidston

Lambston

Pelcomb Bridge

Glanafon

Haverford (Hwlffo

Haroldston West

Sutton

Broadway

Portfield Gate

B4341

Broad Haven

B4327

Dreen Hill

Merlin's Bridge

Uzmasto

Little Haven

Walton West

A4076

Lower Freystrop

Boulsto

Pembrokeshire Coast Path

Talbenny

Solbury

4

Freystrop

St Brides

14

Tiers Cross

Johnston

Hook

Llangwm

SKOMER ISLAND

Wooltack Point

Marloes

B4327

Hasguard

Walwyn's Castle

3

A477

Rosemarket

Ne Mo

St Ishmael's

Sandy Haven

Thornton

Steynton

3

Broad Sound

Herbrandston

Honeyborough

B4325

Houghton

2

Bu

Marloes and Dale Heritage Coast

Hubberston

Waterston

Dale

Great Castle Head

Hakin

Llanstadwell

Neyland

SKOKHOLM ISLAND

Westdale Bay

Dale Point

Milford Haven

Milford Haven (Aberdaugleddau)

Toll

Waterl

Pembroke Dock (Doc Penfro)

East Pennar

Go Hi

St Anns Head

Angle

Angle Bay

Pwllcrochan

B4322

Rhoscrowther

Pembroke (Penfro)

Rosslare Harbour

Hundleton

10

Castlemartin Brook

B4320

Maiden Wells

Freshwater West

B4319

St Twynnells

B4320

Warren

St Petrox

Fres

Castlemartin

Merrion

Stackpole

Linney Head

PEMBROKESHIRE COAST NATIONAL PARK

Bosherston

Pembrokeshire Coast Path

St Govan's Chapel

St Govan Head

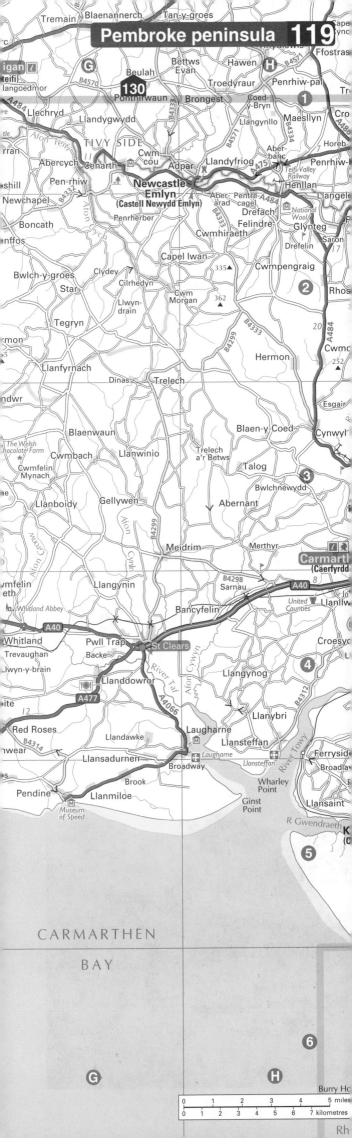

Pembroke 118 D5

Pembroke is an attractive walled town with a 900-year history dating back to its Norman castle, which overlooks the town from its perch on a limestone crag. Surrounded by water on three sides, the castle, built by the Earls of Pembroke, was one of the biggest and most powerful in Wales. A secret underground passage burrows beneath the Great Hall to the harbour. In 1977 Pembroke was designated an Outstanding Conservation Area. In the bustling main street, lined with both Georgian and Tudor buildings there are some fascinating shops, cafés and restaurants. If it's peace you're after, a stroll by the river and mill pond will take you around the castle walls.

Saundersfoot 119 F5

Once a small fishing village, which flourished with finds of high quality anthracite coal, Saundersfoot has since been caught up in near neighbour Tenby's popularity. It's not hard to see why. Set at the foot of a pleasant wooded valley, the village has an attractive harbour alongside wonderful golden sands. The village is a popular centre for fishing, sailing and watersports.

Skomer Island 118 B5

One of a pair of island reserves off the western tip of the Pembrokeshire mainland (the other is Skokholm) Skomer is among Europe's foremost breeding sites for sea birds. Porpoises and dolphins are regular visitors. Skokholm has the first bird observatory built in Britain, founded here in the 17th century. Colonies of guillemots, razorbills and storm petrels live here, along with about 160 grey seal pups, born each year around the beaches

and caves of the island. Skomer is also where 160,000 pairs of Manx shearwaters live. Passenger ferries leave from Martinshaven.

St David's 118 B3

Its cathedral raises St David's to the status of a city, yet it is scarcely more than a village in character and size. Tucked away in a dip next to the substantial ruins of the Bishop's Palace, St David's Cathedral dates from the 12th century but is on the site of a 6th-century monastery founded by David, patron saint of Wales. David was thought to have been born at a point marked by Non's Well, close by on a grassy headland on the coast.

Tenby 119 F5

Sections of its 13th-century wall, notably the fine Five Arches gateway, still stand around this cheerful harbour town and resort whose beaches make it a popular choice of families. Georgian houses crowd around the harbour, where a 19th-century fort can be seen on St Catherine's Island (reached on foot at low tide). The Tudor Merchant's House is a restored building dating from the late 15th century.

Welsh Wildlife Centre 118 F1

The nature reserve here covers woods, meadows, reedbeds and marshes along the River Teifi, as well as a former slate quarry and former railway bed. The diversity of habitats gives rise to an abundance of wildlife, including otters and one of the largest British colonies of Cetti's warbler. The limestone plantlife features rare species such as dotted sedge. For birding make for the treetop hide; for children there's a wildlife adventure playground.

Ice-cream coloured houses cluster around Tenby's harbour

Map labels

Penparc
Cardigan (Aberteifi)
St Dogmaels
Moylegrove
St Dogmaels Moylegrove Heritage Coast
Pembrokeshire Coast Path
Poppit Sands
Gwbr Bay
Bridgend
Llango
Castle
Welsh Wildlife Centre
Monington
Pen-y-bryn
Glanrhyd
Cilgerran
Rhoshill
New
Trwyn-y-bwa
Newport Bay
Bryn-Henllan
Berry Hill
Nevern
Felindre Farchog
Newport
Parrog
Dinas
Tredrissi
Bridell
Pontgarreg
Pontgynon
Castell Henllys
Eglwyswrw
Blaenffo
Whitechurch
Llanfair-Nant-Gwyn
Crosswell
Pentre Ifan
Pontyglasier
Bv
MYNYDD CAREGOG
Penlan Uchaf
Brynberian
PEMBROKESHIRE COAST
Crymmych
Pontfaen
Tafarn-y-bwlch
Hermon
MYNYDD PRESELI NATIONAL PARK
Foel Eryr
311
536 FOEL CWM - CERWYN
Mynachlog ddu
Pentregalar
265
Puncheston
Rosebush
Gors Fawr
368 FOEL DRYCH
Glandwr
The W Chocolate
Tufton
26
Maenclochog
Llandre Isaf
Hebron
Cefn-y-pant
Cy
Henry's Moat (Castell Hendre)
Llangolman
Llanglydwen
Pantymenyn
Woodstock
Wallis
Llys-y-frân Resrc
New Moat
Efailwen
Maesgwynne
Llanycefn
Login
Llys-y-frân
Pen-ffordd
Crosshands
Walton East
Llandissilio
Clarbeston
Clarbeston Road
Bletherston
Llanfallteg
Henllan Amgoed
Gelly
Clunderwen
Llanfallteg West
Cwmfeli Boeth
Wiston
Castle
Bethesda
Commercial
Llawhaden
Robeston Wathen
Redstone Cross
Penblewin
10
Whit
Treva
40
Canaston Bridge
Narberth
B4314
Llanddewi Velfrey
Lampeter Velfrey
Lliwyn-
Picton Castle
Oakwood Theme Park
Bluestone
Crinow
Cold Blow
Melinau
Tavernspite
Red
Minwear
Cross Hands
Templeton
Princes Gate
Martletwy
Yerbeston
Ludchurch
Longstone
Llanteg
Crunwea
Thomas Chapel
Marros
Colby Woodland Garden
Loveston
Reynalton
Begelly
Stepaside
Amroth
Pe
Cresswell
Jeffreyston
Kilgetty
Summerhill
West Williamston
Broadmoor Cross Inn
Pentlepoir
Wiseman's Bridge
Carew Newton
Cross
Redberth
Wooden
East Williamston
Saundersfoot
Carew
Broadfield
Monkstone Point
Milton
Sageston
New Hedges
Carew Cheriton
Manor House
Gumfreston
Tenby (Dinbych-y-Pysgod)
Bishop's Palace
St Florence
Lampeter
Manorbier Newton
Penally
Hodgeston
Jameston
Lydstep
Giltar Point
Manorbier
Lydstep Point
Trewent Point
ole Elidor
Monastery
CALDEY ISLAND
South Pembrokeshire Heritage Coast
ndle Bay
ole Head

The glorious, rocky Pembrokeshire coastline, awarded National Park status, reaches out into the waves of the Atlantic Ocean. Sandy bays, hemmed in by high cliffs, are perfect for watersports – particularly surfing. To the east is the gentler countryside of Carmarthen and the rivers Taf and Towey, an area which gave the poet Dylan Thomas his inspiration.

Haverfordwest Castle stands in a naturally defensive position

Haverfordwest 118 D4

Sited on the Western Cleddau, one of the two wide rivers that flow into the Milford Haven, Haverfordwest was, before the arrival of the railways, a thriving port with barges, small steamships and coasting vessels regularly docking on the quayside. Today Haverfordwest is a thriving market town, the principle shopping centre for the area. Many shops and a café line the quayside. It's worth a visit to the town museum, which is housed in the castle off Church Street. Also worth seeing are the excavated ruins of the Augustinian Priory of St Mary and St Thomas the Martyr, a short walk from the town centre. A 12th-century castle dominates the village from a lofty crag above the river. The substantial walls and keep are an impressive sight, second only to Pembroke in this region.

Laugharne 119 H4

Pronounced larn, this quiet town on the Taf Estuary grew up around 12th- to 16th-century Laugharne Castle, now an imposing ruin. The Welsh poet Dylan Thomas settled here in 1949, and Dylan Thomas' Boathouse and writing shed, where he lived and worked in his final, tragic and alcohol-blighted years, make a poignant visit. Creating the right atmosphere is the paper-strewn desk (with discarded papers on the floor) where Thomas wrote his best-known work, *Under Milk Wood* (1954), basing the town of Llareggub on Laugharne. He and his long-suffering wife Caitlin are buried in St Martin's churchyard.

National Wool Museum 119 H2

The museum is housed in the former Cambrian Mills and has a comprehensive display tracing the evolution of the industry from its beginnings to the present day. Demonstrations of the fleece to fabric process are given on 19th-century textile machinery.

Oakwood Theme Park 119 E4

One of Pembrokeshire's biggest family attractions, Oakwood Park has rides such as the wooden rollercoaster Megafobia, the skycoaster, Vertigo, and the UK's only shoot-and-drop tower, The Bounce, which shoots riders into the air at high speed, and watches them drop. KidzWorld is aimed at younger children, while Techniquest is an indoor science discovery centre.

Dylan Thomas' writing shed, Laugharne

Beacons National Park. Built in about 1300, it was originally an Anglo-Norman stronghold, designed to repel Welsh advances. Even in its ruinous state, its massive towers are still very impressive, while on the south side a sheer 90m drop forms a natural defence. A passageway cut into the cliff leads to a natural cave beneath the fortifications.

Dan-yr-Ogof Caves 121 E4

The National Showcaves, the focus of this complex of attractions in the Brecon Beacons National Park, were discovered by local farmers Jeff and Tommy Morgan in 1912. Their voices are used to guide visitors through the caves, which include the Bone Cave, where 42 Bronze Age skeletons were found, and the Dome of St Paul's in the Cathedral Cave, where waterfalls feed into an underground lake. Elsewhere are a Dinosaur Park, Barney Owl's Adventure Playground (undercover in a converted barn), a replica Iron Age farm, a Shire Horse Centre and Victorian Farm.

Dolaucothi Gold Mines 120 C1

Britain's only known Roman gold mine may date back as early as the Bronze Age. It was also in use from Victorian times until the 1930s. A long guided tour (no children under 5) leads through the most recent site and explores the Roman/Victorian caves and passages. Visitors are kitted out with helmets and lamps for the underground sections, and are encouraged to pan for gold in the mine yard. Roman axe marks can still be seen in the rock at the entrance to the mining passage.

Llandovery 120 D2

A statue of Llewelyn ap Grufydd stands guard on the grassy bank beneath the remains of the 12th-century castle keep. Across the car park from the statue you'll find the Heritage Centre where you can get information about the

Dan-yr-Ogof showcaves

many walks in the area, and discover the myths and history of the region.

National Botanic Garden of Wales 120 B4

When it opened in 2000 this was Britain's first new national botanic garden in nearly 200 years. Essentially a teaching and research facility, the garden is laid out with visitors in mind, with plants along a broad walk linking a Japanese garden, a double-walled garden and a marsh lining the lake and pond. The gardens occupy the estate of a Georgian mansion that has long since vanished, from which time Paxton's Tower, a two-storey triangular eyecatcher, survives.

Tretower Court & Castle 121 H3

The castle is a substantial ruin of an 11th-century motte and bailey, with a three-storey tower and 3m thick walls. Nearby is the Court, a 14th-century fortified manor house which has been altered and extended over the years. The two buildings show the shift from medieval castle to more domestic accommodation over the centuries.

A trip on the Brecon Mountain Railway is a great way to enjoy the National Park

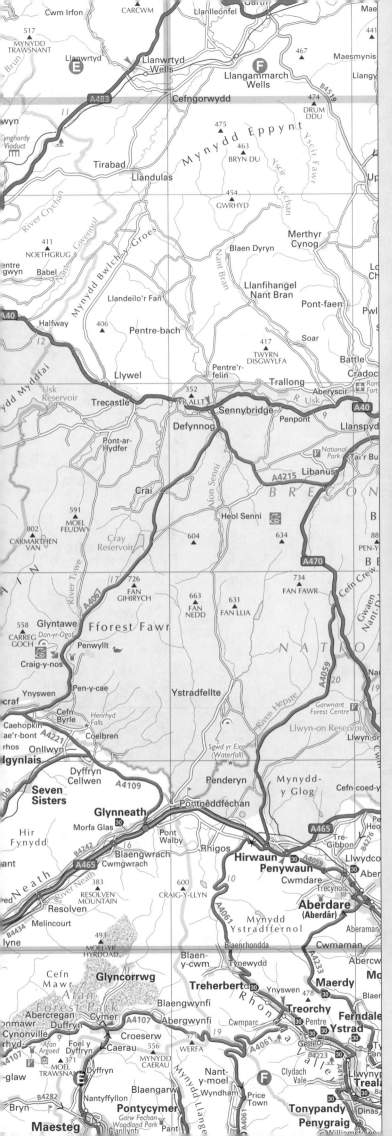

BRECON BEACONS

Four great mountain ranges, the Black Mountain in the west, Fforest Fawr, the Brecon Beacons and the Black Mountains of the east, form the spine of the National Park. The Romans mined for gold here, dramatic show caves have been discovered and remote Carreg Cennen Castle has one of the most spectacular locations in Wales.

Carreg Cennan Castle sits on a limestone crag overlooking rolling farmland

Aberglasney Gardens 120 B3

Aberglasney is a 4ha garden, containing a variety of rare and unusual plants, providing interest throughout the seasons. At its heart is a unique and fully restored Elizabethan/Jacobean cloister and parapet walk, plus the award-winning garden created within the ruinous courtyard of the mansion.

Brecon 121 G3

The town centre's buildings are a mixture of Georgian, Jacobean and Tudor, with a network of narrow streets leading off the Bulwark. The 19th-century Shire Hall with its Athenian-style columns, houses the lively and fascinating Brecknock Museum and Art Gallery, while Brecon's military history is well-recorded and celebrated at the Museums of the Royal Regiment of Wales in the Barracks. Each August, Brecon swings to its own jazz festival, one of Britain's premier jazz events.

Brecon Beacons Visitor Centre 121 F3

The Mountain Centre, as it is now known, is run by the Brecon Beacons National Park Authority and is one of the most popular visitor attractions in the National Park. An informative exhibition offers an introduction to the protected landscape. Food is served in the refreshment lounge and there is a picnic area.

Brecon Mountain Railway 121 G4

Opened in 1980, this narrow-gauge railway follows part of an old British Rail route which closed in 1964 when the iron industry in South Wales fell into decline. The present route starts at Pant Station and continues for 3.5 miles through the beautiful scenery of the Brecon Beacons National Park, as far as Taf Fechan reservoir. The train is pulled by a vintage steam locomotive and is one of the most popular railways in Wales.

Bronllys Castle 121 H2

This is an early Norman castle from the 11th century with inner and outer baileys. The 13th-century round tower still remains on the motte, although the inner bailey curtain wall has vanished.

Carreg Cennan Castle 120 C4

Carreg Cennen perches on an inland cliff on the western side of the Brecon

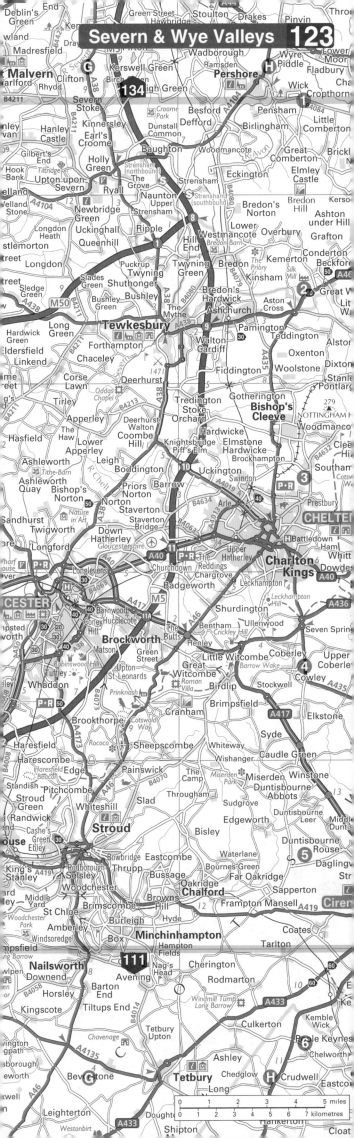

Monmouth Castle was the birthplace of Henry V. East of town rises The Kymin, a hill with fine views and two Georgian follies, the Naval Temple and the Round House (the latter a banqueting hall), both owned by the National Trust.

Painswick 123 G5

This little Cotswold-stone town slopes to the Painswick Brook, where several former textile mills can be seen. Ninety-nine 200-year-old yews clipped into arches and geometric shapes punctuate the almost surreal churchyard, along with an array of 17th- and 18th-century tombstones in a range of shapes and styles – some hexagonal, others triangular or adorned with scrolls. On the edge of town, Painswick Rococo Garden (G4) is a careful re-creation of an exuberant 18th-century design using a painting by Thomas Robins from 1748.

Ross-on-Wye 122 D3

The fine Herefordshire market town of Ross-on-Wye stands on a bluff overlooking a sweeping meander of the River Wye with marvellous views across to the Welsh hills to the west. At the top of the hill in Ross, just beyond the half-timbered and arcaded 17th-century Market Hall is the parish church of St Mary. Ross is one of the main tourist centres for exploring the Wye Valley, but retains its peaceful atmosphere.

Slimbridge 123 F5

The Wildfowl and Wetlands Trust, the inspiration of the English artist and naturalist Sir Peter Scott, was established on the saltmarshes at Slimbridge in 1946. Now equipped with an observation tower and state-of-the-art visitor centre, Slimbridge is the winter home of species such as white-fronted geese and Bewick's swans that migrate every year from Siberia. They pair for life and some pairs have been coming here for over 20 years. The reserve is now home to the largest and most varied collection of wildfowl in the world, including rare and endangered swans, geese, ducks and pink flamingoes.

Pink flamingoes at Slimbridge

Tewkesbury 123 G2

Tewkesbury has a well-preserved medieval townscape dominated by the Abbey Church of St Mary, the eye filled by its great square Norman tower. Inside, one of the most striking features is the set of 14 Norman pillars which support the 14th-century roof. The choir is illuminated by 14th-century stained-glass windows, while around it radiate six chapels containing monuments to the wealthy families which have influenced both the church and the town. Church Street and High Street have numerous timber-framed buildings interspersed with later Georgian façades.

Tintern Abbey 122 D5

William Wordsworth's poem *Composed a Few Miles above Tintern Abbey* was inspired by the majestic ruins of Tintern Abbey. Although turned into a roofless shell during the Dissolution of the Monasteries under Henry VIII, parts of the 12th- to 13th-century Cistercian abbey stand at their original height, notably the abbey church where elaborate window tracery survives. The Cistercians tended to choose beautiful settings for the sites of their abbeys, and this is no exception, with views along the gorge.

Tewkesbury, at the meeting of the rivers Severn and Avon, is a delight to behold

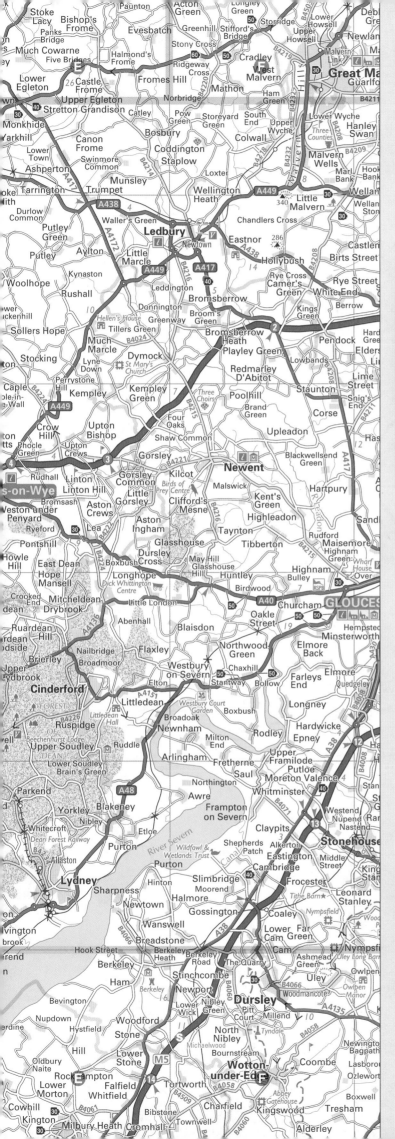

SEVERN & WYE VALLEYS

Ancient forest, rolling hills, meandering rivers and wooded escarpments all combine to produce a unified landscape, while the cities and towns of the area – Gloucester, Hereford, Tewkesbury, Monmouth and Ross-on-Wye – together with a host of picturesque villages, enhance the richness and beauty of this historic region.

This outdoor bookstall is near the old castle walls at Hay-on-Wye

Abergavenny 122 A4

Abergavenny, which is by far the largest town in the upper Usk Valley, occupies a large basin surrounded by three very distinctly shaped mountains: the cone-shaped Sugar Loaf Mountain and the craggy Ysgyryd Fawr in the north; Blorenge in the south. It's also well situated as a base to explore the Black Mountains and the Brecon Beacons. Although it took a pounding after the Civil War, Abergavenny's Norman castle is still worth seeing, as is the museum next door.

Big Pit National Coal Museum 122 A5

The Real Underground Experience, Big Pit is the UK's leading mining museum. It was a real colliery and the place of work for hundreds of men, women and children for over 200 years. It was a daily struggle to extract the precious mineral that stoked furnaces and lit household fires across the world.

Cheltenham 123 H3

A good base for touring the Cotswolds, this Regency town is renowned for its handsome terraces, wrought-iron balconies, leafy thoroughfares, parks, floral displays, horse racing, music festival in July and literature festival in October. The town spreads south along The Promenade, a wide, leafy street with pavement cafés and elegant shops. The Art Gallery and Museum in Clarence Street has an excellent section about the Arts and Crafts Movement. Close by is the Holst Birthplace Museum, which is dedicated to Gustav Holst, composer of *The Planets*. Pittville Park has lakes and a showpiece Pump Room, built in 1825 in the Greek Revival style.

Hay-on-Wye 122 A1

There are only fragmented remains of the old Norman town walls in the Newport Street area, but this would have been a heavily fortified border town since the 13th century when William de Breos built his castle. Today Hay is a vibrant market town known for its 30-plus secondhand and antiquarian bookshops and tourists come from all over the world to visit the annual literary festival. Among a maze of narrow streets you'll discover many fascinating old buildings, including a colonnaded 19th-century butter market, the 16th-century Three Tuns pub, which still has its horse-mounting block outside, and the Victorian clock tower.

Hereford 122 D1

Hereford looks its best in the area towards the River Wye, with a striking Georgian streetscape in Castle Street, and tree-shaded walks in Castle Green and along the river. Dominating the skyline since the 12th century, Hereford Cathedral is built of golden sandstone and was modified during late medieval times. Don't miss the cathedral's chained library and the Mappa Mundi, a unique world map of 1290. To the north, the half-timbered Old House, built in 1621, is one of the city's finest town houses. The Hereford Cider Museum in Pomona Place looks at the world of cider-making.

Monmouth 122 D4

This small market town of Georgian and older buildings stands where the River Monnow flows into the River Wye. The Monnow itself is spanned by a uniquely designed 13th-century fortified bridge. The arcaded Shire Hall dominates the marketplace, Agincourt Square, while

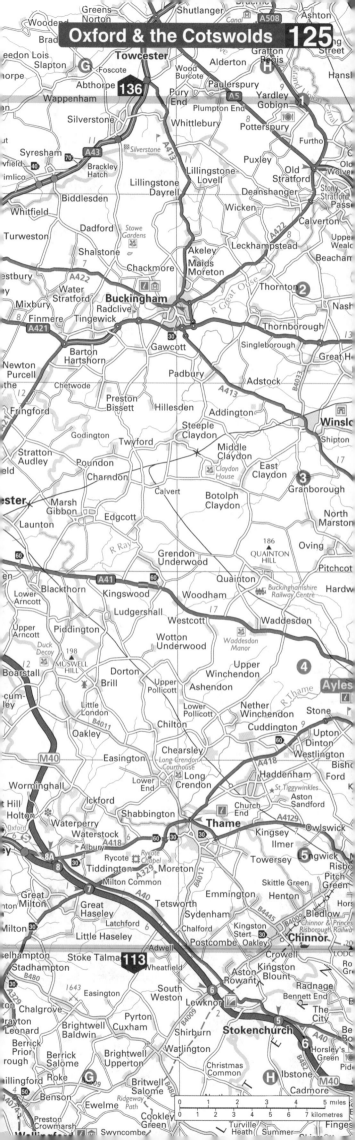

Cirencester 124 A5

During the Roman occupation, Cirencester was Corinium, England's second most important city after London. Now it is a sedate market town, focusing around its Market Place which in turn is dominated by St John the Baptist Church, one of the grandest Cotswold 'wool' churches, built when the wool trade brought great local prosperity during the 15th century. The town's most attractive street, Cecily Hill, leads into Cirencester Park, laid out geometrically in the 18th century. The Corinium Museum celebrates the city's Roman heritage. Craft workshops take place in the Brewery Arts Centre.

*Norths Cotswold Bakery,
Stow-on-the-Wold*

Hailes Abbey 124 A2

Explore the atmospheric ruins of this great medieval pilgrimage abbey, in the midst of the Cotswolds. Built in the 13th-century Hailes became famous when presented with a phial that was said to contain the blood of Christ.

Hidcote Manor Garden 124 B1

Hidcote represents one of the great innovative garden designs, the creation of horticulturist Major Lawrence Johnston between 1907 and 1948. The gardens are made up of a series of structured outdoor 'rooms', each with its own character and separated by walls and hedges of copper and green beech, box, holly, hornbeam and yew. There are outstanding herbaceous borders, old roses and rare or unique plants and trees from all over the world.

Sezincote 124 B2

The Indian-style house at Sezincote was the inspiration for Brighton Pavilion; its charming water garden adds to its exotic aura and features trees of unusual size.

Snowshill Manor 124 A2

From the outside, Snowshill Manor appears to be a traditional Cotswold Tudor manor house, set in walled gardens. Within it reveals the hand of the eccentric sugar plantation owner and architect Charles Paget Wade, who gave the house to the National Trust in 1951. His fascination with craftsmanship extended to collecting a vast range of seemingly unrelated objects such as bicycles, clocks, toys, Japanese samurai armour and such curios as a Georgian iron-toothed man trap.

Stow-on-the-Wold 124 B3

At the heart of Stow is the old market square, surrounded by attractive pubs and coaching inns, shops and restaurants, for Stow's main claim to fame was as a prosperous and busy market town. The old stocks are still in place on the remains of the green in a corner of the square, while in the centre stands the Victorian St Edward's Hall. Overlooking the square is the imposing Norman church of St Edward, which in 1646 played host to 1,000 Royalist prisoners following the final battle of the Civil War, which was fought nearby. A fine private collection of antique toys and other childhood memorabilia can be found in The Toy Museum in Park Street.

Stowe Gardens 125 G2

Stowe is an amazing 18th-century creation, an idealised version of nature and is one of the first and foremost of the great English landscape gardens. Hidden among spectacular views and vast open spaces there are over 40 monuments, temples and secret corners to be discovered.

Waddesden Manor 125 H4

Definitely a château in character, Waddesdon was built in the 1870s by Baron Ferdinand de Rothschild, a member of the 19th-century banking dynasty, for his extravagant house parties. Breathtaking for their opulence, the 45 rooms on view contain 18th-century French furniture and one of the world's finest collections of French decorative arts. The grounds are filled with specimen trees, fountains, grottoes and a rococo revival aviary of exotic birds.

A peaceful corner in the White Garden at Hidcote Manor

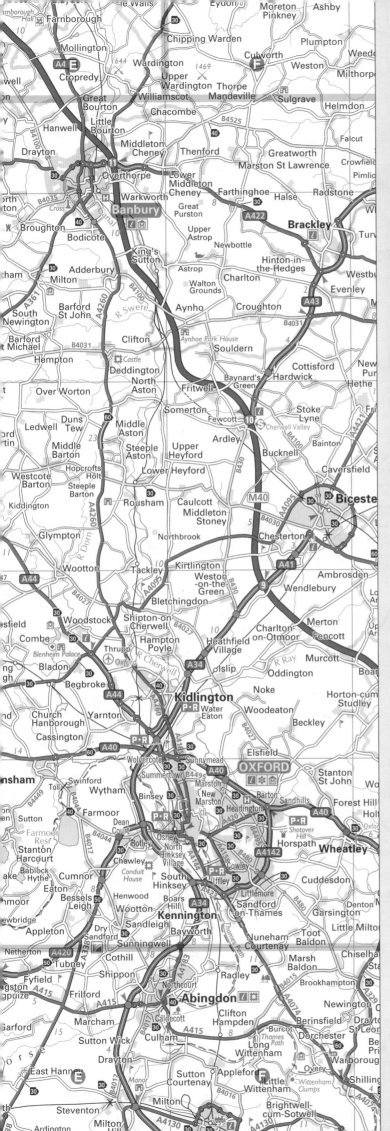

This high limestone plateau is chiefly noted for its beautiful villages. Created from honey-coloured stone and often tucked into delightful wooded valleys, they are enhanced by sparkling streams and contrasted with high, open meadows. To the east is Oxford, one of England's premier university cities.

Blenheim Palace, the home of the Dukes of Marlborough, is an imposing building

Banbury Museum 124 E1

Banbury's museum is situated in an attractive canal-side location in the centre of town. Exciting modern displays tell of Banbury's origins and historic past. The Civil War, the plush manufacturing industry, the Victorian market town, costume from the 17th century to the present day, and Tooley's Boatyard and the Oxford Canal are just some of the subjects illustrated in the museum.

Blenheim Palace 125 E4

One of the largest private houses in Britain and the ultimate in English baroque was designed by Sir John Vanbrugh and Nicholas Hawksmoor and was given by Queen Anne to John Churchill, first Duke of Marlborough, in recognition of his victory over the French at the Battle of Blenheim in 1704. The gilded state rooms overlook lawns and formal gardens laid out by 'Capability' Brown. Beautiful Blenheim Lake, spanned by Vanbrugh's Grand Bridge, forms the focal point of the grounds. In the grounds are a butterfly house, maze and a wooden playground area. A fun miniature railway takes you from the house to the maze and games area.

Bourton-on-the-Water 124 B3

The busiest honeypot in the area is this attractive village, watered by the River Windrush which flows along the main street beneath a succession of five footbridges. The village has a lot to offer in the way of attractions – Birdland is a sanctuary for birds, with a remarkable collection of penguins in stream-side gardens. There is also a Model Village (Bourton in miniature), a perfume factory, a motor museum, the Dragonfly Maze, and a model

railway exhibition, all within walking distance of each other and of the main street. Just off the main street is Bourton's church, St Lawrence's, a mixture of elements, with a medieval chancel, Victorian nave and distinctive domed Georgian tower.

Chedworth Roman Villa 124 A4

Chedworth Villa (National Trust), was in its time one of the largest Roman-British villas in Britain. This, and other items of information are given in the short, well-produced video that is shown every 15 minutes as part of the entry price. Most of the original superstructure of the villa has long gone. What remains are the lower parts of the walls and mosaics featuring, among other things, representations of the four seasons. There is a comparatively recent building in the middle, which is the administrator's house that has a small museum attached at its rear.

Chipping Campden 124 B2

The loveliest village in the Cotswolds is a gilded masterpiece. The main street curves in a shallow arc lined with houses each grafted to the next but each with its own distinctive embellishments. Chipping Campden was a market town, one of the most important of the medieval wool towns in the Cotswolds. Campden's church, at the north end of the town, is perhaps the finest 'wool' church in the Cotswolds, with a magnificent tower and a spacious, almost austere interior. The Gainsborough Chapel houses the fine 17th-century marble tomb of Sir Baptist Hicks and his wife, who built the nearby stone almshouses in 1612, as well as Campden House, which was razed during the Civil War.

much as he left them, with many literary and personal effects evoking the individuality and genius of this great dramatist. The kitchen and outbuildings are evocative of early 20th-century domestic life. Shaw's writing hut is hidden at the bottom of the garden, which has richly planted borders and views over the Hertfordshire countryside.

Shuttleworth Collection
126 D1

In an all-grass aerodrome, this collection features around 40 aircraft from 1909 to 1955. Many are the last survivors of their type, including a 1909 Bleriot, 1931 Tiger Moth and a 1941 Spitfire, kept in full working order. The exhibition includes vintage cars, motorcycles, bicycles and horse-drawn carriages. Flying displays take place once or twice a month, when the museum's airworthy exhibits are flown alongside visiting aircraft, and cars from the collection are given a run.

Whipsnade 126 C4

Occupying parkland on the Chiltern Hills is one of Europe's largest wildlife conservation centres, home to more than 2,500 creatures, including rare and endangered species. Its herd of seven Asian elephants is the largest breeding group in Britain, and free-roaming animals include wallabies and Chinese water deer. Daily demonstrations feature free-flying birds, sea-lion performances and penguin feeding. To get around the park, take the free open-top Safari Tour Bus or alternatively take the Great Whipsnade Railway.

Woburn Abbey 126 B2

Set in a beautiful 1,215ha deer park, Woburn Abbey has been the home of the Dukes of Bedford for nearly 400 years and is currently occupied by the 15th Duke and his family. The Abbey houses one of the most important private art collections in the world including paintings by Canaletto, Gainsborough, Reynolds, Van Dyck and Cuyp and collections of silver, gold and

The gardens at Hatfield House

porcelain. Woburn was the setting for the origin of Afternoon Tea, introduced by Anna Maria, wife of the 7th Duke. An audio tour is available and guided tours on request. There are extensive informal gardens, pottery and a fine antiques centre representing over 70 dealers.

Woburn Safari Park 126 B2

Enjoy a Safari Adventure at Woburn Safari Park and see the beauty of wild animals at close quarters. You can tour the reserves from the safety of your own car and experience the thrill of being alongside white rhino, buffalo, giraffe or look into the eyes of a Siberian tiger. The Leisure Park has indoor and outdoor adventure playgrounds, walkthrough areas with wallabies, squirrel monkeys and lemurs, and a full programme of keeper talks and demonstrations. Don't miss the sea lions or the penguins.

Wrest Park 126 C2

The formal gardens here, originally laid out in the early 18th century, were inspired by the magnificent gardens of Versailles and showcase the fascinating history of gardening styles. An audio tour leads visitors through the 36ha which feature a canal, avenues and a very fine pavilion designed by Thomas Archer.

Whipsnade provides space for animals to roam in natural breeding groups

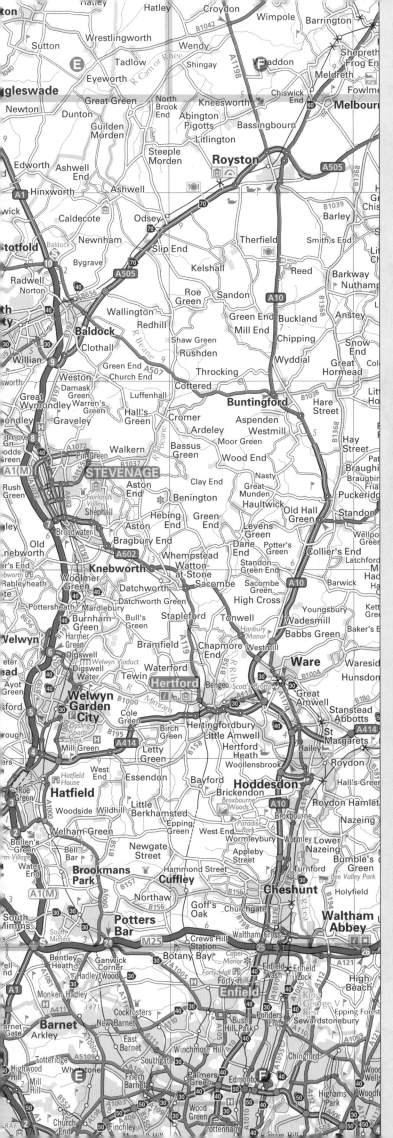

NORTHERN HOME COUNTIES

Welwyn and Hatfield, among the 'new' towns and cities for overcrowded Londoners, stand side-by-side with the great Jacobean palace of Hatfield House and close to modern Luton. Meanwhile Knebworth, to the north, is a time capsule of 500 years of British history. Other places of interest include wild animal parks, beautiful gardens and a unique collection of aeroplanes.

The turrets, domes and gargoyles of magnificent Knebworth House

Audley End House 127 H2

One of England's greatest Jacobean country houses, Audley End House was built between 1605 and 1614 by Thomas Howard, first Earl of Suffolk, on the scale of a great royal palace. It was reduced in size over the next century, with modifications by architects Sir John Vanbrugh and Robert Adam. James I decided it was 'too large for a king'. The interior is largely the influence of the third Baron Braybrooke, who inherited the house in 1825 and filled the many rooms (30 are now open to the public) with furnishings and works of art. The gardens and parkland that surround the house were landscaped by 'Capability' Brown with Palladian bridges and temples.

Gardens of the Rose 126 D5

The Royal National Rose Society's newly revamped Gardens of the Rose were officially opened on 9 June 2007. In addition to a comprehensive collection of roses of all types, the garden boasts a good selection of complementary trees, shrubs, summer bulbs and herbaceous perennials in a garden setting together with a grass maze. A stunning new 72-arch pergola supports a wide selection of climbing roses with clematis and other flowering species. There are three pools containing a variety of marginal plants and water lilies.

Hatfield House 127 E5

A sumptuous 1611 Jacobean house, Hatfield was the childhood home of Queen Elizabeth I. It stands on the site of the Royal Palace of Hatfield, of which

a wing survives. Inside are magnificent state rooms, furniture, tapestries and paintings. Historic mementoes collected over the years by the Cecils, residents for 400 years, include the national collection of model soldiers. The Grand Staircase is a superb example of Jacobean craftsmanship.

Knebworth 127 E3

The country park has a maze, state-of-the-art adventure playground, deer park, gardens designed by Sir Edwin Lutyens and a herb garden designed by Gertrude Jekyll. Since 1974 it has hosted major open-air rock concerts. The house dates from Tudor times but was embellished in 1843 by Victorian novelist Sir Edward Bulwer Lytton into the high Gothic fantasy seen today.

St Albans 126 D5

St Albans has been an important centre since Roman times and the Verulamium Museum tells the story of everyday life in Roman Britain. The Museum of St Albans covers the departure of the Romans to the present day. Built between 1403 and 1412, the Clock Tower is the only medieval town belfry in England. Inside you can hear the great bell Gabriel (also 600 years old), find out about the original clock, the Napoleonic War telegraph station, and see fine Victorian turret clock in action.

Shaw's Corner 126 D4

This Edwardian arts and crafts influenced house was the home of George Bernard Shaw from 1906 until his death in 1950. The rooms remain

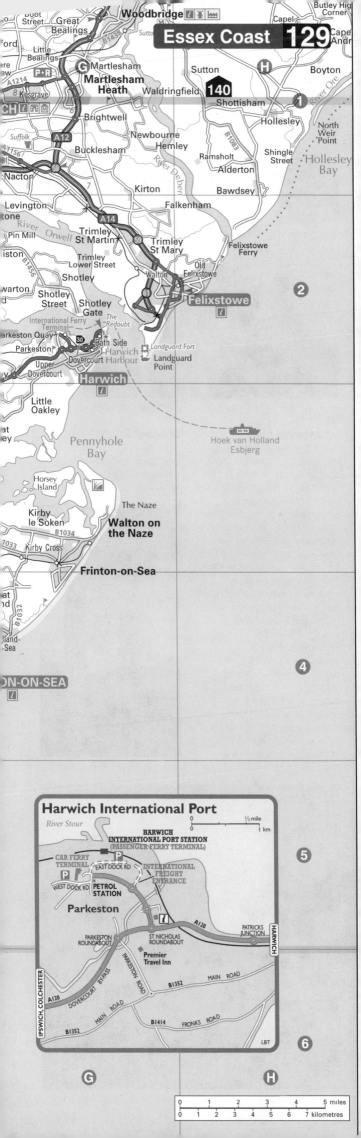

Punch and Judy put on a show on the sands at Clacton-on-Sea

Layer Marney Tower 128 D4

Layer Marney Tower, an astonishing sight in the quiet Essex countryside, is the tallest Tudor gatehouse in the country, built by Henry, first Lord Marney, in the early 16th century. Unfortunately the grand architectural scheme, including a courtyard that would have rivalled Hampton Court Palace, was never completed, and all that stands is one of four sides. Within the grounds are the parish church and a medieval barn where farm animals roam. A wildlife walk passes a large herd of red deer and other livestock.

Paycocke's 128 C3

This timber-framed house is a fine example of a medieval merchant's home. It was completed in about 1505 and has interesting carvings on the outside timbers, including the Paycocke trade sign. Inside there are further elaborate carvings and linenfold panelling. Behind the house is a pretty garden.

St James' Chapel 128 D1

Built mainly in the 13th century, this small thatched, flint-and-stone chapel with lancet windows incorporates some earlier work.

Hedingham Castle's Norman keep

6, used local subjects for his well-loved paintings, among them Flatford Mill, above

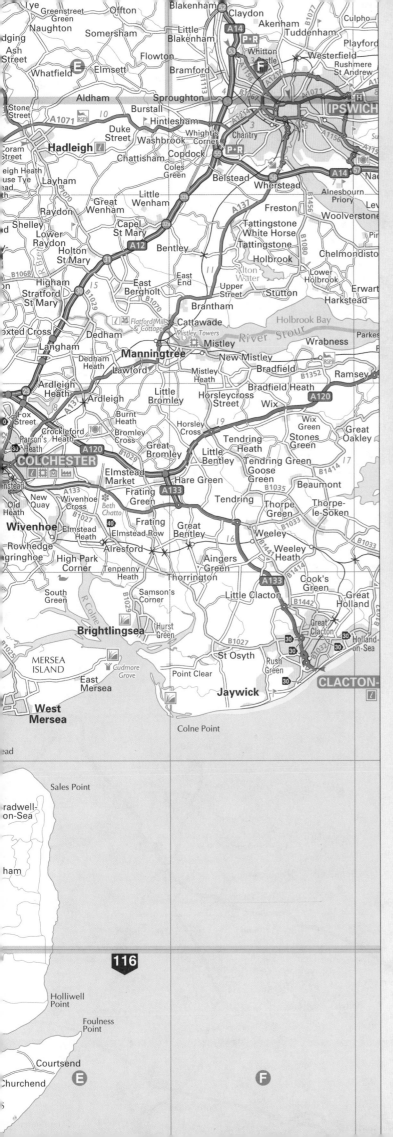

ESSEX COAST

The many different faces of Essex include Roman Colchester and weaving villages such as Coggeshall, with its beautiful timbered wool-merchant's house Paycocke's. In the valley of the River Stour is 'Constable Country' and on the coast the yachting centre of Mersea and the seaside resorts of fun-loving Clacton and sedate Frinton continue to attract visitors.

Paycocke's, built by local wool merchants, is now in the care of the National Trust

Clacton-on-Sea 129 F4
Clacton has golden beaches, a pier, colourful seafront gardens, amusements, watersports, a leisure centre and two theatres – all you would expect from a traditional seaside resort. Annual events include a two-day air show, a carnival and jazz festival.

Colne Valley Railway 128 B2
Many former Colne Valley and Halstead railway buildings have been rebuilt here. Stock includes seven steam locomotives plus 80 other engines, carriages and wagons. Visitors can dine in style in restored Pullman carriages while travelling along the line.

Flatford Mill & Cottage 129 E2
In the heart of Dedham Vale, famous as the location for John Constable's idyllic pastoral paintings, the restored 16th-century Bridge Cottage (National Trust) houses an exhibition on the artist. A riverside tea room provides refreshments.

Harwich Redoubt Fort 129 G2
The 180ft-diameter circular fort was built in 1808 in case of invasion by Napoleon. It has a dry moat and 2.5m thick walls, with 18 rooms for stores, ammunition and quarters for 300 men. The Redoubt is being restored by the Harwich Society, and contains three small museums. Ten guns can be seen on the battlements.

Hedingham Castle 128 B2
This impressive Norman castle was built in 1140. It was besieged by King John, visited by Henry VII, Henry VIII and Elizabeth I, and was home to the de Veres, Earls of Oxford, for over 500 years. During the summer months Hedingham's colourful heritage comes to life with a full programme of special events. There are medieval jousts and sieges with authentic living history displays and encampments.

John Constable, born in East Bergholt in

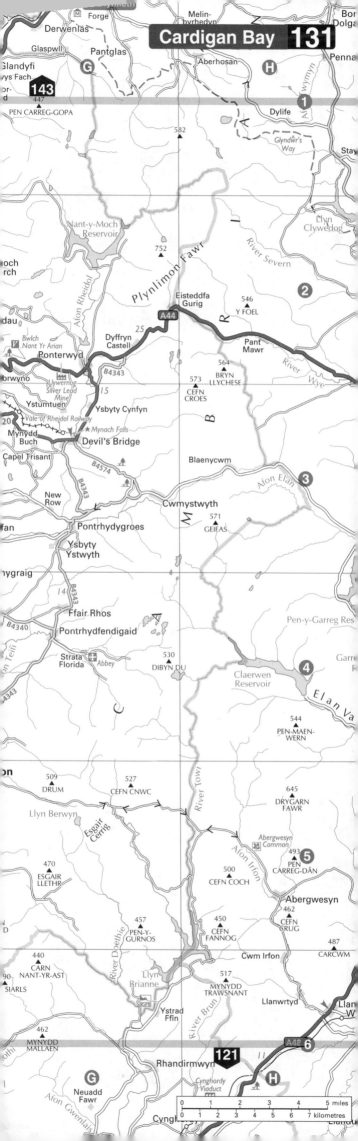

The Vale of Rheidol Light Railway steams between Aberystwyth and Devil's Bridge

farm and outbuildings remain virtually unaltered. The 18th-century estate features the Walled Garden and farm complex, mature woodland and ornamental lake, vast parkland and farmland containing Llanwennog sheep and Welsh Black Cattle. Produce and plants from the walled gardens are sold in the visitor building.

Mynach Falls 131 G3
At Devil's Bridge, coin-operated turnstiles either side of the road allow access to paths into a spectacular wooded gorge where you'll see three bridges, one on top of another (legend has it that the lowest one was built with the help of the Devil). Also here are the spectacular Mynach Falls, which tumble from a great height past the treetops into the depths of the gorge far beneath your feet.

Strata Florida Abbey 131 G4
Little remains of the Cistercian abbey founded in 1164, except the ruined church and cloister. Strata Florida was an important centre of learning in the Middle Ages, and it is believed that the 14th-century poet Dafyd ap Gwilym was buried here.

Vale of Rheidol Railway
131 G3
The Vale of Rheidol narrow-gauge railway, built in 1902, takes passengers on an hour-long journey to Devil's Bridge, revealing spectacular views of the wooded Rheidol Valley along the way.

Ynyslas 131 F1
Seven species of orchid grow in the dunes on this fine section of coast north of Aberystwyth. The reserve juts out into the watery expanses of the Dovey estuary, looking across to Aberdovey and the southern border of Snowdonia National Park. It is fascinating to watch how the dunes are constantly changing as they shift in the wind. The visitor complex explains how they are formed, describes the wildlife and conducts walks in the reserve.

e west coast of Wales, nestles between three hills and two beaches

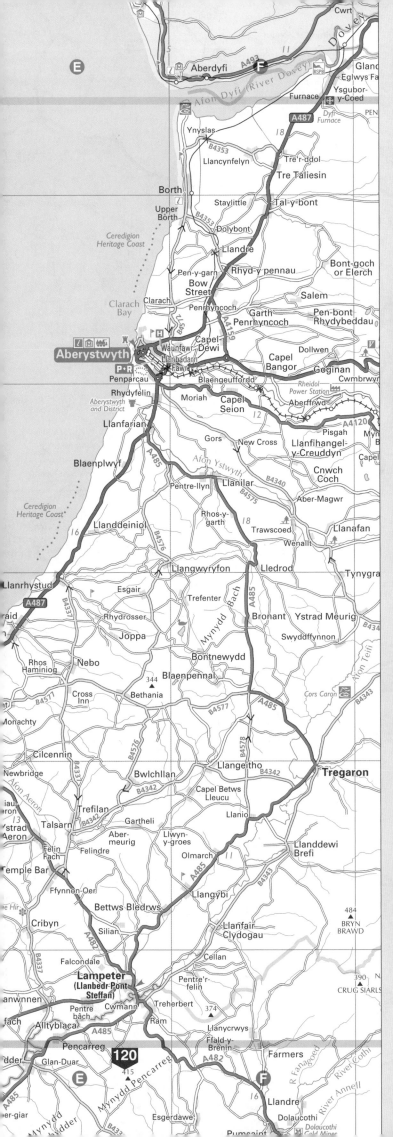

CARDIGAN BAY

Cardigan Bay, Britain's largest bay with jaws 72 miles wide, was Britain's first Marine Heritage Coast and its beaches regularly top the UK list of seaside award winners. Cardigan Bay is backed by the mountains of central Wales from where the River Rheidol dashes down over wild waterfalls to enter the Bay at the university town of Aberystwyth.

The dam at Craig Coch is the highest of the series of dams in the Elan Valley

Aberystwyth 131 E2
Aberystwyth is a lively university town with a strong culture of the Welsh language; Welsh and Celtic manuscripts are displayed in the National Library of Wales on Penglais Hill. Bay-windowed Victorian and Edwardian hotels and guesthouses line the waterfront, which ends at Constitution Hill, where the electric cliff railway (opened 1896) climbs for fine views of Cardigan Bay. On top is the world's largest camera obscura. From the town, steam trains on the Vale of Rheidol Railway wind their way through a wooded valley to Devil's Bridge.

Borth 131 F1
Borth's excellent golden sand beaches and shallow waters are popular with both sailboard enthusiasts and families with young children. The Animalarium has a collection of domestic and farm animals which visitors can pet and feed in the petting barn and there are exotic and endangered species in the larger enclosures.

Elan Valley 131 H4–132 A4
Created between 1893 and 1952 to provide water for Birmingham, this Welsh version of the Lake District has dams and reservoirs within the bleak Cambrian Mountains. Initially the scheme caused controversy as it involved flooding existing communities, yet the lakes are now attractions in themselves. The earlier dams are built in an elaborate Victorian style, and the area is rich in wildlife, including the rare red kite (identified by its large wingspan and forked tail). The Elan Valley Visitor Centre has an exhibition, café and details of walks. There are 12 sites of Special Scientific Interest including meadow, ancient woodland and upland mire.

Felinwynt Rainforest Centre 130 B5
Here you have a chance to wander amongst free-flying exotic butterflies accompanied by the recorded wildlife sounds of the Peruvian Amazon. A waterfall, ponds and streams contribute to a humid tropical atmosphere and provide a habitat for fish and native amphibians. The Centre has an exhibition of the rainforests of Peru and from around the world.

Llanerchaeron 130 D4
Llanerchaeron, a few miles inland from Aberaeron on the Cardigan Bay coast, is centred round a Regency villa designed by John Nash. The self-sufficient country estate, villa, service courtyard, grounds, working organic

Aberystwyth, the principal holiday resort

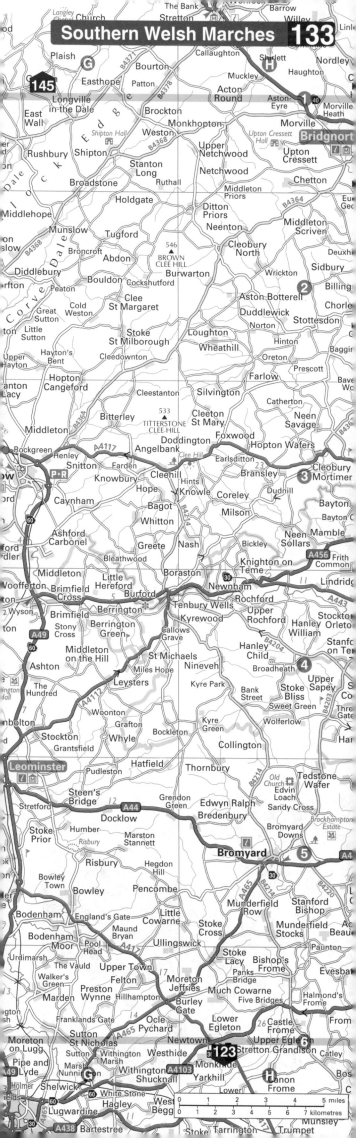

which runs through the park, and an Iron Age fort (Croft Ambrey) may be reached by footpath. There is a fine, restored walled garden, vineyards and family walks

Hergest Croft Gardens 132 D5
From spring bulbs to autumn colour, this is a garden for all seasons. A fine collection of trees and shrubs surrounds the Edwardian house. There's an old-fashioned kitchen garden with spring and summer borders, and Park Wood, a hidden valley with magnificent rhododendrons.

The Judge's Lodging 133 E4
This restored Victorian town house has an integral courtroom, cells and service areas where you can step back into the 1860s, accompanied by an 'eavesdropping' audio tour of voices from the past. Explore the fascinating world of the Victorian judges, their servants and felonious guests at this award-winning, historic house. Various special events take place throughout the year.

Llandrindod Wells 132 B4
Period shop fronts, frilly wrought-iron canopies, and broad avenues lined with villas and hotels assert Llandrindod as one of the best-preserved Victorian spa towns in Britain. Within Rock Park you can sample the rusty-tasting waters that gush from a fountain, or visit the restored Pump Room, while the lake is a popular strolling area. Among many period buildings is the Automobile Palace, an early motor showroom (1909) housing the National Cycle Exhibition, a collection of more than 250 historic bicycles from Victorian examples to more comfortable-looking modern versions. Try to visit in late August, when the whole town dresses in period costume during Llandrindod's Victorian Week.

Ludlow 133 G3
Houses of Georgian brickwork and earlier half-timbering grace the streets of this hilltop town. Broad Street is a particularly harmonious townscape. Ludlow Castle, a border fortress begun in the late 11th century, was enlarged in the 14th century into a palace for the powerful Roger Mortimer. Near the ancient Butter Cross, the Church of St Laurence assumes a practically cathedral-like grandeur, and has a fine set of 15th-century carved misericords (benches in the choir). The town has emerged as a regional foodie capital, with an excellent range of restaurants. The annual Ludlow Festival has drama and music performed in the castle grounds.

Shropshire Hills Discovery Centre 133 F2
This attraction explores the history, nature and geography of the Shropshire Hills, through a series of interactive displays and simulations. These include Landscape of Contrasts, Ancient Landscape, a simulated Balloon Flight, and Land of Inspiration. The Centre has 9ha of meadow lands sloping down to the River Onny for visitors to explore. There is a network of cycle routes and walks and, on summer weekends, a shuttle bus service operates from the Centre which allows visitors to explore the local landscape, hills, villages and market towns. The Centre also houses the Secret Hills Gallery which features craft and artwork displays celebrating Shropshire's creative industry.

Stokesay Castle 133 F2
Stokesay is one of England's best preserved 13th-century fortified manor houses. It has a superb timber-framed Jacobean gatehouse and an impressive great hall with long, Gothic gabled windows. There are delightful cottage gardens.

The Long Mynd ridge, near Church Stretton

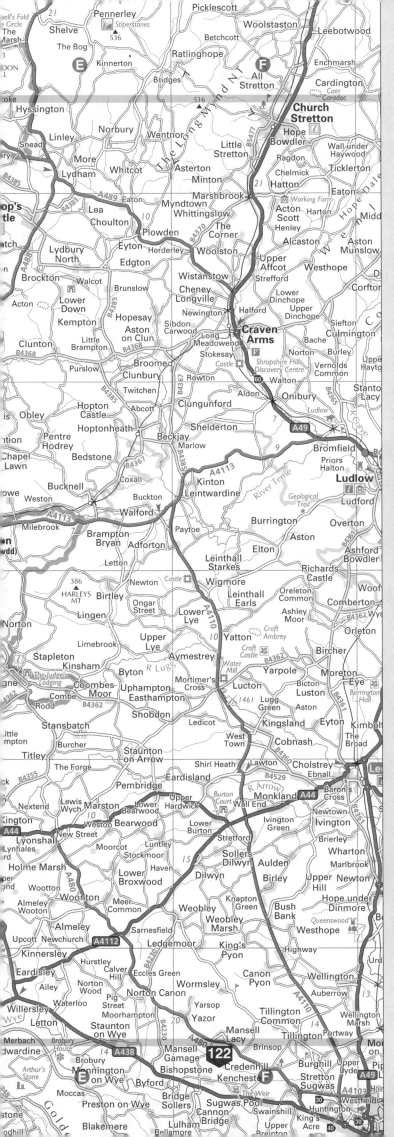

SOUTHERN WELSH MARCHES

In the fertile landscapes of the Welsh Marches the shires of England have gently melded into hill country. Hillside fortresses highlight the times of border conflict and there are great houses and a modern discovery centre, telling the story of the Shropshire Hills, to visit.

Stokesay Castle is set amid peaceful countryside near the Welsh border

Berrington Hall 133 G4
This elegant neo-classical house of the late 18th century was designed by Henry Holland and set in a park landscape by 'Capability' Brown. There is a restored bedroom suite, a nursery, a Victorian laundry and a tiled Georgian dairy. Events are held throughout the year.

Brockhampton Estate 133 H5
This traditionally formed 700ha estate has extensive areas of wood and parkland, with a rich variety of wildlife and over 5 miles of walks. At the heart of the estate lies Lower Brockhampton House, a late 14th-century moated manor house with a beautiful timber-framed gatehouse and ruined chapel.

Burford House Gardens 133 G4
The lawns and borders surrounding the early Georgian mansion lead down to the banks of the River Teme. The gardens contain the National Clematis Collection with around 400 varieties on display, flowering from spring to autumn.

Church Stretton 133 F1
At the foot of Long Mynd, some of the highest and least spoiled uplands in central England, the historic market town of Church Stretton makes a useful base for the area's activities, which include horseback riding, golf and gliding. East of the town, Caer Caradoc is perhaps the area's finest viewpoint, and is capped by the ramparts of an Iron Age hillfort.

Croft Castle 133 F4
Home of the Croft family since Domesday, the walls and towers of this handsome stone castle date from the 14th and 15th centuries, while the comfortable interior is mainly 18th century. Period furnishings and paintings, including works by Gainsborough, are on display. There is a splendid avenue of 350-year-old Spanish chestnut trees

Walking the empty, heather-clad moorlar

plasterwork; the entrance hall, staircase and two principal rooms are shown. The grounds contain charming 18th-century temples, a terrace walk and an obelisk.

Kenilworth Castle 135 F3
No other English castle ruin even approaches 12th-century Kenilworth for sheer size. It has huge sandstone walls, a Great Hall and a mighty Norman keep. Robert Dudley, the Earl of Leicester, transformed it into a Tudor palace, and Elizabeth I, with whom he was having an affair, visited him here in 1575. Sir Walter Scott stayed close by, while writing his novel *Kenilworth* (1821).

Great Malvern 134 A6
Sprawling on the lower slopes of the dramatic Malvern Hills is the 18th-century spa town of Great Malvern. With its rambling houses and steeply climbing streets, the town retains an air of faded gentility. Malvern Priory Church dates back to the 11th century, its great Gothic tower rising high above the town's imposing Victorian buildings. The Malvern Museum is housed in the Abbey Gateway.

Mary Arden's House 135 E5
The childhood home of Shakespeare's mother is 3 miles north of town. To reach the house you can walk along the towpath of the Stratford-upon-Avon Canal or take the train one stop beyond Stratford. The Shakespeare Countryside Museum surrounds the cottage and has displays about life and work here, and Glebe Farm, a working blacksmith's and falconer's.

National Motorcycle Museum 135 F2
The National Motorcycle Museum is recognised as the finest and largest motorcycle museum in the world, with machines always being added to the collection. It is a place where legends live on and it is a tribute to and a living record of this once great British industry that dominated world markets for some 60 years. The museum records the engineering achievements of the last century.

Ragley Hall 134 D5
Built in 1680, Ragley is the family home of the Marquess and Marchioness of Hertford, and has been for nine generations. Set in 160ha of parkland, woodland and landscaped gardens, Ragley has something for all the family. Younger visitors will enjoy Adventure Wood with its swings, trampoline, 3-D maze, rope bridges and wooden fortress. There are 11ha of formal gardens, the Woodland Walk features the Jerwood Sculpture Park, and the 18th-century stable block houses a collection of historic carriages and equestrian memorabilia.

Severn Valley Railway 134 A3
The leading standard-gauge steam railway has one of the largest collections of locomotives and rolling stock in the country. Services operate from Kidderminster and Bewdley to Bridgnorth through 16 miles of picturesque scenery along the River Severn. Special steam galas take place during the year.

Stoneleigh Abbey 135 G3
Like many other abbeys that aren't really abbeys, Stoneleigh is a country house occupying a medieval monastic site. On the guided tour around this Georgian building visitors are taken to the room where Queen Victoria slept, the dining room where she and her husband, Prince Albert, dined in 1858, and the bath that was made specially for her visit. It is also recorded that novelist Jane Austen paid a visit to the house in 1806.

West Midland Safari Park 134 B3
The 4-mile drive through this hugely popular safari park takes about an hour and gives visitors a close encounter with lions, giraffes, zebras and more, as well as with some endangered species such as white rhinoceroses and Bengal tigers. You may also get the chance to feed antelopes. Throughout the day there are live shows that might feature a reptile encounter, feeding the hippos or a sea-lion show. At Pets' Corner younger children can touch and feed the animals, and there are giraffe rides for older children. The leisure park area has traditional rather than ultra-scary rides and is suitable for all members of the family.

Looking down on British Camp, an Iron Age hillfort on the Malvern Hills

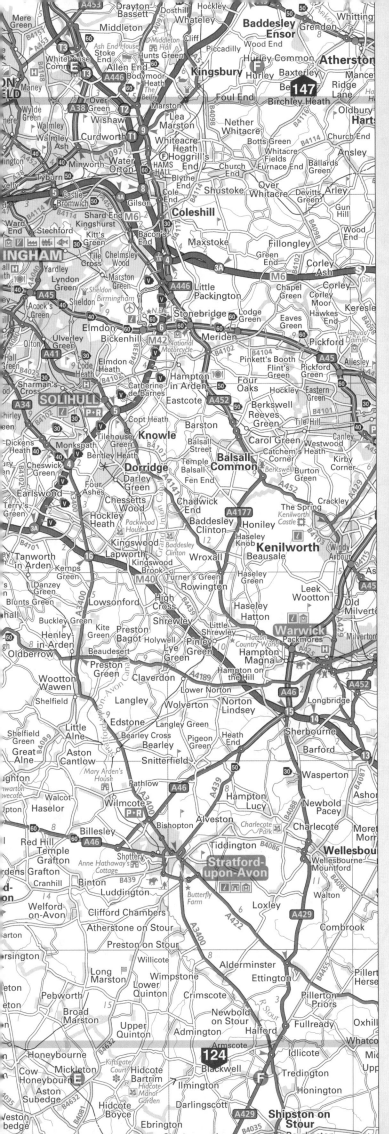

WEST MIDLANDS

This region, dominated by Birmingham and the West Midlands conurbation, has beautiful countryside which extends into leafy Warwickshire known for its stately homes, magnificent castles, and Stratford-upon-Avon forever linked with England's greatest playwright, William Shakespeare. The cities of Birmingham and Coventry have come through the Industrial Revolution to reinvent themselves as thriving cultural and entertainment centres.

A 19th-century windmill at Avoncroft, one of Britain's best-known open-air museums

Anne Hathaway's Cottage 135 E5

Shakespeare's wife lived in this pretty thatched cottage. You can walk along the country lane from Hall's Croft to avoid the traffic. The house stayed in the Hathaway family until the 19th century, and much of the family furniture remains.

Avoncroft 134 C4

More than 20 historic buildings spanning 600 years of history have been rescued and reconstructed on a large open site in the Worcestershire countryside. They range from the venerable to the humble, from 15th- and 16th-century timber-framed buildings to a 1940s prefab of a kind erected hastily across Britain to house those who had lost their homes during bomb raids. The National Telephone Kiosk Collection pays homage to the very British (but now largely superseded) red phone box, while other exhibits include a cock-fighting pit and a working windmill.

Bodenham Arboretum 134 B2

This award-winning arboretum, with over 2,700 species of trees and shrubs, is attractively landscaped in 63ha. The arboretum is incorporated into a working farm. Five miles of paths lead through dells and glades and around lakes, pools and grazing fields.

Charlecote Park 135 F5

This grand country house in the Warwickshire countryside has been the home of the Lucy family and their forbears, the Montforts, for 900 years, although the present rose-pink brick structure dates from 1551. Guests have included Elizabeth I, who slept here for two nights in 1572, and the young William Shakespeare, who is alleged to have been caught poaching on the estate. Herds of fallow deer, red deer and Jacob sheep roam the park; estate buildings open to visitors include the brewhouse, gatehouse, coach house and tack room. The grounds were landscaped by 'Capability' Brown. The Victorian kitchen gives an idea of what life was like below stairs.

Coughton Court 134 D4

This imposing Tudor house is set in beautiful gardens, and has been home to the Throckmortons for hundreds of years. The house contains many family portraits, fascinating furniture, fabrics and ornaments. The estate has two churches, a 19th-century Catholic church, and the parish church of St Peter's. The Throckmorton Family created and maintains the grounds, including the walled garden and the award-winning displays of roses.

Farnborough Hall 135 H6

Farnborough Hall is a classical mid-18th century stone house with notable

Sir Thomas Tresham's Triangular Lodge

Sir Thomas Tresham, and Lyveden remains virtually unaltered since work stopped when he died in 1605. The house has fascinating Elizabethan detail and in the grounds is one of the oldest garden layouts in Britain.

Northampton Museum & Art Gallery 136 C4

Home to the world's largest collection of shoes, Northampton Museum and Art Gallery displays shoes that have been in fashion through the ages, from Ferragamo to Vivienne Westwood. Life and Sole tells the history of footwear, and other displays detail the history of Northampton, and British and Oriental ceramics and glass. There is also a gallery of Italian paintings depicting scenes from the Bible and ancient mythology.

Rockingham Castle 136 D1

Set on a hill overlooking five counties, the castle was built by William the Conqueror. The site of the original keep is now a rose garden, but the outline of the curtain wall remains as do the foundations of the Norman hall, and the twin towers of the gatehouse. A royal residence for 450 years, the castle was granted to Edward Watson in the 16th century, and the Watson family have lived there ever since.

Sandy: RSPB Nature Reserve 137 G4

Sandy is the headquarters of the Royal Society for the Protection of Birds. The house and buildings are not open to the public, but there are waymarked paths through woodlands and sandy heaths with hides for bird and animal observation. There are formal gardens and a specialist wildlife garden which was created in conjunction with the Henry Doubleday Association.

Stanford Hall 136 A3

Stanford is a beautiful William and Mary house, built in 1697 by Sir Roger Cave, ancestor of the present owner. The house contains antique furniture, paintings (including the Stuart Collection) and family costumes. Special events held during the year include car and motorcycle owners' club rallies.

Sulgrave Manor 136 A6

This is a splendid example of a Tudor manor house with a Georgian wing, housing excellent collections of authentic period furniture and fabrics. It is set in pleasant gardens in the English formal style.

Triangular Lodge 136 D2

The Triangular Lodge at Rushden is a delightful Elizabethan folly designed to symbolise the Holy Trinity, with its three sides, three floors, trefoil windows and three triangular gables on each side. Designed and built by Sir Thomas Tresham.

collections of paintings, furniture, china and sculpture are on display.

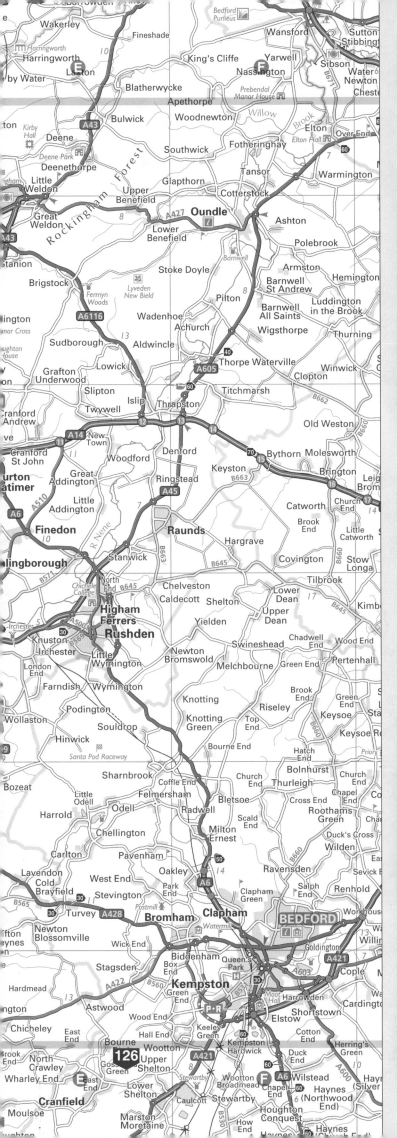

SOUTH EAST MIDLANDS

This region is filled with places of interest including delightful villages and some particularly fine houses, all reflections of its location at the heart of England. The industrial heritage of the area is evident in the great county town of Northampton.

Canons Ashby House, in the care of the National Trust, overlooks formal gardens

Althorp Park 136 B4
Following her death in a car crash in Paris, Diana, Princess of Wales, was buried on a private island in a lake within the grounds of her family home. As home of the Spencers since 1508, Althorp has become something of a shrine to her, and a six-room exhibition celebrates her life. The mansion, modified in the 18th century in Classical style, sits among trees and pastures, and some private apartments are open to the public.

Canons Ashby House 136 A5
Home of the Dryden family since the 16th century, this is an exceptional small manor house, with Elizabethan wall paintings and Jacobean plasterwork. It has restored gardens, a small park and a church, once part of the original 13th-century Augustinian priory.

Lyveden New Bield 137 E2
Lyveden New Bield is an incomplete Elizabethan garden house and moated garden. Building began in 1595 by

Althorp is a classic english stately home set in magnificent gardens and parkland. Ins

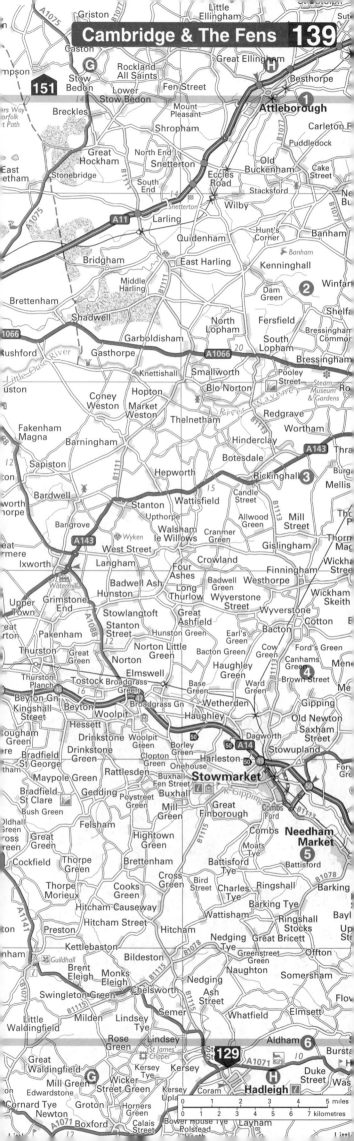

by Stubbs, Lely, Van Dyck and other old masters. The grounds were laid out by John Evelyn, William Kent and 'Capability' Brown, and include a 17th-century church in the style of Wren and a river walk to the restored watermill.

Grimes Graves 139 F1
These unique and remarkable neolithic flint mines are the earliest major industrial site in Europe. Using antlers as picks prehistoric miners sank shafts and tunnels deep into the ground following seams of flint. It is possible to descend by a series of ladders to the bottom of one of the shafts to see how flint was extracted. A small exhibition area illustrates the history of the site.

Kentwell Hall 139 F6
Kentwell Hall is a moated red brick Tudor manor with gardens, woodland walks and a rare breeds farm. Restoration started in 1971 and still continues today. The house and grounds are open to the public at certain times of the year, and recreations of Tudor and 1940s life take place at weekends.

Lavenham Guildhall 139 G6
The Guildhall of Corpus Christi is one of the finest timber-framed buildings in Britain. It was built around 1530 by the prosperous Corpus Christi Guild, for religious rather than commercial reasons. The hall now houses a local history museum telling the story of Lavenham's 15th- and 16th-century cloth trade riches. Visitors can also see the walled garden with its 19th-century lock-up and mortuary.

Thetford 139 F2
In the heart of Breckland, once sparsely populated heathland, is the small historic town of Thetford. During the 11th century Thetford was the Seat of the Bishops of East Anglia and the ruined Cluniac priory is on the outskirts of town. The Ancient House Museum,

an early Tudor timber-framed house with beautifully carved beamed ceilings, now houses an exhibition on Thetford and Breckland life. This has been traced back to very early times, and there are examples from local neolithic settlements. Brass rubbing facilities are available and there is a small period garden recreated in the rear courtyard.

Weeting Castle 139 E2
This ruined 11th-century fortified manor house stands in a moated enclosure. There are interesting but slight remains of a three-storey cross-wing.

Wimpole Hall & Home Farm
138 A5
Wimpole Hall is one of the grandest mansions in East Anglia, and has 145ha of parkland devised and planted by no less than four celebrated landscape designers, Charles Bridgeman, 'Capability' Brown, Sanderson Miller and Humphrey Repton. The house dates back to 1640, but was altered into a large 18th-century mansion with a Georgian façade. The chapel has a *trompe l'oeil* ceiling.

Delightful timber-framed cottages line the streets of Lavenham

Quiet roads lead through Thetford Forest, an area popular with walkers and cyclists

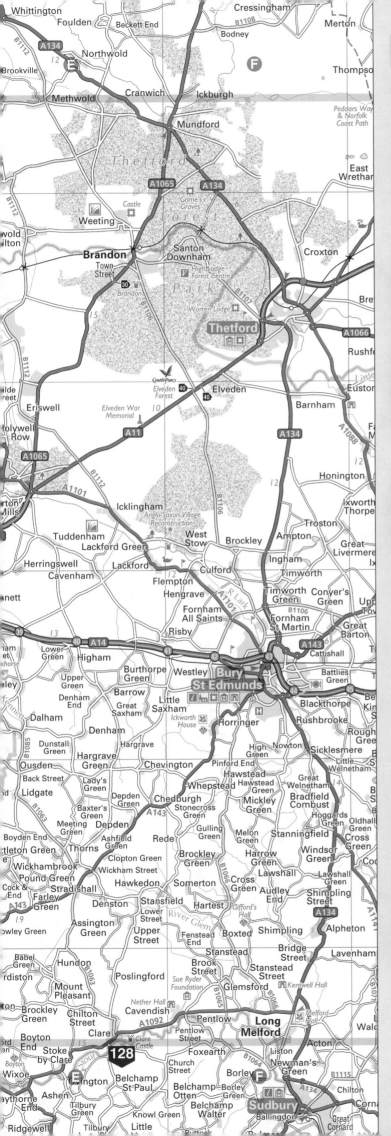

CAMBRIDGE & THE FENS

Outside and beyond Cambridge, renowned for its university, are wide fenland horizons interrupted only by an occasional church spire or the outline of a solitary windmill. Where hills rise out of the flat land there is usually something special built upon them, notably at Ely. The route north from Bury St Edmunds is dominated by the vast Thetford Forest.

Motor cruisers and narrowboats moored on the Great Ouse at Ely

Anglesey Abbey 138 C4
A medieval undercroft has survived from the priory founded here in 1135, but the house dates mainly from 1600. Thomas Hobson of Hobson's Choice was one of the owners. A later owner was Lord Fairhaven, who amassed the huge collection of pictures, and laid out the beautiful gardens.

Anglo Saxon Village 139 E3
The village is a reconstruction of a pagan Anglo-Saxon settlement dated AD 420–650. Seven buildings have been reconstructed on the site of the excavated settlement. There is a visitor centre and a children's play area. A new Anglo-Saxon Centre houses the original objects found on the site. The village is located in the West Stow Country Park with a river, lake, and woodland with many trails and paths.

Bressingham Steam Museum & Gardens 139 H2
Alan Bloom is an internationally recognised nurseryman and a steam enthusiast, and he has combined his interests to great effect at Bressingham. There are three miniature steam-hauled trains, including a 15-inch gauge, running through two and a half miles of the wooded Waveney Valley. The Dell Garden has 5,000 species of perennials and alpines. Foggy Bottom has wide vistas, pathways, trees, shrubs, conifers and winter colour. Other attractions include a steam roundabout and a museum. Various events take place throughout the year.

Duxford Imperial War Museum 138 B6
The Imperial War Museum Duxford occupies a former military airbase. It has Europe's main collection of military and civil aircraft, plus vehicles, submarines and helicopters. The Normandy Experience recreates what it was like for an infantryman landing on D-Day, while an innovative building houses the American Air Museum.

Ely 138 C2
Dwarfing the old-fashioned town that huddles on a rise in the flat farmlands of the Fens, Ely Cathedral dates from the 11th century. The east end was rebuilt in Purbeck marble around 1250, while the collapse of the tower in 1322 necessitated the erection of the breathtakingly delicate lantern tower, lodged on eight oak pillars. In the cathedral precinct is the prestigious King's School, founded by Henry VIII. Combined tickets are available for the cathedral, the attached Stained Glass Museum and Ely Museum, an absorbing local collection in the Old Gaol in Market Street. Also included is Oliver Cromwell's House, the former home in St Mary's Street of the man who defeated Charles I and became leader of the country as Lord Protector in 1653. The riverfront on the Ouse is particularly attractive.

Euston Hall 139 G3
Home of the Duke and Duchess of Grafton, this 18th-century house is notable for its fine collection of pictures,

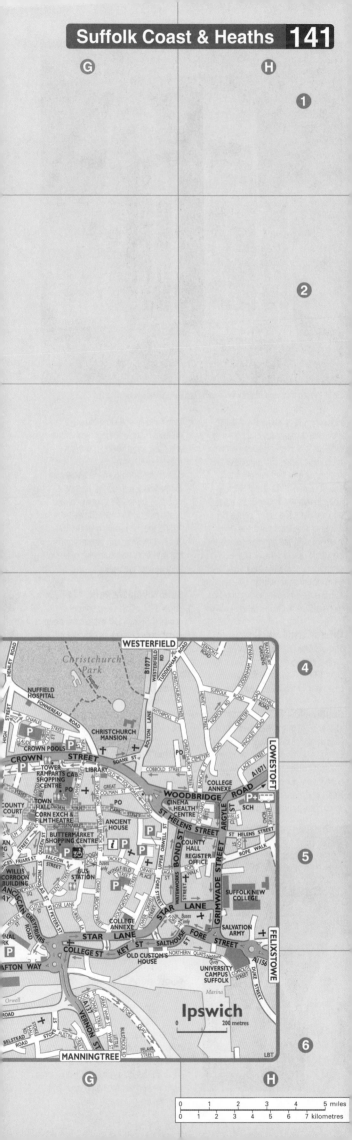

Both the exterior and interior of Orford Castle survive almost intact

hides. Spring is a time for birdsong, including nightingales and booming bitterns. In summer, you can watch breeding avocets and marsh harriers. Autumn is excellent for migrants, and in winter, hundreds of wildfowl visit the reserve. Look out for otters and red deer. The visitor centre has a well-stocked shop and licensed tearoom, and you can find out more about the reserve. There is a programme of events throughout the year, including several for children and families. Self-guided activity booklets help families make the most of a visit.

Orford Castle 140 D5
This great keep of Henry II has three huge towers and commanding views over Orford Ness. The spiral staircase leads to a maze of rooms and passageways.

Southwold 141 E3
The allure of this port-turned-resort is its sedate, old-fashioned character. Groups of brick and colour-washed cottages cluster around greens beneath three landmarks: the lighthouse, Adnam's brewery and the soaring tower of St Edmund's Church.

shore at Southwold

In the middle of town there are art galleries, antiques shops, tea rooms and pubs, most selling the highly esteemed Adnam's ales. Below the Sailors Reading Room – a social club for mariners, with a local history display – some 200 brightly painted beach huts dating from the early 1900s line the beach, near the pier. The Amber Shop and Museum, in Market Place, has examples of amber from all over the world.

Suffolk Wildlife Park 141 E2
Set in 32ha of dramatic coastal parkland, visitors can explore the sights and sounds of Africa at Africa Alive! Giraffes, rhinos, cheetah and hyenas can be seen, and you'll get a bird's eye view of the lion enclosure. Attractions include daily feeding, talks and animal encounter sessions, a magnificent bird of prey display, and free journey round the park with live commentary.

Sutton Hoo 140 B6
In 1939, excavation of an Anglo-Saxon royal burial site led to the discovery of the priceless Sutton Hoo treasure. A warrior's helmet, shield, gold ornaments and Byzantine silver were found close to the sea in the remains of a burial of a 27m ship. The exhibition here examines the 50-year excavation of the site, and aspects of Anglo-Saxon life such as craftsmanship, and life and death in 7th-century England. On display are original finds and a full-size reconstruction of King Raedwald's burial chamber. The burial mounds are a short walk away.

Woodbridge Tide Mill 140 B6
The machinery of this 18th-century mill has been completely restored. There are photographs and working models on display. Situated on a busy quayside, the unique building looks over towards the historic site of Sutton Hoo. Every effort is made to run the machinery for a while whenever the mill is open and the tides are favourable.

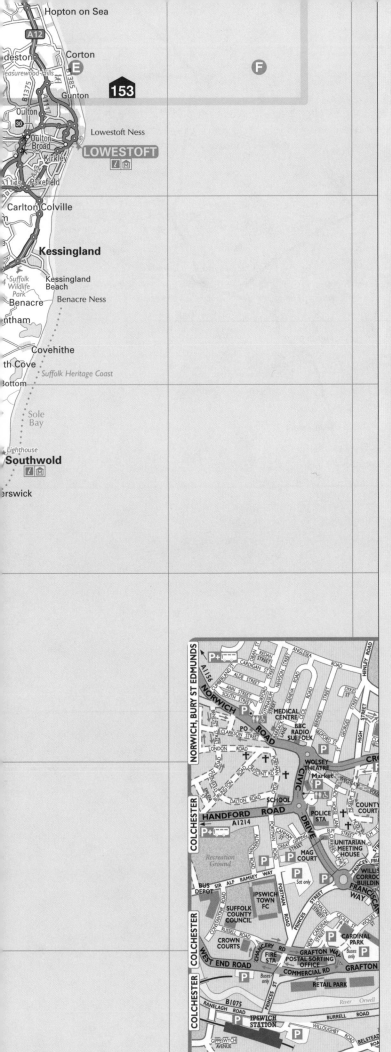

SUFFOLK COAST & HEATHS

Stretching south along the coast from Lowestoft, the Suffolk Heritage Coast, peppered with wildlife-rich estuaries and creeks, is ideal for sailing. Inland there are castles and abbeys to discover along with Sutton Hoo, one of the most important archaeological finds in Britain's history.

An avocet, seen here feeding at Minsmere, is the symbol of the RSPB

Aldeburgh 140 D5

Local fishermen still launch their boats here from the shingle beach and sell the day's catch from their huts. The 14th-century Church of St Peter and St Paul has a stained-glass window commemorating the composer Benjamin Britten, who lived in Aldeburgh from 1947 to 1957. He is buried in the churchyard beside the English tenor Sir Peter Pears, his partner and a co-founder of the internationally renowned annual music festival based around Snape Maltings, inland at Snape, each June. Britten's famous opera, *Peter Grimes*, is based on *The Borough* by the 18th-century Aldeburgh poet George Crabbe which was thought to have been set here.

Easton Farm Park 140 B5

Set on the banks of the River Deben the farm park is home to farm animals including Suffolk Punch horses, ponies, pigs, lambs, calves, goats, rabbits, guinea pigs and poultry.

Framlingham Castle 140 B4

Framlingham, a magnificent example of a late 12th-century castle, was built by Roger Bigod, Earl of Norfolk, as a stronghold and as a symbol of power and status. The castle is noted for its imposing stone walls and crenellated towers with ornate Tudor chimneys.

Ipswich 140 A6

Founded in the 6th century, Ipswich became a prosperous inland port because of its location on the estuary of the Orwell, and in the Middle Ages it was a great trading centre, exporting East Anglian wool. Christchurch Mansion, a wonderful Tudor house was built in 1548 on the site of an Augustinian priory. Set in a beautiful park, it displays period rooms and an art gallery with changing exhibitions and a collection of paintings by Constable and Gainsborough. The Ipswich Museum in the High Street has sections on Victorian Natural History, Suffolk wildlife, Suffolk geology, Roman Suffolk, Anglo-Saxon Ipswich and Peoples of the World.

Leiston Abbey 140 D4

For hundreds of years this 14th-century abbey was used as a farm and its church became a barn. A Georgian house, now used as a school for young musicians, was built into its fabric and remains of the choir, the church transepts and parts of the cloisters still stand.

Minsmere RSPB Nature Reserve 140 D4

Set on the beautiful Suffolk coast, Minsmere offers an enjoyable day out for all. Nature trails take you through a variety of habitats to the excellent

A string of brightly coloured beach huts li...

Ⓐ　　　　　Ⓑ　　　　　Ⓒ　　　　　Ⓓ

153

Clynnog-fawr　Capeluchaf　Nasar

Gyrn-gôch

Pant Glas　19

Lleyn Heritage Coast

Trefor　522
Y GYRN-DDU　A487

Tre'r Ceiri

1

Trwyn y Grolech　564
YR EIFL　Llanaelhaearn　Bryncir

207　Glan-Dwyfach

Carreg Ddu　Llithfaen　PENINSULA

Morfa Nefyn　Porth Nefyn　Pistyll　St Cybi's Well

Porth Dinllaen　Nefyn　Llwyndyrys　Pencaenewydd　Llangybi

Groesffordd　Fron B4354

Edern　Bodfuan　Y Ffor　Rhoslan

Rhos-fawr　B4354　Llanarmon

Porth Ysgaden　LLEYN　Llannor　Llanystumdwy

Rhos-y-llan　A497　Chwilog　13

Tudweiliog　Efailnewydd　Pennarth Fawr Medieval House

Porth Colman　Dinas　371　Abererch

2

Carn Fadrum　B4415　Denio　Pen-ychain

Bryn-mawr　Llaniestyn　Rhyd-y-clafdy

Pen-y-graig　14　Garnfadryn

Llangwnnadl　Meyllteyrn　Penrhos　Pwllheli

Sarn　Botwnnog　Mynytho　St Tudwal's Road

Bryncroes　17　Nanhoron　B4413　Llanbedrog

Rhydlios　Rhoshirwaun　Llandegwning　Trwyn Llanbedrog

Porthoer　Plas yn Rhiw　Llangian

Anelog　Penycaerau　Y Rhiw　Llanengan　Abersoch

Aberdaron　Llanfaelrhys　Sarn Bach　St Tudwal's Island East

3

Uwchmynydd　Porth Ysgo　Bwlchtocyn　Marchros　St Tudwal's Island West

Aberdaron Bay　Porth Neigwl

Bardsey Sound　Porth Geiriad

Lleyn Heritage Coast

St Mary's

BARDSEY ISLAND

4

5

CARDIGAN

6

BAY

Ⓐ　　　　　Ⓑ　　　　　Ⓒ　　　　　Ⓓ

and superb scenery. There is a buffet service on all trains including a licensed bar in corridor carriages.

Harlech Castle 143 E2
The walls and six drum towers of this 13th-century castle stand virtually at their original height. Built as one of Edward I's iron ring of fortresses designed to subdue the Welsh, it is defended by a massive gatehouse and commands views of the sea, the Snowdonia mountains and the Lleyn Peninsula. Fortified steps (open in summer only) lead to the foot of the castle. The song *Men of Harlech* was inspired by a long siege against the castle when it was held by the Lancastrians during the Wars of the Roses.

Harlech Castle, near the centre of town

Penarth Fawr 142 D2
The hall, buttery and screen are preserved in this house which was probably built in the 15th century.

Plas yn Rhiw 142 B3
This is a small manor house, part medieval, with Tudor and Georgian additions. The ornamental gardens have flowering trees and shrubs including sub-tropical specimens, divided by box hedges and grass paths. A stream and waterfall descend from the snowdrop wood behind the house.

Porthmadog 143 E2
Centred around a small harbour and the causeway William Madock built to reclaim land on the Glaslyn estuary, Porthmadog is the most popular holiday resort in Lleyn. Many of the visitors come to take a train ride on one of the two narrow-gauge railways, the Welsh Highland, which will eventually reach Caernarfon, and the Ffestiniog, which takes a scenic route to the lovely slate town of Blaenau Ffestiniog. A short walk leads past Porthmadog's boatyards and over a heavily wooded headland to reach the sheltered and picturesque beach at Borth-y-Guest, a village, where life is taken at a leisurely pace.

Portmeirion 143 E2
The Italian Riviera comes to the shores of Snowdonia in this surreal 20th-century creation, by architect Sir Clough Williams-Ellis, occupying a headland overlooking the Dwyryd estuary. His aim was to show that a beautiful location could be developed without being spoiled. The result is a storybook version of a Mediterranean village in which parts of buildings from elsewhere in Britain have been ingeniously recycled. Portmeirion has a piazza at its heart and buildings that include a belvedere, campanile, pantheon and triumphal arch are overlooked by pastel-hued cottages decorated with carvings and paintings. A Victorian mansion, Castell Deudraeth, houses a restaurant and rooms. Distinctive Portmeirion pottery is sold at the village shop.

Pwllheli 142 C2
Pwllheli, often considered to be the capital of Lleyn, has plenty of facilities, including a magnificent marina, and is considered an international yachting centre. The town is good for shopping and there's a market on Wednesdays.

...hmadog to Blaenau Ffestiniog

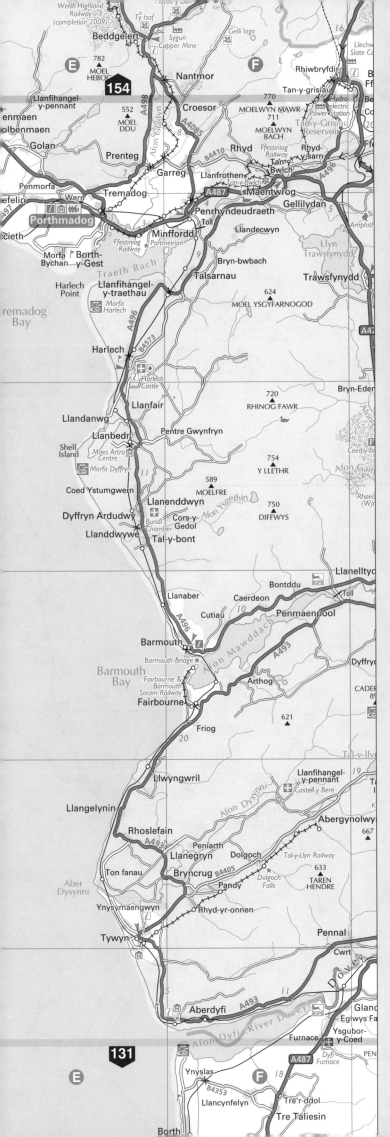

LLEYN PENINSULA & SNOWDONIA

The rocky, westward-pointing finger of the Lleyn Peninsula, has some of the finest beaches in North Wales, while the narrow coastal plains to the south rear up to the cloud-capped foothills of Snowdonia, designated as one of the first and largest of Britain's National Parks.

Pwllheli's long sandy, south-facing beach stretches from Gimblet Rock to Llanbedrog

Barmouth 143 F4

The Snowdonia National Park borders bypass Barmouth on the side of the Rhinog Mountain. The largely Victorian resort built into the rocks has wonderful sands backed by a promenade, funfair and cafés. Those who look for more than a beach holiday and who choose to explore a little further, will find true beauty and majesty in the surrounding mountains and the Mawddach Estuary. The Rhinogydd range, which rises from the backyards of the resort, features some of the finest mountains in Wales. A fascinating web of stairs and alleyways leads from the High Street up to Hen Bermo, the old town, built almost vertically and haphazardly up the cliffs.

Castell y Bere 143 F5

The castle was begun around 1221 by Prince Llewelyn ap Iorwerth of Gwynedd to guard the southern flank of his principality. It is typically Welsh in design with its D-shaped towers. Although a little off the beaten track, the castle lies in a spectacular setting, overshadowed by the Cader Idris range.

Centre for Alternative Technology 143 G5

Within a disused slate quarry on a remote hillside in mid-Wales, a community of half a dozen self-sufficient families has been established to showcase how 'green' energy and alternative technology can be used in various aspects of everyday life. It has been arranged foremost with visitors in mind: a water-powered cliff railway (summer only) carries you up to the site from the parking area. From there you can wander among solar-powered buildings, pumps and turbines, organic gardens and farm animals.

Cymer Abbey 143 G4

The abbey was built for the Cistercians in the 13th century. It was never very large, and does not seem to have been finished. The church is the best-preserved building, with ranges of windows and arcades still to be seen. The other buildings have been plundered for stone, but low outlines remain.

Ffestiniog Railway 143 F1

This narrow gauge steam railway runs for 13.5 miles through Snowdonia National Park, with breathtaking views

The Ffestiniog Railway links the harbour in

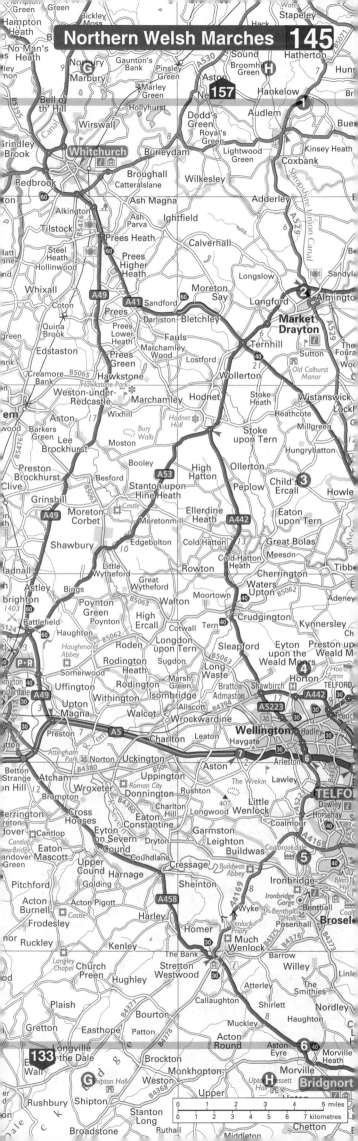

to the ironmasters. Enginuity is a hands-on attraction aimed at children that invites them to try such engineering tasks as stoking a furnace. The Hay Inclined Plane at Blists Hill is an astonishing engineering feat linking two canals by means of a steep tramway.

Llangollen 144 D1

The market town of Llangollen has been hosting, since 1947, the annual International Eisteddfod in July, when performers from all over the world compete in dance, song and instrumental music. The venue is the impressive Royal International Pavilion. Indoor attractions here include the Motor Museum and Canal Exhibition, with cars and cycles dating from 1912 and a display about the building of the canals, and the Llangollen Museum recording the social and industrial history of this fascinating corner of Wales.

Powis Castle's celebrated gardens

Montgomery 144 D6

While none of the border towns of mid-Wales are of great size, Montgomery is scarcely more than a village, yet with imposing Georgian buildings recalling its once greater status as a county town. The finest buildings are in Broad Street, and include the 1748 Town Hall. Overlooking the town are the sparse ruins of the 13th-century castle, well worth climbing for its views. A 16th-century former inn, The Old Bell houses local history displays about the town and the Cambrian Railway.

Pistyll Rhaeadr 144 B3

At the end of a long, sparsely populated valley is this dramatic waterfall (the name means 'waterfall spout'), the tallest in Wales. A narrow ribbon of water drops into a wooded rock basin from a height of 73m, broken in mid-flight by a man-made rock arch placed there to enhance the whole effect. Visitors can walk to the top or watch the spectacle from the picnic area at ground level.

Powis Castle 144 D5

Laid out in the Italian and French styles, the garden retains its original lead statues, an Orangery and an aviary on the terraces. The medieval castle contains one of the finest collections of paintings and furniture in Wales and a beautiful collection of treasures from India.

Shrewsbury 145 F4

Black-and-white Tudor houses and Georgian red brick distinguish the old town of Shrewsbury, on a peninsula tightly enclosed by a great loop of the River Severn, guarded on its landward side by Shrewsbury Castle, which contains the Shropshire Regimental Museum. Examples of half-timbered buildings include Owen's Mansion and Ireland's Mansion, close to the arcaded Old Market Hall of 1596, while the narrow alley of the Bear Steps leads past a timber-framed hall now housing an art gallery.

Pistyll Rhaeadr, where the River Disgynfa cascades into the deep pool below

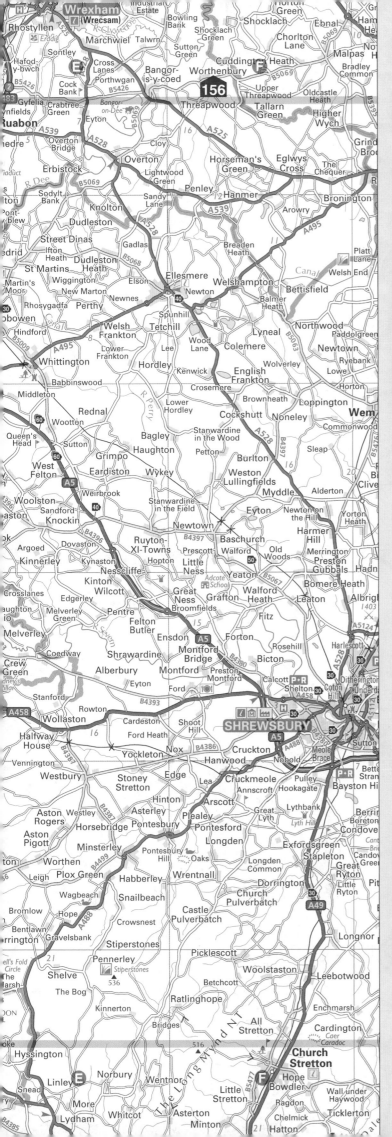

NORTHERN WELSH MARCHES

Shrewsbury is one of the most pleasant English towns; Telford is one of the most modern, but it includes Ironbridge, where the Industrial Revolution first sparked in to life. To the west the first hills of Wales mark the border country around Oswestry.

The Pontcysyllte Aqueduct carries the Llangollen Canal over the River Dee valley

Attingham Park 145 G4
Attingham Park is centred on one of Britain's finest regency mansions, set in a landscaped deer park designed by Humphry Repton. The house is undergoing a major project to revive and re-discover the original lavish decorative schemes, with upstairs rooms open for the first time. The park is an ideal place for a country walk, and there is a programme of events throughout the year.

Bala Lake Railway 144 A2
Steam locomotives which once worked in the slate quarries of North Wales now haul passenger coaches for 4.5 miles from Llanuwchllyn Station (143 H2) along the lake to Bala. The railway has one of the few remaining double-twist lever-locking framed GWR signal boxes, installed in 1896. Some of the coaches are open and some closed, so passengers can enjoy the beautiful views of the lake and mountains in all weathers.

Buildwas Abbey 145 H5
Set beside the River Severn, against a backdrop of wooded grounds, are the extensive remains of this Cistercian abbey founded in 1135. The 12th-century church, a beautiful vaulted and tile-floored chapter house and the crypt chapel can also be seen.

Chirk Castle 144 D2
On a rise in the hills of the northern Welsh borderlands, 14th-century Chirk Castle is one of the few erected by Edward I to survive intact, with its squat towers and forbidding exterior walls. Inside, however, much has changed. The Myddelton family, resident since 1595, added elegant state rooms with Adam-style furniture, tapestries and portraits, a 17th-century Long Gallery, and decorations in a

medieval style by the 19th-century designer Augustus Pugin. The grounds are planted with roses and yews in the formal gardens.

Hodnet Hall Gardens 145 H3
There are over 24ha of brilliantly coloured flowers, magnificent forest trees, sweeping lawns and a chain of ornamental pools which run along the cultivated garden valley providing a habitat for waterfowl and other wildlife. Big game trophies adorn the 17th-century tea rooms and plants are for sale in the kitchen gardens. The house is not open.

Ironbridge Gorge 145 H5
Several outstanding museums stand in the true birthplace of the Industrial Revolution. It was in this valley in 1709 that the ironmaster and engineer Abraham Darby I pioneered the smelting of iron ore with coke rather than charcoal, making the mass-production of metal feasible. The Gorge is dotted with nine sites that all belong to the museum. The largest is Blists Hill Victorian Town, reconstructed on the site of an 18th-century industrial estate, with working factories, shops and workers' cottages staffed by costumed actors and craftspeople. Coalport China Museum occupies what was the Coalport China Works. Close by is the entrance to the Tar Tunnel, where you go underground to see what was a natural source of bitumen when Ironbridge was functioning. Across the river stands the Jackfield Tile Museum and south of Jackfield Bridge is the Broseley Pipeworks. The Museum of the Gorge gives an overview of the development of the gorge, including a scale model of the area as it was in 1796. North of here is the Coalbrookdale Museum of Iron, while the Darby Houses were homes

Lectocetum, Wall was established as a military base in around AD 50 at the junction of two routes, Watling Street and the Rykneld Way, and grew into a busy town, providing overnight accommodation for travelling Roman officials and imperial messengers. The bathhouse is one of the most complete Roman relics of its kind in Britain, and there are also remains of a mansion, where travellers could rest and change their horses.

Lichfield 147 E4

The glory of Lichfield is its cathedral, with its trio of dark sandstone spires soaring over half-timbered houses and the former 17th-century Bishop's Palace in the cathedral close. The west front is adorned with 113 statues, including 24 English kings, while inside its many treasures include an 8th-century illuminated manuscript known as the St Chad's Gospels. Lichfield's most famous son was the man of letters Samuel Johnson; the house where he was born in Breadmarket Street is now The Samuel Johnson Birthplace Museum.

Moseley Old Hall 146 C5

In 1651, the Prince of Wales (later King Charles II), hid at Moseley Old Hall following his defeat at the Battle of Worcester. This romantic and daring story of the uncrowned king's escape is brought to life for visitors who enjoy stories from one of England's most turbulent times. Visitors can see the bed Charles slept on and the priest hole that concealed him. The impressive knot garden is based on a design of 1640.

Shugborough 146 C3

The ancestral home of the earls of Lichfield is a crisply classical 17th- and 18th-century mansion. During the 1740s, rococo plasterwork was added to the sumptuous state rooms. In addition to period furniture, paintings, ceramics and silver, there are photographs by the late Patrick, Earl of Lichfield a cousin of the Queen and a celebrated photographer. You can visit the servants' quarters, kitchen, brewhouse and coach house, plus a Victorian schoolroom and puppet shop. The park has some unusual classical monuments, as well as Park Farm, with an agricultural museum and rare farm breeds.

Snibstone Discovery Park 147 G4

Snibston is a well-designed museum where learning and fun go hand in hand, though not to the detriment of the seriousness of subjects such as conditions down a 19th-century coal mine, where men, women and children worked in sometimes appalling situations. Using former industrial buildings and the Coalville mine buildings, the park mixes indoor and outdoor educational activities, including outdoor science and water playgrounds.

Sudbury Hall 147 E2

Considered one of the finest houses of its period in England, Sudbury Hall dates from the late 17th century. Its greatest qualities are the interiors, with carving by Grinling Gibbons, painted ceilings and murals of mythological subjects by Louis Laguerre, and a spectacular staircase carved by Edward Pierce. The Gallery, one of the longest in England, has an opulent decorative plasterwork ceiling. In the 19th-century service wing, the National Trust Museum of Childhood looks into the world of the child, past and present, with collections of antique toys and dolls. Younger visitors also get the opportunity to play the role of chimneysweep and climb inside a chimney.

Weston Park 146 B4

Built in 1671, this fine mansion stands in elegant gardens and a vast park designed by 'Capability' Brown. Three lakes, a miniature railway, and a woodland adventure playground are to be found in the grounds, and in the house itself there is a magnificent collection of pictures, furniture and tapestries. There is also an animal centre and deer park.

White Ladies Priory 146 B5

Only the ruins are left of this Augustinian nunnery, which dates from 1158 and was destroyed in the Civil War. After the Battle of Worcester Charles II hid here and in the nearby woods before going on to Boscobel House.

Guides and costumed characters bring to life days gone by at Shugborough Hall

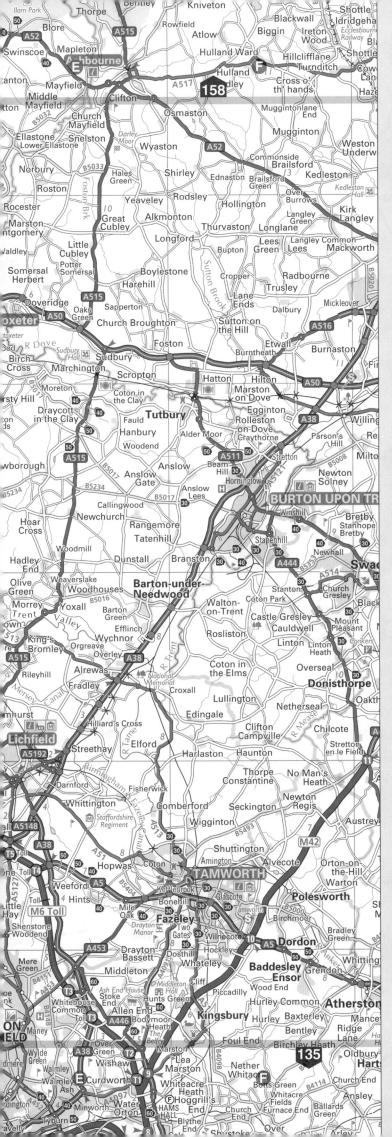

NORTH MIDLANDS

This is a region of beautiful countryside threaded by canals and dotted with wonderful historic houses and it has an industrial heritage that is well worth exploring. Officially designated an Area of Outstanding Natural Beauty, Cannock Chase, once a Norman hunting ground, is the home to fallow and red deer which thrive in the heath and woodland.

The water park at Alton Towers, Britain's most celebrated theme park

Alton Towers 146 D1

As theme parks go, Alton Towers rates as one of Europe's biggest, with plenty of new attractions added each year. There are knuckle-whitening rollercoaster rides such as the unmissable Nemesis, AIR, Ice Show, the Haunted House Strikes Back, Rita: Queen of Speed, and features for younger children such as Adventureland and Old MacDonald's Farmyard. There are also extensive landscaped gardens. Reservations are available for major rides, and are recommended at busy times. Visit near Halloween when some of the rides take place in the dark.

Boscobel House 146 B5

This fully restored and refurbished lodge and famous Royal Oak tree is where King Charles II sought refuge from Cromwell's troops in 1651. The house was built around 1632.

Calke Abbey 147 G3

Despite its name, Calke Abbey is a baroque country mansion mostly built between 1701 and 1703. Little changed over the years, and, occupied by the reclusive Harpur Crewe family up to 1924, it steadily decayed. The National Trust took it over and opened it to the public in 1989, deliberately leaving some of the rooms in their unrestored state. It makes a poignant visit, with the family wealth long gone, the atmosphere is of lost grandeur. The park, designated as a National Nature Reserve and managed for its nature conservation value, has 19th-century glasshouses, an ice house, walled flower garden and an orangery.

Derby 147 G2

Older Derby is well preserved in Friar's Gate and St Mary's Gate, with County Hall dating back to 1660, while the city's industrial past is told in a series of museums. Derby Museum & Art Gallery has a wide range of displays, notably of Derby porcelain, and paintings by the local artist Joseph Wright. The Silk Mill museum is set in a re-built 18th-century silk mill and adjacent flourmill on the site of the world's first modern factory. Displays cover local industries, and include a major collection of Rolls Royce aero-engines from 1915 to the present. A section covers the history of railway engineering in Derby. The building is now part of the Derwent Valley Mills World Heritage Site. Pickford's House Museum of Georgian Life & Costume is set in a house built in 1770 as a combined workplace and family home. It now shows domestic life at different periods, with Georgian reception rooms and service areas and a 1930s bathroom. Other galleries display part of the museum's collections of historic costume and toy theatres. At the Royal Crown Derby Visitor Centre a museum traces the history of the company from 1750 to the present day, while the factory tour demonstrates the making of Royal Crown Derby in detail from clay through to the finished product.

Letocetum Baths 146 D5

As with most Roman remains in Britain, there is little above foundation level to be seen here. Yet the museum and audio-tour help to bring the place back to life. Known to the Romans as

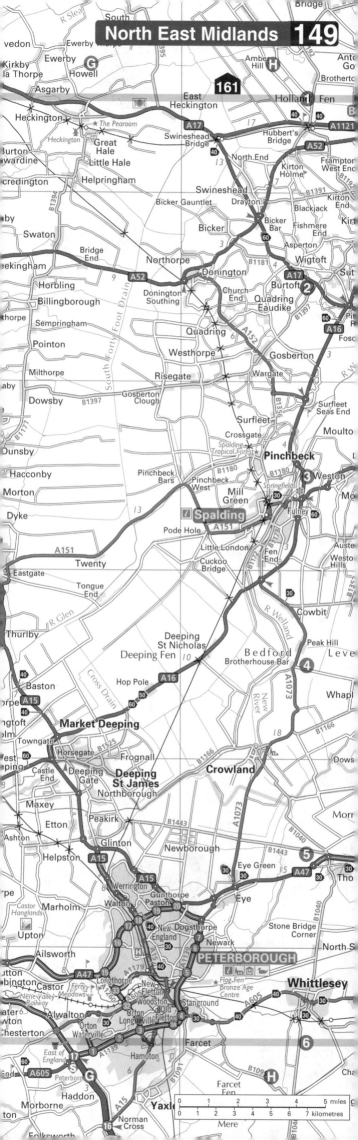

Rutland gallery is a guide to its history. The museum includes a shop and study area. On show in the 18th-century Riding School are displays of archaeology, history and an extensive rural life collection.

Peterborough 149 G6

Peterborough's glory is its magnificent cathedral which has one of the most dramatic west fronts in the country, its three arches an extraordinary creation of medieval architecture. The dramatic Romanesque interior is little altered since its completion 800 years ago. Particular highlights of a visit include the unique painted nave ceiling, the elaborate fan vaulting of the 'new' building, Saxon carvings from an earlier church and the burial places of two queens. An exhibition in the north aisle tells the story of the cathedral.

Peterborough Cathedral

Other attractions in Peterborough include Flag Fen Archaeology Park, with its reconstructed Bronze Age settlement and Iron Age roundhouse, while Railworld focuses on the future of rail transport and how it can meet the challenges of climate change. It features a large model railway, displays on rail history, showcases of rail technology and innovation, an environmental maze, hover trains, and much more.

Prebendal Manor House 149 F6

Dating from the early 13th century, this is the oldest manor in Northamptonshire. There's a 15th-century dovecote and tithe barn museum, and the largest re-created medieval garden in Europe, boasting fishponds, arbours, turf seats, a medieval vegetable garden and a vineyard.

Sacrewell Farm & Country Centre 149 F5

Treasures of farming and the country await discovery at this farm and 18th-century watermill. All aspects of agriculture and country life through the ages are here: listed buildings, working watermill, mill house and farm bygones. Farm animals, tractor rides, mini maze and pedal tractors are just a few of the activities to be experienced. Lamb feeding takes place in March and April

Stamford 149 F5

With golden limestone buildings and cobbled streets opening onto spacious squares, this most attractive of towns is a popular film location for period-costume dramas. Barn Hill offers the best overall view of the houses and medieval churches. To the south is Burghley House, a 240-room Elizabethan mansion built by William Cecil, chief minister to Elizabeth I. The house has a world-famous collection of tapestries, porcelain and paintings and is set in a beautiful deer park designed by 'Capability' Brown.

Woolsthorpe Manor 149 E3

This fine stone-built, 17th-century farmhouse was the birthplace of the scientist and philosopher Sir Isaac Newton. An early edition of his *Principia Mathematica* (1687) is in the house. There is an interactive Science Discovery Centre and an exhibition recounts Newton's childhood at Woolsthorpe.

...ardens and parkland, rises majestically from the flat Lincolnshire landscape

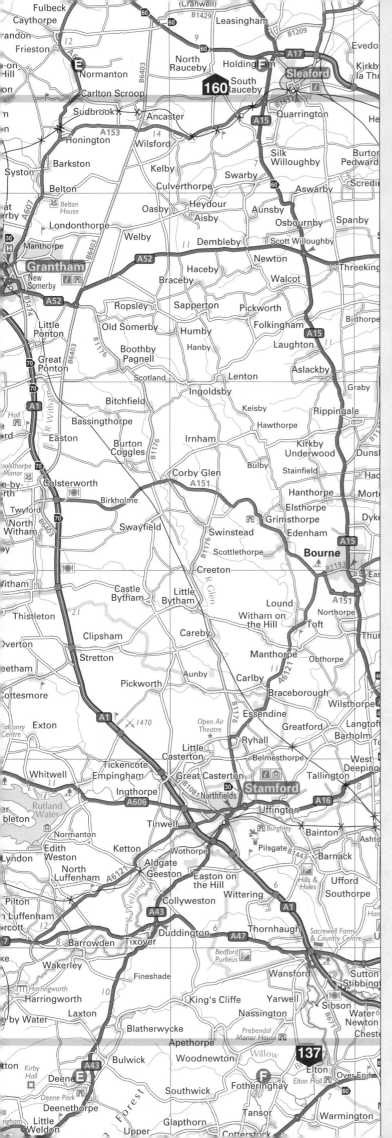

This is an area of beautiful countryside threaded by canals, wonderful historic houses and an industrial heritage that is well worth exploring. Officially designated an Area of Outstanding Natural Beauty, Cannock Chase, once a Norman hunting ground, is home to wild deer that thrive in the heath and woodland.

Belvoir Castle dominates the broad vale which takes its name

Belton House 148 E2

The ground floor of the house has a succession of state rooms, with the Marble Hall as its centrepiece. Splendid furnishings and decorations throughout the house include tapestries and hangings, family portraits, porcelain and fine furniture. The house is situated in beautiful gardens and extensive parkland.

Belvoir Castle 148 D2

Pronounced 'beaver', the castle is a startling Regency-Gothic edifice in pinkish stone, with a jumble of towers and turrets. It has been home to the Dukes of Rutland since 1508, although the present structure, the third on the site, dates from the early 19th century. It contains some opulent interiors, notably the Picture Gallery, including works by Thomas Gainsborough, Nicolas Poussin, Bartolomé Murillo and Hans Holbein. Beneath the castle terrace are the Rose and Statue Gardens; farther away are the lush Duchess's Spring Gardens, restored to their former glory and with plants fed by natural springs close to a summer house.

Grimsthorpe 149 F3

Seat of the Willoughby de Eresby family since 1516, the castle has a medieval tower and a Tudor quadrangular house with a Baroque north front by Vanbrugh. There are eight state rooms, two picture galleries and an important collection of furniture, pictures and tapestries. Other attractions include a family cycle trail, woodland adventure playground and ranger-guided tours of the park by minibus.

Lyddington Bede House 146 D6

The house was once a prominent medieval palace later converted into an almshouse for 12 poor 'bedesmen'. The history of the house is brought to life in an evocative audio tour. Visitors can wander through the bedesmens' rooms and view the Great Chamber with its carved ceiling cornice.

Oakham 148 D5

Oakham's Rutland County Museum is the perfect introduction to England's smallest county. The Welcome to

Grimsthorpe Castle, surrounded by exten

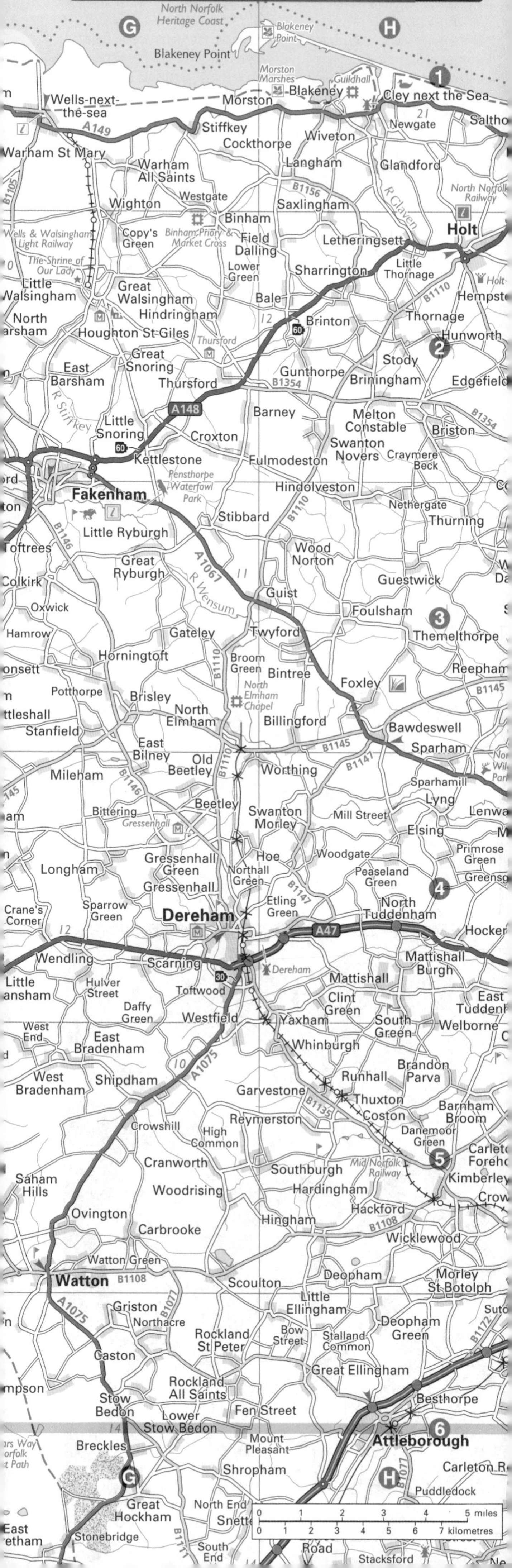

G North Norfolk Heritage Coast **H**

Blakeney Point
Blakeney Point
Morston Marshes
Guildhall
1
Cley next the Sea
Saltho
Wells-next-the-sea
Morston
Blakeney
Newgate
21
A149
Stiffkey
Wiveton
North Norfolk Railway
Warham St Mary
Cockthorpe
Langham
Glandford
Warham All Saints
Westgate
Saxlingham
Letheringsett
Holt
Wighton
Binham
Field Dalling
Sharrington
Little Thornage
Holt
Hempst
Copy's Green
Binham Priory & Market Cross
Lower Green
Brinton
Thornage
Wells & Walsingham Light Railway
The Shrine of Our Lady
Bale
12
Stody
Hunworth
Little Walsingham
Great Walsingham
Hindringham
Gunthorpe
Briningham
Edgefield
North arsham
Houghton St Giles
Great Snoring
Thursford
Barney
Melton Constable
Briston
East Barsham
Thursford
B1354
Swanton Novers
Craymere Beck
Little Snoring
Croxton
Fulmodeston
Hindolveston
B1354
60
A148
Kettlestone
Nethergate
Thurning
Fakenham
Penthorpe Waterfowl Park
Stibbard
Wood Norton
Guestwick
Little Ryburgh
Great Ryburgh
R Wensum
Guist
Foulsham
Themelthorpe
3
Colkirk
Oxwick
Gateley
Twyford
Reepham
Hamrow
Horningtoft
Broom Green
Bintree
Foxley
B1145
Potthorpe
Brisley
North Elmham
North Elmham Chapel
Billingford
Bawdeswell
Sparham
Stanfield
East Bilney
Old Beetley
Worthing
B1145
Sparham
Sparhamhill
Lyng
Lenwa
Mileham
B1146
Beetley
Swanton Morley
Mill Street
Elsing
Bittering
Gressenhall
Hoe
Woodgate
Primrose Green
Longham
Gressenhall Green
Northall Green
Peaseland Green
North Tuddenham
4
Crane's Corner
Sparrow Green
Etling Green
Hocker
Wendling
Dereham
A47
Mattishall Burgh
Little ansham
Scarning
Dereham
Mattishall
East Tuddenh
West End
Tottwood
30
Clint Green
Welborne
East Bradenham
Daffy Green
Westfield
Yaxham
South Green
West Bradenham
Shipdham
A1075
Whinburgh
Brandon Parva
Crowshill
Garvestone
Runhall
Barnham Broom
Saham Hills
High Common
Reymerston
Thuxton
Coston
Danemoor Green
Carleto Foreho
Ovington
Cranworth
Southburgh
Mid Norfolk Railway
Kimberley
Woodrising
Hardingham
5
Crow
Carbrooke
Hingham
Hackford
B1108
Watton
Watton Green
Scoulton
Deopham
Wicklewood
Morley St Botolph
Griston
B1108
Deopham Green
Suto
A1075
Northacre
Little Ellingham
Rockland St Peter
Bow Street
Stalland Common
Gaston
Rockland All Saints
Fen Street
Great Ellingham
B117
Besthorpe
Stow Bedon
Lower Stow Bedon
Mount Pleasant
6
Attleborough
Breckles
Shropham
G
H
Carleton R
Great Hockham
North End Snett
Puddledock
Stonebrstadge
South End
Road
Stacksford

0 1 2 3 4 5 miles
0 1 2 3 4 5 6 7 kilometres

associations of the 15th-century Guildhall of St George are strongest: Shakespeare is said to have performed here. It is now home to King's Lynn Arts Centre who hold a year-round programme of film, performing and visual arts. To the west of King's Lynn is the African Violet Centre.

Norfolk Lavender 150 D2

Norfolk Lavender is England's premier lavender farm, and home to the National Collection of Lavender. There are plants for sale and tours are available (including the distillery) between May and August. There's a Lavender Festival in June.

Oxburgh Hall 151 E5

The outstanding feature of this 15th-century moated building is the 24m high Tudor gatehouse which has remained unaltered throughout the centuries. Henry VII lodged in the King's Room in 1487. A parterre garden of French design stands outside the moat. Rare needlework by Mary, Queen of Scots and Bess of Hardwick is on display. A particular attraction is a 16th-century priests hole, which is accessible to visitors.

Pensthorpe Waterfowl Park 151 G3

Also known as the Natural Centre of Norfolk, this is a great family day out for lovers of nature, conservation, wildlife and the outdoors. Explore the beautiful lakes, nature trails and gardens designed by Chelsea Flower Show gold medallists, and look out for the large collection of cranes in the Conservation Centre. Host of the popular BBC *Springwatch* programme.

Sandringham 150 D3

Sandringham is the Norfolk country retreat of Queen Elizabeth II. It was built in 1870 for the Prince of Wales (later Edward VII). The main ground-floor rooms are much as they were in Edwardian times, while the old stable, coach houses and power house contain a museum of Royal Family possessions. There is free access to the many paths in the surrounding country park.

Thursford Collection 151 G2

This exciting collection specialises in organs, with a Wurlitzer cinema organ, fairground organs, barrel organs and street organs among its treasures. There are live musical shows every day. The collection also includes showmen's engines, ploughing engines and farm machinery. There is a children's play area and a breathtaking Venetian gondola switchback ride.

Wells & Walsingham Light Railway 151 G2

The railway covers the four miles between Wells and Walsingham, and is the longest ten and a quarter inch gauge track in the world. The line passes through some very attractive countryside, particularly noted for its wild flowers and butterflies. This is the home of the unique Garratt Steam Locomotive specially built for this line.

Wisbech 150 B4

Situated in Wisbech town centre, Peckover House is an elegant Georgian brick townhouse with an outstanding walled town garden. Over 70 types of rose grow here, along with a number of notable specimen trees such as Maidenhead Tree and Tulip Tree. The Victorian glasshouses include a fern house, and an orangery with 300-year-old trees that still bear fruit. Visitors can borrow a croquet set and play on the lawn. There is a children's handling collection in the basement.

Norfolk Lavender at Heacham is England's premier lavender farm

This part of East Anglia is full of interest. Charming market towns and villages, great houses, ruined castles and royal residence are waiting to be discovered. The fertile low-lying fens, around the great rectangular bay of The Wash, are the result of a centuries-long battle against water. They are criss-crossed with waterways, including the rivers Nene and Great Ouse, several canals and numerous drainage dykes.

Sandringham House, the Norfolk home of the Royal Family

Castle Rising 150 D3

When it was built in the 12th century, Castle Rising was the largest castle in the country. The roof has gone now, but the grand staircase approach survives in good condition and the keep walls stand at their original height. One of its more famous inhabitants was Isabella of France, the queen of England whose son, Edward III, locked her up here in 1330 following her part in the murder of his father, her husband Edward II. She is said to still haunt the castle.

Gressenhall 151 G4

Gressenhall Farm and Workhouse offers a fascinating journey through the history of rural Norfolk and includes an historic workhouse, a traditional farm, extensive collections, and an adventure playground. The farm has lambs and piglets as well as horses working the fields. Visitors can explore the grounds, gardens and country trails, then take a break in the café.

Holkham Hall 151 F1

Built between 1734 and 1764 by the agriculturalist Thomas Coke First Earl of Leicester, and home to seven generations of his family, this is regarded as one of the greatest examples of the English Palladian style. Beyond its austere, grey façade lies a treasure house of ancient statues, furnishings and paintings by Peter Paul Rubens, Anthony Van Dyck, Thomas

Gainsborough and others. The Bygones Museum, housed in the stable block, is packed with more than 4,000 domestic and agricultural objects, ranging from Victorian money boxes to vintage cars.

Houghton Hall 151 E3

Britain's first prime minister, Sir Robert Walpole, had this Palladian mansion built in the 1720s. The work of architects James Gibb, Colen Campbell and others is complemented by the elaborate interior decoration of William Kent. Bedrooms are decorated in the style of ancient Rome, while the magnificent two-storey hall was inspired by the hall in the Queen's House in Greenwich. In the north office wing the Cholmondeley Soldier Museum has about 20,000 models.

King's Lynn 150 D4

A delightful, bustling town, King's Lynn has many fine and ancient buildings. Visit Town House Museum, a charming museum set in a 19th-century town house, where the everyday life in King's Lynn from medieval times to the 1950s is portrayed in a series of carefully re-constructed rooms. Enjoy collections of historic toys and costumes, and take the air in the delightful garden. Dotted around the displays are colourful games and activities that will keep the children amused. Although it has been used for many purposes, the theatrical

A B C D

1

Buckleburgh
Collection
Sheringham
Weybourne   West
Sheringham   Runton   East Runton
Park   **Cromer**
Upper
Sheringham   Beeston   Norfolk Shire
Bodham   Regis   Horse Centre
West   A148   Overstrand
Beckham   East   Aylmerton   Felbrigg   Sidestrand
                Beckham   Felbrigg   Northrepps   Trimingham
ansthorpe   Gresham   Hall   Crossdale
Castle   Bessingham   Sustead   Metton   Street   Gimingham
Baconsthorpe   Roughton   Southrepps   Mundesley
efield   Thurgarton   Hanworth   Lower   Stow Mill
een 2   Matlask   Aldborough   Alby Hill   Street   Paston
Plumstead   Wickmere   Thorpe   Trunch   Knapton
Green   Calthorpe   Erpingham   Market   Bacton
Little   Wolterton   Antingham   Old Hall   Walcott
Barningham   Saxthorpe   Itteringham   Colby   Suffield   Edingthorpe Happisburgh
     Mannington   Swafield   Witton
     Gardens   Blickling   **North Walsham** Edingthorpe   Whimpwell Green
ty   Oulton   Silvergate   Blickling   Green   Eccles on Sea
     Oulton   Heydon   Hall   Banningham   Spa Common   Ridlington   Hempstead
     Street   Meeting   Ridlington   Ingham   Sea Palling
Heydon   Felmingham   Tungate   House Hill   Street   Corner   Waxham
     3   Southgate   Skeyton   Honing   Calthorpe
Cawston   Tuttington   Corner   Westwick   Crostwight   Happisburgh Street
     Eastgate   Marsham   Aylsham   Bengates   Briggate   Common   Horsey
Great   Brandiston   Burgh next   Worstead   East   Ingham   Horsey
Witchingham   Buxton   Aylsham   Skeyton   Sloley   Ruston   Stalham   Corner
aldeford   Heath   Westgate   Frankfort   Dilham   Horsey
     Hevingham   Street   Buxton   Swanton   Low   Stalham   Windpump
                             Oxnead   Abbott   Smallburgh   Street   Green
Swannington   Lamas   Scottow   Fairstead   Barton   Sutton   Hickling
     Felthorpe   Brampton   Little   Turf   Wood   Hickling Green
Upgate   Stratton   Hautbois   Tunstead   Pennygate   Street   Hill Common Horsey
                             Strawless   Sco Ruston   Crowgate   Neatishead   Catfield   Hickling
Attlebridge   Waterloo   St James   Street   Barton   Heath   Broad
Dinosaur   Coltishall   Threehammer   Irstead   Broad   Catfield   West
     Hainford   Horstead   Belaugh   Common   Sharp   Common   Somerton
Thorpe   Frettenham   Wroxham   Hoveton   Johnson's   Green   Potter   East
Marriott   Horsford   Upper   Street   Ludham   Heigham   Somerton
Taverham   Newton   Crostwick   Street   Bastwick   Martham   Hemsby
     Costessey   St Faith   Horning   Upper   Repps   Ormesby
            Horsham   Bure   Street   Rollesby Broad
on   St Faith   Spixworth   A1151   Woodbastwick Marshes   Broadland   Thurne   Burgh St
ill   Drayton   Conservation   Clippesby Margaret
     4   Aviation   Rackheath   Salhouse   Ranworth   Centre   Pilson   Cargate   Ormesby
Ringland   Norwich   Little   Green   Green   St Michael Billockby
                         New   Plumstead   Panxworth   South   Upton   Thrigby
     Easton   Catton   Rackheath   Blofield   Town   Walsham   Acle   Filby
Royal Norfolk Sprowston Thorpe   Heath   Green   Burlingham   West E
     Hellesdon   End   Great   Hemblington   North
Marlingford New   Plumstead   Witton   Burlingham   Runham
     Costessey   Damgate
     Bowthorpe   **NORWICH**   Blofield   Lingwood   Tunstall   THE BROADS
Bawburgh   Beighton   Burgh
     Little Melton   Thorpe   Stracey Arms   Castle
Colney   St Andrew   A47   Windpump
Wramplingham Lynch   Blofield   Brundall   South   Moulton   Halvergate
High Green   Green   A47 New   Postwick   Strumpshaw   Burlingham   St Mary   Belton
     5   Cringleford Lakenham   Freethorpe
Hethersett   Old   Kirby Bedon   Surlingham   Buckenham   Freethorpe   Wickhampton
Kidd's   Lakenham   Trowse Newton Bramerton   Rockland   Southwood   Common   Berney   Burgh
Moor   Ketteringham New   Armingham   Framingham   St Mary   Cantley   Arms   Castle
Swardeston   Caistor   Pigot   Earl   Hellington Claxton   Limpenhoe   Windmill
rpe   East   St Edmund   Framingham   St Peter   Carleton   Witton Green Pettitts Crafts
Mulbarton   Upper   Yelverton   Earl   Ashby   Langley   Animal Adventure Park Belton
Wymondham Carleton   Dunston   Stoke   St Mary   Street   Hardley
     Bracon   Poringland   Howe   Thurton   Mill Common   Street   Reedham   Browston Green
Silfield   Ash   Saxlingham   Stoke   Hardley
Ashwellthorpe Newton   Thorpe   Holy   Bergh   Thurton   Nogdam End   Fritton
     Wreningham Flotman Saxlingham   Cross   Apton   Brooke   Chedgrave   Norton   St Olave's
A11   Toprow   Nethergate   Shotesham   R Chet   Loddon   Subcourse   Thurlton   Priory
Fundenhall   Flordon   Stubbs   High Green   Norton
oner   Hapton   Saxlingham   Mundham   Green   Hales   Thurlton   A143   St Olaves
Tacolneston   Green   Seething   Thorpe   Herringfleet Somerleyton
     6   Forncett   Kirstead   Raveningham B1136   Haddiscoe
Bunwell   Forncett   Upper Tasburgh Green   Thwaite   Maypole   Burgh
Street   St Mary   St Mary   Woodton   A146   Green   Wheatacre St Peter
Bunwell   Forncett   Stratton   Hempnall   Kirby Cane   Bull's   Aldeby
     Hargate St Peter   St Michael   Fritton   B1527   Stockton   Green
Pottergate   Road Green   Hedenham   Ellingham   A143   Kirby Row Gillingham
Street   Morningthorpe Hemphall   Topcroft   Broome   Geldeston Shipmeadow
Tibenham   Green   Lundy   Topcroft Street Ditchingham   R Waveney
Aslacton   Great Moulton   Green   Shelton   Wainford
                                     Upgate   Green   **Bungay**   Worlingham

A B C D

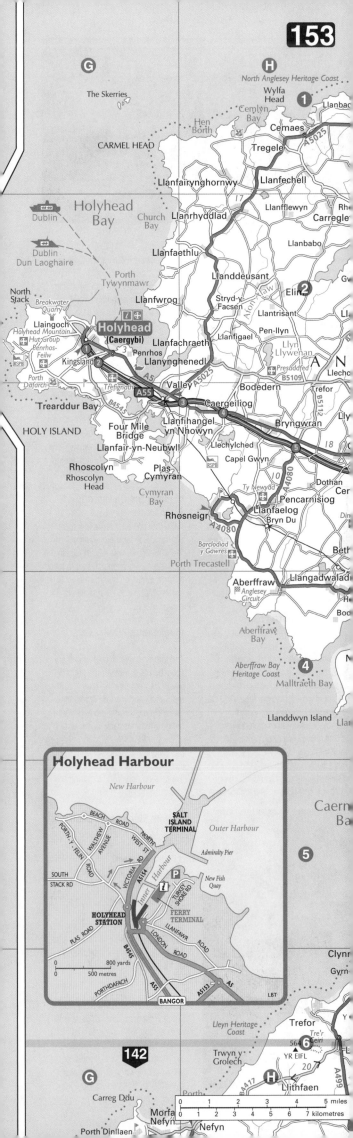

Motor cruisers moored at Horsey Windpump

and the Cromer Lifeboatmen, and the incredible story of the West Runton elephant, Britain's oldest and most complete elephant fossil.

Fairhaven Garden 152 C4
Fairhaven covers 53ha of ancient woodland and water garden with a private broad. In spring there are masses of primroses and bluebells, with azaleas and rhododendrons in several areas. Candelabra primulas and some unusual plants grow near the waterways, and in summer the wild flowers attract butterflies, bees and dragonflies.

Felbrigg Hall 152 A2
Felbrigg is a 17th-century house built on the site of an existing medieval hall. It contains a superb collection of 18th-century furniture and pictures and an outstanding library. A 223ha wood shelters the house from the North Sea and contains waymarked walks and a working dovecot.

Great Yarmouth 153 E5
An important seaside resort that is also a great port, Great Yarmouth has a considerable history. The Victorian seafront promenade is evocative of the traditional English resort, complete with pier and a model village. Time and Tide Museum tells Great Yarmouth's fascinating story, from prehistoric times to the present day using both traditional and interactive technology. Other attractions include the splendid quayside Elizabethan House Museum, a row of 17th-century houses, and the Tolhouse Museum, where you can discover the fate of the thieves, smugglers, witches, pirates and murderers at a time when punishments included transportation or execution.

Horsey Windpump 152 D3
Set in a remote part of the Norfolk Broads, the windpump mill was built 200 years ago to drain the area, and then rebuilt in 1912 by Dan England, a noted Norfolk millwright. It has been restored since being struck by lightning in 1943, and overlooks Horsey Mere and marshes, noted for their wildfowl and insects, as a site of International Importance for Nature Conservation.

Mannington Gardens 152 A2
The moated manor house, built in 1460 and still a family home, forms a centrepiece for the pretty gardens that surround it. Visitors can take in the Heritage rose garden, lakes, a scented garden, a ruined church, and horse graves. Music and theatre events are a regular feature.

Muckleburgh Collection 152 A1
The largest privately owned military collection of its kind in the country, which incorporates the Museum of the Suffolk and Norfolk Yeomanry. Exhibits include restored and working tanks, armoured cars, trucks and artillery of World War II, and equipment and weapons from the Falklands and the Gulf War. There are live tank demonstrations during the school holidays.

Norfolk Shire Horse Centre 152 A1
The Shire Horse Centre has a collection of draught horses and some breeds of mountain and moorland ponies. There are also exhibits of horse-drawn machinery, wagons and carts, and harnessing and working demonstrations are given twice every day. Other attractions include a children's farm, a photographic display of draught horses past and present, talks and a video show.

Pleasurewood Hills 153 E6
Set in 20ha of coastal parkland with rides and attractions for all the family, Pleasurewood Hills has adrenalin-fuelled thrills and spills for the brave and fun rides for children. Shows feature sea lions, parrots, acrobats and clowns.

...ng Gallery

Norwich & The Broads

NORWICH & THE BROADS

From the medieval streets of Norwich it is not very far to the sandy beaches of the Norfolk resorts. Between them come a host of sleepy villages with thatched cottages, the waterways of the Norfolk Broads and an astonishing variety of little churches with round towers.

A traditional merry-go-round at Great Yarmouth Pleasure Beach

Baconsthorpe Castle 152 A2

Discover the extensive ruins of a 15th-century castle, built by Sir John Heydon during the Wars of the Roses. The exact date when the building was started is not known, since Sir John did not apply for the statutory royal licence necessary to construct a fortified house. In the 1560s, Sir John's grandson added the outer gatehouse, which was inhabited until the 1920s, when one of the turrets fell down. The remains of red brick and knapped flint are reflected in the lake, which partly embraces the castle as a moat.

Blicking Hall 152 A3

Flanked by dark yew hedges and topped by pinnacles, the warm red brick front of Blickling is a memorable sight. The grounds cover 22ha and include woodland and a lake, a formal parterre, topiary yew hedges, a Secret Garden, an orangery, and a dry moat filled with roses, camellias and other plants. Inside there are fine collections of furniture, paintings and tapestries, along with a spectacular Jacobean plaster ceiling, and a library of some 12,000 books.

Caister-on-Sea 153 E4

The name Caister has Roman origins, and this was in fact a Roman naval base built around AD 200 and was occupied until the end of the 4th century. The Roman remains include the south gateway, a town wall built of flint with brick courses and part of what may have been a hostel for sailors.

Cromer Museum 152 B1

The museum is housed in five 19th-century fishermen's cottages, one of which has period furnishings. There are pictures and exhibits from Victorian Cromer, with collections illustrating local natural history, archaeology, social history and geology. Discover the scandal of mixed bathing, the daring rescues of Henry Blogg

Blicking Hall, an impressive Jacobean country house, is famed for the plasterwork in th

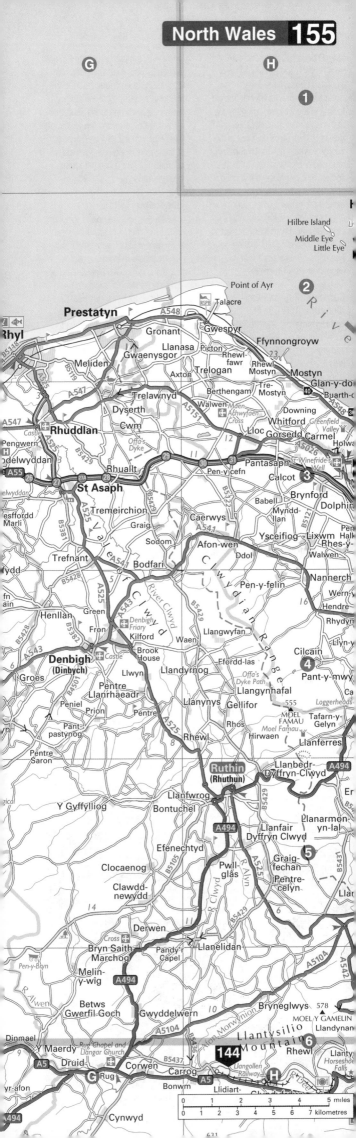

back to 1287 when powerful English king, Edward I, built it as part of his 'iron ring' to repress the rebellious troops of Llewelyn the Great. Great town walls still encircle the old town and the walkway along the top of the walls offers splendid views. At the wall's end, steps descend to the quayside where fishermen sort their nets and seagulls watch out for the scraps. In summer there is a good selection of boat trips, some just around the estuary, others further afield to Anglesey. Among Conwy's other attractions are many fine old buildings including half-timbered Aberconwy House and the equally impressive Plas Mawr.

Conwy Valley Railway Museum 155 D5
The two large museum buildings have displays on both the narrow and standard-gauge railways of North Wales, including rolling stock and other memorabilia. There are working model railway layouts, a steam-hauled miniature railway in the grounds and a 15 inch-gauge tramway to the woods.

Denbigh Castle 155 G4
The castle was begun by Henry de Lacy in 1282 and has an inspiring and impressive gatehouse, with a trio of towers and a superb archway, which is surmounted by a figure believed to be that of Edward I.

Greenwood Forest Park 154 B4
This imaginative forest park in the foothills of Snowdonia offers a sled run down a 70m slide, a jungle boat ride and mini tractors. Other attractions include longbow archery, traditional craft displays, ducks, peacocks, rabbits, an arboretum and gardens, a sculpture trail and a rainforest boardwalk.

Llanberis 154 B4
Llanberis is a busy mountain resort spread out at the foot of Snowdon. From here steam trains on the rack-and-pinion Snowdon Mountain Railway grind their way to the summit, from where you can walk back via a number

of strongly contrasting routes. At a lower level, the Llanberis Lake Railway steams its way along Llyn Padarn. Electric Mountain offers a tour of one of Europe's largest pumped storage stations, hidden deep inside a mountain. In Padarn Country Park, the Welsh Slate Museum paints a vivid picture of the lives of workers in the slate quarries that functioned here from 1861 to 1969.

Llandudno 154 D2
A well-preserved example of Victorian seaside architecture, Llandudno has an elegant seafront, with hotels and guesthouses overlooking a pebble beach and iron-railed pier. Venture by cable-car or steep tramway to Great Ormes Head for fine views over Conwy Bay and the Snowdonia mountains. The Great Orme Mines were dug for copper by Bronze Age settlers around 4,000 years ago and claim to be the oldest metal mines in the world open to the public.

Penrhyn Castle 154 C3
This stately mock-castle overlooking the Menai Strait and Anglesey follows the 19th-century fashion for neo-Norman architecture. Ostentatious in the extreme, it was built by Thomas Hopper between 1820 and 1840 and has more than 300 rooms. The Pennant family flaunted their wealth here (gained from Jamaican sugar, slavery and Welsh slate) with a slate bed which was made for Queen Victoria, stained-glass windows in the great hall, and a grand staircase with ornate lamp-holders, carved masks and encrusted pillars.

Trefriw Woollen Mill 154 D4
The busy clatter of machinery makes it clear that this is very much a working mill, owned by the same family for more than 140 years. Traditional tapestry-style, double-weave products are made on machinery dating from the 1950s and 1960s. Visitors can see the weaving process and the hydroelectric turbines that replaced the waterwheels in the 1930s and 1940s.

The engine pushes the carriage on the Snowdon Mountain Railway

NORTH WALES

The Menai Strait has always made ancient Anglesey a place set apart from the rest of Wales. The dolmen-scattered interior of Anglesey is fringed by steep cliffs and sandy bays, while over on the mainland the narrow coastal plain rises up to the mountains of Snowdonia National Park. The North Wales seaside resorts beckon, along with the splendid medieval castle at Conwy.

Thomas Telford's 1826 suspension bridge leads to Conwy's castle

Beaumaris 154 C3
The coastal town and yachting resort of Beaumaris, on Anglesey, is the island's main focus for visitors. It is dominated by Beaumaris Castle, dating from 1295, the last of Edward I's iron ring of fortresses, a chain of castles built to subdue the Welsh. Although unfinished, the castle is regarded as a perfect example of medieval military architecture, with symmetrical concentric walls designed by James of St George. The 1614 Courthouse is still in use, while Beaumaris Gaol shows how nasty a Victorian prison could be.

Bodelwyddan Castle 155 F3
This 19th-century mock castle, complete with turrets and battlements, is now the Welsh headquarters of the National Portrait Gallery, and houses a large collection of Victorian portraits, including Victorian portraiture photographs. There is plenty of interest here for all ages, with World War I practice trenches, an adventure playground, parkland, walled gardens and a woodland walk.

Bodnant Garden 155 E3
Situated above the River Conwy, with views across the valley to Snowdonia, Bodnant is one of the most visited of all British gardens. By turns formal and informal, it was first planted in 1875 by the Aberconway family whose descendants still run the shop and plant centre. There are Italianate terraces, a huge lily pond and a deep wooded valley known as The Dell. Spring brings shows of daffodils, camellias, magnolias and cherry blossom, while early summer has rich displays of rhododendrons, azaleas and laburnum. Late summer bursts into bloom with roses, clematis and waterlilies.

Caernarfon 154 A4
This market town is dwarfed by the magnificent harbourside Caernarfon Castle, built in 1283 by Edward I to consolidate his conquest of Wales. Edward I's son, the future Edward II, was born here. In 1969 the castle was the setting for Prince Charles's investiture as Prince of Wales. Substantial lengths of the medieval town wall snake through the town. On a hill above the town lie the foundations of the Roman settlement fort of Segontium (founded AD 77), with a museum displaying finds from this far-flung outpost of the Roman Empire. On Caernarfon Airparc, where the RAF Mountain Rescue Service was formed in 1943, is Caernarfon Airworld Museum, an indoor interactive museum with historic and modern aircraft, trial flights and pleasure flights.

Colwyn Bay 154 E3
The chief attraction here is the Welsh Mountain Zoo, overlooking Colwyn Bay, where a pair of snow leopards have been brought in from eastern Europe. A long promenade follows the sweep from Old Colywn to Penrhyn Bay giving access to the beaches, pier and harbour at Rhôs-on-Sea.

Conwy 154 D3
Conwy is a place where history parades itself around every corner. Three fine bridges cross the estuary beneath the castle, allowing both road and the railway into this medieval World Heritage Site. The castle dates

remodelled in 1725 by the Venetian architect Giacomo Leoni, giving the house classical proportions and baroque ceilings. Some of the Elizabethan interiors survive, and contrast strongly with later rooms. In the Saloon, the great woodcarver, Grinling Gibbons, added virtuoso carving. The large grounds have strongly contrasting views, with urban Manchester on one side and the rural Peak District on the other. There is ample scope for walks in the huge deer park, which contains woodland, ornamental gardens and an 18th-century hunting lodge known as The Cage.

Macclesfield 157 H3

Three related attractions tell the story of silk production in the town of Macclesfield. The Silk Museum in Park Lane has exhibits about all aspects of the industry, including the workers' lives, the operation of looms, and manufactured silk. The Heritage Centre on Roe Street, close by, has a collection of silk costumes and displays related to the development of the silk industry in the town. A short walk away is Paradise Mill, a 19th-century silk-producing mill in operation until 1981. Inside, little has been changed, with handlooms that were installed in 1912 still in working order.

National Wildflower Centre
156 C2

Set in a public park on the outskirts of Liverpool, the award-winning National Wildflower Centre promotes the creation of wildflower habitats around the country and provides educational materials, wildflower seeds and interactive facilities. The Centre has demonstration areas, children's activities, a working nursery, compost display and rooftop walk.

Port Sunlight 156 B2

In the industrial Wirral peninsula is this visionary garden village utopia, built in 1888 by the enlightened Sunlight Soap magnate William Hesketh Lever to house his factory workers and now an extremely desirable place to live. No two groups of cottages are quite the same, although black-and-white Tudor and Queen Anne and Elizabethan styles predominate. The Village Trail is a self-guiding walking tour available from the Heritage Centre. At its heart is the Lady Lever Art Gallery, built for the education of the workers, which has paintings by Edward Burne-Jones, Dante Gabriel Rossetti, J M W Turner, John Constable and Joshua Reynolds, as well as Wedgwood ceramics.

Quarry Bank Mill 157 G2

Founded in 1784, Quarry Bank Mill is one of the finest surviving cotton mills of the period. Inside the water and steam-powered mill there are hands-on exhibits and demonstrations that show how traditional spinning and weaving was transformed through the ingenuity of early textile engineers. Using the most powerful working waterwheel in Europe, two mill engines bring the past to life. At the Apprentice House you can discover what home life was like for the pauper children who worked in the mill in the 1830s.

Speke Hall 156 C2

This remarkable timber-framed manor house is set in tranquil gardens and grounds. The house has a Tudor Great Hall, Stuart plasterwork, and William Morris wallpapers. Outside are varied grounds, including a rose garden, bluebell woods and woodland walks. There is live interpretation by costumed guides, and for children a quiz-trail and adventure playground.

Tatton Park 157 F2

The classical Georgian mansion and 405ha park at Tatton stage a lively variety of events throughout the year, including flower shows, antiques fairs, vintage car shows, drama and concerts with fireworks. The house has furniture that was specially made by furniture makers Waring and Gillow of Lancaster, and paintings by Canaletto. The Tudor Old Hall was its precursor. The grounds have plenty to entice, with a Japanese garden, rose garden, fern house, maze and rare-breeds farm, as well as woodland walks and bicycle trails.

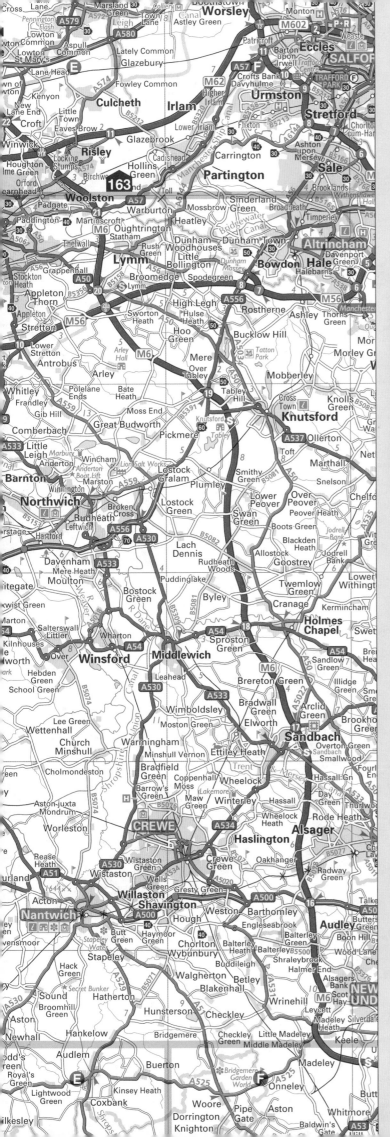

CHESHIRE & THE WIRRAL

This area has much to offer, from the glorious medieval city of Chester, encircled by red sandstone walls, to the vast sprawling cities of Liverpool and Manchester. All have a wealth of museums and galleries and a fascinating array of attractions portraying their rich heritage. To the south grand stately homes set in vast parklands and a giant telescope are part of the Cheshire landscape.

Port Sunlight village was created by soap magnate William Hesketh Lever

Blue Planet Aquarium 156 C3
Aquatunnel, a long moving walkway, enables visitors to get a close-up view of 10 different species of sharks, giant rays and other sea creatures. Divers hand feed the fish and sharks throughout the day and can answer questions via state of the art communication systems.

Cholmondeley Castle Gardens 156 D5
Dominated by a romantic Gothic castle built in 1801 of local sandstone (not open), the gardens are laid out with fine trees and water gardens, a rose and lavender garden, lakeside and woodland walks. Rare breeds of farm animals can be seen in the paddocks.

Erddig 156 B6
For 240 years this 17th-century red-brick mansion was occupied by the Yorke family, but it then fell into near dereliction and was rescued by the National Trust in the 1970s. It is chiefly of interest not for its architecture but for the unusually close bond between its owners and their staff. You enter not through the front door but through the servants' quarters. The house is set in formal gardens overlooking a canal lined with lime trees.

Jodrell Bank 157 F3
Find out about gravity, space travel, radio waves and the movement of the planets at the Science Centre. The main focus is the Lovell Telescope, in operation since 1957 and one of the largest fully steerable radio telescopes in the world. You can zoom in with a remote camera to see what the telescope is receiving through radio waves. Also on site is the second

largest planetarium in Britain after London, and many child-friendly exhibits. Outside, the arboretum has national collections of rowan and apple tree species, and a hide.

Little Moreton Hall 157 G5
Little Moreton Hall is the perfect example of a moated timber-framed manor house. The Long Gallery was the final phase of building, completed 140 years after the Great Hall was begun in the 1440s. Although a visit will probably not last long, this building is a treat for those interested in English architecture.

Lyme Park 157 H2
One of the finest examples of English Palladian architecture, the grey-stone Hall was begun in the 16th century and

Erddig has been restored to how it looked

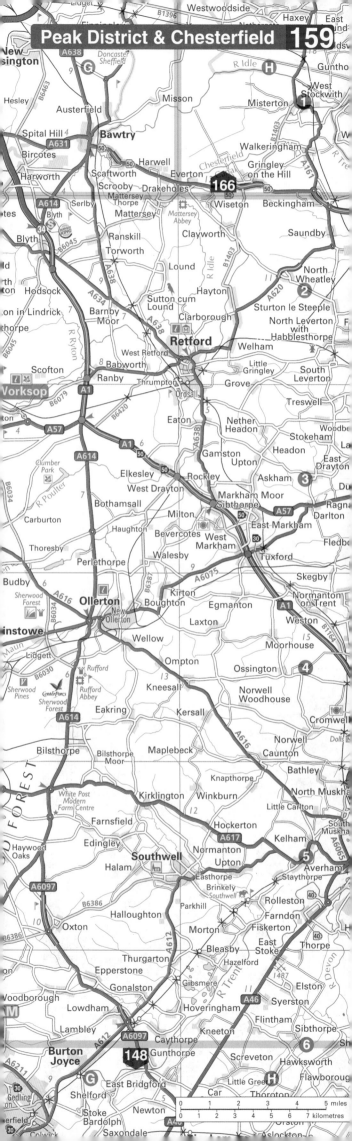

Hardwick Hall 159 E4

Built for the intruiging Bess of Hardwick, properly known as Elizabeth, Countess of Shrewsbury, in the 1590s, this outstanding late 16th-century house strongly evokes life in the Elizabethan period. Much of the original furniture and tapestries remain, and there is needlework by Mary, Queen of Scots, who was held prisoner here for 15 years. The orchard and herb garden lie within the original walled courtyards, while beyond spreads a park grazed by rare breeds of cattle and sheep.

Matlock 158 D4

Matlock is a tourist honeypot, with much to attract visitors. Matlock Bath is the home of the Peak District Mining Museum, which incorporates Temple Mine, an old lead and restored fluorspar mine with a self-guided tour. In the 18th and early 19th century the cream of society took the waters at Matlock Bath, staying in fashionable hotels on the sides of the gorge. Then in 1849 the railway arrived and the place was swamped by day trippers. Today, families come to the Matlocks to visit the popular Gulliver's Kingdom theme park, which is divided into five different worlds each offering many rides and attractions, or to take a cable car up to the Heights of Abraham, with its show caves, nature trail, water gardens and Owl Maze. Regardless of the other attractions, the cable-car ride is worth taking for the magnificent views down the length of the gorge.

Newstead Abbey 159 F5

This beautiful house is best known as the home of poet Lord Byron. Visitors can see Byron's own rooms, mementoes of the poet and other splendidly decorated rooms. The grounds of over 121ha include waterfalls, ponds, water gardens and Japanese gardens. Special events include outdoor theatre and opera, Christmas events and ghost tours.

Sherwood Forest Country Park 159 G4

At the heart of the Robin Hood legend is Sherwood Forest. Today it is a country park and visitor centre with 182ha of ancient oaks and shimmering silver birches. Waymarked pathways guide you through the forest. A year round programme of events includes the spectacular annual Robin Hood Festival.

Southwell 159 G5

The minster is the architectural highlight of this small Nottinghamshire town. Dating from Norman times, the chapter house (begun 1292) has superbly delicate carving, celebrating the foliage of Sherwood Forest in stone. In Upton Road, The Workhouse, the best-preserved building of its kind in Britain, evokes the grim life of the destitute. Opened in 1824 to shelter and feed the sick and poor, the workhouse is typical of the many that once dotted the country.

Worksop 159 F3

A fascinating attraction in Worksop, Mr Straw's House was owned by a tradesman by the name of Mr Straw, who changed virtually nothing in more than 60 years of living here from 1923. After his death it was opened to the public by the National Trust in the mid-1990s. Mr Straw's letters, photographs, clothing, furniture, wallpaper and other household items have been preserved intact, creating a fascinating time capsule.

Glorious rose gardens and herbaceous borders at Haddon Hall

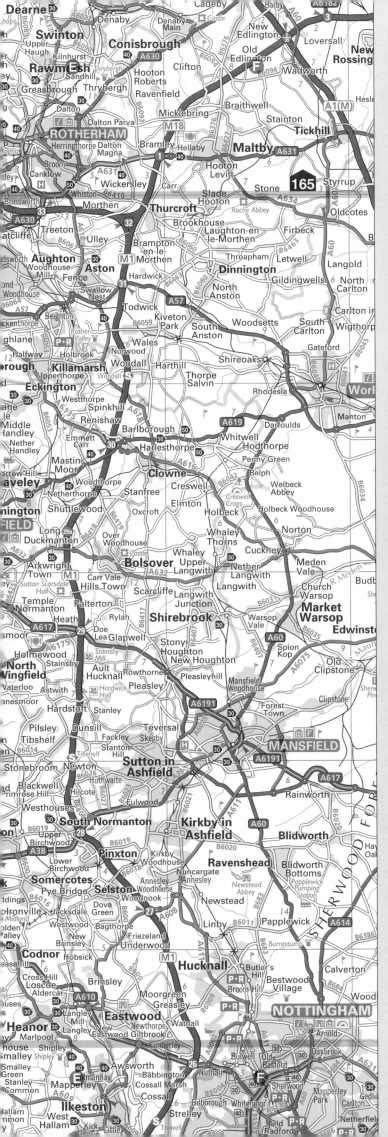

PEAK DISTRICT & CHESTERFIELD

The Peak District was designated England's first National Park, reflecting its importance as a landscape of drama and beauty. Busy with visitors and walkers, yet full of wide-open spaces, it is close to large towns and cities including industrial Sheffield and Chesterfield.

Robin Hood and Little John at the Sherwood Forest Visitor Centre

Buxton 158 A3
Buxton makes an excellent base for exploring the Peak District National Park. This former spa town has a distinctly genteel air, with the old pump room (now an art gallery), well-manicured Pavilion Gardens and its own opera house. Close to St Ann's Well, which dispenses pure water, is the Crescent, built in the 1780s and Buxton's architectural glory. On the southern edge of town, Poole's Cavern is a spectacular show cave with the longest horizontal view of any cave in Britain.

Castleton 158 B2
This busy little village is well situated as a base to explore nearby caverns. The Treak Cliff, Speedwell, Peak Cavern and Blue John Mine 'show caves' are open to the public. All the caves are exciting to explore, even as part of a guided tour. Peveril Castle, perched on Castle Hill, is reached by footpath up a steep and sometimes slippery slope, but the views from the curtain wall are exceptionally good.

Chatsworth 158 C3
Chatsworth is a country house on the grandest scale, with furniture and art to impress, and plenty for children in the grounds. Home of the Duke and Duchess of Devonshire, the original house dates from 1551, but most of what you see was built between 1686 and 1707. The Painted Hall is magnificently baroque, with marble floors, a painted ceiling and a spectacular staircase. The 18th-century landscape 'Capability' Brown laid out the park. There is plenty to explore on the estate, including a cottage garden, a kitchen garden, an excellent farm shop, a maze, and 5 miles of paths leading past rare trees and shrubs, ponds, artful fountains and outdoor sculptures.

Chesterfield 158 D3
Chesterfield's museum tells the story of the town, from its beginnings as a Roman fort through to the Industrial Revolution tracing the development of coal mining and other industries and the arrival of the railways. Chesterfield's most famous Victorian resident, George Stephenson, the 'Father of the Railways' is also featured. The tall spire of St Mary's and All Saints' Church stands crooked and twisted, a unique landmark, famous for the wrong reasons.

Clumber Park 159 G3
Clumber is the 1,500ha estate of a country house that was demolished in 1938. However, several features remain, including an estate village and Gothic Revival chapel. Encompassing forest, parkland, heathland and a huge serpentine lake, the park is large enough for a half day's walking, or you can follow one of several bicycle trails.

Haddon Hall 158 C4
One of the finest examples of an English medieval manor house, Haddon Hall has been in the family of the present owner, Lord Edward Manners, for over 800 years. It was modified between the 12th and 16th centuries, but has changed little since, although ongoing restoration of the house began in 2000. Intricately carved panelling adorns the Long Gallery, and the chapel has 15th-century wall paintings. Outside, the castellations and towers are for picturesque effect rather than defence.

East
Laughton

A159

Scotton
Northorpe

Kirton in
Lindsey

Redbourne

B1206

North End
Moortown

Nettleton
Rothwell
Croxby
A46

Thoresway

Tho

1 Blyton
ckwith
rith

Pilham
Aisby
Yawthorpe

B1205

Grayingham

Blyborough

Waddingham

Snitterby

Brandy
Wharf

B1205

South Kelsey

Thornton
le Moor

Holton
le Moor

Normanby
le Wold

Claxby

Brook

Stain
le V

Ki
le

Corringham

Hemswell

Willoughton

Atterby

Bishop Norton

North
Owersby

South
Owersby

Kingerby
Kirkby
Osgodby

Usselby

Walesby

Gainsborough

A631

Hemswell
Cliff

Harpswell

Spital in
the Street

A631

Glentham

Caenby

Bishopbridge

West
Rasen

Middle
Rasen

A1103

Market Rasen

North
Willingham

Tealby

B1203

B1225

31

Springthorpe

Sturgate

Glentworth

Normanby

Caenby
Corner

Toft next
Newton

Newton
by Toft

A46

Linwood

Legsby

Sixhills

Heapham

Saxby

Owmby

Newtoft

Buslingthorpe

Bleasby

Hainton

Lea

Upton

Fillingham

West Firsby

East Firsby

Faldingworth

Friesthorpe

Lissington

East
Torrington

Knaith
Park

Knaith

A156

Willingham
by Stow

Gate Burton

Ingham

Coates

Hackthorn

Spridlington

Cold
Hanworth

Snarford

Wickenby

Holton cum
Beckering

West
Torrington

Be

East
Barkwith

leborough
Coates

Marton

Stow

Cammeringham

Brattleby

Ryland

Dunholme

Snelland

Fulnetby

Rand

West
Barkwith
Panton

A157

Trent
Port

Thorpe le
Fallows

Aisthorpe

Welton

Swinthorpe

Stainton by
Langworth

Bullington

Wragby

Cottam

A1500

Brampton

Sturton
by Stow

Scampton

Lincolnshire

Scothern

Langton
by Wragby

Low
Langton

Sundown
Adventureland

ampton

Torksey

Bransby

A15

Sudbrooke

Langworth

Apley

Kingthorpe

Church
Laneham
aughterton

Fenton

North Carlton

South
Carlton

Burton

Nettleham

A158

Barlings

Bardney
Limewoods

Gautby

North
Clifton

A156

Saxilby

Riseholme

North
Greetwell

Low
Barlings

Stainfield

B1202

Newton on Trent

Toll

Kettlethorpe

Fossdyke Navigation

A57

Burton
Waters

Reepham

Fiskerton

R Witham

Broadholme

Skellingthorpe

LINCOLN

Cherry
Willingham

South Clifton

Thorney

Harby

Jerusalem

New Boultham

Washingborough

B1190

Bardney

Bucknall

Wigsley

Spalford

Doddington

Hartsholme

Swanpool
Garden
Suburb

Canwick

Heighington

Branston
Booths

B1190

low
rnham

Eagle Moor

Whisby

B1190

Boultham

Bracebridge
Heath

Branston

B1178

Potterhanworth
Booths

Southrey

Stix

A1133

Weecar

Eagle

Road
Transport

Hykeham
Moor

Bracebridge
Low Fields

Potterhanworth

B1202

Sots
Hole

Kirkstead

sthorpe
tton
Trent

Girton

North
Scarle

Eagle Barnsdale

Thorpe on
the Hill

A1434

North
Hykeham

R Witham

Nocton

Wasps
Nest

Martin
Dales

Morton
Hall

South
Hykeham

Waddington

Dunston

Car

Metheringham Delph

sthorpe
arlton-
n-Trent

South Scarle

Swinderby

Haddington

Harmston

B1178

Metheringham

B1189

Martin

B1191

Timberland Delph

Collingham

Witham
St Hughs

Bassingham

Thurlby

Auborn

Coleby

Blankney

Tatters
Bridge

Brough

Norton
Disney

Stapleford

Boothby Graffoe

B1202

Scopwick

Kirkby
Green

Timberland

holme

A46

A1133

Langford

Carlton-le-Moorland

Navenby

A15

B1191

Thorpe
Tilney

Walcott

B1189

inthorpe

Nottinghamshire

Aircraft

R Brant

Wellingore

Ashby de la
Launde

Rowston

Tattersha
Bridge

Do

5 Coddington

A607

Welbourn

Bloxholm

Digby

Billinghay

Newark-on-Trent

Beckingham

Brant
Broughton

Dorrington

North
Kyme

15

New
Balderton
alderton

A17

Stragglethorpe

Leadenham

Ruskington

A153

Anwick

R Slea

South
Kyme

Barnby in
the Willows

Fenton

RAF College
(Cranwell)

Cranwell

B1209

Evedon

Ewerby Thorpe

Ewerby

A1

Claypole

Stubton

Caythorpe

Fulbeck

B1429

Leasingham

Kirkby
la Thorpe

Howell

ham

Brandon

Frieston

Holdingham

Evedon

Dry
Doddington

Hough-on-
the-Hill

Gelston

A607

Normanton

North
Rauceby

South
Rauceby

A17

Sleaford

Asgarby

B1517

Staunton
in the Vale

Long
Bennington

Westbor

Hougham
Marston

Carlton Scroop

Sudbrook

Ancaster

A15

Quar

Heckington

The Pearoom

Heckington

Great
Hale

Little Hale

ilvington

A1

Foston

B B153

Wilsford

C

Silk
Willoughby

Burton
Pedwardine

D

Normanton

Hougham

Honington

Kelby

Swarby

Scredington

Helpringham

voir

Barkston

Belton

Culverthorpe

Aswarby

60

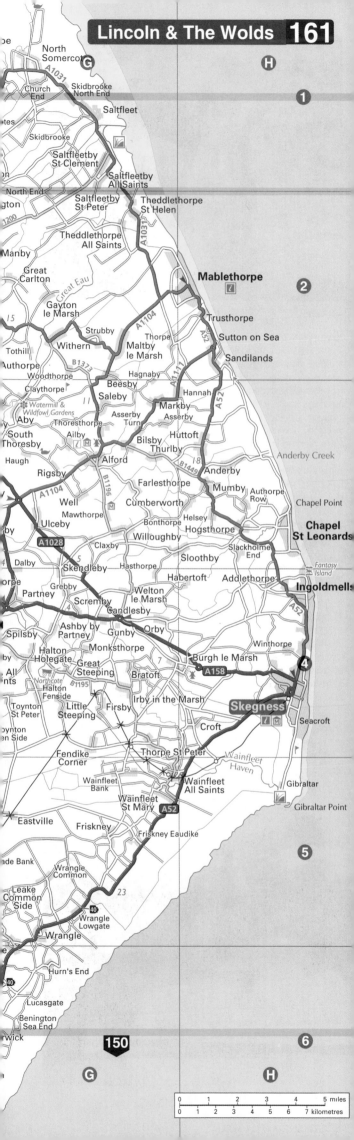

North Somercot
G
H
A1031
1

Church End
Skidbrooke North End
Saltfleet

Skidbrooke

Saltfleetby St Clement

North End
Saltfleetby All Saints

Manby

Saltfleetby St Peter
Theddlethorpe St Helen

A1031

Great Carlton

Theddlethorpe All Saints

Great Eau

Mablethorpe
2

Gayton le Marsh

A1104

Trusthorpe

15

Strubby
Thorpe
A52
Sutton on Sea

Withern
Maltby le Marsh
Sandilands

Tothill
Hagnaby

Authorpe
B1373
Woodthorpe
Beesby
Saleby
Hannah

A1111

Claythorpe
Markby
Asserby

Watermill & Wildfowl Gardens
Thoresthorpe
Asserby Turn
Huttoft

Aby
Ailby
Bilsby
Thurlby

South Thoresby
Alford
B1449
Anderby
Anderby Creek

Haugh
Rigsby
Farlesthorpe
Mumby
Authorpe Row
Chapel Point

Well
B1196
Cumberworth
Chapel St Leonards

Ulceby
Mawthorpe
Bonthorpe
Helsey
Hogsthorpe

A1104
A1028
Willoughby
Slackholme End
Fantasy Island

Dalby
Claxby
Hasthorpe
Sloothby
Addlethorpe
Ingoldmells

Partney
Grebby
Welton le Marsh
Habertoft

A52

Scremby
Candlesby
Orby

Spilsby
Ashby by Partney
Gunby
Winthorpe
4

Halton Holegate
Monksthorpe
Burgh le Marsh
A158

Great Steeping
Bratoft

Skegness

Northcote
B1195
Halton Fenside
Irby in the Marsh

Toynton St Peter
Little Steeping
Firsby
Croft
Seacroft

oynton en Side
Fendike Corner
Thorpe St Peter
Wainfleet Haven

Wainfleet Bank
Wainfleet All Saints
Gibraltar

Eastville
Wainfleet St Mary
A52
Gibraltar Point

Friskney
Friskney Eaudike

5

ade Bank
Wrangle Common

Leake Common Side
23

40
Wrangle Lowgate

Wrangle

Hurn's End

40

Lucasgate

Benington Sea End

rwick

| 0 | 1 | 2 | 3 | 4 | 5 miles |
| 0 | 1 | 2 | 3 | 4 | 5 | 6 | 7 kilometres |

The ground floors of the towers can be seen at Bolingbroke Castle

Newark-on-Trent 160 A5
The Newark Millgate Museum is home to diverse social history collections and features fascinating exhibitions with recreated streets, shops and houses in period settings. The mezzanine gallery, home to a number of temporary exhibitions, shows the work of local artists, designers and photographers.

Sibsey Trader Windmill 161 F5
Built in 1877, this restored mill with complete gear, six sails and fantail is in working order today. The tea room sells produce made from the mill's organic, stone-ground flour.

Skegness 161 H4
Skegness is one of several popular seaside resorts along the coast. Skegness Natureland Seal Sanctuary houses seals, penguins, tropical birds, an aquarium, reptiles, pets' corner and free-flight tropical butterflies. Natureland is well known for its rescue of abandoned seal pups, and has successfully reared and returned a large number of them to the wild.

The hospital unit incorporates a public viewing area, and a large seascape seal pool with underwater viewing.

Tattershall Castle 161 E5
This large fortified house was built in 1440 by Ralph Cromwell, Treasurer of England, and has a keep 30m high. Restored in 1911–14, it contains four great chambers with large Gothic fireplaces, tapestries and brick vaulting. There are spectacular views from the battlements and there is a museum in the guardhouse.

Watermill & Wildfowl Gardens 161 G3
Situated in lush countryside not far from the sea, the Watermill & Wildfowl Gardens is home to of many species of wild birds and waterfowl. There is a pleasant woodland area with walks and plenty of places to enjoy a picnic. The mill displays milling and agricultural memorabilia and the bakery exhibits tell the history of milling and baking at Claythorpe Mill up until the 1970s when production came to an end.

at Lincolnshire Aviation Heritage Centre

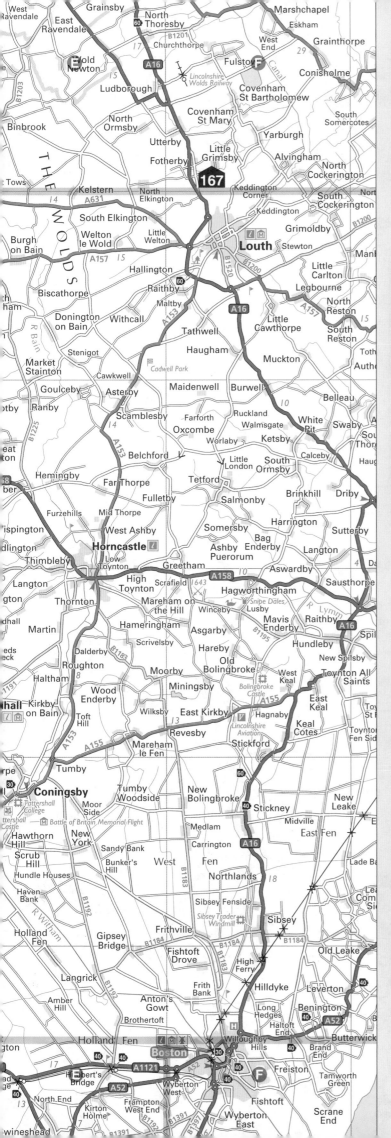

LINCOLN & THE WOLDS

Lincoln and its surroundings are fascinating. The city has one of the great cathedrals of the world, an impressive castle and narrow cobbled streets lined with ancient buildings. All of this stands on a high ridge above fenland and the rolling countryside of the Lincolnshire Wolds which extends to the coast with its long sweeping beaches and popular seaside resorts.

Fairground attractions on the seafront at Skegness

Battle of Britain Memorial Flight 161 E5

Here you can view the aircraft of the Battle of Britain Memorial Flight, comprising the only flying Lancaster in Europe, five Spitfires, two Hurricanes, a Dakota and two Chipmunks. Because of operational commitments, specific aircraft may not be available.

Bolingbroke Castle 161 F4

The remains of 13th-century Bolingbroke Castle, birthplace of Henry IV in 1367, are surrounded by a large moat. The remains of a hexagonal curtain wall, with a twin-towered gatehouse and some towers can be seen. The castle was slighted after the Civil War.

Lincolnshire Aviation Heritage Centre 161 F4

At this former World War II bomber airfield at East Kirkby visitors can see one of only four remaining Lancasters in the UK. It can be can be powered up and is able to taxi under its own steam. The hangar for the Lancaster also features a display of RAF vehicles and aviation artefacts relating to World War II. The other main exhibit is a Spitfire. The Control Tower, restored to its operational status, recreates sounds of a night operation against Berlin.

Mablethorpe 161 H2

Mablethorpe is a charming resort with a long sandy beach backed by a wide promenade. A Sand Train runs along the beach to the northern end of the resort where the seal sanctuary cares for injured seals and other animals.

Market Rasen 160 D2

This small, bustling market town, on the River Rase on the western edge of the Lincolnshire Wolds, is surrounded by rich farmland. Market Rasen racecourse, in a lovely rural setting, is best known as a premier summer jumping track. The town is good for shopping and, of course, the market still thrives on Tuesdays (auction), Fridays and Saturdays.

The Avro Lancaster Bomber NX611 on dis

Splendid half-timbered Rufford Old Hall is home to the Hesketh family

Preston 163 E2

Harris Museum and Art Gallery, situated in an impressive Grade I listed Greek Revival building contains extensive collections of fine and decorative art, while the city's history is covered in The Story of Preston. Football fans will want to visit The National Football Museum which is packed with great footballing moments, stories and objects.

Rufford Old Hall 162 D3

Rufford is one of Lancashire's finest Tudor buildings, and is where a young William Shakespeare is believed to have performed for its owner, Sir Thomas Hesketh. Visitors can wander around the house and view the fine collections of furniture, arms, armour and tapestries. The gardens contain topiary and sculptures, and there are woodland and canal walks.

Samlesbury Hall 163 F1

This well restored half-timbered manor house, built during the 14th and 15th centuries, is set in 2ha of beautiful grounds. Sales of antiques and collectors' items, craft shows and temporary exhibitions are held throughout the year.

Towneley Hall 163 H1

This 14th-century country house, home of the Towneley family for over 500 years, contains Burnley's art gallery and museum. It is set in the town's largest park where there are sculpture trails, woodland walks, play areas and ornamental gardens.

Turton Tower 163 G3

This historic house, which incorporates a 15th-century tower house and Elizabethan half-timbered buildings, displays a major collection of carved wood furniture. Outside there are Victorian follies and a traditional English country garden.

Wigan 162 E4

Along the redeveloped Leeds and Liverpool Canal, Wigan Pier Experience is an archive of an industrial town. The Way We Were exhibition offers a taste of what life was like in Wigan in 1900 through re-creations that include a Victorian classroom, a coal mine and a variety theatre. All the sites are interactive, with actors dressed in period costume helping to create the full experience: slouch in the classroom and you'll be told to sit up straight.

largest working examples of its type, is part of the Wigan Pier Experience

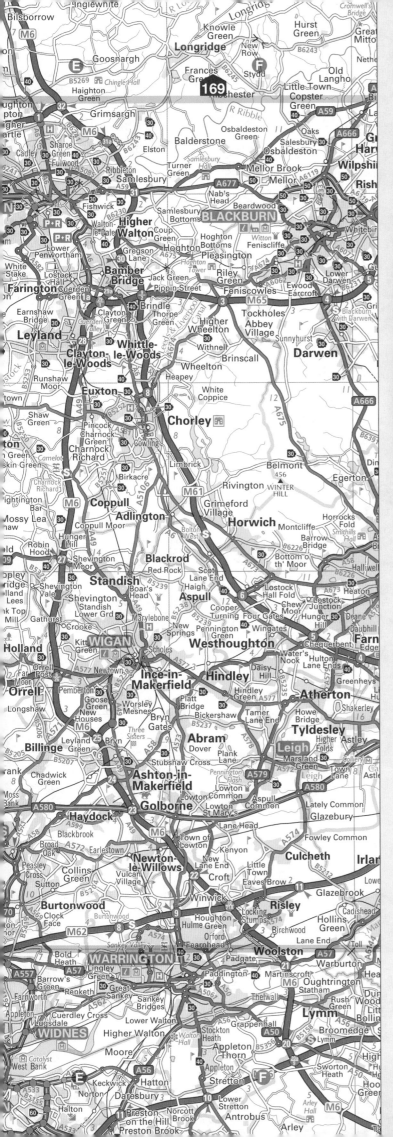

MERSEYSIDE & MANCHESTER

Many of the North's great cities have revitalised themselves in recent years with proud museums to their industrial heritage and new uses for redundant sites. But they are not far from an unspoilt coastline and peaceful landscapes dotted with grand houses.

There is a successful breeding herd of Père David's deer at Knowsley Safari Park

Chorley 163 E3
Astley Hall Museum & Art Gallery in Chorley is a charming Tudor/Stuart building set in beautiful parkland. It retains a comfortable 'lived-in' atmosphere, with pictures and pottery on display, as well as fine furniture and rare plasterwork ceilings.

Camelot 163 E3
Camelot is a medieval fantasy theme park with five magic lands to discover. Attractions include jousting tournaments, big rides such as a looping rollercoaster and a go-carting circuit, plus carousels, a farm and gardens.

Heaton Hall 163 H4
Set in 240ha of rolling parkland on the edge of Manchester, Heaton Hall was designed by James Wyatt for Sir Thomas Egerton in 1772. The house has magnificent period interiors decorated with fine plasterwork, paintings and furniture. Other attractions include a unique circular room with Pompeian-style paintings, and an original Samuel Green organ still in working order. Attractions in the grounds include a Tram Museum, sports pitches, stables, farm and animal centres, and a horticultural centre.

Knowsley Safari Park 162 D5
A 5-mile drive through the reserves enables visitors to see lions, tigers, elephants, rhinos, monkeys and many other animals in spacious, natural surroundings. There is a children's amusement park, reptile house, pets' corner plus sea-lion shows. Other attractions include an amusement park and a miniature railway.

Martin Mere 162 D3
One of several Wildfowl and Wetlands Trust sites in the UK, Martin Mere is a wetland habitat for birds, with swans, ducks and geese from every corner of the world. Winter is a particularly good time to visit, when thousands of pink-footed geese, and whooper and Bewick's swans can be seen under floodlighting in the evening.

The Trencherfield Mill steam engine, one

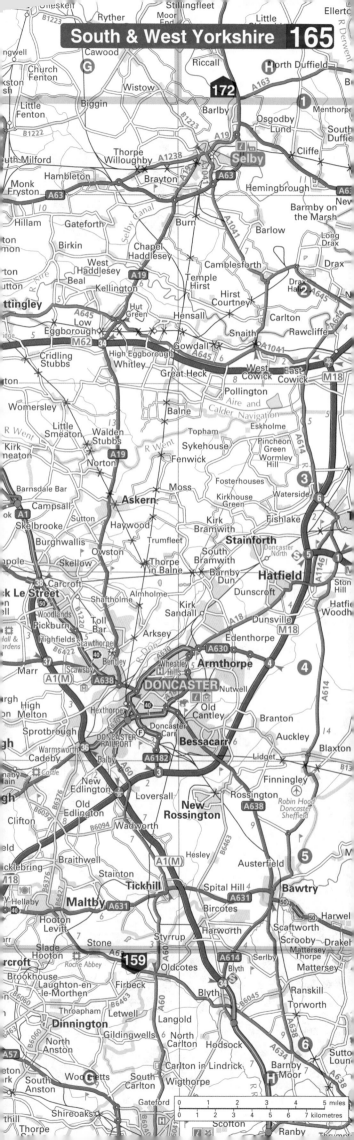

century. You can walk from Hebden Bridge to Heptonstall via the packhorse bridge and the steep cobbled lane known as The Buttress.

Holmfirth 164 C4

Best known for its *Last of the Summer Wine* connections, the town of Holmfirth is a gem. Fine stone farmhouses and cottages on the upper slopes of the valley tell a tale of prosperity with the expansion of the cotton mills in the mid-19th century. Holmfirth has to be explored at a gentle pace, because most of the streets are steep. From Victoria Bridge in the middle of the town it is possible to wander up Penny Lane, round the back of the church where the surrounding hills peep out between chimney-pots and sooty walls, and down cobbled lanes worn shiny and smooth by a million clogs.

Huddersfield 164 C3

Tolsen Memorial Museum portrays the history of Huddersfiled. Displays show the development of the cloth industry and there is a collection of horse-drawn vehicles, together with natural history, archaeology, toys and folk exhibits.

Magna 165 F5

Housed within a massive former steel works Magna, the UK's first science adventure centre, offers an exciting exploration of Earth, Air, Fire and Water. Visitors can create their own adventure through hands-on interactive challenges.

National Coal Mining Museum 164 D3

This museum offers a unique opportunity to go 140m underground down one of Britain's oldest working mines. Take a step back in time with one of the museum's experienced local miners who guide parties around the underground workings, where models and machinery depict methods and conditions of mining from the early

Yorkshire Sculpture Park

1800s to the present day. Other attractions include the Hope Pit, pithead baths, a Victorian steam winder, a nature trail and adventure playground. Wear sensible footwear and warm clothing.

Nostell Priory 165 F3

The interior of the mansion is the main draw, with plasterwork by Robert Adam and James Paine and furniture by Thomas Chippendale. There are paintings by Flemish artist Pieter Breughel the Younger and an 18th-century dolls' house, complete with original fittings and scaled-down Chippendale furniture. Outside, enjoy the scented rose garden and the lakeside walk to the Menagerie Garden.

Yorkshire Sculpture Park 164 D3

The sculpture park was set up in 1977 and was a pioneer in placing sculpture outdoors. A trail takes visitors on a tour of the highlights, and there are plenty of places for picnicking. There are permanent and changing exhibits in this expansive parkland, with works by some of the leading figures of the last 100 years, including Dame Barbara Hepworth, Dame Elisabeth Frink and Sir Anthony Caro, plus gallery space for smaller exhibits.

Hebden Bridge takes its name from the old packhorse bridge over Hebden Water

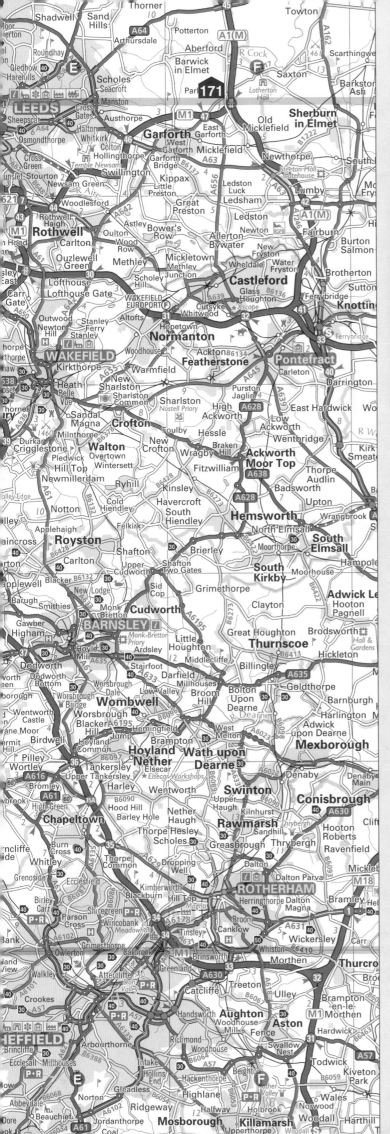

Some of the most important cities of the Industrial Revolution lie on the fringe of the Peak District National Park, very close to the high moorland landscape of the North.

Holmfirth is famous as the backdrop for the TV series Last of the Summer Wine

Bradford 164 C1

Bradford played a major role in the wool trade during the Industrial Revolution and legacies of this past include fine, gritstone buildings and early Victorian architecture. The main attraction is the National Museum of Photography, Film and Television, housed in a curved, glass-walled building. Inside are five floors of interactive displays on all forms of visual media, including an IMAX cinema. You can learn more about the city's past in the Bradford Industrial Museum, housed in the former Moorside Mills northeast of the city itself.

Brodsworth Hall & Gardens 165 G4

This Victorian country house has survived largely intact. Displays portray how the serving classes fared below stairs and how their masters lived in the opulent 'upstairs' apartments. Outside, visitors can enjoy a leisurely stroll around the extensive newly restored gardens.

Conisbrough Castle 165 G5

The white, circular keep of this 12th-century castle is a spectacular structure. Made of magnesian limestone, it is the oldest of its kind in England. Recently restored, with two new floors and a roof, it is a fine example of medieval architecture and was the inspiration for Sir Walter Scott's classic novel *Ivanhoe*.

Doncaster Museum & Art Gallery 165 G4

The wide-ranging collections include fine and decorative art and sculpture along with ceramics, glass and silver, and displays on history, archaeology and natural history. The historical collection of the Kings Own Yorkshire Light Infantry is housed here. The By River and Road gallery details the history of the Doncaster area.

Glossop 164 B5

Textiles breathed life into Glossop; there was water power and coal a-plenty and a workforce who came from Stockport and Manchester. At the turn of the 19th century there were more than 56 mills. The heart of Glossop is Norfolk Square, which still has a prim elegance and is surrounded by interesting shops, including a small heritage centre. There are some fascinating nooks and crannies hidden away in the fabric of the place. Just beyond the housing estate of Gamesley lies the remains of the Agricolan Roman fort of Melandra Castle, while to the north of the town, near Howard Park, is Mouselow or Castle Hill, with important Bronze Age and Iron Age associations.

Halifax 164 B2

In the heart of the Pennine Hills, Halifax became a powerhouse of the textile industry during the Industrial Revolution. The focus of its pre-industrial heritage is Piece Hall, built as a woollen market in 1779, with 350 small rooms set on a series of colonnaded tiers around a vast open space. Today, the hall has small gift shops, cafés, a market and open-air concerts. The main tourist attraction is Eureka! The Museum for Children, aimed at 3- to 12-year-olds, where children can learn about themselves and the world.

Hebden Bridge 164 A2

This spectacular little Pennine town is set in the steep-sided valley of Calderdale, with double-decker houses – one house at the top entered from one street, another underneath entered from a street below – clinging tenaciously to the hillsides. Heptonstall, above Hebden Bridge, became the local focus for hand-weaving in the pre-Industrial age, but was overtaken by the large mills in Hebden Bridge during the 19th

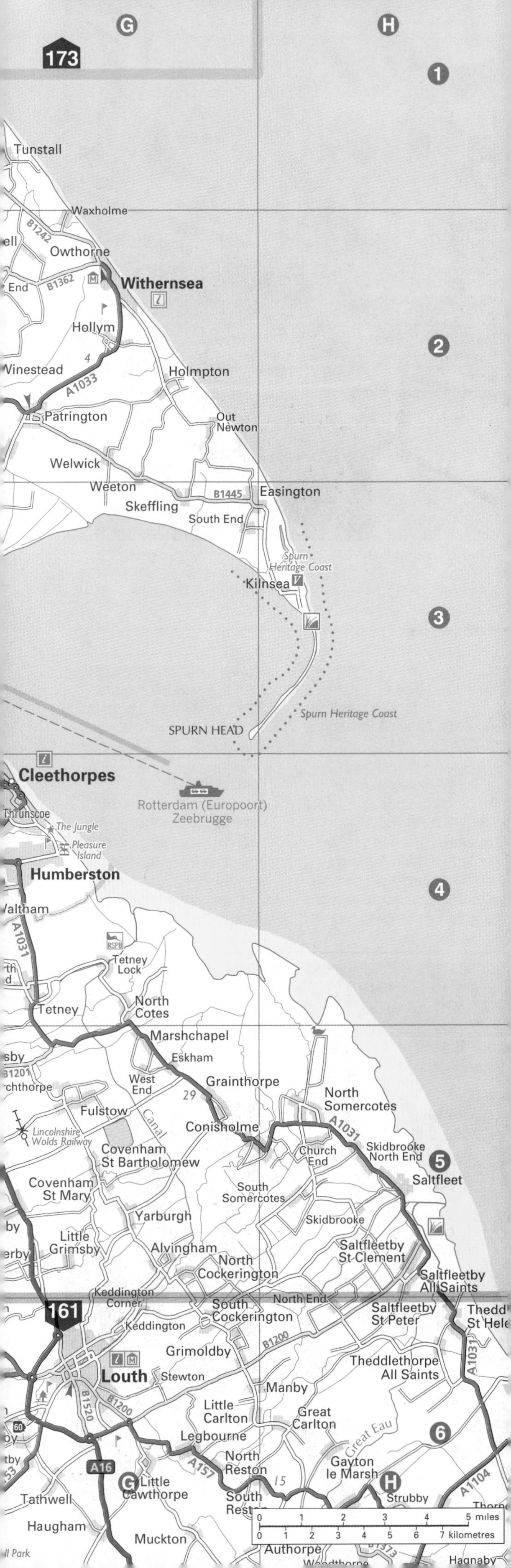

173

Tunstall

Owthorne

Waxholme

End

Withernsea

Hollym

Winestead

Holmpton

A1033

Patrington

Out Newton

Welwick

Weeton

B1445

Easington

Skeffling

South End

Spurn Heritage Coast

Kilnsea

SPURN HEAD

Spurn Heritage Coast

Cleethorpes

Thrunscoe

The Jungle

Pleasure Island

Rotterdam (Europoort)
Zeebrugge

Humberston

Valtham

A1031

RSPB

Tetney Lock

Tetney

North Cotes

Marshchapel

Eskham

B1201

chthorpe

West End

29

Grainthorpe

Fulstow

Conisholme

North Somercotes

A1031

Covenham St Bartholomew

Church End

Skidbrooke North End

5

Saltfleet

Covenham St Mary

South Somercotes

Yarburgh

Skidbrooke

Alvingham

Saltfleetby St Clement

Little Grimsby

North Cockerington

Saltfleetby All Saints

Keddington Corner

South Cockerington

North End

Saltfleetby St Peter

Thedd St Hele

161

Keddington

B1200

Grimoldby

Stewton

A1031

Theddlethorpe All Saints

Louth

Manby

B1520

B1200

Little Carlton

Great Carlton

A16

Legbourne

Great Eau

A157

North Reston

Gayton le Marsh

6

A1104

by

G

Little Cawthorpe

South Reston

15

H

Strubby

Tathwell

Muckton

Haugham

l Park

Authorpe

Woodthorpe

Hagnaby

Lincolnshire Wolds Railway

Grimsby Fishing Heritage Centre tells the story of local fishermen and their boats

point for thousands of migrating birds in the spring and autumn. The area is also a nature reserve managed by the Yorkshire Wildlife Trust and, in addition to the birds, visitors can expect to see seals and butterflies.

Thornton Abbey & Gatehouse
167 E3

The ornate fortified gatehouse of Thornton Abbey is one of the finest in Britain. Built by one of the wealthiest English Augustinian monasteries in the 14th century, it protected the abbey's treasures and provided lodgings for the abbot and his guests. Within the grounds stand the remains of a beautiful octagonal chapter house.

Waterways Museum
166 A2

The museum tells the story of the port of Goole, the transportation of coal and the lives of the barge families. Discover the Humber keels and sloops, and Goole's shipbuilding history through the objects, photos and memories of Goole people.

Withernsea   167 G2

Withernsea is a lively resort offering traditional seaside attractions. The lighthouse in the centre of town brings local history to life with displays on shipwrecks, RNLI lifeboats and HM Coastguard. From the top of the lighthouse there are fine views over the town and along the coast.

…d later rooms, has an imposing lodgings' tower

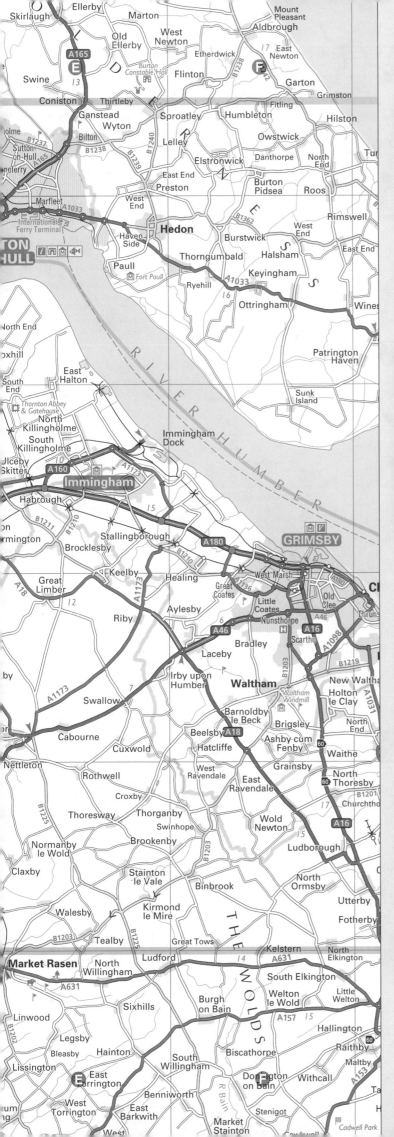

HUMBERSIDE & NORTH LINCS

The Lincolnshire Wolds are a haven of peace and solitude, rich in wildlife and scant in population. Miles of sandy dunes run south from Grimsby at the mouth of the River Humber and there are nature reserves and trails across all points along the coast.

This lighthouse, now disused, once protected shipping passing Spurn Head

Gainsborough Old Hall   166 B5

This complete medieval manor house dates back to 1460–80 and contains a remarkable Great Hall, an original kitchen and a variety of room settings. Richard III, Henry VIII, the *Mayflower* pilgrims and John Wesley all visited the Old Hall.

Gainsthorpe Medieval Village   166 C4

The earthwork remains of a deserted medieval village, one of the best-preserved examples in England, are clearly visible as a complex of grassy humps and bumps.

Grimsby Fishing Heritage Centre   166 F3

Situated next to Alexandra Dock and just a few minutes from the town centre, this museum re-creates Grimsby's maritime history. Visitors can sign on as a crew member for a journey of discovery, and experience the harsh reality of life on board a deep sea trawler built inside the Centre. Through interactive games and displays, the challenge is to navigate the icy waters of the Arctic in search of the catch.

Normanby Hall   166 B3

A whole host of activities and attractions are offered in the 120ha of grounds that surround Normanby Hall, including riding, nature trails and a farming museum. Inside the Regency mansion the fine rooms are decorated and furnished in period style. Outside there are self-guided nature trails, extensive woodland and a deer park.

Pleasure Island   167 G4

Pleasure Island is packed with over 70 rides and attractions. There are white-knuckle rides and family shows and an indoor themed area for younger members of the family.

Spurn Heritage Coast   167 H3

This long, curving stretch of shingle and sand arcing into the mouth of the Humber River is a stopover

Medieval Gainsborough Old Hall, with Tud

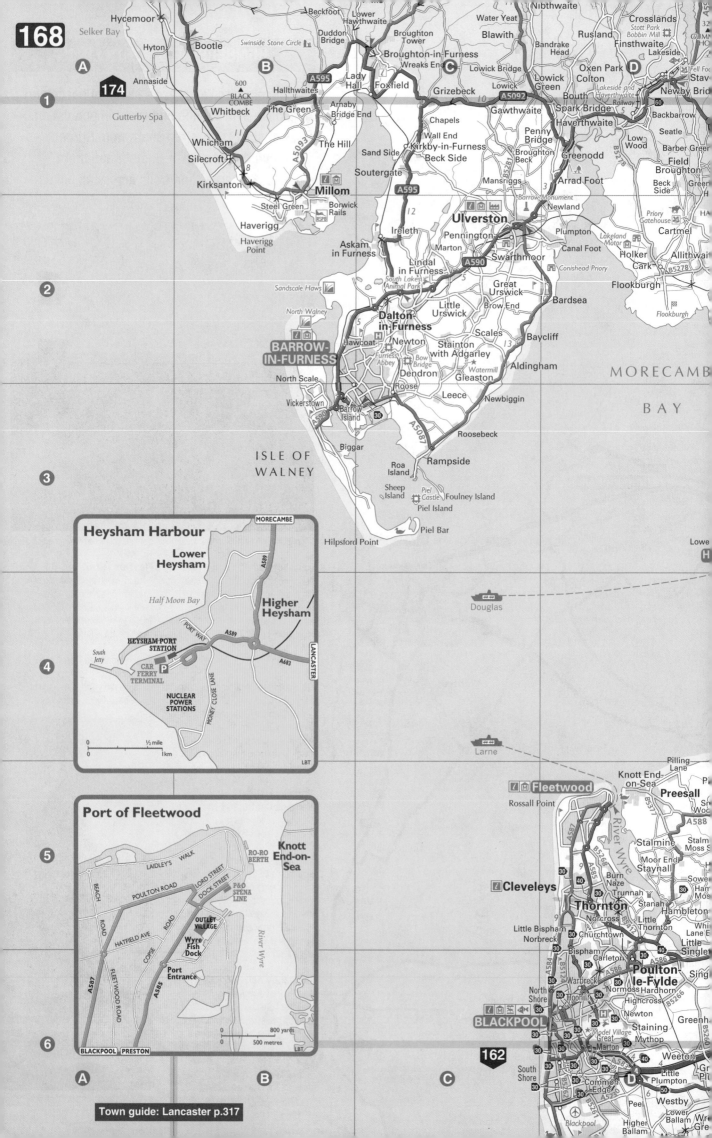

A · B · C · D

1 · 2 · 3 · 4 · 5 · 6

A · B · C · D

174

Selker Bay
Hycemoor
Hyton
Annaside
Bootle
Whitbeck
Gutterby Spa
Whicham
Silecroft
Kirksanton
Steel Green
Haverigg
Haverigg Point
Borwick Rails
Millom
The Green
Hallthwaites
The Hill
Sand Side
Soutergate
Arnaby Bridge End
Lady Hall
Foxfield
Duddon Bridge
Broughton Tower
Wreaks End
Broughton-in-Furness
Grizebeck
Chapels
Wall End
Kirkby-in-Furness
Beck Side
Mansriggs
Pennington
Marton
Swarthmoor
Lindal in Furness
Askam in Furness
Sandscale Haws
North Walney
North Scale
BARROW-IN-FURNESS
Vickerstown
Biggar
Hawcoat
Newton
Furness Abbey
Bow Bridge
Dendron
Roose
Dalton-in-Furness
Little Urswick
South Lakes Animal Park
Great Urswick
Scales
Stainton with Adgarley
Gleaston
Watermill
Leece
Newbiggin
Aldingham
Bardsea
Brow End
Bay cliff
Roosebeck
Rampside
Roa Island
Sheep Island
Piel Castle
Foulney Island
Piel Island
Piel Bar
Hilpsford Point

ISLE OF WALNEY

MORECAMB(E) BAY

Beckfoot
Lower Hawthwaite
Water Yeat
Blawith
Nibthwaite
Crosslands
Stott Park Bobbin Mill
Rusland
Finsthwaite
Lakeside
Bandrake Head
Broughton Beck
Lowick Bridge
Lowick Green
Lowick
Bouth
Gawthwaite
Spark Bridge
Haverthwaite
Lakeside and Haverthwaite Railway
Oxen Park
Colton
Newby Bri(dge)
Backbarrow
Low Wood
Seatle
Penny Bridge
Greenodd
Arrad Foot
Newland
Barrow Monument
Ulverston
Plumpton
Canal Foot
Conishead Priory
Lakeland Motor
Holker
Cark
Cartmel
Allithwai(te)
Flookburgh
Priory Gatehouse
Barber Green
Field Broughton
Beck Side

A595 · A5092 · A590 · A5087 · A5093

Heysham Harbour

MORECAMBE
Lower Heysham
Half Moon Bay
Higher Heysham
HEYSHAM PORT STATION
CAR FERRY TERMINAL
NUCLEAR POWER STATIONS
South Jetty
PORT WAY
MONEY CLOSE LANE
LANCASTER
A589 · A683

0 — ½ mile
0 — 1 km
LBT

Douglas

Larne

Lowe

H

Port of Fleetwood

Knott End-on-Sea
RO-RO BERTH
P&O STENA LINE
LAIDLEY'S WALK
LORD STREET
DOCK STREET
POULTON ROAD
BEACH ROAD
HATFIELD AVE
COPSE ROAD
FLEETWOOD ROAD
OUTLET VILLAGE
Wyre Fish Dock
Port Entrance
River Wyre

A587 · A585

800 yards
500 metres
BLACKPOOL PRESTON
LBT

Fleetwood
Knott End-on-Sea
Rossall Point
Pilling Lane
Preesall
River Wyre
Stalmine
Stalm Moss
Moor End
Staynall
Cleveleys
Burn Naze
Trunnah
Stanah
Hambleton
Thornton
Norcross
Little Thornton
Sowe
Ham
Mos
Little Bispham
Norbreck
Churchtown
Whi
Lane
Little
Single
Bispham
Carleton
Hardhorn
Poulton-le-Fylde
Sing
Warbreck
Normoss
Highcross
Newton
Staining
Greenh(alg)h
North Shore
Hoohil
Marton
BLACKPOOL
Model Village
Great Marton
Mythop
Staining
South Shore
Common Edge
Peel
Weeton
Little Plumpton
Westby
Weston
Higher Ballam
Lower Ballam

A587 · A588 · A585 · A586 · A5268 · B5377 · B5412 · B5261

162

Town guide: Lancaster p.317

town's most notable features with three graceful arches striding over the water.

Lakeland Motor Museum
168 D2

The Lakeland Motor Museum is set in extensive outbuildings within the grounds of Holker Hall, the home of the Cavendish family. Here you will find a fascinating collection of historic cars and other vehicles, dating from the early days of motoring to the present. In the Hall you are free to explore the rooms unhindered by ropes and barriers. The 10ha of formal gardens and woodland are justifiably renowned.

Leighton Hall 169 E2

Early Gillow furniture is displayed among other treasures in the fine interior of this neo-Gothic mansion. Outside, a large collection of birds of prey can be seen, and flying displays are given each afternoon. There are also fine gardens, a maze and a woodland walk.

Levens Hall 169 E1

The beginnings of the Hall can be traced back to a grim medieval pele tower which was later incorporated into a more elaborate Elizabethan building to create a comfortable family home. As fine as the house is, the most famous feature is outdoors – the topiary garden, in which yew trees were clipped into a variety of shapes. The designs we see today, probably the finest examples in the country, are much as they were designed three centuries ago.

Millom 168 B1

Sitting on its own peninsula overlooking the estuary of the River Duddon, Millom is well off the beaten track. The Millom Folk Museum is housed in the imaginatively redeveloped railway station. The museum has vivid reminders of the town's iron-mining days, including an impressive full-scale reconstruction of an iron-ore drift mine. The lagoon, adjacent to the Duddon Estuary, is an RSPB reserve attracting breeding wildfowl, waders and the rare natterjack toad.

RSPB Leighton Moss Nature Reserve: Silverdale 169 E2

The largest remaining reed bed in northwest England, this reserve covers 130ha, and is home to birds such as breeding bitterns, bearded tits and marsh harriers.

Ulverston 168 C2

Ulverston is sufficiently off the beaten track to maintain an unhurried air, though Thursdays and Saturdays find the market square thronged with stalls. Overlooking the town, is a 27.4m copy of the Eddystone Lighthouse – a monument to Sir John Barrow, Ulverston-born in 1764. A founder member of the Royal Geographical Society, his story is told in the town's heritage centre. The Laurel and Hardy Museum is a haphazard collection of Laurel and Hardy memorabilia, assembled here because Stan Laurel was born in Ulverston in 1890.

Whalley Abbey 169 H6

The ruins of a 14th-century Cistercian abbey are set in the delightful gardens of the Blackburn Diocesan Retreat and Conference House, a 17th-century manor house with gardens reaching down to the River Calder. The remains include two gateways, a chapter house and the abbot's lodgings and kitchen. The manor house is not open to the public.

Vintage cars and other motor vehicles on display at the Lakeland Motor Museum

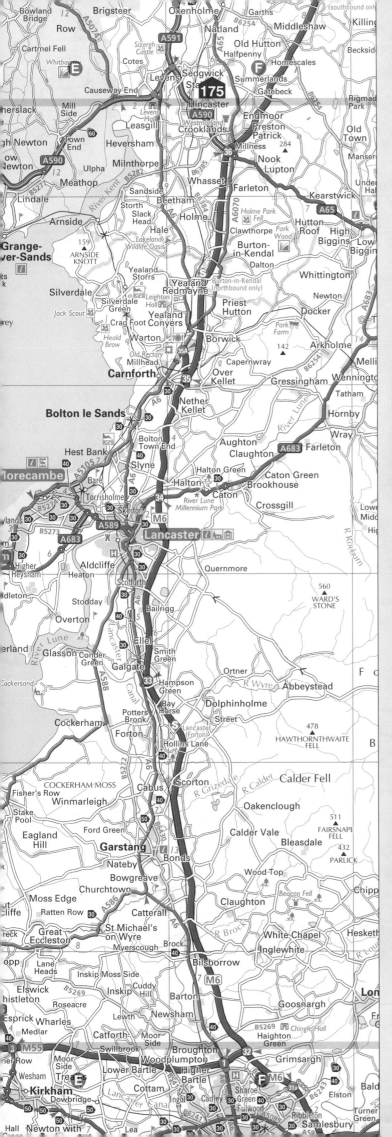

BLACKPOOL & MORECAMBE BAY

A mild climate and seemingly endless sands have made Morecambe Bay popular with generations of holidaymakers who enjoy the genteel pleasures of its seaside towns. To the south is big brash Blackpool while to the north, visible across the bay, are the bleaker beauties of the Lake District.

Donkeys on the beach near Blackpool Tower

Barrow-in-Furness 168 B3
For a fascinating overview of Barrow's shipbuilding industry head for the Dock Museum. Sitting astride a deep dry dock, the museum tells how Barrow became a major force in maritime engineering. Other exhibits focus on older shipbuilding traditions. Located in a peaceful valley between Barrow and Dalton are the majestic red sandstone remains of beautiful Furness Abbey which once housed a wealthy monastic order. View the fine stone carvings and visit the exhibition to find out more about the powerful religious community that was once based here.

Blackpool 168 D6
What Blackpool does, it does extremely well: donkey rides, amusement arcades and big rides. During the 19th century, local factory workers traditionally came here for their annual week's holiday to enjoy the famous promenade, the long sandy beach and its theatres. Blackpool Tower, a scale copy of Paris's Eiffel Tower, dates from this time and you can still visit the Grand Theatre. Blackpool Pleasure Beach is the main draw. The original Big Dipper was opened here in 1923 and is still going strong. The best time to visit is in the autumn, when you can see the famous Blackpool Illuminations, huge moving tableaux of fairytales and brilliantly lit trams.

Cartmel 168 D2
Cartmel has a large and magnificent church which once belonged to a 12th-century Augustinian priory. When the monastery itself was disbanded by the Dissolution in 1536–37 the priory

church was saved. Much of the stone from the priory was re-used to build the village, and the only other tangible relic of monastic times is the gatehouse (now a heritage centre) that forms one side of the little market square. The Cartmel of today is a pretty little village, worth exploring in its own right as well as for its gem of a church.

Grange-over-Sands 169 E2
Looking out over Morecambe Bay is the charming little resort of Grange-over-Sands, with its ornamental gardens, promenade and relaxed ambience. Thanks to the Gulf Stream, Grange enjoys a congenially mild climate, a factor which helps to explain why so many people find the town a pleasant place in which to spend their retirement years.

Haverthwaite 168 D1
Haverthwaite is the southern terminus of the Lakeside and Haverthwaite Railway. Originally a branch of the Furness Railway, the line used to carry goods and passengers from Ulverston to connect with the Windermere steamers at Lakeside. Today it is run as a recreational line, using steam-hauled trains. As in the railway's heyday, the scenic journey can be combined with a leisurely cruise on Windermere.

Kirkby Lonsdale 169 G2
This tiny market town is a delightfully unspoilt place, whose charms have been recognised by artists and authors, from Constable and Turner to Ruskin and Wordsworth. On the edge of town, the medieval Devil's Bridge spans the River Lune. It is one of the

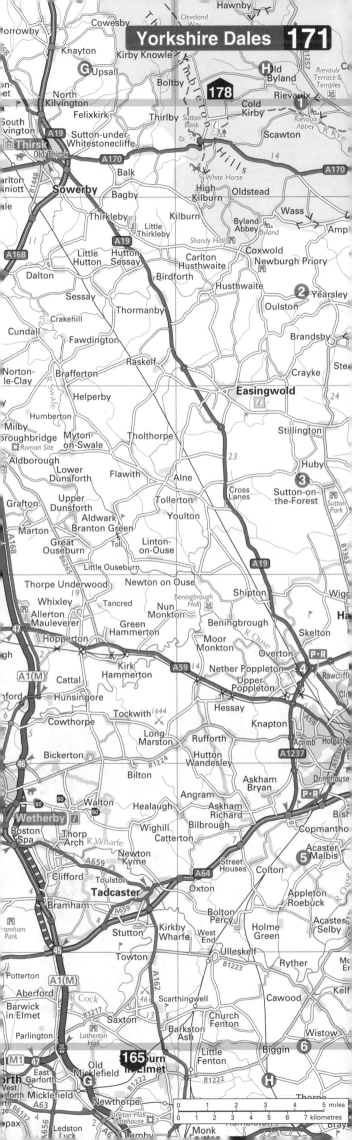

earls of Harewood) by John Carr in 1759. Much of the furniture is by Thomas Chippendale from nearby Otley. There's plenty to enjoy outside, with an adventure playground, a rose garden, lakeside walks, a Spiral Meadow in the kitchen garden and a Bird Garden with over 100 species of bird. Don't miss Thomas Chippendale's lavishly carved and gilded State Bed.

Haworth 170 C6

When Haworth was home to the Brontë family in the 19th century, it was still a textile-manufacturing village. The steep, cobbled streets are surrounded by wild moorland, and the look of the village has changed little since the Brontës lived here, despite the gift shops and tea rooms. Haworth Parsonage was the lifelong family home of the Brontës. An intensely close-knit family, the Brontës saw the parsonage as the heart of their world and the moorland setting provided them with inspiration for their writing. The house contains much personal memorabilia, including the furniture Charlotte bought with the proceeds of her literary success, Branwell's portraits of local worthies, Emily's writing desk and Anne's books and drawings.

Malham National Park Centre 170 A3

The Yorkshire Dales National Park Centre has maps, guides and local information together with displays on the remarkable natural history of the area, the local community and the work of conservation bodies.

Saltaire 170 D6

Now a World Heritage Site, Saltaire is a remarkable Victorian factory village. It was built in the 1850s by the philanthropic wool baron Sir Titus Salt to house his workers in decent conditions around his colossal Italianate woollen mill. A school, hospital, two churches, Sunday school, washhouse and shops were all part of Salt's design. Today, Salt's Mill has shops, businesses and the 1853 Gallery, the world's largest permanent collection of paintings by the local artist David Hockney. Walk along the back streets of Saltaire to see how the more fortunate 19th-century mill workers lived.

Skipton 170 B4

The Gateway to the Dales is at its liveliest on market days – Monday, Wednesday, Friday and especially Saturday. The broad, tree-lined main street is full of shops and old pubs, with ginnels (cobbled alleys) running off on either side. Retaining turrets and battlements, Skipton Castle dates from Norman times. It played a significant role in the Wars of the Roses and endured a three-year Parliamentarian siege during the Civil War, after which it had to be partly rebuilt.

Rievaulx Abbey 171 H1

Rievaulx Abbey was founded in 1132 and became one of England's wealthiest monasteries before its dissolution in 1538. Visitors can explore the magnificent romantic ruin set in a tranquil wooded valley of the River Rye and find out about monastic life with the help of the audio tour and exhibition.

Rievaulx Terrace & Temples 171 H1

This curved terrace, half a mile long, overlooks the abbey, with views of Ryedale and the Hambleton Hills. It has two mock-Greek temples, one built for hunting parties, the other for quiet contemplation. There are also remarkable frescoes by Borgnis, and an exhibition on English landscape design.

◄ moving of England's ruined monasteries

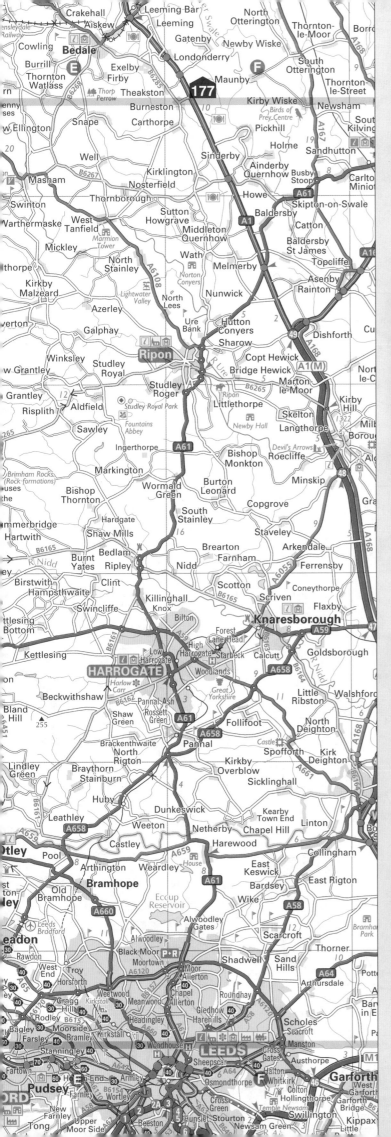

YORKSHIRE DALES

The Yorkshire Dales is a landscape of gorges and waterfalls, wide valleys and slow rivers, strange rock formations, potholes and underground passages. Harrogate lies at the outer edge of the dales and moors, while the major cities of Leeds and historic York are also part of this region.

Brimham Rocks, standing in high, open moorland

Beningbrough Hall 171 H4

Beningbrough was built around 1716. It houses 100 portraits from the National Portrait Gallery in London. Ornately carved wood panelling is a feature of several of the rooms. There is also a fully equipped Victorian laundry and walled garden.

Brimham Rocks 171 E3

Aspiring rock climbers beat a path to this vast series of strange rock formations scattered across nearly 400ha of elevated moorland on the edge of the Yorkshire Dales. The sculptural effects of wind, ice and rain have produced a series of gritstone towers and pinnacles, some appearing to balance precariously on the flimsiest foundations. Look for the Dancing Bear, David's Writing Desk and the Idol.

Fountains Abbey and Studley Royal Park 171 E3

Fountains Abbey, now a World Heritage Site, was established in 1132. Henry VIII closed it down during his dissolution of the country's monasteries in 1539, yet it has survived as Britain's largest abbey ruin and you can still see the church tower, dating from around 1500, soaring above the Norman nave, and can wander among the remains of the monastic quarters. Studley Royal Park is a remarkable creation of geometric pools, follies and a landscape of rocky outcrops dating from the 18th-century. The gardens include the sweeping lawn as an approach to the abbey and Anne Boleyn's Seat, a viewpoint above the valley has a framed view of the ruins.

Grassington 170 C3

Grassington is the major tourist centre in Upper Wharfedale, with a large number of guesthouses, shops and eating places radiating out from its cobbled market square. It also has a National Park Centre, near the village centre, and the Upper Wharfedale Folk Museum, a tiny but enjoyable collection housed in two 18th-century former lead-miners' cottages, which explores the history of mining in the area.

Harewood House & Bird Garden 171 F5

This showpiece country house was designed for the Lascelles family (the

Rievaulx Abbey, perhaps the most beautit

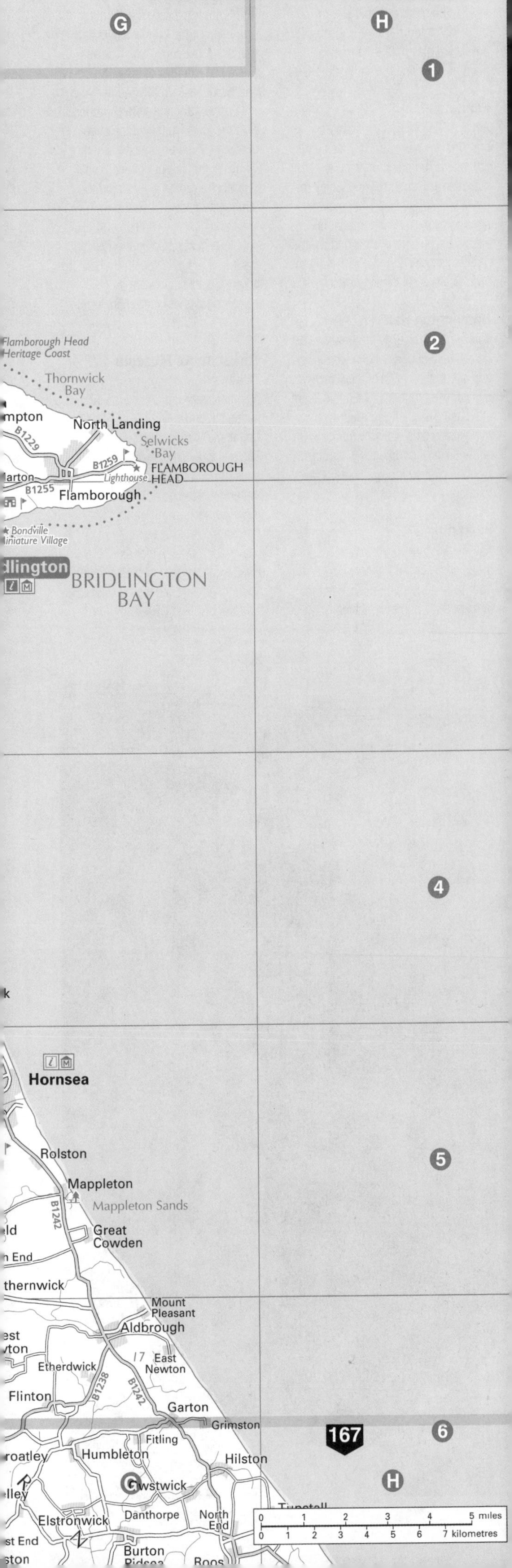

G

H

1

2

Flamborough Head
Heritage Coast
· · · *Thornwick*
Bay
mpton
North Landing
Selwicks
·Bay
B1229
B1259   ★ FLAMBOROUGH
arton   *Lighthouse* HEAD
B1255
Flamborough ·

★ *Bondville*
iniature Village · · · ·

dlington

BRIDLINGTON
BAY

4

k

Hornsea

5

Rolston

Mappleton
Mappleton Sands

ld   Great
n End   Cowden

thernwick

Mount
Pleasant
Aldbrough
est
ton   17 East
Etherdwick   Newton
B1238 B1242
Flinton   Garton

Grimston
roatley   Fitling
lley   Humbleton   Hilston

167   **6**

wstwick   H

Elstronwick   Danthorpe   North
st End   End
ston   Burton
Pidcon   Roos   Tunstall

0	1	2	3	4	5 miles
0	1 2	3	4 5	6	7 kilometres

formal Italianate Temple of the Four Winds, the great Pyramid and the huge Mausoleum. There is also an adventure playground, farm shop, plant nursery and holiday park.

Flamingo Land 172 B1
Set in 152ha of North Yorkshire countryside with over 100 rides and attractions there's something for everyone at Flamingo Land. Enjoy the thrills and spills of 12 white-knuckle rides and take a stroll through the extensive zoo where you'll find tigers, giraffes, hippos and rhinos. The theme park also has six family shows.

Nunnington Hall 172 A2
This large 16th- to 17th-century house, built of honey-coloured stone and set on the banks of the River Rye, has panelled rooms and a magnificent staircase. The Carlisle collection of miniature rooms with tiny furnishings and musical instruments, is on display. There is changing programme of temporary exhibitions.

Pickering 172 B1
The market town of Pickering lies just to the south of the National Park. Overlooking the market place is the large parish church dedicated to Saints Peter and Paul. Inside are fine 15th-century frescoes, illustrating scenes from the lives of saints and martyrs. Pickering Castle is a well-preserved example of an early earthwork castle refortified in stone during the 13th and 14th centuries. There is an exhibition in the chapel. Beck Isle Museum offers fascinating glimpses into the more recent past. Successive rooms are devoted to different aspects of bygone life in town and country; you can visit the cobblers, gents' outfitters and even the bar of a public house. Outbuildings house a blacksmith's forge, wheelwright and a collection of old farming implements.

Yorkshire Air Museum 172 A5
This award-winning museum and memorial is based around the largest authentic former World War II Bomber Command Station open to the public. There is a restored tower, an air gunners museum, archives, an Airborne Forces display, Squadron memorial rooms, and much more. Among the exhibits are replicas of the pioneering Cayley Glider and Wright Flyer, along with the Halifax Bomber and modern jets like the Harrier GR3, Tornado GR1 and GR4.

The chalk cliffs rises to dizzy heights near Bempton

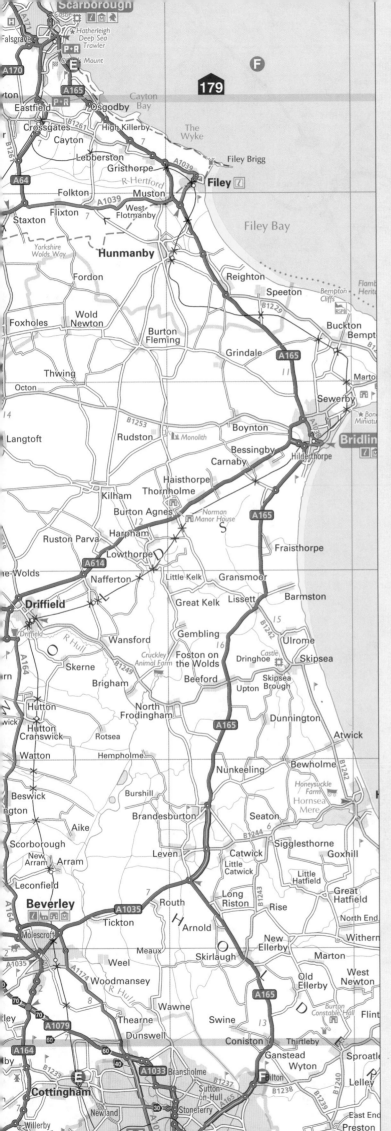

YORKSHIRE WOLDS

The chalky escarpment of the Wolds is cut by deep and winding dry valleys. The North Sea coast has miles of sandy beaches around the holiday resorts of Filey, Bridlington and Hornsea, contrasting with the dramatic chalk cliffs at Flamborough Head. Finally, the wonderfully complete medieval city of York, is crammed with historic treasures and outstanding museums.

Castle Howard is an imposing baroque country house

Bempton Cliffs 173 F2

One of the major bird sites on the east coast, these sheer 120m chalk cliffs are home to more than 200,000 breeding seabirds. There are five safe viewing points and a visitor office, run by the RSPB. Bird species (depending on the season) include puffins, guillemots, razorbills, kittiwakes, fulmars and migrating birds. It is one of the country's most important breeding sites for Britain's largest seabird, the gannet, with several thousand nests. Also look out for seals and porpoises. A footpath follows the coast to the east round the spectacularly indented cliffs of Flamborough Head.

Beverley 173 E5

Beverley is one of the best-looking old market towns in the north of England. The main attraction is its architecture. It has streets lined with mostly 18th- and 19th-century houses, two market places and the North Bar of 1409, a rare early brick gateway. Beverley Minster dates mostly from the 13th century. It is a large, long building with twin towers and an interior full of light and elaborate carving. Though smaller, St Mary's Church, at the other end of the town, is equally impressive. The carving of a rabbit in St Michael's Chapel, with a pilgrim's staff and pouch, is reputedly the inspiration for the White Rabbit in Lewis Carroll's *Alice's Adventures in Wonderland* (1865).

Burnby Hall Garden 172 C5

The two lakes in this garden have an outstanding collection of 80 varieties of hardy water lilies, designated a National Collection. The lakes stand within 4ha of beautiful gardens including heather beds, a rock garden, a spring and summer bedding area, woodland walk and Victorian garden. The Stewart Museum contains sporting trophies and ethnic material gathered on Major Stewart's worldwide travels.

Burton Constable Hall 173 F6

This superb Elizabethan house was built in 1570, but much of the interior was remodelled in the 18th century. There are magnificent reception rooms and a Tudor long gallery with a pendant roof: the contents range from pictures and furniture to a unique collection of 18th-century scientific instruments. Outside are 80ha of parkland, landscaped by 'Capability' Brown, with oaks and chestnuts, and a lake with an island.

Castle Howard 172 B3

A ruler-straight road leads through the great estate of this palatial baroque house, the first building to be designed by the playwright and architect Sir John Vanbrugh, in 1699, with the assistance of the vastly more experienced Nicholas Hawksmoor. The domed hall and wide façades are familiar to millions of Britons through the 1981 television adaptation of Evelyn Waugh's *Brideshead Revisited*. Visitors can take a tour through rooms decorated with Howard family heirlooms, and paintings by Peter Paul Rubens, Canaletto and Hans Holbein. There are exhibitions dedicated to the filming of *Brideshead Revisited*, the building of the house, and the role of women at the house over the centuries. The gardens feature the

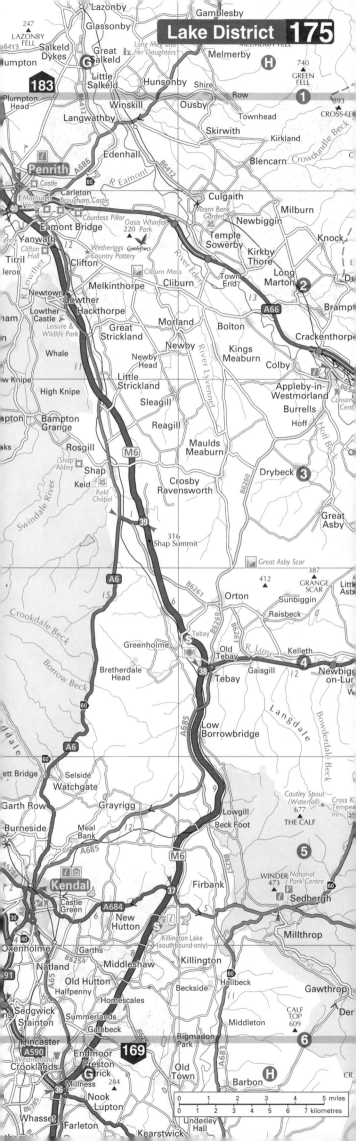

Set in the beautiful village of Troutbeck, 17th-century Townend is a solid, stone-built house with huge chimneys typical of the area

displayed in its individual film set. One of the oldest museums in the county is the Keswick Museum and Art Gallery, which has a good display on Lakeland's literary connections.

Lake District Visitor Centre
175 E4

On the northeast shore of Windermere is Brockhole, a fine house in gardens that shelve down to the lake shore. Built for a Manchester businessman, the house has, since the late 1960s, been the National Park Visitor Centre. Brockhole is an excellent first stop for visitors new to the Lake District. There are gardens, displays, exhibitions, an adventure playground and a calendar of events.

Ravenglass 174 B5

The small Cumbrian village of Ravenglass is best known as the home of the Ravenglass and Eskdale Railway. This delightful narrow-gauge railway used to carry iron ore from the Eskdale mines to the coast; now the engines carry passengers up the valley. There are seven stations along the line, all offering opportunities for scenic walks with the option of taking a later train back down to Ravenglass. The terminus, at Dalegarth, is just a short walk from the tiny village of Boot.

Rheged 175 F2

Rheged – Upland Kingdom Discovery Centre, on the A66, interprets the history of the area through film and a range of innovative techniques. It is also home to the National Mountaineering Exhibition.

Sizergh Castle 175 F6

This beautiful medieval castle/manor house extended in Elizabethan times, has many fine features including a series of exceptional oak-panelled rooms. The gardens, with lovely views over the lower Lakeland fells, are well worth exploring.

Townend 174 F4

The best-preserved building in the Troutbeck valley is Townend, a fine example of a yeoman farmer's house.

Townend offers a fascinating glimpse into what domestic life was like for Lakeland's wealthier farmers, with low ceilings, original home-carved oak panelling and furniture, and stone-flagged floors.

Whitehaven 174 A3

Whitehaven has a small fishing fleet and its harbour is a conservation area with several monuments to its past mining history, which finally died out in 1986. The Beacon, a lighthouse-style building on West Strand, offers visitors an insight into the history of the town and harbour using audio-visual presentations and exciting displays.

Windermere 175 F5

The town of Windermere grew up around its railway station and gradually spread along the lakeside into Bowness where visitors can take a boat trip on England's largest lake via Waterhead and Lakeside (linking to the steam trains of the restored Lakeside–Haverthwaite Railway). The World of Beatrix Potter, another popular attraction in Bowness, uses the latest technology to bring to life the stories of Peter Rabbit, Jemima Puddleduck and many other characters. At the Windermere Steamboat Museum, on the A592 Bowness to Ambleside road, you will find a fascinating collection of craft, mostly steam-powered launches from the Victorian and Edwardian eras.

Locally produced colouring pencils

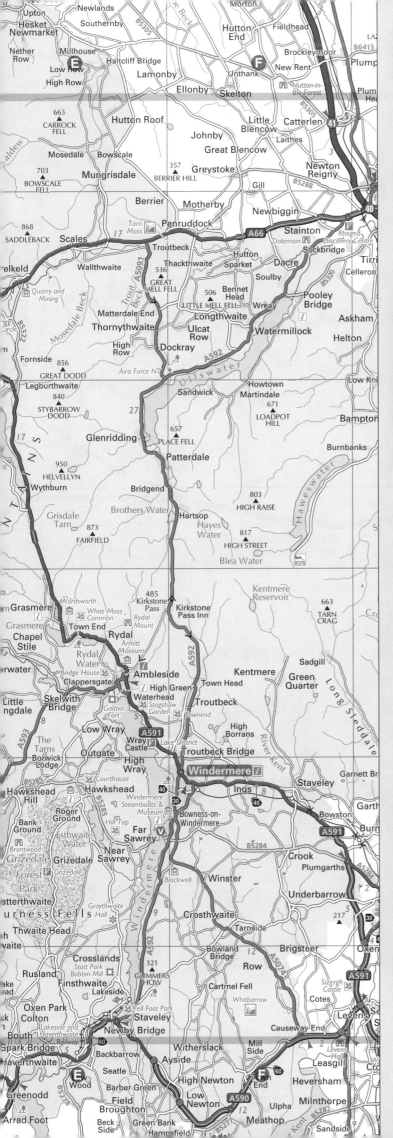

LAKE DISTRICT

Despite its popularity, most of this beautiful north-west corner of England retains its air of emptiness and remoteness. Narrow passes, soaring mountains, plunging waterfalls and lakes of every shape and size create a landscape which has inspired poets, writers and artists for 200 years.

Derwent Water, south of Keswick, can be explored by ferry and rowing boat

Coniston 175 D5

Overlooked by the bulk of The Old Man of Coniston, 803m, and near the northern tip of Coniston Water, the village enjoys a superb setting. The story of copper mining, slate quarrying and farming, as well as the lives of celebrities such as John Ruskin, Arthur Ransome and Donald Campbell, are told in the Ruskin Museum. A short stroll from the centre of Coniston brings you to the shore of the lake where a public slipway allows the launching of boats.

Grasmere 175 E4

The village of Grasmere is set in a valley surrounded by hills, and is a short stroll from Grasmere lake. Literary pilgrims have flocked to Grasmere since William Wordsworth produced some of his finest romantic poetry here. Wordsworth's home, Dove Cottage, is open to the public, and an adjacent coach house has been converted into the Wordsworth Museum.

Hardknott Pass & Roman Fort 174 D4

When you gaze down from the remains of the fort at the western end of the Hardknott Pass (393m) it is easy to see why the Romans chose this site. Hardknott Fort enjoys a commanding position down into the green valley of Eskdale. Hardknott Pass is one of the most spectacular roads in the country; a few of the hairpin bends are as steep as 1-in-3.

Hawkshead 175 E5

Hawkshead is an intriguing maze of tiny thoroughfares, alleyways, courtyards and 17th-century whitewashed houses. The 15th-century parish church has wall frescoes, but its main charm is its position on a knoll overlooking the village. A more recent attraction is the National Trust's Beatrix Potter Gallery, in the middle of the village, where you will find displays of Beatrix's original drawings, and information about her life as author, artist, farmer and pioneer of the conservation movement.

Kendal 175 G5

Kendal, the gateway to the Lakes, is famous for its mint cake, the essential standby of hillwalkers. Narrow enclosed yards, where the weavers lived and worked survive behind the shop fronts of Stricklandgate and Highgate. Near the parish church is Abbot Hall, an art gallery, showing works by the many artists who were inspired by the Lakeland landscape. The Museum of Lakeland Life and Industry, also at Abbot Hall, brings recent history to life, with reconstructed shops, room settings and a farming display. At the opposite end of town the Kendal Museum has fascinating displays of geology, archaeology and natural and social history.

Keswick 174 D2

Keswick is a natural centre for mountain climbers, country walkers and more leisurely tourists alike. The Cumberland Pencil Museum, a delightfully quirky specialist collection, shows that even the humble pencil has a fascinating history. The Cars of the Stars Motor Museum features celebrity TV and film vehicles. Some notable exhibits to look out for are James Bond's DB5 Aston Martin, Harry Potter's Ford Anglia and Del Boy's Robin Reliant. Each vehicle is

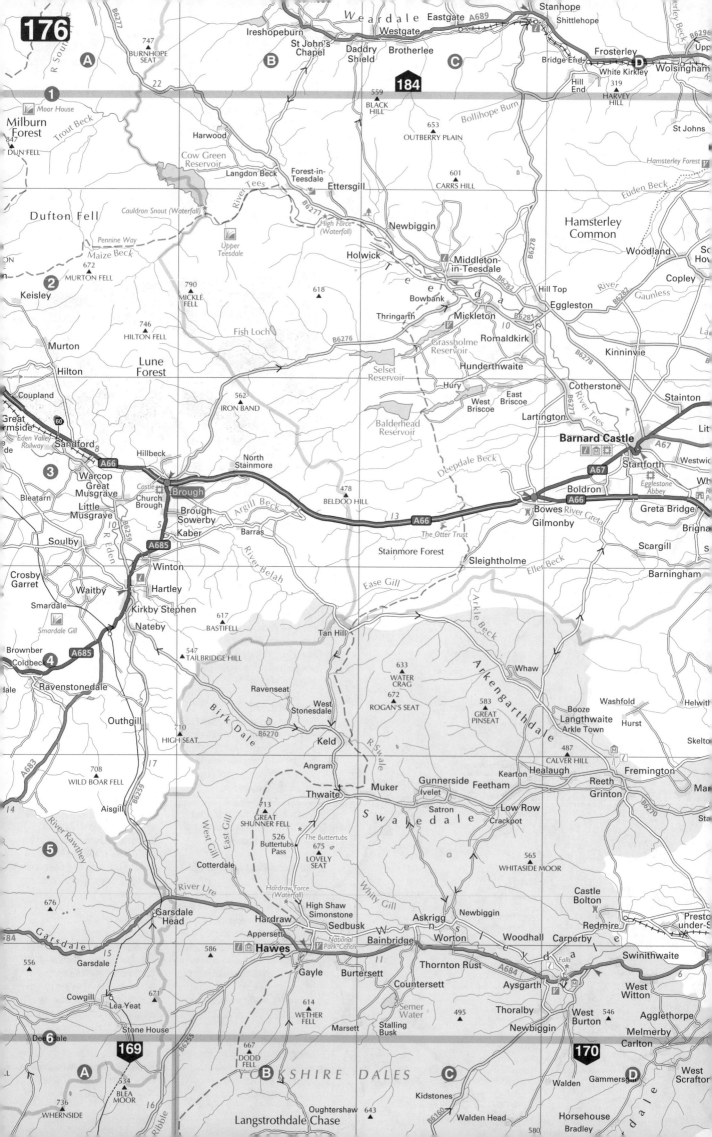

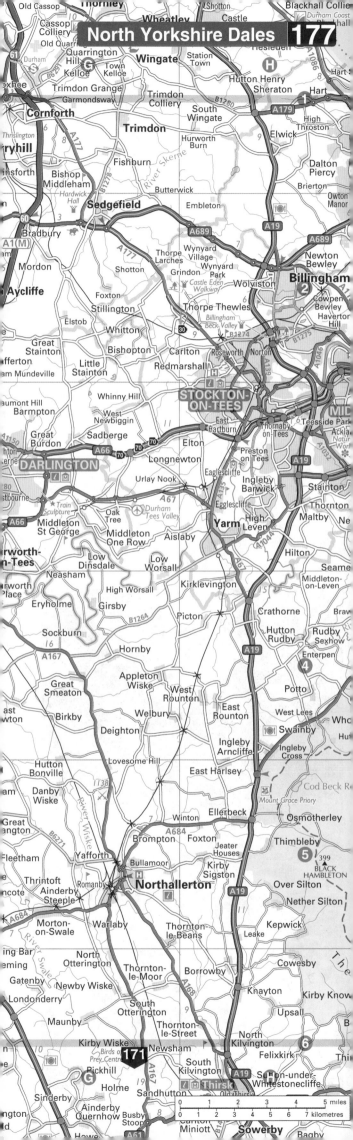

such as knitting and peat cutting. Just across from the Station Yard is the entrance to Outhwaite and Son, rope-makers, where visitors can see how the rope is produced.

Kirkby Stephen 176 A4

This unspoilt town stands at the foot of Mallerstang, a dale which stretches south, half-in and half-out of the Yorkshire Dales National Park. The parish church, described as the 'Cathedral of the Dales', is one of the region's hidden gems, containing many fine features including the Loki Stone, a 10th-century Anglo-Danish cross carved with the features of the Norse God, Loki.

Mount Grace Priory 177 H5

The best-preserved Carthusian priory in England is set in beautiful woodland. A reconstructed and furnished monk's cell and a herb garden offer a glimpse into the solitary life of a monk. The gardens are a haven for wildlife.

Reeth 176 D5

Reeth is an attractive centre for tourism, with general shops, craft shops, pubs, a few hotels and guesthouses, and the dale's most important museum. The Swaledale Folk Museum, which also acts as an information centre for visitors, is hidden away behind the post office on the far eastern side of the Green. Inside there are particularly good displays on the dale's main industries over the years: farming and lead-mining.

Richmond 177 E4

Richmond is one of the most tempting historical towns in the Yorkshire Dales. Off cobbled Trinity Church Square, one of England's largest market places, is a steep knot of unspoiled streets such as Frenchgate and Newbiggin Broad, mainly with refined Georgian buildings, and two surviving medieval gateways. Perched on a precipitous bank above the fast-flowing River Swale, Richmond Castle dates from 1071; within it, Scollard's Hall (1080) may be Britain's earliest surviving domestic building. Still very much in use, the Georgian Theatre Royal has the oldest unaltered interior (1788) in Britain. The museum displays original playbills and painted scenery made in 1836. The Green Howards Museum traces the history of the regiment from the late 17th century onwards. Take one of the walks outside of the castle and down to Richmond Falls on the River Swale.

Upper Teesdale 176 B2

Spring gentians and orchids are among the rare post-Ice Age vegetation in this tundra-like part of the northern Pennine Hills. However, the real drama of the valley lies to the west. High Force, a spectacular 21m waterfall, is part of the Raby Castle estate and is at its most raging after a heavy rainfall. Take the 10-minute walk down through woodland from the B6277. Cauldron Snout waterfall, near the vast reservoir of Cow Green, is spectacular as it tumbles down the hillside.

The village of Hardraw is famous for its spectacular waterfall

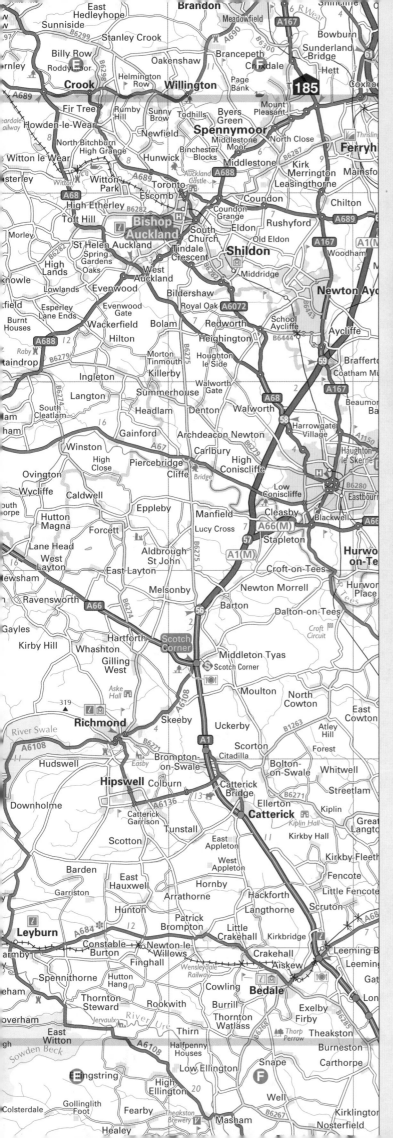

NORTH YORKSHIRE DALES

Swaledale is the grandest of the Yorkshire dales, its rugged dramatic beauty is more appealing to some than the prettier and busier Wensleydale. At its eastern end stands Richmond, a busy market town with a castle on the banks of the River Swale.

Hawes, seen here at first light, is the main town of Upper Wensleydale

Barnard Castle 176 D3
This historic market town is named after the substantial ruins of its 11th-century castle, used as a stronghold of the Balliol family. On the edge of town, the Bowes Museum of fine arts occupies an unexpectedly grand building, built in 1869 in the style of a French château. The icon of the collection is the Silver Swan, a unique life-size, musical automaton that plays every day. Just outside the town are the scant, but charming remains of Egglestone Abbey, a small medieval monastery.

Castle Bolton 176 D5
Castle Bolton is another of Yorkshire's well-preserved medieval castles. Work began on the castle in 1378 for the Scrope family. The magnificent four corner towers that rise to 30.5m give an indication of the grandeur of the original building. There were eight halls, each acting as independent household units inside the castle. Bolton Castle's most notable resident, albeit unwillingly, was Mary, Queen of Scots, who was imprisoned here in July 1568 for six months. The bedchamber in which she is thought to have stayed can be seen, and has been decorated in appropriate style, as have many other parts of the castle.

Darlington 177 F3
Housed in Darlington's carefully restored North Road Station, the railway museum's prize exhibit is *Locomotion No 1*, which pulled the first passenger train on the Stockton to Darlington railway and was built by Robert Stephenson & Co in 1825. Several other steam locomotives are also shown, together with models and other exhibits relating to the Stockton & Darlington and the North Eastern Railway companies.

Easby Abbey 177 E4
Set beside the River Swale, this Premonstratensian Abbey was founded in 1155 and dedicated to St Agatha. Extensive remains of the monks' domestic buildings can be seen.

Hardraw Force 176 B5
Hardraw Force has the longest free drop of any waterfall in England, said to be around 30m. To reach the Force you must pass through the Green Dragon pub, paying a small entrance fee as you do so. The volume of water from the fall is not great, and it is therefore best visited after heavy rain.

Hardwick Hall 177 G2
Built for Bess of Hardwick, properly known as Elizabeth, Countess of Shrewsbury, in the 1590s, this outstanding late 16th-century house evokes life in the Elizabethan period. Much of the original furniture and tapestries remain, and there is needlework by Mary, Queen of Scots, who was held prisoner here for 15 years. The orchard and herb garden lie within the original walled courtyards, while beyond spreads a park grazed by rare breeds of cattle and sheep.

Hawes 176 B6
Family businesses make up the shops in the main street in Hawes, and it is certainly the place to stock up on good local produce, especially on the busy Tuesday market day when stalls line the streets. For a taste of Wensleydale cheese, and the chance to watch it being made, head for the Wensleydale Creamery with its flourishing visitor centre. The Dales Countryside Museum, in the Station Yard, (which also contains a Tourist Information Centre and a National Park Centre) has first-class displays on life in the Dales, particularly on small local industries

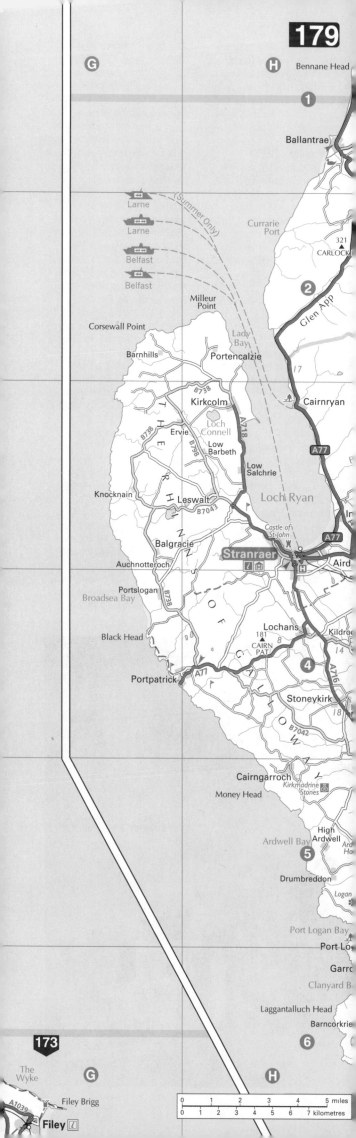

G
H Bennane Head

1

Ballantrae

Larne
Larne
Belfast
Belfast

(Summer Only)

Currarie Port

321
CARLOCK

2

Glen App

Milleur Point

Corsewall Point

Lady Bay

Barnhills
Portencalzie

17

B738
Kirkcolm
Cairnryan

Ervie
Loch Connell

A718
B798
Low Barbeth

A77

Knocknain
Low Salchrie

Leswalt
B7043
Loch Ryan

THE RHINZ OF GALLOWAY

A77

Balgracie
Castle of St John

Auchnotteroch
Stranraer
Aird

Portslogan
Broadsea Bay
B738

Black Head
Lochans
Kildroc

181
CAIRN PAT
8

4
14

A716

Portpatrick
A77
Stoneykirk

18

B7042

Cairngarroch
Kirkmadrine Stones

Money Head

High Ardwell
Ardwell Bay
Ard Ho

5

Drumbreddon

Logan

Port Logan Bay

Port Lo

Garro

Clanyard B

Laggantalluch Head

Barncorkrie

6

173

The Wyke

G
H

A1039
Filey Brigg
Filey

0	1	2	3	4	5 miles
0	1 2 3	4	5	6	7 kilometres

cottages and red-tiled roofs leading down the main street and almost into the sea. There is a good stretch of sandy beach and a rocky foreshore; children love to investigate the little rock pools left in these scars by the receding tide.

Scarborough 179 F6

A headland occupied by the ruins of 12th-century Scarborough Castle divides the two curving sandy bays of Scarborough, while the oldest part of town huddles beside the fishing harbour in South Bay. Claiming to be Britain's first seaside resort, Scarborough's attractions, apart from the sandy beaches and boat trips around the bay, include a Sea Life and Marine Sanctuary, an art gallery and the Rotunda William Smith Museum of Geology.

Staithes 178 C3

This perfectly preserved Yorkshire fishing village is divided into two by Cowbar Beck and the steep-sided gorge through which it runs. The little harbour, and the mouth of the beck, are still full of the traditional fishing cobles which today go to sea mainly for crabs and lobsters; you can buy them freshly caught in the village. Painters and photographers are attracted in droves to the village. James Cook lived here before realising his ambition to go to sea, though the draper's shop where he worked was washed away by the sea. To the north of Staithes are Boulby Cliffs. At more than 200m they are the highest, if not the most dramatic, on England's east coast and offer excellent views. Close by is the Boulby Potash Mine, the deepest mine in Europe.

The Moors Centre 178 C4

The Moors Centre represents the public face of the National Park. Here you can discover what makes the North York Moors so special and the unique habitats that the moors supports. The Centre hosts exhibitions and a wide variety of events, including guided walks. A number of waymarked walks explore the immediate environs; longer walks start from the car park.

Whitby 179 E3

Whitby is a blend of fishing port and Victorian seaside resort, set along the slopes of the deep valley of the River Esk. Prominent among the boats that pack the harbour are the traditional flat-bottomed fishing cobles. High above the town the 13th-century ruins of Whitby Abbey are reached by 199 steps. The visitor complex gives a vivid audio-visual guide from the days of the abbey's 7th-century founder, St Hilda, to its shelling by German warships in World War I. The abbey, steps and graveyard of St Mary's Church feature in Bram Stoker's classic novel *Dracula* (1897).

A statue of the great explorer Captain James Cook looks over the town from the West Cliff. He was born close by in Marton and his ships were built at Whitby; the house where he lodged in Grape Lane while an apprentice is now the Captain Cook Memorial Museum, telling the story of his life and voyages of discovery. Whitby Museum has a collection of fossils, natural history, Whitby jet and seafaring memorabilia, while The Dracula Experience provides a blood-curdling encounter with Whitby's fictional past.

...Bay is a tumble of brightly painted cottages leading down to the sea

E   F

Scarborough map

North Bay

CASTLE
ROMAN SIGNAL STATION
ANNE BRONTE'S GRAVE
ST PETER'S (RC)
ST MARY'S
FIRE STA
YMCA
METH CENTRAL HALL
SCHOOL
COVERED MKT
EASTBOROUGH
RNLI
HARBOUR OFFICE
FISH QUAY
LUNA PARK
TOWN HALL
FUTURIST CINEMA & THEATRE
LIGHTHOUSE & YACHT CLUB
LIBRARY
OLYMPIA LEISURE (SUPERBOWL)
RADIO YORK
ROTUNDA MUS
ART GALLERY
WOOD END MUSEUM OF NATURAL HIST
THE SPA COMPLEX

South Bay

Scarborough

0   200 metres

LBM

Whitby
Abbey
Saltwick Bay
Stainsacre
High Hawsker
Low Hawsker
Ness Point or North Cheek
Raw
Robin Hood's Bay
Fylingthorpe
Robin Hood's Bay
Old Peak or South Cheek
A171
20
Ravenscar
Staintondale
Shire Horse Centre
Cloughton Newlands
Hayburn Wyke
Harwood Dale
Cloughton
Cloughton Wyke
A165
Cromer Point
Burniston
Broxa
Silpho
Cleveland Way
Langdale End
Hackness
Suffield
Newby
Scalby
Wrench Green
Everley
Scarborough
Castle
Falsgrave
Hatherleigh Deep Sea Trawler
Oliver's Mount
Forest Park
River Derwent
Sea Cut
West Ayton
East Ayton
A170
Eastfield
A165
Cayton Bay
Sawdon
Irton
Osgodby
Hutton Buscel
Seamer
Crossgates
High Killerby
Rust
Wykeham
Cayton
Snainton
Brompton
Lebberston
Gristhorpe
A64
R. Hertford

From the sharp escarpments in the west to the towering cliffs and sandy beaches on the east coast, the North York Moors offer a rich variety of landscapes and attractions to please everyone.

The 24 massive stone arches of the Ribblehead Viaduct cross the valley floor

Great Ayton 178 A3

Great Ayton is bisected by the clear waters of the picturesque River Leven. The village was home to Captain Cook from the age of 8 to 16 when he left to work in Staithes and the school he attended is now a museum devoted to his life and achievements. The 12th-century All Saints' Church, now redundant, is open to visitors in the summer months. The interior is quite simple, with walls of rough-hewn stone, and enough original architectural detail to keep most lovers of old churches engrossed. Behind Great Ayton is the famous profile of Roseberry Topping the conical peak, a distinctive landmark for miles around.

North Yorkshire Moors Railway
178 D4–C6

The Pickering–Whitby line was built in 1836 after consulting with George Stephenson. The line closed in 1965 and was reborn eight years later as the North Yorkshire Moors Railway, a recreational line manned by volunteers. Railway buffs can spend some time admiring the gleaming old locomotives at Grosmont station, which has been convincingly restored to how it may have probably looked a century ago; there is also public access to the engine sheds. Grosmont is the northern terminus of the railway, offering connections with main line services on the Esk Valley line between Middlesbrough and Whitby.

Ormesby Hall 178 A3

An attractive 18th-century mansion, Ormesby Hall has a fine stable block attributed to John Carr of York. Inside the Hall there is fine plasterwork, carved wood decoration and 18th-century portraits. The Old Wing houses a permanent model railway exhibition.

Robin Hood's Bay 179 E4

To visit Robin Hood's Bay be sure to leave your car at the top of the hill, where there are large car parks. The road down to the beach is a cul-de-sac and visitors' cars are barred. Apart from the access road, the houses – which cling precariously to the side of the cliff – are reached by narrow alleyways and steps. The result is a jumble of whitewashed

The pretty little fishing village of Robin Ho

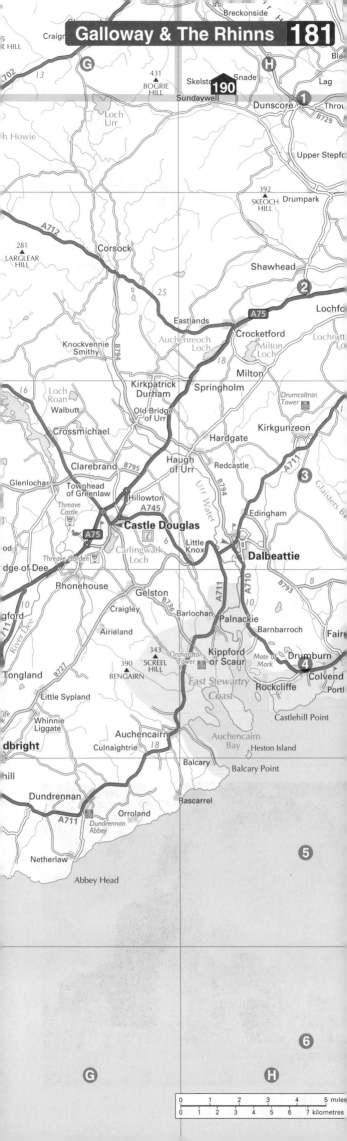

Breckonside

Craign
R HILL
702

G

431
BOGRIE
HILL

Skelston
Sundaywell

Snade

190

H

Lag

1

Dunscore

Throu
B729

Bla

Loch
Urr

h Howie

Loch
Urr

Upper Stepfo

392
SKEOCH
HILL

Drumpark

A712

Corsock

281
LARGLEAR
HILL

Shawhead

2

25

Eastlands

A75

Crocketford

Lochfo

Lochru
Lo

Knockvennie
Smithy

B794

Auchenreoch
Loch

Milton
Loch

Milton

Drumcoltran
Tower

16

Loch
Roan

Walbutt

Kirkpatrick
Durham

Springholm

Kirkgunzeon

18

Crossmichael

Old Bridge
of Urr

Hardgate

Redcastle

A711

Glaisters b

Clarebrand

B795

Haugh
of Urr

B794

Urr Water

3

Glenlochar

Townhead
of Greenlaw

Hillowton

A745

Edingham

od

Threave
Castle

Castle Douglas

Little
Knox

Dalbeattie

A75

Threave Garden

Carlingwark
Loch

A711

A710

B793

8

dge of Dee

Rhonehouse

Gelston

B736

Barlochan

Palnackie

Barnbarroch

Fair

River Dee

B711

10

Craigley

Airieland

343
SCREEL
HILL

Orchardton
Tower

Kippford
or Scaur

10

Mote of
Mark

Drumburn

4

Colvend

Portl

gford

Tongland

B727

390
BENGAIRN

East Stewartry
Coast

Rockcliffe

Castlehill Point

Little Sypland

Whinnie
Liggate

Auchencairn

Auchencairn
Bay

Heston Island

dbright
ife

Culnaightrie

18

Balcary

Balcary Point

hill

Dundrennan

Rascarrel

A711

Orroland

Dundrennan
Abbey

5

Netherlaw

Abbey Head

G

H

6

Kirkcudbright 181 F4

This pretty harbour town (the name is pronounced 'Kirkoobree') lies southwest of Castle Douglas. The street plan is medieval, the gap-toothed castle ruin at its heart 16th-century, and its fame as a centre for painters dates from 1901, when artist and 'Glasgow Boy' E A Hornel settled here. Broughton House, on the High Street, where he lived and worked, is now a gallery and museum. More paintings by Kirkcudbright artists can be seen in the Tolbooth Art Centre. Other items, including book illustrations and pottery, are on show at the Stewartry Museum on St Mary Street.

Bruce's Stone, Glen Trool

Logan Botanic Garden 179 H5

This frost-free corner of the Rhinns of Galloway, in the far southwest, serves as an annexe for tender plants from the Royal Botanic Garden in Edinburgh, and is a plant-lover's delight. Exotic species from the southern hemisphere thrive on the acid soil, including palm-like cordyline, trachycarpus and the ever-popular tree ferns (Dicksonia). Feature plants include Himalayan poppies and South African proteas, and there are bright floral displays throughout summer in the walled garden. The rhododendrons and primulas of the woodland garden are perhaps more familiar to local gardeners.

Orchardton Tower 181 H4

This charming little tower house dates from the mid-15th century. It is, uniquely in Scotland, circular in plan. A door at ground level leads to a cellar with a vaulted roof, while a spiral staircase leads to the parapet from where there are fine views.

Threave Garden 181 G3

Threave is the National Trust for Scotland's investment in the future – a teaching garden, where horticulturalists come to learn and try out new ideas. Glorious in its own right, it offers a mixture of established splendours such as a vast walled garden, alongside less formal, more experimental areas. Threave House dates from 1872, and was the heart of an estate that today covers 480ha of prime countryside. In early spring there are around 200 different varieties daffodil in bloom while the herbaceous borders are a delight in summer.

Whithorn Story 180 D5

It took an Act of Parliament in 1581 to stop the pilgrims from flocking to Whithorn. Royals and commoners were drawn to the shrine of St Ninian, Scotland's first Christian missionary, who built a stone church here in AD 397. He followed it with a priory, but the existing ruins are from a later, 12th-century construction. Excavations have turned up stone carvings and smaller, more personal treasures left by the pilgrims; ongoing archaeological work is uncovering the remains of a 5th-century village. The centre includes audio-visual presentations and access to the main sites.

Wigtown 180 D4

Wigtown brands itself as Scotland's Book Town. The neat buildings in black and white that line the broad main street have an upbeat air, and more than 20 specialist and antiquarian booksellers and many other related outlets offer a wide choice for literary browsers.

16th-century chapter house

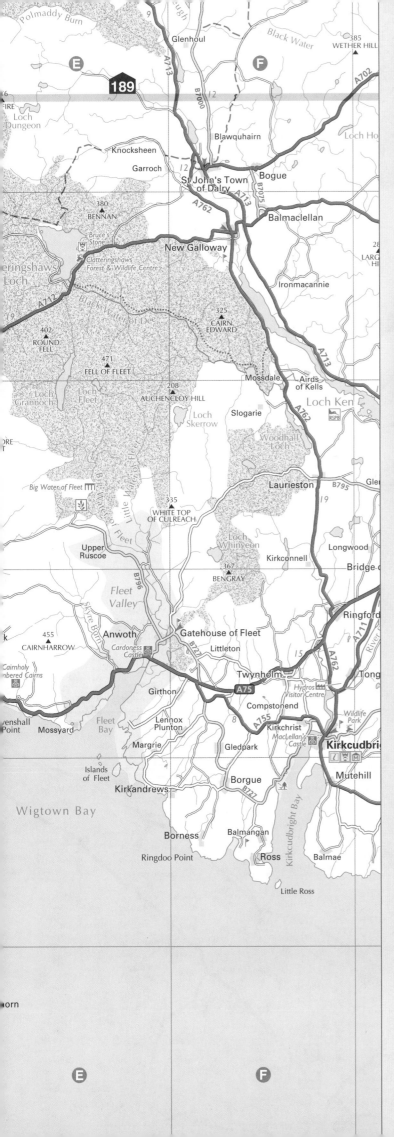

E

GALLOWAY & THE RHINNS

The hilly, hammerhead peninsula at the end of the Solway coast known as the Rhinns of Galloway is a peaceful region with stunning scenery and a mild climate encouraging tender plants to flourish. To the east are the Galloway Hills an area of open moorland, vast tracts of forest, wilderness, lochs and picnic spots.

The pretty artists' town of Kirkcudbright is best explored on foot

Castle Kennedy Gardens
180 A3
Landscaped with terraces and avenues, these stunning 18th-century gardens are uniquely situated between two lochs. As well as rhododendrons, rare plants, a walled garden and the romantic ruined Castle Kennedy, there is a tearoom, gift shop, plant centre and seasonal children's activities.

Gem Rock Museum 180 D4
The Gem Rock at Creetown is the leading independent museum of its kind in the UK, and is renowned worldwide. Crystals, gemstones, minerals, jewellery and fossils, the Gem Rock displays some of the most breathtaking examples of nature's wonders. Fire in the Stones, an audio-visual presentation, illustrates the creation of the stones and how they are turned into beautiful works of art.

Glenluce Abbey 180 A4
The abbey, founded for the Cistercians in 1192 by Roland, Earl of Galloway, stand in a beautiful setting overlooking Luce Bay. The remains include a vaulted chapter house. An exhibition displays objects found at the abbey.

Glen Trool 180 C2
The Galloway Forest Park covers around 76,000ha of wild moorland and loch. While much of it is given over to commercial conifer forestry, Glen Trool remains an area of outstanding natural scenic beauty, with semi-ancient oak woodland that is seen at its best in the autumn. From the visitor centre east of Glentrool village, walking and bicycling routes lead through the park, and the Southern Upland Way long-distance path also passes nearby. Bruce's Stone, at the end of the road by the loch, commemorates a victory by Robert Bruce against an English force in 1307. Don't miss the panoramic view from the Bruce Memorial car park at the end of the road.

Glenwhan Gardens 180 A4
Enjoying spectacular views over the Mull of Galloway and Luce Bay, Glenwhan is a beautiful 5ha garden set on a hillside. There are two lakes, alpines, scree plants, heathers, conifers, roses, woodland walks and fascinating garden sculpture.

The remains of Glenluce Abbey include a

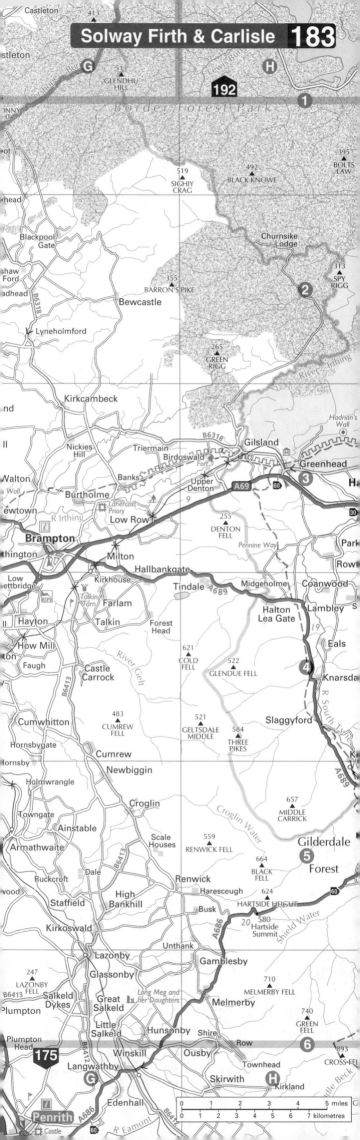

Castleton
413
G
513
GLENDHU
HILL
Tewis Burn
H
192
1

Liddesdale Burn

stleton

Border Forest Park

ONNY
II
head

395
BOLTS
LAW
519
SIGHTY
CRAG
492
BLACK KNOWE
313
SPY
RIGG

Blackpool
Gate
shaw
Ford
adhead
B6318

Churnsike
Lodge

355
BARRON'S PIKE
Bewcastle
2

River Irthing

nd
265
GREEN
RIGG

Kirkcambeck
B6318
Hadrian's
Wall

II
Nickies
Hill
Triermain
Gilsland
M
Walton
Birdoswald
Fort
Greenhead
H
Banks
Upper
Denton
A69
60
3
Wall
ewtown
Burtholme
Low Row
Lanercost
Priory
9
30
R Irthing
255
DENTON
FELL
Pennine Way
Park
Row
Brampton
Z
Milton
Hallbankgate
thington
Low
ettbridge
Kirkhouse
Tindale
A689
Midgeholme
Coanwood
7
RSPB
Farlam
Halton
Lea Gate
Lambley
Hayton
Talkin
Talkin
Tarn
Forest
Head
19
Eals
How Mill
621
COLD
FELL
4
ton
Faugh
Castle
Carrock
River Gelt
522
GLENDUE FELL
Knarsda
B6413
483
CUMREW
FELL
521
GELTSDALE
MIDDLE
584
THREE
PIKES
Slaggyford
R South Tyne
Cumwhitton
Hornsbygate
Cumrew
Newbiggin
A689
ornsby
Holmwrangle
Croglin
657
MIDDLE
CARRICK
K
Towngate
Croglin Water
Gilderdale
Ainstable
Scale
Houses
559
RENWICK FELL
5
Armathwaite
B6413
Renwick
664
BLACK
FELL
Forest
Ruckcroft
Dale
Haresceugh
624
60
wood
Staffield
High
Bankhill
Busk
HARTSIDE HEIGHT
Shield Water
Kirkoswald
A686
20
580
Hartside
Summit
Unthank
Gamblesby
710
MELMERBY FELL
247
LAZONBY
FELL
Lazonby
B6413
Glassonby
Melmerby
B6413
Long Meg and
her Daughters
Salkeld
Dykes
Great
Salkeld
740
GREEN
FELL
Plumpton
Little
Salkeld
Hunsonby
Shire
Row
6
175
Winskill
Ousby
893
CROSS FE
Plumpton
Head
Langwathby
G
Townhead
H
Skirwith
Kirkland
Edenhall
Middle Beck
Penrith
Z
A686
60
Castle
R Eamont

0	1	2	3	4	5 miles
0	1	2	3	4	5	6	7 kilometres

Hutton-in-the-Forest 182 F6

This beautiful house, set in woods that were once part of the medieval forest of Inglewood, has been in the ownership of the Inglewood family since 1605. The house consists of a 14th-century pele tower with later additions, and contains a fine collection of furniture, portraits, tapestries and china, a 17th-century gallery and cupid staircase. The walled garden has a large collection of herbaceous plants, and there are 19th-century topiary terraces, a 17th-century dovecote and a woodland walk with impressive specimen trees.

National bard Robert Burns

Lanercost Priory 183 G3

Standing close to Hadrian's Wall are the atmospheric ruins of this Augustinian priory founded in the 12th-century. Information panels detail the history of the priory and its later conversion to a grand mansion.

Maryport 182 B6

This is an attractive coastal town with Victorian docks and a modern marina. The Lake District Coast Aquarium, on the quayside, is one of the best places to see some of the varied marine life of the Irish Sea. The Maritime Museum tells the story of the docks and also houses an information centre.

New Abbey 182 A3

Sweetheart Abbey is a most romantic name, and the picturesque ruins which dominate this unassuming little Galloway community tell a sad tale of devotion. The Cistercian abbey was founded in the 13th century by Devorgilla, Lady of Galloway and wife of John Balliol. After he died she carried his heart in a casket with her for the next 20 years, and then was buried with it before the high altar of the abbey church here. Nearby, New Abbey Corn Mill is an 18th-century water-powered mill for grinding oatmeal, preserved in full working order. Shambellie House Museum of Costume is set in a mid-19th century house, typical of its period. Rooms are brought to life by tableaux of clothed figures, covering different periods. The main location for the National Museum of Scotland's costume collection, the museum is a must for fashion enthusiasts.

Ruthwell 182 C3

Ruthwell Savings Banks Museum is housed in the building where savings banks first began. The museum traces their growth and development from 1810 up to the present day, and portrays the life of Dr Henry Duncan, father of savings banks, and restorer of the Ruthwell Cross. The carved cross, now in a specially built apse in the parish church, dates from the 7th or 8th centuries. Two faces show scenes from the Life of Christ; the others show scroll work, and parts of an ancient poem in Runic characters.

Thomas Carlyle's Birthplace 182 C2

Thomas Carlyle, the great social historian, was born in this house in 1795. Three rooms contain many of his personal possessions and provide an insight into life in a 19th-century Scottish town.

d and Lady Inglewood, is surrounded by magnificent woodland

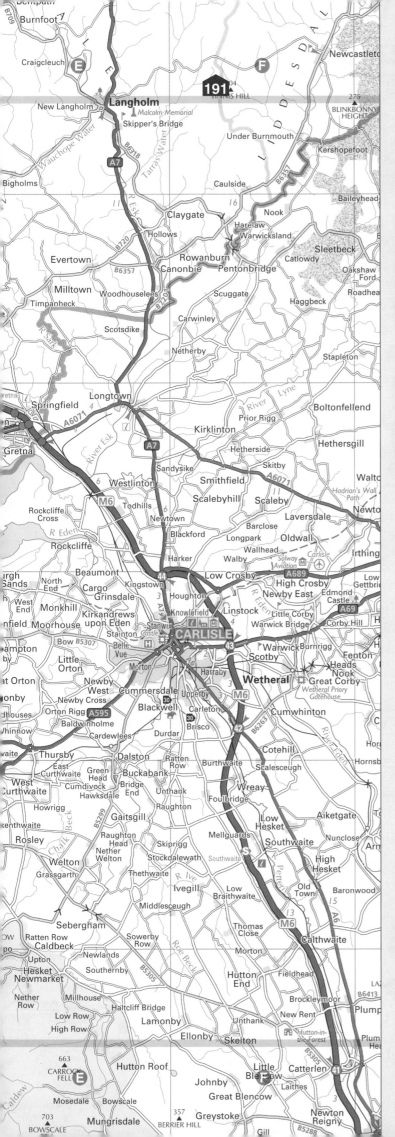

SOLWAY FIRTH & CARLISLE

The Solway coast is one of Scotland's best-kept secrets with sandy beaches, rocky coves and clifftop paths. Inland is the lowland farm country around Dumfries, famous for its connections with the celebrated Scottish poet Robert Burns. To the east is the border town of Carlisle and further east again the start of Hadrian's Wall.

The south corner tower of triangular Caerlaverock Castle

Birdoswald 183 H3

A visitor centre at Birdoswald introduces you to Hadrian's Wall and the Roman Fort. This unique section of Hadrian's Wall overlooks the Irthing Gorge, and is the only point along the Wall where all the components of the Roman frontier system can be found together. The visitor centre isn't just about the Romans though, it also covers the border raids in the Middle Ages, and recent archaeological discoveries.

Caerlaverock Castle 182 B3

The remains of three huge round towers mark out the corners of this ruined, triangular castle of pink sandstone, once the fortress home of the Maxwell family. It is set close to the Solway shore some 8 miles southeast of Dumfries; two sides were protected by an arm of the sea, while the third had a moat, earthworks and a mighty gatehouse to ward off attack. The castle dates from the 13th century, and saw plenty of action before extensive rebuilding in the 15th. In the 1630s it was remodelled for more comfortable living, and an outstanding feature from this time is the ornately carved façade within.

Dumfries 182 A2

Dumfries is in an idyllic setting on the broad tree-lined banks of the River Nith. Drop into the Robert Burns Centre, in the town's 18th-century watermill, which tells the story of Burns' last years spent in the busy streets and lively atmosphere of Dumfries in the 1790s. Robert Burns House, where he died in 1796, displays many of his original letters and manuscripts. Old Bridge House Museum built in 1660 is the oldest house in Dumfries, while the

exhibitions in Dumfries Museum & Camera Obscura, situated in and around the 18th-century windmill tower, trace the history of the people and landscape of Dumfries & Galloway. You'll find the Camera Obscura on the top floor of the windmill tower.

Gretna Green 183 E3

Gretna Green's fame rests on its location on the border, and its historical association with runaway lovers from England. Several sites claim to be the original location where, under Scottish law, marriages could simply be declared in front of witnesses – and that was that.

Hutton-in-the-Forest, the historic home o

A replica bus transports visitors around Beamish Open Air Museum

houses an art gallery and library. Hexham makes a good base for exploring the most impressive parts of Hadrian's Wall.

Killhope Lead Mining Centre 184 B5

Equipped with hard hats and lamps, visitors can explore the working conditions of Victorian lead miners. The lead mine and the 19th-century crushing mill have been restored to look as they would have done in the 1870s, and the waterwheel has been restored to working order.

Souter Lighthouse 185 H3

When it opened in 1871, Souter was the most advanced lighthouse in the world, and warned shipping off the notorious rocks in the river approaches of the Tyne and Wear. Painted red and white and standing at over 45m high, it is a dramatic building. Hands-on displays and volunteers help bring it to life and visitors can explore the lighthouse including the engine room and lighthouse keeper's cottage.

Sunderland 185 G4

Sunderland Museum and Winter Gardens has wide-ranging displays and many hands-on exhibits covering the archaeology and geology of Sunderland, the coal mines and shipyards of the area and the spectacular glass and pottery made on Wearside. Other galleries display works by L S Lowry and wildlife from all corners of the globe. The Winter Gardens are an horticultural wonderland where the exotic plants from around the world can be seen in a spectacular glass and steel rotunda. Housed in a striking modern building, the National Glass Centre celebrates the unique material and explains its history.

Tynemouth 185 G3

From its position overlooking one of the area's prettiest beaches, Blue Reef Aquarium is home to a dazzling variety of creatures. Visitors can enjoy close encounters with seals, seahorses, sharks, stingrays, giant octopuses, frogs, otters and hundreds of other aquatic life forms on a journey through a transparent underwater tunnel. Set on a steep headland is Tynemouth Priory & Castle, both a fortress and a religious site.

Washington 185 F4

In a parkland setting, on the north bank of the River Wear, Washington Wetland Centre is where you'll find a wonderful collection of exotic wildfowl from all over the world. Sitting next to Washington's Holy Trinity Church, Washington Old Hall was the home of George Washington's ancestors from 1183 to 1613. The house is filled with period furniture, and contains displays on George Washington and the history of American Independence.

Angel of the North, the landmark steel statue which stands on a hilltop above Gateshead, was designed by sculptor Antony Gormley

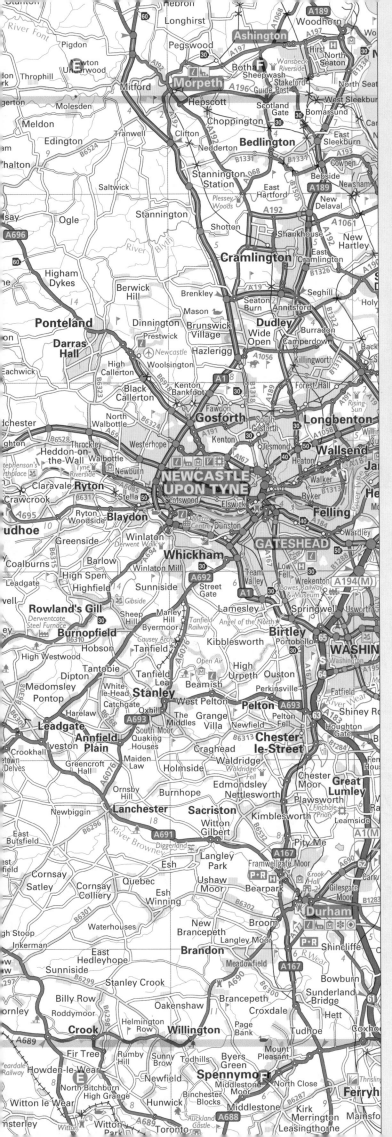

HADRIAN'S WALL & TYNESIDE

On the border between England and Scotland, where warfare was endemic until the mid-18th century, this beautiful landscape and its sparse settlements bear the marks of continual violence. Most striking of all is Hadrian's Wall marking the northern boundary of the Roman Empire.

Hadrian's Wall snakes its way across the countryside

Beamish Open Air Museum
184 F4

A painstaking reconstruction of a northern town from a bygone era, full of buildings transported from other places, Beamish is filled with details of past times. Its aim is to tell the story of the people of northeast England between 1825 and 1913. Costumed staff welcome visitors to shops stocked with period goods, and to the pub and newspaper office. You can take part in a lesson in the village school, ride on an electric tram, visit the dentist's surgery, catch a replica 1825 steam train and visit a factory.

Belsay Hall, Castle & Gardens
184 D2

The beautiful, austerely classical Greek Revival Hall, built from stone from its own quarries, was designed by Sir Charles Monck in 1807. The magnificent 12ha gardens include formal terraces, long borders, a winter garden and a spectacular quarry garden where a series of ravines house many rare and exotic plants. Within the grounds are the ruins of a 14th-century castle.

Finchale Priory 185 F5

Dating from the 13th century, these beautiful priory ruins are in a wooded setting beside the River Wear. It can be reached from Durham via a pleasant riverside and woodland walk.

Hadrian's Wall 184–5

Hadrian's Wall was built between AD 122 and 128 on the orders of the Roman emperor Hadrian to control trade over the border. The B6318 road, which runs parallel to it for part of the way, follows the line of the Roman military way that served the regular forts and observation turrets along the Wall. Today it is a World Heritage Site.

In many places the Wall has long since disappeared, but there are well-preserved sections between Chollerford (C2) in the east and Haltwhistle (A3) in the west. At Housesteads Roman Fort (A3) the latrines have seating for 12 soldiers and a water channel for sponges (used in place of toilet paper). Close to here is Vindolanda Fort (A3), with reconstructions of part of the Wall and buildings, and a museum displaying local excavations. The Mithraic Temple at Carrawburgh (B2) has the remains of a place of worship for the soldiers, dedicated to the god Mithras. Chesters Fort (C3) was a cavalry fort with the remains of the bathhouse (look for the niches where clothes were placed), headquarters and barracks. Corbridge Roman Site (C3) is a former Roman garrison town and was the supply base for the Roman invasion of Scotland in AD 80, with some well-preserved granaries. For an idea of Roman-style bathing, visit the reconstructed bathhouse at Hadrian's outpost, Segedunum Roman Fort at Wallsend (F3). A 35m tower gives a superb view of the remains of the fort itself. At South Shields, Arbeia Roman Fort (G3) has a reconstructed gatehouse and re-created scenes of camp life. At the west end of the Wall, the finest monument is Birdoswald Fort (183 H3).

Hexham 184 C3

Hexham, a market town on the River Tyne, is dominated by its abbey church. Begun by St Wilfrid in about AD 675, it contains the crypt built by the saint, but otherwise dates mostly from 1180 to 1250. Moot Hall, near the marketplace, is a miniature castle pierced by a gateway, erected in the late 14th century as the entrance to barracks for the local garrison; it now

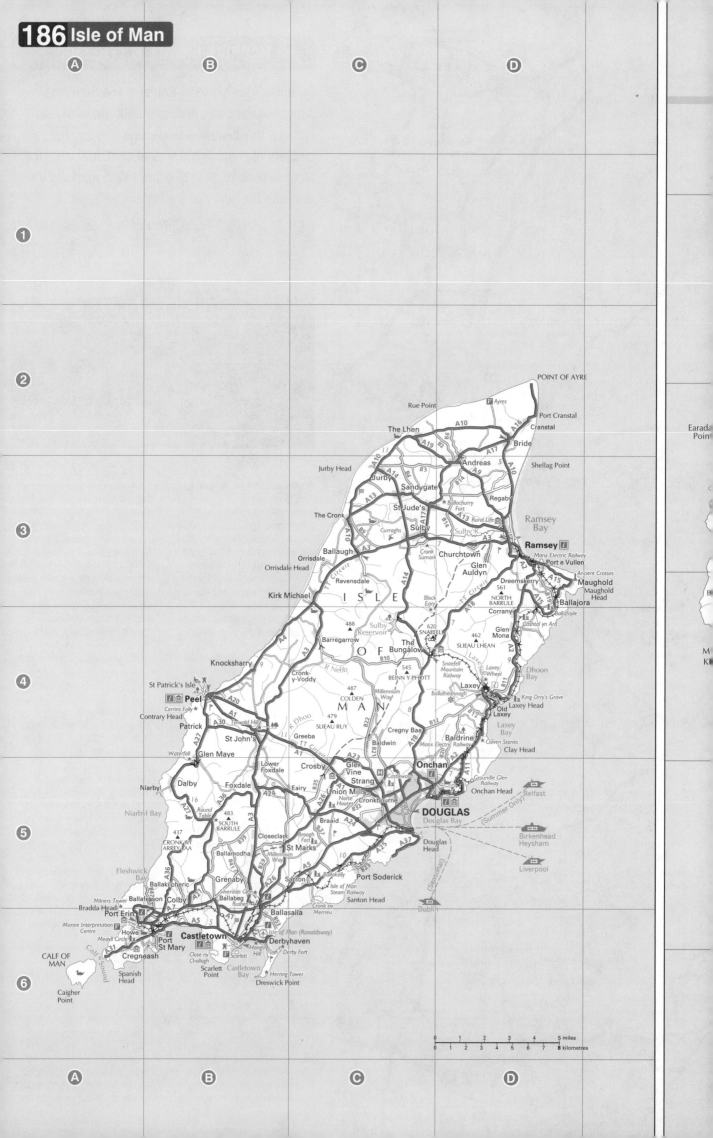

POINT OF AYRE

Rue Point

A10

The Lhen
Port Cranstal
A16
Cranstal

A19
B6
Bride
B3
Andreas
A9
Shellag Point

Jurby Head
A14
A17
A10
Jurby
Sandygate
A13
B14
Ballachurry
Fort
St Jude's
A13
Rural Life
Ramsey
Bay

The Cronk
A17
Sulby
Sulby R.
A3
Ramsey
Manx Electric Railway
A9
Churchtown
Port e Vullen

Ballaugh
A3
Cronk
Sumark
Glen
Auldyn
A15
Ancient Crosses
Orrisdale
A14
561
Dreemskerry
Maughold
Orrisdale Head
TT Circuit
Block
Eary
A18
NORTH
BARRULE
Maughold
Head
Ravensdale
ISLE
TT Circuit
Corrany
Ballafayle
Ballajora

Kirk Michael
488
Sulby
Reservoir
620
SNAEFELL
462
Glen
Mona
Cashtal yn Ard

Barregarrow
OF
The
Bungalow
SLIEAU LHEAN
B10
Laxey
A2

Knocksharry
R. Neb
545
BEINN Y PHOTT
Snaefell
Mountain
Railway
Laxey
Wheel
Dhoon
Bay

St Patrick's Isle
MAN
Cronk-
y-Voddy
487
COLDEN
Millennium
Way
Ballaheannagh
Laxey
King Orry's Grave

Peel
A20
A3
R. Dhoo
479
Old
Laxey
Laxey Head
Contrary Head
Corrins Folly
A1
SLIEAU RUY
B22
Cregny Baa
Laxey
Bay

Patrick
A30
Tynwald Hill
A18
Baldrine
Cloven Stones
Greeba
A1
Baldwin
Manx Electric Railway
Clay Head

Waterfall
St John's
TT Circuit
A23
Glen
Vine
Onchan
A11

Glen Maye
Lower
Foxdale
Crosby
Strang
Castletown

Niarbyl
Dalby
Foxdale
A24
Eairy
B35
Union Mills
Norse
Houses
B32
Cronkbourne
Groundle Glen
Railway
Onchan Head
Belfast

Niarbyl Bay
A27
Round
Table
483
SOUTH
BARRULE
Braaid
A24
DOUGLAS
Douglas Bay

437
CRONK NY
ARREY LAA
Closeclark
Brough
Fort
B37
A25
A37
Douglas
Head
Birkenhead
Heysham

Fleshwick
Bay
A36
St Marks
Millennium
Way
A5
10
Liverpool

Ballamodha
B30
Ballakelly
Santon
Port Soderick

Ballakilpheric
A3
Grenaby
A26
Santon
Isle of
Man
Steam Railway
Santon Head

Bradda Head
Milners Tower
Ballafesson
Colby
Ballabeg
Rushen
Ballasalla
Cronk ny
Merriu

Marine Interpretation
Centre
Port Erin
A5
A47
Isle of Man (Ronaldsway)
Dublin

CALF OF
MAN
Howe
Meayll Circle
Port
St Mary
Castletown
Derbyhaven
Derby Fort

Cregneash
A31
A7
Close ny
Chollagh
Hango
Hill
Castletown
Bay
Herring Tower

Spanish
Head
Scarlett
Point
Scarlett
Dreswick Point

Caigher
Point

Earada
Point

M
K

0 1 2 3 4 5 miles
0 1 2 3 4 5 6 7 8 kilometres

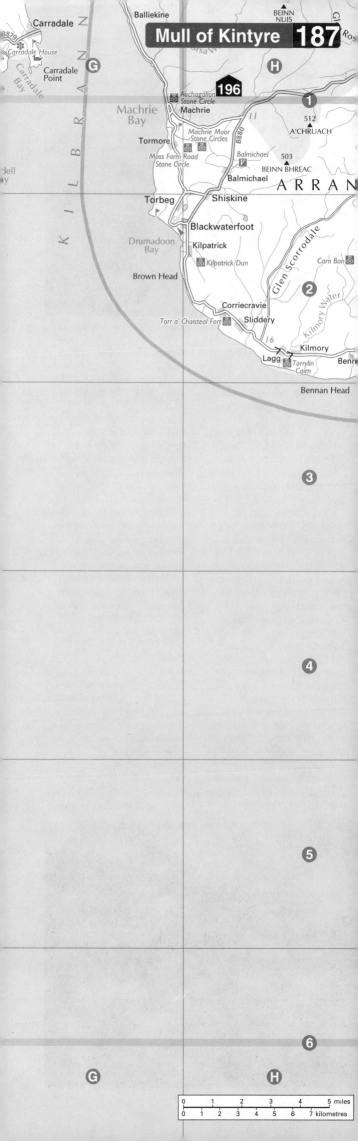

Carradale

Balliekine

BEINN
NUIS

Glen Ros

3879

Carradale House

Carradale
Point

G

H

196

Auchagallon
Stone Circle

Machrie

1

Machrie
Bay

Tormore

Machrie Moor
Stone Circles

512
A'CHRUACH

Moss Farm Road
Stone Circle

Balmichael

503
BEINN BHREAC

Balmichael

A R R A N

Torbeg

Shiskine

Blackwaterfoot

Drumadoon
Bay

Kilpatrick

Kilpatrick Dun

Glen Scorrodale

Carn Ban

2

Brown Head

Corriecravie

Kilmory Water

Torr a' Chaisteal Fort

Sliddery

16

Lagg

Kilmory

Torrylin
Cairn

Benn

Bennan Head

3

4

5

6

G

H

| 0 | 1 | 2 | 3 | 4 | 5 miles |
| 0 | 1 | 2 | 3 | 4 | 5 | 6 | 7 kilometres |

The Snaefell Mountain Railway, Isle of Man, runs from Laxey to Snaefell's peak

Park (C3) where a large variety of animals and birds can be seen. A walk-through enclosure lets visitors explore the world of wildlife, including local habitats along the Curraghs nature trail.

Peel (B4), on the west coast, makes a characterful base for a stay on the island. Peel Castle, a great natural fortress with an imposing curtain wall, is set majestically on St Patrick's Isle at the mouth of the harbour.

At the Cregneash Village Folk Museum (A6) visit the village information centre where you can experience what life was really like in a Manx crofting village during the early 19th century. Visitors can stroll around this attractive village and see Manx Four-horned Loghtan sheep grazing along with other animals from the village farm.

Castletown (B6) has one of Europe's best-preserved medieval castles in Castle Rushen, a limestone fortress rising out of the heart of the old capital of the island. Set at the mouth of the harbour is the Nautical Museum, which portrays Manx maritime life and trade in the days of sail. At the Old House of Keys visitors can learn about the long and often turbulent history of Manx politics and are invited to participate in a lively debate with interactive Members of Tynwald, the Manx parliament.

Kintyre 187

Despite swift, modern access down its western side provided by the A83, Kintyre still has the feeling of a world apart. The eastern road is much slower, allowing time to enjoy the views to the island of Arran. Campbeltown (F2), at the southern end of Kintyre, remains an important service centre for the farming community of the peninsula. Further south is Southend (E4), a small village with sandy beaches and a golf course. The Mull of Kintyre (E4) is the lumpy southern tip, looking across to Northern Ireland, barely 12 miles away. Continue round the coast and you come to Machrihanish Bay (E2), a mecca for watersports enthusiasts such as surfers and kayakers as well as holidaymakers and locals, and another golf course.

Machrie 187 G1

Across Kilbrannan Sound lies the southwestern tip of Arran where the legacy of much earlier settlers may be seen in the stone circles on Machrie Moor (H1). The standing stones date from the Bronze Age but there is also evidence that the site was previously occupied in the neolithic era.

Close by you'll find the Arran Butterfly Farm Park at Tormore (G1) and the Balmichael Visitor Centre (H1).

e harbour

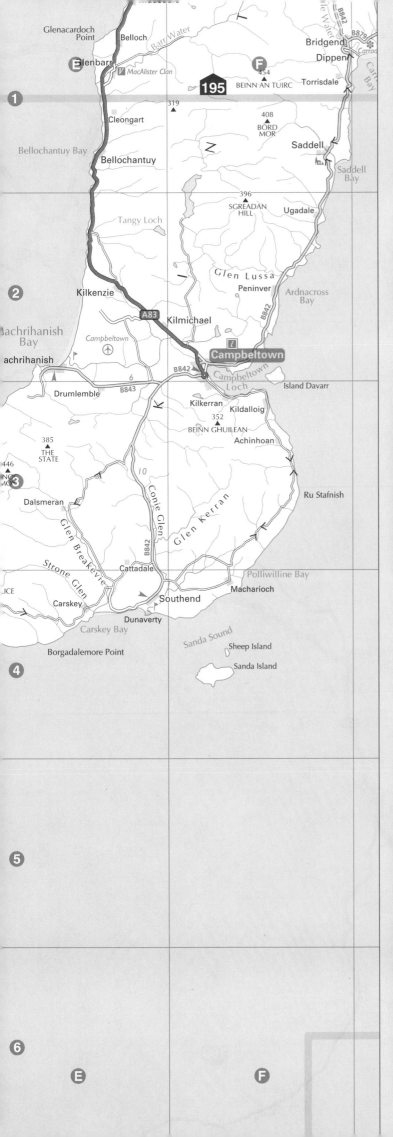

Best known perhaps for the annual motorcycle races – the Isle of Man Tourist Trophy (TT), held on various courses for almost a century – the Isle of Man is a curious fragment of the British Isles. The Mull of Kintyre is a landscape of hills, lochs, rivers and forests on the extreme west coast of Scotland, and across the Kilbrannan Sound lies Arran with its mysterious stone circles.

Three red sandstone pillars on Machrie Moor, Arran

Isle of Man 186

Measuring 33 miles by 13 miles and in the Irish Sea off the northwest coast of England, the landscape has much to interest the visitor: sandy beaches, dramatic moors and mountains, and a generous smattering of Celtic crosses, standing stones and ancient burial grounds. The capital, Douglas (D5), has a Victorian waterfront, horse-drawn trams and the Manx Museum, the Island's treasure house, where the Story of Man provides an exciting introduction to the island's history. Galleries depict natural history, archaeology and the social development of the Island. The

Isle of Man Steam Railway runs from Douglas to Port Erin (A6) in the south, passing through magnificent countryside and the Manx Electric Railway also runs from here to Ramsey (D3).

Built in 1854, the Great Laxey Wheel (D4), designed to pump water from the lead and zinc mines is a masterpiece of Victorian engineering. Snaefell (C4) is the Isle of Man's highest mountain, and running up it, from Laxey (D4), is Snaefell Mountain Railway, Britain's oldest working mountain railway. A miniature railway runs on Sundays.

Adjacent to the reserve area of the Ballaugh Curraghs is Curraghs Wild Life

The pretty fishing port of Tarbert, on Kintyre, has rows of colour-washed cottages fac

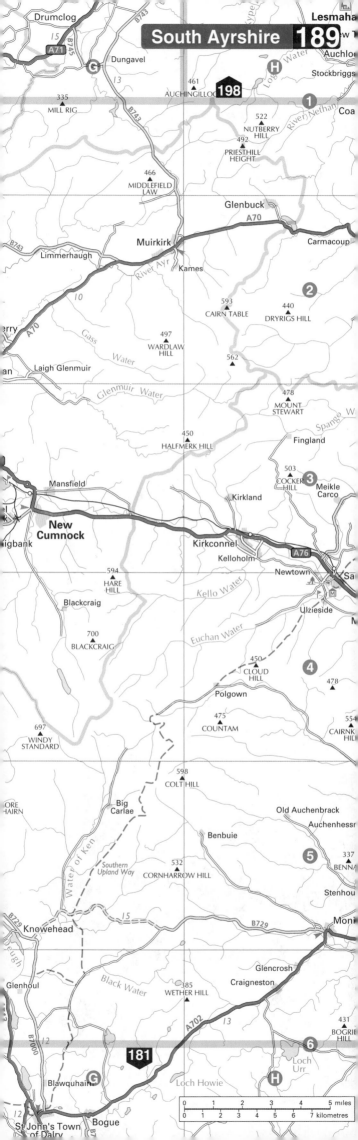

Drumclog

Lesmaha

New

Auchlo

B743

A71

15

Dungavel

G

198

Stockbriggs

461

AUCHINGILLOC

1

Coa

335

MILL RIG

13

B743

522

NUTBERRY
HILL

492

PRIESTHILL
HEIGHT

River Nethan

466

MIDDLEFIELD
LAW

Glenbuck

A70

Carmacoup

Muirkirk

Limmerhaugh

River Ayr

Kames

2

593

CAIRN TABLE

440

DRYRIGS HILL

B743

10

erry

A70

Gass

497

WARDLAW
HILL

562

Water

Laigh Glenmuir

Glenmuir Water

478

MOUNT
STEWART

Spango W

an

450

HALFMERK HILL

Fingland

Mansfield

503

COCKER
HILL

3

Meikle
Carco

Kirkland

**New
Cumnock**

Kirkconnel

A76

igbank

Kelloholm

Newtown

Sa

594

HARE
HILL

M

Kello Water

Ulzieside

Blackcraig

Euchan Water

M

700

BLACKCRAIG

450

CLOUD
HILL

4

478

697

WINDY
STANDARD

Polgown

475

COUNTAM

554

CAIRNK

598

COLT HILL

ORE
HAIRN

Big
Carlae

Old Auchenbrack

Auchenhessr

Benbuie

5

337

BENNA

Water or Ken

Southern
Upland Way

532

CORNHARROW HILL

Stenhou

B729

15

B729

Mon

Knowehead

 leugh

Glencrosh

Craigneston

Glenhoul

Black Water

385

WETHER HILL

A702

13

431

BOGRII
HILL

B7000

12

6

181

Loch
Urr

G

Blawquhairn

Loch Howie

H

St John's Town
of Dalry

12

Bogue

B

| 0 | | 1 | | 2 | | 3 | | 4 | | 5 miles |
| 0 | 1 | 2 | 3 | 4 | 5 | 6 | 7 kilometres |

A life-size statue of Tam o'Shanter on display in the Statue House, Alloway

1777 to 1792 for the powerful Kennedy family, who had dominated this part of Ayrshire since the 12th century. Highlights include the graceful oval staircase and the Circular Saloon. The top floor was granted to General Eisenhower in 1945, for his lifetime, as a thanks from the people of Scotland for American help during World War II; there are photographs and mementoes of his visits.

Sanquhar 189 H4

Sanquhar Tolbooth Museum is housed as you might expect in the town's fine 18th-century tollbooth. It tells the story of the mines and miners of the area, its earliest inhabitants, native and Roman, the history and customs of the Royal Burgh of Sanquhar and local traditions.

Souter Johnnie's Cottage
188 C4

'Souter' means cobbler and the village cobbler who lived in this 18th-century cottage was the inspiration for Burns' character Souter Johnnie, in his ballad

Tam o'Shanter. The cottage is now a Burns museum and life-size stone figures of the poet's characters can be seen in the restored ale house in the cottage garden.

The Burns Memorial in Alloway

setting surrounded by verdant parkland

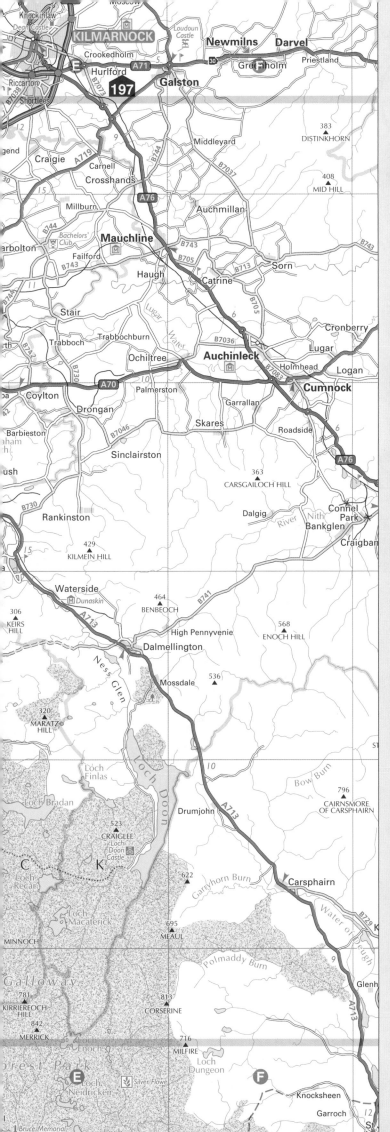

SOUTH AYRSHIRE

This stretch of coastline is the playground for Glasgow and industrial southwest Scotland, with sandy beaches, first-class golf links and the promise of lively nightlife in the vibrant resort of Ayr. The undulating landscape of rich farmland is peppered with noble castles.

You'll need to book months ahead if you want to play a round at Royal Troon

Alloway 188 D3
Robert 'Rabbie' Burns is Scotland's most famous poet and songwriter, and his birthday (25 January) is celebrated worldwide at haggis suppers. He was born into poverty, in 1759, in a tiny cottage in Alloway. With the nearby museum and other buildings in the park opposite, it is the focus of the Burns National Heritage Park. *Tam o' Shanter* is a ballad telling the story of drunken Tam, making his way home on his mare, and spying on a party of witches. Sculptor James Thom created vivid statues, now housed in the Statue House, which bring the ballad characters to life. The Burns Monument is a venue for events, and there are views over his beloved Alloway from the roof. There's an audio-visual presentation at the Tam o' Shanter Experience, and you can see the stone bridge, the Auld Brig o' Doon, which featured in his poetry.

Bachelors' Club 189 E2
In this 17th-century thatched house, Robert Burns and his friends formed a debating club in 1780. Burns attended dancing lessons and was initiated into freemasonry here in 1781. The house is furnished in the style of the period.

Crossraguel Abbey 188 C4
Crossraguel Abbey is one of the best preserved and most interesting of the many abbey ruins across Scotland. The 13th-century Cluniac monastery was founded by Duncan, Earl of Carrick and the abbey church, abbot's house and an imposing castellated gatehouse can be seen.

Culzean Castle & Country Park 188 C3
Culzean (pronounced 'Cullane') is the National Trust for Scotland's most popular property. That's partly thanks to the surrounding country park, 228ha of wild gardens and leafy woodland riddled with trails. You can discover a walled garden, an aviary, a deer park and lots of follies dotted around the park. The golden stone castle, romantically set right at the edge of the cliffs, is handsome rather than beautiful, with baronial towers and a castellated roofline. It is reached via a bridge, and rises high above a terraced garden. Inside, is an 18th-century show home, the masterpiece of Scottish architect Robert Adam, who worked on it from

Culzean Castle is stately mansion in a clif

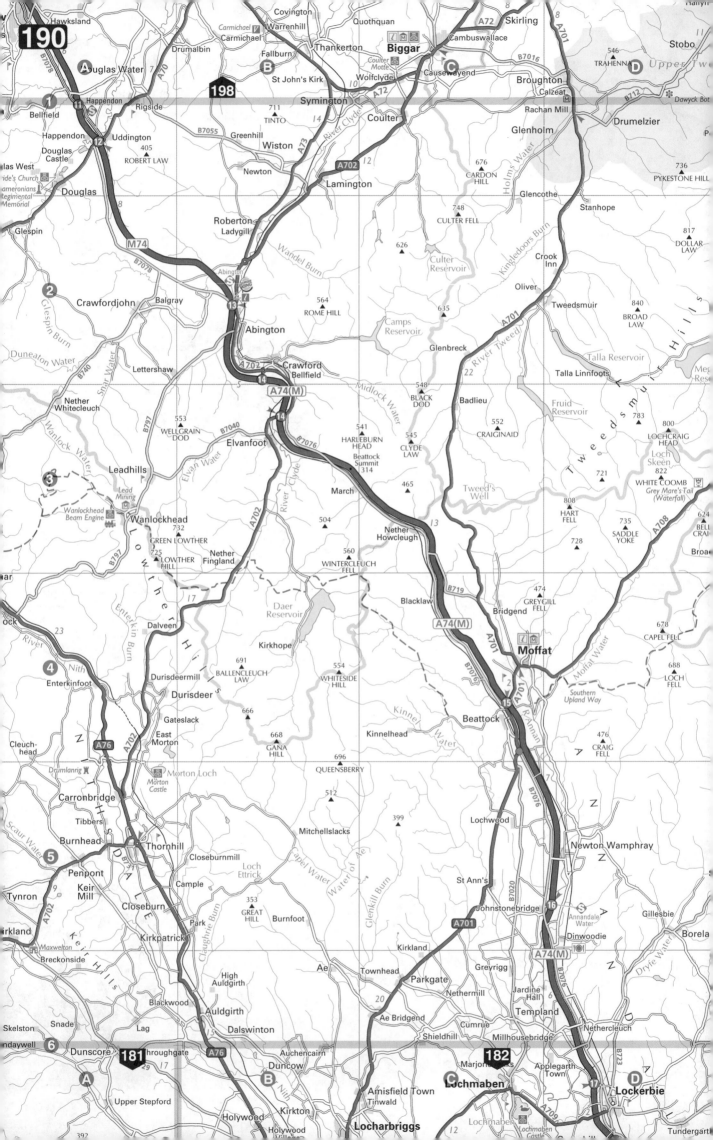

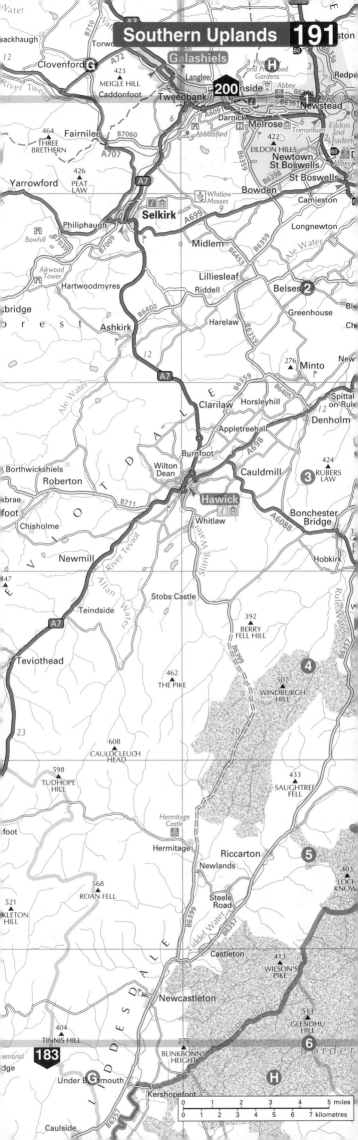

The imposing fortress of 14th-century Hermitage Castle

building in the 14th century and remodelled it to the massive and forbidding structure seen today.

Melrose 191 H1

The Romans built a massive fort here, by a bridge over the River Tweed, and called it Trimontium after the three peaks of the nearby Eildon Hills. There's little left to see, but the Three Hills Roman Heritage Centre in the middle of this compact Borders town sets it all into context. The more visible history of Melrose dates from 1136, when David I founded the pink sandstone abbey which lies just below the town centre. Severely battered by the English in the 14th century, it was later rebuilt, and then robbed of its stones by the Douglases who used them to build a house. Repairs in the 19th century were at the instigation of novelist Sir Walter Scott; the ruins are majestic and the stone carving outstanding – take time to look upward to identify saints, dragons, flowers and a pig playing the bagpipes. The burial spot of Robert the Bruce's heart is marked by an engraved inscription. Otherwise, Melrose is a genteel town to explore, with an excellent bookshop and Priorwood Gardens, dedicated to the art of growing flowers which can be dried.

Moffat 190 C4

A beautiful Victorian spa town, Moffat is set on the banks of the River Annan amid spectacular walking country. Station Park, with its colourful floral displays, boating lake and children's playground, is an ideal place to sit and watch the world go by. Moffat Woollen Mill in the town is famous for its knitwear and woven products.

Traquair 190 F1

Traquair, a beautiful old castle, started out as a royal hunting lodge at the time of James III – its 'modern' extensions were made in 1680, and today it presents a serene, grey-harled face to visitors. Part of Traquair's sense of mystery comes from its connections with the doomed Stewart cause: Mary, Queen of Scots stayed here in 1566 (her bed is now in the King's Room), and the famous Bear Gates have not been opened since 1745, when 'Bonnie' Prince Charlie last rode through. There are secret stairs to the hidden Priest's Room, and touching relics of a time when Catholics were persecuted in Scotland.

Wanlockhead 190 A3

Drive up to Wanlockhead, Scotland's highest village at 424.6m above sea level, set amid the windswept, heathery domes of the Lowther Hills, and you arrive in a different world. A heritage trail from the Museum of Lead Mining Visitor Centre leads around the settlement to show the workings of a community where generations of miners toiled to extract lead. You can wander into Straitsteps Cottages for a taste of family life here in 1740 and 1890, and discover the little lending library, founded in 1756. Best of all, you can follow a miner into the hillside, down the workings of an old lead mine, to see how the men really worked.

Wanlockhead has been a lead-mining town since the Roman times, and remains of 18th- and 19th-century workings can still be seen

The map contains the following place labels:

Kings Muir, Kirkton Manor, Kirkburn, Cardrona, Kailzie, A72, Walkerburn, Blackha, A72, B7062, Robert Small's Printing Works, Innerleithen, Traquair, River, 12, MINCHMUIR, 566, 742, DUN RIG, B709, 9, Yar, A708, 12, Yarrow, Yarrow Water, 696, BLACK LAW, Yarrow Feus, 629, Douglas Burn, Gordon Arms Hotel, Sundhope, 513, Ettrickbridg, B7009, E t t r i c k F o r, Cappercleuch, St Marys Loch, Gilmanscleuch, 15, Tibbie Shiels Inn, 6, 466, MOSSBRAE HEIGHT, pelhope, Loch of the Lowes, B709, Tushielaw Inn, Hellmoor Loch, 22, Hopehouse, B711, Redfordgreen, Borth, hill, Ettrickhill, Ettrick, Buccleuch, 16, Borthwickbrae, Burnfoot, 498, LAW KNEIS, Deanburnhaugh, C, Hoscote, 550, BLACK KNOWE, Borthwick Water, 423, CRIB LAW, 347, E, 443, THE PIKE, B709, 16, T, 417, Falnash, Caerlanrig, Te, White Esk, 476, STOCK HILL, Rae Burn, 23, Davington, Mosspaul Hotel, Johnstone, Samye Ling Monastery, 594, WISP HILL, Fort, Eskdalemuir, Clerkhill, Burnfoot, Megget Water, B723, E S, 492, BROAD HEAD, A7, Castle O'er, Effgill, 521, ARKLETON HILL, Georgefield, Arkleton, Kirkstile, 13, Bentpath, B709, 331, HART FELL, Burnfoot, Water of Milk, 450, CAULDKINERIG, Craigcleuch, E, L, New Langholm, Langholm, Malcolm Memorial, Skipper's Bridge, orrie, E, F, Wauchope Water, A7, B7068, 319, GRANGE FELL, hill, B7068, 252, Bigholms, Tarras Water, B6318

SOUTHERN UPLANDS

This area is characterised by rolling hills with medieval abbeys, stately homes and small stone-built towns tucked into their folds. Nestling at the foot of the Eildon Hills is Melrose, where the heart of Robert the Bruce is buried.

Melrose Abbey is a magnificent ruin with lavishly decorated masonry

Abbotsford 191 H1

Sir Walter Scott, best known for epic romantic poems such as *The Lady of the Lake*, and novels including *Ivanhoe*, built his home in 1812 on the banks of the River Tweed. It is filled with historical curiosities, some of which – like the condemned criminals' door from the old Tolbooth in Edinburgh – are built into the fabric of the house. View the great man's library, the gracious dining room with windows looking down to the river, and a bristling armoury, its walls covered with guns, knives and other paraphernalia. Don't miss Scott's collection of knick-knacks of the famous, including Rob Roy's purse, James IV's hunting bottle and a pocket book worked by Flora MacDonald.

Bowhill 191 G2

The house contains an outstanding collection of pictures, including works by Van Dyck, Canaletto, Reynolds, Gainsborough and Claude Lorraine. Memorabilia and relics of people such as Queen Victoria and Sir Walter Scott, and a restored Victorian kitchen add further interest. Outside, the wooded grounds are perfect for walking.

Drumlanrig 190 A5

This imposing 17th-century mansion is one of several homes of the Duke of Buccleuch, one of the wealthiest landowners in Scotland. Four square towers guard the corners, each topped by little turrets that give this castle its unmistakable skyline; the famous view is the one up the straight avenue as you approach. Inside, admire the wooden panelling and carved oak staircase; the art collection is internationally famous. Outside you can wander through the formal gardens, visit the craft workshops and forge, and rent a bicycle to explore the grounds.

Grey Mare's Tail 190 D3

The spectacular waterfall tumbles straight down for 61m, over the lip of a hanging valley, its source, Loch Skeen, invisible from below. Steep paths lead to the top of the falls (stout footwear essential), with a view of wild loch and upland scenery that makes the climb worthwhile.

Hermitage Castle 191 G5

The dark sandstone walls of this lonely Border fortress loom high above the marshy ground beside the river known as Hermitage Water. The lack of windows indicates that this was never a homely castle, rather a grim place for fighting and foul deeds. The Douglas family took over a simple rectangular

The Bear Gates of Traquair House

G
North Northumberland
Heritage Coast

H

1

Staple
Sound

Inner
Sound

eston

Seahouses

North Sunderland

Beadnell

Swinhoe

*Beadnell
Bay*

Newton-by-the-Sea

Brunton

Christon
Bank

Embleton

*Embleton &
Newton Links*

Dunstan
Steads

*Embleton
Bay*

Dunstanburgh Castle

Dunstan

Craster

Stamford

*Howick
Hall*

Howick

Cullernose Point

Littlehoughton

Longhoughton

Boulmer

Denwick

Hawkhill

Seaton Point

Lesbury

Bilton

Hipsburn

Alnmouth

Bilton
Banks

High
Buston

*Alnmouth
Bay*

A1068

Low
Buston

Birling

Warkworth Castle
& Hermitage

Warkworth

Gloster Hill

Amble

○ Coquet Island

Togston

Acklington

High
Hauxley

Radcliffe

Broomhill

South
Broomhill

60

East Chevington

Druridge Bay

Red Row

Chevington Drift

West
Chevington

Druridge

*Druridge
Bay*

Stobswood

Widdrington

*North Northumberland
Heritage Coast*

Widdrington
Station

Cresswell

A1068

Tritlington

Ulgham

Ellington

Linton

Lynemouth

ebron

nghirst

A189

Beacon Point

Woodhorn

Ashington

A197

Woodhorn Demesne

Pegswood

A197

Hirst

North
Seaton

Newbiggin-by-the-Sea

Bothal

*Wansbeck
Riverside*

Stakeford

Sheepwash

Morpeth

A196

Guide Post

North Seaton Colliery

Hepscott

West Sleekburn

Scotland
Gate

185

Choppington

Bomarsund

Cambois

Clifton

East
Sleekburn

North Blyth

H

Nedderton

G

Bedlington

Stannington
Station

A068

Bebside

A189

Newsham

0   1   2   3   4   5 miles
0 1 2 3 4 5 6 7 kilometres

2

4

5

6

Kielder Water 192 A5

Kielder Water, at 9 miles long, is the largest man-made lake in Europe, and the huge Kielder Forest – the largest wooded area in Britain – comes down to its shore. Tower Knowe Visitor Centre on the southern shore is a mine of information, and you can sail the water on the ferry from here. There is also an exhibition about the area's history, as well as shops, eating places and picnic sites – as there are at Leaplish Waterside Park and at Kielder Castle Visitor Centre at the northwest end.

Morpeth 193 G6

Morpeth's town centre has attractive alleys and courtyards, and some fine old buildings, including the Town Hall by Vanbrugh, rebuilt after a fire in the 19th century, and the Clock Tower in the middle of Oldgate, erected in the early 17th century. In the bridge chapel (the Chantry) with its tea room and Tourist Information Centre, more than 40 craftsmen display their work. St Mary's Church is where you will find the best example of stained glass in the whole of Northumberland, dating, like the church, from the 14th century.

Rothbury 193 E4

One of the main tourist centres of Northumberland, Rothbury is an attractive town, with stone buildings spreading outwards from an irregularly shaped green and a medieval bridge over the River Coquet. The town suffered from William Wallace's army in the 13th century, and proclaimed the Old Pretender as James III in the 18th, but since the 19th century it has developed as a holiday centre. The parish church is worth visiting for a glimpse of the font – its bowl dates

Dunstanburgh Castle

from 1664, but stands on part of the 9th-century Rothbury Cross, decorated with vigorous Celtic-inspired designs.

Wallington House & Gardens 193 E6

Wallington is the largest country estate protected by the National Trust. With 5,260ha that include the entire village of Cambo, the main attraction is the country house set among woods and gardens. There is a Pre-Raphaelite central hall, a small museum of curiosites and a display of dolls' houses. There are plenty of walks exploring the historic landscape, and a walled garden.

Warkworth Castle & Hermitage 193 G4

The magnificent eight-towered keep of Warkworth Castle stands on a hill high above the River Coquet, dominating all around it. A complex stronghold, it was home to the Percy family, which at times wielded more power in the North than the King himself.

Warkworth Castle crowns a hilltop above the River Coquet

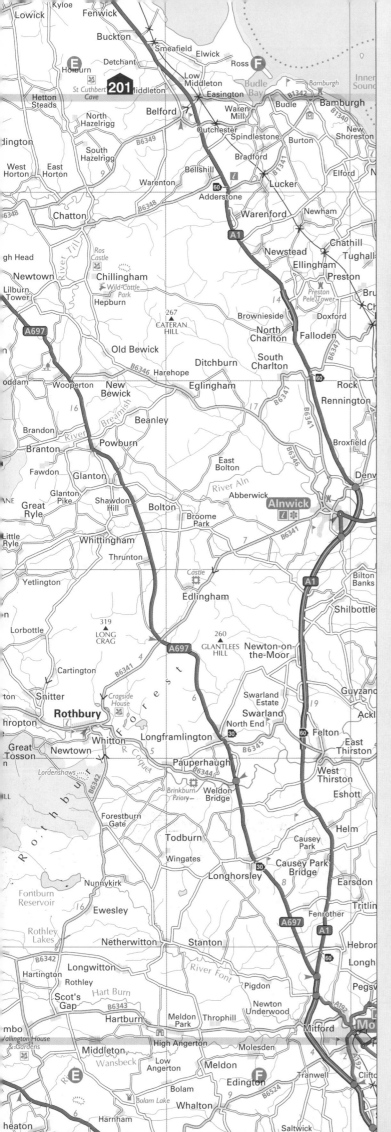

NORTHUMBRIA & THE BORDERS

Once the scene of constant border warfare between the Scots and the English, this area is now a haven of peace and tranquility. Much of the landscape is protected as part of the stunning Northumberland National Park. Amid all this are busy border towns, great medieval abbeys, castles and large country estates.

Kielder Water is surrounded by vast coniferous plantations and moorland

Alnwick 193 F3
The castle at Alnwick (pronounced 'Annick') has been the stronghold of the powerful Percy family since 1309. They went on to become the Earls of Northumberland, and then in the 18th century, the Dukes of Northumberland. The medieval interior glows with fine woodwork and marble and is filled with treasures, including paintings by Canaletto, Titian, Van Dyck and Andrea del Sarto, while the castle grounds are famous now as Hogwarts in the Harry Potter films. The town's cobbled market place bustles with life, and there are plenty of shops selling local produce, crafts and antiques.

Cragside House 193 E4
The aptly named Cragside was the home of Victorian inventor and landscape genius, Lord Armstrong, and sits on a rocky crag high above the Debden Burn. Crammed with ingenious gadgets it was the first house in the world to be lit by water-powered electricity. In the 1880s it also had hot and cold running water, central heating, fire alarms, telephones, and a passenger lift. In the estate there are 40 miles of footpaths to explore.

Dunstanburgh Castle 193 G2
You will have to walk to see Dunstanburgh Castle, as the ruin stands on an outcrop of rock on a lonely stretch of coast, one mile from the road. A particularly memorable approach is from the fishing village of Craster, from where the walk is about twice as far along the coast path. The site was fortified during the Iron Age, although the present structure was begun in 1314 by Thomas, Earl of Lancaster. Built to protect a small harbour, it was originally bounded on three sides by the sea (and by a moat on its fourth).

Jedburgh 192 A2
Jedburgh lies on the old main road into Scotland, and has witnessed many conflicts – in fact, so frequently was the town's castle attacked, rebuilt and attacked again that it was finally demolished in 1409. The broken tower and red sandstone walls of the ruined abbey still dominate the town. Jedburgh also has one of the great medieval Border abbeys (along with Kelso, Dryburgh, and Melrose), and the shepherding skills of the monks were the basis on which the town's weaving industry and wealth grew.

Jedforest Deer & Farm Park 192 A3
Birds of prey and deer are to be found on this working farm, 5 miles south of Jedburgh. Eagles, owls and hawks display daily. Look for the ranger-led activities on farming and the environment. For children there are indoor and outdoor play areas and special activities.

Kelso 192 B1
Kelso is one of the most elegant of the border towns. A poignant fragment is all that remains of Kelso Abbey, destroyed by the English in 1545. Nearby is the handsome five-arched bridge over the River Tweed built by John Rennie in 1803. From the parapet there is a fine view across to Floors Castle, the largest inhabited house in Scotland, a monument to the wealth and privilege of the Dukes of Roxburgh. Fine art, tapestries and French furniture are all on view.

202

ORONSAY

Oronsay
Rudha
Bàn
Dubh Eilean
Eilean
Ghurdmail
Colonsay-Port Askaig

J U R

Rudh' ant-

ISLAY

Rudha
Bholsa

363
SGARBH
BREAC

Rudha' a' Mhàil

Nave Island
Ardnave
Point
Gortantaoid
Point

Loch a'
Chnuic Bhric

Bunnahabhain

316
GUIR-
BHEINN

Ton Mhòr

Kilnave

Sanaigmore

Finlaggan

Port
Askaig

Feolin Ferry

Kiells

Loch
Finlaggan

Eilean Mòr

Lecht Gruinart

Rudha Lamanais

Loch
Gòrr

B8018

Gruinart

B8017

Ballygrant

A846
8

Loch
Ballygrant

Cabra

DU
BHE

Saligo Bay

Loch Lossit

Gileann Mòr

Coul Point

Loch
Gorm

Sunderland

B8018

Machir
Bay

Kilchoman

266
BEINNE
DUBH

Am Fraoc
Eilean

Bridgend

Gartachossan

Bruichladdich

Loch
Indaal

A847

Kilchiaran Bay

Bowmore

429
SGÒRR NAM
FAOILEANN

McArthur's
Head

15

Port
Charlotte

Kilennan Burn

471

231
BEINN TART A'MHILL

Lossit Bay

River Laggan

490
BEINN BHEIGER

Rudha Li

Nereabolls

RHINNS OF ISLAY

A847

Duich R.

A846

B8016

454
BEINN URARAIDH

Loch Uraraidh

Ardtalla

Claggain
Bay

Rudha na
Faing

Portnahaven

Port Wemyss

L a g g a n

Islay

Glenegedale

Kintour

Ardmo
Point

Orsay

RHINNS
POINT

B a y

Kildalton
Cross

346
BEINN SHOLUM

Eilean
a' Chuirr

Rudha Mòr

Kintra

Rudha na
Gainmhich

Port
Ellen

A846

Ardbeg
Lagavulin

165
MAOL BUIDHE

Laphroaig

Texa

3

T H E   O A

Risabus

Lower
Killeyan

RSPB

Kinnabus

American
Monument

Loch
Kinnabus

MULL
OF OA

Rudha nan Leacan

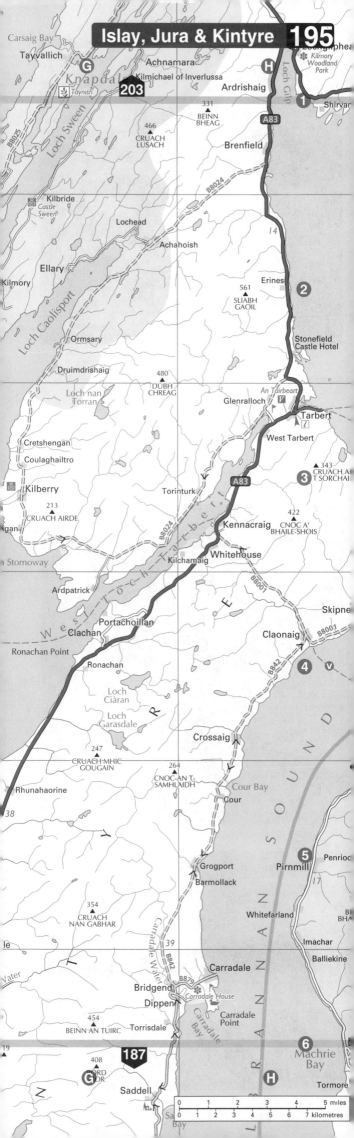

Carsaig Bay
Tayvallich

G

Loughphea

❀ Kilmory
Woodland
Park

Loch Gilp

Knapdale
Achnamara
Kilmichael of Inverlussa

↓ Táynish

203

H

Ardrishaig

1

Shirvan

A83

331
BEINN
BHEAG

Brenfield

B8025

Loch Sween

14

466
CRUACH
LUSACH

Kilbride
Castle
Sween

Lochead

Achahoish

Erines

2

Ellary

Kilmory

Loch Caolisport

561
SLIABH
GAOIL

Ormsary

Stonefield
Castle Hotel

Druimdrishaig

Loch nan
Torran

480
DUBH
CHREAG

An Tairbeart

Glenralloch

Tarbert

Cretshengan

Coulaghailtro

West Tarbert

Kilberry

213
CRUACH AIRDE

Torinturk

A83

3

343
CRUACH A'
T SORCHAI

422
CNOC A'
BHAILE-SHOIS

Kennacraig

Stornoway

Kilchamaig

Whitehouse

Ardpatrick

E

B8001

Skipne

Portachoillan

Claonaig

B8001

Clachan

Ronachan Point

Ronachan

West Loch Tarbert

B842

4

V

Loch Ciàran

Loch
Garasdale

R

Crossaig

247
CRUACH MHIC
GOUGAIN

264
CNOC AN T-
SAMHLAIDH

Rhunahaorine

Cour Bay

Cour

38

Grogport

Barmollack

5

Pirnmill

Penrioc

354
CRUACH
NAN GABHAR

Whitefarland

17

Imachar

Balliekine

B
BHA

le

Carradale Water

39

B842

Carradale

Z

Bridgend

B879

Carradale House

Dippen

Carradale
Point

Carradale
Bay

454
BEINN AN TUIRC

Torrisdale

6

Machrie
Bay

19

408
ORD
OR

187

G

H

Saddell

Sa
Bay

Tormore

| 0 | 1 | 2 | 3 | 4 | 5 miles |
| 0 | 1 | 2 | 3 | 4 | 5 | 6 | 7 kilometres |

Port Askaig is one of the gateways to Islay

South Jura 194–5

This beautiful but little-known island has a population of around 200 people and 6,000 deer. Standing stones and cairns date habitation here back to 7000 BC. The coastline features caves and cliffs, raised beaches and long stretches of white sand. Many rare species of plants, birds and mammals flourish on the island including otters, and Small Isles bay at Craighouse (E3) has a colony of seals which can often be seen basking on the rocks in front of the Manse. The Paps of Jura (E2) offer opportunities for climbing and hill walking – stout walking boots are a must. The views from the top take in Islay, Colonsay, Mull, Scarba and Northern Ireland.

The High Cross of Kildalton is one of Islay's treasures

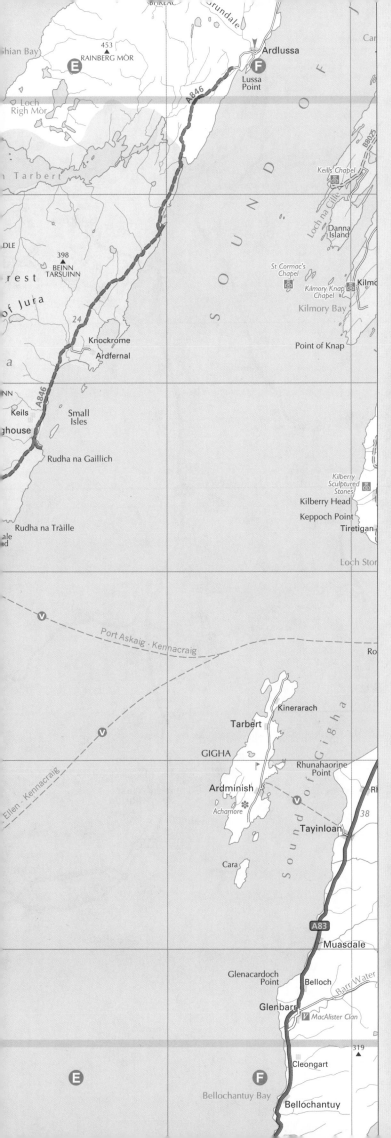

Islay, Jura and Gigha are part of a small chain of islands down Scotland's rugged western shoreline, each with its own character and community life. The peninsula of Kintyre has long been a playground for the Scots, particularly Glaswegians. All are accessible by ferry, for a short trip or longer exploration. Outdoor pursuits include walking, fishing and sailing.

The lighthouse at Port Ellen on Islay

Gigha 195 F4

Gigha, off Kintyre, is a small island with sandy beaches, rich wildlife, fort remains and standing stones. It is famous for the gardens of Achamore House, noted for their camellias, azaleas and rhododendrons.

Islay 194

Islay is a working island with seven distilleries, the excellent Museum of Islay Life at Port Charlotte (B4), and an annual festival of music and whisky. Loch Finlaggan, west of Port Askaig (D3), was the base for the Lordship of the Isles in the 14th and 15th centuries, and is now an extensive archaeological site. Around 110 species of bird breed on Islay, including the chough, a black crow-like bird with startling red legs and beak.

And an estimated 50,000 geese overwinter here from Greenland and Iceland. Several annual festivals attract visitors to the island including the Festival of Malt and Music in May. Cycling, fishing and hill walking are popular pastimes.

Kintyre 195

In 1098 Norse king Magnus Barelegs hauled his ship over the narrow neck of land at Tarbert to claim the beautiful Kintyre peninsula for an island. Tarbert (H3) is an appealing little port, busy with yachts and small fishing boats. The A83 travels down the west coast giving views over to Gigha while the B842 goes down the east coast to the quiet village of Carradale (H6), with a heritage centre devoted to the story of Carradale and Kintyre.

The distinctive Paps of Jura dominate the southern part of the island

Carrick
Largiemore

435
CRUACH
CHUILCEACHAN

A

River Ruel

Glenmassen

B

Glen Massen

643
CLACH
BHEINN

664
BEINN
RUADH
Ardentinny

Benmore
Younger

C

STRONCHULLIN
HILL

548

Coulport

Glen Fruin

D

Shandon

B833

203

432
CRUACH NAN
CUILEAN

601
SGORACH MÒR

Benmore

Rashfield

Ardbeg
Kilmun
Blairmore

Clynder

Rhu

Rosneath

Glendaruel

Kilmodan
Sculptured Stones

Otter Ferry

Ballimore

Stronafian

B836

Glen Lean

Clachaig

A815

A880
Kilmun

Strone

Cove

Kilcreggan

1

Loch Long

Loch Long

Holy Loch

2

Fearnoch

Kilfinan

Drum

454
BEINN
BHREAC

A8003

606

611

CRUACH NAN CAPULL

Glenkin

Sandbank

Ardnadam

Hunter's
Quay

Firth

Gourock

204

ilfinan
Bay

Loch Riddon

Glenstriven

A885

Kirn

Ashton

B833

Kilfinan

B8000

A886

505
BEINN
BHREAC

Ardentraive

Colintraive

Altgaltraig

Loch Striven

391
KILMARNOCK
HILL

Ardhallow

503
BISHOP'S
SEAT

Dunoon

Cloch
Point

A770

Larkfield

Braeside

30

A78

Lyle
Hill

Chrisswell

Loch
Thom

Gryff
Reserv

Port
Driseach

Rhubodach

Kyles of Bute

Kilmarnock

Lunderston
Bay

Ardgowan

Inverkip

Shielhill

Cornalees Bridge

Garvock

Auchenlochan

Tighnabruaich

Kames

Millhouse

Glenan Bay

Blair's
Ferry

207
CNOC NA
CARRAIGE

B U T E

267
KAMES HILL

A886

8

Ardmaleish

Ardyre Point

Port Bannatyne

322
BEINN
RUADH

Knockdow

Dunan

Innellan

A815

Toward

Wemyss Bay

Upper
Skelmorlie

Skelmorlie

Routenburn

Noddsdale Water

441
CREUCH
HILL

Portavadie

Kilbride
Bay

Ardlamont

Ardlamont
Bay

Kildavanan

Kilbride

St Colmac

Ardbeg

Toward
Quay

A815

6

A78

Knock Castle

522
HILL OF
STAKE

3

Kildavaig

Ettrick
Bay

Ardscalpsie
Bay

Rothesay

Castle

St Mary's
Chapel
(ruin)

Ardencraig

B878

A844

B881

Loch
Ascog

Ascog

Kerrycroy

Quarter

Skelmorlie Aisle

Vikingar!

Largs

483
IRISH
LAW

Ardlamont
Point

Inchmarnock

Ballanlay

A844

Meikle
Kilmory

Loch Fada

8

Mount Stuart

Bruchag

GREAT
CUMBRAE
ISLAND

Kelburn

Kelburn
Country Centre

A760

14

Chapel

Skipness Point

Midpark

Stravanan
Bay

Kingarth

B881

Kilchattan

Kilchattan
Bay

Millport

B896

B899

B896

Fairlie

Camphill
Reservoir

371
COCK
LAW

4

Cock Of Arran

Lochranza

Castle

Glen Catacol

Glen Chalmadale

A841

8

Garrochty

Garroch Head

St Blane's
Church

Sound of Bute

Little
Cumbrae
Island

Fairlie Roads

Hunterston
Power Station

12

Portencross

Farland Head

B7048

Crosbie

Blackshaw

Munnoch

Drakemyre

B781

B780

ol

North Arran

834
CAISTEAL ABHAIL

Sannox

**West
Kilbride**

Seamill

A78

B7047

Dalgarven

B714

Kilwinnir

5

Loch
Tanna

874
GOATFELL

Corrie

Glen Iorsa

Glen Rosa

792
BEINN
NUIS

orsa Water

6
Merkland Point

Brodick Castle, Garden
& Country Club

Brodick
Bay

A841

Ardrossan

Horse Isle

A78

A738

Steve

Arde

Saltcoats

6

A R R A N

agallon
e Circle
chrie

Strathwhillan

FIRTH

Irvine
Bay

187

A'CHRUACH

A

A841

4

B

Clauchlands Point

C

OF

D

achrie Moor
Stone Circles

B880

503
BEINN

Margnaheglish

CLYDE

Balmichael

Balmichael

Town guide: Glasgow p.314

Lamlash
Bay

Holy Island

(Summer Only)

(Winter Only)

A760

be seen today dates from the 18th and 19th centuries, but there are a few earlier remains.

Dunoon 196 C2
On the grassy headland between the town's two bays are the remains of the 13th-century royal castle and below is the 1896 statue of Burns's love, Highland Mary, erected to mark the centenary of the poet's death. Dunoon is busiest each year during late August for the Cowal Highland Gathering, when more than 150 pipe bands from all over the world compete for prestigious trophies.

Brodick Castle on Arran

Greenbank Garden 197 G4
This garden was gifted to the National Trust for Scotland as a demonstration piece, to inspire suburban gardeners and show just what can be grown in a heavy clay soil. Set in a frost pocket, with 1ha of walled garden and extensive policies (grounds) beyond, Greenbank prides itself on being very much a garden that normal people can aspire to. That may be a little optimistic, given that it contains over 3,500 different plants.

Irvine 197 E6
Irvine is a modern town with two particularly good attractions for visitors. A whacky science centre dedicated to inventions, and an outpost of the Scottish Maritime Museum, are set on the old harbourside. The Big Idea is a high-tech centre built on the site where Swedish explosives expert Alfred Noble launched the British Dynamite Company. Track your progress through the exhibits with a unique iButton, try building your own invention and enjoy a ride through the history of explosions – great for kids. The maritime museum is an altogether calmer affair, with a collection of moored ships and a tour of a shipyard worker's tenement.

National Museum of Rural Life Scotland 197 H4
Take in the sights, sounds and smells as you explore this 70ha farm. Discover what life was like for country people in the past and how this has shaped Scotland's countryside today. Try milking 'Clover' by hand, hitch a ride on our farm explorer, meet the horse, sheep, cows and hens.

Newark Castle 197 E2
The one-time house of the Maxwells, Newark Castle dates from the 15th and 17th centuries. The courtyard and hall are preserved. Fine turrets and the remains of painted ceilings can be seen, and the hall carries an inscription of 1597. The castle enjoys views across the Clyde.

Paisley Museum & Art Galleries 197 F3
Pride of place here is given to a world-famous collection of Paisley shawls. Other collections illustrate local industrial and natural history, while in the art gallery the emphasis is on 19th-century Scottish artists and an important studio ceramics collection.

Rothesay 196 B3
Bute has been the holiday playground for generations of Glaswegians, most of whom arrive at Rothesay on the ferry from Wemyss Bay. Standing on the Firth of Clyde, Rothesay has a late 19th-century atmosphere created by its solid, mostly Victorian houses and decorative Winter Gardens, but much more ancient are the impressive ruins of the moated and circular 13th-century Rothesay Castle, where some restoration took place in the 19th and 20th centuries. Also worth a visit are Bute Museum and Ardencraig garden.

Vikingar! 196 D4
Vikingar! is a lively reminder that the Norse had a major impact in the shaping of Scotland. The centre tells of the Vikings in Scotland from the early invasions to final defeat at the Battle of Largs in 1263, using models, impressive audio-visual effects and suitably hairy actors to re-create the Viking world. Take in the Homestead, with its Viking smells, and the Hall of the Gods. There's an entertaining film show with shouting and sword-clanging, and the Hall of Knowledge has replica carvings, information boards and a touch-screen computer.

Dunoon Castle looks out over the Victorian pier on the Clyde

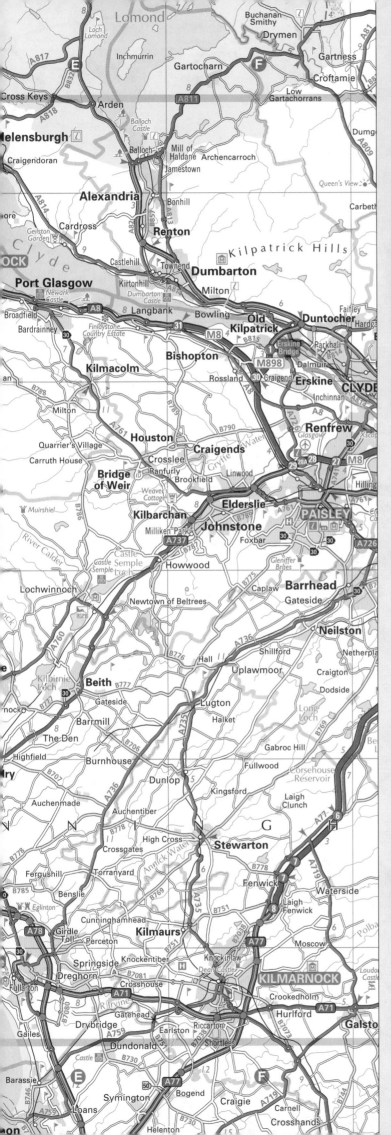

GLASGOW & THE CLYDE

Glasgow, famed for leading the Industrial Revolution, is now known for its vibrant arts and entertainments scene and superb museum and galleries. Part of its charm is that the hills and open countryside and the resorts and islands of the Firth of Clyde are so accessible.

The David Livingstone Centre features displays on the life of the explorer

Brodick Castle 196 B6
Red sandstone Brodick Castle is Arran's biggest single attraction. It dates from the 13th century and was a stronghold of the Dukes of Hamilton. It has an extensive collection of porcelain and silver, some 19th-century sporting pictures and trophies, and a beautiful country park with meadows and woodland. The gardens include a world-renowned collection of rhododendrons.

Burrell Collection 197 G3
This priceless collection of 9,000 pieces of art from around the world was given to Glasgow in 1944 by Sir William Burrell. You'll find August Rodin's *The Thinker* in the Courtyard. Intriguing old stone doorways lead into different parts of the museum. In the Ancient Greece and Rome section, look for fragments of delicate Roman mosaics. Don't overlook the Islamic Art section at the farthest end of the museum, dripping with Oriental carpets. The corridor between the café and the entrance is aglow with medieval glass, suspended along the windows that form the outer skin of the building.

Clydebuilt 197 G3
On the south bank of the River Clyde, home of the Scottish shipbuilding industry, visitors can discover how Glasgow's famous ships were built, from the design stages through to the launch. There are also displays on the textile and cotton industries, iron and steel, and tobacco. Hands-on activities allow you to operate a real ship's engine, become a ship's riveter, and steer a virtual ship up the Clyde.

David Livingstone Centre 197 H4
Share the adventurous life of Scotland's greatest explorer, from his childhood in the Blantyre Mills to his explorations in the heart of Africa, dramatically illustrated in the historic tenement where he was born. Various events are held throughout the season.

Dumbarton Castle 197 E2
The castle, set on Dumbarton Rock above the River Clyde, dominates the town (the capital of the Celtic kingdom of Strathclyde) and commands spectacular views. Most of what can

A lifeboat is part of the collection at Irvine's Scottish Maritime Museum

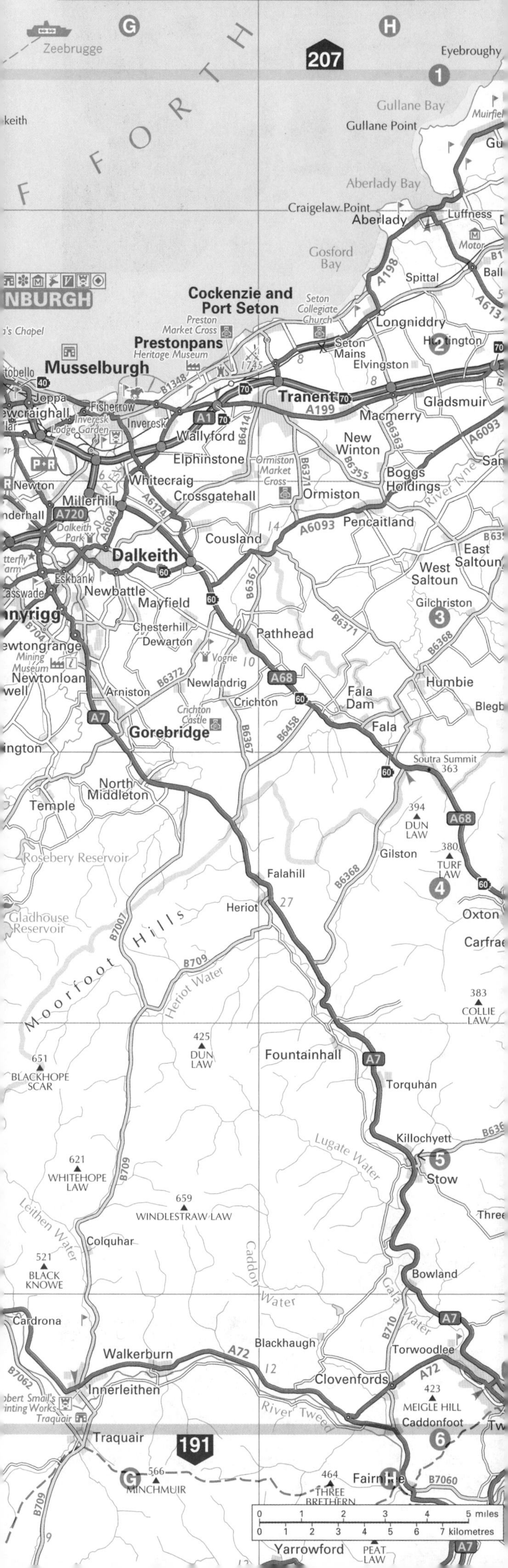

G H

207
Eyebroughy
1
Zeebrugge
keith
Gullane Bay
Gullane Point
Muirfiel
Gu
F FORTH
Aberlady Bay
Craigelaw Point
Aberlady
Luffness
Motor
B1
's Chapel
Cockenzie and
Port Seton
Seton
Collegiate
Church
Gosford Bay
Spittal
A198
Ball
A613
NBURGH
Preston
Market Cross
Prestonpans
Heritage Museum
Seton
Mains
Longniddry
H ington
2
70
tobello
Musselburgh
Joppa
Fisherrow
Inveresk
Elvingston
A1 70
Tranent
A199
Macmerry
Gladsmuir
wcraighall
lar
Lodge Garden
Inveresk
Wallyford
New
Winton
A6093
San
P+R
Newton
derhall
A720
Whitecraig
Elphinstone
Ormiston
Market
Cross
Boggs
Holdings
River Nine
Crossgatehall
Ormiston
Millerhill
Dalkeith
Park
A6124
Cousland
14
A6093
Pencaitland
East
Saltoun
B63
West
Saltoun
tterfly
arm
Dalkeith
60
Gilchriston
3
casswade
Eskbank
Newbattle
Mayfield
B6368
nyrigg
Newtongrange
60
Chesterhill
Dewarton
Pathhead
B6371
Humbie
Blegb
Mining
Museum
well
Arniston
B6372
Newlandrig
A68
Fala
Dam
A7
Crichton
Castle
Crichton
60
Fala
ington
Gorebridge
B6458
B6367
Soutra Summit
363
North
Middleton
60
Temple
394
DUN
LAW
A68
Roseberry Reservoir
Gilston
380
TURF
LAW
4
60
Falahill
B6368
Oxton
Gladhouse
Reservoir
Heriot
27
Carfrae
Moorfoot Hills
B7007
B709
Heriot Water
383
COLLIE
LAW
651
BLACKHOPE
SCAR
425
DUN
LAW
Fountainhall
A7
Torquhan
B6368
621
WHITEHOPE
LAW
B709
Killochyett
5
Stow
Leithen Water
659
WINDLESTRAW LAW
Three
Colquhar
Caddon Water
521
BLACK
KNOWE
Bowland
Gala Water
Cardrona
B710
A7
B7062
Walkerburn
A72
Blackhaugh
12
Torwoodlee
obert Smail's
inting Works
Innerleithen
Clovenfords
A72
Traquair
423
MEIGLE HILL
Caddonfoot
6
Traquair
191
464
THREE
BRETHREN
Fairn H e
B7060
Tw
G
566
MINCHMUIR
0 1 2 3 4 5 miles
0 1 2 3 4 5 6 7 kilometres
9
Yarrowford
PEAT
LAW
A7

Visit the village store at New Lanark World Heritage Village

canal, through a tunnel, and back down on the wheel.

Hopetoun House 198 D2
Hopetoun House is a splendid early 18th-century mansion built by William Bruce and William Adam, with 40ha of parkland giving great views of the two Forth bridges. Stuffed with fine paintings, original furniture, tapestries and rococo details, the house is still the home of the Marquis of Linlithgow.

Lauriston Castle 199 F2
The castle is a late 16th-century tower house with 19th-century additions, but is most notable as a classic example of the Edwardian age. It has a beautifully preserved Edwardian interior with the feel of a country house, and the spacious grounds are very pleasant.

Malleny Garden 199 E3
The delightful gardens are set round a 17th-century house (not open to the public). Shrub roses, a woodland garden, and a group of four clipped yews, survivors of a group planted in 1603, are among its notable features. The National Bonsai Collection for Scotland is also at Malleny.

New Lanark World Heritage Village 198 B5
Robert Owen purchased the cotton mills here in 1799 and established a utopian society – a model community with improved conditions for the workers and their families. There was a school, day nursery, institute for adult education and a village store run by a cooperative. The

site slowly declined, but in 1973 the New Lanark Conservation Trust started to restore it, with the results seen today. Don't miss the walk to the three waterfalls upstream.

Peebles 199 F5
The broad main street of this bustling Borders town always seems to be busy, its small shops and family businesses doing a brisk trade. Visitors come here to shop and enjoy the authentic ambience of a pleasant country town. Walks, trails and cycleways lead into the wooded countryside, starting with a gentle walk upstream from the park along the River Tweed to Neidpath Castle, a 14th-century tower set high above the river.

Robert Smail's Printing Works 199 G6
These buildings contain a Victorian office, a paper store with reconstructed waterwheel, a composing room and a press room. The machinery is in full working order and visitors may view the printer at work and experience typesetting in the composing room.

Royal Yacht *Britannia* 198 F2
A visit to *Britannia*, now in Edinburgh's historic port of Leith, starts in the visitor centre where you can discover *Britannia*'s fascinating story. Then step aboard for a self-led audio tour which takes you around five decks giving you a unique insight into what life was like for the Royal Family, officers and the crew.

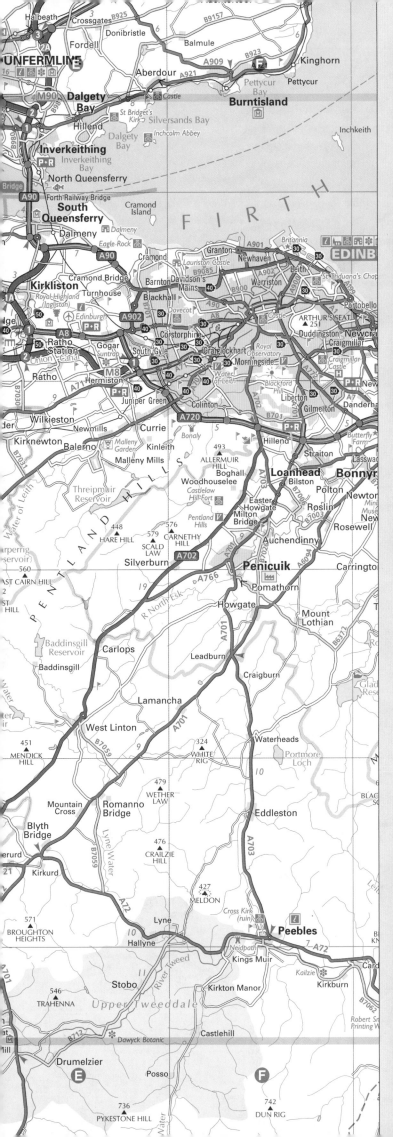

EDINBURGH & PENTLAND HILLS

Edinburgh, Scotland's capital, has everything a capital city should have – a castle, a royal palace, national collections of art, splendid museums, excellent shopping and fine architecture. To the south, the Pentland Hills attract walkers, cyclists and those seeking solitude and wide open spaces.

Well-preserved Craigmillar Castle has a tower house, courtyard and gardens

Biggar 198 D6

The bustling Borders town of Biggar has a broad main street and a wide central square surrounded by local shops and tea rooms. The town's heritage is preserved in a range of interesting museums, well signed from the centre. These include Gladstone Court with its re-creation of an indoor 'street' of shops, and the Greenhill Farmhouse Museum, linked to the 17th-century persecution of the Covenanters.

Craigmillar Castle 199 F2

At the core of this splendid medieval castle is a stout 15th-century L-plan tower house with walls up to 2.7m thick. Defensive features include massive doors, a spiral turnpike stair, narrow passageways and two outer walls to fend off English attackers. Mary, Queen of Scots fled here after the murder of Rizzio. The plot to murder Darnley, her second husband, was also hatched here.

Dawyck Botanic Garden 199 E6

From the landscaped walks of this historic arboretum an impressive collection of mature specimen trees can be seen, some over 40m tall. Notable features include the Beech Walk, Swiss Bridge, a fine estate chapel and stonework terracing produced by Italian craftsmen in the 1820s.

Falkirk 198 B2

The main attraction here is the Falkirk Wheel, a unique 35m structure. It opened in 2002 to link the canals that run across the middle of Scotland, replacing 11 locks which had been dismantled in 1933. The wheel is a cross between a lock and a lift, a state-of-the-art method of raising and lowering boats between the two different levels of the Forth & Clyde Canal and the Union Canal. Watch from the glass-sided visitor centre as the great structure rotates, and take a 40-minute boat ride up onto the higher

The Falkirk Wheel is an exceptional feat of modern engineering

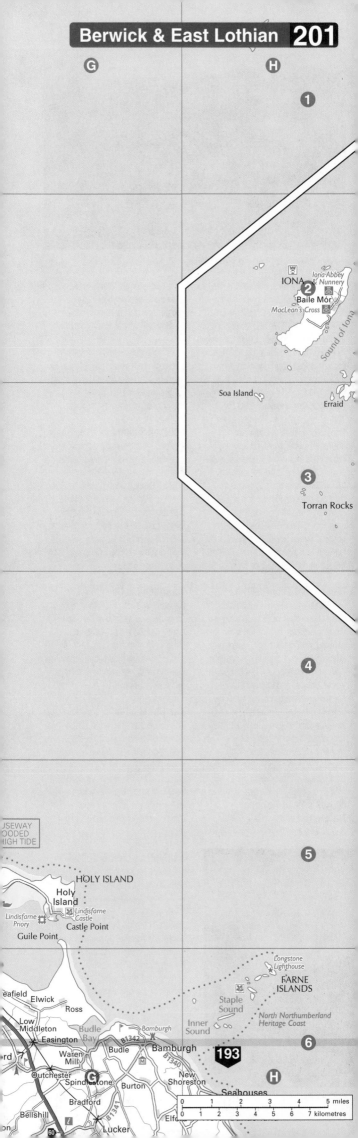

G   **H**

1

2

IONA
Iona Abbey & Nunnery
Baile Mór
MacLean's Cross
Sound of Iona

Soa Island

Erraid

3

Torran Rocks

4

5

CAUSEWAY
FLOODED
AT HIGH TIDE

HOLY ISLAND
Holy
Island
Lindisfarne
Priory
Lindisfarne
Castle
Castle Point
Guile Point

Longstone
Lighthouse

FARNE
ISLANDS

Staple
Sound

North Northumberland
Heritage Coast

eafield Elwick
Ross

Low
Middleton Budle
Easington Bay Bamburgh
Waren Budle
Mill Bamburgh
Inner
Sound

6

rd
Outchester **G** Spindlestone Burton
Bradford
Bellshill 60 Lucker

New
Shoreston
Seahouses
H

193

Elf

| 0 | 1 | 2 | 3 | 4 | 5 miles |
| 0 | 1 | 2 | 3 | 4 | 5 | 6 | 7 kilometres |

There are spectacular clifftop walks along St Abb's Head

museum beside the ruins of 12th-century Lindisfarne Priory recounts the life of the early monks. Lindisfarne Castle was built in the 1540s and restored in 1903 by the architect Sir Edwin Lutyens; its interior is a combination of the 16th century, comfortable Edwardian furnishings and Lutyens' quirks.

Manderston House 200 D4

This grandest of grand houses gives a fascinating picture of Edwardian life above and below stairs. Completely remodelled for the millionaire racehorse owner Sir James Miller, the architect was told to spare no expense, and so the house boasts the world's only silver staircase. The state rooms are magnificent, and there are fine formal gardens, with a woodland garden and lakeside walks. Manderston has been the setting for a number of films.

Museum of Flight 200 A2

The Museum of Flight is situated on 25ha of one of Britain's best preserved wartime airfields. The museum has four hangars, with more than 50 aeroplanes, plus engines, rockets and memorabilia. Items on display include two Spitfires, a Vulcan bomber and Britain's oldest surviving aeroplane, built in 1896; recent exhibits also include a Phantom jet fighter, and a Harrier jump-jet. The Concorde Experience (pre-booking required) explores the story of this historic plane through the lives of those who worked or travelled on it.

St Abb's Head National Nature Reserve 201 E3

Seabirds nest in their thousands here.

It's a wild and beautiful landscape at any time of year, with the spectacular cliffs of soft red sandstone, sculpted by wind and waves, reaching 100m above sea level. Fulmars, kittiwakes, guillemots, puffins and razorbills are the most prominent breeding species, and when they are in residence in late spring, the cliffs become an astonishing vertical city.

Scottish Seabird Centre 200 A1

There are breathtaking panoramic views over the Firth of Forth and the sandy beaches of North Berwick from the Scottish Seabird Centre. In the Discovery Centre visitors can see wildlife close up with amazing live cameras – puffins spring-cleaning their burrows, gannets with fluffy white chicks, seals sunning themselves and occasional sightings of dolphins and whales.

Tantallon Castle 200 A1

Situated on a rocky headland the formidable stronghold of Tantallon Castle was once the 14th-century stronghold of the Douglas Earls of Angus. Highlights include the massive stone curtain wall and the replica gun in the east tower.

The Hirsel 200 D5

The grounds of The Hirsel, seat of the Home family, can be explored by following the colour-coded routes through the estate which lead to places such as Dundock Wood, at its best in May and June. The focal point is the museum which gives an insight into how people lived and worked in days gone by.

Thirlestane Castle 200 A5

Thirlstane is one of the most sumptuously decorated great houses in Scotland. A simple pink sandstone tower house was transformed in 1670–76 for the Duke of Lauderdale, Secretary of State, by architect William Bruce and master craftsman Robert Mylne. Curious semi-circular stair-towers punctuate the outer walls, but the remarkable feature is the plasterwork of the ceilings, created by Dutch masters. Deep garlands of flowers and foliage are adorned with gilded highlights. The informal riverside grounds, with their views of the grouse moors, include a woodland walk, picnic tables and an adventure playground.

puffins and other birds

BERWICK & EAST LOTHIAN

The rolling Lammermuir Hills, one of Scotland's remaining untouched wilderness areas, rise from the plains of East Lothian and run down to the Scottish Borders. The coast sweeps south to Northumberland and historic Berwick-upon-Tweed, with a chain of strong castles and the heartland of Christianity at Holy Island, and amid all this history are nature reserves and rocks sheltering birds.

Tantallon Castle is protected by the sea on three sides

Berwick-upon-Tweed 201 E4
Positioned near the Scottish border, Berwick was for long under threat of invasion and is guarded by Britain's only complete set of 16th-century ramparts, which you can walk around in their entirety. Here, three great bridges span the River Tweed, the Royal Border Railway Bridge, the Royal Tweed Bridge and the Berwick Bridge. Berwick itself reveals its quirky side within the walls, a place full of unexpected levels and grey stone houses. Prominent in the town, Berwick Guildhall houses the Cell Block Museum in the Town Gaol. Berwick Barracks, the earliest surviving in Britain, date from the early 18th century and contain The King's Own Scottish Borderers Regimental Museum and the Berwick Museum and Art Gallery.

Haddington 200 A2
This handsome, businesslike market town is set in prime agricultural country on the River Tyne. It was granted the status of a royal burgh in the 12th century and later became the county town for East Lothian. Protestant reformer John Knox was born here in c1505. The original medieval town was laid out to a triangular street plan which can still be traced along High Street, Market Street and Hardgate. Painted in bright, warm colours, the 18th-century Georgian buildings of the High Street create a pleasing and harmonious façade. The graciously proportioned Town House was built by William Adam in 1748.

Hailes Castle 200 A2
The castle ruins stand in a picturesque setting beside the River Tyne. They incorporate a 13th-century fortified manor house which was extended in the 14th and 15th centuries. There is a surprising amount to explore, including the vaulted kitchens and, above them, the largest surviving space which is believed to be the chapel.

Holy Island 201 G5
Joined at low tide by a causeway to the mainland, Holy Island (known as Lindisfarne before 1082) retains the sense of isolation that drew monks and hermits here from early medieval times onwards. You need to take note of the signs for safe crossing times. The most famous monk was St Cuthbert (died AD 687), bishop of the monastery. The

St Abb's Head is a major breeding groun[d]

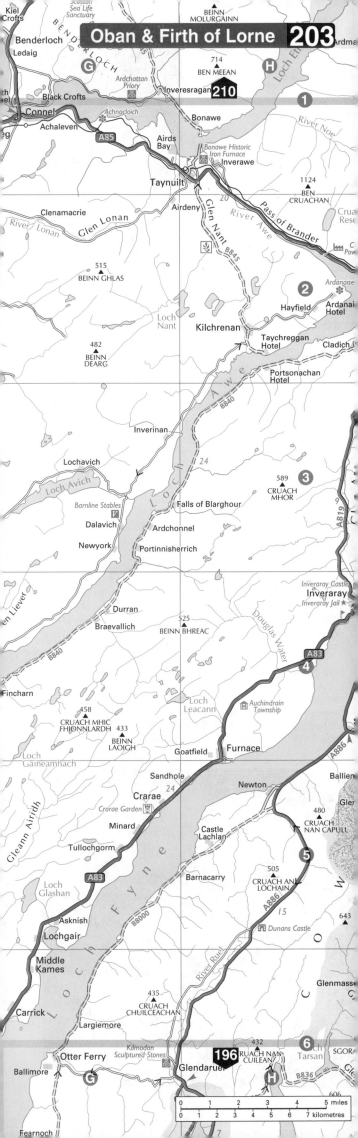

Clyde and Crinan canals.) To the north of the town, Inveraray Castle is a splendid 18th-century mansion with pepperpot towers and a delightfully decorative interior.

To the south is Auchindrain Township, a former crofting settlement which now gives visitors an experience of Highland life. Its houses have original furniture and the barns are equipped with old implements.

Iona 201 H2

Fionnphort is the access point for Iona, a magical island known since the 6th century AD as the cradle of Christianity in Scotland. Most visitors make straight for the abbey, but spare time for the remains of the 13th-century priory, built for Augustinian nuns. St Columba founded his monastery here in AD 563, and from it Christianity radiated throughout Europe. Now home to the Iona Community, the abbey welcomes pilgrims from around the world. Beside it is the ancient burial ground of Scottish kings, including Duncan and Macbeth. Excursions take in the island of Staffa, with its spectacular hexagonal basalt columns, and Fingal's Cave.

Kilmartin 203 F5

The peaceful green glen which leads to the hamlet of Kilmartin is littered with piles of silvery boulders, the remains of burial cairns dating from around 3000 BC which form one of the most remarkable collections of early monuments in Britain. Learn more at Kilmartin House, the archaeological museum by the church. To the south, the great rocky outcrop of Dunadd was the capital of the 6th-century Scottish kingdom of Dalriada: look for the footprint-shaped impression in the exposed stone on the top of the rock.

Lochgilphead 202 F6

Lochgilphead was once the centre of herring fishing on Loch Gilp, with a wooden pier that stretched across the bay, but the fish mysteriously vanished before World War I. Kilmory Castle gardens were partly laid out by Joseph

Visitors can tour Iona's abbey, its church and cloisters

Hooker, first director of Kew Gardens, and are full of rare rhododendrons.

Oban 203 F2

A busy railhead and ferry port for the Western Isles, Oban developed as a holiday resort in the 19th century. The bustling harbour is the start point for local tours to the islands. It is on a curving bay sheltered by the low island of Kerrera, and dominated by the circular folly of stone arches on the hillside behind. This is McCaig's Tower, erected by John Stuart McCaig, a banker and philanthropist, in 1897 as a family memorial and to relieve local unemployment. Unfortunately McCaig died before it could be completed. Today it provides a superb viewpoint. Oban is also a popular touring centre, with good shops on the main roads of Corran Esplanade and George Street. The distillery in the middle is a pleasant diversion on a wet day.

Rare Breeds Farm Park 203 F1

Children can meet, feed, stroke and touch the geese, llamas, alpacas, rabbits, donkeys, deer, cattle, ducks and pigs at this farm park designed especially for children. There are woodland walks and picnic areas.

...oked by the arches of McCaig's Tower

OBAN & FIRTH OF LORNE

Great sea lochs spread their narrowing fingers inland, creating isolated and island-bound communities and havens for wildlife. There is ancient history to discover at Kilmartin and Iona and a sheltered garden at Crarae. Oban is the main touring centre of the area.

Temple Wood stone circle near Kilmartin

Bonawe Iron Furnace 203 H1

The furnace is a restored charcoal blast furnace for iron smelting and making cast iron. It was established in 1753 and worked until 1876. The works exploited the Forest of Lorne to provide charcoal for fuel.

Crarae Garden 203 G5

This hillside garden, on the shores of Loch Fyne, was the creation of Lady Grace Campbell. Her work was continued by her son, Sir George Campbell, who began the transformation of a narrow Highland glen into a Himalayan gorge in 1925. Today it is cared for by the National Trust for Scotland, and has more than 400 species of rhododendron and azalea. This is primarily a woodland garden, with paths winding through eucalyptus and other trees.

Crinan Canal 203 F5

Today you are most likely to see pleasure craft negotiating the canal's 15 locks, but its original purpose was to enable merchant traffic to and from the Western Isles to avoid the hazardous voyage around the Mull of Kintyre. From the basin at Ardrishaig, where it leaves Loch Fyne, the canal hugs the wooded hillsides as it climbs up to its highest point of 19.4m. On the hills above Cairnbaan are reservoirs that constantly replenish the water down in the canal as it descends underneath the unusual hand-wound rolling bridge at Dunardry (1 mile west of Cairnbaan). Beyond this the landscape opens out into the flat marshland near to the River Add estuary. The canal ends at the picturesque haven of Crinan Harbour.

Inveraray 203 H4

Spread out along a bay near the head of Loch Fyne, Inveraray was for centuries the capital of Argyll. The tall brown stone tower of All Saints' Episcopalian Church is famous for its peal of 10 bells and has panoramic views from the top. The town's courthouse and jail of 1820 are now host to an entertaining and interactive exhibition about prison life. The three-masted schooner *Arctic Penguin*, moored in the small harbour, includes an exhibition about local-born novelist Neil Munro, author of the humorous Para Handy tales. (Para Handy was the roguish skipper of a 'puffer', or small steamboat, which plied the Forth &

The calm waters of Oban's harbour are o

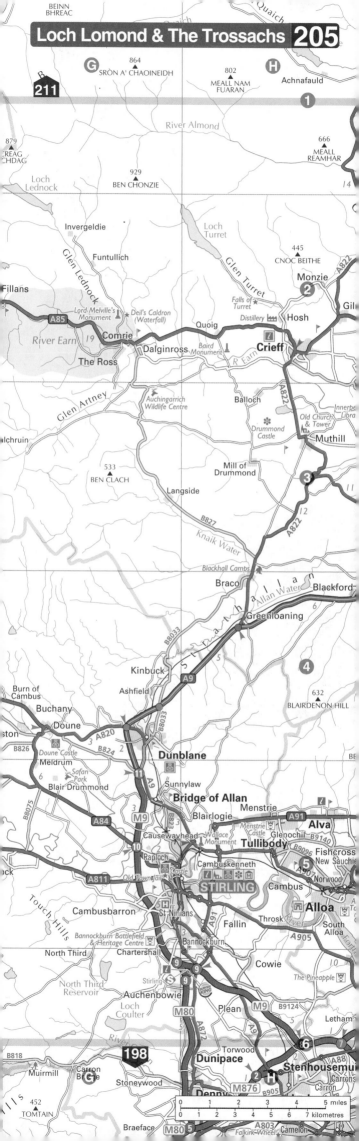

larger English army at the Battle of Bannockburn in 1314 with an exhibition on The Kingdom of the Scots as well as an audio-visual show recounting the story of this most vital battle of the Wars of Independence. Outside there's a commemorative Rotunda and the Borestone traditionally Bruce's command post – as well as a magnificent statue of the King on his warhorse.

The east side of Doune Castle

Benmore Botanic Garden
204 A6

From the formal gardens, through the hillside woodlands, visitors can follow the paths to a stunning viewpoint with a spectacular outlook across the garden and the Holy Loch to the Firth of Clyde and beyond. Among many highlights are the stately conifers, the magnificent avenue of giant redwoods, and an extensive magnolia and rhododendron collection.

Blair Drummond Safari Park
205 G5

At this safari park to the west of Stirling, visitors can drive among animals, including elephants, giraffes, lions and camels, which roam free. The pets' farm has llamas, donkeys and ponies, and there are sea-lion shows, a boat safari and an adventure playground.

This converted church in the centre of Callander houses the Rob Roy and Trossachs Visitor Centre

Callander
204 F4

Callander is a bustling little town, the eastern gateway to the Trossachs. The architecture of its long main street reflects the town's heyday in the late 19th century as a holiday resort, and today it is lined with interesting shops. In the square, the former church is occupied by the tourist information office with, upstairs, the audio-visual Rob Roy Story. Rob Roy MacGregor was a folk hero and outlaw, who took refuge with his clansmen in the Trossach hills.

Crieff
205 H2

The old town of Crieff lies west of Perth on the very edge of the Highlands, and its shops buzz with visitors in high summer. It's a hub for activities including fishing, bicycling, watersports on nearby Loch Earn, and walking in the surrounding hills – Knock Hill, signposted from the town centre, offers

the best views. Crieff Visitor Centre tells the story of ancient drovers' roads. To the west of the town, the Glenturret Distillery dates from 1775 and claims to be Scotland's oldest.

Doune Castle
205 G4

It would be easy to pass through the village of Doune and miss the castle – look out for signs which lead down a narrow road to this substantial grey ruin, hidden in the trees on a curve of the River Teith. Built by the powerful regent of Scotland, Robert Stewart, Duke of Albany, in the late 14th century, it is comparatively simple in construction, with a main block of buildings set with a courtyard, and contained by a great curtain wall.

Killin
204 E1

The village of Killin lies at the western end of Loch Tay, in the ancient district of Breadalbane, and is a popular touring, walking and fishing centre for the area. It has its own attractions, notably the Falls of Dochart, which run through the heart of the village. The surrounding hills abound with legends, which are brought to life at the Breadalbane Folklore Centre in St Fillan's Mill. The preserved, 19th-century farmhouse, Moirlanich Longhouse, is north of the village.

Loch Lomond
204 C5

Some 24 miles long, the loch is a watersports' playground littered with 38 islands. It narrows to the north, where the mountains become bigger and bleaker. Ben Lomond, on the eastern shore, is a popular 'Munro' hill climb at 973m. Luss, off the A82, is the prettiest village to explore. The Loch Lomond Shores Visitor Centre at Balloch (C6) explains the geology and history of the region. This is popular hiking country, with plenty of waymarked trails and a lovely stretch of the West Highland Way long-distance path, which runs down the eastern shore of Loch Lomond.

The Trossachs
205 E4

The Trossachs is the area to the east of Loch Lomond, including the wooded hills of the Queen Elizabeth Forest Park, and the peak of Ben Venue (729m). Some of the best scenery is around Loch Katrine, with easy walking and a steamboat ride among tree-clad islands.

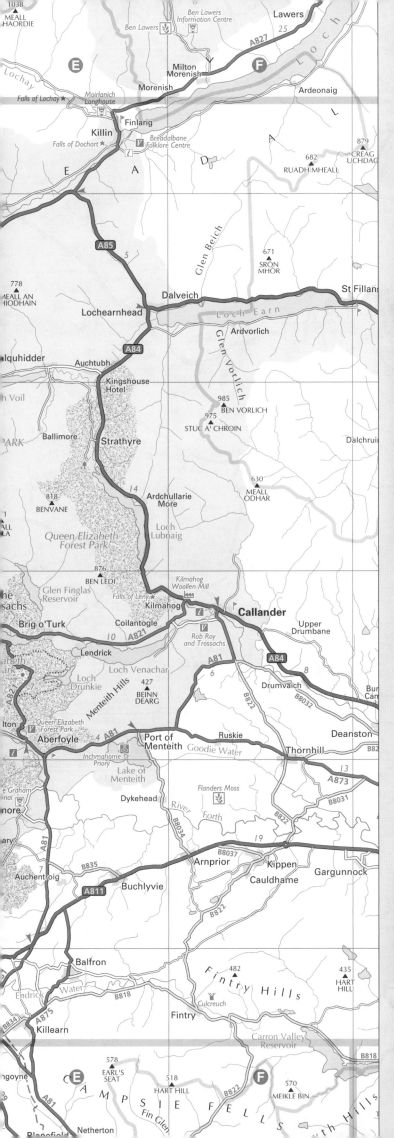

LOCH LOMOND & THE TROSSACHS

Close to the Lowland cities there is a stirring Highland landscape of lochs, mountains and forests in the homeland of Rob Roy MacGregor and the characters of Sir Walter Scott, in whose footsteps the first tourists enthusiastically came. Today the area is a designated National Park.

Ben Venue reflected in the clear waters of Loch Achray in the Trossachs

Aberfoyle 205 E4

Aberfoyle is surrounded by the pine trees of the Queen Elizabeth Forest Park, and the extensive visitor centre 1 mile to the north has information about the many walking routes in the area. This little stone-built town bustles at the heart of the Trossachs, its Scottish Wool Centre, signposted from the main road, attracting a steady flow of visitors throughout the year, to enjoy the lively Sheep Show and the shopping.

Alloa Tower 205 H5

Beautifully restored, the tower, completed in 1467, is the only remaining part of the ancestral home of the Earls of Mar. The structure retains rare medieval features, notably the complete timber roof structure and groin vaulting. A superb loan collection of portraits of the Erskine family includes paintings by Raeburn.

Auchengarrich Wildlife Centre 205 G3

This extensive wildlife park is set in 40.5ha of the Perthshire hills, with animals such as Highland cattle, llamas, chipmunks, beavers, rabbits, porcupines and meerkats. It also has Scotland's largest collection of waterfowl including both ornamental and game birds. There's a huge play barn for the children.

Bannockburn 205 G5

The Heritage Centre, on the outskirts of Bannockburn, commemorates King Robert the Bruce's victory over a much

Enchanting Benmore Botanic Garden is surrounded by dramatic scenery

An ordinary farmhouse hid the entrance to the Secret Bunker

Abbey was a powerful Benedictine house, founded by Queen Margaret in the 11th century. A modern brass in the choir marks the grave of King Robert the Bruce. The monastery guest house became a royal palace, and was the birthplace of Charles I. Visit the Andrew Carnegie Birthplace Museum to learn about the handloom weaver's son, born here in 1835, who created the biggest steel works in the USA and then became a philanthropist on a huge scale.

Falkland Palace 206 D4
Stuart monarchs used this handsome Renaissance-fronted fortress in the heart of Fife as a hunting lodge and cosy retreat. The palace dates to the 15th century, with major additions between 1501 and 1541. Mary, Queen of Scots, spent part of her childhood here. A series of rooms reflects the different periods of occupation, including the Chapel Royal and the King's Room. The gardens are outstanding.

Kellie Castle 207 G4
The oldest part dates from about 1360, but it is for its 16th- and 17th-century domestic architecture (designed by Sir Robert Lorimer) that Kellie Castle is renowned. It has notable plasterwork and painted panelling, and there are also interesting Victorian gardens.

Lochleven Castle 206 C4
Near the western shore of Loch Leven, the stark grey, roofless tower of Lochleven Castle stands on a small island, accessible by boat from Kinross. This 15th-century fortress gained notoriety as the prison of Mary, Queen of Scots, after her defeat in 1567. After her forced abdication she escaped and sought refuge with Elizabeth I of England, who promptly imprisoned her again. The castle was abandoned in the mid-18th century. Loch Leven is a nature reserve noted for its huge over-wintering flocks of pink-footed geese, with the Royal Society for the Protection of Birds' Vane Farm Visitor Centre on its southern shore.

Mills Observatory 207 E1
The observatory was built in 1935, and has a Victorian 10-inch Cooke refracting telescope among its instruments. The gallery has displays on astronomy and space exploration; visitors can view a safe projection of the sun on bright days. There are open nights during the winter months.

Perth 206 C2
Perth is a lively city at the centre of a prosperous farming community, its compact core offering great shopping and bohemian cafés that spill on to the pavements. The Perth Mart visitor centre is housed within the old cattle market – come in February or October for the pedigree bull sales, the biggest of their kind in all Europe. Balhousie Castle, along the edge of the North Inch Park, houses the Black Watch Regimental Museum. Open-top bus tours from the train station are a good way to see the town, linking attractions such as the Art Gallery and Museum, and the 12th-century St John's Kirk, and travelling as far as Scone Palace, 2 miles to the north.

Scone Palace 206 C2
This sumptuously furnished stately home dates mainly from the 19th century. In the grounds is a tartan maze, and the Moot Hill, the earliest crowning place of Scottish kings. The Stone of Scone, or Stone of Destiny, on which kings were crowned, was originally here, but is now held for security in Edinburgh Castle.

Scotland's Secret Bunker
207 G4
The purpose of the bunker was to house a self-supporting military community and seat of government in the event of the Cold War getting out of hand. Now you can explore the eerie chambers, complete with original communications equipment, and the cramped dormitories where as many as 300 personnel would have slept in rotation.

FIFE & KINROSS

Throughout the Middle Ages St Andrews was the spiritual capital and became Scotland's seat of learning. It is best known today for golf. The coastline here is dotted with a string of little fishing villages with quaint cottages around secluded harbours. To the north is the Firth of Tay and the ports of Perth and Dundee, while Dunfermline in the south is on the Firth of Forth.

The three-masted RRS Discovery *is berthed at Discovery Point, Dundee*

Anstruther 207 G4
Anstruther is a resort town and former herring port, where seafront shops sell fish and chips and colourful beach toys. The Scottish Fisheries Museum is housed in historic waterfront buildings around a central courtyard, and illustrates the past and present life of Scottish fishermen and their families. The town also has a history of smuggling, which centred on the Dreel burn and the 16th-century Smuggler's Inn.

Dundee 207 F1
The focus of Dundee's waterfront is Discovery Point, centring on a famous heroine of polar exploration, the three-masted RRS *Discovery*, which was built here in 1900–01. The story of her planning and construction is told in the museum alongside, with models, audio clips and objects that bring the city's shipbuilding to life. On the other side of the train station, Sensation: Dundee is a tribute to modern research. It's a hands-on science centre dedicated to understanding the five senses. At the heart of the city is a former jute factory, the Verdant Works. The tour takes in the origin of the fibre (grown in India), the manufacture and uses of jute, and its considerable impact on the people of Dundee.

Dunfermline 206 C6
The city's volunteer-run Abbot House Heritage Centre propels the traveller through time introducing a range of characters from Dumfermline's past: Scotland's royal saint, Braveheart's Wallace and Bruce, Scotland's Chaucer, steel magnate Andrew Carnegie and a whole panoply of kings, ending with the birth of ill-starred Charles I. Dunfermline

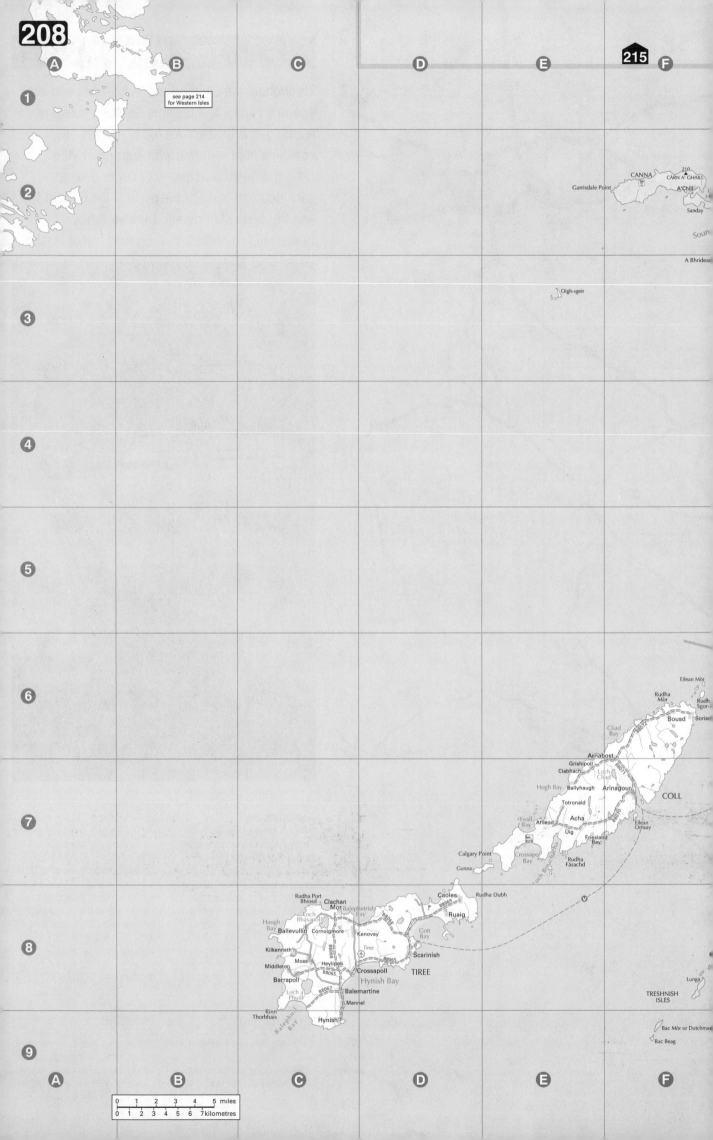

A   B   C   D   E   **215** F

1

see page 214
for Western Isles

2

CANNA
CARN A' GHAILL   210
Garrisdale Point   A'Chill
Sanday

Soun

A Bhridea

3

Oigh-sgeir

4

5

Eilean Mòr

6

Rudha
Mòr   Rudh
Sgor
Sorisd
Cliad
Bay   Bousd
Arnabost
Grishipoll
Clabhach   Loch
Cliad   Arinagour
Hogh Bay   Ballyhaugh   COLL
Totronald
Feall
Bay   Arileod   Acha
Uig   Eilean
Ornsay
Friesland
Bay

7

Calgary Point   Crossapol
Bay   Rudha
Fàsachd
Gunna   Loch Breachacha

8

Rudha Port
Bhiosd   Clachan
Mòr   Balephetrish
Bay   Caoles   Rudha Dubh
Haugh
Bay   Loch
Bhasapoll   Ruaig
Ballevullin   Cornoigmore   Kenovay   Gott
Bay
Kilkenneth   Tiree
Moss   Scarinish
Middleton   Heylipoll   TIREE
Barrapoll   Crossapoll
Hynish Bay
Loch a   Balemartine   Lunga
Phuill   TRESHNISH
Rinn   Mannel   ISLES
Thorbhais   Balephuil
Bay   Hynish

9   Bac Mòr or Dutchma

Bac Beag

A   B   C   D   E   F

Boats moored by the brightly painted houses in Tobermory, Isle of Mull

Eigg 209 H4

Eigg, with its high spine of pitchstone porphyry called the Sgurr, has a small pier-side complex including a restaurant and craft shop. In 1997 the island was famously bought by its occupants, in a landmark venture.

Mallaig 209 K3

Mallaig grew to prominence after the arrival of the railway in 1901, which provided swift access south for fishing catches. That was during the herring boom – now prawns are the mainstay. At the end of the road, Mallaigvaig looks across to the hills of Knoydart, one of the remotest areas of Scotland.

Mull & West Highland Narrow Gauge Railway 209 L9

The first passenger railway on a Scottish island opened on Mull in 1983. Both steam and diesel trains operate on the ten-and-a-quarter inch gauge line, which runs from Craignure to Torosay Castle. The 1.25-mile line offers dramatic woodland and mountain views taking in Ben Nevis, Glen Coe and the Isle of Lismore.

Rùm 209 G3

Once cleared as a private sporting island, Rùm is now a nature reserve owned by Scottish Natural Heritage, and is home to red deer, feral goats and some 100,000 Manx shearwaters which nest in the hillsides. About 30 people live in the small east-coast settlement based around the deserted Edwardian castle at Kinloch, which offers hostel facilities but is otherwise not open to view.

Staffa 209 G9

Many visitors will know of Staffa because of composer Mendelssohn's 'Fingal's Cave' overture. He came to this extraordinary island in 1829, to visit the cavern on its south side. Here, the dark volcanic basalt has cooled and formed its characteristic six-sided columns, making it look like a massive cathedral organ. The enormous interior of Fingal's Cave is also like a cathedral. Weather permitting, boat trips to Staffa allow visitors time ashore.

Tiree 208 D8

To the west of Mull is the island of Tiree. With no woodland and only three sizeable hills on the relatively flat landscape there is nothing to obscure the view. The only sounds you are likely to hear are bird calls and the waves crashing on the endless white beaches made of crushed shells. Rare birds, including corncrakes and little terns, are often seen here.

the cliffs by Mallaig

MALLAIG & INNER HEBRIDES

Mountains, sea lochs and a multitude of small islands ringed with sandy bays form a landscape of wild, untouched beauty.

Ardnamurchan, the most westerly point on the British mainland, is marked with a lighthouse

Ardnamurchan 209 J6

You can go no further west on mainland Britain than Ardnamurchan Point, with its spectacular views over to Mull, Coll and Tiree. A lighthouse stands guard on here with access inside in summer – it's a good place for spotting seals and otters, if you're lucky. The whole Ardnamurchan peninsula, with its rocky hills and desolate moorland, gale-blown trees and pretty heather-capped promontories, has an 'end-of-the-world' feeling. The main road mostly hugs the northern shore of Loch Sunart (L6), rich in birdlife, and you can take a minor road to Ardnamurchan's north coast as the main road passes round Beinn nan Losgann, or continue to the little crofting village of Kilchoan (H6), where a ferry goes to Tobermory on Mull. The 13th-century Mingary Castle (J6), built on its sheer cliff to guard the entrance to Loch Sunart, is the place where King James IV finally accepted the submission of the Lord of the Isles in 1495; Hanoverian troops built barracks inside it 350 years later.
Make a detour to Sanna Bay (H6) for views to Muck, Rùm and Canna and for superb wild flowers by the beach.

Armadale 209 K2

Armadale, on the Isle of Skye, can be reached by ferry from Mallaig. The Castle Gardens and Museum of the Isles are set in the heart of a Highland estate, once part of the lands of Clan Donald. The warming effect of the North Atlantic Drift allows exotic trees and plants to flourish in the 16ha of gardens. Also here is the Museum of the Isles which takes visitors through 1500 years of the history of the area once known as The Kingdom of the Isles.

Canna 208 F2

Canna, one of the Small Isles and an early Christian settlement site, is owned by the National Trust for Scotland. Its most famous feature is Compass Hill where iron in the basalt rock can upset compasses within a radius of 3 miles.

Coll 208 F7

It is the unspoiled beaches, the peace and quiet, the low-lying landscape and the flora and fauna that attract visitors to Coll. Birders flock here, the RSPB has established a nature reserve on the southwest of the island to help protect the corncrake. There is no public transport on the island but you can hire a bike from several places in Arinagour.

Watching the sunset over Rùm and Eigg, f

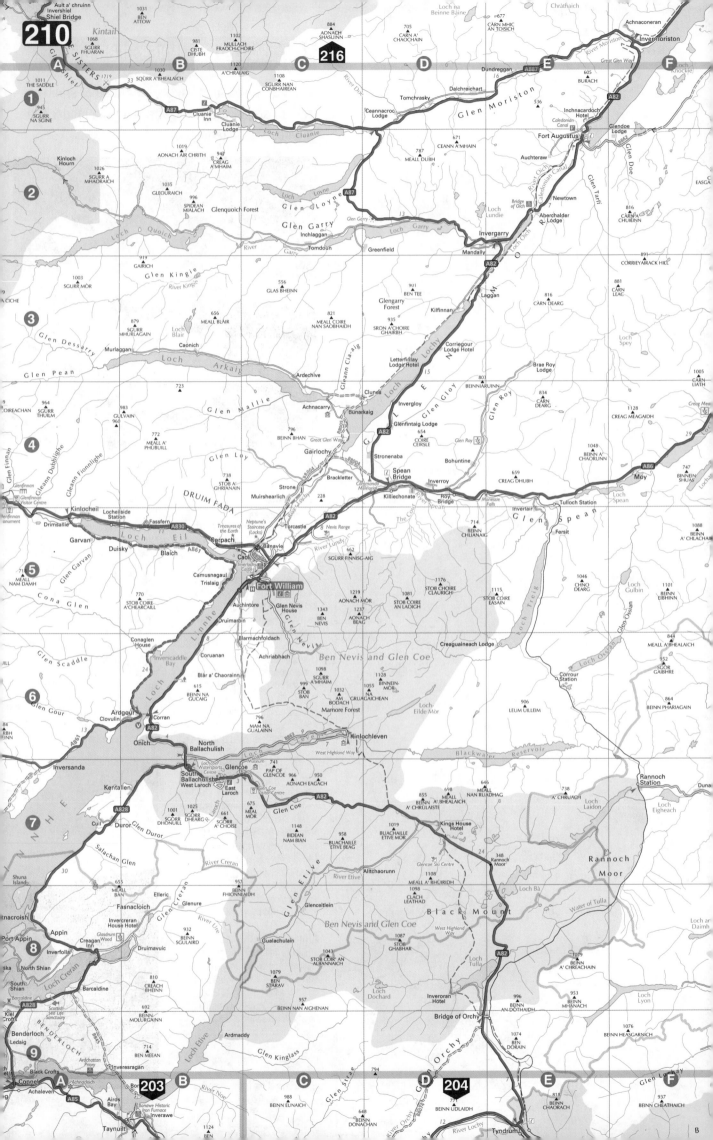

Ruthven Barracks were built just south of Kingussie to subdue the Jacobite rebellion

disaster at Culloden. The occasion is recalled by a pillar monument topped by the statue of a kilted soldier, built here in 1815, which provides a focus for the magnificent view down the loch. The National Trust for Scotland has an informative visitor office near by.

Highland Folk Museum 211 J2
An early 18th-century farming township with turf houses has been reconstructed at this award-winning museum. A 1930s school houses old world maps, little wooden desks and a Coates library. Other attractions include a working croft with rare breed animals and tailor's workshop. Vintage buses run throughout the site.

Highand Wildlife Park 211 K2
As you drive through the main reserve you can see awe-inspiring European bison grazing alongside wild horses, red deer and Highland cattle plus a wide variety of other species. In the walk-round forest, woodland and moorland habitats prepare for close encounters with animals such as wolves, capercaillie, arctic foxes, wildcats, pine martens, otters and owls.

Newtonmore 211 J3
Newtonmore has a reconstructed 18th-century village, including a tailor's workshop, a church and a school. Living history actors bring things to life, including traditional farming skills and crafts such as weaving and wood carving.

Pitlochry 211 L7
This bustling town in the wooded valley of the River Tummel is based around one long main street, lined with shops and eating places. It's been a popular holiday resort since the 19th century, and has two distilleries. There's a view from the footbridge to the salmon ladder, installed as part of the hydroelectric dam system along the river. Learn more about this at the Scottish Hydro Electric Visitor Centre, which gives free access to a fish observation window, as well as a paying exhibition.

Ruthven Barracks 211 J3
The impressive Ruthven Barracks, dramatically set on a grassy mound, formerly the site of a castle, were built in 1718 in order to subdue the Highlands, following the 1715 rebellion. Despite being set on fire by the fleeing Jacobite army in 1746, there are still considerable remains. The garrison here guarded General Wade's military road, leading from Glen Truim in the south.

Scottish Sea Life Sanctuary 210 A9
Set in one of Scotland's most picturesque locations, the Scottish Sea Life Sanctuary provides dramatic views of native undersea life including stingrays, seals, octopuses and catfish. There are daily talks and feeding demonstrations and during the summer young seals can be viewed prior to their release back into the wild.

Glenfinnan Monument on Loch Shiel, where 'Bonnie' Prince Charlie raised the standard in 1745

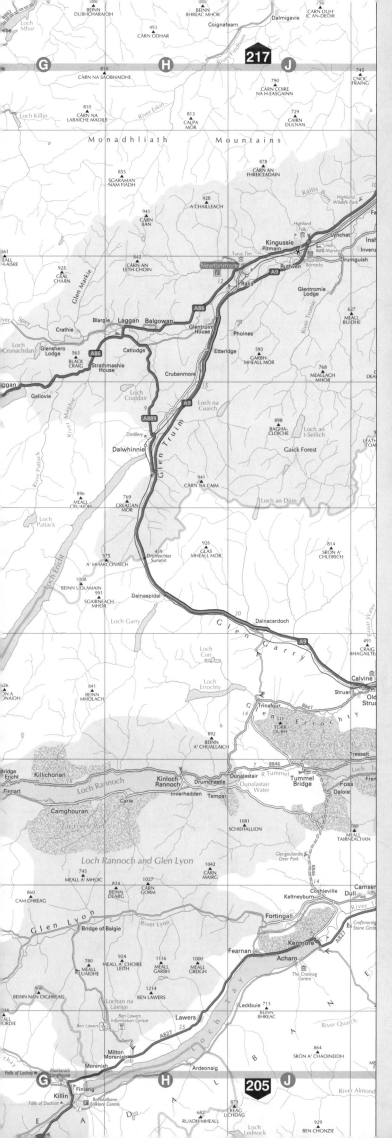

BEN NEVIS & THE GRAMPIANS

Sparkling lochs, some of Scotland's highest mountains, including the towering Ben Nevis, and the grim story of the massacre at Glen Coe combine to make this area one of the country's most popular tourist spots. The winter sports boom has brought benefits to summertime visitors, with cable-car access to some of the mountains.

Buachaille Etive Beag reflected in the still waters of Lochan na Fola in Glen Coe

Aviemore 211 K1

The once-sleepy, remote railway station settlement of Aviemore was developed in the 1960s as a ski destination, and while it has never been able to rival the brash attractions of the continental resorts, it manages to hold its own as an activities centre for the Cairngorms National Park. Its arcaded main street is a reminder of an earlier time, but there is now a good range of outdoor shops and places to eat and relax.

Blair Castle 211 K6

Blair Castle is at the heart of the Atholl Estates set amid glorious Highland scenery. The castle has been the ancient seat of the Dukes and Earls of Atholl for almost 740 years and it is home to the Atholl Highlanders, Europe's only remaining private army. There are 30 splendid rooms open to visitors, who can also explore the historic gardens and grounds which include a deer park, pony trekking centre, farm tours and woodland.

Dunkeld 211 M8

With the exception of the diminutive 13th-century cathedral, the original settlement of Dunkeld was destroyed by the Jacobites after their victory at Killiecrankie in 1689. It was rebuilt, with terraced houses packed tightly into just two main streets, Cathedral Street and High Street, with a tidy little square, the Cross. By the partly restored cathedral stands the Parent Larch, a tree imported from Austria in 1738 and the parent of many of the trees in the nearby forests, planted between 1738 and 1830 by the Dukes of Atholl.

Fort William 210 C5

Fort William's location on a road and rail junction at the head of Loch Linnhe and the foot of the Great Glen makes it a convenient touring base for the northwest of Scotland, and its position makes it popular with walkers and climbers. Fort William's biggest attraction lies to the east: the rounded bulk of Ben Nevis (1,343m), Britain's highest mountain. Conditions at the top can be arctic on the best of days, and walkers should take all necessary precautions before attempting to climb it.

Glencoe 210 C7

The Glencoe and North Lorn Folk Museum is set in two heather-thatched cottages in the main street of the village of Glencoe. It houses items connected with the MacDonalds and the Jacobite risings and local domestic and farming exhibits. Glen Coe itself has stunning scenery and some of the most challenging climbs and walks in the Highlands. Red deer, wildcats, eagles and ptarmigan are among the wildlife. It is also known as a place of treachery and infamy. The MacDonalds of Glencoe were hosts to a party of troops who, under government orders, fell upon the men, women and children, in a bloody massacre in 1692. The Visitor Centre tells the story.

Glenfinnan 210 A4

On 19 August 1745, Prince Charles Edward Stuart ('Bonnie' Prince Charlie) raised his standard here at the top of Loch Shiel, a rallying cry to supporters of his father's claim to the throne of Scotland. It was the start of the Stuarts' final campaign, which would end in

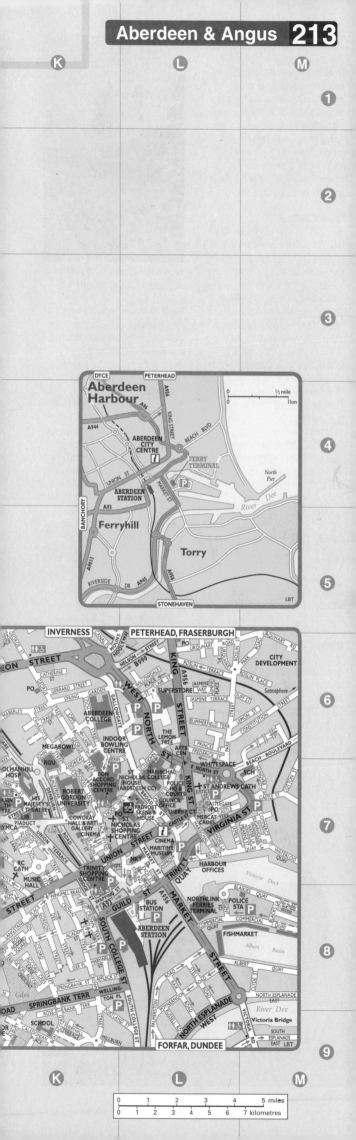

Crathes Castle 213 G3

The castle, dating from 1553, is a great example of a baronial-style tower house, famous for its Jacobean ceilings, boldly painted with figures, designs and mottoes. The interior of the castle presents the comfortable setting of mellow furnishings, oak-carved panels and family portraits, while outside in the garden there are massive hedges of Irish yew topiary and deep herbaceous borders.

Drum Castle 213 G2

The great 13th-century Square Tower is one of the three oldest tower houses in Scotland and has associations with King Robert the Bruce. The handsome mansion, added in 1619, houses a collection of Irvine family treasures. The grounds contain the 40ha Old Forest of Drum, a natural oak wood, and a walled rose garden.

Edzell Castle & Garden 212 E6

The 16th-century castle has a remarkable walled garden built in 1604 by Sir David Lindsay. Flower-filled recesses in the walls are alternated with heraldic and symbolic sculptures of a sort not seen elsewhere in Scotland. There are ornamental and border gardens and a garden house.

Forfar 212 D7

The Meffan, in the centre of town is, a lively art gallery and museum. Here you can discover the Forfar Story on a walk down a cobbled street full of shops, ending up at a witch-burning scene. Carved Pictish stones and a diorama of an archaeological dig complete the vibrant displays.

Glamis 212 C8

Glamis Castle is the family home of the Earls of Strathmore and Kinghorne and has been a royal residence since 1372. It was the childhood home of the late Queen Mother, the birthplace of her daughter the late Princess Margaret, and the setting for Shakespeare's play *Macbeth*. Though the castle is open to visitors it remains the home of the Strathmore family. Each year there are Highland games, a transport extravaganza, the Scottish Prom

Edzell's walled gardens were designed to provide a retreat from the castle

Weekend, and a countryside festival. In the village itself, a row of stone-roofed, late 18th-century cottages houses a collection of domestic equipment and cottage furniture.

Kirriemuir 212 C7

Kirriemuir is a proud little town built of red sandstone. It is associated with writer J M Barrie, whose most famous creation was Peter Pan, the boy who never grew up. Barrie was born here, the son of a handloom weaver, and his birthplace on Brechin Road is now an evocative museum. The town's position makes it the natural gateway to the great Glens of Angus, the long valleys which stretch north into the open moorland of the Grampian Mountains.

Montrose 213 G7

The harbour town of Montrose lies at the mouth of the South Esk River on Scotland's eastern seaboard, with fabulous golden sands exposed at low tide. Its prosperity grew in the 18th century, largely on the back of trade with continental Europe, and some of its architecture echoes the style and elegance of Edinburgh's New Town. A vast, shallow inland sea trapped behind the harbour, the Montrose Basin is important for migrant birds. The House of Dun (F7), on its northern shore, is a mansion of 1730 designed by architect William Adam, and greatly restored by the National Trust for Scotland.

grounds of Glamis Castle

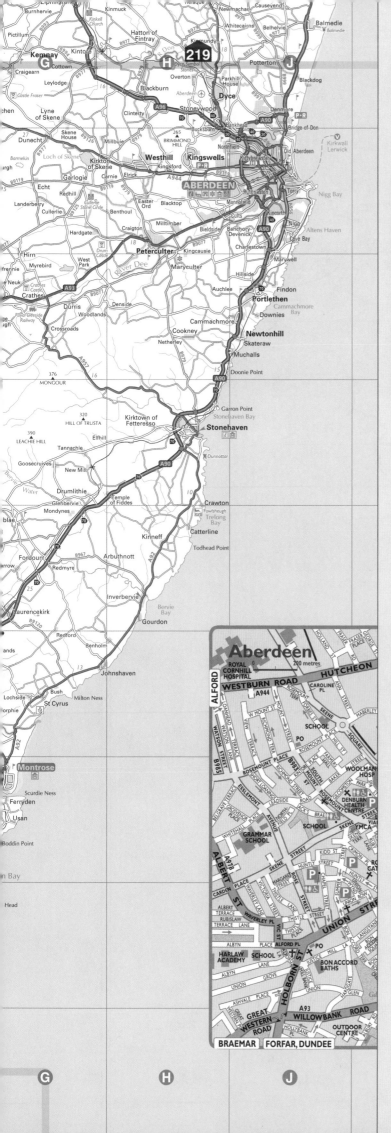

ABERDEEN & ANGUS

Scotland's northeast focuses on Aberdeen, but away from the bright lights and glittering granite buildings is a mellow countryside bristling with strongholds of the past – stone circles, castles and historic houses.

The substantial ruins of Arbroath Abbey are located close to the centre of Arbroath

Aberdeen 213 J2

Scotland's third city was once its biggest seaside resort, thanks to the miles of golden sands which stretch north from the mouth of the River Don. Today Aberdeen has a businesslike air and is better known as the oil capital of Europe. In the late 18th century, the town expanded, and many of Aberdeen's finest granite buildings in the New Town date from the 19th century. Architect Archibald Simpson is associated with many, including the Union Buildings and Assembly Rooms Music Hall on Union Street. Provost Ross's House, on Shiprow (1593), houses the lively Aberdeen Maritime Museum, where visitors can discover what it is like to live and work on a massive North Sea oil platform. The Aberdeen Art Gallery on Schoolhill has an outstanding collection of 18th- to 20th-century paintings.

Arbroath 212 F8

Arbroath Smokies, textiles and engineering feature at the Arbroath Signal Tower Museum housed in the 1813 shore station of Stevenson's Bell Rock lighthouse. The Declaration of Arbroath, declaring Robert the Bruce as king, was signed at the 12th-century Arbroath Abbey on 6 April 1320. The abbot's house is well preserved, and the church remains are also interesting.

Balmoral Castle 212 B3

Queen Victoria and Prince Albert first rented Balmoral Castle in 1848, and Prince Albert bought the property four years later. He commissioned William Smith to build a new castle, which was completed by 1856 and is still the Royal Family's Highland residence. Explore the exhibitions, grounds, gardens and trails as well as the magnificent Castle Ballroom.

Brechin 212 F6

In Brechin's Pictavia Visitor Centre you can find out about the ancient pagan nation of the Picts, who lived in the north nearly 2000 years ago. Visitors can learn about Pictish culture, art and religion through film, interactive displays and music. There are also nature and farm trails, a pets' corner, and an adventure playground in the adjacent country park.

Castle Fraser 213 G1

This magnificent turreted tower house was built between 1575 and 1636. The original structure was remodelled at that time to give it the distinctive Z-plan by the addition of a square tower at one corner and a round one at the opposite corner. The changes were made by the 6th Laird, Michael Fraser, and the castle remained in that family until the 20th century. Family portraits are displayed inside, along with a rich collection of carpets and drapes. The surrounding estate is extensive, with waymarked walks and a walled garden.

A statue of James VI of Scotland stands in

Pastel-painted houses crowd along the harbour in Portree, Skye

scenic road to Elgol (K9). Fine restaurants and Scottish islands don't always go together, but Skye offers some excellent dining. At Carbost (H7), the Talisker Distillery produces a fragrant, peaty single malt whisky.

Isles of Lewis & Harris 214

Lewis and Harris are joined by a narrow neck of land but retain strong individual identities. They share a strong Gaelic culture and a traditional observance of the Sabbath – so plan ahead if you're here on a Sunday, as restaurants, shops and petrol stations may be closed. Lewis (D3), the northern part, has great undulating blanket peat moors scattered with lochs, and a surprising density of population for such an isolated place. Stornoway (E3) is the administrative centre, a busy fishing port and the only real town on the island. Good roads lead through the crofting communities which hug the shore, and to the mountainous southwest corner, where the white sands of Uig (C3) compete with green islands to steal the view. The island has many prehistoric monuments and monoliths, of which the avenue and circle of 13 stones at Callanish (D3), dating to around 3000 BC, is outstanding. Just up the coast, Dun Carloway Broch is an excellent example of a stone-built circular Iron Age dwelling. Situated on the island of Great Bernera (C2) is a reconstructed Iron Age house, which can be compared with the evocative 19th-century Blackhouse at Arnol (D4).

Harris (C5), the southern sector, is the most beautiful of the Outer Hebrides, with high mountains and deep-cut bays. The subtle browns, greens and smoky greys of the landscape are reflected in the island's most famous export, Harris Tweed, a hand-woven wool cloth of high quality made here since the 1840s. At Rodel (C5), St Clements Church dates from c1500, and has curious sculptures on the stone tower.

North Uist 214

Part of the chain of the Outer Hebrides, North Uist (A6), Benbecula (B7), South Uist (B8), Eriskay (A9) and Barra (A9) are linked by a series of causeways and ferry crossings. They are characterised by low, peaty ground glittering with a thousand trout-stocked lochans (small lakes), with big bare hills and beaches of sparkling white shell sand to the west. North Uist is particularly rich in standing stones and other prehistoric remains, signs that these islands have been inhabited for over 4,000 years. Communities are widely scattered and surprisingly numerous, for crofting on the fertile machair (sea meadow) is still viable in the 21st century.

The Kildonan Museum on South Uist (A8) reveals the history of the people here, and also has a welcoming café. The ruined croft house that was the birthplace of Jacobite heroine Flora Macdonald, is signed from the main road near the museum. The islands provide vital wetland habitat for birds including corncrakes, red-necked phalaropes, geese and mute swans, with major reserves at Balranald (A6) and Loch Druidibeg (A8).

The Sound of Eriskay (A9), now crossed by a stone causeway, is where the whisky-laden SS *Politician* foundered in 1941, giving novelist Compton Mackenzie the idea for his comic tale Whisky Galore (1947); the classic film was shot on neighbouring Barra in the following year.

The steep and winding route to remote Applecross crosses a spectacular pass

OUTER HEBRIDES & ISLE OF SKYE

The group of islands off the west coast of Scotland is steeped in history and legend and everywhere there are constant reminders of the past – cairns and tombs and forts.

Applecross 215 M6

The strung-out settlements on this remote west-coast mainland peninsula only became fully accessible by road in the 1970s. Today this winding single-track road is the slow, scenic route between Kishorn and Shieldaig. It takes in the dramatic mountain pass of Bealach-Na-Ba, or Pass of the Cattle, to the south, and the southern shore of Loch Torridon to the north. In between, acid moors and hummocks stretch to mountains inland, with the scattered remains of deserted villages along the coast, overlooking Raasay and Skye. Applecross Bay is a welcoming curve of pinkish sand, with an excellent little inn noted for its seafood.

Isle of Skye 215

Skye is the largest and best known of the Inner Hebrides, its name woven into the story of 'Bonnie' Prince Charlie's flight after the Battle of Culloden in the 18th century, and the loss of a way of island life and emigration to the New World in the 19th century. Every view of the island is dominated by the Cuillin (pronounced coolin) Hills (J8), jagged mountains that reach their highest peak in the south with Sgurr Alasdair (1,009m). These are the Black Cuillin,

distinct from the scree-covered granite of the lower Red Cuillin, but all are challenges for climbers. In the north of the island, ancient lava flows have produced sheer cliffs, with crags and pinnacles such as the Old Man of Storr (K5). On the Trotternish peninsula (J4) are the unusual rock formations of the Quiraing. The harbour town of Portree is the focus of island life, and its Aros Experience offers the best introduction to Skye's natural history.

The Skye Bridge (M8) sets one massive concrete foot firmly on the little 2.4ha island of Eilean Ban, a nature reserve run by a charitable trust for the local community. Access is via the Bright Water Visitor Centre on the pier at Kyleakin (M8), which has information on local wildlife and history.

The western side of Skye is wilder, with the long fingers of Waternish (G5) and Duirnish (F6) stretching to the Outer Hebrides. Dunvegan (G6) is the family seat of the MacLeods, and claims to be Scotland's oldest inhabited castle, occupied since the 13th century. Among its treasures is the Fairy Flag, a now tattered scrap of cloth, with apparently potent powers to rescue the clan at times of peril. Broadford (L8) is the main place in the south, with access to the magnificently

Storm clouds gather over an exposed croft at Carinish on North Uist

Town guide: Inverness p.316

Fort George 217 K5

Built following the Battle of Culloden as a Highland fortress for the army of George II, this is one of the outstanding artillery fortifications in Europe and still an active army barracks.

Glen Affric 216 E8

This peaceful valley is one of the best-loved beauty spots in the Highlands. Its scenery combines forest and moorland, river and loch with mighty mountains such as Carn Eige (1,182m). A narrow road leads up from Cannich (F7) to the River Affric parking area, passing the Dog Falls and a beautiful picnic area at Loch Beinn a Mheadhoin on the way up. Footpaths are marked, and for serious hikers a trail leads through to Kintail.

A 1,265ha area of native woodland, incorporating fragments of ancient Caledonian pine forest, has been established. Crested tits and crossbills may be seen year-round in the woods, while golden eagles and capercaillie are rarer sightings.

Highland Museum of Childhood 217 G5

Located in a renovated Victorian railway station of 1885, the museum tells the story of childhood in the Highlands amongst the crofters and townsfolk; a way of life recorded in oral testimony, displays and evocative photographs.

Inverewe Garden 216 A2

The influence of the North Atlantic Drift enables this remarkable garden to grow rare and sub-tropical plants. At its best in early June, but full of beauty from March to October, Inverewe has a backdrop of magnificent mountains and stands to the north of Loch Maree.

Landmark Forest Heritage Park 217 M8

This woodland-themed park, combines serious information about the natural world with activities such as a giant water slide. The Ancient Forest leads you through a venerable wood of Scots pines, with a treetop walkway and wildlife feeding area favoured by red squirrels.

Loch Ness 217 H8

Loch Ness is believed by some to hide a fishy monster, with the first recorded sighting back in the 6th century AD. Find out about more recent searches and their results at Drumnadrochit's Loch Ness 2000 visitor centre (H8). Urquhart Castle, which overlooks the loch, dates mainly from the 14th century.

Torridon 216 B5

Torridon is a spectacular wilderness of massive, bare mountains. The bulk of Beinn Eighe looms above the lonely pass between Shieldaig and Kinlochewe. This was Scotland's first national nature reserve, celebrated with a visitor centre north of Kinlochewe, and seen at its best from Loch Clair. To the west, Liathach is rated by many climbers and hill walkers as Scotland's finest mountain. The mountains are for serious walkers only, but there's a more accessible path along the north shore of Loch Torridon to Red Point. The National Trust for Scotland has a small visitor centre on the approach to Torridon village, with video footage showing the wildlife of the area.

Ullapool 216 D1

The white-painted houses of this small town stretch along a spit of land on the shore of Loch Broom. Despite its frontier feeling, Ullapool has a dignified air brought about by its neat grid of streets. Tourism has replaced fishing as the mainstay, and as the last settlement of size on the route up the northwest coast, it is usually busy with visitors in summer. The MV Summer Queen cruises to the Summer Isles. South of Ullapool are the breathtaking Corrieshalloch Gorge (E3) and the Falls of Measach.

Dog Falls in Glen Affric is on the route of a popular walk

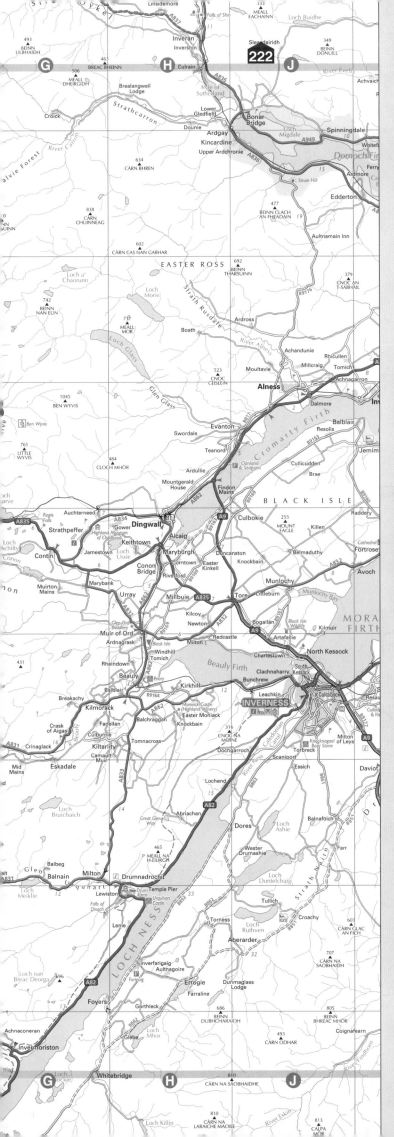

INVERNESS & WESTER ROSS

The sea, lochs and the mountains all converge on Inverness, beautifully set beside the Moray Firth and at the northeastern extremity of the Great Glen. This is a region of castles and gardens, heritage parks and deep lochs, and the desolation of Culloden which tells of the crushing of the Jacobite clans.

Eilean Donan Castle is in a dream setting of loch and mountains

Black Isle 217 JA

Neither black nor an island, the Black Isle is the broad and fertile peninsula bordered by three firths or river estuaries: Cromarty, Beauly and Moray. Wild sea cliffs tip down to low-lying ground in the west, with a central wooded ridge of Ardmeanach. The harbour town of Cromarty occupies the northeast point (K4). Its history is told in the Courthouse Museum on Church Street. Cromarty's most famous son was Hugh Miller, a geologist and fossil collector, his statue stands above the town, and his thatched cottage is a museum.

Cawdor Castle 217 L5

The name of Cawdor evokes Shakespeare's *Macbeth*. It has a central tower dating back to 1454, a drawbridge, and proud turrets and wings that proclaim later additions. It is the home of Angelika, the Dowager Countess of Cawdor, and the presentation of family portraits and treasures within is refreshingly relaxed and even light-hearted.

Culloden 217 K6

A cairn recalls this last battle fought on mainland Britain, on 16 April 1746, when the Duke of Cumberland's forces routed 'Bonnie' Prince Charles Edward Stuart's army. The battlefield has been cleared of vegetation leaving it much as it would have looked on the day the battle took place, and in summer there are living history enactments. This is a most atmospheric evocation of tragic events. An exciting visitor centre explores the impact of the battle.

Dornoch 217 K2

A stone marks the spot near the golf course in Dornoch where, in 1727, Janet Horne was tarred, feathered and burned. Accused of changing her daughter into a pony, she was the last witch in Scotland to be executed. Today the town is known for its world-class golf course, sandy beaches and dolphin-watching expeditions. The cathedral, once the seat of the bishops of Caithness, dates from the 13th century.

Eilean Donan Castle 216 A8

Probably the most photographed castle in Scotland, Eilean Donan is perched on a rock near the northern shore of Loch Duich, and joined to the mainland by a bridge. There has been a fortification on the site since the 13th century, and a MacRae stronghold was destroyed here by government troops in 1719. The perfect castle as seen today, complete with stone walls up to 4.3m thick, is the result of rebuilding between 1912 and 1932.

K   L   M

1

2

3

Rosehearty
Pittulie
Sandhaven
Castle Lighthouse & Museum
Kinnaird Head
Fraserburgh
Peathill
Kirktown
Fraserburgh Bay
Cairnbulg
Inverallochy
Maggie's Hoosie
Whitelinks Bay
Percychorner
Pitblae
A90
B9031
Coburby
Mid Ardlaw
St Combs
Memsie
A98
Memsie Cairn
Rathen
Newburgh
Lonmay
Crofts of Savoch

4

234 WAUGHTON HILL
Strichen
Crimond
Blackhill
Loch of Strathbeg
Rattray Head
New Leeds
Leys
Denhead
Backfolds
Kirktown
St Fergus
Fetterangus
Rora
A981 A950
Deer Abbey
Dunshillock
River Ugie
Inverugie
Buchanhaven
Peterhead
Maud
Old Deer
Mintlaw
Longside
A950
Peterhead Bay
Blackhill of Clackriach
Bulwark
Stuartfield
Inverquhomery
Drymuir
Millbreck
Nether Kinmundy
Hillhead of Cocklaw
Burnhaven
Nethermuir
Clola
Blackhill
Stirling
Buchan Ness
Boddam
Kinnadie
Lendrum Terrace

5

6

Inkhorn
Kinknockie
Longhaven
Coldwells
Ardallie
A90
Auchiries
Bullers of Buchan
Arthrath
Muirtack
Hatton
North Haven
Slains
Ythanbank
Birness
Bogbrae
Chapel Hill
Cruden Bay
Bay of Cruden
Whinnyfold
The Skares
Artrochie

7

Ellon
P+R
Kirkton of Logie Buchan
Collieston
Kirktown of Slains
Esslemont
Logierieve
Forvie
Udny Station
Newburgh
A90
Cultercullen
Foveran
A975
Delfrigs

8

Causeyend
Belhelvie
Balmedie
Balmedie

9

K 213

Potterton
Denmore
A90
Bridge of Don

0 1 2 3 4 5 miles
0 1 2 3 4 5 6 7 kilometres

and a chance to see inside the vast bonded warehouses where the spirit matures. The multimedia exhibition and interactive presentations communicate the unique history, and traditions of Glenlivet Scotch Whisky. A complimentary dram is offered on return from the tour.

Haddo House 219 J7
It is a splendid Palladian-style mansion built in the 1730s to designs by William Adam. Home to the Earls of Aberdeen, the house was refurbished in the 1880s in the 'Adam Revival' style. The adjoining country park offers beautiful woodland walks.

Huntly Castle 218 F6
The original medieval castle was rebuilt a number of times and destroyed, once by Mary, Queen of Scots. It was rebuilt for the last time in 1602, in palatial style, and is now an impressive ruin, noted for its ornate heraldic decorations. It stands in wooded parkland.

Kildrummy Castle 218 E9
An important part of Scottish history, at least until it was dismantled in 1717, this fortress was the seat of the Earls of Mar. Now it is a ruined, but splendid, example of a 13th-century castle, with four round towers, hall and chapel all discernible. Some parts of the building, including the Great Gatehouse, are from the 15th and 16th centuries.

Macduff Marine Aquarium 219 H4
Exciting displays feature local sea life. The central exhibit, unique in Britain, wholds a living kelp reef where divers feed the fish. Other displays include an estuary exhibit, splash tank, rock pools, deep reef tank and ray pool. Young visitors especially enjoy the touch pools. There are talks, video presentations and feeding shows throughout the week.

Pitmedden 219 J8
The outstanding attraction here is Pitmedden Garden, a fine 17th-century walled garden planted on an extravagant scale. Five miles of box hedging form six parterres each filled

Towering Sueno's Stone is encased in protective glass

with 40,000 plants to produce a brilliant display during the summer months. Herbaceous borders provide a colour throughout the season. There is a Museum of Farming Life and a woodland walk leads visitors around the estate.

To the north is Tolquhon Castle. Now roofless, this late 16th-century quadrangular mansion encloses an early 15th-century tower. There is a fine gatehouse and a splendid courtyard.

Pluscarden Abbey 218 B5
This remarkable monastery is the only medieval foundation in Britain still used for its original purpose. Lying in a green valley it is the permanent home of 27 Benedictine monks, and a haven of spiritual retreat for both men and women. The monastery was founded in 1230 for the French Valliscaudian order by Alexander II, and during the Reformation in the 16th century was gradually abandoned. In 1943 Benedictine monks from Prinknash Abbey in Gloucestershire started to restore it, and in 1974 it received the status of abbey. Today the white-habited monks work in the grounds and workshops and care for the abbey buildings. These focus on the massive abbey church, where ancient stonework and frescoes contrast with modern stained glass.

...5 and set in extensive grounds with woodland walks, is today a cultural arts centre

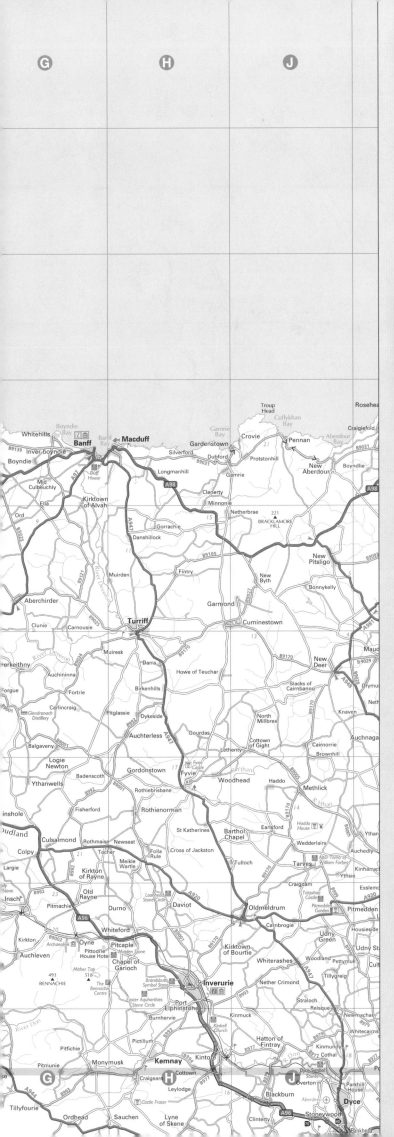

NORTH ABERDEENSHIRE & MORAY

The pure clear waters of the River Spey are at the heart of Scotland's whisky trade, with more distillers in Speyside than any other area.
On the rugged coastline the busy fishing ports, such as Peterhead and Fraserburgh, are the centre of the fishing industry.

Glenfiddich, above, features on Speyside's Malt Whisky Trail

Deer Abbey 219 K6
The remains of the Cistercian abbey, founded in 1218, include the infirmary, Abbot's House, refectory and kitchen. Like the abbey church, most of the buildings to the west and north of the cloister are simply lines of stone in the grass. To the north is a display of carved structural stonework found during investigations of the abbey. The University Library at Cambridge now houses the famous *Book of Deer*, one of the oldest documents in Scottish history.

Duff House 219 G4
Tucked away in an apparently quiet corner of Banff, Duff House is the principal outstation of the National Galleries of Scotland, providing the perfect, glittering backdrop to a wealth of paintings including portraits by the Scottish painters Raeburn and Ramsay, and paintings of the Italian, Dutch and German schools of art. The house itself is a grand mansion designed by architect William Adam for the 1st Earl of Fife. It was started in 1735, but unfortunately the Earl's pride in his new house was seriously dented when a crack appeared in the structure, and he never lived there.

Forres 218 A5
The ancient market town of Forres on the River Findhorn was once plagued by witches. William Shakespeare made full use of this in *Macbeth* (c1606), when he set scenes with the three 'weird sisters' in the area. Three more witches are commemorated with an iron-bound stone in the town. A huge glass box protects Sueno's Stone, on the eastern outskirts. This is a Pictish cross-slab which stands 6m tall and is believed to date from the 9th or 10th century (free access). The sandstone is intricately carved in five sections with vivid scenes from an unidentified and

bloody battle. To the south of Forres, the Dallas Dhu Historic Distillery is preserved by Historic Scotland.

Glenfarclas Distillery 218 C7
Established in 1836, Glenfarclas Distillery is proud of its independence. There is a guided tour illustrating their whisky's history and production, followed by a dram in the splendour of the Ships Room or a chance to browse in the gift shop.

Glenfiddich Distillery 218 D6
Set close to Balvenie Castle, the distillery was founded in 1887 by William Grant and has stayed in the hands of the family ever since. Visitors can see the whisky-making process in its various stages, including bottling, and then sample the finished product.

Glenlivet Distillery 218 B8
The visitor centre includes a guided tour of the whisky production facilities

Duff House, designed by William Adam in

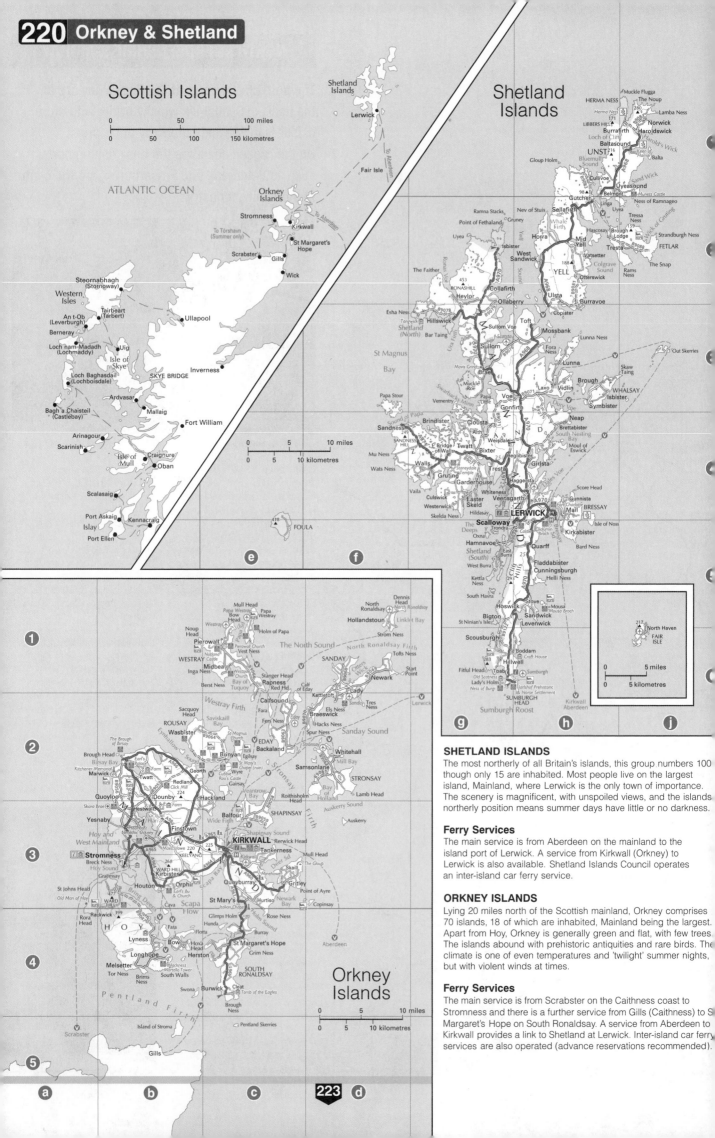

SHETLAND ISLANDS

The most northerly of all Britain's islands, this group numbers 100 though only 15 are inhabited. Most people live on the largest island, Mainland, where Lerwick is the only town of importance. The scenery is magnificent, with unspoiled views, and the islands northerly position means summer days have little or no darkness.

Ferry Services

The main service is from Aberdeen on the mainland to the island port of Lerwick. A service from Kirkwall (Orkney) to Lerwick is also available. Shetland Islands Council operates an inter-island car ferry service.

ORKNEY ISLANDS

Lying 20 miles north of the Scottish mainland, Orkney comprises 70 islands, 18 of which are inhabited, Mainland being the largest. Apart from Hoy, Orkney is generally green and flat, with few trees. The islands abound with prehistoric antiquities and rare birds. The climate is one of even temperatures and 'twilight' summer nights, but with violent winds at times.

Ferry Services

The main service is from Scrabster on the Caithness coast to Stromness and there is a further service from Gills (Caithness) to St Margaret's Hope on South Ronaldsay. A service from Aberdeen to Kirkwall provides a link to Shetland at Lerwick. Inter-island car ferry services are also operated (advance reservations recommended).

The neolithic village of Skara Brae is one of Orkney's most-visited sites

treasure of World Heritage status. You have to bend double to walk through the 14.5m entrance passage before you emerge into the beautifully formed inner chamber. While the contents are long gone, the structure itself has survived undamaged, barring some runic graffiti left by passing Vikings. Nearby is the Ring of Brodgar, a magnificent stone circle.

The lighthouse perched on the clifftop at Cape Wrath was built in 1828

Northwest of Kirkwall, Skara Brae is the site of a village inhabited between 3100 and 2500 BC. The sands subsequently encroached and covered the houses, which lay undiscovered until a storm in 1850 revealed stone structures. Excavations showed six similar houses linked by passageways. As you walk around the site, you look down into the houses from above. Slabs of stone created hearths, cupboards in the walls, bed surrounds, clay-lined troughs in the floor, and even a dresser. Orkney's second town, Stromness, boomed in the early 19th century. The winding main street is paved and cobbled; follow it all the way to its southern end, to the maritime displays in the Stromness Museum on Alfred Street.

Shetland Islands 220

The capital is the harbour town of Lerwick (h4) where traditional knitwear is the thing to buy. The Shetland Museum in a splendid building on Hays Dock is a terrific introduction to the islands. Complex layers of history were uncovered at Jarlshof Prehistoric and Norse Settlement, near Sumburgh (h6), when a storm dislodged the covering turf. The obvious survivor is the shell of the 17th-century Laird's House, which overlies a broch. Around it are the remains of a Viking farm with a communal longhouse. Further layers have revealed a settlement from the 2nd century BC, and a 14th-century medieval farm. The double-skinned circular tower of Mousa Broch (h5) dates from 100 BC to AD 300, and is the best-preserved example of its kind in Scotland. Access in summer is via a small passenger boat from Leebitton, in Sandwick. A tiny grass-covered island off the southwest coast, St Ninian's Isle (g5) is a green jewel. It is joined to the land by a curved tombolo of silvery shell sand, which permits access except during the highest tides of the year, and is a lovely area for walks.

St Ninian was the first Christian missionary to reach Shetland, and the ruins of a 12th-century church still stand. In 1958 a hoard of intricately worked Pictish silver was discovered, buried under the nave. The treasure is now in the Museum of Scotland in Edinburgh, but replicas can be seen in the Shetland Museum in Lerwick. The nature reserve at Herma Ness (j1), on Unst, is home in the summer to 100,000 screaming seabirds which nest on and around the cliffs. There's a regular ferry service from Yell to Unst.

dramatic landscape

① ② ③ ④ ⑤ ⑥ ⑦ ⑧ ⑨

(map labels)

Old Man
of Stoer

Clash

Bay of C

Rhu
Coigach

Rubha Mòr
Reiff

Achna

Altandhu

Eilean Mullagrach

Isle Ristol

Polbain

Glas-leac Mòr   SUMMER ISLES

Tanera
Beg

Badentarbat
Bay

Steòrnabhagh
(Stornoway)

Tanera
Mòr

Glas-leac Beag

Horse
Island

Priest
Island

Eilean Dubh

Greenstone
Point

Cailleach Head

Leac

Rudha Beag

Scoraig

Mellon
Udrigle

Stattic Point

Little

Rudha Reidh

Cove

Mellon
Charles

Ormiscaig

Laide

GRUINARD
ISLAND

Badluachrach

A832

Gruinard
Bay

Badcau

WEST SUTHERLAND, ORKNEY & SHETLAND

Orkney, a green and fertile group of islands, played a key role in both world wars, while Shetland, the most northerly part of Britain, has a culture that is more Viking than Scottish. West Sutherland is a vast, empty expanse, treeless and often windswept. Most visitors are drawn by Cape Wrath with its chill winds and the roar of the pounding waves.

Lerwick's main thoroughfare passes in front of the harbour which is lined with sandstone buildings dating from the 18th century

Cape Wrath 221 M1

The far northwestern corner of Scotland feels like another country, with silvery light reflected from the grey quartzite mountains, and everywhere emptiness and space. If you want to get to Cape Wrath, prepare for a short ferry ride over the Kyle of Durness, then a minibus ride across the bleak moor called The Parph. The road passes between the peaks of Sgribhisbheinn and Fashven to reach the sheer Clo Mor cliffs and the remote lighthouse, built in 1828, which blinks out over the Atlantic.

Knockan Crag 221 L8

North of Ullapool the habitation is sparse and the landscape becomes altogether bigger and wilder, with giant, bare mountains looming out of bleak, bitter moorland. Knockan Crag National Nature Reserve offers access to this fine, dramatic countryside in all its glory. The visitor centre, which has interactive displays on the landscape and the geology of the area and details of two circular trails, is a good place to start.

There is a further extensive nature reserve at Inchnadamph (M6). From this point the road leads round the shores of Loch Assynt, past the rocky ruins of Ardvreck Castle. Beyond this place is the popular harbour of Lochinver (K6). This links up with a narrow and very scenic road from Loch Lurgainn.

Orkney Islands 220

This low-lying group of more than 90 islands and skerries lies 20 miles off the northern coast of Scotland. Today these islands ring with Norse-sounding placenames, although Picts and Celts pre-dated the Vikings by at least 4,000 years, leaving extraordinary signs of their presence at Maes Howe (b3) and Skara Brae (b3). Hoy (b4) is the second largest of the Orkney islands. Its best-known feature is the columnar stack of red sandstone, known as the Old Man of Hoy. The heather-covered hills of Cuilags and Ward Hill offer excellent walking country, with views over Scapa Flow. This sheltered natural harbour was home to the Royal Navy during both world wars, and was the site of the scuttling of the German fleet after the end of World War I. Learn more at the fascinating Scapa Flow Visitor Centre and Museum at Lyness (b4). A group of Italian prisoners of war confined on the islands during World War II created the Italian Chapel in two Nissen huts. The buildings of Kirkwall's (c3) narrow, paved streets date from the 16th to the 18th centuries. Dominating everything is St Magnus Cathedral on Broad Street, begun by Earl Rognvald in 1137 and completed in the 15th century. A 7m grassy mound in a field to the south of Loch of Harray, on the road from Stromness to Finstown, is Maes Howe. Under the turf lies a chambered grave dating from around 2800 BC that is a

The visitor centre at Knockan looks out ove

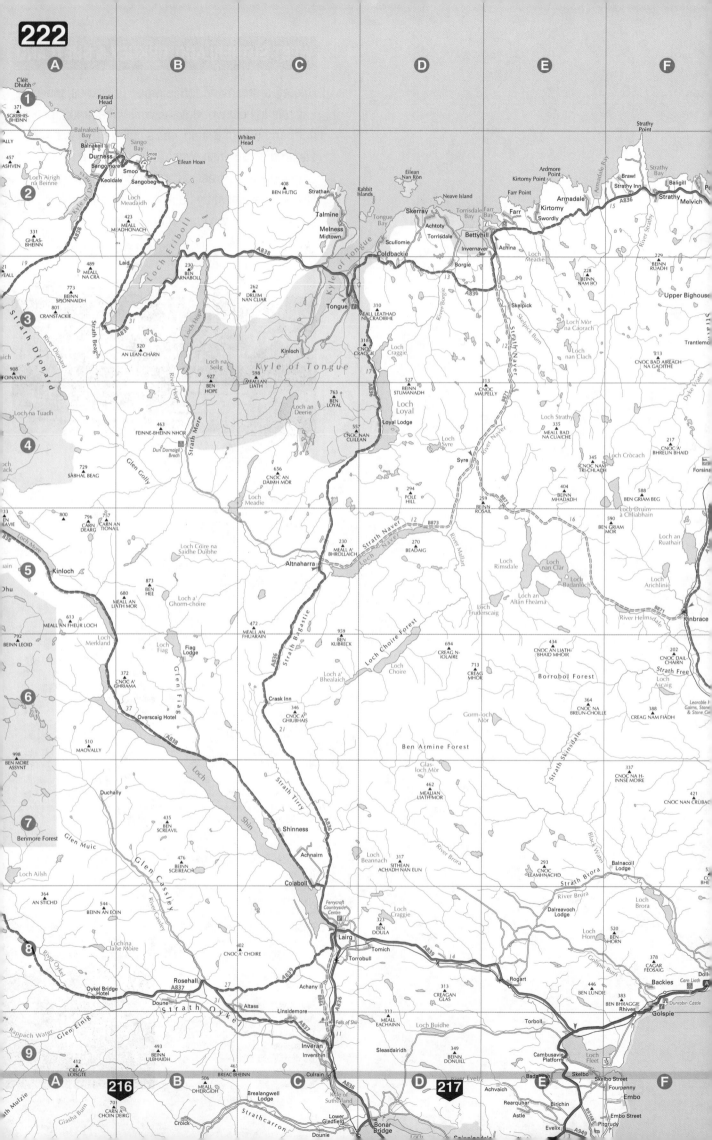

PENTLAND FIRTH

K   L   M

St John's Point
St Margaret's Hope

DUNCANSBY HEAD

1

Scarfskerry
Castle of Mey
Gills Bay
Brough
Loch Mey
Gills
Kirkstyle
Huna
John o' Groats
Muckle Stack
Rattar
Mey
Barrock
Canisbay
Stacks of Duncansby
St John Loch
Dunnet
Inkstack
Brabstermire
Skirza

2

astlehill
Castletown
Greenland
Loch Heilen
Gill Burn
Freswick
Freswick Bay
Ness Head
Tain
Slickly
Auckengill
Bowermadden
Kirk Burn
Nybster
220
Bower
Lyth
Sortat
Howe
Brough Head
Halcro
16
Mireland
Keiss
17
illock
Kirk
Loch of Wester
Sinclair Bay

3

Loch Watten
Killimster
Reiss
Castle Girnigoe & Sinclair
Noss Head
Watten
A882
Winless
Sibster
Ackergill
Staxigoe
Bilbster
Haster
Milton
Janetstown
Wick
Papigoe
Wick Bay
Badlipster
Newton
Old Wick
South Head
Loch Hempriggs
Whiterow
Castle of Old Wick

4

Tannach
Thrumster
145 BALLHARN HILL
Grey Cairns of Camster
212 Loch of Yarrows
Sarclet
HILL OF YARROWS
Cairn o'Get
Ulbster
Whaligoe
ER HILL
Roster
Hill o'Many Stanes
Whaligoe Steps
Bruan
Upper Lybster
Mid Clyth
Halberry Head

5

Swiney
Occumster
Clyth Ness
Invershore
Lybster
Forse
Lybster Bay
Latheron
town

6

7

8

9

K   L   M

0 1 2 3 4 5 miles
0 1 2 3 4 5 6 7 kilometres

Set amid beautiful gardens, Dunrobin Castle has been home to the Earls and Dukes of Sutherland since the 13th century

John o' Groats 223 L1

In popular imagination, John o' Groats is the most northerly point on the British mainland, 874 miles from Land's End in Cornwall. It is named after a Dutchman, Jan de Groot, who lived here in 1509, and his octagonal house overlooks the wild waters of the Pentland Firth. There are craft studios, souvenir shops and a café or two to mark the location, and good walks to the spectacular wind-blown cliffs of Duncansby Head.

The late Queen Elizabeth, the Queen Mother, restored the nearby Castle of Mey as a holiday home. It contains an appealing blend of kitsch, comfort and grandeur.

Lairg 222 C8

Lairg, a small rural village in central Sutherland, is an ideal touring base for visiting the remote north. At the Falls of Shin, to the south, visitors can see the Atlantic salmon battle upstream to return to Loch Shin and their spawning grounds. There are several woodland walks from the visitor centre, which also has a restaurant, gift shop and an adventure playground.

Smoo Cave 222 B2

Between Durness and the inlet of Loch Eriboll is Smoo Cave, reached by a steep path down to the cavern, where the high arched mouth opens into three chambers accessed by paths, bridges and walkway. There are pools within the cave, and dripping limestone has created a Gothic collection of stalactites and stalagmites.

Strath Naver 222 E3

This remote valley has a forlorn air, the landscape dotted with broken walls and the grassy mounds of small homesteads. Its name is resonant with the period of the Highland Clearances, and in particular with the clearing of his land by the Duke of Sutherland and his callous factor (land agent), Patrick Sellar, between 1812 and 1819, to make way for sheep farming. It was a time when the crofters were forced to leave their homes inland to eke a living on the inhospitable coast, or join the emigration to the New World. The story is well told at Strathnaver Museum near Bettyhill (E2). In the valley, there is a well-marked trail at the former village of Rosal.

Thurso 223 J2

The thriving little town of Thurso, where a good salmon river pours through the little harbour into the bay, has long been a gateway to Orkney. It is also a point of departure for those embarking on the scenic route taking in the north and west coasts via Durness and Ullapool.

Wick 223 L3

The Heritage Centre is a fascinating local museum. It tells of the town's heyday as one of the busiest herring ports in the world, when the harbour bristled with boats and the population was swelled by migrant workers from the west coast and Ireland. Some of the boats and whole rooms are preserved here, and you can see the old smokehouse for curing fish. At the core of the museum is the outstanding Johnston collection of photographs which form a vivid record of life in the town between 1863 and 1977.

To the south is the ruin of the best-preserved Norse castle in Scotland, Castle of Old Wick. Dating from the 12th century this spectacular site is on a spine of rock projecting into the sea, between two deep, narrow gullies. Visitors must take great care and wear sensible shoes.

The much-photographed signpost at John o' Groats points the way to Land's End some 874 miles away

NORTH OF SCOTLAND

The lonely northern coast offers a rich variety of scenery, from tall storm-lashed cliffs to gentle sandy bays. Inland, scattered ruined cottages remain, testimony to a more populous past before the Clearances, when landlords drove people from the land in favour of more profitable sheep.

A deserted croft sets the scene near Bettyhill, Strath Naver

Dunbeath 223 J6

The village of Dunbeath was built to cash in on the herring boom in the early 1800s, with up to 100 boats operating from the harbour here. The herring boom is long gone and the harbour is much less active now, but you can learn about Dunbeath's past in the Heritage Centre. Just north of Dunbeath is the Laidhay Croft Museum, recreating the experience of a crofting life now largely gone. The museum gives visitors a glimpse of a long-vanished way of life.

Dunnet Head 223 J1

Dunnet Head is the most northerly point on mainland Britain and on a clear day it commands extensive views from Cape Wrath at the northwestern tip of mainland Scotland to Duncansby Head, at its closer northeastern tip, though it is Hoy and Orkney to the north that command most attention. There are many lochans on the tussocky headland, along with structures from World War II built to defend the naval base at Scapa Flow in Orkney. Also here is the lighthouse built in 1832.

Dunrobin Castle 222 F8

Looming above its gardens like a French château, Dunrobin Castle has 189 rooms, making it the largest mansion in northern Scotland. It dates back to c1275, but its outward appearance is overwhelmingly Victorian, thanks to extensions between 1845 and 1850 by Sir Charles Barry, the architect of the Houses of Parliament.

Helmsdale 223 H7

Gold fever struck this little harbour in 1868, when gold was discovered in the Strath of Kildonan and up to 3,000 prospectors set up a shanty town. The excitement was brought to a halt by the local landowner, the 3rd Duke of Sutherland, but you can still buy gold panning equipment in the town today and try your luck.

Helmsdale grew up in the early 19th century as a resettlement site for crofters who had been moved from farther inland to make way for large-scale sheep farming in an episode which became known as the Highland Clearances — learn more at the Timespan Heritage Centre on Dunrobin Street.

Fishing boats and lobster pots on a grassy area in front of the ruins of old St Peter's Kirk in Thurso

A An Tiaracht
Tearaght Island

AN BLASCAOD MÓR
GREAT BLASKET
ISLAND

Beiginis
Beiginish

Blasket
Centre

Killurrihy
514

Cuan
Fionntrá

Daingin
184

An Dún Meánach
Doonmanagh

Aglish

284

Acres Point

B 290

Inis na Bró
Inishnabro

1·75

Inis Mhic Aoibhleáin
Inishvickillane

1·35

Bealach an
Bhlascaoid
Blasket
Sound

Sliabh an Iolair
Mount Eagle

CEANN SLÉIBHE
Slea Head

Fán
Fahan

Pointe na Páirce
Parkmore Point

Ventry
Harbour

Ballymacadoyle
Hill

21

An Bhuaic

Pointe na
Reanna
Reenbeg
Point

Ceann an
Daimh
Bull's
Head

Ceann na
Mine Airde
Minard
Head

Inch Point
Illaunstoo

DINGLE BAY
Bá an Daingin

Rossbehy
Creek

Caragh Bric

Ross Behy

R564

Glenbeigh
Wood

Glen
Glea

Seefir

Glanbehy
Bridge

228

Canglass Point

King's Head

Feakelecally

N70

Mount Foley
252

The Kerry
Way

Kells

Glenesh
Wood

668

651

Been Hill

Bunglas

14

Beenreagh

Coomaglaslaw
Lake

Beenreagh

Knocknadobar

688

13

Fóilmore
Bridge

Teeromoyle

Mullaghnarakill

662

772

714

606

Coomasaharn
Lake

Beal

DOULUS HEAD

Killelan
Mountain

267

Slievagh
207

Coomduff

IVERAGH

Teermoyle

Meenteog

Macklaun

686

Colly

Dr

466

CAHERSIVEEN
Cathair Saidhbhín

Reenadrolaun
Point

Beginish
Island

Valencia
Harbour

Knight's Town

Caunoge
Cánóg

Keelnagore

Cnocrua
Knockroe

Coill na gCorr
Keelnagore

495

Knocknagapple

Ballaghisheen
Forest

547

Knocknacu

Fogher Cliff

Chapeltown

VALENCIA ISLAND

Beennakryraka
Head

Aghnagar
Bridge

Cillín Liath
Killeenleagh

497

Faill an Locha
Foillclogh

Derreen

Cro Oireach
Dromarágh

Loch Dhoire Ianna
Derriana Lough

An Cnoc Maol
Knockmoyle

Loch Thuairín Uí
UIBH

682

Skellig
Experience

R565

R565

20

Portmagee Channel

Cill Ó Luaigh
Killoluaig

An tImleach Mór
Emlaghmore

676

Knocknagantee

Portmagee
An Caladh

397

BRAY HEAD

Dromgour

Derreen

8

Máistir Gaoithe
Mastergeehy

Loch Chluáin Eachlann
Cloonaghlin Lough

Tul

Baile na hAbhann
Ballynahow

An Trian Iarach
Teeranearagh

Moing Uí Dhúda
Muingydowda

Loch na Móna
Lough Namona

River

Cill Urlaí
Killurly

R567

Sallahig

Caherbarnagh

Loch Uisce na Mac Tire
Lough Iskanamacteery

Lomanagh

Oileán na gCánóg
Puffin Island

LOCH LUÍOCH
Lough Currane

673

650

Coomcallee

BÁ FHÍONÁIN
St Finan's Bay

Baile an Sceilg
Ballinskelligs

AN COIREÁN
Waterville

Loch na
nGrág

An Sceilg Bheag
Little Skellig

Bólas
Bólus

Oileán
an Chapaill
Horse Island

An Baile Breac
Ballybrack

509

Esknaloughoge

377

Derreenauliff

Ceann Duibhchealla
Ducalla Head

409

BÁ NA SCEALG
Ballinskelligs Bay

Árd Caorach
Ardkearagh

Mullach Bog
Mullaghbeg

542

The Kerry
Way

Illaunleagh

Skellig Michael

Sceilg Mhichíl
Skellig Michael

CEANN BHÓLAIS
BOLUS HEAD

Ceann Muice
Hog's Head

499

Cnoc an Iolair
Eagles Hill

Bunnow Harbour

Cahernageeha
Mountain

Castle Cove

N70

Illaundrane

Binn Uí Ruairc
Beenarourke

304

Cathair Dónall
Caherdaniel

Nedanone

RIVER

Dog's

Derrynane

Oileán na
Mainistreach
Abbey Island

Derrynane Bay

Daniel's Island

KENMARE

Dúinis
Deenish
Island

Ceann an Uain
Lamb's Head

Ardgroom

Dhá Dhrom

Lough
Fadda

An Scairbh
Scariff Island

Kilcatherine Point

Inishfarnard

Gortgarriff

COULAGH BAY

Eyeries
Na hAoraí

R57

Crumpa

Ardacluggin
Point

Urhin

Travara Bridge

Kealinc

MOUNTAI

C

B

Cod's Head

19

R575

Knocknagallaun

SLIEVE MISKISH

376

488

Knockgour

Baile Chaisleáin
Bhéarra

BEARA
PENINSULA

Allihies
Na hAllichí

Ballydonegan

Gour
Bridge

R572

The Bull

Garnish
Point

Cable
Car

Garnish
Bay

Lackacroghan
760

Firkeel

8

Gahermore

Fair
Head

DURSEY ISLAND

Ballynacallagh

The Béara Way

Kilmichael

The Cow

DURSEY
HEAD

White Ball Head

Black
Ball Head

Crow Head

The Calf

ATLANTIC OCEAN

TRALEE, LIMERICK

HBI

Kerry County
Airport

N22

N22

NORTH RING ROAD

N22

CORK

St FINAN'S
HOSPITAL

CONVENT

ST MARGARET'S ROAD

ROCK ROAD

FITZGERALD
STADIUM

DISTRICT
HOSPITAL

N71

PORT ROAD

KILLORGLIN

Deenagh River

N72

CONVENT

SCHS

NEW ROAD

SCH

LIBRARY

ST ANNE'S ROAD

HIGH STREET

OLD LEWIS RD

COURT-
HOUSE

Fair Hill

CORK

CORK

COLLEGE

CATHEDRAL

SCHOOL

FRIARS MACOIL

NEW STREET

MAIN ST

COLLEGE ST

EAST AVE RD

BUS &
RAIL
STATION

Killarney

National
Park

CATHEDRAL
PL

BEECH ROAD

PO

TOWN
HALL

COUNTESS ROAD

N71

MUCKROSS ROAD

ROSS ROAD

Race Course,
Ross Castle

Killarney

200 metres

200 yds

© Govt of Ireland 2008

KENMARE

WOODLAWN ROAD

R Y

K L RATHMORE M
An Ráth Mhór
Scrahanfa
Gneeveguilla
Gullaun Cullen
Raheen

MILLS
Sráid a
Barraduff N72 R582 Ballydaly
N72 R570 Headfort Claragh
Mountain
450
229 N22 Glenflesk Caherbarnagh
The Paps 682
528 577 Knocknabro BAILE BHUIRNE
Poulgorm Knocknagowan Ballyvourney
Bridge
Clonkeen DERRYNASAGGART MOUNTAINS Baile Mhic Íre
CNOIC DHOIRE NA SAGART Ballymakeery
Carrigawaddra N22 Clondrohi
Coomagearlahy Mullach an Ois Lissacresig
Mullaghanish
Morley's Bridge Cúil Aodha Re na nDoiri
Inchee Bridge Coolea Reananerree
Cill na Martra
Barnastooka Doire Fhinín Killnamartery
An Leaca Bhán Derryfineen
Lackabaun
Kilbarry
Carran Béal Átha Turnaspidogy Rossmore
Knockantooreen an Ghaorthaidh
Bealick Ballingeary Inchigeelagh RIVER LEE
Gougane Barra Inse Geimhleach
Forest Park Caolmhagh Bohane's
Kealvaugh Cross Roads Kil
Conigar Doughill Gortnahoughtee Baul
Cappaboy Mountain Carrigarierk Glan
Beg Douce Cross Roads
Mountain Carrigmount Tullagh Shanlaragh
Gortloughra Shanacrane Togher
Bridge Inchicahan
Maulavanig Cahermuckee Cousane Farnanes Derrynacaheragh Cross Roads
Cousane Gap
Kealkill Barrboy DUNMANWAY
Maughanaclea Dún Mánmhaí
Hills Coomleagh Nowen Hill Coolkellure
Pierson's Ardrah Sillahertane
Bridge Barnagowlane Mullaghmesha Milane Hill Clubhouse
Ballylickey Leitry Bridge Cross Road
Glandart Ceancullig Clashnacrona
BANTRY Forest
Beanntraí Trawlebane Moyny Curraghalicky
Bridge Lake
Sprat Hill Dromore Bawnboy DRIMOLEAGUE Curraghalicky
Drom Dhá Liag Drinagh Kippagh
Cullomane Bridge
Cross Roads Caheragh Derryclogh Reavouler
Killeenleagh Bridge Carrigfadda
Ballyourane Driminidy Carrigbaun Reanascreena
Rea Cross Roads
Cross Roads Carrigeeny
Derreenard Maulatrahane Connonagh
Skeagh Milleen Leap ROSS CA
Aghadown Bridge An Léim Ros O
N71 Glandore Ballyvireen
Kilcoe SKIBBEREEN Cuan Dor Bridge
An Sciobairín Rinneen UNIONHALL Cregg
Church Bréantrá Glandore
Cross Myross Harbour
Kilkilleen Creagh CASTLETOWNSHEND Rabbit Island
Inishbeg Baile an Chaisleáin
Bawnlahan Horse Island
Ringarogy Barloge Scullane Point
Island Gokane
BALTIMORE Point Toe Head
Dún na Séad The Stags
Kilmoon Kedge Island

han Point

K L M

0 1 2 3 4 5 miles
0 1 2 3 4 5 6 7 kilometres

Bantry House is set against a steep hillside overlooking Bantry Bay

beaches and rare plants. Clear Island is a stop-off point for migratory birds, and its observatory is well established. Distinctive features are the buoys and snaking black lines of the mussel- and oyster-culture industries.

Sheep's Head Peninsula
225 G7

This fertile peninsula lies between Dunmanus and Bantry bays and its main town, Durrus (J6), gives its name to a distinctive local cheese. Low rocky hills in the east give way to a rugged shoreline, and there are great views to the north and south from the Seefin Pass above Kilcrohane (H7). Yachts moor in Ahakista Bay (H7), and it feels like a prosperous, tranquil backwater.

Skelligs 224 B4

The jagged islands off the end of Iveragh Peninsula are Great Skellig, or Skellig Michael, and Little Skellig, the second largest gannetry in the world.

Skellig Michael, the more distant of the pair has a lighthouse from 1820. Christian monks sought refuge here in the 6th century but abandoned it in the 11th century. Hundreds of precipitous steps lead up to their beehive huts. Visit on a cruise from the excellent Skellig Experience Visitor Centre on Valencia Island (C3), just over the bridge from Portmagee.

Valencia Island 224 C3

Valencia, just off the tip of the Iveragh Peninsula, makes an interesting detour from the Ring of Kerry. It is 11km long and has its own signposted Ring drive and a coastal walk, both offering great views. On the eastern end of the island is the Georgian village of Knight's Town.

To reflect the road signs of each country, distances and speed limits are shown in miles and mph in Northern Ireland, and kilometres and km/h in the Republic of Ireland.

A pool and an arched folly grace Garinish Island's Italian gardens which were landscaped in the 20th century

The dramatic scenery of Ireland's southwest corner, with its long, rocky peninsulas, often overshadows the delightful river valleys inland. Coastal walks and drives and easily accessible islands offer extensive views and great opportunities to explore.

The large white structure of Balitmore Beacon, also known as Lot's Wife, stands at the entrance to Baltimore Harbour

Baltimore 225 K8

This once wealthy fishing village is sheltered from the Atlantic by a headland. Today, visitors come for the rocky bays and seabirds, for access to the islands of Roaringwater Bay and to drive to the headland for extensive views.

Bantry House 225 J6

On the southwestern edge of bustling Bantry town, this pink and white house makes the best of its views over the wooded islands of Bantry Bay. The mansion dates from 1700 and is filled with items collected by the family. The house stands on the third of seven terraces, a feature of the extensive formal gardens. Highlights include the Italianate garden and the Wisteria Circle.

Beara Peninsula 224 E6

The rugged massif of the Caha Mountains forms the spine of this large peninsula, with Hungry Hill (685m) its highest point. It is crossed by the scenic Healy Pass and encircled by the Beara Ring Drive. You can walk the Beara Way (197km) or follow a 171km bicycle route. Castletown Bearhaven (F6) is the main town, a fishing port on the south side sheltered by the hills of Bear Island. The Call of the Sea Visitor Centre, on the north edge of the town, is good for children. Allihies is an artists' town, and its beach of crushed quartz is the spoil from the old copper mines. Dursey Island (D6) lies just off the western tip, linked to the mainland by cable car.

Cahersiveen 224 D3

Cahersiveen is superbly set on the estuary of the Valencia River. The Heritage Centre is in a square keep with odd baronial towers, looking towards the harbour.

Drombeg Stone Circle 225 M7

At this Bronze Age site, east of the coastal village of Glandore, 17 stones form one of the best prehistoric circles in the country. During excavations in the 1950s the cremated remains of a body were found buried in an urn in the middle of the circle. The remnants of two round huts stand to the west of the circle, with a lined pit from AD 368.

Glengarriff 225 J5

Ferries for Garinish Island leave from Glengarriff, a small leafy town with a nature reserve to the north, sheltering ancient woodland. The Glengarriff Bamboo Park on the eastern edge has 30 species of bamboo. Garinish, or Ilnacullin, is the site of a wondrous Italianate garden.

Mizen Peninsula 225 G8

This rugged peninsula stretches between Dunmanus and Roaringwater bays, with the high point of Mount Gabriel at its landward end, and 23m high cliffs at its seaward end. Ballydehob (J7) has a disused 12-arch tramway viaduct. Schull (J7) is an amiable fishing village, with the Republic's only planetarium. At the peninsula's tip, beyond Goleen (H8) and the beaches of Barley Cove, lies Mizen Head (G8), accessed by a bridge, and site of the Mizen Head Visitor Centre.

Roaringwater Bay 225 J7

In the far southwest corner of Ireland, Roaringwater Bay is around 12km long and up to 8km wide. Of the 15 islands within the bay, Sherkin and Clear Island are the largest. Sherkin, a 10-minute boat ride from Baltimore, has a 15th-century abbey, a ruined castle, good

A footbridge spans the River Lee in Cork

paintings, and the Sculpture Room, there is a modern space for temporary shows. Whatever time of year you visit Cork City Gaol Heritage Centre, it's always bone-cold inside the walls of the grim structure on a steep hillside. Cells are furnished in 19th- to early 20th-century style, and the audio tour and audio-visual presentation bring it all to life.

Fota Wildlife Park 226 E3
More than 90 species of exotic animals live in this wildlife park, east of Cork city. It was established in 1983 to breed endangered species, and the cheetahs are a particular success story, with more than 150 cubs born here. Ostriches, giraffes, zebras, kangaroos and ring-tailed lemurs are some of the animals in the 28ha of lush countryside. Opulent Fota House, with famous gardens and arboretum, is a neo-classical mansion dating from 1825.

Jameson's Old Midleton Distillery 226 F3
Midleton is a small town dominated by the silver-grey spire of its cathedral and the massive bulk of the distillery, which took over whiskey production in 1975. The original 1825 distillery has been restored. A gleaming copper still stands before the Visitor Centre, and a 10-minute film followed by a 50-minute guided tour (largely out of doors) give an insight into the history and skills of whiskey manufacture. The tour ends with a whiskey tasting.

Kinsale 226 D5
Smart little Kinsale is known as a culinary oasis, bolstered by the prestigious annual Gourmet Festival. It has interesting little shops, elegant small hotels and restaurants to suit all tastes. The modern harbour, bristling with sailing masts, is popular for diving and fishing trips. Wading birds occupy the mudflats, and swans complete the idyllic scene.

Timoleague 226 B6
Timoleague is known for its abbey on a bend of the Argideen. The substantial ruin dates from 1312. Of the two later churches in the village, the Church of the Ascension reflects in miniature the square tower of the abbey; the Catholic church has a 1929 window by artist Harry Clarke. The formal castle gardens, with terraces and herbaceous borders date from the 1820s.

Youghal 227 H3
This venerable harbour and market town is at the mouth of the Blackwater River on a broad, sandy bay. Guided walks from the Heritage Centre explore fascinating facets of the town. Fox's Lane Folk Museum is dedicated to domestic gadgets from 1850–1950.

To reflect the road signs of each country, distances and speed limits are shown in miles and mph in Northern Ireland, and kilometres and km/h in the Republic of Ireland.

…ey Castle on a guided tour

CORK

Cork is a vibrant, modern, industrial and university city close to the coast. The surrounding area includes pretty villages, busy towns and sandy beaches. The region is popular for sailing and fishing.

Welcoming craft shops line the streets of Kinsale

Ardmore 227 J3

Golden sands and a stone pencil-tower mark this coastal village at the western end of the scenic South Coast Drive, and the start of St Declan's Way, which stretches to Cashel on an old pilgrimage route. St Declan chose Ardmore for a church in the 5th or 6th century, and he is believed to be buried in the small oratory in the churchyard. The biggest remains are those of the 12th-century cathedral.

Blarney Castle 226 D3

Blarney Castle is a romantic 15th-century ruin set in landscaped gardens. Entry through the thick stone walls is via a double outer door, complete with murder hole and right-handed spiral staircase to confound attackers. Many visitors come to kiss the Blarney Stone, which is said to impart eloquence. To explore the gardens follow the path south from the tower. A grotto, artfully constructed beneath a giant yew, is named the Witches' Kitchen. Nearby the Wishing Steps lead down to a murky pool.

Clonakilty 226 A6

This lively little market town was once known for linen manufacture but is now best remembered for its associations with patriot Michael Collins, whose statue stands on Emmet Square. Collins was born 8km west at Sam's Cross, and you can learn more on the 1921 Trail at the Arigideen Valley Heritage Park, at Castleview. Just east of the town are the attractive Lisselan Estate Gardens and there is a sandy beach at Inchydoney Island (A7).

Cobh 226 E4

Cobh is a seaside resort with brightly painted Regency frontages above little shops and restaurants. Inside St Colman's Cathedral note the rose window framed by dummy organ pipes, and the mosaic floors. The Queenstown Story Heritage Centre tells the story of the convicts who passed through Cobh on their way to Australia, and the people who emigrated to the US and Canada from here. RMS *Titanic* called into Cobh on 11 April 1912, taking on final passengers before heading west. The daily Titanic Trail walking tour highlights the town's links with the notorious liner.

Cork 226 D3

Cork is second only to Dublin for the quality and variety of its shopping, and exploring is easy in such a compact district. The outstanding Crawford Art Gallery is housed in a redbrick building, erected in 1724. As well as rotating exhibitions from the permanent collection of

Visitors can learn about the treasures in B

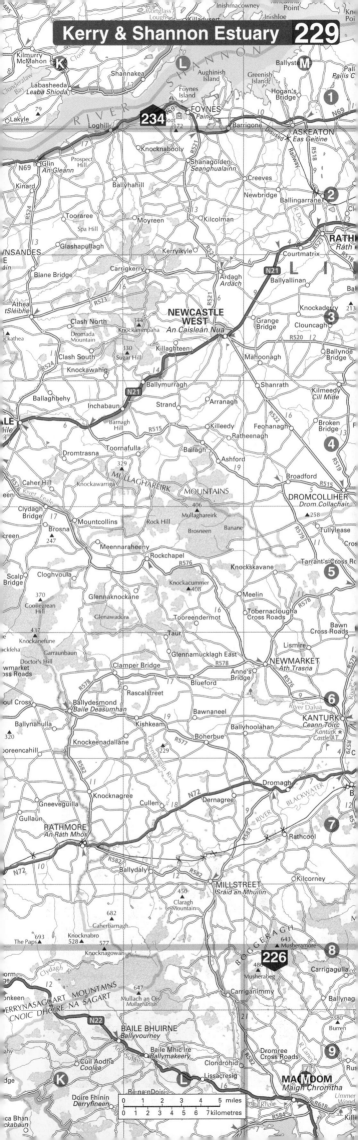

Brandon Mountain (C5) to the west. In the middle are green valleys becoming more stony towards the western tip and Dunquin (B6). There are rocky cliffs at Slea Head (B7) and Brandon Head (C5), and sandy bays on the north shore around Castlegregory (E5), and on the north-west tip around Ballyferriter (B6). One of the best viewpoints is at the top of the Connor Pass (C6), reached by a hair-raising narrow, winding road. The Slea Head Drive is a scenic loop from Dingle; follow it clockwise for the best views. The Dingle Way long-distance path goes from Tralee for 179km around the peninsula.

Gap of Dunloe 229 G8
The Gap is a deep cleft in the mountains to the west of Killarney National Park. A rough road winds through the ravine and over the pass between the mountains, through the park's most wild and romantic scenery. You can drive only as far as Kate Kearney's Cottage (pub, restaurant and souvenirs); then it's a walk of 11km to the other side, but in summer most people go by jaunting car or on horseback. The road brings you down to the shores of the Upper Lake and Lord Brandon's Cottage café, from where you can catch a boat (in summer) through the lakes to Ross Castle.

Inch 228 E6
Inch Strand, the most famous beach in Ireland, stretches 5km south of the R561 to Inch Point. To the east, a ridge covered with marram grass shelters the shallows of Castlemaine Harbour, beloved of oystercatchers, ringed plovers and other waders. A lifeguard is on duty in summer.

Killarney 229 H7
This seasoned holiday town fills to bursting in summer. The Catholic cathedral, St Mary's, dating from 1842, has been restored. Scenic walks lead from the western end of New Street to Lough Leane and the lakeside tower of Ross Castle. A square stone keep, with the remains of curtain walls, the castle dates from the late 15th century. It was the last castle to stand out against Cromwell's armies, falling at last in

1652. Nearby, you can rent a boat and row to Inisfallen Island, with its monastic remains.

Listowel 229 H3
Listowel has an imaginative literary museum and was once home of the world's first monorail. The museum, Seanachí (pronounced 'Shanakey'), meaning storyteller, is in a fine Georgian house on the town square. The Lartigue Monorail of 1888 ran between Listowel and Ballybunion.

Muckross Estate 229 H8
The Muckross Estate lies within Killarney National Park. At its heart is the Victorian mansion of Muckross House, with its extensive gardens, a crafts centre and the Traditional Farms – three working farms, dating from the 1930s, complete with animals. The house was designed in 1843, and its interior is comfortably and richly furnished. Highlights include the room where Queen Victoria stayed in 1861 and items of Killarney inlaid furniture.

Tralee 229 G5
The county town of Kerry is known for its Rose of Tralee International Festival – a week-long party and beauty pageant that attracts more than 200,000 visitors in August. The town sprawls on the flatlands east of Tralee Bay and has excellent sandy beaches nearby at Banna (F4) and Derrymore (F5). The town's medieval history is told at the Kerry County Museum in the Ashe Memorial Hall.

Ventry 228 B6
The Celtic and Prehistoric Museum's six small rooms contain a fabulous collection of antiquities from across the globe. They include a nest of fossilised dinosaur eggs, a mammoth skull with 3m tusks, fished from the North Sea, Stone Age hand-tools of chipped flint and Bronze Age brooches.

To reflect the road signs of each country, distances and speed limits are shown in miles and mph in Northern Ireland, and kilometres and km/h in the Republic of Ireland.

Gallarus Oratory (AD 800), an early Christian church at Smerwick, Dingle Peninsula

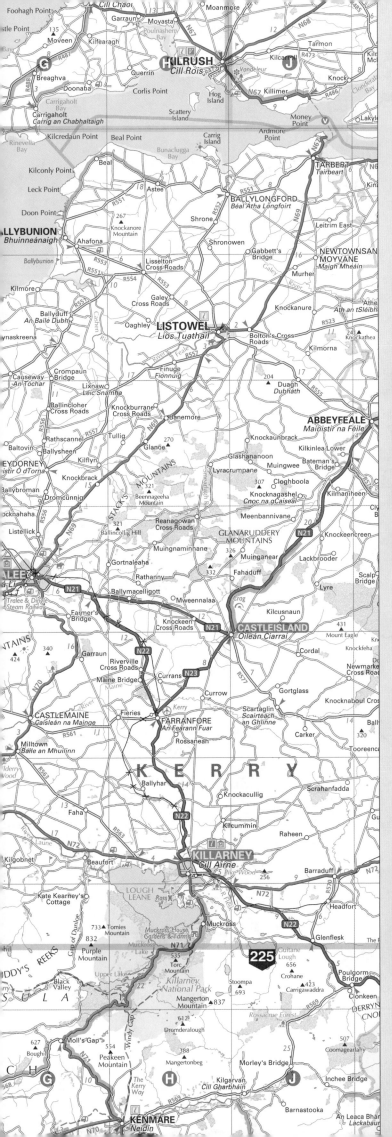

The dramatic scenery of County Kerry in the island's southwestern corner makes them among the most visited regions of Ireland. Ireland's longest river, the Shannon, defines the northern boundary of County Limerick while the Dingle Peninsula lies west of Tralee with rugged mountains, stunning seascapes, and fascinating ancient forts and beehive huts.

The view over to Great Blasket Island from Slea Head on the Dingle Peninsula

Ardfert Cathedral 228 F4

In the low-lying coastal landscape north of Tralee, locally born St Brendan founded a monastery in the 6th century. Nothing remains, but the three medieval churches here, and the 13th-century friary to the east demonstrate the importance of this ecclesiastical site. The main structure, just north of Ardfert village, is the battlemented and roofless cathedral, which dates from the 13th to the 17th centuries.

Blasket Islands 228 A7

The green humps of the Blasket Islands lie off the western end of the Dingle Peninsula. They have captured a special place in Irish consciousness for their remarkable literary heritage depicting their world apart. The village on Great Blasket was abandoned in 1953, but in summer you can visit by ferry from Dunquin (B6), and even stay overnight: there's a café and weaver's workshop, the sandy beach of Trágh Bhán and colonies of seals.

Crag Cave 229 J5

At 3.81km, Crag Cave is one of the longest surveyed cave systems in Ireland. It is a spectacular world, where pale forests of stalagmites and stalactites, thousands of years old, throw eerie shadows around vast echoing caverns complemented by dramatic sound and lighting effects. Tours of the caves last about 30 minutes.

Dingle 228 C6

Dingle started out as the site of a fort and trading port, developed into a fishing town, and is now the main tourist centre for visitors to the peninsula. Its narrow streets are busy in summer, but there are good pubs, craft and antiques shops, and diving, sea-angling, sailing and dolphin-watching. Waterborne tours leave from the western quay. Along the seafront, the Dingle Oceanworld Aquarium celebrates local marine life.

A leisurely way to explore

Dingle Peninsula 228 B5

It is the mountains that first define the Dingle Peninsula: the Slieve Mish mountains to the east and the high peaks of Mount Eagle (B7) and

rich area, and Athassel is a stony ghost of one of the biggest and best. This was one of the wealthiest monasteries in Ireland until its destruction in 1447 (go among the ruins at your own risk). The Rock of Cashel is the best ruined monastic site in the area, visible for miles, and a microcosm of an age when archbishops behaved like kings. The rock was actually the seat of Munster kings from the 4th century. In 1101 King Muircheartach Ua Briain presented the site to the Church, and it remained in use until the mid-18th century, when its decaying buildings were abandoned in favour of St John's Church in the town below. At the foot of the Rock of Cashel, a 4th-century stone fort, Brú Ború Heritage Centre is dedicated to the study and celebration of native Irish music, song, dance, story telling, theatre and Celtic studies.

Clonmel 231 J4

Clonmel dates from the 12th century, and the best way to see its historic buildings is via the Heritage Trail (tourist office leaflet). Highlights include the arcaded Main Guard of 1684 and the blue-painted Town Hall on Parnell Street. A literary festival in September recalls a number of famous local authors.

Jerpoint Abbey 231 M2

The highlights of this 12th-century Cistercian ruin are the Romanesque carved figures in the chapels of the north and south transepts. The Gothic tower, cloister and roofless nave date from the 14th and 15th centuries. A little visitor centre explains the significance of the carvings and traces the history of high crosses in the area.

Lough Gur 230 C2

Some 3,000 years ago neolithic farmers picked out the prettiest spot in County Limerick for their settlement: crescent-shaped Lough Gur. The site has been thoroughly excavated, and its story is told in the snug thatched replica longhouse and roundhouse above the lake. The ruined castle visible from the parking area dates from 1500, and is private. Nearby are a wedge tomb and the Grange stone circle. More ancient sites can be seen from the lakeside.

Michelstown Caves 230 F5

The entrance to this spectacular natural wonder is very low key. If it weren't for the flagstaff outside the farmhouse, it would be easy to miss. A grey metal door in the rock leads to the 88 concrete steps that descend into a wonderland created over millions of years by dripping water depositing limestone to form the translucent stone curtains, stalactites, stalagmites and even sideways-growing halectites. For 1km, successive caverns open out, revealing ever more fantastic formations, and culminating in the Tower of Babel.

Waterford 231 M5

Merchant's Quay runs beside the River Suir, with shops, hotels and other buildings facing the water. These include the handsome old Granary of 1872 housing the tourist office and Treasures Exhibition at the western end, and the circular medieval Reginald's Tower at the eastern end. The main shopping area lies in the warren of small streets behind Merchant's Quay. The Catholic Cathedral of the Most Holy Trinity of 1793, lit inside by 10 exquisite crystal chandeliers, is equally elegant. Waterford Crystal is famed throughout the world. Visit the factory where that crystal is made and afterwards visit the gallery and shop with new appreciation of the skill of the glassblowers.

To reflect the road signs of each country, distances and speed limits are shown in miles and mph in Northern Ireland, and kilometres and km/h in the Republic of Ireland.

s above the limestone ridges of The Rock of Cashel

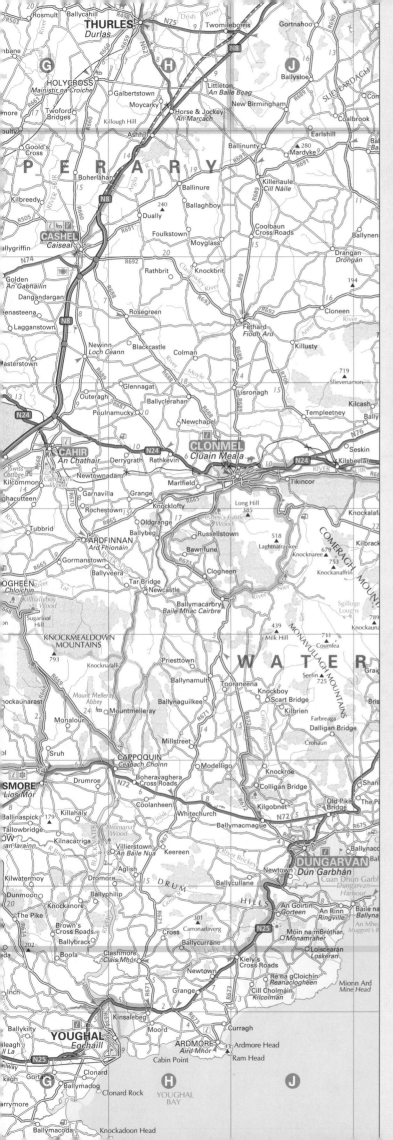

TIPPERARY

Bustling Waterford, on the south bank of the River Suir, is famous for its crystal glassworks, while the surrounding county has pretty harbours, fishing villages and market towns. Inland, bordering the Midlands and the East, County Tipperary is ringed by low mountains that form the backdrop to attractive river valleys, historic towns such as Clonmel and Caher, and the Rock of Cashel.

The visitor centre at Lough Gur tells the story of neolithic farmers

Adare 230 A2

Adare's status in medieval times can be seen in the several ruined abbeys within it. Holy Trinity Abbey was founded in 1230 for monks of the Trinitarian Order, and its low square tower dominates the high street. The Augustinians built a friary on the riverbank opposite the castle around 1314, and the elegant church was restored and reopened as the parish church in 1937. The extensive ruins of a Franciscan friary of 1464 lie in the parkland of Adare Manor, a 19th-century mansion which is now a hotel. The massive remains of the 1326 Desmond Castle lie on the north bank of the River Maigue, a short walk from the middle of the town.

Ahenny High Crosses 231 L4

There is a remarkable dignity and remoteness about this pair of wheel crosses standing 2.5m high in a graveyard on a green hillside. Perhaps it's the conical capstones, which bring to mind the statues of Easter Island, or the dominance of the high central spoke. The pinkish sandstone of these monuments was carved in the 8th century AD. Moss and lichen mellow the effect of the intricate Celtic motifs, spirals and geometric designs carved onto every surface; human figures can be made out on the bases.

Caher 231 G4

This busy little 18th-century town has two main attractions. Caher Castle stands on a crag beside the River Suir. It is one of the best-preserved Norman castles in Ireland, with keep, tower and outer wall largely intact. The Swiss Cottage is a great contrast – a

thatched rustic building with stickwork verandahs, set in parkland, built in 1810 to designs by John Nash.

Cashel 231 G2

At the Bolton Library on John Street is a monk's encyclopaedia of 1168 and the smallest book in the world. The Folk Village, in a row of thatched cottages on Dominic Street, re-creates 18th-century rural life and has displays on Republican history. The handsome Cashel Palace Hotel was originally the archbishop's palace of 1732. The broken remains of abbeys are scattered throughout this

High on the skyline, St Patrick's cathedral

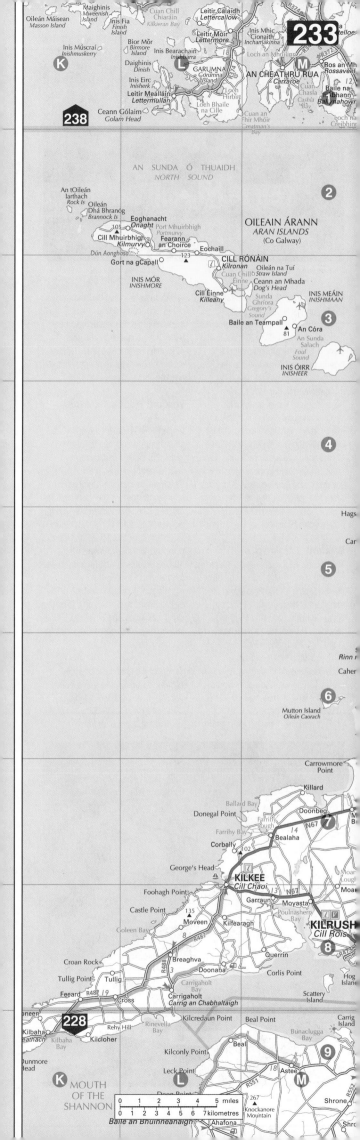

The county town of Wexford

ancestral home. Since the 1960s, this has ensured a steady stream of visitors. The John F Kennedy Memorial Park, opened in 1968, 12km south of town, is a 252ha arboretum that's best in spring and autumn. On the impressive *Dunbrody* Heritage Ship, a full-scale reproduction of a New Ross emigrant vessel of the 19th century, guides in period costume explain the harsh conditions on board. Dunbrody Abbey and Dunbrody Castle have a good visitor centre. There is an intriguing yew hedge maze with 1,550 yew trees and a museum. In addition there is a golf pitch-and-putt course, a local craft centre and Dunbrody Abbey Cookery School.

Wexford 232 E4
The Vikings established Wexford as a port and shipbuilding town in the 8th century. In the Middle Ages it was an important English garrison town, but when Cromwell arrived in 1649 the rebellious spirit of the townspeople cost them dearly and several hundred were executed on the Bullring. Rebelliousness continued, however, and in 1798 a republic was declared here. The long, narrow main street runs parallel with the quay. Little obvious remains of the old town, the

Westgate tower being the sole survivor of the 14th-century walls. Nearby are the ruins of Selskar Abbey, built by Henry II in penitence for the murder of Thomas Becket. The opera festival every October attracts performers and devotees from all over the world.

Wexford Wildfowl Reserve
232 E4
Behind the sea wall on the north side of Wexford Harbour lies the North Slobs, 3m below high tide level. This wetland area was drained from marshland in the 19th century to form a farming landscape, but its meadows and drainage channels also provided an ideal habitat for birdlife. In winter you might see 29 different species of duck and 42 types of wader. The 10,000 Greenland white-fronted geese form as much as one-third of the world's total population and the pale-bellied Brents also arrive on a globally significant scale. The Reserve's 100ha include a series of accessible hides for visitors to observe the birds.

To reflect the road signs of each country, distances and speed limits are shown in miles and mph in Northern Ireland, and kilometres and km/h in the Republic of Ireland.

A replica of the Dunbrody, *used by those emigrating from Ireland in the 19th century*

G   **H**   **J**

URTOWN
e na Cúirte
chapel

Roney Point

237

garrett

Cahore Point

rin
oads

Rosslare Europort

0		400 m
0		400 yds

Rosslare Bay

Pier

LIFEBOAT STATION

Rosslare Harbour

ROSSLARE EUROPORT STATION

P

FERRY TERMINAL

LC

POST OFFICE

N25

St George's Channel

CHERBOURG, FISHGUARD, PEMBROKE, ROSCOFF

i

ROSSLARE, NEW ROSS

HBI

DUBLIN

WATERFORD PLUNKETT STATION

N9 (N24)

Rice Bridge

DOCK ROAD

Waterford

Golf Course

ROCKSHIRE ROAD

BISHOPSGROVE

RD

ROCKSHIRE CL

ARD MHUIRE

Marymount

NEW ROSS

N25

FOUNTAIN ST

ABBEY ROAD

SCH

BUS STATION

P

P

MERCHANT'S QUAY

DOMINICAN CHURCH

MUS

i

PO

ARTS CENTRE

CLOCK TOWER

ST PATRICK'S CHURCH

HOLY TRINITY CATHEDRAL (RC)

River Suir

Marina

BLACKFRIARS ABBEY

CUSTOM HO

THE GLEN

GARDA STATION

P

CINEMA

BARRON STRAND ST

PO

SHOPPING CENTRE

FRENCH CHURCH

BALYBRICKEN GREEN

PATRICK STREET

SCH

LIBRARY

PETER ST

CITY HALL

REGINALD'S TOWER

THEATRE

ROSE LANE

CHRIST CHURCH CATH

THE MALL

CORPORATION OFFICES

P

SPRING GARDEN ALLEY

NEWGATE

NEW ST

JOHN ST

BEAU STREET

LOMBARD ST

JOSEPH QUAY

SOUTH QUAY

WILLIAM STREET

FIRE STATION

COURT HOUSE

CANADA ST

SCHOOL

PO

N25

MANOR ST

SCH

WATCH TOWER

John's Bridge

Hardy's Bridge

John's

R684

2008

CORK

P

Peoples Park

DUNMORE EAST

HBI

G   **H**   **J**

SOUTH EAST IRELAND

See how early settlers lived at the Irish National Heritage Park and, beyond the historic city of Wexford, discover sandy beaches which give way to river estuaries – havens for wildlife.

Studying the information board at the thatched hut, Irish National Heritage Park

Enniscorthy 232 D2

If you are unsure of the details of the 1798 rebellion in the south of Ireland, the Enniscorthy 1798 Centre puts the whole period in perspective. The culmination is a reconstruction of the eventual showdown on Vinegar Hill, where the Crown's forces stormed the rebels' headquarters, defended by 20,000 pikemen. There is a more traditional museum in the Norman castle close to the pedestrian-only middle of town.

Hook Head 232 B7

County Wexford points a finger into the crashing waters of the Atlantic Ocean at Hook Head. The lighthouse at the end of the peninsula is one of the oldest working lighthouses in the world. Records show its origins to be in the 5th century AD and its red sandstone base dates from 1172. The Head is a strange place. A walk along the water's edge reveals blow holes and dangerous rocky ledges. It's no place for a swim: even on calm days there can be freakishly large waves. Two abbeys were founded at the base of the peninsula. Dunbrody, dating from 1182, lies in open meadows by a tributary of the Barrow River. Tintern (B5), founded in 1200 by Cistercians, is more impressive. At the head of a tidal creek, it is reached down a gravel road and retains its nave, chancel chapel, cloister and tower. A tour of Hook Head should also include Duncannon (B6), a seaside resort with a huge sandy beach and an excellent star-shaped fort from the 16th century, and Slade, where the ruins of a 15th-century castle guard a tiny fishing harbour.

Irish National Heritage Park 232 D4

On the edge of Wexford, just off the northern bypass, the Irish National Heritage Park is a good place to stop. In 14ha of reclaimed marsh and swamp, 9,000 years of Irish history have been re-created through a series of full-scale models. There's a Mesolithic site with its dolmen and camp, a Bronze Age area showing how a cist burial would have looked, and a ring fort, a common feature of the Irish landscape. You can see how a monastic settlement would have looked, with its high cross, oratory and water mill, visit a crannóg, reconstructed on an island in the marsh, and appreciate the craft of the Viking shipbuilders who settled in this area.

Johnstown Castle 232 E5

The site is a little confusing, being also the home of an agricultural college and an array of government departments, but at its heart lies the fabulously Gothicised castle, and the agricultural and famine museums, established in the castle's stable block. The foyer is as close inside the castle as visitors can get, but you can wander in its 20ha of gardens, see the peacocks, walled garden and ornamental lakes. The agricultural museum re-creates country trades and scenes from the last 200 years.

New Ross 232 B4

The wharfside warehouses of this old inland port are being redeveloped. Narrow streets wind up the steep riverbank to the Three Bullet Gate, a remnant of a once extensive town wall. Cromwellian destruction might have seen the end of the town were it not for the proximity of the Kennedy

Lower Shannon **235**

Kilmacduagh Monastic Site
234 E3

Kilmacduagh monastic site, founded around 610 by St Colman MacDuagh, stands against a backdrop of the domed limestone hills of The Burren. The most striking feature today is the 11th-century round tower, which leans noticeably. The roofless cathedral nearby predates the coming of the Normans to Ireland, though it was rebuilt in graceful Gothic style in the 14th century. Nearby is the Abbot's House or Bishop's Castle, a two-floor, square block of a fortified tower house. Also on the site are O'Hyne's Abbey, founded in the 10th century, and St John's Oratory, a lovely little building that might date back to St Colman's time.

The round tower at Kilmacduagh

Kilrush 233 M8

There's an attractive Georgian air to Kilrush, a laid-back little town near the mouth of the Shannon Estuary. On Merchant's Quay you'll find the Scattery Island Centre with an exhibition about the monastic site on the island, 1.5km from Kilrush. At the centre you can reserve a boat ride to the island, where there is a fine round tower and the remains of several medieval churches mark the site of St Senan's monastery. Other attractions of Kilrush are its horse fair in November, and the beautiful Vandeleur Walled Garden.

Limerick 234 F8

There are two medieval highlights here: King John's Castle, dating from 1200, whose great drum towers loom above the river. Inside, interactive exhibits bring the story of the castle to life. The second is square-towered St Mary's Cathedral, parts of which date back to 1168. The Hunt Museum, in a Georgian customs house of 1765, has an eclectic collection spanning 9,000 years.

Roscrea 235 M5

In the centre stands a huge 13th-century golden-towered castle, with a Queen Anne mansion and formal walled garden within the high curtain wall. The Roscrea Castle Complex Heritage Centre and Damer House has exhibitions about the town's history and there's a heritage walk taking in the weathered 12th-century wheel cross and round tower of St Cronin's, and the tower of a 15th-century Franciscan friary.

The Burren 234 C3

The Burren rises as a cluster of grey domed hills with terraced sides whose western feet slope to the sea at Galway Bay. Villages scatter the fringes: Ballyvaughan (C3), Doolin (A4), Lisdoonvarna (B4) and Kilfenora (B4) with its Burren Visitor Centre. One main road, the N67, crosses the interior from Ballyvaughan to Lisdoonvarna. There are no settlements here, but this is where many of the most interesting historical sites are found. Aillwee Cave (C3) leads you into the subterranean world of The Burren, a honeycomb of caverns and passages. You'll see stalactites and stalagmites, glittering calcite, caverns of church-like size, and an underground waterfall. The Burren Way, one of Ireland's official 'Waymarked Ways', runs for 45km from Ballyvaughan to Liscannor (A5). Old country roads, tracks and walled boreens take you across the hills and valleys to Doolin. From here a coastal path leads to the Cliffs of Moher (A4).

Thoor Ballylee 234 E3

William Butler Yeats restored the 16th-century tower house that became his country retreat and preferred writing spot. You can wander through the four floors, viewing Yeats's first editions and memorabilia.

To reflect the road signs of each country, distances and speed limits are shown in miles and mph in Northern Ireland, and kilometres and km/h in the Republic of Ireland.

Wedge tombs can be found on the limestone uplands of The Burren

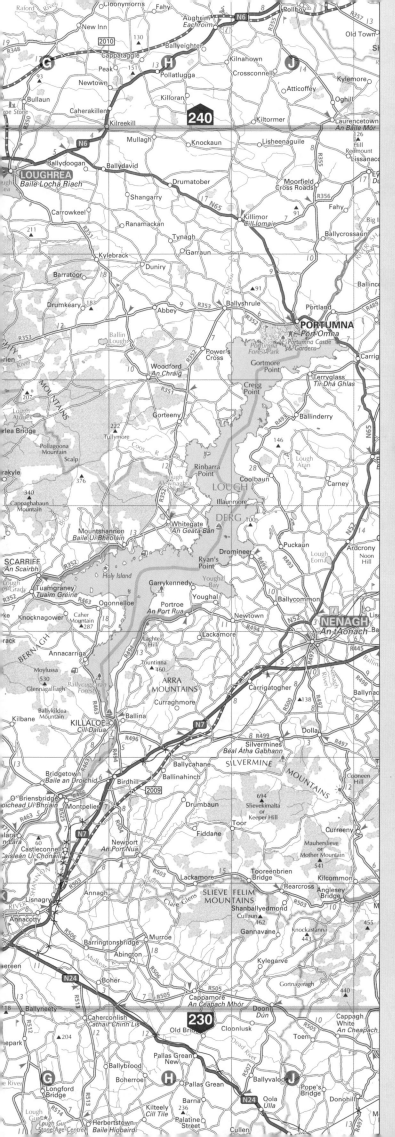

LOWER SHANNON

North of the Shannon, County Clare is home to the stark limestone plateau called The Burren and the towering Cliffs of Moher. Limerick, Ireland's fourth-largest city, has a historic hub with fine churches, museums and galleries. Many castles, both ruined and restored, dot the rolling landscape that leads to lovely beaches on the coast. Offshore are the largely Irish (Gaeilge)-speaking Aran Islands.

A Celtic cross overlooks the waters on the island of Inishmore, Aran

Aran Islands 233 M2

All three islands share the same distinctive landscape of bleak grey limestone, void of grass in most parts but supporting sheets of wild flowers. Irish is spoken throughout the islands, but principally on isolated Inishmaan (M3), where you'll find plenty to photograph. Inishmore (L3) has the most striking archaeological remains, the largest village, Kilronan (L3), has more visitors than the other two islands put together. There's an excellent Heritage Centre and island museum in Kilronan, and you can buy genuine Aran sweaters in the craft shop before taking a pony-and-trap or minibus tour of the island. The main attraction is Dún Aengus (L2), a large Iron Age stone fort perched on the edge of a cliff. Inisheer (M3), easily reached from Doolin (A4), is small enough to walk in a morning, and there's a cheerful pub.

Birr and Birr Castle Demesne 235 L3

The Parsons family settled at Birr in 1620, and as the Earls of Rosse they directed the fortunes of the area from then on. During the 18th century they laid out a model Georgian town but the chief attraction is undoubtedly Birr Castle Demesne. The castle itself, founded in 1170 and altered in the succeeding centuries, is still the private residence of the Earl and Countess of Rosse (not open to the public). The family has developed the grounds as a public attraction, with woodland walks, formal and informal gardens and water features. The demesne is also home to the National Birds of Prey Centre.

Bunratty Castle and Folk Park 234 E7

The folk park re-creates a corner of 19th-century Ireland with reconstructed buildings and workplaces, some incorporated into a 'village street'. These include cottages and farmhouses occupied by costumed guides; and, at the other end of the social scale, the fine Georgian country residence of Bunratty House. Garden-lovers will be delighted by the restored walled garden of Bunratty House, and by the other gardens which reflect their parent dwelling: cottage garden, farmhouse garden and so on. A tall tower house, Bunratty Castle, built around 1425, has been restored, and fitted out with rare and appropriate furniture, paintings and tapestries.

Cliffs of Moher 234 A4

A towering layer-cake of shale, sandstone and silt forms a great rampart facing Galway Bay. In summer this is generally crowded with visitors, here for the superb views of the Aran Islands and along the Clare coastline south-west to Loop Head.

Craggaunowen Bronze Age Project 234 E6

Craggaunowen is one of the best 'step-into-the-past' open-air sites in Ireland. Costumed guides interpret the realities of the 5th and 6th centuries in the re-created buildings here.

The round tower at Glendalough, a 7th-century monastic site

They were designed in 1909 by Sir Edwin Lutyens and planted by Gertrude Jekyll. The well-tended landscape includes fine terraces and garden 'rooms' – themed areas enclosed within 'walls' of neatly clipped hedges.

Kildare 236 F2

This is racing territory: more than 140 registered stud farms breed world-class flat-racing horses, and in Punchestown and The Curragh County Kildare has two of the country's leading racecourses. For this reason, Kildare town's principal attractions are related to the National Stud. Next to the Stud are the renowned Japanese Gardens.

Kilkenny 236 D8

Kilkenny rose to prominence in the 13th century. James Butler, Third Earl of Ormond, bought the castle here in 1391, and his family stayed until 1935, extending and improving the property in the 17th and 18th centuries. The 20ha parkland includes a formal rose garden as well as mature woodland and a children's playground. Off the servants' corridor the Butler Gallery of Contemporary Art houses exhibitions by international artists and sculptors. A walk around Kilkenny reveals some interesting buildings. The Courthouse has a 19th-century classical frontage on a fortified medieval house, which once served as a prison and Rothe House, built in 1594, is now home to a small museum.

Powerscourt 237 L2

The most memorable feature of Powerscourt is the view from the terrace, over a broad sweep of wooded garden to the peak of the Great Sugar Loaf on the horizon. This superb vista is the set piece of a house and garden originally designed in 1731. The house was gutted by fire and stood virtually derelict until 1996, when an exhibition space was created and the ballroom carefully restored. Today, a visit to the house exhibition is a peculiar mix of building history and stately home, but the gardens are the attraction. Elsewhere the estate has turned its attentions to retail outlets, and these occupy the west wing along with a restaurant, cafés and gift shops. Part of the estate, but 5km away, is the Powerscourt Waterfall, Ireland's highest at 106m.

Rock of Dunmase 236 D4

Rising dramatically from the flattish County Laois countryside, the Rock of Dunamase is covered in the broken walls and towers of a castle. It was built during the mid-12th century and lasted until Cromwell's men blew it up in 1650. You can climb the three steeply sloping wards to reach the broken keep, from where there are stunning views.

To reflect the road signs of each country, distances and speed limits are shown in miles and mph in Northern Ireland, and kilometres and km/h in the Republic of Ireland.

Powerscourt Gardens are a blend of formal plantings, sweeping terraces and lakes

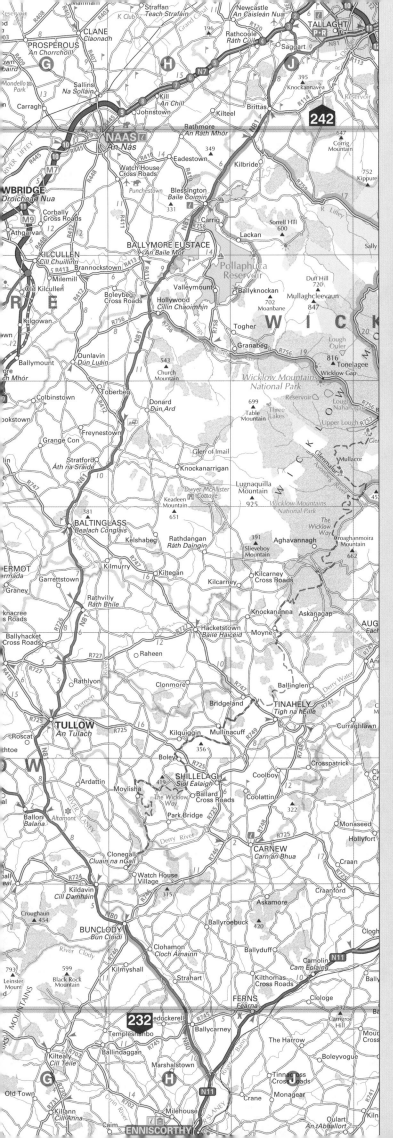

KILKENNY & WICKLOW MOUNTAINS

West of Dublin, Ireland's famous racehorses are bred in the pastures of County Kildare, home of the National Stud. South of the capital are the Wicklow Mountains, with Powerscourt Gardens and the monastic site of Glendalough, while inland are a fine castle and medieval sites.

A horse and her foal in the fields of the National Stud near Kildare

Abbeyleix 236 C5
Abbeyleix is a handsome Georgian town and at Abbeyleix Heritage House you can learn about the town's development from its origins as a huddle of houses around a 12th-century Cistercian monastery. There's also a display on the town's long-defunct carpet industry.

Avoca 237 L6
High-quality mohair and cashmere garments and beautiful throws are manufactured in the tiny weaving shed at the Old Mill on the edge of the village. Established in 1723, it is one of the oldest factories in continuous use in Ireland. Visitors can get a feel for the clatter of the weaving shed before visiting the factory shop. The village itself was the setting for the BBC series *Ballykissangel*.

Bray 237 L2
Bray sits on a long sweep of beach at the south end of Killiney Bay. It is home to the National Sea Life Centre. On the slopes of the Little Sugar Loaf, holding out against the advances of new housing, Killruddery House and Gardens have been in the Brabazon family since 1618. The gardens were designed in French classical style in the 1680s and the 17th-century house was redesigned in Elizabethan style in 1820.

Carlow 236 F6
Carlow is unremarkable, although there is good shopping off its wide square. Away from the heart of town is a pleasing tangle of early 19th-century streets, but its castle lies stranded in wasteland. The courthouse building is a striking replica of the Parthenon, and was supposedly intended for Cork City until a mix-up of documents gave Carlow one of its grandest buildings. About 3km out of town is the Browneshill Dolmen. A surfaced track leads from a little parking area to the array of stones that dates from 2500 BC.

Emo Court 236 D3
Architect James Gandon designed the Earl of Portarlington's grand neo-classical mansion in 1792 and the family lived here until 1920. The interior is full of fine plasterwork and *trompe l'oeil* decoration and the gardens are delightful.

Glendalough 237 K4
At Glendalough are the ruins of St Ciaran's Church, and those of St Kevin's Church. A double arch by the Glendalough Hotel leads you into the churchyard where the remains of the cathedral stand, its 9th-century nave and chancel now roofless. The 12th-century Priest's House contains carvings of St Kevin, and the round tower would have served as a belfry, lookout tower and treasury. On the far side of the churchyard, the 10th-century St Mary's Church may have housed St Kevin's tomb. Beyond the Lower Lough, another group of important sites includes the 10th-century Reefert Church, with its tombs of local chiefs, and St Kevin's Cell, the beehive-style hut where the settlement began. On the cliffs on the south side of the lough, the peculiar Teampull na Skellig is a platform cut into the rock, the site of the early 'Church of the Rock'. Nearby St Kevin's Bed is a Bronze Age burial site. The Visitor Centre also acts as an information outlet for the Wicklow Mountains National Park. It's at the entrance to the glen, just beyond the site of the Trinity Chapel.

Heywood Gardens 236 C5
Nothing remains of Heywood House but the gardens are remarkable.

A   B   C   D   E   F

1

2

CLEW BAY

Bills Rocks

Carrickfadda
Ballytoohy
Kinnacorra
Kinatevdilla
CLARE ISLAND
462
Portnakilly

LOUISBURGH
Cluain Cearbán
Old Head
Kilsallagh
Aghany
Emlagh Point
R378
Formoyle
Mullagh
Killeen
Killadoon
Cregganbaun
Kinnadoohy
270
Glenkeen Bridge
SHEEFFRY

3

INISHTURK
Inis Toirc
Caher Island
Dromore Head
189
Ballybeg Island
Inishdalla
Barnabaun Point
761
MWEELREA MOUNTAINS
Doo Lough
Roonah L
Delphi

4

INISHBOFIN
Inis Bó Finne
Davillaun
Tonakeera Point
Inishdegil More
INISHSHARK
Inis Airc
86
Inishlyon
Inishbroon
Crump Island
Renvyle Point
Rusheenduff
Renvyle
Glassillaun
Ben Creggan
817
Mweelrea
Ben Gorm
R335
LEENANE
An Líonán
Shark Head
Inishgort
Cashleen
Gowlaun
Garraun
Lough Fee
618
Meall Dubh
High Island
Friar Island
Tully Lough
Tully Mountain
355
Tully Cross
Altnagaighera
Kylemore Abbey
SLÉIBHTE MAUMTURK

5

Cleggan
An Cloigeann
Aughrusbeg Lough
Ballynakill Harbour
Letterfrack
Leitir Fraic
Diamond Hill
Kylemore Lough
666
R344
Claddaghduff
Ballynakill Lough
Moyard
N59
Connemara National Park
Lough Nahillion
727
Binn Bhán
Benbaun
Cruagh
Omey Island
Iniskturk
Kill
Lough Auna
633
Bencullagh
NA BEANNA BEOLA
THE TWELVE PINS
711
Loch Inagh
Eeshal Island
CLIFDEN
An Clochán
Owenglin River
N59
Binn an Choire Mhóir
Bencorr
Talbot Island
Errislannan Point
Drinagh
Clifden Bay
Salt Lake
Derrylea Lough
Derryclare Lough
Sraith Salach
Recess

6

Knock
Ballinaboy
Mannin Bay
R341
Lough Erlaghnabeeny
Ballynahinch Lake
R341
Loch Ghleann Dá Loch
Inishdugga
Lough Nadirkmore
Toombeola
R342
Cashel
An Caiseal
Inishkeeragh
Ballyconneely
Baile Conaola
Doonreaghan
Bun na hAbhann
Bunnahown
Chapel Island
Horse Island
298
ROUNDSTONE
Cloch na Rón
14
SLYNE HEAD
Illaunurra
Dog's Bay
Bertraghboy Bay
Glinsce
Glinsk

An Más
Mace Head
Carna
An Más
166
Cill Chiaráin
Kilkieran

Maighinis
Mweenish Island
Inis Fia
Finish Island
Leitir Cal
Letterfrack
Leitir Móir
Lettermullan

Oileán Máisean
Masson Island
Inis Bearachaín
Inishbarra
GARUMNA
Gorumna Island

An tOileán
Iarthach
Rock Is
Oileán
Dhá Bhranóg
Brannock Is
Cill Mhuirbhigh
Kilmurvy
Eoghanacht
Onaght
Port Mhuirbhigh
Portmurvy
Fearann an Choirce
Eochaill

233

AN SUNDA Ó THUAIDH
NORTH SOUND

E   F

© Govt of Ireland 2008

N59, CLIFDEN

Galway

Shantalla

UNIVERSITY COLLEGE HOSPITAL A & E

UNIVERSITY COLLEGE

CATHEDRAL OF ST NICHOLAS & OUR LADY ASSUMED INTO HEAVEN (RC)

River Corrib

CINEMA

SHOPPING CENTRE

THE PLAZA

HEALTH CENTRE

200 metres
200 yds

Nun's Island

COURTHOUSE

TOWN HALL

COUNTY BUILDINGS

ST MARY'S COLLEGE

Salmon Weir Bridge

FRANCISCAN FRIARY

King's Gap

LYNCH ST STONE

NICHOLAS CHURCH

EYRE SQUARE SHOPPING CENTRE

BROWNE'S GATEWAY

Kennedy Park

Eyre Square

LYNCH'S CASTLE

GARDA

TAIBHDHEARCH THEATRE

Wolfe Tone Bridge

SPANISH ARCH & CITY MUSEUM

FIRE STATION

GALWAY TECHNICAL INSTITUTE

GALWAY STATION

JF KENNEDY MEMORIAL GDN

BUS & RAIL TERMINUS

Docks

Aran Islands Ferry

CASTLEBAR, SLIGO   DUBLIN, LIMERICK   DUBLIN

SPIDDAL

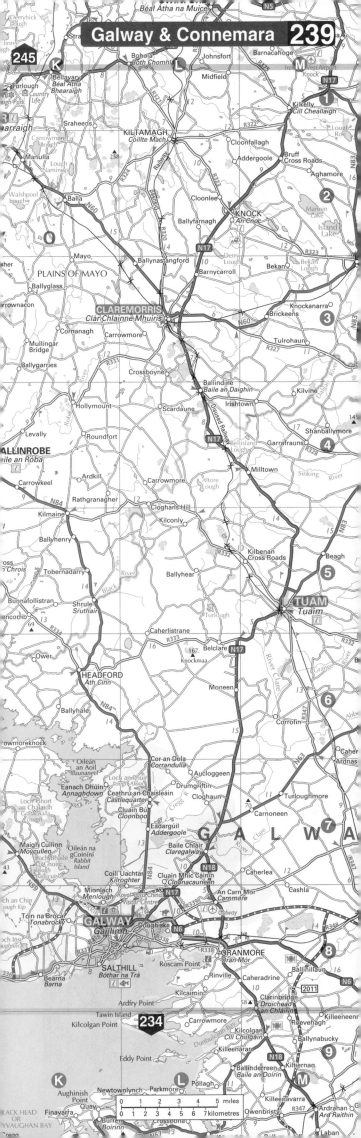

Westport House

Killary Harbour 238 E4

Killary Harbour, lying between counties Galway and Mayo, forms the northern boundary of Connemara. The fiord-like inlet is 45m deep, and mountains rise dramatically on both sides – south the 550m bulk of the Maumturks (Sléibhte Mhám Toirc); north the flanks of Mweelrea (819m) and Ben Gorm (750m). At the eastern end lies Leenane, huddled under the mountains; here the Leenane Sheep and Wool Museum displays spinning and dyeing techniques and provides information on rare breeds.

Kylemore Abbey 238 E5

Kylemore Abbey, grey and impressive, dominates Pollacappul Lough just east of Letterfrack. The house was built as a grand Gothic country seat in the 1860s, and in the late 19th century was the heart of a 5,600ha estate. After World War I it became a convent for Belgian nuns who now run a school here. It's not open to the public, but the beautiful Walled Garden is a major attraction.

Northern Connemara 238

The N59 runs from Clifden (D5) to Leenane (F4) through northern Connemara, with side roads leading north to a beautiful coast of deeply indented bays. Letterfrack (E5), a neat little 19th-century village, is home to the Connemara National Park Visitor Centre. North of Letterfrack there are some superb white sand beaches, Rusheenduff (D4) and Glassillaun (E4) being especially striking. Out at Renvyle Point (D4), the Renvyle House Hotel was the country retreat of Dublin surgeon and man of letters Oliver St John Gogarty who entertained W B Yeats, George Bernard Shaw and other Irish literary luminaries.

Twelve Pins and the Mamturks 238 E5–F5

Much of the drama and beauty of Connemara derives from the mountain ranges that rise from the central bogs of the region: the amorphous mass of the Maumturks, and on their western flank the more shapely peaks of the Twelve Pins. Guided walks in the mountains, including the ascent of Benbaun (at 727m the highest of the Twelve Pins), are offered by Connemara Walking Centre (Clifden) and the Connemara National Park Visitor Centre; you can also climb 438m Diamond Hill by a waymarked track. Bisecting the Twelve Pins/Maumturks massif is the outstandingly beautiful Inagh valley with its long lake. The N59 road encircles the mountains, while the R344 runs through the Inagh valley.

Westport 239 H2

The delightful town of Westport was laid out for the Marquess of Sligo in the 1780s. At the top of Bridge Street there's a tall clock tower; on the Octagon, at the top of James Street, a column supports a statue of St Patrick, whose holy mountain of Croagh Patrick is visible from the outskirts of town. Westport House was completed in 1779 and contains beautiful ceilings and a collection of furniture, silver, glass and pictures. The grounds include a log flume, miniature train and pedal-yourself boats on the lake. The Westport Arts Festival in September brings a variety of lively activities to town. Westport is also excellent for traditional music session pubs.

To reflect the road signs of each country, distances and speed limits are shown in miles and mph in Northern Ireland, and kilometres and km/h in the Republic of Ireland.

Brightly painted shopfronts catch the eye in Galway

GALWAY & CONNEMARA

Lively Galway city is set on Galway Bay. Between here and Clifden stretches Connemara, with its rugged sea coasts, mountains and heathlands. Westport is the main town in County Mayo, home to Croagh Patrick and the miraculous shrine of Knock.

A marble statue of St Patrick on the summit of Croagh Patrick

Clew Bay 238 E2

There may not be 365 islands in Clew Bay, as locals claim, but there are certainly a lot of them. Clew Bay is a beautiful bay, lined with sandy beaches at Mulrany on the north and between Louisburgh and Murrisk on the south.

Clifden 238 D5

The only town in Connemara, Clifden has everything you could want from music pubs to excellent walks. Its focus is the town square and twin thoroughfares of Main and Market streets, teeming with visitors in summer. The town comes fully alive in mid-August when it hosts the Connemara Pony Show

Cong 239 J5

Most visitors come to Cong to see the famous abbey, but the village of stone houses and waterways, between loughs Corrib and Mask, is a delightful place – this is where John Ford shot most of his 1952 film *The Quiet Man*. The thatched Quiet Man Heritage Cottage on Circular Road has a display on the archaeology and history of the area. Cong Abbey consists of a range of 12th-century grey limestone buildings with elaborately carved pillars.

Connemara beaches 238

Western Connemara is famed for its small but wonderful white sand beaches. Among the best are those near Roundstone (E7); Gorteen Bay (Port na Feadóigne) and Dog's Bay (D7); around Ballyconneely (D6) at Creggoduff and Mannin; between Claddaghduff and Omey Island (C5); and northern Connemara – Renvyle Point (D4), Rusheenduff (D4) and Glassillaun (E4).

Croagh Patrick 239 G2

In AD 432 St Patrick preached at the summit of Croagh Patrick and banished all the snakes from Ireland. The cone-shaped peak that overlooks Clew Bay is Ireland's holy mountain, with a steepish path up from Campbell's Bar in Murrisk to a saddle at 450m, then a knee-cracking scramble up a very steep boulder slide to the summit chapel at 762m. The reward is a superb view.

Galway 239 K8

Galway is a great city to explore on foot. Lynch's Castle, an impressive 15th-century tower house (now a bank), is well provided with sculptures, as is the Collegiate Church of St Nicholas. Behind Lynch's Castle a 17th-century window marks the spot where in 1493 Mayor James Lynch Fitzstephen personally hanged his own son for murdering a visiting Spaniard. Across the street you'll find No 8 Bowling Green, the home of Nora Barnacle before she eloped with James Joyce in 1904. It is now the Nora Barnacle House Museum. On Quay Street is Thomas Dillon's Claddagh Gold jewellery shop, with a small museum telling the story of the Claddagh Ring, Galway's famous love token. Behind the Tudor-era Spanish Arch is the new Galway City Museum, a fascinatingly unfocused collection of mementoes where a highlight is the Claddagh Exhibition.

The ruined Monk's Fishing House is part of Cong's abbey buildings

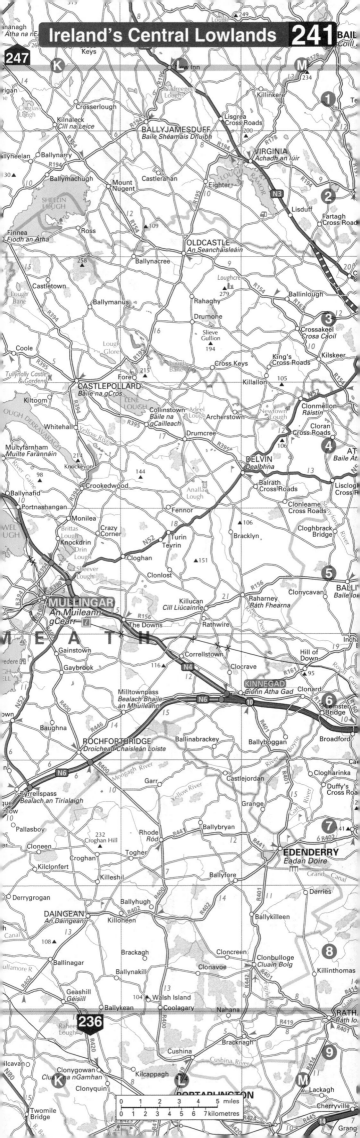

247

M

K

1

Keys

Low Inn

Killinkere

Crosserlough

Kilnaleck
Cill na Leice

Nadreegeel Lough

Lisgrea Cross Roads

Lisgrea

R178

Ballynarry

R194

Ballymachugh

Mount Nugent

Castlerahan

Eighter

VIRGINIA
Achadh an Iúir

N3

2

Lisduff

SHEELIN LOUGH

Ross

R154

▲109

Fartagh Cross Road

Finnea
Fiodh an Átha

OLDCASTLE
An Seanchaisleán

Loughcrew

R154

Ballinlough

Castletown

258 ▲

Ballynacree

Rahaghy

279 ▲

Drumone

Crossakeel
Crosa Caoil

3

Ballymanus

Slieve Gullion
194

Cross Keys

King's
Cross Roads

Kilskeer

Coole

R395

Lough Glore

Lough Bane

Killallon

105

N52

Tullynally Castle
& Gardens

Fore

215

Clonmellon
Ráistín

Kiltoom

CASTLEPOLLARD
Baile na gCros

Whitehall

R395

Collinstown
Baile na gCailleach

Adeel Lough

Archerstown

Newtown Lough

Cloran
Cross Roads

4

AT
Baile At

Multyfarnham
Muilte Farannáin

214

Knockeyon

98

Drumcree

R395

DELVIN
Dealbhna

13

Lisclog
Cross R

Ballynafid

Portnashangan

Crookedwood

144

Fennor

Balrath
Cross Roads

Clonleame
Cross Roads

Cloghbrack
Bridge

Monilea

Crazy
Corner

N52

Turin

Tevrin

▲106

Bracklyn

Knockdrin

Cloghan

▲151

Clonlost

R156

Clonycavan

5

BALLI
Baile Ío

MULLINGAR
*An Muileann
gCearr*

Sheever Lough

Killucan
Cill Liúcainne

21

Raharney
Ráth Fhearna

M E A T H

Gainstown

The Downs

R156

Rathwire

Inch

19

Hill of
Down

Gaybrook

Correllstown

116▲

N4

Clocrave

R161

95

Milltownpass
*Bealach Bhaile
an Mhuileann*

N6

10

KINNEGAD
Cionn Átha Gad

Clonard

6

Leinster
Bridge

Baughna

R446

ROCHFORTBRIDGE
Droichead Chaisleán Loiste

Ballinabrackey

Ballyboggan

Broadford

N6

R400

Mongagh River

Garr

Castlejordan

R401

Clogharinka

Duffy's
Cross R

Tyrrellspass
Bealach an Tirialaigh

Grange

Pallasboy

Cloneen

232
Croghan Hill

Rhode
Ród

Togher

R441

Ballybryan

R441

7

41

R402

Kilconfert

Croghan

Killeshil

Ballyfore

EDENDERRY
Éadan Doire

Derrygrogan

Ballyhugh

R402

R401

Derries

DAINGEAN
An Daingean

Killoneen

Ballykilleen

R402

108▲

Brackagh

Cloncreen

Clonbulloge
Cluain Bolg

8

Killinthomas

Ballinagar

Ballynakill

Clonavoe

R442

R401

Geashill
Géisill

104

Walsh Island

Nahana

RATH
Ráth Ío

R419

9

Ballykean

Coolagary

236

R420

Cushina

Bracknagh

Cushina River

Clonygowan
Cluain na nGamhan

Kilcappagh

L4

M

Lackagh

Cherryville

Twomile
Bridge

Clonquin

PORTARLINGTON

R424

Grang

0	1	2	3	4	5 miles	
0	1	2	3	4	5	6	7 kilometres

O'Rourke's Tower lies to the left beyond the copy of the Cross of the Scriptures. Ahead is the copy of the South Cross, with the cathedral just beyond it. At the far side of the site you can follow a marked path for 450m to the Nuns' Church.

Fore 241 L3

The village is famous for the legendary Seven Wonders of Fore, evidence of which lies in the fields on the outskirts. The wonders include 'water that flows uphill' and the 'mill without a race' – the ruin of a mill that is said to have been founded here by St Fechin in a waterless place; the stream, flowing uphill, appeared with a stroke of his staff. 'The stone raised by St Fechin's prayers' is the massive lintel of a 12th-century church, which reputedly rose into place on the saint's prayers. The 'anchorite in a stone', is actually the cell of 17th-century hermit within a mausoleum.

Kilbeggan 241 J7

Kilbeggan is a good example of the kind of wayside settlement that grew into a flourishing town by virtue of its position on the Grand Canal. Locke's Distillery on Main Street was in production for a full 200 years, until 1957, and is now a fine museum of whiskey. Exhibits include an old steam engine and a working millwheel. You can still buy Locke's whiskey – among the range sold here, are bottles of Locke's single malt, which nowadays is made at Cooley's Distillery in Co Louth.

Lough Ree 240 F5

Islands dot this mighty 25.5km stretch of water, superb for both boating and fishing. You can rent boats and fishing tackle at various outlets around the lake. Athlone has several tackle shops and day-boat and cruiser rental companies. Check at the marina which islands you can land on (your craft will need an anchor, and a rowing dinghy). The most rewarding island is Inchcleraun (E5) where you can

A Celtic cross at Clonmacnoise

explore the 12th-century Clogás Oratory with its bell tower.

Strokestown Park and Famine Museum 240 E2

Strokestown Park is a fine, predominantly 18th-century Palladian building, where a conducted tour takes you through family rooms and down into the kitchens. The Famine Museum that occupies the old stable block is arranged in a series of rooms. The Walled Garden provides a quiet place to walk.

Tullynally Castle & Gardens 241 K3

Tullynally Castle has been the seat of the Pakenham family (now Earls of Longford) since 1655, and they still live in the house that was rebuilt during the 19th century into a full-scale Gothic castle. The tour takes family and domestic rooms. Outside are lovely gardens and grounds.

To reflect the road signs of each country, distances and speed limits are shown in miles and mph in Northern Ireland, and kilometres and km/h in the Republic of Ireland.

…tified house was remodelled as a Georgian mansion, then a Gothic revival castle

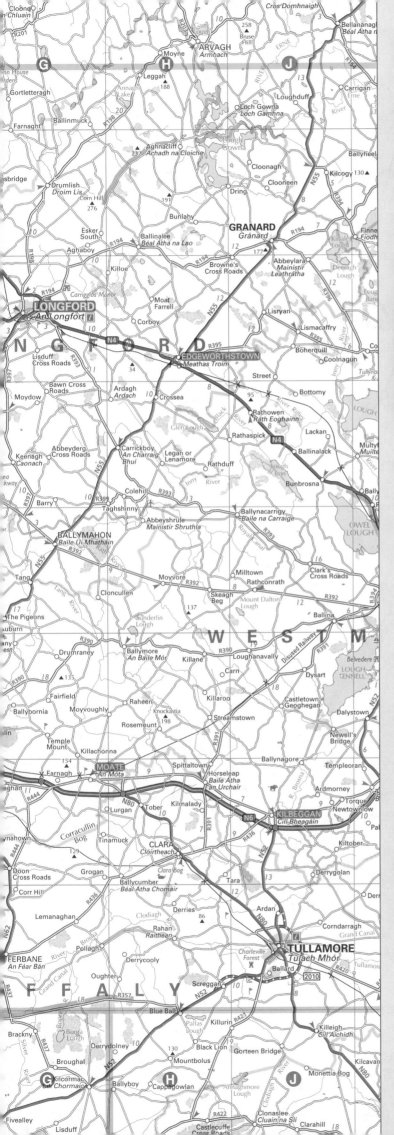

IRELAND'S CENTRAL LOWLANDS

The defining features of the landlocked Midlands are its many loughs (lakes) that dot the landscape and its vast stretches of bogland. The region's largest town is Athlone, and Tullynally is the country's largest castle, while Clonmacnoise is one of Ireland's finest ecclesiastical sites.

Grey and forbidding Athlone Castle on the River Shannon

Athlone 240 F6

Athlone is a lively base for boating and fishing on the River Shannon. The best place for a pint, a tune and all the local information, is Sean's Bar on Main Street, an establishment of great character. The excellent Castle Museum and Visitor Centre in the keep of Athlone Castle offers an eclectic display of bygone implements of rural life and agriculture. From the battlements there's a good view of the town and the River Shannon towards Lough Ree.

Belvedere House 241 K6

With its fine plasterwork ceilings and decoratively carved woodwork, this 18th-century fishing and hunting lodge and gardens make an enjoyable excursion. Pride of place among the many follies in the grounds goes to the Jealous Wall, a large sham castle frontage, complete with turrets, Gothic arches and 'shattered' windows.

Clonalis House 240 B2

Clonalis House is a late Victorian Italianate country house. Its interest lies in the antiquity of its owners, the O'Conors, once the Kings of Connacht. Ruaidri Ua Conchobair (Rory O'Conor) reigned from 1166–1186 as the last High King of Ireland. You can see the great stone on which the O'Conor chiefs have been inaugurated since pre-Christian times, and the harp that belonged to Turlough O'Carolan (1670–1738), the blind harpist, composer and poet known as the last of the traditional court bards.

Clonfert Cathedral 240 E8

The first impression of Clonfert Cathedral is that it is small, but it is an architectural gem with some masterful stonework. The site was originally occupied by a monastery founded in

ad 563 by St Brendan the Navigator. The Cathedral of St Brendan was built around 1160 and later additions include a 13th-century chancel, and a 15th-century tower. St Brendan's monastery was destroyed in 1541. A 1900s restoration accounts for its excellent state of repair and continued use for worship.

Clonmacnoise 240 F7

Clonmacnoise lies on a great bend of the River Shannon. You enter through the Visitor Centre, essential to your appreciation of Clonmacnoise. The monastic site lies immediately east of the Visitor Centre, with the Round Tower and churches huddled compactly together inside their surrounding wall. As you enter the site,

Tullynally Castle: the original 17th-century

K   L   M

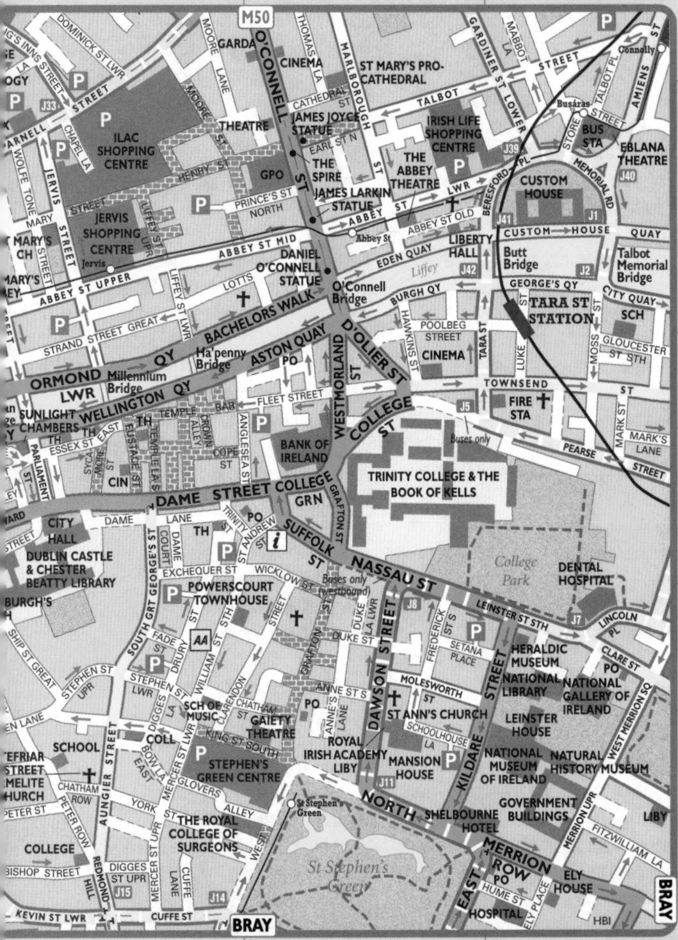

M50
O'CONNELL STREET
GARDA STA
DOMINICK ST LWR
MOORE LANE
MARLBOROUGH STREET
GARDINER STREET LWR
AMIENS ST
CINEMA
ST MARY'S PRO-CATHEDRAL
CATHEDRAL
JAMES JOYCE STATUE
TALBOT STREET
IRISH LIFE SHOPPING CENTRE
Connolly
ILAC SHOPPING CENTRE
THEATRE
GPO
EARL ST N
THE SPIRE
THE ABBEY THEATRE
Busáras
BUS STA
ÉBLANA THEATRE
JERVIS SHOPPING CENTRE
PRINCE'S ST NORTH
JAMES LARKIN STATUE
ABBEY STREET LWR
ABBEY ST OLD
CUSTOM HOUSE
MEMORIAL RD
CUSTOM — HOUSE QUAY
Talbot Memorial Bridge
ABBEY ST MID
DANIEL O'CONNELL STATUE
EDEN QUAY
LIBERTY HALL
Butt Bridge
CITY QUAY
GLOUCESTER ST STH
ABBEY ST UPPER
LOTTS
O'Connell Bridge
BURGH QY
GEORGE'S QY
MOSS ST
MARK'S LANE
STRAND STREET GREAT
BACHELORS WALK
Ha'penny Bridge
ASTON QUAY
POOLBEG STREET
TARA ST STATION
TARA ST
FIRE STA
ORMOND QY LWR
Millennium Bridge
WELLINGTON QY
FLEET STREET
TOWNSEND
PEARSE STREET
SUNLIGHT CHAMBERS
TEMPLE BAR
WESTMORLAND ST
D'OLIER ST
CINEMA
DAME STREET
COLLEGE ST
COLLEGE GRN
BANK OF IRELAND
TRINITY COLLEGE & THE BOOK OF KELLS
College Park
DENTAL HOSPITAL
CITY HALL
DAME LANE
SUFFOLK ST
NASSAU ST
HERALDIC MUSEUM
DUBLIN CASTLE & CHESTER BEATTY LIBRARY
POWERSCOURT TOWNHOUSE
WICKLOW ST
Buses only (westbound)
DUKE LA LWR
FREDERICK STREET
SETANA PLACE
LINCOLN PL
NATIONAL LIBRARY
SOUTH GRT GEORGES ST
GRAFTON STREET
DUKE ST
DAWSON STREET
CLARE ST
NATIONAL GALLERY OF IRELAND
SCH OF MUSIC
GAIETY THEATRE
ANNE ST S
ST ANN'S CHURCH
MOLESWORTH STREET
LEINSTER HOUSE
ROYAL IRISH ACADEMY LIBY
SCHOOLHOUSE LA
KILDARE STREET
NATIONAL MUSEUM OF IRELAND
NATURAL HISTORY MUSEUM
STEPHEN'S GREEN CENTRE
MANSION HOUSE
THE ROYAL COLLEGE OF SURGEONS
NORTH
GOVERNMENT BUILDINGS
LIBY
St Stephen's Green
SHELBOURNE HOTEL
MERRION ROW
ELY HOUSE
St Stephen's Green
EAST
PO
HUME ST
ELY PLACE
HOSPITAL
HBI
BRAY
BRAY
5
6

Dún Laoghaire

HOLYHEAD

0   400 m
0   400 yds

West Pier
Western Marina
Harbour
Car Ferry Terminal Entrance
Eastern Marina
FERRY TERMINAL
East Pier
Old Harbour
STA
LIFEBOAT STATION
N31
DUNLEARY ROAD
CROFTON ROAD
Scotsman's Bay
LONGFORD PLACE
DÚN LAOGHAIRE TOWN CENTRE
QUEEN'S ROAD
YORK ROAD
PATRICK ST
MULGRAVE ST
GEORGE'S ST UPP
R119
R118
PARK RD
HBI

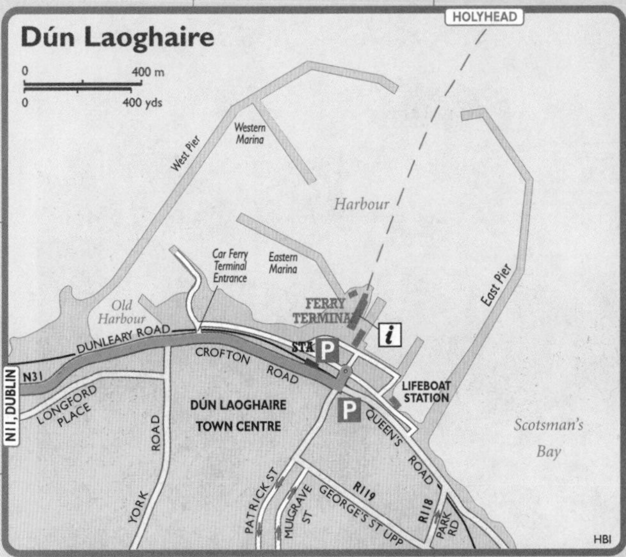

K   L   M

0 1 2 3 4 5 miles
0 1 2 3 4 5 6 7 kilometres

made to world literature. With four Nobel laureates, it's an impressive record. First editions here include Joyce's *Ulysses* and Bram Stoker's *Dracula*.

At the Guinness Storehouse exhibits take you through the process from water, Irish barley, hops and yeast to the finished product. You get a free pint in the seventh floor Gravity Bar where the views are impressive

The National Museum safeguards some of Ireland's most precious and important treasures – gold and silverware found in bogs, caves and burial mounds and memorabilia from the 20th-century struggle for independence.

The Victorians restored St Patrick's Cathedral, the largest church in Ireland. Until the 1920s it stood amid slum housing, outside the old city walls. Today it overlooks a little park. The church belongs to the Protestant Church of Ireland.

No visit to Dublin is complete without visiting Trinity College Library to see the intricate beauty of the Book of *Kells*, and the similarly ornate books of *Durrow* and *Armagh*.

Dún Laoghaire 242 F8

Part modern port facility and part seaside resort, Dún Laoghaire is where the Holyhead car ferries have berthed since 1966. A walk along the piers is a popular seaside stroll of a couple of hours each, and affords splendid views. The spire of the former Mariners' Church dominates the town; it now contains the National Maritime Museum. Among its exhibits are a longboat seized from a French raiding party in 1796 and the original optic, worked by clockwork and still functioning, from the Baily lighthouse on the Howth peninsula.

Howth Head 242 F7

The peninsula of Howth Head forms the northern arm of Dublin Bay. A waymarked path stretches for 8km around the head itself, passing the Baily lighthouse, and makes an invigorating walk (catch a bus back). On the northern side of the head, Howth town is a fishing port, its harbour facing the rocky islet of Ireland's Eye. Boat trips to view its puffin colony, Martello tower and 6th-century monastic ruins are available. Little remains of St Mary's Abbey, but about 1km to the west, signs to the Deer Park Hotel also lead to the grounds of Howth Castle (not open), famous for their azaleas and rhododendrons, and the National Transport Museum with restored trams, buses, fire engines and other vehicles.

Kells 242 A3

Kells wouldn't get much attention were it not for its connections with the famous book, now in Trinity College, Dublin. St Columcille (St Columba) established a monastic settlement here in AD 550, of which only a well-preserved oratory building (St Columcille's House) remains. It's tucked away beyond the church and you'll need to get the keys, as a sign instructs, before you can visit. The churchyard contains a round tower and some good high crosses, but the best, the Market Cross, with its graphic depictions of biblical stories, stands under a shelter outside the Old Courthouse. Here, in the Heritage Centre, touch-screen computers allow you to view pages of a virtual Book of Kells and there are replicas of other valuables to be found in the National Museum.

Monasterboice 242 D2

What you'll find here is a neat, working cemetery, a splendid round tower, without its cone, and a set of truly magnificent high crosses. There are some extant walls from a large church building, probably originating from the 8th or 9th century. It is the crosses that draw people, and these are among the best in Ireland. The Cross of Muiredach is an elaborate wheel head cross from the 10th century. On its base the inscription translates as 'A prayer for Muiredach by whom was made this cross'.

To reflect the road signs of each country, distances and speed limits are shown in miles and mph in Northern Ireland, and kilometres and km/h in the Republic of Ireland.

*fices and ceremonial accommodation dating from many different periods

(map of Dublin with numerous street and landmark labels)

Dublin

0 — 200 metres
0 — 200 yds

© Govt of Ireland 2008

LAMBAY
ISLAND
Reachrainn

Eye
easáin

TH
adair

Holyhead
Douglas-
(Seasonal)

Liverpool
Birkenhead
Holyhead

IN

Holyhead

EYSTONES
Clocha Liatha

DUBLIN & BOYNE VALLEY

The Republic of Ireland's vibrant capital has lively pubs, restaurants and nightclubs, and numerous historical and contemporary attractions. North of Dublin are the ancient sites of the Boyne Valley, and outstanding monastic ruins.

The entrance to the megalithic passage tomb at Newgrange, Brú na Bóinne

Brú na Bóinne (Bend of the Boyne) 242 D3

Brú na Bóinne is the name given to a large group of neolithic remains in the Boyne Valley. The huge, white-fronted passage tomb of Newgrange is the best known, but the nearby mounds of Knowth and Dowth were probably of equal importance historically. These great tombs are over 5,000 years old. There are over 50 lumps and bumps with ritual significance around Brú na Bóinne. Of the three major tombs, you can visit the interiors of Knowth and Newgrange on organised tours, but visitor numbers are restricted to 700 a day. Arrive early and be prepared to wait for a place.

Drogheda 242 D3

Viking traders established this port town in AD 911. Its name 'Droichead Atha' means 'bridge by the ford', though it was not bridged until the Normans came in the 12th century. The north side of the river has the main shopping area and medieval remains such as St Lawrence's Gate, a four-floor barbican, and Magdalene Tower, a remnant of a Dominican friary from 1224. On the south side of the river, accessed from the riverside by steep steps, is the Millmount fortification. A Martello tower crowns an Anglo-Norman motte from the 12th century (guided tour only). A museum, craft centre and restaurant are in the next-door barracks, and there are splendid views. There's a Heritage Centre and more medieval defences near Millmount.

Dublin 242 E7

The Dublin Castle complex is a mix of vice-regal classicism, medieval buildings, modern offices and a world-renowned museum, the Chester Beatty Library and Gallery of Oriental Art, which contains a collection of early religious manuscripts including fragments of 2nd-century biblical tracts and 9th-century Koranic texts. On view at the castle itself are the fine State Apartments, its Undercroft, and its Chapel Royal, a neo-Gothic gem of a church built in 1814.

In a substantial northside Georgian town house, the Dublin Writer's Museum reflects the contribution the city has

Dublin Castle is now an assembly of court.

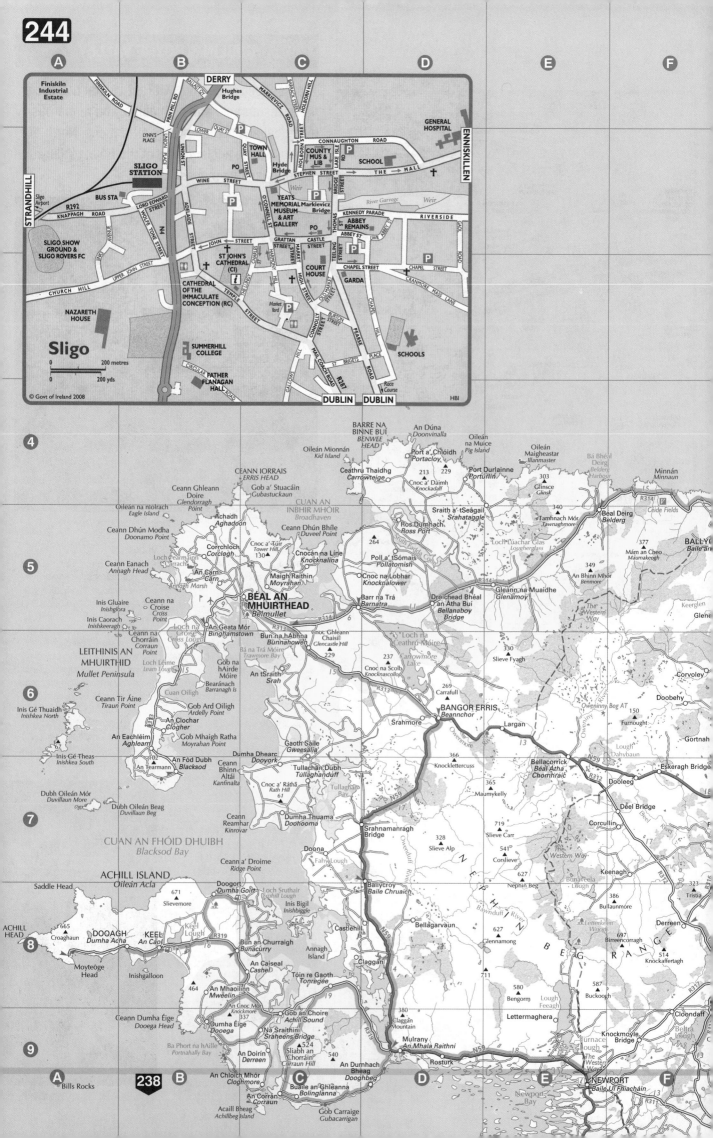

peninsula, where you may spot the rare red-necked phalarope. The western or Atlantic coast of the peninsula has a succession of beautiful sandy (and seaweedy) strands.

Nephin Beg Mountains 244 E8
The Nephin Beg Mountains are the loneliest in Mayo if not in the whole of Ireland. In these unpopulated, roadless mountains you can leave busy urban life behind. The waymarked Bangor Trail, a long-distance path that runs for 45km from Bangor Erris south to Newport through the heart of the range, is a true challenge for strong and determined walkers.

Skreen Churchyard 245 L5
At first glance there's nothing very special about the tombs scattered in the tangle of undergrowth in Skreen churchyard. But take your time here and you'll discover some fine pieces of stone carving. Most are the work of the Diamond family, a dynasty of stonemasons that has been living and working locally for more than 200 years.

Sligo 245 M5
Sligo is extremely walkable, with a tight grid of central streets containing most of the attractions. The handsome redbrick Yeats Memorial Building is the headquarters of the Yeats Society, which is dedicated to promoting the work and reputation of Ireland's national poet, William Butler Yeats. Sligo Art Gallery on the upper floors, mounts 15 to 20 exhibitions a year. The bronze sculpture of W B Yeats was erected on Stephen Street by the people of Sligo in 1989 to commemorate the 50th anniversary of the poet's death. A former presbytery is home to Sligo County Museum,

Bronze sculpture of W B Yeats in Sligo

which gives an enjoyable run-through of local history via photographs and objects. The main attraction is the Yeats Memorial Room, a small room with formal and informal photographs, as well as letters and his 1923 Nobel Prize for literature. The Niland Gallery, based on a collection started by Sligo's late county librarian Nora Niland, has a dazzling range of art, with Irish artists predominating. Pride of the gallery is its definitive collection of paintings, watercolours and drawings by Jack B Yeats, brother of poet William. The 13th-century Dominican Sligo Abbey, under an arched tower, is in a remarkably good state of preservation.

To reflect the road signs of each country, distances and speed limits are shown in miles and mph in Northern Ireland, and kilometres and km/h in the Republic of Ireland.

Lissadell House offers an insight into Ireland's political, artistic and literary history

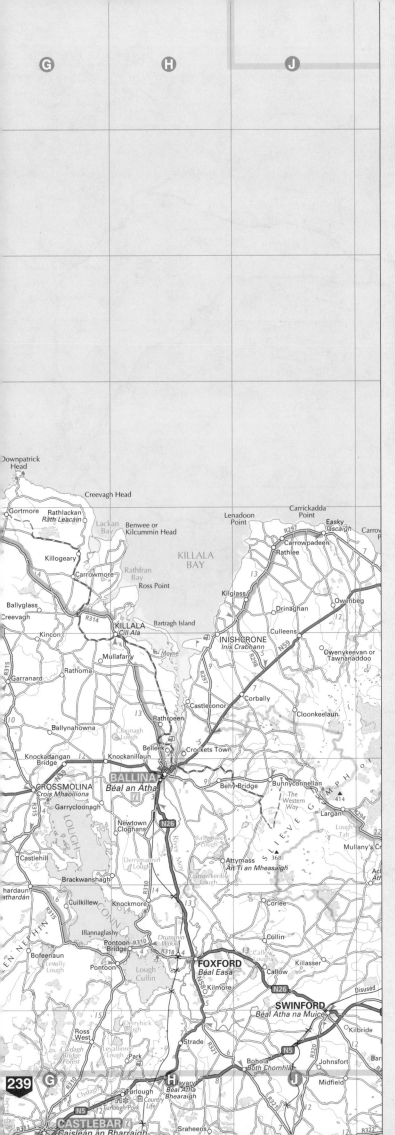

SLIGO & NORTH MAYO

From Sligo town visit County Sligo's picturesque coastline, mountains, lakes and forests that inspired the poet W B Yeats. There are also many prehistoric sites to discover.

Carrowmore, the largest cemetery of megalithic tombs in Ireland, has monuments built of crude granite boulders

Achill Island 244 B8

Achill Island is connected to the mainland by Michael Davitt Bridge. The narrow coast road signposted 'Atlantic Drive', which runs south along the sound, is the best introduction to the island. It passes the austere 15th-century Carrickildavnet Castle. Next to the castle stands the ruin of Kildownet church. The 'Atlantic Drive' turns north for a beautiful run up the wild west coast. Towards the top of the island you reach the village of Keel, with its long beach and spectacular view of the Cliffs of Minaun. The road ends at Keem Strand, a lovely unspoiled beach in a deep bay with a memorable cliff walk. One of Achill Island's remarkable sites is the deserted village of roofless houses on the southern slope of Slievemore.

Carrowmore Megalithic Cemetery 245 M5

In low-lying country west of Sligo town are scattered burial sites known as the Carrowmore Megalithic Cemetery. The oldest of the tombs may date back more than 7,000 years to early Stone Age times, making this the oldest and largest prehistoric burial site in Ireland. Over centuries many of the tombs have been robbed of their stone; others were dug into out of curiosity or in hopes of unearthing buried treasure, but around 30 are still easily identifiable. The dates of burial items recovered from the graves span 3,000 years and include the remains of human bones burned in cremation. Creevykeel court tomb is signposted off the N15 at Cliffony (246 A3). In contrast to the older and cruder Carrowmore tombs, this structure of 3000–2000 BC is a sophisticated mound with several chambers.

Céide Fields 244 F4

Céide Fields Visitor Centre has been designed in a pleasing pyramid shape to blend with the landscape. A display explains how climate change and forest clearance around 3000–2000 BC allowed blanket bog to creep in and smother a Stone Age agricultural landscape. A guided tour across the bog shows the excavations, which have revealed walls of massive stones built in straight lines.

Lissadell House 245 M4

Lissadell House, though somewhat grim and grey from the outside, is one of the most romantic Great Houses in Ireland, thanks to its associations with Ireland's 'national poet' W B Yeats and with the celebrated nationalist leader Constance Gore-Booth, Countess Markievicz. The Gore-Booth family had lived at Lissadell on the northern shore of Drumcliff Bay since 1604, and Sir Robert Gore-Booth built the present neo-classical house there in 1832. The house and grounds saw decades of neglect during the 20th century, and though the grounds are still in a bit of a tangle, you can tour the restored rooms of the house.

Mullet Peninsula 244 B6

The peninsula is one of the wildest and least-populated corners of Ireland. The low-lying, isolated Mullet, composed mostly of mountain and bog, is a Gaeltacht area, so you will hear only Irish spoken in the peninsula's sole village of Binghamstown. The eastern or landward side of the Mullet cradles Blacksod Bay (B7) and is sandy in parts, but also spread with mudflats. Birding is sensational here, as it is by Termoncarragh Lake (Loch Tearmainn Carrach, B5) at the head of the

Cruising Lough Erne, one of the largest freshwater lakes in the UK

huge variety of birdlife gives endless opportunities for birding.

Enniskillen 246 F4

Enniskillen is the bustling capital town of County Fermanagh. Attractions include Castle Barracks with its regimental and county museums; the Cole Monument in Forthill Park, commemorating one of Wellington's generals, from the top of which there's a splendid view over the town; and Blakes of the Hollow, a pub with great traditional music.

Florence Court 246 E5

The Cole family, later Earls of Enniskillen, built Florence Court early in the 18th century within sight of rugged Cuilcagh Mountain. The beauty of its wooded parkland looking to the mountains is still its greatest asset. Inside you can admire superb plasterwork and antique Irish furniture.

Knockmany Chambered Cairn 247 J3

At the end of your uphill walk from the parking area is an ugly modern structure, but it protects the Bronze Age passage tomb of Knockmany, its stones superbly incised with whorls, spirals and cupmarks. It's also adorned with graffiti cut over the centuries, hence the locked gate through which you are obliged to stare at them. However, you can climb to the roof skylight for a better view. The vista from the hilltop is quite wonderful; it's said you can see seven counties from here.

Lough Erne 246 D2–247 G6

The monastery established by St Molaise in the 6th century stands on Devenish Island (F4). Here you'll find a tall round tower, built by monks around 1120, the ruins of the beautiful little 15th-century abbey church and a fine High Cross. In Caldragh cemetery on Boa Island (E2), reached by causeways on the A47, stands the 'Janus Man', a stumpy figure, thought to be 2,000 years old. Near him is his swollen-headed brother the 'Lusty Man'. On the causeway islands and shores of Upper Lough Erne are fine carvings of definite Christian tradition. Lough Erne is wonderful for wildlife, with a good overview from Explore Erne's (C3) displays. Three country parks around Lower Lough Erne provide lakeside and woodland walks and Castle Caldwell Forest Park (D3) offers good birding. Castle Archdale Forest Park (E3) has a boating marina, fine gardens, and an exhibition about the World War II flying boats based here. At Lough Navar Forest (D3) an 11km scenic drive ends at the spectacular Cliffs of Magho viewpoint. Ireland's best collection of antique Irish lace is displayed at Sheelin Lace Museum.

Marble Arch Caves 246 E5

Tours here start with the caving and mineral display in the visitor centre, then a spectacular subterranean route takes you by boat and on foot through the caverns, including the 'Moses Walk' through a subterranean river. Stalagmites, stalactites, glistening sheets of calcite and rock minerals are all revealed by lamplight.

To reflect the road signs of each country, distances and speed limits are shown in miles and mph in Northern Ireland, and kilometres and km/h in the Republic of Ireland.

Intricate lattice-work crafted by hand at Belleek Pottery

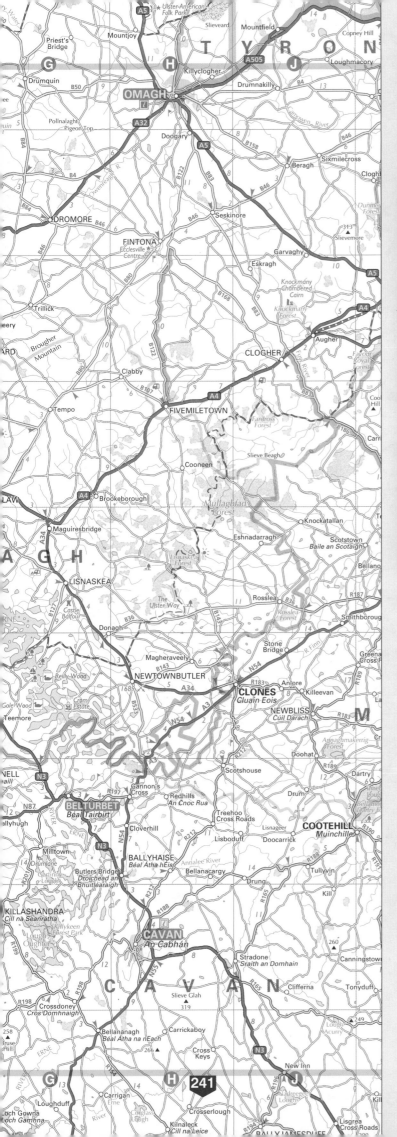

LOUGH ERNE & IRON MOUNTAINS

Two major cities occupy this region, the historic city of Armagh and Enniskillen, the main city of County Fermanagh. This lakeland county has many attractions set around Lough Erne.

Enniskillen Castle, floodlit at night, is reflected in the waters of Lough Erne

Armagh 247 M4
The city's two great cathedrals are the most eye-catching and significant buildings in town. The Anglican Cathedral of St Patrick is the smaller and older of the two. Its largely 19th-century exterior of pink sandstone conceals parts of a mid-13th century cathedral, which was preceded by other churches going back to AD 444 when St Patrick built the first church on this site. Across the valley on Cathedral Road are the two huge rocket-like towers of the Roman Catholic Cathedral of St Patrick. The interior is an unrestrained Gothic burst of mosaic, marble and golden angels on the wing. On English Street near the neat Georgian Mall, St Patrick's Trian has displays covering the city's links with the saint and the story of the city itself. Life in Armagh in the 18th century is entertainingly re-created at the Palace Demesne.

Belleek Pottery 246 C3
Since the late 1850s Belleek Pottery has concentrated on high-quality products, especially white Parian ware. On the factory tour you see a fascinating process and get the chance to talk to the highly skilled potters and hand-painters. The basket ware, a lattice of finely meshed clay strings, is probably the best known of Belleek products. The visitor centre explains the history and technicalities, and there is a showroom and shop.

Boyle 246 A8
Boyle is a handsome town with a mixture of Georgian and Victorian architecture. By far the most important and striking building is Boyle Abbey, standing beside the River Boyle. Founded in 1148 by the Cistercian community, the remains of the old monastery cloister garden, kitchens and refectory are in an excellent state of preservation, as is the abbey church itself. King House is a wonderful place for children, with storytelling, activities and dressing-up; adults can watch audio-visual displays on the history of the King family and the area, and also on the Great Famine. Frybrook House, a well-preserved Quaker house, dates from the mid-18th century.

Castle Coole 246 F4
The family who built this great Palladian mansion still live here. One of Ireland's finest and grandest country houses, with its huge portico and long arcaded wings, Castle Coole was designed by James Wyatt and finished in 1798.

Crom Estate 247 G6
A variety of woodland and the presence of Upper Lough Erne in so many of the views make Crom Estate an ideal spot for walking all year round. Paths lead to Crom Old Church, and the ruin of Crom Old Castle of 1611. With luck you'll see some of the resident deer, and the

K L M

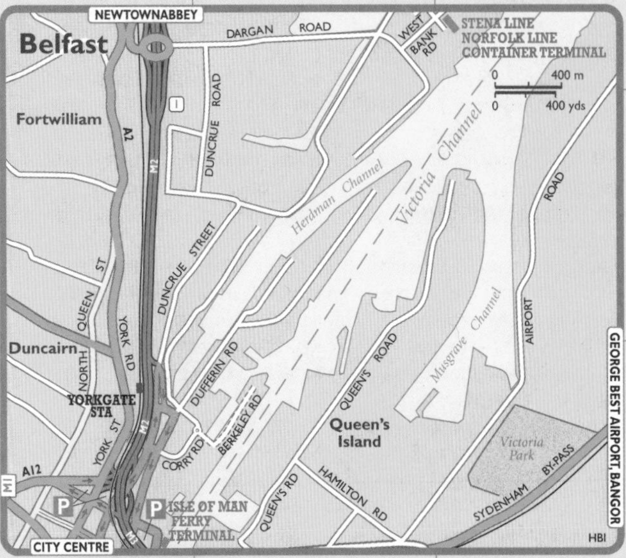

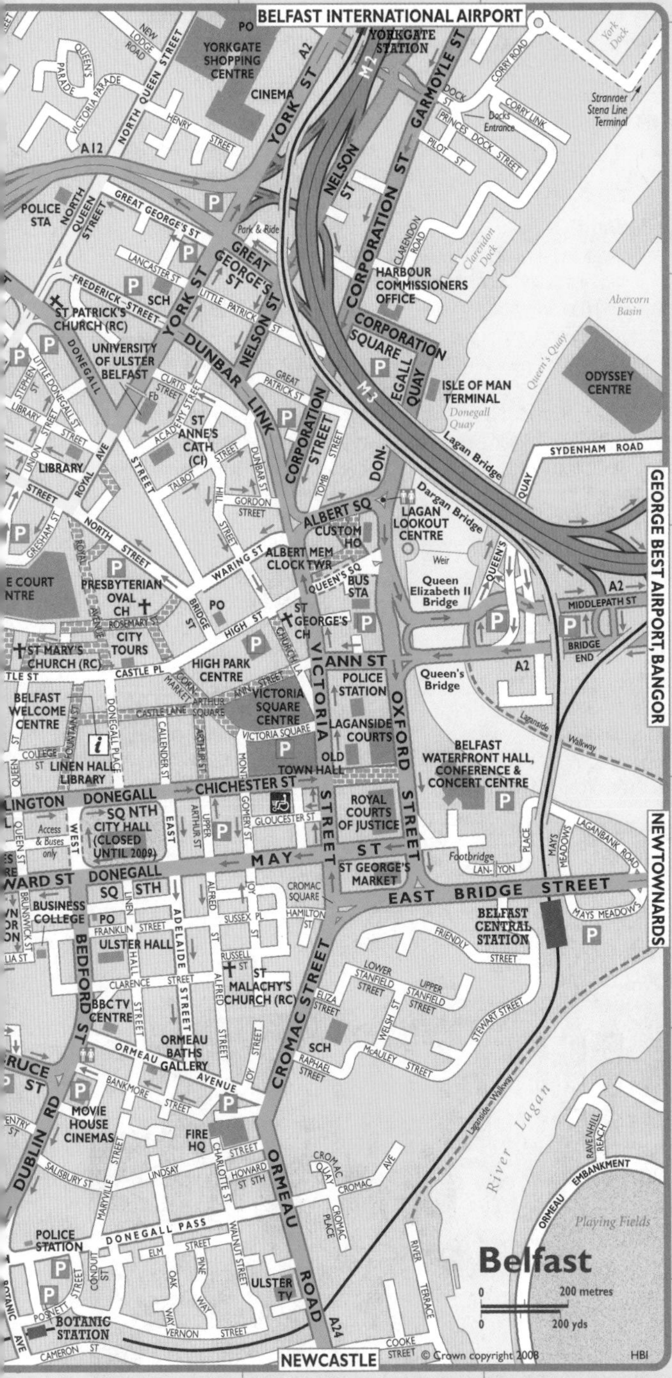

NEWTOWNABBEY
Belfast
DARGAN ROAD
WEST BANK RD
STENA LINE
NORFOLK LINE
CONTAINER TERMINAL
0 400 m
0 400 yds
Fortwilliam
A2
M2
DUNCRUE ROAD
DUNCRUE STREET
Herdman Channel
Victoria Channel
ROAD
QUEEN ST
NORTH QUEEN
YORK RD
Duncairn
DUFFERIN RD
QUEEN'S ROAD
Musgrave Channel
AIRPORT
GEORGE BEST AIRPORT, BANGOR
YORKGATE STA
BERKELEY RD
CORRY RD
Queen's Island
Victoria Park
YORK ST
A12
M1
M3
SYDENHAM BY-PASS
HAMILTON RD
QUEEN'S RD
ISLE OF MAN FERRY TERMINAL
CITY CENTRE
HBI

BELFAST INTERNATIONAL AIRPORT
PO
YORKGATE SHOPPING CENTRE
YORKGATE STATION
CINEMA
NORTH QUEEN STREET
HENRY STREET
YORK ST
NELSON ST
CORPORATION ST
GARMOYLE ST
CORRY ROAD
CORRY LINK
Docks Entrance
PRINCES DOCK STREET
PILOT ST
York Dock
Stranraer Stena Line Terminal
A12
A2
M2
POLICE STA
GREAT GEORGE'S ST
Park & Ride
CLARENDON ROAD
Clarendon Dock
HARBOUR COMMISSIONERS OFFICE
LANCASTER ST
SCH
LITTLE PATRICK ST
ST PATRICK'S CHURCH (RC)
FREDERICK STREET
CORPORATION SQUARE
EGALL QUAY
UNIVERSITY OF ULSTER BELFAST
DUNBAR LINK
Abercorn Basin
Queen's Quay
ODYSSEY CENTRE
ISLE OF MAN TERMINAL
Donegall Quay
M3
ST ANNE'S CATH (CI)
CORPORATION STREET
DON.
Lagan Bridge
SYDENHAM ROAD
LIBRARY
ROYAL AVE
TALBOT ST
GORDON STREET
ALBERT SQ
CUSTOM HO
Dargan Bridge
LAGAN LOOKOUT CENTRE
QUAY
GEORGE BEST AIRPORT, BANGOR
NORTH STREET
WARING ST
ALBERT MEM CLOCK TWR
QUEEN'S SQ
BUS STA
Weir
QUEEN'S
Queen Elizabeth II Bridge
A2
MIDDLEPATH ST
E COURT NTRE
PRESBYTERIAN OVAL CH
ROSEMARY ST
BRIDGE ST
PO
HIGH ST
ST GEORGE'S CH
CITY TOURS
BRIDGE END
ST MARY'S CHURCH (RC)
CASTLE PL
HIGH PARK CENTRE
ANN ST
Queen's Bridge
A2
POLICE STATION
VICTORIA SQUARE CENTRE
LAGANSIDE COURTS
Laganside Walkway
BELFAST WELCOME CENTRE
CASTLE LANE
VICTORIA SQUARE
BELFAST WATERFRONT HALL, CONFERENCE & CONCERT CENTRE
COLLEGE
LINEN HALL LIBRARY
OLD TOWN HALL
VICTORIA STREET
OXFORD STREET
DONEGALL
CHICHESTER ST
LINGTON
SQ NTH
CITY HALL (CLOSED UNTIL 2009)
GLOUCESTER ST
ROYAL COURTS OF JUSTICE
Access & Buses only
MAY ST
ST GEORGE'S MARKET
Footbridge
LAGANBANK ROAD
MAYS MEADOWS
NEWTOWNARDS
DONEGALL SQ STH
WARD ST
CROMAC SQUARE
EAST BRIDGE STREET
HAMILTON ST
BUSINESS COLLEGE
PO
FRANKLIN STREET
SUSSEX PL
BELFAST CENTRAL STATION
MAYS MEADOWS
ULSTER HALL
FRIENDLY STREET
BEDFORD ST
ST MALACHY'S CHURCH (RC)
LOWER STANFIELD STREET
UPPER STANFIELD STREET
CLARENCE STREET
STEWART STREET
BBC TV CENTRE
ELIZA STREET
ORMEAU BATHS GALLERY
CROMAC STREET
SCH
McAULEY STREET
ORMEAU AVENUE
RAPHAEL STREET
BANKMORE STREET
DUBLIN RD
MOVIE HOUSE CINEMAS
FIRE HQ
Laganside Walkway
River Lagan
RAVENHILL REACH
ORMEAU EMBANKMENT
SALISBURY ST
LINDSAY
HOWARD ST STH
CROMAC QUAY
CROMAC AVE
CROMAC PLACE
ORMEAU ROAD
Playing Fields
POLICE STATION
DONEGALL PASS
ELM
OAK
PINE
WALNUT STREET
RIVER TERRACE
Belfast
0 200 metres
0 200 yds
ULSTER TV
A24
BOTANIC STATION
VERNON STREET
CAMERON ST
BOTANIC AVE
NEWCASTLE
COOKE STREET
© Crown copyright 2008
HBI

K L M

0 1 2 3 4 5 miles
0 1 2 3 4 5 6 7 kilometres

famous pub in Belfast', has also been restored. The classic 19th-century Botanic Gardens beside the river contain two pieces of High Victorian glass-and-cast-iron architecture: the great Glasshouse of 1839–40 with its Cool Wing full of bright plants, and its steamy Stove Wing and mighty central dome. There's more steam in the nearby Tropical Ravine, with a gallery looking down through a miniature tropical rain forest. Displays in the Ulster Museum include Stone and Bronze Age implements, jewellery and religious icons of the Dark Ages and medieval Ireland, and machines and mementoes of Ulster's industrial heritage of shipbuilding, textiles and heavy industry. Consecrated in 1904, St Anne's Cathedral is an impressive church built of stone from all 32 counties of Ireland. Highlights include the 'Occupations of Mankind' carvings on the capitals of the nave pillars and the modern stained glass of the east window. To the north, the city rises up to Cave Hill, with Belfast Castle on its lower slopes. This splendid Victorian 'Scottish Baronial' edifice, built for the third Marquess of Donegall in 1870, contains a small Heritage Centre on its top floor.

Castle Ward 249 G4
Castle Ward is an intriguing monument to an ill-matched couple. Lord Bangor took one half and designed a severely restrained Classical frontage and set of front rooms, while his wife ordered a feast of exuberant Strawberry Hill Gothic to the back of the house. The result is both eccentric and delightful. In the grounds you'll find a farmyard with a sawmill, the original 16th-century fortified tower, the Strangford Lough Wildlife Centre and a high-tech adventure playground.

Castlewellan Forest Park
248 E5
This beautiful forest park occupies the estate of the Annesley family in the northern foothills of the Mountains of Mourne. Special features are the National Arboretum of rare trees and plants from all over the world, which surrounds an 18th-century garden; a long lake; the Grange Yard, an early 18th-century farmstead; and many miles of footpaths.

Gosford Castle and Forest Park
248 A4
The grand mock-Norman castle, built of grey granite in the 1820s–50s now stands empty. It features as 'Castlemallock' in The Valley Of Bones, in Anthony Powell's saga A Dance to the Music of Time. Today the estate forms the Gosford Forest Park with an arboretum and walled garden, and waymarked trails through the paddocks and woods.

Mount Stewart 249 G2
Mount Stewart, on the eastern shore of Strangford Lough, is the home of the Stewart family, Marquesses of Londonderry. There are tours of the house, but the estate is especially known for its gardens, laid out between the 1920s and the 1950s with verve, imagination and eccentricity by Edith, Lady Londonderry. Water gardens, formal gardens, woods and dells lead on to the 'Land of the Fairies', and also to the Temple of the Winds, a Georgian banqueting hall on a hillock looking out over Strangford Lough.

Struell Wells 249 G4
Each of the many springs in this green valley has a reputation for healing. During the 18th century Struell Wells became a major place of healing and of pilgrimage. Enthusiasm was spurred by the story that St Patrick had spent a night in the freezing water of the drinking well known as The Tub. From The Tub, with its domed roof, the water flows through the Eye Well (said to cure eye diseases) to reach a pair of 19th-century bathhouses.

To reflect the road signs of each country, distances and speed limits are shown in miles and mph in Northern Ireland, and kilometres and km/h in the Republic of Ireland.

BELFAST & THE ARDS OF DOWN

Belfast, Northern Ireland's capital with attractive city buildings, is situated on the southern tip of Belfast Lough amid hills and mountains. The surrounding area contains large estates and forest parks.

Mount Stewart House and Gardens

Ards Peninsula & Strangford Lough 249 G1–H4

East of Belfast, the Ards Peninsula stretches south for some 25 miles and is edged with a fine sweep of coastline with some pretty small towns and villages. Strangford Lough is a giant tidal inlet, 19 miles long, between the Ards Peninsula and the mainland. A twice-daily flush of tides pours through a tiny gap only 500 yards wide at Portaferry (G3). The lough, managed by the National Trust, contains 70 islands and vast mudflats and sandbanks, exposed at low tide. Birding is first class and it is a haven for wildlife. For a memorable view, climb the 122 steps to the top of Scrabo Tower (F1) at the summit of Scrabo Hill Country Park, off the A21 south east of Newtownards. From the viewing platform you have a view over the peninsula and lough, south to the Mountains of Mourne and east across the sea to the Scottish hills.

Belfast 248 E1

Belfast is very easy to negotiate – most of the main attractions are within a few minutes' walk of each other. The heart of Belfast is Donegall Square, whose broad pavements and flowerbeds surround the giant City Hall. The great green dome of the City Hall (opened in 1906) is a prime Belfast landmark. Patterned Italian marble and elaborate stucco greet you in the hall, from where tours of the building begin. The Grand Opera House is a splendid example of a late Victorian music hall. The restored and refurbished Grand Opera House puts on a wide variety of entertainment and Crown Liquor Saloon, 'the most

Flower beds in front of Stormont

Londonderry / Derry

City centre inset map labels

BUNCRANA, MOVILLE

Londonderry Derry

0   200 metres
     200 yds

COLERAINE

LIMAVADY RD

DUNGIVEN

St Eugene's Cath (RC)
SCH
CREGGAN ST
FRANCIS STREET
GREAT JAMES STREET
LITTLE JAMES ST
SWIMMING BATHS
WILLIAM ST
SACKVILLE ST
CUSTOM HOUSE
PO
QUAYSIDE SHOPPING CENTRE & MULTIPLEX CINEMA
CAVEDOWN ROAD
HARBOROUGH STREET
LITTLE DIAMOND ST
FREDERICK STREET
CHAMBERLAIN ST
GUILDHALL
SHIPQUAY GATE
BUS STATION
EASTWAY
BEECHWOOD AVENUE
WESTLAND
FAHAN STREET
TOWER MUSEUM & O'DOHERTY FORT
River Foyle
Bogside
LONE MOOR ROAD
LINEWOOD STREET
BEECH WOOD
ROSSVILLE ST
BUTCHER GATE
RICHMOND SHOPPING CENTRE
MILLENNIUM FORUM
Prince's Quay
KING ST
BLIGH'S LANE
NULLAMORE DRIVE
ELM WOOD ST
APPRENTICE BOYS HALL
CENTRAL LIBRARY
BOND'S HILL
A6
SCHS
STANLEY'S WALK
ROYAL BASTION (CITY WALLS)
BISHOP'S PALACE
PALACE
FOYLESIDE SHOPPING CENTRE
Foyle Street Urban Park
CLOONEY TERRACE
UNION ST
Celtic Park Recreation Ground
LECKY ROAD
ST COLUMB'S WALK
DOUBLE BASTION (CITY WALLS)
DEANERY
ST COLUMB'S CATH
FERRYQUAY GATE
DUNGIVEN RD
LOWER VIOLET ST
GASYARD CENTRE
BRANDYWELL PARK
COOKE STREET
SCH
BISHOP GATE
COURT HOUSE
FOUNTAIN ESTATE
CARLISLE ROAD
i
SIMPSON'S BRAE
PRIMROSE AVE
BRANDON TERRACE
CNOC FOLA
BLOODY FORELAND
BARRACK STREET
LONG TOWER ST
UPPER FOUNTAIN ST
ABERCORN ROAD
JOHN ST
Abercorn Quay
LONDONDERRY STATION
Waterside Quay
MALVERN TERRACE
CHAPEL ROAD
HATSBANK PK
KNOCKDARA PK
SCHOOL
SOUTHWAY
ANNE ST
CARRIGANS LANE
BISHOP STREET
IVY TERRACE
FOYLE ROAD
A40
FOYLE VALLEY RAILWAY CENTRE
Craigavon Bridge
Two level bridge
SPENCER ROAD
DUKE ST
MARGARET ST
FOUNTAIN HILL
SCH
SCH
A5
LETTERKENNY
© Crown copyright 2008
STRABANE
DUNMORE TERRACE
HBI

WATERSIDE LINK

FOYLE EMBANKMENT

Regional map labels

TORAIGH
TORY ISLAND
An Baile Thiar / West Town
CAIN
TO

Na Mic Uí gCorra / The Stag Rocks
Inis Oirthir / Inishsirrer
Gabhla / Gola Island
Gola / Bá Ghaoth Dobhair
GAOTH DOBHAIR / Gweedore
Mín Lá / Meenl
R257

Inis Meáin / Inishmeane
Ba Ghaoth Dobhair
Doirí Beaga / Derrybeg
431
Taobh an Leith / Tievealehid

Inis Sionnaigh / Inishinny
Min an Chladaigh / Meenaclady
Bún na Leaca / Brinlack

Uaigh / Owey Island
Inis Fraoigh / Inishfree Lower
An Bun Beag / Bunbeg
Gaoth Dobha / Gweedore
R258

An Chruit / Cruit Island
Bá Inis Fraoigh / Inishfree Bay
Rinn na Feirste / Rinnafarset
R259
Muir / Mon

Donegal
Croithlí / Crolly

Cionn Caslach / Kincaslough
Anagaire / Annagary
GLENVI
NA

ÁRAINN MHÓR / **ARAN ISLAND**
AILT AN CHORRÁIN / Burtonport
NA ROSA / The Roses
Loch an Iúir / Loughanure
Loch an Iúir
Crocknafarra
AT

An Leadhb Gharbh / Leabgarrow
Inis Mhic an Doirn / Rutland Island
Mín Beannaid / Meenbannad
Loch Mile / Lough Meela
PAR

Inis Caorach / Inishkeeragh
Inis Fraoigh Upper / Inishfree Upper
Loch Crathar / Lough Graghy
Loch Chró / Lough na nGarr
Cnoc na

An Tearmann / Termon
R259
AN CLOCHÁN LIATH / Dunglow

Cionn na Cruaiche / Crohy Head
An Machaire / Maghery
Loch an Eala Mór / Lough Kincasla-More
An Dúchoraidh / Doocharry

Min na Croise / Meenacross
R252

Roaninish
Bá Thrá Éanach
An Dumhaigh / Dooey Point
Derry Loughlan / Forest
Loch Mhic Néill / Lough Macnoil

BÉAL AN BHEARA / Gweebarra Bay
Leitir Mhic an Bhaird / Lettermacaward

Dunmore Head
Inishkeel

Dawros Head
Portnoo / Port Nua
Naran
Clooney
Derkbeg Hill
Fintown Railway
R261

Rossbeg
Kiltooris Lough
Máas
N56
Lough Aderry
13

Inishbarnog
Sheskinmore Lough
Lough Machugh
Heritage Centre
GLENTIES / Na Gleannta
R253
Anna

LOUGHROS MORE BAY
Loughros Point
Loughros Beg Bay
Kilrean
R253
Crockbrack

An Tor Mór / Tormore Island
472
Sliabh Thuaidh / Slievetooey
ARDARA / Ard an Ratha
Ivy Bridge
Carnaween

Sturróg / Sturall
Cruach an Chuilinn / Croaghacullion
Common Bridge
Binbane

Cionn Ghlinne / Glen Head
Father McDyer's Folk Village & Heritage Centre
Mín na Croise / Meenacross
R230
Glengesh Pass Forest
Maol Mosóg / Mulmosog Mountain
R262

Ceann Ros Eoghain / Rossan Point
R263
Gleann Cholm Cille / Glencolumbkille
R230
Gleann Cheise
Killin Hill

Málainn Mhóir / Malin More
Loch Onna / Lough Inna
Mín an Aoire / Meenaneary
Crocknapeast
Croagh

Bá Mhálainne / Malin Bay
473
Maol na nDamh / Mulnanaff
Bungosteen Bridge
Frosses / Na Frosa

Málainn Bhig / Malin Beg
Sliabh Slieve
An Charraig / Carrick
Crownasillagh Forest
494
Inver / Inbhear
Milltown
N56

Reachlainn Uí Bhirn / Rathlin O'Birne Island
Liag League / Teelin / Teileann
595
Crownarad
Bruckles
Dunkineely / Dún Clonnaola

Cill Charthaigh / Kilcar
Largy
KILLYBEGS / Na Ceala Beaga
Inver Bay

Cionn an Charrain / Carrigan Head
Cionn Mhucrois / Muckros Head
Fintragh Bay
Drumanoo Head
Carntullagh Head
McSw
Doorin Point

Inishduff

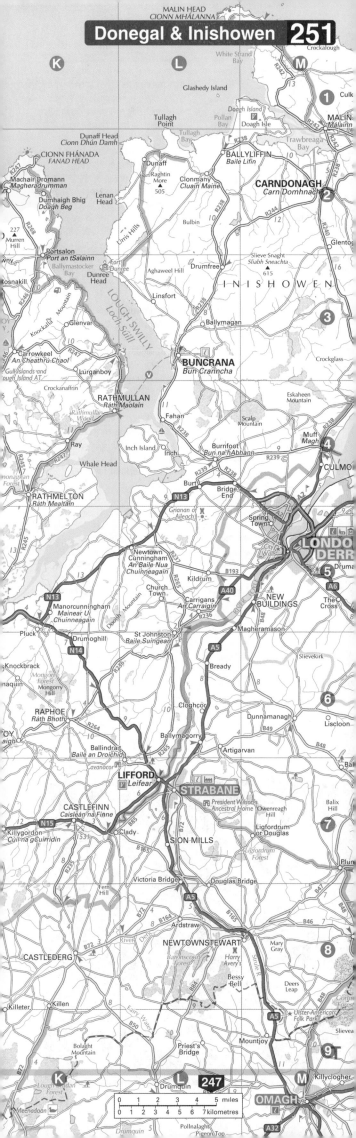

MALIN HEAD
CIONN MHÁLANNA

Crockalough

White Strand
Bay

K

L

M

1

Glashedy Island

Culk

R242

13

Doagh Island

Pollan Bay

MALIN
Maláinn

Tullagh
Point

Doagh Isle

R242

R238

Dunaff Head
Cionn Dhún Damh

Tullagh
Bay

Trawbreaga
Bay

CIONN FHÁNADA
FANAD HEAD

Dunaff

BALLYLIFFIN
Baile Lifín

10

R247

Raghtin
More
505

Clonmany
Cluain Maine

CARNDONAGH
Carn Domhnach

2

Machair Dromann
Magheradrumman

R244

12

Lenan
Head

Bulbin

R240

R238

R268

Dúmhaigh Bhig
Doagh Beg

Urris Hills

10

Glentoc

227
Murren
Hill

Portsalon
Port an tSalainn

Fort
Dunree

Drumfree

INISHOWEN

Slieve Snaght
Sliabh Sneachta
615

16

Ballymastocker
Bay

Dunree
Head

Aghaweel Hill

Crockglass

R246

Knockalla
Mountain

Linsfort

Ballymagan

3

osnakill

10

Glenvar

Eskaheen
Mountain

Carrowkeel
An Cheathrú-Chaol
Gull Islands and
ough Island AT.

Lurganboy

10

LOUGH SWILLY
Loch Súill

BUNCRANA
Bun Cranncha

Crockanaffrin

RATHMULLAN
Ráth Maolain

11

Muff
Magh

R238

4

Scalp
Mountain

CULMO

Ray

Fahan

R238

Burnfoot
Bun na hAbhann

R239

Whale Head

Inch Island

Inch

R239

Burt

R239

R228

A2

LONDO
DERR

RATHMELTON
Ráth Mealtáin

R245

Bridge
End

N13

Grianan of
Aileach

Spring
Town

City
Walls

5

Drum

Newtown
Cunningham
An Baile Nua
Chuinneagain

R237

Kildrum

B193

A40

NEW
BUILDINGS

A6

The
Cross

N13

13

R265

Church
Town

Carrigans
An Carraigín

R236

Magheramason

Manorcunningham
Mainear Uí
Chuinneagain

Pluck

R265

4

St Johnston
Baile Suingean

A5

Slievekirk

N14

Drumoghill

R236

Bready

6

Knockbrack

Mongorry
Forest
Mongorry
Hill

Cloghcor

Dunnamanagh

B49

Liscloon

naquin

RAPHOE
Ráth Bhoth

R264

Ballymagorry

Artigarvan

B48

Bá

OY
aigh

10

R265

LIFFORD
Leifear

7

Ballindrait
Baile an Droichid

Cavanacor

STRABANE

President Wilson's
Ancestral Home

Owenreagh
Hill

Balix
Hill

CASTLEFINN
Caisleán na Finne

B85

B72

Ligfordrum
or Douglas

Killygordon
Cúil na gCuirridín

N15

12

153

Clady

SION MILLS

Ligfordrum
Forest

R235

B165

Fern
Hill

Victoria Bridge

Douglas Bridge

B47

Plun

B72

B164

Ardstraw

B165

A5

CASTLEDERG

B72

NEWTOWNSTEWART

Baronscourt
Forest

Harry
Avery's

Mary
Gray

8

Bessy
Bell

Deers
Leap

Killeter

Killen

Fairy Water

B84

Ulster-American
Folk Park

A5

Slievea

Bolaght
Mountain

Priest's
Bridge

Mountjoy

9

B72

K

L **247**

M

Killyclogher

Meenedoon

Drumquin

OMAGH

A32

of the friary, by the River Eske, try to picture the learned Michael O'Clery and his assistants compiling their 'Annals of the Four Masters'. This wonderful document (copies are in Dublin's National Library) is a vivid history of the island from 2958 bc (40 years before Noah's Flood) until ad 1616. The Donegal Railway Heritage Centre recalls a now defunct scenic local line, with a simulator and rail exhibits.

Errigal Mountain 251 G4

At 752m Errigal is the highest of Donegal's many mountains, and its peak catches the eye because of the way its naked quartzite gleams like snow. Approaching along the N56/R251 from Gweedore (F4) you see the rugged screes, corries and cliffs of the mountain's west face at their most formidable. It is in fact an easy mountain to climb if you are sensibly shod, reasonably fit and prepared for a sudden change in the weather. Wonderful views over the lakes and mountains of Donegal reward your effort.

Glencolumbkille 250 C8

There's something special about the atmosphere in Glencolumbkille, tucked away in a hidden cleft. This peaceful green valley is where St Columba (born in Donegal in ad 521) established a monastery. There's a Folk Village Museum with traditionally built and furnished thatched homes. Walkers can follow An Turas Cholmcille, Columba's Journey, for 5km around 15 stations or sacred sites, to reach St Columba's Chapel, Bed and Well.

Inishowen 251 M3

The diamond-shaped Inishowen peninsula is flanked by Lough Foyle and Lough Swilly. Many visitors travel up through Inishowen to stand on Malin Head (L1), the most northerly point of Ireland and a place that sets the tone of wildness and the prevailing view of mountain, moor and rugged coastline. Once you get down to west-facing beaches such as White Strand Bay (L1), Pollan Bay (L1), Tullagh Bay (L2) and Crummie's Bay, near Dunree Head (K3) you're likely to have them to yourself.

President Wilson's Ancestral Home 251 L7

James Wilson was aged 20 when he emigrated to America from this little whitewashed cottage in 1807; his grandson, Woodrow Wilson became President of the United States. You can see the family's box beds, and furniture typical of the period, and you get the chance to chat to members of the Wilson family, who still live next door.

Slieve League 250 C9

Seen from the little parking bay high on a windy ledge at Bunglass, the Slieve League cliffs are hugely impressive – a great wall of multihued rock that plunges 595m into the sea below. Walkers with a head for heights can teeter along the very narrow 'One Man's Path' to the summit of Slieve League, but not in windy conditions or when the ground is slippery.

Ulster American Folk Park 251 M9

The site is divided into Irish and American areas, linked by a reconstruction of one of the ships in which Irish emigrants journeyed to the New World. Costumed guides work as their ancestors would have worked, and are always ready to explain and to answer questions. The park's large collection of original buildings come from all over Northern Ireland and from America.

To reflect the road signs of each country, distances and speed limits are shown in miles and mph in Northern Ireland, and kilometres and km/h in the Republic of Ireland.

DONEGAL & INISHOWEN

County Donegal borders Northern Ireland and Donegal town is one of the biggest settlements in this large but sparsely populated region. The stunning Atlantic coastline is studded with rocky inlets, towering cliffs and deserted beaches. Inishowen is a remote and underpopulated region of the county. The walled City of Derry, in County Londonderry, has a fine stretch of coast.

The conical shape of the white quartzite Errigal mountain

Arran Island 250 D5
The Arran Island ferry from Burtonport takes just 20 minutes. Most visitors come for the day, but it's best to stay overnight -- especially in August, during the annual festival, which is centred on the eastern side, in the bars and shops of Leabgarrow. From here you can wander narrow lanes towards the rugged west coast, or turn aside to climb one of the three modest peaks for the view.

Derry/Londonderry 251 M5
It's easy to find your way around Derry. The wide River Foyle shapes the east boundary, while 'old Derry', the walled city, forms a neat rectangle whose four radiating streets converge on the central market square. There's a good Craft Village within the angle of Butcher Street and Shipquay Street, where small workshops rub shoulders with cafés, wine bars and trendy eateries. On Waterloo Street you'll find great traditional and modern music in the bars. However, the chief visitor attraction is undoubtedly the splendid city walls. You can climb to the top and make the circuit of 1 mile, with splendid views. A Walls Walk starting at Shipquay Gate should begin with a visit to the florid Guildhall. Inside, fine stained-glass windows depict the city's history. Cannon on the walls are reminders of the defence of the city in 1688–89 when the Catholic army of King James II laid siege. At Bishop's Gate you can descend from the walls to see St Columb's Cathedral and its treasured relics of the Great Siege.

Donegal 251 G9
Although it's the county town, Donegal is a modest little place with small-scale streets overshadowed by the gabled walls and turrets of Donegal Castle. Looming up on its rocky knoll is Donegal Castle, a great Jacobean mansion built in 1623 on what remained of a 15th-century fortress of the O'Donnell clan. You can tour the castle, which is furnished in mid-17th century style. In the ruins

The Slieve League Cliffs

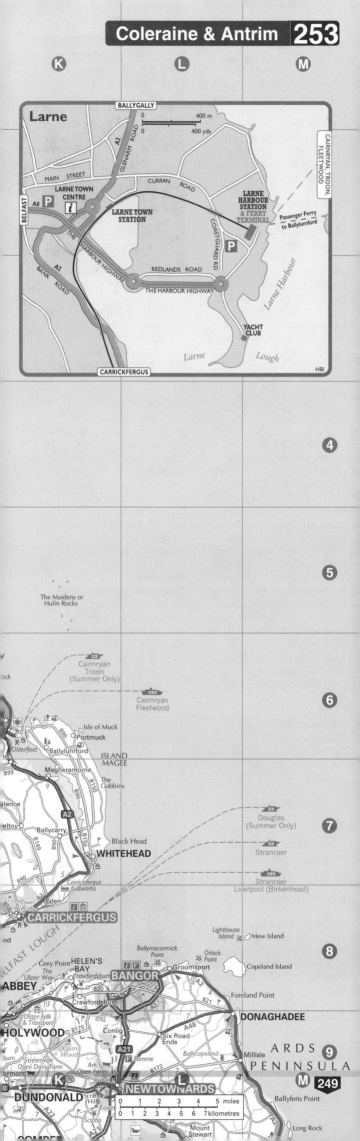

K L M

Larne

BALLYGALLY

GLENARM ROAD

A2

0   400 m
0   400 yds

MAIN STREET

CURRAN ROAD

BELFAST

A8

P

LARNE TOWN CENTRE

LARNE TOWN STATION

THE HARBOUR HIGHWAY

COASTGUARD RD

LARNE HARBOUR STATION & FERRY TERMINAL

CAIRNRYAN, TROON, FLEETWOOD

Passenger Ferry to Ballylumford

A2

BANK ROAD

REDLANDS ROAD

P

THE HARBOUR HIGHWAY

Larne Harbour

YACHT CLUB

Larne   Lough

CARRICKFERGUS

HBI

4

5

The Maidens or Hulin Rocks

6

Cairnryan Troon (Summer Only)

Cairnryan Fleetwood

ock

Olderfleet

Isle of Muck
Portmuck

Ballylumford

ISLAND MAGEE

B90

B90

Magheramorne

The Gobbins

B99

ilenoe

A2

eltoy

Ballycarry

B149

B90

B150

Black Head

WHITEHEAD

Douglas (Summer Only)

Stranraer

7

B90

Carrickfergus Gasworks

Town Walls

Eden

Stranraer
Liverpool (Birkenhead)

CARRICKFERGUS

nd

BELFAST LOUGH

Lighthouse Island   Mew Island

8

Grey Point   HELEN'S BAY

The Ulster Way   Crawfordsburn

ABBEY

BANGOR

Ballymacormick Point

Orlock Point

Groomsport

Copeland Island

Foreland Point

B20

Crawfordsburn

A2

B21

DONAGHADEE

Ulster Folk & Transport

Open Dairy Farm

HOLYWOOD

B170

Conlig

A48

A21

Six Road Ends

Cairn Wood

Ark Open Farm

Somme

Ballycopeland

Millisle

ARDS

9

Streamvale Open Dairy Farm

ormont

B172

PENINSULA

burn

K   L

Scrabo Hill

NEWTOWNARDS

M   249

DUNDONALD

A22

Scrabo Tower

0   1   2   3   4   5 miles
0 1 2 3 4 5 6 7 kilometres

Ballyferis Point

Mount Stewart

Long Rock

Dunluce Castle 252 E2

The poignant ruin of Dunluce Castle stands on the edge of the cliffs – so close that during a 1639 storm the kitchens fell into the sea and the kitchen workers were killed. Dunluce is associated with many stories – the most romantic concerns its recapture from the English in 1584 by the owner, Sorley Boy MacDonnell, whose men had been hauled 60m up the cliffs in baskets.

Giant's Causeway 252 E2

A World Heritage Site, the Causeway is a hump-backed promontory, formed of the wave-eroded stubs of 37,000 mostly hexagonal basalt columns created some 60 million years ago when lava from an undersea volcano cooled rapidly on contact with cold sea water. Taller columns can be seen in the cliffs behind. Legend says that the hero-giant Fionn MacCumhaill laid down the Causeway as a stepping stone, so he could stride across the Sea of Moyle to his giantess girlfriend's cave in the Hebridean island of Staffa, where there are similar columns.

Glens of Antrim 253 G4

Only a short drive away from the crowded Antrim coast you'll find peace and quiet amid beautiful scenery of basalt cliffs, green valleys and dense woodland. Waymarked walks for all tastes and abilities in Glenariff Forest Park (H5) take you past water in motion: fast mountain rivers, streams, rapids and waterfalls. The nine Glens of Antrim form one of Ireland's most beautiful landscapes. Great water-cut clefts in Antrim's coastal shelf, they tend to be U-shaped and high-sided, in some cases (notably Glenariff, H4) with imposing cliffs forming their upper flanks. Narrow roads wind up one glen and down the next, so that you can spend a very enjoyable day cruising the glens in low gear.

Old Bushmills Distillery 252 E2

Bushmills is the oldest distillery in the world; it started production in 1608, and has been distilling superb malt whiskeys ever since. The buildings, with their pagoda-style roofs, are a pleasure to look at. The tour takes you past the huge round mash tuns where the wash bubbles and ferments, and the great stills shaped like gleaming copper onions. At the end of the tour you can sip a complimentary dram and buy a bottle of whiskey.

Portstewart 252 D3

This trim little Victorian seaside resort sits on a gracefully curving waterfront. Its chief attraction is the sandy beach, stretching for 3km west of the town and cared for by the National Trust.

Rathlin Island 253 G1

It's a good idea to rent a bicycle to explore the island, which measures 8km by 5km. At the west end, the Kebble Cliffs National Nature Reserve is the largest and most remarkable cliff-nesting site in Northern Ireland.

Carrickfergus Castle

The cliffs are home to some quarter of a million seabirds during the nesting season (Apr–end Aug). Rathlin also has an excellent small museum on the harbour, the Boathouse Centre, run by the islanders.

Springhill 252 D8

The Conyngham family, who came from Scotland, built Springhill around 1690 and created a comfortable home. Furniture was made by estate workers from the Conynghams' own timber, and the Georgian library and gunroom, with historic weaponry display, retain 18th-century wallpaper. In the former laundry is a collection of bygone costumes, and there are walks through the wooded grounds.

Ulster Folk & Transport Museum 253 K9

The Folk Museum explores Ulster history and everyday life through reconstructed buildings, which include thatched cottages and farmhouses, a flax mill, a school and a rural Orange Hall. The Transport Museum consists of a number of galleries of beautifully maintained exhibits – gleaming steam locomotives, horse-drawn carriages, penny-farthings and racing bicycles, motorcycles and a horse-drawn tram.

To reflect the road signs of each country, distances and speed limits are shown in miles and mph in Northern Ireland, and kilometres and km/h in the Republic of Ireland.

A waterfall in Glenariff

COLERAINE & ANTRIM

The coast of County Antrim has some of Ireland's most spectacular scenery, including the famous Giant's Causeway with its dramatic cliffs and volcanic rocks, as well as quaint fishing villages and Carrickfergus Castle.

The volcanic basalt rock of the Giant's Causeway

Ardboe High Cross 252 E9
Situated at Ardboe Point, on the western shore of Lough Neagh, is the best example of a high cross to be found in Northern Ireland. Marking the site of an ancient monastery, the cross has 22 sculpted panels, many recognisably biblical, including Adam and Eve and the Last Judgment. It stands over 5.5m high and dates back to the 10th century.

Ballycastle 253 G2
Looking like an old-fashioned, Georgian seaside resort, Ballycastle makes a convenient base for exploring the Antrim coast and glens. To get the most out of your explorations, you can learn all about the area's history and culture in the Ballycastle Museum. Lammastide (the last Monday and Tuesday of August) is the best time to be here, for the Ould Lammas Fair. Held since 1606, it is a great social event, with music, dancing, street entertainment, food markets and more.

Carrick-a-rede Rope Bridge
252 F2
Carrick-a-rede rope bridge was originally a scary flywalk with a single guide-rope, slung 25m in the air by salmon fishermen to reach their offshore fishing station. The National Trust has made it more stable, but it still sways enough to raise the hairs on your neck.

Carrickfergus Castle 253 K8
Carrickfergus is the southern gateway to the Antrim coast, and its great grey Norman stronghold makes an impressive introduction. Carrickfergus Castle was built on its shore promontory in 1180 to guard Belfast Lough. Its strategic position has always made it liable to attack and siege, but it has survived remarkably intact. Tableaux, effigies and explanatory plaques tell its story to visitors.

Downhill Estate 252 C3
The collection of buildings and ruins on the cliffs near Castlerock is all that remains of the 18th-century glories of the Downhill Estate, laid out in 1783–85 by the Protestant Bishop of Londonderry, Frederick Hervey, the fourth Earl of Bristol. The ruin of the Bishop's Palace of Downhill, its walled garden and icehouse lie near the Lion Gate (topped with leopard sculptures) entrance.

Dungiven Priory 252 B6
The chancel of the 12th-century Augustinian Dungiven Priory holds one of the finest medieval tombs in Ireland, that of Cooey-na-Gal, a chieftain of the O'Catháin clan. His effigy, with sword and battleaxe, lies under a canopy of carved foliage. In niches under the tomb stand six guardians in the act of drawing their swords.

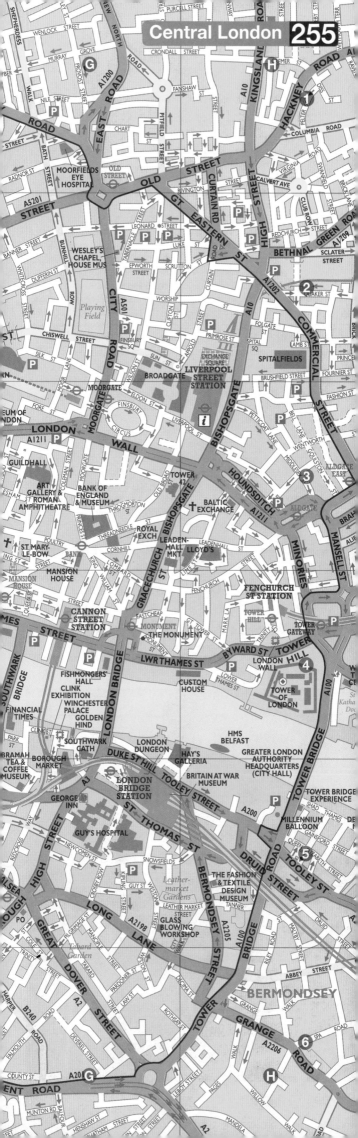

more than 500 works complemented by a changing programme of blockbuster art exhibitions. One of Europe's largest aquariums, the London Aquarium occupies three floors and represents a variety of watery environments.

Covent Garden 254 D4
A former fruit and vegetable market was turned into the present Piazza, with shops, stalls, eating places and street entertainers. There's still a daily market, with a wonderful range of crafts, jewellery, clothing, accessories and antiques. To the northeast of the Piazza is the magnificently refurbished Royal Opera House. On the opposite side is the former Flower Market, now London's Transport Museum. The Theatre Museum, on Russell Street, has collections to please any thespian, and nearby are two of the area's famous theatres, the elegant Theatre Royal Drury Lane and the Lyceum.

Globe Theatre 255 F4
The original Globe was one of Britain's first purpose-built theatres, erected by a company that included Shakespeare in 1599. It was destroyed by fire in 1613. A project began in 1969 to create an accurate, functioning reconstruction, using materials, tools and techniques closely matching those of Elizabethan times, but it was 1997 before it was finished. The theatre is built of unseasoned oak and held together with 6,000 oak pegs. It is crowned with the first thatched roof to be built in the city. In the middle, an elevated stage and an open-air yard are bordered on three sides by covered tiers of benches that seat 1,500.

Houses of Parliament 254 D6
Despite their appearance, the Houses of Parliament, which form the main part of the Palace of Westminster, are 19th-century buildings. The original medieval palace, virtually destroyed by fire in 1834, was replaced in Elizabethan style. The famous clock tower housing Big Ben (the hour bell) was completed in 1858. The Jewel Tower was used to store Edward III's treasures. For a guided tour of the Houses of Parliament, UK residents should contact their Member of Parliament. Anyone is able to attend debates in both the House of Commons and the House of Lords (join the queue outside St Stephen's Entrance and expect to wait one to two hours during the afternoon).

Hyde Park 254 A5
Hyde Park was opened to the public in the 17th century. Members of the Household Cavalry exercise their horses along Rotten Row and at 10.30am and 12pm you can watch them riding to and from the Changing the Guard ceremony at Buckingham Palace. The city's greenery extends west into Kensington Gardens, the grounds of Kensington Palace. The Serpentine Gallery hosts changing exhibitions of contemporary art. Close by, the Diana, Princess of Wales Memorial Playground opened in 2000. Queen Victoria's beloved husband, Prince Albert, is commemorated in the dazzling Albert Memorial.

London Eye (The Millennium Wheel) 254 D5
The world's largest observation wheel offers the best overview of London from 135m above the Thames. The capsules have unobstructed views from large windows and the wheel is in constant, very slow motion. Reservations are recommended, especially at peak times.

, London Eye offers a leisurely overview of the sights

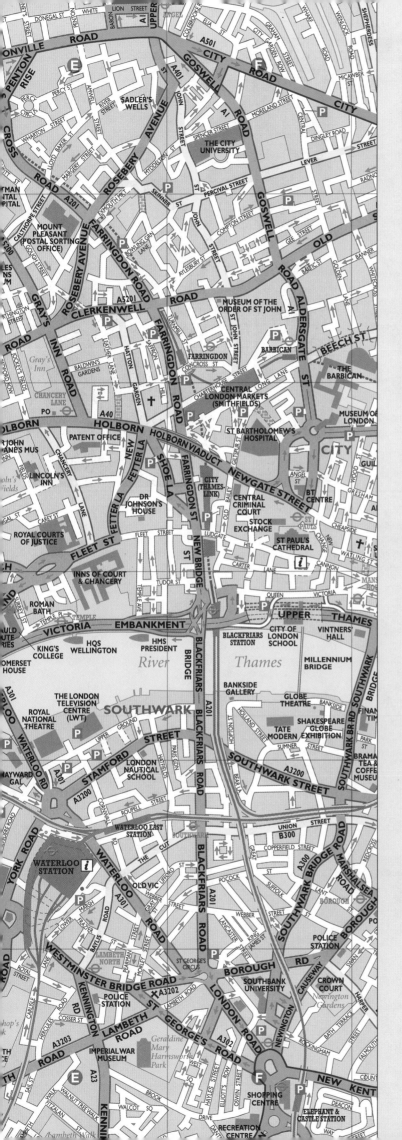

CENTRAL LONDON

London is a bustling metropolis with some of the best monuments, museums and galleries in the world. It's worth buying a London Pass as it includes free entry to over 60 attractions and allow you to jump the queue at selected ones.

Looking across the Thames to the Houses of Parliament

British Museum 254 D3

Britain's largest museum has more than 4 million objects on display in around 90 galleries. It is unrivalled for the variety and quality of its treasures, the result of more than 200 years of collecting, excavation and unashamed looting. The imposing, neo-classical building is entered via the Great Court. The curved glass canopy has created a huge, light space and it's worth lingering here to enjoy the sculpture displays. At the heart of the court is the circular Reading Room. Among the museum highlights are the Rosetta Stone, which provided a key to decipher Egyptian hieroglyphics. The Elgin Marbles still cause passionate debate: these frieze reliefs, carved between 447 and 431 BC, were taken by Lord Elgin, then British ambassador in Constantinople, from the Parthenon in Athens. The Sutton Hoo Ship treasures are from an Anglo-Saxon royal burial ship that survived intact in Suffolk. Rows of preserved Egyptian mummies have a gruesome fascination.

Buckingham Palace 254 B5

You enter the palace through the Ambassadors' Court and go through the dramatic Grand Hall to climb the curving marble of the Grand Staircase, with its gilt-bronze balustrade, to the first-floor State Rooms. Visitors can see a total of 20 rooms of decorative magnificence with superb hangings and furniture. Other attractions are the Queen's Gallery, with an important collection of paintings, and the nearby Royal Mews.

Charles Dickens Museum
255 E2

Charles Dickens lived in Doughty Street in his twenties and it was here he worked on his first full-length novel,

The Pickwick Papers, and later *Oliver Twist* and *Nicholas Nickleby*. Pages of the original manuscripts are on display together with valuable first editions, his marriage licence and many other personal mementoes.

County Hall 254 D5

The former headquarters of the Greater London Council houses two major attractions. Laid out in a labyrinth, Dalí Universe is dedicated to surrealist artist Salvador Dalí. It features a permanent exhibition of

One of the city's most popular attract

Madame Tussaud's & Stardome
254 A2

Madame Tussaud's world-famous waxwork collection was founded in Paris in 1770. It moved to England in 1802 and found a permanent home in London's Marylebone Road in 1884. The 21st century has brought new innovations and new levels of interactivity. Listen to Kylie Minogue whisper in your ear, become an A-list celeb in the 'Blush' nightclub, and take your chances in a high-security prison populated by dangerous serial killers. Madame Tussaud's has recently been combined with the Stardome (formerly the London Planetarium) which offers a celebrity themed entertainment venue.

Museum of London 254 F3

Laid out in a striking building near the Barbican, the Museum of London is the world's largest urban history museum and Europe's biggest archaeological archive. Most impressive is the Roman London Gallery, which explains the development of Londinium. Large models illustrate the city's growth, and a huge array of ordinary items shows how people lived and worked.

Royal Academy of Arts 254 C4

Burlington House was built as a Palladian mansion for the Earl of Burlington in around 1720. Since 1768 it has been the Royal Academy of Arts, England's first formal art school. Sir Joshua Reynolds was the first president, and John Constable and J M W Turner were among the first students. Today the Royal Academy hosts major exhibitions of art from international collections. The Royal

Academy Summer Exhibition is a popular show of work by both amateurs and professionals.

St Paul's Cathedral 255 F3

Sir Christopher Wren's masterpiece is a dramatic combination of vast, airy spaces and elaborate decoration. Eight pillars support the huge dome. The acoustics are such that someone standing on the opposite side of the gallery will hear your whispers clearly after several seconds' delay. The frescoes on the dome depict scenes from the life of St Paul. The Golden Gallery runs around the outer dome, a breathtaking 85m from the cathedral floor. A hole in the floor gives a dizzying view down. The Chancel is a riot of 19th-century Byzantine-style gilding. A marble effigy of poet John Donne stands in the south choir aisle. This is one of the few effigies that survived the Great Fire of London in 1666, and you can make out scorch marks on its base.

Sir John Soane's Museum
255 E3

Sir John Soane, Professor of Architecture at the Royal Academy of Arts, arranged his eccentric and eclectic collection of art and objects for the benefit of his students, filling every inch of space in his house. You'll find yourself wandering among Classical and Renaissance statues and busts, marbles and bronzes, urns, altars, antique gems, odd bits of demolished London buildings, Indian ivory-inlaid furniture, Peruvian ceramics, cork models of Greek temples, Napoleonic medals and thousands of architectural drawings. The Picture Room is a highlight: hinged screens allowed Soane to fit more than 100 works into this small room.

Tate Modern 255 F4

Tate Modern, housed in the restored Bankside Power Station, is one of the world's leading museums of modern art. Every year there are three additional special loan exhibitions and several shows focusing on a single artist, theme or period. The permanent themed displays always include works by the most influential artists of the 20th century, covering significant periods and movements, with combinations of film media, installations, painting, photography and sculpture.

Tower Bridge 255 H5

London's best-known bridge links the Tower of London and the south bank of the River Thames. The hydraulically operated bascules are the main draw, designed to allow tall ships to sail through and still lifted more than 900 times a year. The neo-Gothic towers are an attraction in themselves. Climb to the upper walkways and engine rooms, where an exhibition details the

Nelson's Column in Trafalgar Square

The imposing West Front of Westminster Abbey

controversies that preceded the eventual construction of the bridge, opened in 1894.

Tower of London 255 H4

In previous centuries, prisoners accused of treason would enter the Tower of London by boat through Traitors' Gate – some taking their final journey. Today the visitors' entrance is through the Middle Tower. At the heart of the Tower is its oldest medieval building, the White Tower, thought to date from 1078. There's an exhibition about small arms from the Royal Armouries collection, and spiral stairs lead to the gloriously simple Chapel of St John the Evangelist. First stop for many visitors is the Jewel House, where displays tell the history of the Crown Jewels before reaching the treasury, where the jewels are kept. The famous prisoners incarcerated and executed here over the years provide the human interest. The high-ranking prisoners were kept in the 13th-century Beauchamp Tower. Tower Green was the main focus for suffering and heroics, and was where Anne Boleyn, among others, was beheaded.

Trafalgar Square 254 D4

One of the world's most famous squares sits at the northern end of Whitehall, commemorating Admiral Lord Nelson's victory against Napoleon and the French at the 1805 Battle of Trafalgar. Nelson towers on his column in the middle of the square, guarded by four bronze lions. Steps lead up to the Corinthian portico of the church of St Martin-in-the-Fields, at the northeastern corner of the square. Officially the parish church of

Buckingham Palace, St Martin's has strong royal connections. To the north of the square, the National Gallery's collection of Western European art, dating from 1250 to about 1900, is arranged by period.

Wallace Collection 254 A3

Founded by the 1st Marquis of Hertford, the Wallace Collection was bequeathed to the nation in 1897 and came on public display three years later. This is one of the world's finest collections of art ever assembled by one family. The collection is shown in the family home, a tranquil oasis just a few minutes from Oxford Street. There are paintings on display by Titian, Canaletto, Rembrandt, Rubens, Hals, Fragonard, Vélazquez, Gainsborough and many more. There are also collections of porcelain, furniture and armour. Many events and exhibitions throughout the year, contact for details.

Westminster Abbey 254 D6

The largest surviving medieval church in London has been the setting for all royal coronations since 1066, and its mausoleum commemorates 3,300 of the nation's most famous historical figures. You enter by the north transept, then turn left to take a one-way clockwise tour of the church and cloisters. The main part of the chapel, with its fan-vaulted ceiling, is an impressive setting for the royal tombs arranged around the altar and aisles. The south transept, also known as Poets' Corner, is where great poets, authors, artists and actors are honoured with memorials.

BATH

It is difficult to imagine a more beautiful city than Bath – great architecture, plenty to see and compact enough to explore on foot – and its World Heritage Site status has ensured its preservation. The city is built from eye-pleasing honey limestone and has a striking setting amid seven hills, where the Cotswolds meet the Mendip Hills, and on the banks of the River Avon and the Kennet and Avon Canal. The hills can make walking tiring, but you are more than compensated by the views. With more than 20 museums and historic sites, a huge choice of accommodation and plenty of specialist shops – including a daily antiques market in Bartlett Street (B1) – there is definitely something for everyone. In between sightseeing, you can take in vibrant street entertainment from any number of cafés. Most visitors make for the Roman Baths and Pump Room (C3) in the centre: from the Georgian elegance of the Pump Room you suddenly walk into Roman times in the finest bathhouse site in Britain. Nearby is Bath Abbey and to the north the Building of Bath Museum (C1) relates the fascinating story of how the Georgian city was created.

Bath is found on atlas page 111 E5

BRIGHTON

Brighton had humble beginnings as a fishing village but is now probably Britain's liveliest seaside resort, raucous but bohemian, with top arts and clubbing venues and some fanciful Regency architecture. The Royal Pavilion (C3) is an oriental extravaganza bristling with Indian-style minarets and onion domes. Its carefully restored interior, famous for sumptuous décor and elaborate *chinoiserie*, makes it one of the most extraordinary palaces in Europe. Across the gardens is the former royal stable block, now housing the Dome (C2) concert hall and the Brighton Museum and Art Gallery, with lively exhibits on Brighton's social history, and collections of art nouveau furniture and 20th-century fashion. Behind the elegant sweep of Regency seafront terraces are The Lanes (B3), a warren of narrow streets and alleys with smart antiques, gifts and designer clothing shops, cafés, restaurants and galleries. Down on the seafront, Brighton Pier (C4) pulsates with seaside amusements and Brighton Sea Life Centre (D4) has an underwater tunnel that allows close viewing of sharks and other marine life.

Brighton is found on atlas page **95 D2**

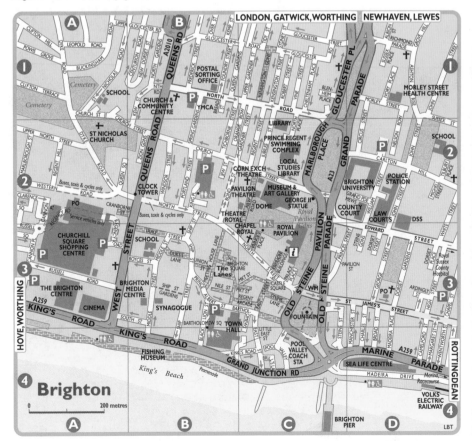

BIRMINGHAM

While lacking the townscape of other major historic cities, Birmingham does have notable pockets of interest. Around its intricate canal network, new walkways, shops and public areas have been created.

Gas Street Basin (B4), where narrowboats are often moored, makes a good starting point for waterside walks along the canal's towpaths. Birmingham's obvious central point is around Victoria Square (D3) and Centenary Square (C4), by the Grecian former Town Hall. Close by is the eclectic Birmingham Museum and Art Gallery (C3) with one of the world's largest collections of Pre-Raphaelite paintings. A canalside stroll leads north from the centre to the Jewellery Quarter (B1), which retains much Victorian character and is still the focal point for jewellery-making; there are great numbers of specialist workshops operating on a small scale. The Museum of the Jewellery Quarter, on the north end of Vyse Street (A1), occupies the extraordinarily antiquated workshops of Smith and Pepper, in operation from 1899 to 1981 for the manufacture of bangles. In that time, virtually nothing changed, and when the factory closed down it was left untouched until it became a museum. Birmingham noticeably lacks green space and trees, and

so the Birmingham Botanical Gardens in Westbourne Road, Edgbaston (134 D2), can be a welcome contrast. This is the foremost plant collection in the Midlands, with four glasshouses, themed gardens and aviaries. Dedicated shoppers, and even those who prefer to

browse, should head to the city's large shopping complexes. The most well known, and the biggest, is the Bullring (E4) with around 160 outlets ranging from multi-floor stores to small, individual shops. A visit to Cadbury World (134 D2) in Bournville is a must for chocoholics.

Stone steps lead up towards Birmingham's 19th-century Council House, with its central portico and friezes

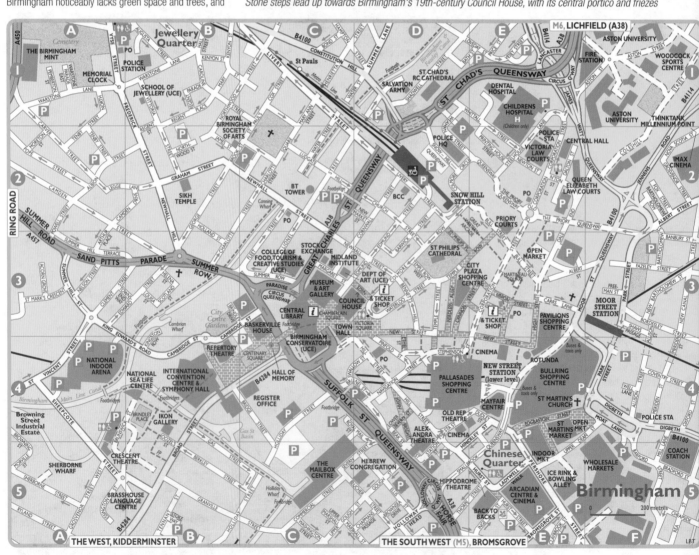

Birmingham
Birmingham is found on atlas page **134 D2**

CAMBRIDGE

Modern industry may be the first sight of Cambridge as you enter from the flat countryside that surrounds it, so the dense and incongruously beautiful core of this historic city may be a very nice surprise.

The obvious starting point for a visit is King's Parade (C3); climb the tower of the University Church (also known as Great St Mary's) for a rare high-level view. On one side is the classical Senate House, where university students receive their degrees, next to Gonville and Caius College. In the other direction, Market Hill hosts a bustling market. Don't miss King's College Chapel, known for its Chapel Choir, whose annual Christmas Eve carol service attracts crowds who start waiting outside at dawn. It's well worth catching a choral evensong. The chapel was built between 1446 and 1515. It is perhaps the greatest example of the uniquely English late Gothic Perpendicular style, typified by its wedding-cake fan vaulting that made it the largest single-span vaulted roof of its time. By the altar is Peter Paul Rubens' masterpiece *The Adoration of the Magi*, donated by Major A E Allnatt in 1961. Trinity is the largest college in Cambridge, founded in 1546 by Henry VIII, and its Great Court is the largest of the courtyards at both Cambridge and Oxford universities. One of Trinity's other major features is the Wren Library – designed by Sir Christopher Wren and completed in 1695 – which

houses almost 60,000 historic books and manuscripts, including the original manuscript of *Winnie the Pooh* by A A Milne (a Trinity student). Trinity's neighbour, and the second-largest college, is St John's, founded in 1511. Its notable features include the elegant turreted gatehouse, the Bridge of Sighs and the 13th-century School of Pythagoras. The best of the rest include: Queens', with its half-timbered Cloister Court and matchstick-like Mathematical Bridge; Emmanuel's garden; Jesus, with cloister-like seclusion and an impressive chapel; and Clare, an elegant Renaissance creation with a stone bridge.

Among the large stretches of greenery spread around the city are The Backs, (B3, the area along the river that gives classic back-door views of Queens', King's, Trinity, Clare and St John's colleges, and glimpses into their gardens), where you can go punting, Jesus Green and Parker's Piece. Around Jesus Lock are the college boathouses, where you can watch crews rowing on the river, possibly in training for the Oxford v Cambridge boat race. To the south of the city centre, off Hills Road (D5), the University Botanic Garden has mature trees, a scented garden, rockeries and several national collections of species. Two of Cambridge's best museums are free: The Fitzwilliam Museum (C5) in Trumpington Street, has a collection of fine jewellery, porcelain, furniture and glass, paintings by Paul Cézanne, Picasso, Peter Paul Rubens, John Constable and William Blake, watercolours by J M W Turner and prints by Rembrandt. In contrast,

intimate little Kettle's Yard (B1) is a stylish gallery offering a marriage of 18th-century furnishings, antique Oriental rugs and avant-garde art.

The quadrangle at Trinity College, Cambridge

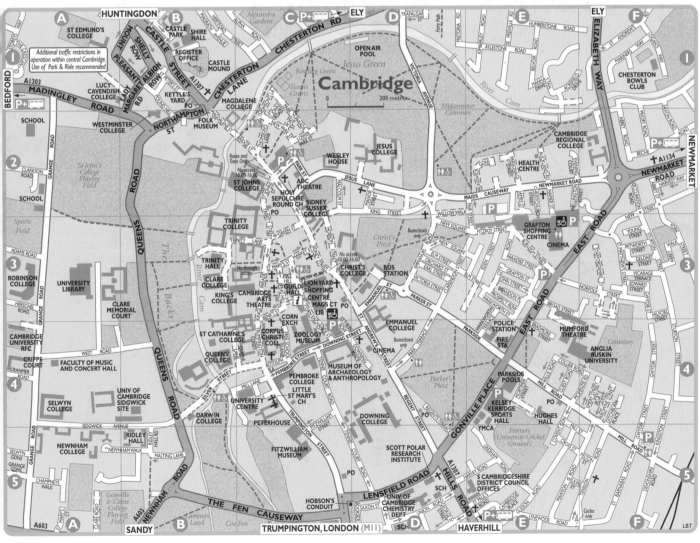

Cambridge

Cambridge is found on atlas page **138 B5**

Bristol is found on atlas page **110 C4**

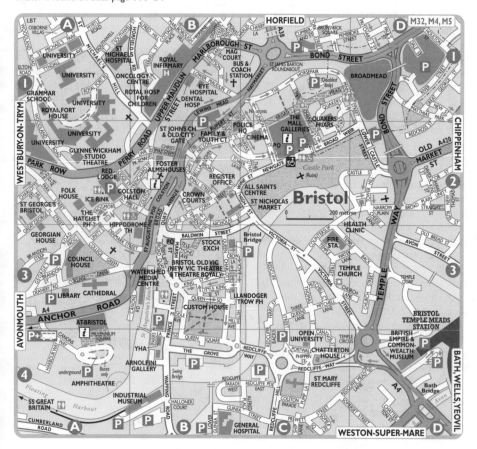

BRISTOL

A strong sense of maritime past pervades the premier city in southwest England, where a huge millennium facelift has created tree-lined avenues and turned Queen Square into a traffic-free haven. Maritime wealth endowed Bristol with imposing churches, notably the 13th-century St Mary Redcliffe (C4) and the cathedral (C2), with a Norman chapter house. The former docks are now busy with places to eat and family attractions. In the Harbourside area are At-Bristol (A3), covering the Imagarium (planetarium), Wildwalk (a journey through evolution) and the science and technology museum, Explore. At Great Western Dock (A4) is the SS *Great Britain*, the world's first steam-powered ocean liner, built by Isambard Kingdom Brunel. In the original Temple Meads station built by Brunel, the British Empire and Commonwealth Museum evokes Britain's Empire days. The Old City (B2) is now home to banks and restaurants; meanwhile the West End around Park Street (A2) is the hip area, with funky shops. Clifton Suspension Bridge is the symbol of the city and probably Brunel's best-known design.

Canterbury is found on atlas page **117 E6**

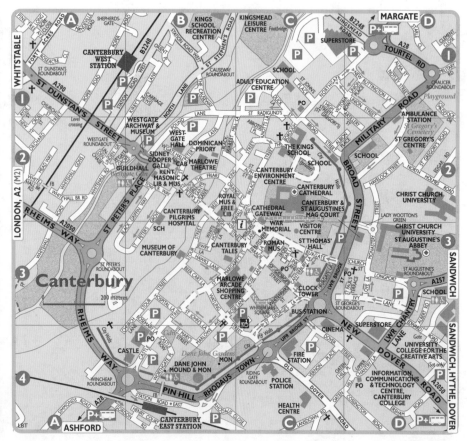

CANTERBURY

Much remains of the medieval city that grew up catering to millions of pilgrims who journeyed each year to the shrine of the English saint, Archbishop Thomas Becket. Thomas Becket was murdered in Canterbury Cathedral (C2) in order to please King Henry II, in 1170. The cathedral, approached via the ornate 16th-century Christ Church Gate, dates from around 1070. Its main glory is the 12th- and 13th-century stained glass featuring pilgrim scenes. In the northwest transept a stone marks the spot where Becket died. Several charitable hospitals founded in medieval times to accommodate pilgrims include Eastbridge Hospital and the Poor Priests' Hospital, within which is the Museum of Canterbury (B3), charting 2,000 years of the city's history. Medieval city walls enclose three sides of Canterbury and its narrow, crooked alleys are lined with timbered leaning buildings. One of the original 14th-century gates, Westgate (B2), on St Peter's Street, still survives. The underground Roman Museum in Long Market houses the remains of a Roman house and re-created interiors. Outside the old city are the ruins of St Augustine's Abbey (D3), burial place of the missionary who brought Christianity to Britain.

CARDIFF

From its beginnings as the site of a Roman fort on the River Taff, Cardiff grew up as a village protected by a Norman castle and, later, a modest harbour town. Cardiff is now the home of the National Assembly for Wales. The heart of the city has handsome Victorian and Edwardian shopfronts and arcades, a 19th-century covered market and gleaming civic buildings. The focus of the city is Cardiff Castle (A2), a Norman fortress dating from Roman times which was transformed into a neo-Gothic extravaganza in the 19th century. The buildings of the Civic Centre, built in the 19th and 20th centuries, are laid out on broad avenues. In front is the elaborate City Hall and the National Museum and Gallery (B1), with an Evolution of Wales exhibition and the largest collection of Impressionist and post-Impressionist paintings outside France. Cardiff's docks have become vibrant Cardiff Bay, fringed with restaurants, bars and shops. Among the attractions are Techniquest, a science discovery complex and planetarium; arts and crafts exhibitions; Butetown History and Arts Centre; and the Pierhead Building, with a display about the National Assembly for Wales. The Millennium Centre hosts opera, ballet and musicals in a dramatic modern building.

Cardiff is found on atlas page **109 G4**

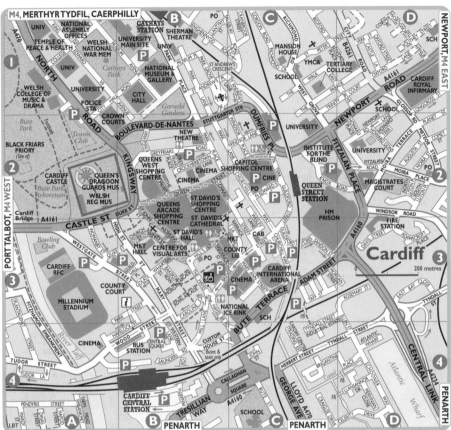

Carlisle is found on atlas page **183 F4**

CARLISLE

Carlisle is a border city, with a wide pedestrianised marketplace at its heart. Its name is derived from the Celtic word *caer* meaning fort. Scottish and English names and accents mingle freely in its covered market and malls, though there is little today to hint at the troubles the city has faced. It was last besieged in 1745 by 'Bonnie' Prince Charlie's Jacobite army. Chief among the city's assets are the castle (A2), the striking red sandstone cathedral (B2), and the Tullie House Museum and Art Gallery (A2), which dramatically portrays much of the city's turbulent past as a Roman frontier settlement and as a border town. The cathedral was first built in the 12th century, but has had several periods of rebuilding. Look especially for the 14th-century stained glass and the 16th-century altarpiece and the Treasury with a display of silver. Carlisle is the terminus for the scenic Settle–Carlisle railway.

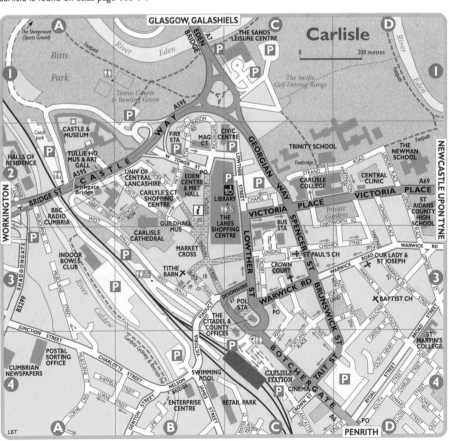

Chester is found on atlas page **156 C4**

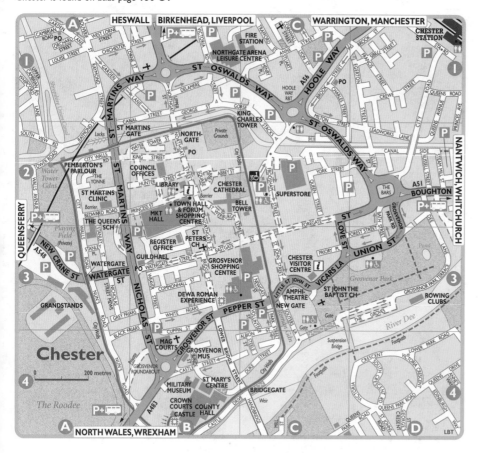

CHESTER

A Roman city called Deva, then a medieval port and cathedral city, and, after the River Dee silted up, a place where prosperous Georgian merchants settled: Chester has many layers of history. You can walk along or beside the most complete medieval city walls in Britain to get an overview of the city. One of the original city gateways is Eastgate; just to the south, the wall passes the partly excavated site of the largest Roman amphitheatre in the country. The best Roman remains are in the Grosvenor Museum (B4), with Roman tombstones and other displays on the city's history. The Dewa Roman Experience (B3), beneath the site of the original Roman fort, evokes Roman Chester with a re-created street complete with the sounds, sights and smells of Roman life, as well as excavations and artefacts. Central Chester is a crossing of two main streets: along these run the Rows, two tiers of arcaded shopping streets, one above the other. The black-and-white buildings at The Cross are 19th-century Tudor replications, but Chester has many original examples of half-timbered architecture.

Colchester is found on atlas page **129 E3**

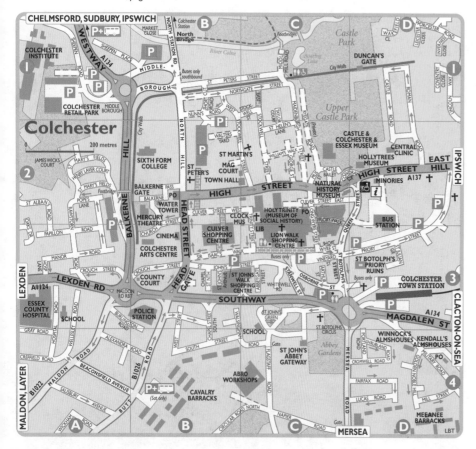

COLCHESTER

An important Roman city that was their capital in England before its destruction by rebels led by Boudicca, Colchester is today a thriving garrison town. The centre is undergoing regeneration but there are plenty of remains and buildings to interest the historian. The main attraction is the castle (C2), built in the 11th century by the Normans, on the site of a Roman temple. There is now a museum here. Ruins include St John's Abbey (C4) and St Botolph's Priory (D3). During the Civil War a small Royalist force was besieged in the town by the Parliamentarians for several weeks until they surrendered. The Victorians, too, left their mark on the city in the form of notable public, as well as residential, buildings. Other attractions are the Natural History Museum (C2) and Tymperleys Clock Museum (C2). There is a university here, which ensures a good range of clubs, pubs and cafés, which are supplemented by two theatres, arts and music venues and sports facilities. Families can visit Rollerworld and, a few miles west of the city, Colchester Zoo and the East Anglian Railway Museum with rides and events.

COVENTRY

On 14 November 1940 a bomb destroyed the medieval cathedral at Coventry. Its ruins now stand alongside the new cathedral (C2), designed by the Scottish architect Sir Basil Spence and consecrated in 1962. Widely regarded as a masterpiece of modern architecture, Spence's edifice shows that contemporary style can still produce a feeling of spirituality. It has a great sense of internal space, height, peace and light, and is further distinguished by a parade of modern works of art. Most notable are the tapestry *Christ in Glory* by Graham Sutherland, bronzes by Sir Jacob Epstein and the Great Baptistry Window by John Piper. Don't miss the West Screen, a wall of glass engraved with saints and angels. The wartime bombing led to the rebuilding of much of the city centre but two medieval gates remain. An impressive stand of the old city walls remains between the Cook Street and Swanswell Gates. The reconstructed 15th-century Black Swan Terrace has been restored to show the life of a weaver in those times. There are examples of all forms of road vehicles at Coventry Transport Museum (C2), up to the most modern. Next to the city walls (C1,) garden lovers will be delighted by Lady Herbert's Garden and the adjacent Garden of International Friendship.

Coventry is found on atlas page **135 G3**

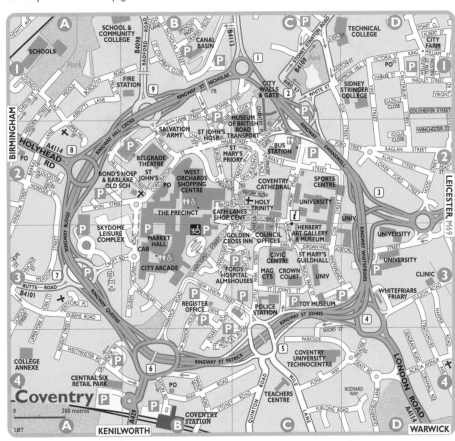

DONCASTER

Doncaster is a vibrant centre with strong manufacturing industries, an important railway hub and even has an international airport. Doncaster Museum and Art Gallery (C3) has wide-ranging displays on natural history, archaeology and art as well as local history. In the same building is the Regimental Museum for the King's Own Yorkshire Light Infantry. Cusworth Hall, Museum and Park, east of the city centre, have undergone a large renovation. It is worth going when the Hall is open to see the life of a manor house. The Victorian Corn Exchange (B2) now hosts a lively and popular market, which attracts visitors from around the surrounding area, as does Lakeside discount shopping village. AeroVenture, just south of the city, attracts aircraft enthusiasts and their families with its range of exhibits. Families are also to be found at The Dome, east of the city centre, with its swimming pools, ice-rink and climbing wall. The Dome is near the famous Doncaster racecourse, which holds races on around 30 days each year.

Doncaster is found on atlas page **165 G4**

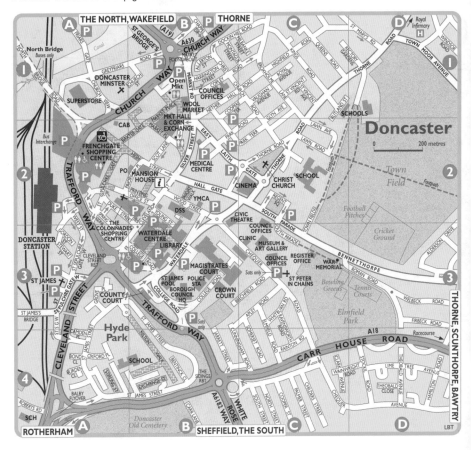

Dover is found on atlas page **106 C2**

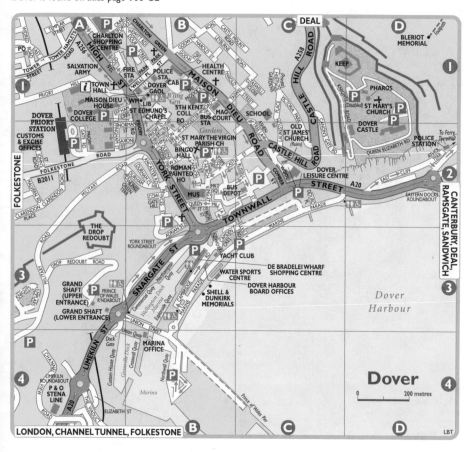

DOVER

Dover is the main port for ferries departing for France and has long been at the forefront of the defence of the country. Dover Castle (D2) is England's oldest fortress, whose history spans the Iron Age to the Cold War. On clear days you can see the coast of France from this giant fortress, perched on the famous White Cliffs and commanding the shortest sea crossing between England and the Continent. Within the ramparts of an Iron Age fort, the Romans built a lighthouse, which still stands, while in the Saxon period the earthworks were re-used for a town. The Church of St Mary in Castro within the castle walls is one of the most complete Saxon churches in southern England. The castle saw dramatic action during World War II. In 1940 it was from the underground tunnels here that Vice Admiral Ramsay and Prime Minister Sir Winston Churchill masterminded the evacuation from Dunkirk. The tour of the Secret Wartime Tunnels re-creates Britain at war through sounds, smells and archive film clips.

Durham is found on atlas page **185 F5**

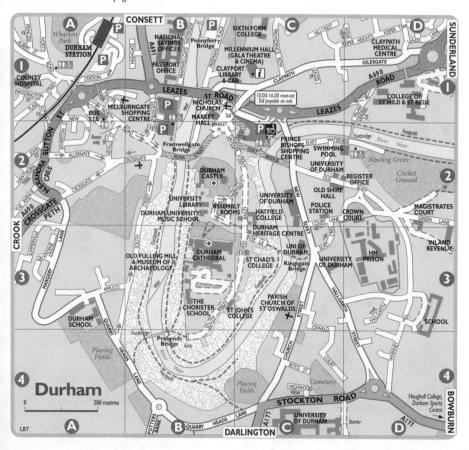

DURHAM

Durham is a World Heritage Site with a magnificent cathedral and captivating views. The heart of this university city is compact, historic and largely traffic-free. High on the cliff above the River Wear, the mighty three-towered cathedral (B3) was built mostly over 40 years from 1093 and both rounded Norman and pointed Gothic arches can be seen. Huge cylindrical pillars are carved with geometric designs, while at the east end lies the body of St Cuthbert. The Bishop's throne is the most elevated in Britain – the prince-bishops of Durham were a law unto themselves, and even the king needed permission to enter their lands. The cloisters and precincts represent the most complete survival of a medieval monastery in England; off the cloister, the Treasury has relics of St Cuthbert. On the opposite end of the hilltop is the Norman castle (B2), whose great circular keep contains the Gallery and Chapel, and the medieval Great Hall. There is also a series of 18th-century state rooms. In an attractive cobbled street, the Durham Heritage Centre (C3) in St Mary le Bow Church in North Bailey tells the city's story.

AA Town plans and guides

EDINBURGH

The Old Town has historic routes such as Grassmarket and Canongate and a medieval network of alleys. More breathing space can be found in the striking Georgian streets of the New Town.

Edinburgh Castle (C3) towers over the city from its volcanic rock. Bronze Age people settled on the top around 850 BC, and by the Middle Ages it was a fortified site and royal residence. The Half Moon Battery is the defensive wall and walkway on the east side. Since 1861 a field gun has boomed out here Monday to Saturday at precisely 1pm to enable mariners to fix the time. The Crown Room displays the ancient regalia of Scotland, locked away after the parliamentary union with England in 1707 and unearthed by Sir Walter Scott in 1818. The Stone of Destiny, on which Scottish kings were crowned, is also here. The Scotch Whisky Heritage Centre (C3) is below the castle.

Filled with works of art from the Royal Collection, the Palace of Holyroodhouse (F2) sits at the foot of the Royal Mile (F2–C3) and is the Queen's official residence in Scotland, which means it may be closed at short notice. The state rooms, designed for Charles II and hung with Brussels tapestries, are particularly good.

In the city, the entertaining Museum of Scotland (D3) showcases the Scottish collections from the Royal Museum (D3) next door. It is a superb, well-explained collection

that covers the shaping of Scotland through geology and glaciation, what is known of the lives of the earliest settlers in Scotland and the founding of Scottish identity. The National Gallery of Scotland (D2) has a collection of 20,000 paintings, sculptures and drawings. The main focus is paintings by Europe's great masters but Scottish artists are displayed in their own section downstairs.

The New Town (C2) covers 1sq mile to the north of Princes Street, and is characterised by broad streets of grand, terraced houses with large windows and ornamental door arches. The Georgian House (B2), on Charlotte Square's north side, is a meticulous re-creation of an 18th-century home, down to the Wedgwood dinner service on the dining table.

The Royal Mile (F2-C3) is the name of the long street that links Edinburgh Castle with Holyrood Palace. About 60 narrow closes lead off on either side; Lady Stair's Close, near St Giles' Cathedral (D3), is the best known and leads through to The Writers' Museum (D3). Drop into the Museum of Edinburgh (F2) to get a feeling of the interiors of these old houses. The 1490 John Knox House (E2) is where John Knox, the founder of the Church of Scotland, preached.

A sweeping, living sculpture of grassy terraces and ponds is the first thing you see as you arrive at the National Gallery of Modern Art and Dean Gallery, west of the city centre. Works by Pablo Picasso and Barbara Hepworth are part of the superb permanent collection

here. Across the road the Dean Gallery's collection majors on Dada and the Surrealists, and the Scottish sculptor Eduardo Paolozzi.

The tower of the Balmoral Hotel on Princes Street

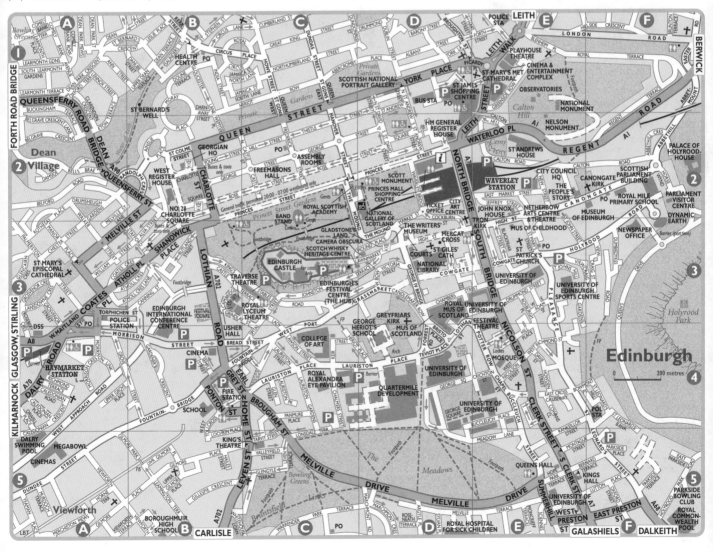

Edinburgh

Edinburgh is found on atlas page **199 F2**

AA Town plans and guides

GLASGOW

Known as a gritty but friendly city, Glasgow has some handsome architectural treasures, along with regenerated cultural pursuits. Make sure you look up – much of the finest architecture is above street level.

The main attraction at Glasgow Science Centre, on the south bank of the Clyde just west of the city centre, is the Science Mall, with four floors of 500 interactive exhibits. The other main elements on the site are the IMAX theatre, and the dizzying 122m viewing tower designed to turn 360 degrees in the wind. William Hunter was a Glasgow-trained physician who left his scientific collections to his old university. The Hunterian Museum and Art Gallery, to the northwest, was opened for show in 1807, making this the oldest public museum in Scotland. The magnificent art collection, in a separate building on campus, originates from Hunter's own purchases of 17th-century Flemish, Dutch and Italian masters. There's also a coin collection and displays of geology and archaeology, including Roman finds from Scotland.

Set on Glasgow Green (E5), The People's Palace is a museum that captures the character of the city by presenting its social history, including a re-created tenement home. Charles Rennie Mackintosh was born in Glasgow, and at the age of 16 was apprenticed to a firm of architects. He was an outstanding student, praised for the originality of his work, a distinctive fusion of the flowing lines of art nouveau with the simplicity of the Arts and Crafts Movement. He left his mark on Glasgow, with principal points of interest forming the Rennie Mackintosh Trail. The Glasgow School of Art (B1) was founded in 1845. Mackintosh won the competition to design the new building at 167 Renfrew Street in 1896. It is known as his masterpiece and still looks fresh and modern over 100 years later. The Willow Tearooms, in Sauchiehall Street (C2), offer a restored Mackintosh interior upstairs in the Salon de Luxe. The House for an Art Lover is a fantasy, designed in 1901 without the imposed limitations of budget or client, by Mackintosh and his wife, Margaret MacDonald. At the university's Hunterian Gallery, Mackintosh House is the exquisite re-creation of the interior of the home that the Mackintoshes made together, with original furniture, as it appeared in 1906.

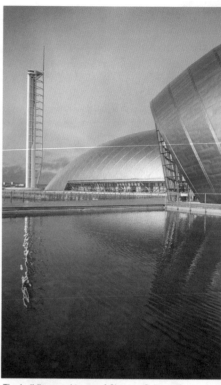

The buildings and tower of Glasgow Science Centre

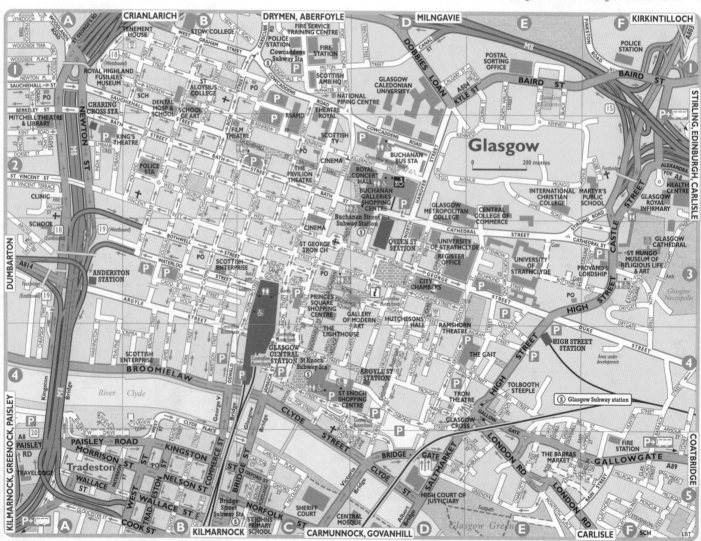

Glasgow

Glasgow is found on atlas page **197 G3**

GLOUCESTER

The county town of Gloucestershire is set in an area of great natural beauty, with the Malvern Hills and the Forest of Dean in close proximity. The jewel of Gloucester's compact historic heart is the cathedral (B2), housing the tomb of Edward II, magnificent medieval stained glass in its east window, and 14th-century fan vaulting in its cloisters – little wonder it was used in the filming of *Harry Potter and the Philosopher's Stone*. Cathedral Green is fringed by buildings from the 15th to the 18th centuries, and the transformed Victorian docks have shops, bars, restaurants and cafés in the preserved warehouses. The National Waterways Museum (B4) in the docks charts the story of Britain's waterways. Don't miss a trip along the historic canal within the docks aboard the *Queen Boadicea II*. Among the museums are the City Museum and Art Gallery (C3) and the Folk Museum (B2). Beyond the city centre, Robinswood Hill Country Park (123 G4) is superb for walks and wildlife and south of the city is the Great Witcombe Roman Villa (123 G4), good remains with an extensive bath house.

Gloucester is found on atlas page **123 G4**

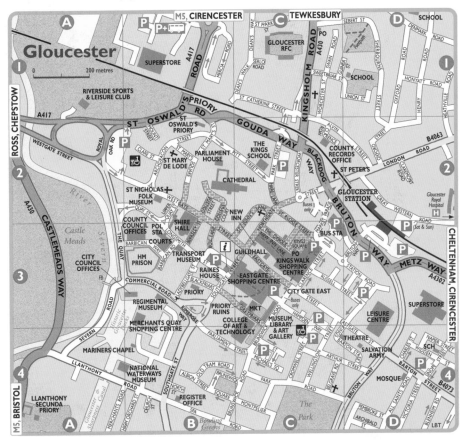

KINGSTON UPON HULL

The large port of Kingston upon Hull (or Hull, as it is usually known) is only patchily inviting at first look. World War II bombing devastated large areas of the city. Much investment has gone into rejuvenating the waterfront. The best areas are the narrow cobbled High Street (D2), with old warehouses, Victorian shopping arcades, a lively covered market and the streets around the vast Holy Trinity Church (C3). There is also still considerable activity along the quaysides as trawlers land their catches. The Deep is billed as 'the world's only submarium'. It puts the marine world into chronological context, from the Big Bang onwards, and has all kinds of marine life and push-button gadgets. Hull's other museums include the lively trio of Wilberforce House (D2), the home of slavery abolitionist William Wilberforce; Streetlife (D2), a transport museum; and the more sober Hull and East Riding Museum (D3), with re-creations of an Iron Age village and a well-displayed Roman section. The charmingly old-fashioned Hull Maritime Museum (B2) has details on the city's history of whaling, fishing and shipping, and nearby is the equally absorbing Ferens Art Gallery (B3).

Kingston upon Hull is found on atlas page **166 D2**

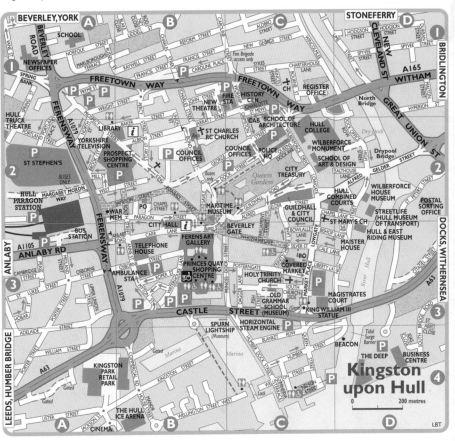

Harrogate is found on atlas page **171 F4**

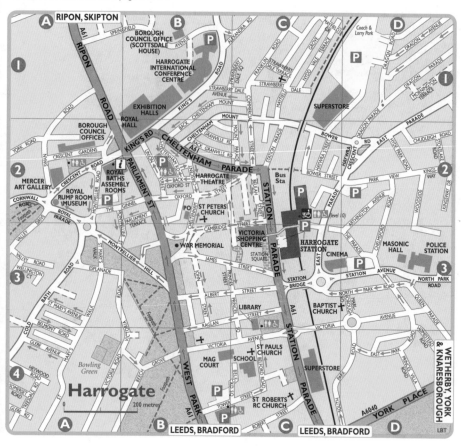

HARROGATE

Its spa days may have declined, but Harrogate still exudes style, with Victorian buildings and hotels ranged around the expansive 80ha green known as The Stray. You can stroll through the lushly planted Valley Gardens (A3) and go boating on the lake. Then sample the waters from Europe's strongest sulphur well at the Royal Pump Room Museum (A2), or look into the former Promenade Room that now houses the Mercer Art Gallery (A2). The 1897 Royal Baths (A2) in Crescent Road still have the original Turkish baths, decorated appropriately in Moorish style with plush tiles, in addition to saunas and solariums. Harrogate is a leading events venue and the annual Antiques Fair attracts dealers from around the world. Harlow Carr Botanical Garden (171 E4) is one of the show gardens of the north. Don't leave without having afternoon tea at Betty's Tearoom on Parliament Street (B2), a Harrogate institution.

Inverness is found on atlas page **217 J6**

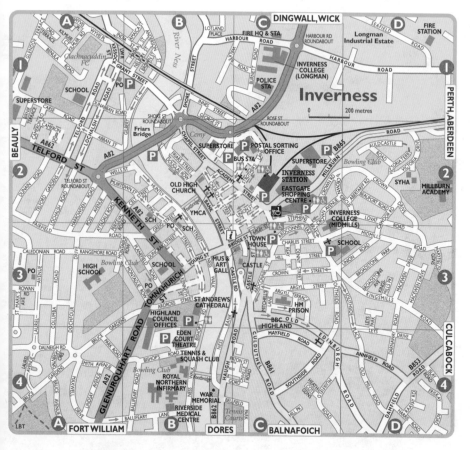

INVERNESS

The administrative capital of the Highland region, Inverness flaunts its city status with an air of bustle and building projects. It is a service town for the surrounding area, and fills in summer with visitors planning their expeditions to more remote places and enjoying the shops and restaurants.

Three important roads meet just north of here: the A96 from the northeast, the A9 from the south, and the A82 which runs up the side of the Great Glen. It is also the northern end of the Caledonian Canal, where the River Ness flows into the Moray Firth.

Inverness's lack of antiquities is due, the locals will tell you, to the Highlanders' habit of burning the town down at regular intervals after English Parliamentarian leader Oliver Cromwell built a fort here in 1652. The architecture of the town is predominantly 19th century, including the red sandstone castle with its monument to Flora MacDonald, who helped 'Bonnie' Prince Charlie to escape in 1746 after his defeat at nearby Culloden Muir. The drum tower hosts the Castle Garrison Encounter, with costumed actors playing out scenes of Hanoverian army life at that time.

LANCASTER

Once an important port for the slave trade, much of Lancaster's character comes from the Georgian buildings of this unhappy period, though there was much traffic in mahogany, tobacco, rum and sugar, too.

Lancaster Castle (A2), built around 1200 and strengthened in the 15th century, dominates the city and is still used as a crown court and prison, but some sections are open to the public, including the cells where the Pendle Witches were imprisoned. The shopping centre (B3) contains many historic buildings including the Judges' Lodging (B2), now a museum featuring the finely crafted furniture of the local family, the Gillows. The Grand Theatre, in St Leonard's Gate (C2), was built in the 18th century and the restored building hosts a full range of entertainments. Lancaster University has a number of facilities that open to the public, including the Ruskin Library and the Rare Book Archive. Williamson Park, southwest of the city centre, houses The Butterfly House and there is a woodland walk.

Lancaster is found on atlas page **169 E3**

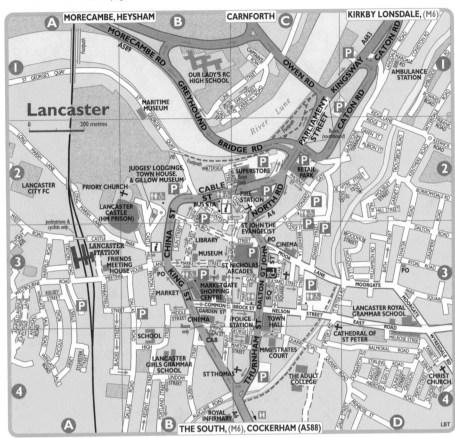

LEEDS

After a large expansion in the 19th century, Leeds is once again one of the fastest-growing cities in England, and displays true northern grit alongside a cultural renaissance. The classical Town Hall (B2) is one of Britain's grandest, and the Victorian glass-roofed arcades and elliptical Corn Exchange (C4) are period gems as well as bustling shopping venues. Nightlife, music and theatre are other major draws. The City Art Gallery (B3) has an impressive range of 19th- and 20th-century paintings and sculptures. Next door is the Henry Moore Institute with major exhibits from 1850 to the present. A dynamic waterfront culture of pavement cafés and specialist shops has grown up along the River Aire (C4) and the Leeds–Liverpool Canal. South of the River Aire, the Royal Armouries Museum houses the national collection of arms and armour. Outstanding among the other more outlying attractions is Leeds Industrial Museum, within Armley Mills. The museum now tells Leeds' story as one of the world's great industrial cities. Temple Newsam, east of the city, is a large 16th-century house with rich collections of fine art, as well as Europe's largest working rare breeds farm.

Leeds is found on atlas page **164 D1**

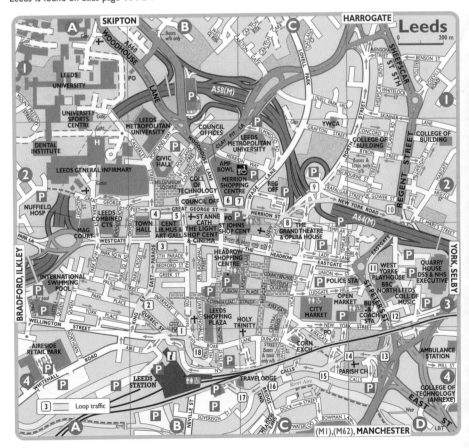

Leicester is found on atlas page **148 A5**

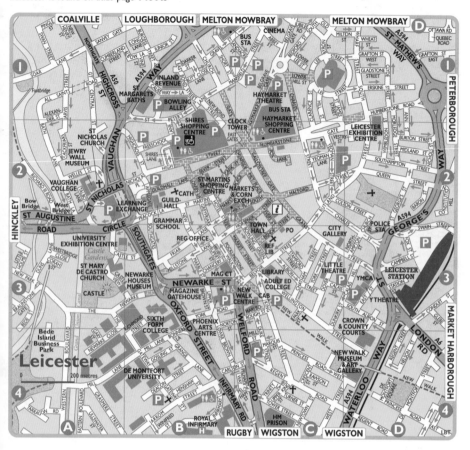

LEICESTER

The city expanded in the 19th century with the growth of industry and the centre has a range of Victorian buildings reflecting its role as a county town and important manufacturing centre. Leicester is one of the country's oldest cities and was a settlement before the Romans moved here and founded a new city. Behind the massive fragment of the Roman Jewry Wall and a Roman Baths site of the 2nd century AD is the Museum of Leicestershire Archaeology (A2), which covers finds from the earliest times to the Middle Ages.

Discover Leicestershire's social history at Newarke Houses (B3) where the displays show everyday life and social change throughout the county. Wygston's House Museum of Costume (B2) houses selections from the county's extensive collections of costumes and textiles. The exhibits include a recreation of a 1920s draper's shop and fashionable outfits from 1805 to the present day. New Walk Museum and Art Gallery (D4) is a major regional venue housing local and national collections. One of the leading visitor attractions is the National Space Centre, northeast of the city centre, with six themed galleries of interactive exhibits and audiovisual experiences, as well as rockets and space capsules.

Lincoln is found on atlas page **160 B3**

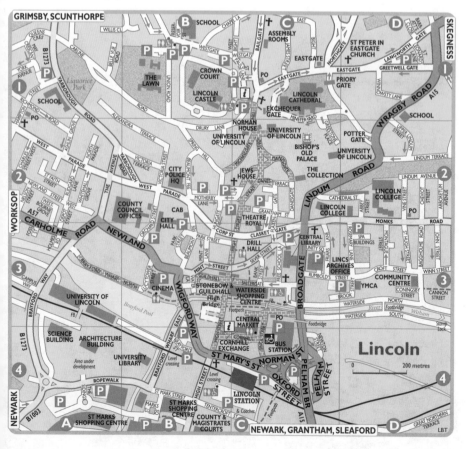

LINCOLN

Lincoln is visible for miles around in the low-lying landscape, with its castle and majestic twin-towered cathedral prominent on a high hill. From the modern pedestrianised shopping streets at the foot of the hill, a walk up appropriately named Steep Hill leads into Minster Yard and Lincoln Cathedral (C1), mostly dating from the 13th and 14th centuries and in the top league of England's ecclesiastical architecture. Highlights include the elaborate west façade, stained-glass rose windows and 14th-century carved choir stalls. Close by are the Bishop's Palace (C2), and Lincoln Castle (B1), dating from Norman times and retaining gateways, towers and a 19th-century prisoners' chapel. Museum attractions include the free Usher Gallery in Lindum Road (C2), with fine and decorative arts and memorabilia of the locally born poet Alfred, Lord Tennyson, and the Museum of Lincolnshire Life, just north of the city centre.

LIVERPOOL

One Mersey waterfront, two cathedrals, four Beatles and several superb museums put Liverpool in a class of its own. Its days as one of the great ports of the British Empire have long gone, but the grandeur of its architecture echoes the boom years – Liverpool has more landmark buildings than any English city outside London and was designated European Capital of Culture 2008.

Walk from Lime Street Station (D2), past neo-classical St George's Hall, along Dale Street (C2) and Water Street (B3) to the waterfront. Here is the 1911 Royal Liver Building (B3), a main landmark, with the famous sculptural Liver Birds perched high on the 10-storey tower. The red-brick Albert Dock (B4), dating from 1846, was imaginatively restored in 1988 into gift shops, cafés and major museums. Fans can visit the Beatles Story, dedicated to the world-famous group. There's a mock-up of The Cavern club, the white piano on which John Lennon composed *Imagine*, and other memorabilia. At either end of Hope Street (E4) are the two cathedrals. The vast, sandstone Anglican Liverpool Cathedral (E5) was started in 1904 but inaugurated in

1978, to Giles Gilbert Scott's design; its tower can be seen from north Wales. The concrete Roman Catholic Metropolitan Cathedral (F3) was built in 1967 and is sometimes affectionately known as the Mersey Funnel. It was designed by Frederick Gibberd, and is brilliantly lit by blue stained-glass windows.

The Walker Art Gallery (D2), on William Brown Street, houses one of the UK's best provincial art collections, including works by local artist George Stubbs, noted for his paintings of horses. The impressive Maritime Museum (B4), in Albert Dock, gives an insight into the

city's maritime past. Next door, Tate Liverpool houses an excellent collection of modern art. Just beyond Albert Dock is the Museum of Liverpool Life (due to open 2010), where you can learn more about what makes this city tick – from the character of the residents to music and sport. From Albert Dock, the Magical Mystery Tour Bus goes to Strawberry Fields, Penny Lane and the Cavern, locations closely associated with the Beatles. Other tours take in the childhood homes of John Lennon and Sir Paul McCartney where the group often rehearsed.

The Royal Liver Building (centre) on the waterfront is one of Liverpool's most famous landmarks

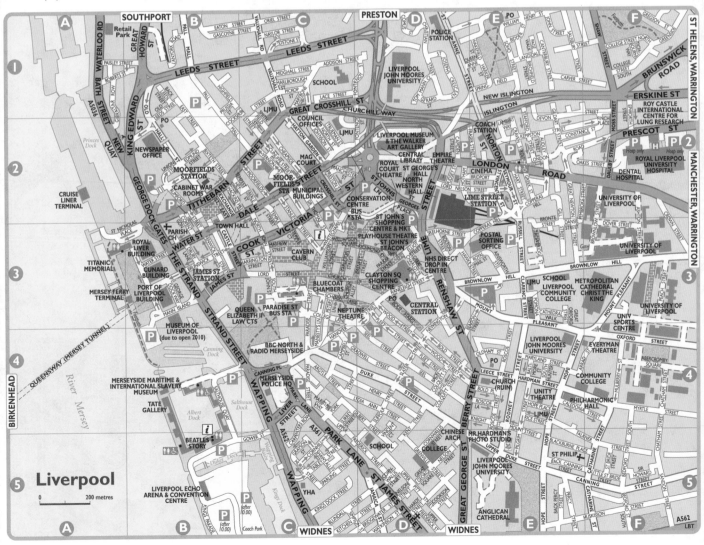

Liverpool

Liverpool is found on atlas page **162 C5**

MANCHESTER

Manchester grew from a small town in the late 18th century to become one of the most important cities of the Industrial Revolution. It made its money from cotton, earning it the nickname Cottonopolis. Waves of decline and rebuilding followed, culminating in Manchester's successful hosting of the 2002 Commonwealth Games, which created entire new areas.

Great buildings, such as the neo-Gothic Town Hall (D3), and the Royal Exchange (D2, the former Cotton Exchange), speak of the wealth of the late 18th century, and you are free to wander around these buildings. The top attraction is Urbis (D1), housed in a shimmering glass building near the cathedral. Inside, state-of-the-art interactive displays and exhibits lead you through a journey exploring life in different cities of the world. Now restored and given a striking new stone and glass extension to the original, stone-built, porticoed Victorian building, the Manchester Art Gallery (D4) can finally show off its artistic wealth, which includes a great collection of modern pieces as well as its noted Pre-Raphaelite paintings. The first floor is home to the Manchester Gallery, with works by L S Lowry and others. In the Castlefield district, the Museum

of Science and Industry (B4) is an excellent free visit, with Robert Stephenson's 1830 locomotive *Planet*. Salford Quays, southwest of the city centre, houses two major free tourist attractions. Within a gleaming steel-built structure, The Lowry encompasses theatres and galleries, including an exhibition of Lowry paintings,

with some of his earlier, iconic images of matchstick men in the streets of industrial Manchester. Across a footbridge is the Imperial War Museum North (designed by architect Daniel Libeskind), an ingenious building made of three shards of fractured steel symbolising the world torn apart by conflict.

The Lowry Centre, at the heart of the redeveloped Salford Quays

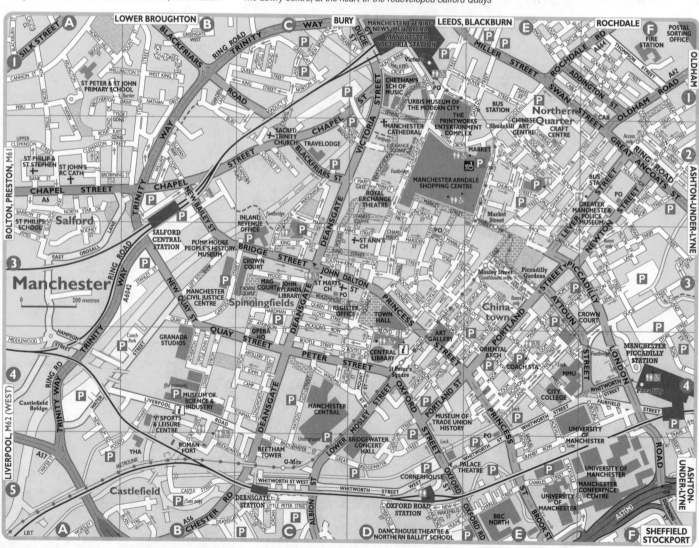

Manchester

Manchester is found on atlas page **163 H5**

NEWCASTLE UPON TYNE

The locals of this resurgent city compensate for the biting North Sea winds with a natural warmth and exuberance. The River Tyne provides some of Newcastle's key landmarks. The Tyne Bridge (C4) has as its companions the High Level Bridge (1849), with two decks, the Swing Bridge (1876) and the Gateshead Millennium Bridge (D4), dating from 2000. The bridges join Newcastle to Gateshead, where a major attraction is the huge Baltic Centre for Contemporary Art (D4). This lively arts complex includes The Sage theatre and arts venue. Newcastle dates from Roman times, and the 'new castle' – of which the keep and chapel survive – was begun in 1080. Early legacies of the boom years as a coal port include elegant Victorian architecture by John Dobson in Grey Street (D3). Around here is the main shopping area, with the indoor Grainger Market (C3) offering all kinds of goods. The city, known for its lively nightlife, has enough cultural highlights to justify a visit. The Laing Art Gallery (C2) focuses on 19th-century art. The Hancock Museum (B1) on Barras Bridge is a leading natural history museum. Two of Newcastle's liveliest attractions are the Centre for Life (A4) and the Discovery Museum (A4).

Newcastle upon Tyne is found on atlas page **185 F3**

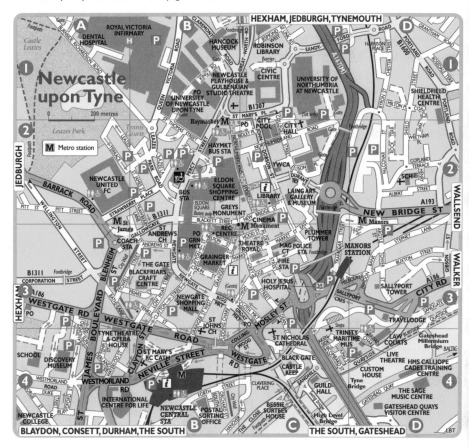

NORWICH

Norwich is found on atlas page **152 B5**

Norwich is one of Britain's most complete medieval cities. Outstanding among the jumble of old streets is cobbled Elm Hill (C1), full of antiques, crafts and specialist shops. Northeast in the city is the cathedral (D1), founded in 1096 and with a 15th-century spire rising to 96m. It has a magnificent stone-vaulted roof with 1,106 carved stone bosses depicting the Bible story. Southwest of the cathedral is the busy market place, a maze of narrow alleyways with stalls selling just about everything six days a week. Norwich's newest public building is the architecturally acclaimed Forum (B3), home to Origins, an interactive journey through 2,000 years of Norwich and Norfolk's history. The Royal Arcade is where you'll find Colman's Mustard Shop and Museum. The Bridewell Museum (C2) chronicles local trades and industries. Looking down on the marketplace, 12th-century Norwich Castle (C3) has a fine museum and art gallery. Don't miss the Dragon Hall (D4), a 15th-century merchants' hall in King Street or The Sainsbury Centre for the Visual Arts, an outstanding art collection in a modern building by architect Norman Foster, at the University of East Anglia, 3 miles west of Norwich.

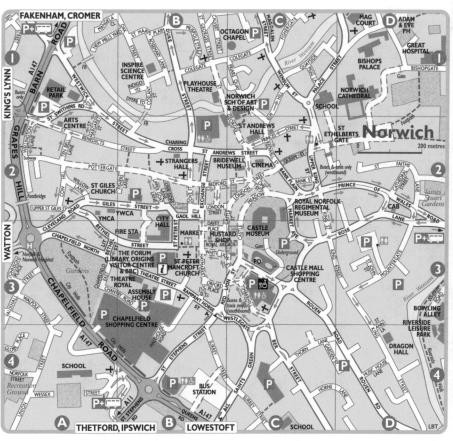

OXFORD

Oxford is a beautiful city of honey-coloured Cotswold stone. The university's colleges stand in cloistered seclusion and can be hard to identify as they are not clearly signed, but between them display a wonderful array of architecture. Don't miss the back lanes and alleys. The high street, known as The High, runs from Carfax Tower (C4) east to Magdalen Bridge (E4) over the River Cherwell.

At the beginning of a visit to Oxford, it's a good idea to get your bearings from the rooftops. You can climb St Michael's Church Saxon Tower (C3) in Cornmarket Street, the city's oldest building. Or survey the city from Carfax Tower, a remnant of the 14th-century St Martin's Church, at the busy crossroads known as Carfax, the city's focal point. Another excellent vantage point is the University Church of St Mary the Virgin (D3), High Street, dating from 1280. Climb the 36.5m tower to the external viewing gallery. Founded in 1524, Christ Church (D4), Oxford's largest and most visited college has the biggest quadrangle, and its chapel, Christ Church Cathedral (predating the college), is England's smallest cathedral. The Ante Hall is Hogwarts Hall in the Harry Potter movies.

Christ Church Picture Gallery has a collection of 300 paintings, including works by Tintoretto, Leonardo da Vinci, Michelangelo and Carraccis.

The Thames and Cherwell slice through remarkably verdant land close to central Oxford. The tree-lined Cherwell is the place for punting and provides almost rural views of Magdalen College (F5) one of the richest and most spacious colleges, founded in 1458 and set in its own deer park. University rowing crews train on the Thames (D5), also known here as the Isis. Stroll through the Oxford Botanic Garden (E4), founded in 1621 and the oldest of its kind in Britain, to Christchurch Meadow (E5) and the confluence of the rivers, or rent a punt or rowing boat from Magdalen Bridge or the Cherwell Boathouse in Bardwell Road.

In Radcliffe Square (D3) is an eye-catching architectural group belonging to the university. The Sheldonian Theatre (D3), built 1664–1668, was the first major architectural work by architect Sir Christopher Wren, who was Professor of Astronomy at the time. The interior assumes the shape of a Roman theatre and its grand ceremonial hall is used for university functions and concerts. Close by, the Bodleian Library (D3) is one of six copyright libraries in the UK, entitled to receive a copy of every book published in the country. The circular domed Radcliffe Camera (D3) of 1737–49, is a reading room for the library. Britain's oldest public museum (opened in 1683), the Ashmolean (C2) houses Oxford University's priceless collections from the time of early man to the 20th century. Come here to see material about early cultures in Europe, Egypt and the Near East, and an antiquities department covering everything from the Stone Age to Victorian times. On a separate site in Beaumont Street (B2), the Cast Gallery has a staggering 100,000 casts (not all on show at one time), which together give a privileged overview of classical sculpture. The University Museum (D1) nearby has fascinating collections on natural history.

Looking over All Souls College from the top of St Mary's Tower in Oxford

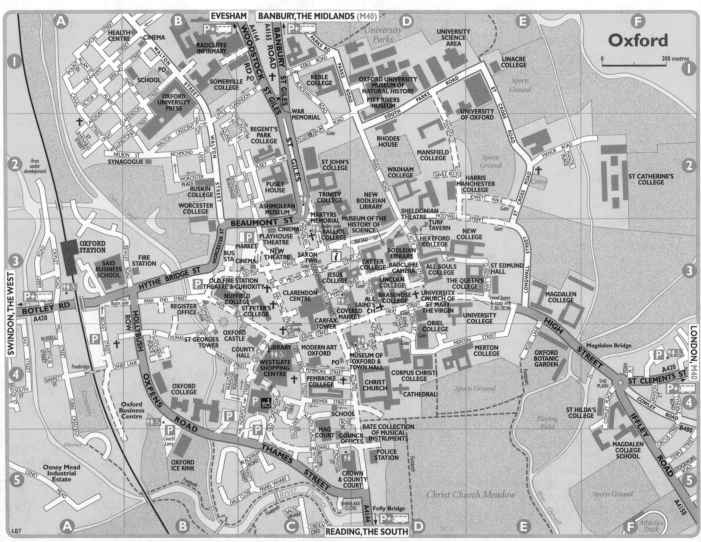

Oxford
Oxford is found on atlas page **125 F5**

NOTTINGHAM

Built on sandstone hills at a crossing point of the River Trent, Nottingham is renowned for its association with the 13th-century outlaw Robin Hood. Although not the most attractive of cities, Nottingham has a real buzz, with a vibrant mix of bars, pubs and clubs serving a large number of students from Nottingham University. The city has a long history and underwent expansion in the Victorian era. The Castle Museum and Art Gallery (A4) includes the Story of Nottingham gallery and has underground tours through passages cut below the city (in which Ye Olde Trip to Jerusalem pub is built). For more underground tours, visit the City of Caves beneath the Broadmarsh Shopping Centre (B3), dug out over the centuries. The Galleries of Justice (C3) in Shire Hall vividly re-enact a trial in a Victorian court and the grim hardship of life in a prison cell. The city's links with Robin Hood are evident in the names of streets and in The Tales of Robin Hood (A3) attraction near Nottingham Castle (A4).

Nottingham is found on atlas page **148 A2**

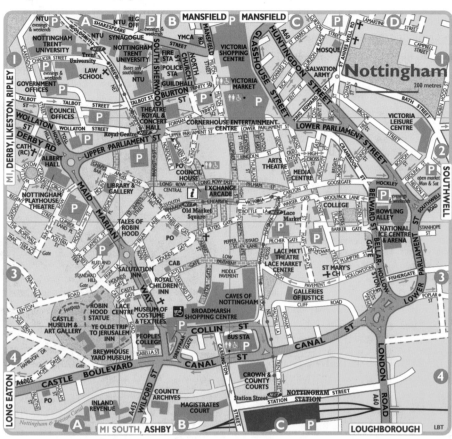

St Andrews is found on atlas page **207 G3**

ST ANDREWS

This attractive, breezy city has a sandy bay and a narrow harbour, and Scotland's oldest university, founded in 1413 and where Prince William was a student. St Andrews is also the home of the Royal & Ancient Golf Club (A1), founded in 1754 and still the ruling authority on the game. Check out the history of the game at the British Golf Museum (A1) on Bruce Embankment. Near the gaunt ruins of the cathedral (D2) stand the remains of the 12th-century St Rule's Tower. Climb the spiral stairs of the 44m tower for views that reveal the medieval grid of the city streets. The two main roads are North Street, leading to St Andrews Links (golf course), and South Street, with the city gateway of 1589, the West Port. North along the shore lie the spectacular ruins of the castle (C1), rebuilt in 1390, where a battle and siege took place in 1546. The visitor centre tells the story. Don't miss the bottle-shaped dungeon in the castle.

AA Town plans and guides

PORTSMOUTH

At first sight Portsmouth may not seem a great place for a day out. But it has pockets of huge historic interest, mostly around the waterfront. It has been a naval base since the 12th century and the hub of one of the most powerful sea-borne fighting forces in history.

A couple of minutes' walk from Portsmouth Harbour station is the Historic Dockyard (A1) with its celebrated warships. Naval officers guide you round Nelson's flagship HMS *Victory* to recall the appalling conditions on board and see the spot where Nelson died in battle in 1805. Close by is the world's first iron-clad battleship, HMS *Warrior* (A2), launched in 1860. Rescued in 1982 after sinking in 1545, Henry VIII's warship *Mary Rose* (A1) features a rich array of finds that provides an unrivalled time capsule of Tudor life. Also in the dockyard, the Royal Naval Museum charts the history of British maritime defence. Don't miss the 45-minute cruise from the Historic Dockyard to see modern warships, or a sail out to Spitbank Fort.

In the town, soaring high over the shops and restaurants of the Gunwharf Quays (B3) development, the 256m Spinnaker Tower (A3) opened in 2005 to give the best viewing platform on the south coast: the glass

floor on one level gives a dizzying sense of being on top of things, while from the top level you are exposed to the bracing fresh air. At the end of the High Street lies Old Portsmouth (A4), an area of cobbled streets lined with Tudor and Georgian houses and pubs. These streets were once full of press gangs seeking new naval recruits, whom they forced to join a leaving

ship. Southsea Castle, to the south on Clarence Esplanade, was built in 1595 to protect Portsmouth against French invasion. Next door, the D-Day Museum and Overlord Embroidery records the largest invasion force ever gathered: for D-Day (6 June 1944). Its focal embroidery measures 110m and encompasses several panels.

Step aboard Nelson's flagship, HMS Victory, *at Portsmouth's Historic Dockyard*

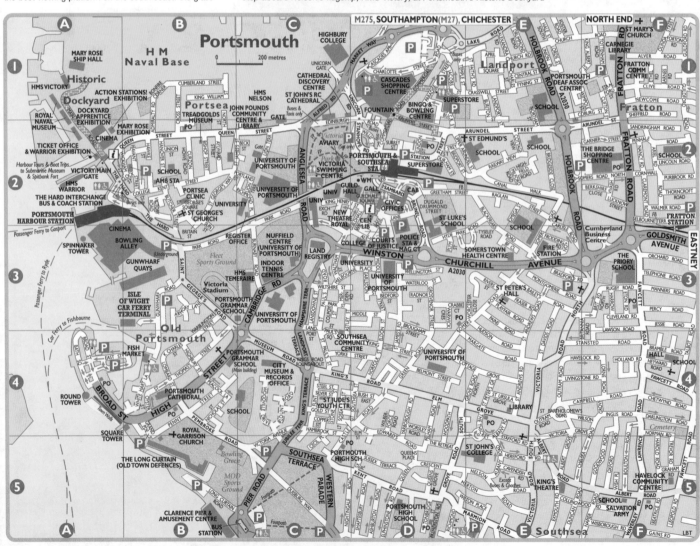

Portsmouth

Portsmouth is found on atlas page **93 E3**

SALISBURY

England's tallest spire, 123m, announces Salisbury Cathedral (B4) from miles around. The city has a compact centre dominated by its cathedral and Cathedral Close. Started in 1220 and completed in only 38 years, the cathedral is uniformly Early English. In the north aisle a dial-less clock from 1386 is probably the oldest mechanism in working order in the world. The miniature fan-vaulted roof in the Audley chantry chapel is adorned with ancient roundels, while the cloisters are the largest of any English cathedral. The library over the East Walk contains one of the four original copies of the Magna Carta of 1215. Outstanding in a city that is well endowed with fine streets is Cathedral Close whose houses date from the 14th to 18th centuries. Among them is Mompesson House (B3), a fine example of Queen Anne-style architecture. Another house contains the Salisbury and South Wiltshire Museum (B4), with archaeology galleries presenting the area's rich prehistoric heritage, including Stonehenge. Alongside the impressive architecture are green swathes of parkland. The spacious Market Square (C3) has a lively market on Tuesday and Saturday.

Salisbury is found on atlas page **101 E3**

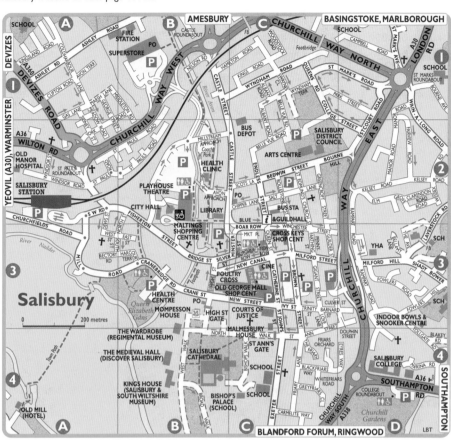

SHEFFIELD

Getting around Sheffield is easy if you use the Supertram service, which rumbles around the city centre. Until 1997 Sheffield was as far from a visitor destination as you could imagine. Then came the film *The Full Monty*, a tale of unemployed steelworkers-turned-male strippers, set in Sheffield and suddenly the city emerged into the limelight. The Millennium Gallery (C3), with four different galleries under one roof, has exhibitions drawn from the collections of Britain's national galleries and museums, including the Victoria & Albert Museum and Tate Gallery. Also here is the Ruskin Gallery with its wonderful array of treasures by Victorian artist and writer John Ruskin. Among Sheffield's other museums Weston Park, west of the city centre, and Bishops' House, south of the city, are well worth a visit. Graves Gallery (C3) displays works by Turner and Cézanne. Plenty of green spaces mean that you can visit gardens and parks and Sheffield Botanical Gardens, southwest of the city, has glass pavilions. Sheffield Cathedral (B2) was built on the site of an Anglo Saxon church and contains fine Tudor memorials.

Sheffield is found on atlas page **158 D2**

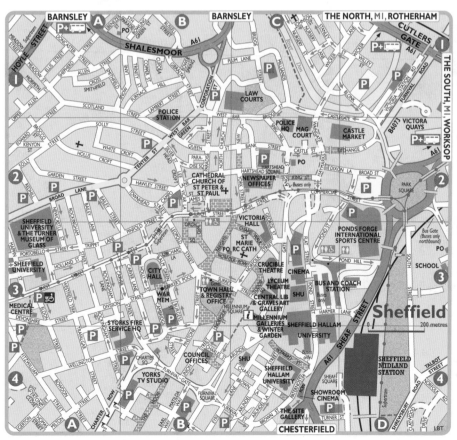

AA Town plans and guides

Southampton is found on atlas page **101 H5**

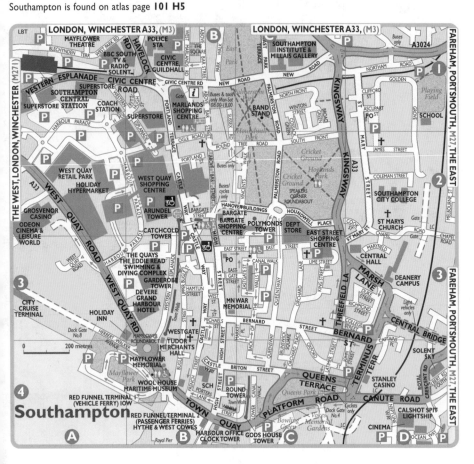

SOUTHAMPTON

Between the modern office blocks and shopping streets, fragments of the old town that was largely destroyed during World War II can be found, including a large section of the medieval town wall and its 13 remaining towers. A self-guiding walking tour follows its route – look out for Walk the Southampton Walls signposts and plaques. The city's museums reveal the diverse history of this major port from medieval prosperity to the golden age of transatlantic travel. The Medieval Merchant's House (B4) has been restored and furnished to look as it might have done in 1290, while Solent Sky (D4) in Albert Road South tells the history of aviation in the Solent area, including the achievements of R J Mitchell, designer of the Spitfire. The Titanic Voices Exhibition in the Maritime Museum (B4) in Town Quay has some haunting recordings of the crew and passengers of the ill-fated ship *Titanic*. On its maiden voyage from Southampton in 1912, this supposedly unsinkable ship went down, with the loss of more than 1,000 lives. With a plethora of waterfront bars and restaurants, Town Quay and Shamrock Quay (B4) are among the city's liveliest spots.

Stirling is found on atlas page **205 G5**

STIRLING

Stirling Castle's position high on a rocky outcrop (A2) has given it a prominent role in Scottish history. The castle, where Mary, Queen of Scots spent her childhood, served as a royal palace. Mary was crowned in the Chapel Royal in 1543. The town was of particular importance in the Wars of Independence fought against England. Notable Scottish victories include Stirling Bridge (1297), fought at the Old Bridge, when William Wallace (c1270–1305) cleverly split the opposing army, and Bannockburn (1314), when Robert the Bruce took charge. Both men are commemorated as local heroes, Wallace with the National Wallace Monument on the hill of Abbey Craig, and Bruce with a heritage centre on the field of Bannockburn, below the castle. Argyll's Lodging (B2) gives an insight to life in 17th-century Stirling and it's fascinating to tour the reconstructed rooms. For a more harsh view of the past visit the Old Town Jail (B3) and take a tour of this forbidding institution.

STRATFORD-UPON-AVON

Even without the Shakespeare connection, Stratford is a very appealing town on the River Avon, with many historical buildings. Many of the buildings have Georgian frontages, but the 15th-century almshouses are timber-framed, and the King Edward VI School is thought to be where Shakespeare was educated. The site most visitors head for first is Shakespeare's Birthplace (C2) in the middle of town. Whether this marks the Bard's true birthplace is open to question, but it has become his shrine. Since his birth in 1564, this half-timbered Tudor house has changed, but the interior has been refurbished to give a good impression of the young Shakespeare's life. Halls' Croft (B4), New Place and Nash's House (C3) all have Shakespeare connections. The Royal Shakespeare Company (RSC) has three venues here, the Royal Shakespeare Theatre, the Swan and the Other Place (C3). There is a fine range of small individual shops in the town centre.

Stratford-upon-Avon is found on atlas page **135 F5**

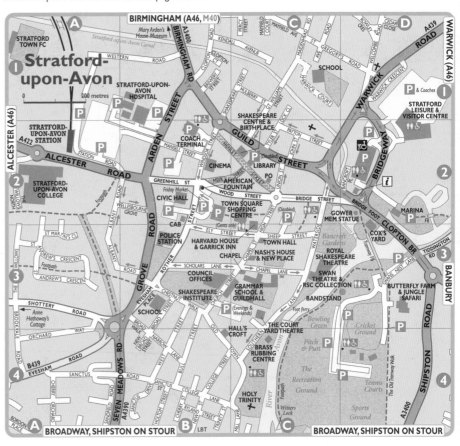

WARWICK

Many visitors to Warwick Castle (C3) unfortunately miss the town of Warwick itself, which was given a handsome makeover after a disastrous fire in 1694. As a result, it has some of the finest 18th-century streetscapes in England. Predating the fire are two medieval gateways, the old houses in Castle Lane (C3), the 15th-century Beauchamp tomb in the Church of St Mary (B2) and, near the West Gate, Leycester Hospital (B3). The last of these is a wonderfully complete group of half-timbered buildings (mostly 16th century). Visitors can look into the chapel, courtyard and great hall. Architecturally, Warwick Castle is one of the finest examples of a medieval castle in England, with its exteriors dating back to the 14th and 15th centuries. The castle is owned by the Tussaud's Group and is run as a modern tourist attraction. The interior was thoroughly upgraded in the 17th to 19th centuries, and the private apartments are furnished as they would have been in 1898. The Kingmaker is an exhibition devoted to the castle's most significant and influential owner, Richard Neville, Earl of Warwick.

Warwick is found on atlas page **135 F4**

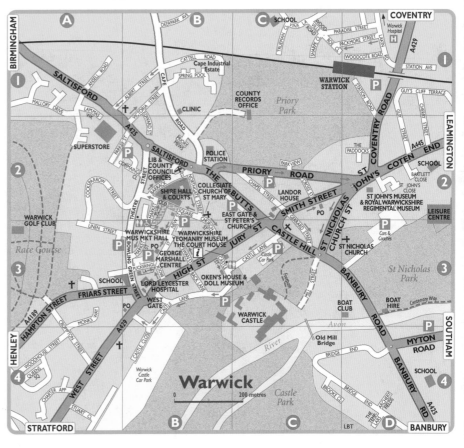

Winchester is found on atlas page **101 H4**

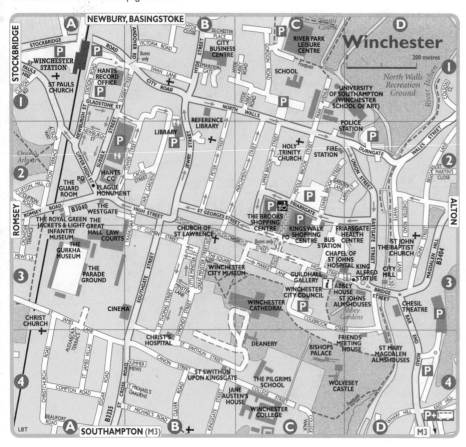

WINCHESTER

England's ancient capital and seat of the Anglo-Saxon kings, Winchester has a compact and historic central area that you can easily explore on foot. The city came to prominence under Alfred the Great, who made it the capital of his Wessex kingdom in the 9th century. The highlight of the city is its medieval cathedral (C3), dating from 1079 to 1404, in Norman to Perpendicular styles. Close by are the free City Museum (B3) and Winchester College (C4), founded in 1382 and Britain's oldest and one of its most prestigious schools. Near Westgate (A2), the Great Hall (A3), built in 1235, is all that survives of the city's 13th-century Norman castle. You can visit King Arthur's Round Table – a resplendent medieval fake. The Hospital of St Cross is a 12th-century almshouse (D4), still home to 25 monks and reached by a tranquil walk across water meadows; by ancient tradition, Wayfarer's Dole (bread and beer) is still given to anyone who asks for it at the porter's lodge.

Windsor is found on atlas page **114 A4**

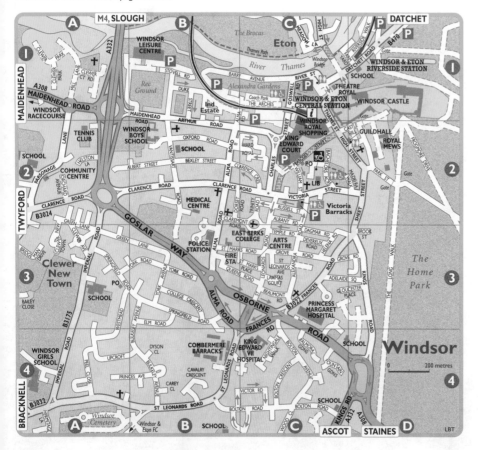

WINDSOR

Windsor is easily explored on foot and has plenty of attractions to fill a whole day. In addition to the obvious lure of its castle (D1), Windsor is also well stocked with shops. Windsor Castle towers above the town. It is the largest inhabited castle in the world and has been one of the principal residences of the sovereigns of England since William the Conqueror built it. Much of the present-day structure, however, dates from the 19th century. There are several buildings to visit within the castle complex. St George's Chapel, begun in 1475 by Edward IV and completed in 1509, is a masterpiece of Perpendicular Gothic architecture. The baroque State Apartments, restored following the fire of 1992, are hung with works from the Royal Collection, the world's finest private art collection. It is worth exploring Windsor's shops and noteworthy buildings. The Guildhall (D2) was designed by Sir Christopher Wren. Farther up the High Street you will pass the 19th-century parish church of St John the Baptist. From here you can continue up Park Street to the Long Walk (D3), which skirts Windsor Home Park.

WORCESTER

The city of Worcester is a mix of the sublime and the mundane: amid some insensitive 20th-century development are fine streets of Georgian mansions and timber-framed buildings. The cathedral (B4) has a superb crypt, cloister and monuments, including that of King John and the 14th-century Beauchamp tomb. The Royal Worcester Porcelain Works (C4) dates from 1751 and offers a factory tour and a museum, where examples of this delicate china are on display in period settings. During the Battle of Worcester in 1651, Charles II made his headquarters near the cathedral at the 11th-century Commandery (C4), which now houses the Civil War Visitor Centre, focusing on the trial of Charles I and Cromwell's campaign. Another famous person associated with this area is the British composer Edward Elgar, whose statue stands near the cathedral. He was born outside the city at Lower Broadheath, at what is now the Elgar Birthplace Museum (134 B5).

Worcester is found on atlas page **134 B5**

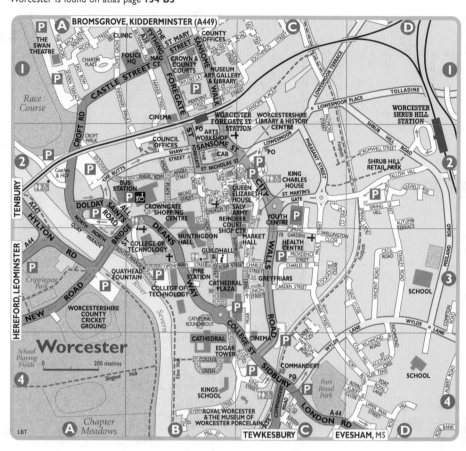

York is found on atlas page **172 A4**

YORK

This strikingly beautiful city straddling the River Ouse is one of Britain's premier sights. York has a multitude of museums and buildings spanning a range of historic periods. Much of the city's compact heart is pedestrianised, so it's a great place to explore on foot, taking in its wealth of shops and vibrant street performers. Among the most evocative streets are the Shambles (C2), originally a street of butchers' shops and retaining overhanging, jettied, timber-framed buildings, and Stonegate (B2), where shop signs and frontages span several centuries. Also look for York's distinguished clutch of medieval churches (some no longer used for services). Arguably the finest is Holy Trinity (C2) with its inward-facing box pews and late 15th-century stained glass. York Minster (C1) is Europe's largest Gothic cathedral north of the Alps, with two towers, richly traceried windows and a massive west front. Among the museums, York Castle Museum (C4), Jorvik Viking Centre (C3), The Yorkshire Museum (B1) and the National Railway Museum, just west of York Railway Station (A2), are superb. The Museum Gardens (A1) make a great picnic spot, with medieval and Roman remains scattered around.

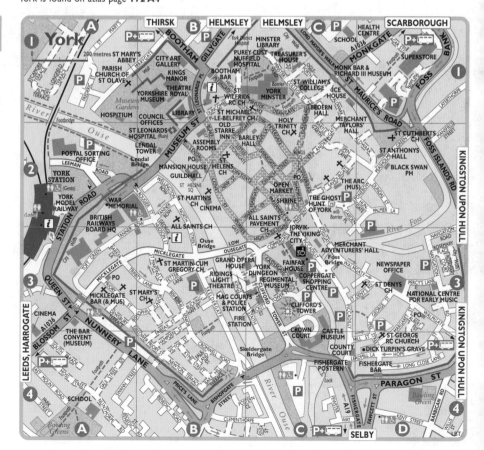

AA Town plans and guides

Motoring guide

This section of the atlas has been put together to help you enjoy worry-free motoring. We have included simple checks on how to avoid the risk of breakdown and we give advice on where to stop and what to do if you do breakdown. Car tyres, satellite navigation and tips on driving in floods and standing water are all covered along with common sense, eco-driving tips to help reduce fuel consumption, CO_2 emissions and pollution.

CONTENTS

SAFETY & SECURITY

CAR TYRES

The right tyres, in good condition and correctly inflated, are vital for braking and cornering safety. Regular checks and maintenance will help to prolong the life of the tyres and keep you on the right side of the law too.

Basic legal requirements

- Tyres must be compatible with others on the car and generally in good physical condition.
- Tyres must be correctly inflated to the vehicle manufacturer's recommended pressure.
- Tread depth must be above the legal minimum, which for passenger cars in Britain and Ireland is 1.6mm throughout a continuous band in the centre three-quarters of the tread and around the entire circumference.
- You don't have to carry a spare and it doesn't have to meet the legal requirements while it's stowed away. It may, however, affect the level of breakdown assistance to which you are entitled if you do not carry a serviceable spare.

Tyre life is influenced by many factors:
Driving style – aggressive cornering and braking increases wear
Position – front tyres wear faster because of movement through steering and driven tyres wear more quickly
Speed – high-speed driving increases temperature and hastens wear
Load – excess loading increases wear
Pressure – both under inflation (through increased flexing and temperature) and over inflation (through reduced contact area) increase wear
Alignment – incorrect wheel alignment results in rapid and uneven wear, as can excessive wear to suspension components, such as shock absorbers.

Though the legal limit is 1.6mm, tyre performance – particularly wet grip – gets worse as the tread wears. Check tread depth more frequently once it reaches 3mm and replace tyres before the tread wears below 2mm.

Tyre pressures

Check pressures every two weeks with the tyres cold using a reliable and accurate tyre pressure gauge. Correct tyre pressure is important for several reasons:
Tyre life – under or over inflation increases wear

Fuel economy – under inflation increases fuel consumption
Safety – under or over inflation will affect grip and braking performance
Ride – over inflation can result in a harsh, uncomfortable ride.

Non-standard spare wheels

The handbook and spare tyre itself will carry clear information about the operating restrictions – maximum speed and distance – which you must stick to for safety reasons. This means that, unlike a standard spare, skinny spares must be considered an emergency, get-you-home solution only. The original car tyre should be repaired or replaced as soon as possible.

LOADING YOUR CAR

How to pack without endangering your passengers

Follow these few simple rules when you pack the car to help ensure you get home safely without endangering yourself, your family or other road users.

- Check the handbook and adjust tyre pressures if necessary to suit the heavier load. Remember to adjust them back again after the trip.
- Drive defensively – handling and performance will be affected by any load and stopping distances will be increased.
- Don't exceed the Maximum Authorised Mass / Maximum Permitted Weight – this is the technically permissible maximum weight of the vehicle based on the capability of tyres, suspension, etc. It includes everything in / on the car (the payload), the driver and passengers and is normally shown on the VIN plate and / or in the handbook.

Inside the car

Make sure everything's secure.

- Items sliding around or tipping over whenever you brake or turn will be irritating at best, dangerously distracting at worst.
- Empty boxes or plastic crates can be useful in the boot to stop smaller loads sliding around or shopping bags spilling at the first corner.
- Keep the parcel shelf clear, any loose item can become a dangerous projectile in a crash.
- Keep the front foot-well clear – loose items rolling about on the floor are distracting and potentially very dangerous if they get caught under the driver's feet or the pedals.

Keep larger / heavier items low down

Not only does this make packing easier – put the bigger things in first and then pack the smaller items around them – but it also helps to keep the centre of gravity lower to minimise the affect on handling.

Heavy items in the boot should be pushed tight up against the back of the back seat to reduce the risk of them bursting through in a crash. Pushing heavy items as far forwards as possible gives better weight distribution and handling too.

Can you still see?

Try to avoid packing above the line of the seat backs so that you retain a clear view to the rear – anything packed higher than this is at risk of flying forwards in a crash. Consider using a roof rack or roof box for lighter / more bulky items to leave more room inside.

Passengers come first

If you have to fold seats to get a large or awkward load in the car, then leave passengers and collect them later rather than risk carrying them unrestrained. Install child restraints first – it might be more difficult once you've packed everything else. Leave plenty of room for children – items packed in tight around them is sure to make for an unhappy journey.

On the roof

Roof racks are a great way of carrying very large or awkward items. Check the handbook to make sure that the load, including the weight of the roof rack itself, doesn't exceed the maximum permitted roof load – generally limits are low and easily exceeded by a couple of items of flat-pack furniture, for example. Ensure that loads are securely attached – In Britain, the *Highway Code* states simply that 'you must secure your load and it must not stick out dangerously'. Secure fixings holding the front and rear of the load down are important. Don't forget the extra height and distribute weight safely.

DRIVING IN FOG

According to the *Highway Code*, in Britain you must use headlights when visibility is seriously reduced – generally when you cannot see for more than 100m or the length of a football pitch. Take extra care in conditions where visibility is seriously reduced:

- Use dipped headlights at all times and windscreen wipers and demisters.
- Familiarise yourself with your front and rear fog lights – know how to switch them on and off – and use them when appropriate.
- Beware of other drivers not using headlights.
- Drive only as fast as conditions allow and maintain a greater distance between you and the car in front (follow a three-second rule) – tailing someone's rear lights can give a false sense of security and is dangerous.
- If the road has street lights on, then you probably don't need fog lights on.
- Be able to stop within the distance you can see clearly – this is particularly important on motorways and dual carriageways, as vehicles are travelling faster.
- Do not accelerate to get away from a vehicle that is too close behind you.
- Check your mirrors before you slow down.
- At a junction with limited visibility, stop, wind down the window, and listen for traffic. When it is safe to emerge, do so positively and do not hesitate in a position that puts you directly in the path of approaching vehicles.

SATELLITE NAVIGATION

Follow the tips below to get the most out of your satnav and avoid trouble at the same time.

- You're driving, not the satnav. You can't blame the satnav if you commit an offence or have an accident. Watch the road – not the satnav.

- What you see must take priority over what the satnav says. If the road looks wrong, don't take it.

- You know what you're driving, the satnav probably doesn't. If you have a large vehicle, or a trailer, you can't be sure that the road is suitable for you just because the satnav tells you to go down it. Watch for signs.

- A satnav can give all sorts of information about where you are going, much of which you don't need.

- Put the satnav in a sensible place. It should be in your line of sight, but should not create a blind spot. Put it where it won't injure anyone in an accident.

- Don't try to programme the satnav while driving. You know it will take one hand from the wheel, two eyes from the road and a brain from driving.

- Use all the satnav's features. On a complicated, busy roundabout, it is unwise to take your eyes off the road to look at the satnav, and much better to receive spoken instructions.

- Check the route is practical before you start. Is the satnav taking you to the right Farnborough? Hampshire, Warwickshire or Kent? If you put in the wrong destination, it will take you to the wrong destination.

- Update the satnav regularly. It needs to know about new roads, new one way systems and generally keep itself up to date.

- Remember, thieves like satnavs too. If it's detachable, always take it out when you leave the car. Mounts or suction cap marks also attract thieves.

OLDER DRIVERS

There is no safe or unsafe age for a driver. Both physical and mental conditions can take their toll.

Older people are more likely to suffer serious injury in accidents – always wear seat belts and use safety features in the car.

In Britain, it is a driver's responsibility to ensure fitness to drive. All drivers must advise the DVLA at Swansea of medical conditions that will affect their driving. Doctors should advise when a patient needs to do this, but always ask if a new condition is diagnosed, or treatment given. Have regular eye tests.

Drivers over 70 have to reapply for their licence every three years – there is no test or medical, but a medical declaration has to be submitted.

Many older drivers restrict themselves on how and where they drive – this self-regulation is a sign of responsibility, not one of ineptitude, and should be encouraged. Don't drive in situations that cause anxiety.

If you've got a licence and are fit to drive, keep driving – it is very hard to take up driving again after several years off,

as traffic conditions change. Listen to other people. A second opinion can help. Do neighbours or friends feel safe if they have a lift with you?

FLOODS AND STANDING WATER

Only drive through water if you know how deep it is.

Drive slowly and steadily to avoid creating a bow wave. Allow oncoming traffic to pass first and test your brakes as soon as you can after leaving the water.

Don't try driving through fast-moving water, such as at a flooded bridge approach – your car could easily be swept away.

Driving fast through standing water is dangerous – tyres lose contact with the road and you lose steering control. This is known as aquaplaning.

Watch out for standing water, trying to avoid it if you can, and adjust your speed to the conditions. If you do experience aquaplaning, hold the steering wheel lightly and lift off the throttle until the tyres regain grip.

Driving through water at speeds above a slow crawl can result in water being thrown onto pavements, soaking pedestrians or cyclists. You could face a hefty fine and between three and nine penalty points if the police believe you were driving without reasonable consideration to other road users.

Driving fast through standing water can cause expensive damage – the air intake on many cars is low down at the front of the engine bay and it only takes a small quantity of water sucked into the engine to cause serious damage. All engines are affected but turbo-charged and diesel engines are most vulnerable.

As you drive slowly through standing water keep the engine revving by slipping the clutch, otherwise water in the exhaust could stall the engine.
If you breakdown in heavy rain don't prop the bonnet open while you wait for the patrol to arrive – the engine will be more difficult to start again if the electrics are all rain-soaked.

BREAKDOWN ADVICE

TOP TEN BREAKDOWN CAUSES

Many of these problems can be fixed at the roadside, but most can be avoided with the correct preventative care.

Flat or faulty battery

- Most problems are caused by terminals and clamp connections or by a loss of voltage, often caused by constant use on short journeys without regular recharging.
- At every service, check that the terminals have been cleaned and protected from corrosion with a layer of petroleum jelly or grease. Clamps and connections must be secure.
- If you seldom make a long journey, a fortnightly overnight charge prolongs battery life.
- Modern maintenance-free batteries need no top-up.

Lost keys

- Many modern cars have a transponder key to prevent theft.
- If you lose the key, recovery to an authorised dealer is usually the only answer.
- Even a dealer may take several days to obtain a replacement, so always carry a spare set of keys.

Flat or damaged tyres and wheels

- Know the correct pressures for different speeds and loads, and adjust accordingly.
- Kerb impact can damage sidewalls and, possibly, wheel rims. Both can result in slow leaks. Consult a specialist tyre dealer if any damage is visible.
- When checking tread depth, look for uneven tyre wear – the wheels may be misaligned.
- Look at the spare tyre. A worn or flat spare won't be of use in an emergency.
- Check that the jack and wheel-removal tools are in good condition and that the key or removal tool for locking wheel nuts is accessible.

Alternator faults

- Persistent battery problems and dim headlights when the engine is idling can indicate alternator / generator faults.
- Belts driving the alternator may also operate the radiator fan and

water pump. A red ignition warning light plus a rapid rise in engine temperature could indicate a broken belt. Stop immediately.

Starter motor

- Though usually robust, starter motors can fail.
- Good, regular garage maintenance should highlight potential faults.

Distributor cap

- Moisture and dirt are the chief enemies of this vital ignition-system component.
- A crack in the cap's insulation may be almost invisible but can be sufficient to allow high ignition voltage to leak away, especially in damp weather, so there may be no ignition spark.
- Replace the cap at the car manufacturer's recommended intervals. If the weather protection covering the cap splits, replace it.

Fuel problems

- Fill up at the start of your journey to avoid running out of fuel.
- Every year more than 100,000 motorists put the wrong fuel in their car – petrol in diesel engines or vice versa. In these cases the car will have to be recovered to a garage. Draining the tank and disposing of contaminated fuel is expensive. See also Misfuelling, on page 336.

Clutch cables

- The clutch cable is under high stress. Abrasion can weaken the wire strands until they break.
- Temporary repairs can often be made at the roadside, but replacement at the first signs of wear is the best answer.

Spark plugs

The spark plug is a much-neglected part of the ignition system.
Make sure that you replace plugs at the manufacturer's recommended service intervals.

HT leads

- High-tension (HT) leads and their connections can deteriorate with age. Water and dirt enter cracks in the insulation, reducing the ignition voltage.
- Damp-repellent sprays are only a temporary solution.
- Ask your garage to check the condition of the leads and replace as necessary.

WORRY-FREE MOTORING

Avoid the risk of breakdown by having your car serviced at recommended intervals. Making the following ten checks regularly will also help you to enjoy safer, worry-free motoring.

Tyres

- Know the correct tyre pressures for your car and check them at least fortnightly using a good-quality gauge or garage air line.
- Look for cuts on sidewalls. If any one tyre needs regular top-ups, it may have a slow puncture.
- Don't forget to check the spare as well.

Toolkit

- Check the handbook for the location of the basic toolkit for the car. It should contain at least a jack and wheel removal tools.
- Familiarise yourself with the jacking points used to lift the car safely.
- If locking wheel nuts are fitted make sure that the toolkit includes the key or removal tool.

Engine oil

- Check the dipstick at least every fortnight and before any long journey.
- Have the oil and filter changed at recommended service intervals.
- High oil consumption can indicate engine problems.

Water

- Check the coolant level regularly and top up as necessary – but only when the engine is cold.
- Have the antifreeze concentration checked before winter.
- Antifreeze not only prevents the coolant from freezing but also prevents the build-up of corrosion within the cooling system and so is important all year round.

Wipers

- Wiper blades wear down over time and smear the windscreen if they become worn. Replace them at least once a year for best performance.

Screenwash

- Check and top up regularly – it's a legal requirement that the system works.
- Use a good screenwash additive through summer and winter – water alone won't clear oily road grime and freezes more readily in winter.

Windscreen

- Inspect the screen regularly for stone damage and always replace a cracked or chipped screen as soon as possible.
- Any damage may impair vision or distract attention.
- Minor chips can grow and crack the glass, but many chips can be repaired by a windscreen specialist.

Lights

- Check all lights weekly. Don't forget indicators, brake and fog lights.
- Clean lights regularly. In bad weather wipe them over with a damp cloth during driving breaks.

Power steering

- Ensure that the fluid reservoir is checked at every service, and check it yourself once a month.
- Top up only using the correct hydraulic fluid as advised in the car handbook.

Bodywork

- Deal promptly with damage to bodywork to prevent rust setting in.
- Many cars have extended bodywork warranty schemes, which may require annual inspection at the dealer. Check that any previous owner has kept records up-to-date.

IF YOU BREAKDOWN – WHERE TO STOP AND WHAT TO DO

On a motorway

Motorway hard shoulders are for emergency use only. You should only stop if it is a real emergency and you have no other choice. It's best to try to drive to a safer place off the motorway if you can, rather than stopping on the hard shoulder.

You must not stop on the hard shoulder to:

- go to the toilet
- use a mobile phone
- check a route or map.

If an emergency forces you to stop, pull on to the hard shoulder and stop as far to the left as possible, with your wheels turned to the left. Leave your sidelights on and use your hazard flashers.

Try to stop near an emergency telephone (situated at approximately 1-mile intervals along the hard shoulder).
Leave the vehicle by the left-hand door

and ensure all your passengers do the same. Leave any animals in the vehicle or, in an emergency, keep them under proper control on the verge. If you have reflective jackets in the vehicle, wear them. Do not use a reflective triangle.

Ensure that passengers keep away from the carriageway and hard shoulder, and that children are kept under control.

Do not attempt even simple repairs. Walk to an emergency telephone on your side of the carriageway (follow the arrows on the posts at the back of the hard shoulder) – the telephone is free of charge and connects directly to the police. Use these in preference to a mobile phone. If you must use a mobile phone (for AA breakdown in the UK call 08457 887766 in the Republic of Ireland call 1800 66 77 88.) make sure you can describe your location – there are reference numbers on all telephones and marker posts.

Give full details to the police; also inform them if you are a vulnerable motorist, such as a woman travelling alone.

Return and wait near your vehicle well away from the carriageway and hard shoulder. It is best to retreat up the bank, or behind a barrier if this is possible.

If you feel at risk from another person, return to your vehicle by a left-hand door and lock all doors.

Leave your vehicle again as soon as you feel this danger has passed. Before you rejoin the carriageway after a breakdown, build up speed on the hard shoulder and watch for a safe gap in the traffic. Be aware that other vehicles may be stationary on the hard shoulder.

If you cannot get your vehicle onto the hard shoulder
- Do not attempt to place any warning device on the carriageway.
- Switch on your hazard warning lights.
- Leave your vehicle only when you can safely get clear of the carriageway.

If you have a disability which prevents you from following the advice above
- Stay in your vehicle.
- Switch on your hazard warning lights.
- If you have a car or mobile telephone, contact the emergency services and be prepared to advise them of your location.

ON OTHER ROADS

Get your vehicle off the road if possible and warn other traffic by using your hazard warning lights, particularly if your vehicle is causing an obstruction.

If you have a reflective jacket, put it on. If you have any fear that your vehicle may be struck by other traffic make all your passengers get out of the car and get well away from the traffic.

Question whether it is safe for you to fix the car or whether you need professional help.
If it is safe and you have one, put a warning triangle or other permitted warning device on the road at least 45m behind your broken down vehicle on the same side of the road. Always take great care when doing this.

Keep your sidelights on if it is dark or visibility is poor.

Do not stand (or let anybody else stand), between your vehicle and oncoming traffic.

At night or in poor visibility do not stand where you will prevent other road users seeing your lights.

Use your mobile phone, or any other available phone, to summon assistance. Make sure you know where you have broken down.
For AA breakdown in the UK call 0800 887766 or, if calling from a mobile, 08457 887766. For rescue service in the Republic of Ireland call 1800 66 77 88.

If you have used a warning triangle remember to retrieve it, with care, when the breakdown is over.

FUEL AND THE ENVIRONMENT

HOW TO GET THE MOST OUT OF THE FUEL YOU BUY

Whatever car you have there are a number of simple things you can do to reduce energy use (fuel consumption), CO_2 emissions and pollution. These simple, common sense, eco-driving tips really will make a difference. You'll save money on your fuel bills too.

MISFUELLING

If you've put the wrong fuel in your car, don't turn on the ignition or start the engine as this will circulate the contaminated fuel and increase the risk of damage.

Petrol in Diesel
If the car's still under warranty you should check with the franchised dealer regarding the correct remedial action – some manufacturers advise that seals and filters should be renewed even if the engine has not been run.

Diesel in Petrol
This is much less common because the standard diesel nozzle at fuel stations is larger than the fuel filler neck on modern petrol cars – you have to be pretty determined and patient to misfuel with diesel as a result.

AA Fuel Assist
AA Fuel Assist is a specialist roadside service that drains, flushes and replenishes vehicle fuel systems on the spot, saving the customer both time, money and inconvenience.

AA Fuel Assist is available in the UK to the general public as well as to AA members and will attend any vehicle providing the Fuel Assist van has enough capacity in its tanks.

The service (Monday to Friday, 8am–8pm) not only retrieves the contaminated fuel but ensures that it is recycled through a waste management company with the end product being used to power cement kilns and furnaces for example.

An appointment system is in place. Bookings and enquiries 0870 240 3985 (opening hours 7:30am–7pm). Dedicated, trained technicians – who only do fuel

drains, not general breakdowns – arrive within an hour, on average.

MAINTENANCE

Regular Servicing – get the car serviced regularly (according to the manufacturer's schedule) to maintain engine efficiency.

Engine oil – make sure you use the correct specification of engine oil (refer to the handbook)

Tyre pressures – check tyre pressures regularly and before long journeys. Under-inflated tyres create more rolling resistance and so use more fuel. Getting tyre pressures right is important for safety too. Refer to the handbook as pressures will normally have to be increased for heavier loads.

BEFORE YOU GO

Lose weight – extra weight means extra fuel so if there's anything in the boot you don't need on the journey take it out and leave it at home.

Streamline – roof racks / boxes create extra wind resistance and so increase fuel consumption. If you don't need it take it off. If you do, pack carefully to reduce the extra drag.

Don't get lost – plan unfamiliar journeys to reduce the chance of getting lost – use this atlas, try the AA Route Planner or consider a satnav if you regularly drive unfamiliar routes. Check the traffic news before you go too.

Combine short trips – cold starts are inefficient so it pays to combine errands such as buying the paper, dropping-off the recycling, or collecting the kids into one trip rather than making multiple short trips.

Consider alternatives – if it's a short journey (a couple of miles or so) consider walking or cycling rather than taking the car – fuel consumption is worse when the engine's cold and pollution will be greater too until the emissions control system gets up to normal temperature.

ON THE WAY

Leave promptly – don't start the engine until you're ready to go. This avoids fuel wastage due to unnecessary idling and

ensures that the engine warms up as quickly as possible. In winter months, scrape ice rather than leave the car idling for a long period to warm up.

Easy does it – drive smoothly, accelerate gently and read the road ahead to avoid unnecessary braking.

Decelerate smoothly – when you have to slow down or to stop, decelerate smoothly by releasing the accelerator in time, leaving the car in gear.

Rolling – If you can keep the car moving all the time, so much the better. Stopping then starting again uses more fuel than keeping rolling.

Change up earlier – change gear as soon as possible without labouring the engine – try changing up at an engine speed of around 2000 rpm in a diesel car or around 2500 rpm in a petrol car. This can make such a difference to fuel consumption that all cars in the future are likely to be fitted with Gear Shift indicators that light a lamp on the dashboard to indicate the most efficient gear change points.

Cut down on the air-con – air-conditioning adds to the load on the engine and so increases fuel consumption and CO_2 emissions. Use it only when necessary rather than leaving it on all the time. You should run it at least once a week throughout the year though to maintain the system in good condition.

Turn it off – any electrical load increases fuel consumption, so turn off your heated rear windscreen, demister blowers and headlights, when you don't need them.

Stick to the limits – drive at or within the speed limit – the faster you go the greater the fuel consumption and the greater the pollution too. In Britain according to the Department for Transport driving at 70mph uses up to 9 per cent more fuel than at 60mph and up to 15 per cent more than at 50mph. Cruising at 80mph can use up to 25 per cent more fuel than at 70mph.

Don't be idle – if you do get caught in a queue avoid wasting fuel by turning the engine off if it looks like you could be waiting for more than three minutes.

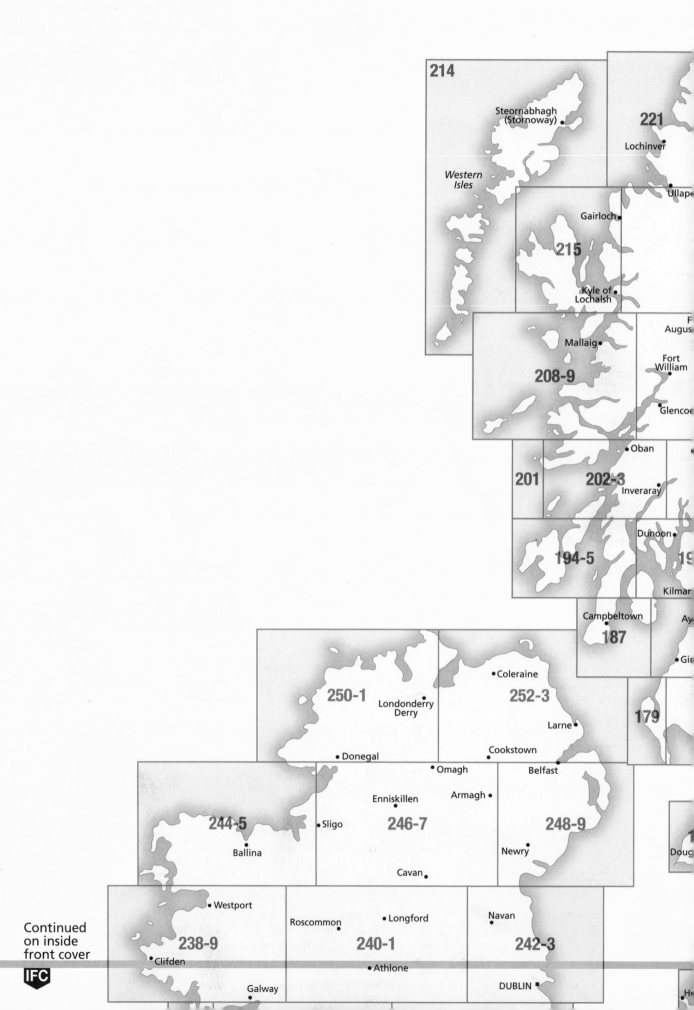

214

221
Lochinver

Steornabhagh
(Stornoway)

Ullap

Western
Isles

Gairloch

215

Kyle of
Lochalsh

F
Augus

Mallaig

Fort
William

208-9

Glencoe

Oban

201

202-3

Inveraray

Dunoon

194-5

19

Kilmar

Campbeltown

Ay

187

Gir

Coleraine

250-1

252-3

Londonderry
Derry

Larne

179

Cookstown

Donegal

Omagh

Belfast

Enniskillen

Armagh

244-5

246-7

248-9

Sligo

Newry

Ballina

Doug

Cavan

Westport

Navan

Roscommon

Longford

238-9

240-1

242-3

Clifden

Athlone

Galway

DUBLIN

H

Continued
on inside
front cover

IFC